HOGARTH

by the same author

GEORGE ELIOT

ELIZABETH GASKELL

MACMILLAN DICTIONARY OF WOMEN'S BIOGRAPHY
(editor)

CULTURAL BABBAGE: TECHNOLOGY, TIME AND INVENTION
(edited with Francis Spufford)

HOGARTH

A LIFE AND A WORLD

Jenny Uglow

faber and faber

First published in 1997
by Faber and Faber Limited
London WC1N 3AU

Typeset by Agnesi Text, Hadleigh
Printed in England by Butler and Tanner Ltd, Frome

A CIP record for this book
is available from the British Library

ISBN 0–571–16996–1

This book is for Steve

Contents

EVENING
1748–1762

NIGHT
1762–1764

PREFACE

Picturing a World

A strutting, consequential little man.
BENJAMIN WEST, President of the Royal Academy

How I want thee, humorous Hogart!
Thou, I hear, a pleasant rogue art.
Were but you and I acquainted,
Every monster should be painted . . .
Draw them so that we may trace
All the soul in every face.
JONATHAN SWIFT, after seeing *The Rake's Progress* (1736)

My picture was my Stage and men and women my actors . . .
WILLIAM HOGARTH (*c.* 1763)

THIS IS WHAT I first loved in Hogarth. He drew ordinary, flawed people in everyday settings and told powerful stories, bawdy and violent, appealing and grim. He eyed his city, its posturing rich and flailing poor. Any day, stuck in a London queue, you can glance over your shoulder and think, 'My God, those faces look exactly like a Hogarth crowd.' Unlike the stiff, serenely proud folk of aristocratic portraits, his men and women have squashed, pulled-about faces, big noses, straggly hair and precarious wigs; you can see how their clothes button up (or fall apart), how they take their medicine, sing, smoke, scheme and gamble and live and die. Yet although they seem solid and real, Hogarth's prints are also distant and strange, and this too is part of their appeal.

Like a sharp-elbowed, awkward-angled peg, Hogarth refuses to fit neatly into any slot. He was an artist of flamboyant talent; a satirist with an unerring eye; an ambitious, pragmatic professional; a visionary who changed British art; a stubborn, difficult, comic, vulnerable man. His name conjures an epoch – 'The Age of Hogarth', 'Hogarth's England', 'Hogarth's London'. His daring was matched by his versatility. After the black-and-white prints, whose monochrome satire touches on cruelty, his paintings are a revelation, both in

ix

their vibrant colour and their emotional range. He painted the great and good but also the common people – the middle-class wife, the merchant, the shrimp-seller, children, his servants, his friends. His portraits have the same directness as his prints, but seem the work of a painter of more delicate perceptions, in love with texture and tone and nuanced surface.

Never content, Hogarth wanted to excel at everything – at engraving, at portraiture and at history-painting, highest of the arts – and he couldn't, quite. As a painter he lacks the elegant clarity of Ramsay, the stateliness of Reynolds, the vivacity of Gainsborough's brushwork. But his paintings reveal his *artistry*, his strong theatrical sense and brilliant formal use of space, line and colour. Here, as in the prints, he enjoys visual puns and clues. He excels at the telling detail – from the small child dropping her fan in the early *A Performance of The Indian Emperor*, to the surreal cascading crockery, frozen in mid-air with the tea still spurting from the tea-pot, in *A Harlot's Progress*, or the brick flying through the window with an almost audible 'whoosh' in *An Election Entertainment*.

Tables overturn, chairs balance at the moment of toppling, houses crash into the street, liquid streams from unexpected heights. That sense of risk, of aspiration and sudden, tumbling fortunes, of being pissed on from above while pits open below, is another vein threading through Hogarth's work and life. As Hazlitt said, he painted no indifferent, unimpassioned pictures of humanity; he was comically rich and exuberant, 'carried away by a passion for the *ridiculous*'. He did not show folly or vice

'in its incipient, or dormant, or *grub* state; but full grown, with wings, pampered into all sorts of affectation, airy, ostentatious and extravagant. Folly is seen at the height – the moon is at the full; it is "the very error of our time".'[1]

Hogarth was not an isolated genius. His satire sprang from a rich graphic culture already in place in London, but he pushed its possibilities further than any of his peers. His story sequences of the Harlot and the Rake and *Marriage A-la-Mode* were something absolutely new, little 'ballad operas' blending old plot lines with topical allusions, as familiar as morality plays and as fresh as the scandal in the morning papers. The satirical and the polite conduct a lively running argument in every aspect of his art. He also broke all the art-world taboos, disdaining academic divisions, turning directly to the public, cutting past the connoisseurs. Shocking his peers, he was the first artist to advertise, to shout his wares in the press, to bypass the dealers and printsellers by selling his own work. After Hogarth nothing could be quite the same. In the world of prints he was a hinge between the old popular art and the modern, easing open the door to mass production and pointing forward to the cartoonist and the modern comic strip.

Yet although Hogarth seems so open and accessible, many details of his work are elusive, full of references and jokes that his contemporaries could read in a way lost to us. And although he insisted men and women should judge with their own eyes, not according to rules, this must be set against the profound and problematic rethinking of culture and art that was taking place at the time. The more I looked at Hogarth's prints and paintings, the more intrigued I became. I wanted to write about the man, but also to crack the codes and understand the different audiences he was addressing – to use the voices of his own age and the rich fund of art history so that we could *all* 'read' his pictures – and this required a picture wider than the individual life, a broad shading of events, manners, beliefs and arguments taken for granted at the time. In the course of my quest I have often taken heart from the fact that Hogarth himself would have no truck with the idea of 'idle curiosity' – to him curiosity was active and positive, powerful and pleasurable. He gives me leave to trespass.

Hogarth's domain was London: Smithfield, Covent Garden, Leicester Square. His precarious childhood, oddly like that of Dickens, gave him both a vivid sympathy for the poor and a fierce determination never to be one of them. His connections (and his criticisms) spread beyond London and Britain to Europe and outward to the colonies, built on slavery and convict labour. All the great arguments of his time run through his work: the nature of British liberty, the dangers of mercantilism and luxury, the duty of the rich to the poor.

He was born in 1697, in the reign of William and Mary, and died in 1764, Serjeant-Painter to the young George III. His early manhood saw the South Sea Bubble and the rise of Walpole; his final years the Seven Years War and the triumph of Pitt. He lived in a time of commercial and imperial expansion, of trade with (and wars over) India, the West Indies, North America. And if such expansion implies stability, there was also great turbulence: war abroad and riots and Jacobite rebellion at home. Thousands gathered at Tyburn on public hanging days and highwaymen were heroes. The street scenes and fairground crowds that Hogarth drew always have a hint of violence in reserve.

Yet if the early eighteenth century was greedy and cruel, with an ever widening gulf between haves and have-nots, the new polite society increasingly cultivated the cults of feeling and benevolence. As an artist, an aspiring 'gentleman' and a sturdy patriot, Hogarth was involved with the new

1 The Cities of London and Westminster, and the Borough of Southwark (1756)
1 Smithfield, 2 Covent Garden, 3 St Martin's Lane,
4 Leicester Fields, 5 Charing Cross, 6 Foundling Hospital,

7 Bedlam, 8 Westminster, 9 St James's Palace,
10 St Paul's, 11 Tottenham Court Road, 12 towards Tyburn

philanthropic movements; he was a Governor of St Bartholemew's Hospital, of the Foundling Hospital and of Bedlam. His work also shares the excitement of the intellectual and scientific exploration that flowered across Europe. In his early years Newton's *Optics* was published, and Newcomen's steam engine invented; his middle age was the epoch of Voltaire and Rousseau, of Hume and Canaletto and Handel; his late years of Boulton and Watt and Josiah Wedgwood. His own milieu embraced artisans and merchants, aristocrats and writers, doctors and actors. In London – in literature, art, music and the theatre – old forms cracked under the pressure and, like his close friends Henry Fielding and David Garrick, Hogarth was in the vanguard of change. Every decade brought contentious cultural battles, in which he played a noisy part.

After the Act of Union with Scotland in 1707 there was, after all, a new 'British' nation – and what was the culture of this nation to be? Collectors and young aristocrats flocking back from the Grand Tour brought a cosmopolitan gloss to British life, but the Continental wars also fostered a backward-looking nationalism, with powerful doses of Francophobia and anti-Catholic prejudice. Europe seemed to threaten old British freedoms and livelihoods: 'No French bottle-makers! No lowering of wages to 4d a Day and Garlick!' shouted the mob.[2] Hogarth often seems on the side of these placard-bearing 'patriots'. When he began his career, foreigners dominated the London art scene, but by the late 1740s, largely through his efforts, there was a recognizable British school. Yet his position was complex: in Paris he could behave like a xenophobic lager lout but in London he worked with French artists and engravers and was intimately linked with the spread of French rococo styles. While his prints satirize affectation, he clearly favoured the project of 'politeness', working to free artists from the rule of the market and place them on a par with gentlemen and men of learning.

Hogarth's patriotism and his fights about the status of British art and the rights of the artists are as gripping as the stories in his prints. Again and again, one has to use the word 'first': he pushed through the first copyright act for engravers; he won the first public exhibition spaces; he led the move to start the school of art in St Martin's Lane, the forerunner (though to Hogarth's fury) of the more exclusive Royal Academy.

In his emulation and ambition, and in his independence and mockery, he focused the tensions of his day. The influential writers and statesmen of early eighteenth-century Britain aspired to the model of Augustan Rome, the civic dignity and 'virtue' that fostered Horace and Virgil, and Hogarth, like other artists, felt the power of this ideal. But he used his eyes, and his native wit. He could see that there were beggars at the gates of London's great, that glittering salons held old chamber pots and fine silks cloaked foul linen. Pomposity invites subversion. The great imaginary heroes of this age are not epic figures. They are often outsiders, castaways, servants, rogues or wanderers, orphans and illegitimate children, whose comic trials criticize their society and query the very nature of the self: Defoe's Crusoe and Moll Flanders, Swift's Gulliver, Gay's Polly and Macheath, Fielding's Joseph Andrews and Tom Jones, Smollett's Roderick Random, Sterne's Tristram Shandy – and Hogarth's Harlot and Rake.

'A picture is worth a thousand words'; 'Every picture tells a story'. Sometimes I turn these clichés over like pebbles in my pocket, soothed by their roundness and solid certainty. I forget the rivers of time that burnished them, the ancient strata they come from – even the place I first picked them up. Hogarth himself believed that a picture was worth many volumes of print. True, and not true. Every picture (even a still life) may *suggest* a story but it is the viewer who *tells* the tale, frames the narrative and fills the gaps. True, the brain takes in more information, more quickly, through the eye, but we still need words to name, order, analyse what we see.

Cultural critics often call ours a visual age, citing the dominance of television, film, comics and advertising, but perhaps the force of pictures was even stronger in previous centuries, when literacy was limited. In Protestant Britain, in the sixteenth and seventeenth centuries, paintings and sculptures in churches were destroyed for their very power by the Puritans. In Hogarth's day, pictures spoke in many voices, through trade cards and emblem books, shop signs and woodcuts on broadsheet ballads. And then, as now, people all displayed 'pictures' of themselves, wittingly or unwittingly. From barrow boys to bishops, faces, clothes and body language tell subtle stories about status and sense of self – and sometimes appearances mislead as much as they inform. Hogarth was staggeringly astute at deciphering, remembering and rephrasing such messages to make particular points, and as a printmaker he was also swift to exploit the wide appeal of the pictured world. And all his work moves back and forth between *word* and image: speech bubbles, captions, commentaries, written keys, mottoes and texts are a central part of his graphic art.

In a sense, Hogarth was a very literary artist, but his work requires a different kind of 'reading'. Even the most fundamental similarities seem suspect. Westerners allegedly read pictures rather like print, their eyes running across the image from the left (but starting at the bottom, not the top of a 'page'), then circling up into the centre and then 'out' at the right. Yet, if tested, everyone seems to differ – some seize on a central point, some on a detail, some on an incident in the right-hand corner: it makes one very diffident about saying how 'we' see a picture. However much an artist, like a novelist (or a biographer), manipulates our point of view, it seems we are far freer before an image than before a text.

The problem of 'reading' becomes even more difficult when writing about Hogarth, since engravings are often (but not always) a mirror image of the original paintings. So when you know the prints of *Marriage A-la-Mode*, it is disconcerting to stand in front of the painting and find the young wife glinting and pointing her toe in the opposite side of the picture. She seems the wrong way round. And if one *does* read from left to right, following the relationships across the frame, then which is the 'true' story? And if the painting was conceived as a blueprint for the print, then which is the 'true' original?

Hogarth enjoyed playing with the tricksy world of the eye, the unreal realism of pictures. His famous self-portrait *The Painter and his Pug*, for example (plate VIII) should perhaps be labelled a still life not a self-portrait – *nature morte*, not *vivante*. It is a painting of a painting, an oval stretched on the canvas with the nails still showing. In these receding dimensions, the pug who sits in front of the painting is more 'real' than his 'painted' master. And, as so often in Hogarth's work, gestural words complicate the image – Milton, Shakespeare and Swift on the books' spines, the enigmatic 'line of beauty' on his palette. The idea of a true likeness, though still important, succumbs to a freighted presentation of self.

It is tempting but insidious to use the present tense when describing pictures: 'The children are standing,' we say, as if this is a timeless present, when even the concept of 'childhood' might mean something different to the artist than to us. Yet the pictures *are* present, the children do still stand before us, in paint or in print, and I have often used this time-free present. Facts are facts, but all images carry the imprint of their creator and their time and, from his own day onwards each generation has invented its own Hogarth. I have set out to portray the man, explore his stories, and see how he and his contemporaries pictured their world, both literally and metaphorically. But my approach too is coloured by my own concerns, framed by the scholarship and assumptions of today.

Hogarth left few personal documents: a couple of letters, a sheaf of rough notes. He published one theoretical book in 1753, *The Analysis of Beauty*, and planned another, about painting and sculpture. At the end of his life, to go with his collected prints, he tried to write a short autobiography, which endures only in angry scraps and bits, muddled fits and starts. He did not lie, but his notes were composed in the heat of argument, full of bitter self-justifications, and his omissions are as significant as his emphases. After Hogarth's death, Horace Walpole wrote a brilliant, brief appraisal, and over the next thirty years a 'life' was slowly pieced together as anecdotes were collected to accompany catalogues of his prints. The first was *Biographical Anecdotes of William Hogarth* (1781), compiled by John Nichols, helped by the difficult and often malicious George Steevens. In 1790 John Ireland wrote a two-volume commentary, which appeared as *Hogarth Illustrated*, adding a third volume in 1798 which wove a narrative life from Hogarth's own papers. More anecdotes and rare prints were published in *Graphic Illustrations of Hogarth* by Samuel Ireland (no relation) in 1794 and 1799.[3] Ending this sequence, Nichols's son, J. B. Nichols, published *Anecdotes of William Hogarth* in 1833, adding extracts and essays by Lamb, Hazlitt and others.

Victorian scholars added little to the store of knowledge about Hogarth's life, but twentieth-century studies began with Austin Dobson's biography in 1907. Over the years, scholars, curators and researchers into individual works unearthed new details; in the late 1940s came A. P. Oppé's *The Drawings of William Hogarth*, and R. B. Beckett's *Hogarth*, the first attempt to catalogue his paintings. In the next two decades original manuscripts were edited and published: Charles Mitchell's *Hogarth's Peregrination*; Joseph Burke's edition of *The Analysis of Beauty*, Michael Kitson's of the unpublished *Apology for Painters*. In 1965, Ronald Paulson published the detailed catalogue of *Hogarth's Graphic Works* (since substantially revised), and six years later his two-volume critical biography, *Hogarth: His Life, Art and Times* (now expanded in three volumes). This at last provided an authoritative life, based on archival research. Other works followed, including David Bindman's vivid short study and Mary Webster's informative account. The wider perspective was developed by exhibitions spread over three decades, the Tate *Hogarth* show of 1971, curated by Lawrence Gowing; *Rococo: Art and Design in Hogarth's England* at the Victoria and Albert Museum in 1984, and *Manners and Morals: Hogarth and British Painting, 1700–1768* at the Tate in 1993. In 1997, three hundred years after Hogarth's birth, there are exhibitions of prints at the British Museum, the Sir John Soane's Museum and at Hogarth House, Chiswick, paintings at the Tate and *Marriage A-la-Mode* at the National Gallery. In addition, around all these works cluster constellations of individual books, articles and catalogues. I owe an enormous debt to all these scholars.

*

xvii

I should add a note here about the early sources, and dates. Under the old calendar, which was abandoned in 1752, the year began on Lady Day (25 March), not on 1 January; hence the proper convention is to use both years for the early months, say, February 1732/33. I have simplified this, and written 1733. I have not, however, modernized spellings or punctuations. Eighteenth-century styles can differ wildly, and in each case my text follows the manuscript or text cited in the notes. This means readers will encounter a dazzling diversity of capitals and commas, spellings and stops. The engraver George Vertue, whose packed notebooks are a much used source, preferred full stops to commas; in his manuscripts Hogarth often used none at all – and if a word *sounded* right, that was fine. Sometimes he ran on so fast that whole words are missing. But, after all, I was first drawn to Hogarth precisely because of his vitality and overflowing detail, his ability to catch life at full tilt. Hearing his words and reading his pictures, we can try, across time, to catch him in flight too.

MORNING

1697–1732

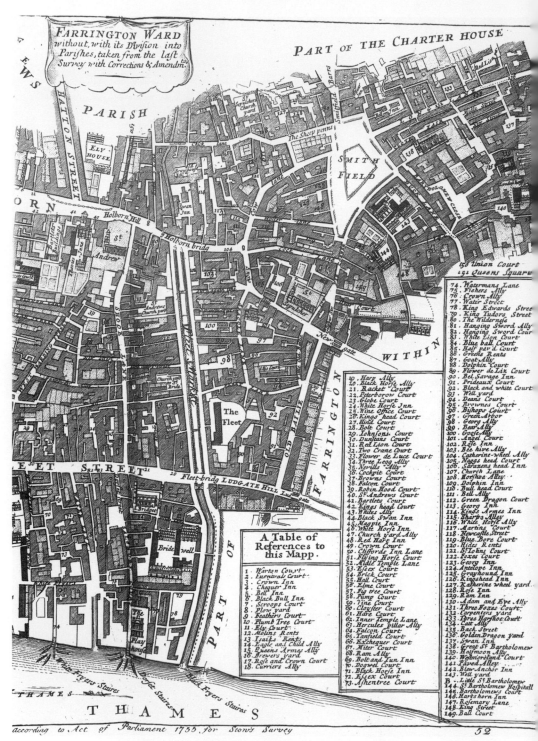

2 The Ward of Faringdon Without (1756)

1

Smithfield Muses

Books and the man I sing, the first who brings
The Smithfield *muses to the ear of Kings.*
ALEXANDER POPE, *The Dunciad*, 1728

IF YOU CROSS the open space of Smithfield, heading north towards the long sheds of the market, and cast a look over your shoulder, suddenly the golden cross on the top of St Paul's Cathedral glints over the roofs of St Bartholomew's Hospital to the south. Cutting down that way, where Bartholomew Close opens into the curving lane of Little Britain, the whole dome swings into sight, blocking the view, swelling above its columns and classical pedestal. On a clear March day, with a touch of snow in the wind, the great curves and angles of the dome stand stark, catching the glinting sun. In a July noon, it hangs and shimmers, sailing above the jostling streets, the cranes on the building sites, the jams at the traffic lights, the black-glass office building where the Fleet prison stood, the granite-like front of the Central Criminal Court at the Old Bailey. The City grows, is demolished, rises again, brick and glass and concrete. So it grew and was demolished and rebuilt through all the years of Hogarth's childhood. No map will quite do, for no map moves so fast.

Bartholomew Close, where William Hogarth was born, escaped the Fire of London. Further west, in September 1666, the flames leapt the Fleet Ditch and roared towards the Strand, but here they only licked the alleys south of Smithfield, blackening the north-east side of St Sepulchre's Church as they burned out. The fire had sparked and rolled across the City, from Pudding Lane to Pie Corner. God's curse on gluttony, said some. Here in Giltspur Street, where the Fortune of War pub used to stand, the statue of the fat Golden Boy still perches above the pavement, hugging his round stomach, warning against greed. Some claimed the Fire was started by Papists and that Frenchmen had been seen throwing fireballs into houses; a poor, deranged Huguenot who 'confessed' was hanged at Tyburn. On the other hand, foreigners such as the Dutch saw the conflagration as a judgement on

3

England's arrogance, showing her 'that God is the only master of the elements, by punishing her, as Lucifer was punished, with the torments of fire'. The official Parliamentary Inquiry split the blame as 'due to the hand of God upon us, a great wind and a season so very dry'. Seven-eighths of the City was lost; thirteen thousand buildings, including eighty-four churches. Men, women and children fled along the waterside and crowds huddled on distant slopes to watch London burn.[1]

The Fire, and the Plague that came before it, and the Civil Wars before that, lived on in the memory of Londoners, as it would for those not yet born, as signs of their precarious world. The Monument to the Great Fire, completed in 1677, rises firmly at the side of one of Hogarth's earliest prints, its inscription damning not incendiary papists, but the wolfish speculators of the South Sea Bubble. Fire, pestilence and greed devoured the people. But behind the Monument, in this print, hovers the shadowy outline of St Paul's, a reminder that grandeur can rise from ashes.

Although worshippers used the new cathedral from 1697, weaving their way through the scaffolding, it was not finally completed until 1710, when Hogarth was thirteen. By then new streets had long since risen around it. Even the new lanes were fourteen feet wide, to allow two drays to pass. But when Hogarth was born, on 10 November 1697, 'next doore to Mr Downinge's the printers', he opened his eyes on to an older world.[2] These houses, untouched by fire, were old and shadowy, built of lath and timber and plaster, with projecting gables and odd angles, slanting window frames and peeling plaster. Hogarth learned to crawl and walk and clamber on sloping floors and crooked stairs.

Bartholomew Close is an oddly shaped courtyard south-east of Smithfield's wide market place. The Close is wedged between the hospital and the old priory church of St Bartholomew the Great, with curving lanes stretching round the buildings to the east, and a crooked dog's-leg alley called Middlesex Passage, which angles round the back of the church. City workers and doctors still use this passage as a short cut to Cloth Fair and the Rising Sun pub, and children's voices still echo here, bouncing off high buildings.

Coming out of the lanes, the elongated diamond of Smithfield seems vast, dizzying. Distances slide as the eye adjusts from narrow to wide, dark to light. The sloping angles and strange perspectives of Hogarth's prints, which often seem those of the playhouse or the prison, also derive from this rough square, a natural stage set, with its isolated figures or swelling crowds. The space, like Hogarth's art, has an in-built contradiction, ruled simultaneously by butchery and healing: by London's greatest meat market and one of London's greatest hospitals. Brick, flesh and blood.

4

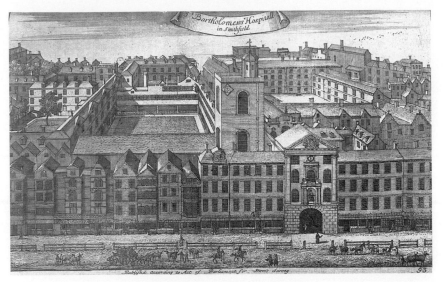

3 St Bartholomew's Hospital (1756)

St Bartholomew's Hospital still dominates the square's southern side as it did in Hogarth's time. In 1704, when Hogarth was seven, the Hospital could house nearly four hundred patients, and 'cured and discharged' over two thousand people – burying one hundred and sixty-five. It was a source of civic pride, its benefactors coming from the great City guilds, the Drapers, Brewers, Merchant Taylors, Grocers and Goldsmiths, and also from poorer trades, plasterers and clothworkers. Some gave £500, some £5, which was still a month's wages from an artisan. Untouched by the Fire (although it lost much income from City properties) it was fronted by narrow four-storey houses, with half-moon windows, gabled roof spaces above and small shops below. Behind lay interlocking courtyards and, in 1691, 'repaired and beautified', it acquired a new ward, standing on 'Piers and Pillars, under which are Shops that front the Common Passage', the Long Walk leading down to Christ's Hospital.[3]

The square itself had a turbulent, violent history. Here in the market place, in 1381, Wat Tyler was stabbed by the Lord Mayor, his body lugged into the hospital and dragged out again by the mob. Here, under Mary Tudor, Protestant martyrs were burned at the stake, chained to face the church. In 1700, apart from the odd stabbing or brawl, the blood that stained the cobbles was that of beasts, not of men. In a typical year, says Strype's *Survey*, 70,000 oxen and cows were sold, 540,000 sheep, 200,000 calves, 200,000 hogs and 52,000 pigs. Every Monday and Friday, country drovers rose before dawn to

5

bring their herds and their flocks into the city. Children woke to the bellowing of livestock and the shouting of men. Great spirals of dust, sand and sawdust flew up over the roofs, clouding the early sun, as animals pounded and scuffed in their pens. On Friday afternoons came the horses, amid a barrage of bargains and bets and chinking coin and swearing of deals.[4]

By the late seventeenth century, the tangled streets east of the market – Cloth Fair, Barley Mow Passage, Cloth Court, Rising Sun Court, Half-moon Court, King Street – the site of an old textile trade, were occupied by small merchants, artisans and shopkeepers. Hogarth's father, Richard, a school-teacher and writer, had moved to Bartholomew Close about seven years before, taking lodgings with John and Anne Gibbons near the narrow passage through to Middlesex Court. This was convenient for the booksellers and printers in Duck Lane and Little Britain, and in the roads running down to Paternoster Square and St Paul's, but he may also have been drawn here because he was a Nonconformist, and the Close was home to many dissenters. The other inhabitants – 'a joiner, a tobacconist, a baker, an upholsterer, a tailor, a plasterer, a stonecutter, and a painter' – are all listed on a Nonconformist Register.[5] In Middlesex House, butting on to the church, with a window in its gallery peering directly into the nave, was a small Presbyterian meeting house. The persecution under James II, when worshippers kept look-outs and scurried through secret doors at threats of trouble, had supposedly ended with the 'Glorious Revolution' of 1688, when William and Mary took the throne, and the Toleration Act of 1689 allowed dissenters to establish meeting houses unmolested.

William III was himself a Dutch Calvinist, and his name was shared by this latest Hogarth son, born in the week of celebrations between the King's birth-day and his triumphant return from the Continent, after the Peace of Ryswick. But toleration was far from secure. Meeting houses were tempting targets in a riot and it was as well to keep in with Anglicans. William's birth was entered in the Nonconformist Register, but he was baptized in St Bartholomew the Great on 28 November 1697. The family crossed the Close into Little Britain, their baby swaddled against the autumn chill, hurried under the Tudor gateway, across the rough space where the cloisters once stood, and in through the west door, where the old stone font stood. The wooden cover, carved with tonsured monks, was heaved up on a rope. As the cold water was sprinkled on the baby's brow, the pale November light would have played on the squat, rounded arches of the apse and the tomb of St Rahere, who founded this Priory in 1123 in the swamps outside the city. Since the Reformation, like a rocky outcrop in the urban sprawl, the walls of the church

6

had become encrusted with buildings. The few remaining cloisters became stables. The south transept was a blacksmith's forge, with the anvil so close to the walls that the hammering sounded through the services and smoke blew into the choir. The Lady Chapel was first a house, and then a printer's shop, where Benjamin Franklin would work as an apprentice in the 1720s. All this was part of the eroded patchwork of history that Hogarth inherited.

Hogarth's father, Richard, was an outsider in London. When he came south from Westmorland in the late 1680s, he was an energetic young man in his mid-twenties, determined to make a living as a writer and teacher. Ten years later he was still in Smithfield, and in November 1690 he had married his landlord's eldest daughter, Anne Gibbons, aged twenty-nine, two or three years his senior. The Gibbons had nine children and although older siblings moved away Anne stayed at home, helping with the family business and caring for the younger children. This stage had now passed: the two youngest, still at home, were Mary, aged sixteen, and John, fourteen and on the verge of his apprenticeship. The Hogarths stayed in Anne's parental home, and after her father died in 1692, they lived on there with Widow Gibbons and her boarders. For the next few years Richard ran his school here, supplementing his income by working for the booksellers.

Life had proved hard. Three children were born to the Hogarths in their first four years of marriage, all dying within a few months: John, Elizabeth and Anne. Richard, born in 1695, was healthier. William looked stronger still. The family crowded into the old house, three generations living side by side. Life for such families, who were not destitute but far from rich, was simple and plain: the children might sleep separately from their parents but siblings shared a bed, closed off by heavy curtains to keep out the draughts; rough rugs and straw matting covered the floors. They washed (rarely) in basins or at a pump in the yard. Most cooking was done on an open range, or taken to the bakers' ovens, and the common diet was starchy and substantial – bread, beef, beer and cheese, and broths of peas and beans. Despite the many London markets, fresh vegetables were scorned and scurvy and rickets were common. Infants such as William were fed gruel and broth, bread and rice with milk. Illness spread easily, and the rats and mice behind the wainscoting helped to carry disease.

Bartholomew Close was no slum, but the circumstances must still have felt harsh to Richard Hogarth, who had come to the city with high hopes. At the end of his life, Hogarth remembered his father with bitter sadness. He had been born around 1663, three hundred miles to the north, the third son of a farming family in the Vale of Bampton, a fertile valley between the Ullswater fells and the northern ridges of the Pennines. (Local shepherds still meet here each autumn to reclaim the sheep separated from their flocks during summer on the heights.) Although Bampton is a small village, Westmorland was renowned for its grammar schools and the one here was famous, as was the school founded by Archbishop Grindal at St Bees, on the windy Cumberland coast. Richard might have gone to either; he had a good classical education and ran a small school before leaving the sheep-nibbled turf to make his way in London.[6]

Roads had much improved and regular coaches to the North doubled in number after the Restoration; it now took less than a week to reach the capital, but Richard still faced about a hundred hours of travelling. In summer the carts lumbered through dust clouds; in winter they jolted across flooded pot-holes and frozen ruts; overturned wagons and broken wheels were common, robberies scarcely less so. Approaching the capital, the route became increasingly crowded with carriers and market wagons, migrant workers and young apprentices, until, at last, breasting the hill at Finchley, London stretched below, wreathed in a fog of sea-coal smoke, the river curving to the south with the matchstick masts of ships riding the tide. Then the vista disappeared as the road straggled down through villages, market gardens and stable yards through the desert of rubbish dumps, encampments and brick kilns that ringed the city. Those kilns, hastily thrown up for rebuilding after the Fire, would smoke on for a century as the streets and squares rushed ever outwards, eating the lost fields.

Although London was choked and noisy, the late 1680s seemed a good time to come; Protestantism and the populace had triumphed and the times appeared full of opportunity. But this was a limited perception. True, unlike countries on the Continent, after 1688 Parliament did share power with the monarchy, but Parliament itself was almost completely composed of the landed élite. Its members intended to keep it that way, whichever party held power, whether Whig under William and Mary, or, after 1701, Tory under Anne. Entrenchment and stability were the keywords. The structures of royal authority were replaced by the convenient arrangements that the great magnates made among themselves: slowly the webs of patronage wove like iron into the dealings of government, local as well as national.

Money, however, counted now as much as land: merchants and bankers played an essential role in funding William's wars, supporting his determination to prevent French dominance in Europe. The constitutional revolution was followed by a financial one, with the founding of the Bank of England and the National Debt and the birth of the Stock Market in the 1690s. The City became ever more powerful: England was not only a nation under arms (in the Nine Years War, 1689–97, and the War of the Spanish Succession, 1702–13) but a nation living on credit. Public opinion, too, gained increasing sway after the ending of the Licensing Act in 1695 brought an explosion of satires, pamphlets, newspapers and tracts, and a whirlwind of arguments over religion, the role of the state, the rights of the individual.[7]

During the reign of William and Mary many British institutions came into being, from regular sessions of Parliament to a free press. There was a greater spirit of tolerance, a more sophisticated sense of the visual, affected by William's Dutch culture, an emphasis on 'civility' and polite 'wit', rather than Jacobean rough humour or Restoration scurrility. And unpopular though they were, William's wars brought a fervour of patriotism unsurpassed since Elizabethan days. Gradually the uneasy, shifting accord between aristocratic, City and professional interests was welded within a new social stratum, 'polite society' or 'the Town'.

This era has been splendidly described as a gateway to domestic modernity, 'a time when we learned to live peaceably in brick houses, to grow flower bulbs in pots, to dine off blue-and-white china dishes, to drink tea, chocolate and coffee, to take toast and marmalade at breakfast and to read the newspapers'.[8] But on the fringes, life was less placid and profitable. Without access to influence the ranks were closed. Compare the position of Richard Hogarth to that of two Westmorland friends who travelled south around the same time, Thomas Noble, four years his junior, from Butterwick, near Bampton, and another local youth, Edmund Gibson. Both were from well-off families; both were on their way to Oxford; both joined the Church and both flourished. Richard, by contrast, would spend his life in Smithfield, crossing and recrossing the square mile like a rat in a maze, from Bartholomew Close to St John Street, from St John's Gate to the Fleet, from the Old Bailey to Long Lane. The London road could carry one down, as well as up, the social scale. In Hogarth's *A Harlot's Progress*, in 1732, a country girl gets off the York coach, her doom foretold as an old bawd greets her. Behind her, facing the other way, a nervous, shortsighted clergyman is reading a letter of recommendation: it is addressed to Edmund Gibson, now the powerful Bishop of London.

Richard's hopes, like Gibson's and Noble's, had rested on his scholarship, but he had no university to provide networks and contacts, no private income, no aristocratic patrons. He was independent, outspoken, with a streak of dogmatism, lightened by brusque humour. All these traits

9

4 Detail from *A Harlot's Progress*, plate I (1732)

show in the book he published in May 1689, an introduction to Latin, Greek and English, *Thesaurarium Trilingue Publicum*.[9] It was aimed at children or, as his friend Thomas Noble said in an introductory letter, to correct 'the infinite mistakes that occur thro bad spelling, which is so common, even in these days, especially amongst women, and those that are more ignorant'. Richard was inventive and lively. He split words into syllables to aid spelling and used games and puns as well as rules. In short commonplaces he drove home lessons of determination, integrity and prudence: 'Wholesome precepts containing several Vertues necessary to be instilled into young people'. Wise men, he says, should find their principles and stick to them: only fools swerve between thrift and extravagance, gravity and conceit:

'A prudent Man carries all his Treasure within him; what Fortune gives she can take, therefore he so providently orders the Matter as to leave nothing to her Mercy: He stands firm, and keeps his Ground against Misfortunes without so much as changing Countenance: he will not Murmur at any thing that comes to pass by God's Appointment.'[10]

Beneath the platitudes a feeling lingers, that men must brace themselves for setbacks.

Six months later Richard published *Gazophylacium Anglicanum*, an abridgement of an English dictionary of 1671. In the preface he made it clear he was a good classicist but was deliberately avoiding Latinate words because

10

they made such books high-flown (and high-priced). But, as if embarrassed, he explained that he undertook this task 'to save my Time from being worse employed', apologized for the book's unevenness, due to it being squeezed between 'my other more necessary Business', and claimed it was printed from a 'foul copy'. A touchy pride, very like his son's, sounded in his plea that the 'discreet reader' would overlook faults without carping: 'and as for the Ignorant and Envious, I value not their Censures'.[11]

Richard was right to be on his guard, for such dictionaries and abridgements were part of the standard mix of pedantry and popularism later sneered at as typical of 'Grub Street'.[12] Not all publishers and booksellers were exploitative opportunists, but many hired writers at pitiful rates to feed the new public greedy for education and political debate, and also for scandal and sensation. Thirty years later Hogarth's friend Henry Fielding wryly conjured up the scene, by now a standard joke. In *The Author's Farce*, at the house of Mr Bookweight, we find 'Dash, Blotpage, Quibble, writing at several tables'. Dash does ghosts and murders; Blotpage does poetry and criticism; Quibble does the politics. 'I love to keep a controversy warm,' says Bookweight. 'I have had authors who have writ a pamphlet in the morning, answered it in the afternoon, and compromised the matter at night.' Others arrive, like Mr Scarecrow, with a libel against the ministry in one hand and a translation of the *Aeneid* (cribbed from Dryden) in the other, and the plight of the classicist is shown in Mr Index, who comes to present his bill:

BOOKWEIGHT: What's here? – 'For adapting the motto of *Risum teneatis amici* to a dozen pamphlets at sixpence per each, six shillings. For *Omnia vincit amor et nos cedamus amori*, sixpence. For *Difficile est satyrum non scribere*, sixpence'.* Hum, hum, hum. Ah. 'A sum total, for thirty-six Latin mottos, eighteen shillings; ditto English, seven, one shilling and ninepence; ditto Greek, four, one shilling.' – Why, friend, are your Latin mottos dearer than your Greek?

INDEX: Yes marry they are, sir. For as nobody now understands Greek, so I may use any sentence in that language to whatsoever purpose I please.[13]

Richard never quite reached these depths: the booksellers valued his scholarship, but they made use of it, and he was sliding towards becoming a hack. ('Hackney author' was another new slang term, aligning writers with

---

* The mottoes, all clichés but very apt ones, are from Horace, Virgil and Juvenal: 'Could you refrain from laughing, my friends?', 'Love conquers all, and we must yield to love' (Dryden), and 'It is hard not to write satire.'

11

'hackney drivers' of public coaches and with prostitutes or 'hackney drabs'.) Nor did Richard gain much status as a teacher. Many cheap schools sprang up in the late seventeenth century as Londoners became keen to give learning to their offspring. Conservatives were dismayed and condemned them loudly: 'too many little Parish Nurserys of the Latin Tongue,' wrote the respected teacher Lewis Maidwell, lamenting falling standards in 1705.[14] Yet the school and his writing were all Richard Hogarth had. In the year of William's birth, he was correcting Latin for a publisher, chasing more successful friends to promote his own textbooks, and wooing patrons – but none was forthcoming.[15]

Private sorrows were added to these professional struggles. Of all the Hogarths' children, only William and his sisters Mary and a second Anne (born in 1699 and 1701) would grow up to be adults. This catalogue of deaths was the shared history of many families. Even the great did not escape, but infant mortality was particularly high in areas like Smithfield. The wards that ringed the City of London were crime- and disease-ridden, looping like a poisoned necklace up from the Thames by Rag Fair east of the Tower, to Moorfields and Cripplegate in the north, then down through Clerkenwell, Smithfield and Newgate to meet the river again at Blackfriars. Dotted down the western side of this arc lay the major gaols: from the 'new Prison and New-Bridewell' of Clerkenwell to Newgate, the Fleet and Ludgate, almost touching each other, and then down to the old Bridewell in Blackfriars.

Newgate, just south of Smithfield, behind the hospital, formed part of the theatre of Hogarth's early years. It had been 'magnificently' rebuilt after the Fire: with terrible irony, the east front was decorated with figures of Justice, Fortitude and Prudence, the west front with those of Liberty, Peace, Security and Plenty. From its gate, about every six weeks, began the long procession to Tyburn, turning west into Snow Hill past St Sepulchre's. The condemned were woken in their cells at midnight, by twenty slow rings of the handbell, to hear a long exhortation on sin and repentance. In the morning, as the carts passed the church to the clang of the steeple bell, the public was beseeched: 'All good people pray heartily to God for these poor Sinners, who are now going to the Death, for whom this great Bell doth toll'. Then they rolled on, across Holborn Bridge, towards the crowds and the gibbet.

Holborn Bridge spanned the Fleet Ditch. Despite the much vaunted building works that widened it into a canal in the 1670s, bringing barges up to Holborn, the Ditch was scummy, solid and stinking, fed not only by nearby brooks, but by all the narrow gutters, or kennels, that ran down the middle of the alleys. Down it rolled a flotsam of sewage, carcases (occasionally human as well as animal) and offal chucked in by the 'tripe dressers, sausage makers and catgut spinners' of Field Lane.[16] Pushed and pulled by the rhythm of the river tides, wrinkling the scum and sucking refuse from the crumbling walls, the slime oozed to Blackfriars. A shower, as Swift famously described, could turn its sluggish stream into a torrent:

> Sweepings from Butchers' Stalls, Dung, Guts and Blood,
> Drown'd Puppies, stinking Sprats, all drench'd in Mud,
> Dead Cats and Turnip-Tops come tumbling down the Flood.[17]

Smithfield was not all dung, guts and blood. For two weeks every August, the market exploded with festivity. 'Shews of all sort gave me uncommon pleasure when an Infant and mimickry common to all children was remarkable in me,' wrote Hogarth.[18] The streets of London were full of fortune-telling booths, performing animals, jugglers and puppet plays; every passer-by was drawn into the audience. But the greatest of all the shows of London was Smithfield's Bartholomew Fair.

In the dog-days of summer the market place flowed with people, rich and poor. The melting, sweating, human tide was swept this way and that, wreathed in the smell of roast pigs and burnt crackling, old clothes and foul breath, tobacco, coffee and ale, its ears assaulted 'with the rumbling of Drums, mix'd with the Intolerable Squeakings of *Cat-calls*, and *Penny Trumpets*, made still more terrible with the shrill belches of *Lottery-Pick-Pockets*, thro' Instruments of the same Metal with their Faces'.[19] The cries of nut-sellers and fruit-vendors fought with those of showmen whipping up an audience for waxworks, rope-dancing and music booths, conjuring tricks, acrobats and drolls. Once inside the booths, the impatient fairgoers, sitting on rickety benches or at trestle tables, crunched walnuts and damsons, handed round baskets of plums, pears and peaches, flirted and joked and heckled with cries of 'Show, Show, Show, Show!' until the players arrived.

Bartholomew Fair was a byword for immorality and in 1697 the Lord Mayor had published an ordinance against 'obscene, lascivious and scandalous plays, comedies and farces, unlawful games and interludes, drunkenness etc'.[20] But the shows were soon back. Actors from the Haymarket and Drury Lane joined the strolling players, closing down the smart theatres for the weeks of the Fair. The choice of play, like the crush, was overwhelming, as the French tourist Sorbière noted in 1698. When he came out of the rope-dancing (which he found admirable), he says,

'I met a man that would have took off my Hat, but I secur'd it and was going to draw my Sword, crying out "Begar! Damn'd Rogue! Morbleu!" &c., When on a sudden I had a hundred people around me, crying "Here, Monsieur, see *Jepthah's Rash Vow*"; "Here, Monsieur, see *The Tall Dutchwoman*", "See *The Tiger*", says another; "See *The Horse and No Horse* whose Tail stands where his head should do"; "See *The German Artist*, Monsieur"; "See *The Siege of Namur*, Monsieur": so that betwixt Rudeness and Civility, I was forc'd to get into a Fiacre, and with an air of haste and a full trot, got home to my lodgings.'[21]

Other fairgoers lingered, not always at the plays. In the cloisters of the hospital gamblers bent over the tables in upstairs rooms, while below, in the colonnades, prostitutes and punters haggled, whispered and joked. According to Ned Ward, the tavern-keeper and hack writer who drew this sweating bustle so memorably in *The London Spy*, the women gave as good as they got. A man famed as a wonderful 'Similizer', says Ward,

'steps up to a very pert lady. who, as I suppoze was not for his Turn, and claps his bare Hand in her neck: *Dear Madam*, says he, *You are as Cold as a Cricket in an Ice-House*: She turning short about look'd upon him, and reply'd, "*If you please to clap your Fiery-face to my Back-side, 'twill be the ready way to warm me*": At which smart return, all that heard it fell a Laughing.'[22]

Laughter and humiliation, illusion and reality merged in the flesh. Bearded women, Siamese twins, giants and dwarfs, 'monsters' and freaks mingled with the costumed devils and heroes of the plays, the attenuated moral emblems of medieval religious drama. The old play of *The Creation of the World* came complete with Noah's Ark, flying Angels, Dives rising out of Hell, and – in 1702 – 'with the addition of the Glorious Battle obtained over the French and Spaniards by the Duke of Marlborough'. The Fair was present and past, dream, desire and trickery, its pickpockets cunning as its conjurors, its audiences dupes to both. It could itself become the stuff of a morality play: in Hogarth's *Taste of the Town*, the name of Conjuror Fawkes – a famous Bartholomew Fair figure – hangs over the door as the people troop into the masquerade. The sign, claiming 'Faux – Dexterity of hand', glances at the 'dexterity' of Robert Walpole and the chicanery of politics and politeness. The Fair, as much as the schoolroom, gave Hogarth his emblems and his themes.

Many of the shows – however amateur and chaotic – depended on the visual for their effect. Painting, scenery, pictures and costume combined, at least in the hope of the showmen, to make audiences surrender to the drama. One of the most famous hits of Hogarth's childhood was Elkanah Settle's ambitious droll *The Siege of Troy*, acted at the Fair in 1707, when he was ten. It was repeated in later seasons, pirated by the puppet shows, and staged again at Southwark Fair in 1715 and 1716. In the centre of *Southwark Fair* (1734) – in which everything, not only Troy is on the brink of 'falling' – Hogarth shows the sign of the Wooden Horse, its belly open, its ladders at the ready.

5 Detail from *Southwark Fair* (1734)

Hogarth's prints often have the same exuberant mingling of the popular and the mythic, the gross and the visionary that characterized these Bartholomew spectaculars. 'Enter *Mob* drunk,' runs one of Settle's notes,

15

followed by a scene where the cobbler's wife soothes her drunken husband, who staggers home bawling out a catch. This takes place not in a London street, but before the walls of Troy, and those walls were a miracle of the scene-painter's art, 'consisting of ten Pieces of uniform Painting', which will shortly collapse in flames – as London had. This is the stage direction:

'. . . the Soldiers run up and down the Streets, seemingly setting the Town on Fire, whilst near forty Windows or Portholes in the several Paintings all appear on Fire, the Flames catching from House to House, and all perform'd by Illuminations and Transparent Paintings seen scattered through the Scenes.'[23]

These backdrops, which must have thrilled a ten-year-old, and the play as a whole became reference points in the long-running argument about 'high' and 'low' art. Settle (the last official City laureate) also organized the great procession for the Lord Mayor's Show in mid-November with its chariots and pagan deities, saints and satyrs, and in 1728 Pope made him into one of the most important figures in his *Dunciad*, master of the tawdry and the grandiose. Two years earlier, in 1726, in one of those cross-linking moments typical of the close, dense, argumentative London culture, the playwright and poet John Gay wrote jokingly to the Countess of Burlington of how he and William Kent (largely responsible, under Burlington's patronage, for popularizing the Palladian style) had spent a Friday night at Bartholomew Fair watching *The Siege of Troy* 'and thought ourselves very happy'.

'I think the Poet corrected Virgil with great judgement in the Poetical justice which he observ'd; for Paris was kill'd upon the spot by Menelaus, and Helen burnt in the flames of the town before the Audience. The Trojan Horse was large [as] life and extreamly well painted; the sight of which struck Kent with such astonishment, that he prevaild with me to go with him the next day to compare it with the celebrated paintings at Greenwich. Kent did not care to reflect upon a Brother of the Pencil; but if I can make any judgment from hums, & hahs, and little hints, he seem'd to give the preference to Bartholomew Fair.'[24]

Gay's glee comes from an in-joke: the famous Painted Hall at Greenwich represented twenty years' work on the part of Kent's older rival, the history painter Sir James Thornhill – whom the guide had insisted on calling 'Cornhill'. This guide or 'show-man' so garbled the pictures' allegories that *they* turned into a Bartholomew droll: "Tis proof that a fine puppet-show may be spoild and depreciated by an ignorant interpreter.' Some high art, Gay implies, could be thoroughly low.

16

Sir James Thornhill, the Greenwich paintings and the Pope–Burlington–Kent view of art would later play their part in the life of Hogarth, now a small, stocky figure, weaving his way through the Smithfield mob. And the mob itself would be one of his great subjects. In the atmosphere of the Fair, where the normal becomes transformed by art, the stage a world and the world a stage, the crowd is part of the drama. When Hogarth depicts shows, he often seems as intrigued by the spectators as by the action, whether it be the ranked audience of *The Beggar's Opera* or the *Sleeping Congregation* in church, the aristocratic family watching their children act *The Indian Emperor* or the crowds in *Industry and Idleness*, their mouths equally agape at a Tyburn execution or at a Lord Mayor's procession. It is as if, working in a visual – as in a dramatic – medium, nothing truly exists unless it is shown as *being* seen. Even in intimate interiors, couples are watched, and implicitly commented upon, by the portraits on their walls, which are themselves gazed on in their turn. 'Reading' these prints, we set our reactions against those we see: through the audiences within them, which reach out to include ourselves, Hogarth's narratives force their implications far beyond the pictures' frames.

At the Fair the crowd was a kaleidoscopic jumble of rank, age and occupation and commentators were often fascinated by the way this confused variety was mysteriously welded into a 'public'. Feeling the urge to impose at least *some* sort of order, Ned Ward's narrator, a countryman being shown round by an old schoolfellow, turns individuals into types, immediately making them ripe for satire:

'Some companies were so very oddly mix'd, that there was no manner of coherence between the Figure of any One Person and another: One perhaps should appear in a Lac'd-Hat, Red-Stockings, Puff-Wig, and the like, as Prim as if going to the Dancing-School. The next a Butcher, with his Blue-Sleeves and Woollen Apron, as if just come from the Slaughter-House. A Third, a Fellow in his Yorkshire Cloth-Coat, with a Leg laid over his Oaken Cudgel, the Head of which being a Knot of the same Stuff, as Serviceable as a Protestant Flail, and as big as a Hackney Turnip. Another in a Soldiers Habit, and look'd as Peery as if he thought every fresh Man that came in a Constable. These mixed with women of as different appearances: one with a straw hat and Blue-Apron, with Impudence enough in her face to dash a Begging Clergyman out of Countenance . . . Another Dress'd up in Hood, Scarf and Top-Knot, with her cloaths hung on according to the Drury-lane mode, as if she could shake 'em off and leap into Bed, in the Twinkling of a Bed-Staff. A third, in a white Sarsnet-Hood, and a Posie in

17

her Bosom, as if she was come from the Funeral of some good Neighbour that Died in Child-Bed; and amongst the rest, a Girl of about a Dozen Years of Age . . .'[25]

6 *The Laughing Audience* (1733)

This is just like a Hogarth crowd, a mass made up of individuals. And often, in his crowd scenes, there are children – quarrelling over dolls, playing in the corners of prison cells, sleeping under booths in the streets. They inhabit his portraits too, at once innocents moulded by their elders, and figures of anarchic energy, questioning and disturbing.[26] A ragged boy plays with fire, a merchant's daughter overturns the holy water at a baptism, even

18

aristocratic boys leap and play while their elders stare calmly out at us, seated in solemn politeness.

The Hogarth children grew up in the shadow of the Hospital, the din of the market, the troubling exhilaration of the Fair. In 1701, when William was four and his elder brother Richard six, they moved from Bartholomew Close across Smithfield to a house at the end of St John Street, which runs into the market from the north. Soon they moved again, just round the corner to St John's Gate, the old gatehouse of the Knights of St John of Jerusalem. This was their home for the next seven or eight years. From here they looked north into a spacious square, a respectable oasis between Smithfield and the narrow, crooked lanes of Clerkenwell, the thriving suburb which

7 Detail from *Hudibras's First Adventure* (1726)

19

had grown up since the fire, home of clock- and watchmakers, and of Hockley-in-the-Hole with its bear garden and bare-knuckled boxers. In 1709 the Hockley proprietor, Christopher Preston, fell into the ring with his bears and was killed, but the shows went on – and six years later, for 2s 6d, you could see a contest between wrestling women, or between a dog and a man, or a combined show of bull- and bear-baiting.[27] One of Hogarth's plates of *Hudibras* shows a huge, forlorn bear, with his great head pulled down by the chain in his nose, bleared eyes and splayed hindlegs. His squashed-nosed keeper leans back into the cudgel-bearing crowd, but the sad bear speaks of man's hubristic urge to control nature, and of the cruelty that can go with 'entertainment'.

By the time William was seven, he had a 'show', of a more civilized kind, in his own house. By January 1704 Richard Hogarth had started a new venture, indicated by an advertisement in the *Post-Man*, a newspaper circulated round the coffee houses:

'At *Hogarth's* Coffee House in St John's Gate, the mid-way between Smithfield Bars and Clerkenwel, there will meet daily some learned gentlemen, who speak Latin readily, where any Gentleman that is either skilled in that Language, or desirous to perfect himself in speaking thereof will be welcome. The Master of the House, in the absence of others, being always ready to entertain Gentlemen in the Latin Tongue.'[28]

'In the absence of others' sounds ominous, but the idea was not as bizarre as it appears: beneath the guise of learned gentleman conversing in a long-dead language, Richard was actually offering oral Latin lessons to adults. The general term 'daily' was soon changed to every day at four o'clock, a definite time which left Richard free to teach in local schools. His coffee-house pupils would be the same kind of people he had addressed his early books to, aspiring young lawyers, doctors, clerks and merchants who wished to toss off a Latin phrase to show their cultured status, and develop correct styles of formal speaking and writing. The ideals of the seventeenth-century Latinists, who wanted to make this a universal tongue, still persisted in English schools, and the coffee houses that had opened in almost every street of London towards the end of the previous century often had strong educational, and Puritan, overtones. Defining the 'character' of one coffee house, a contemporary pamphlet described a babble of voices pronouncing on theology and Euclid, denouncing theatres, balls and masques, quoting classics and moderns, arguing about everything from science to taxes:

A third's for a Lecture, a fourth a Conjecture,
A fifth for a Penny in the Pound.

Other men discuss news or philosophy:

'Pedantry is rife and even the 'prentice boy "*doth call for his coffee in Latin*", and learned quotations, apt or otherwise, trip off the tongue so freely that "'twould make a poor Vicar to tremble".'[29]

(Ned Ward's view of coffee-house customers was less solemn: 'Some going, some coming, some scribbling, some talking, some drinking, others jangling, and the whole room stinking of tobacco like a Dutch barge or a boatswain's cabin'.)[30]

Coffee houses, originating in Venice, had spread to England from Europe in the mid-seventeenth century and flourished during the Commonwealth as sober alternatives to taverns, where all could enter for a penny fee. Inside, rank was laid aside:

Now being enter'd, there's no needing
Of complements or gentile breeding,
     For you may sit you any where
There's no respect of persons there.[31]

These egalitarian sentiments were suspect once the monarchy was restored, but Charles II's attempt to close down the coffee houses in 1675 failed in the face of public protest, revealing how powerful they already were in the culture of town and city. By 1700 many had a particular clientele, ranging from famous establishments like Will's, where Dryden sat in his special chair among the 'Wits', to Child's in St Paul's churchyard, where doctors and clergymen gathered, or Jonathan's in Exchange Alley, where dealers in stocks and shares set up shop to show their independence of the Royal Exchange. With their mix of philosophy, politics, speculation and intrigue, they were perfect places to find out what was going on; in the first issue of Addison's new journal in March 1711 his Mr Spectator declares, to show his knowledge of the town,

'Sometimes I am seen thrusting my Head into a Round of Politicians at *Will's*, and listening with great Attention to the Narratives that are made in those little Circular Audiences. Sometimes I smoak a pipe at *Child's*; and whilst I seem attentive to nothing but the Post-Man, overhear the Conversation of every Table in the Room.'[32]

They were also centres for post (to the annoyance of the government): Swift picked up Stella's letters at the St James', telling her how he longed to see 'her little hand-writing in the glass frame at the bar of St. James's Coffee-house'.[33]

Although most coffee houses were simple places, in back alleys or over shops, they still acted as a centres for the men (not for the women) of the local community. Richard's advertisement had announced that a 'Society of Trades' would meet every Monday night 'in the Great Room over the Gateway, for promoting their respective Trades'. Prints show the coffee being brewed in a great pot behind a rough bar, while boys run between the trestle tables with coffee pots, cups, and glasses. A child in the background, or helping out, would see a wide range of people and hear the news: gossip about the Queen's devotion to the Duchess of Marlborough, exultation at the capture of Gibraltar in 1704, dismay at British defeat at Almazar or disputes over the Act of Union with Scotland in 1707. And spread about the tables or hung on racks or pinned to the wall would be papers and broadsheets – replete with woodcuts and rich, mixed, satirical prints.

Richard Hogarth, however, wanted his establishment to have a learned, literary tone. In June 1707, the *Daily Courant* ran another notice, on behalf of a 'Mr George Daggastaff', asking,

'Any gentleman or Lady that is desirous of having any Short Poem, Epigram, Satyre &c if they please to communicate the Subjects to the Authors of the Diverting Muse, or the Universal Medley, now in the Press and will be continued Monthly, or if they have any Song or Poem of their own that is New and Entertaining,'

to leave them at Mr Hogarth's Coffee House.[34] That particular Smithfield muse vanished without trace. Perhaps, like other schemes of Richard's, it was a good idea that never quite got off the ground. But thirty years later the room where the Trades Society met was the site of Edward Cave's presses for *The Gentleman's Magazine*. Here, in 1737, the young Samuel Johnson worked, so poor that he signed his letters '*impransus*' – 'supperless'. This district linked Smithfield to Cripplegate, the ward that contained the original Grub Street and, by the 1730s, Grub Street (in its metaphorical sense) ran down to St John's: Charles Ackers the printer worked in St John's Close, Dr Thomas Birch lived in St John Street; the dissolute Richard Savage, imprisoned for murder in Newgate in 1727 before a controversial acquittal, haunted the Cross Keys Inn opposite the Gate.

*

22

As Richard Hogarth struggled to make a living, more children were born: Anne in 1701, Thomas in 1703, Edmund in 1705. But that last year also brought the death of the eldest son, Richard, at the age of ten. He was buried in the churchyard of St James, just north of St John's Gate, on 17 December 1705. William was now eight, old enough to feel the loss: in those days children were not kept away when sickness struck. Rooms were darkened, parents wept, and local women came in to lay out small bodies. Bereft of his older brother, he had to adjust to a new role as the eldest child, with his sisters Mary and Anne, aged six and four, and the two-year-old Thomas and infant Edmund.

The wider family was still close by. From the coffee house he could cross the square to his grandmother, who had moved, with his aunt Mary and her husband Timothy Helmesley, across the lane into the parish of St Bartholomew the Less, the little church within the hospital walls. There he could see his cousins, Richard Helmesley, about his own age, little John, aged four in 1707, and soon new additions, Timothy and Frances, born in 1708 and 1710. This family too had suffered, and both these babies were named after older children who had died. Other Gibbons relations, like his uncles John and William, also lived near by. If he wanted to go further he could cross the City to London Bridge with its leaning houses, where felons' heads still mouldered on poles for all the world to see. Near by, Edmund Hogarth, Richard's brother, lived. This uncle, a prosperous victualler, seems to have had little fondness for his brother's family – he cut them out of his will in 1719, leaving Anne Hogarth 'one Shilling if lawfully demanded & nothing else of mine'.[35]

A web of kinship was superimposed on the grid of streets and lanes, steeples and taverns and shops. The streets, it appears, held more attractions than the schoolroom. Hogarth's education remains a puzzle: in later life, in the company of more accomplished scholars, he was mocked for lack of learning, but he had a natural speed of thought and an ability to make quick, witty connections: his prints are full of classical mottoes and tags, biblical and historical allusions. Later, he could certainly read French.[36] And his early reading inevitably included the great popular works, spiritual and satiric, such as Bunyan's *Pilgrim's Progress* and Butler's *Hudibras*.

Although Hogarth himself wrote that he 'learnt to draw the letters of the alphabet with great correctness', he put the stress on the drawing, not the letters. Artists create their own myths, but it rings true when he says that he filled the margins of his copy books with doodles, and that his school writings were 'more remarkable for the ornaments which adorned them than for the Exercise itself'. He never suggested that his schooling was harsh and narrow

23

or that he was beaten for this scribbling; the ornaments could indeed have been part of the lessons. His father was an original spirit and it has been suggested that Hogarth might have been taught on the lines recommended by the influential seventeenth-century teacher Jan Comenius, who believed, like Richard Hogarth, in teaching Latin and the vernacular at the same time, and also in using pictures to impress ideas.[37] Image and caption, design and idea, always work together in Hogarth's prints. But in his childhood the pictures won. Blockheads with better memories could beat him in lessons, he said, but he took pride in having 'naturally a good eye', and after 'an early access to a neighbouring Painter drew my attention from play', he remembered, 'evry opportunity was employd in attempt at drawing'.[38]

When he looked back, Hogarth claimed it was not books that taught him, but the people whom he watched, drew and imitated: 'mimickry common to all children was remarkable in me'. But the streets of Smithfield could be threatening as well as diverting. Prejudice and panic ran like the sewage and blood in the open gutters. In 1709, around William's twelfth birthday, the renegade High Church Tory Dr Henry Sacheverell was asked to preach the annual sermon in St Paul's commemorating both the Gunpowder Plot and the landing of William of Orange. In violent, incoherent language he rounded on the 'enemies' of the church, from Catholics and Dissenters ('a confederacy in iniquity') to the Whig government itself. When he was impeached for 'scurrilous and seditious sermons' mobs of supporters followed his carriage armed with crowbars and staves. Five thousand strong, they tore through the streets, burning and ravaging Dissenting meeting houses.[39] That November, and for several years after, the old processions in defence of the established Church of England, a 'Solemn Mock Procession of Pope and Devil' threaded through the city, as they had after the Popish Plot a generation before, with their leering monks, demon masks and burning effigies.[40] In the following elections, riots spread across the country: when four Tory candidates won in the City of London, the crowds broke every window that was not illuminated for their victory.

This High Church Tory blaze was fuelled by pamphlets and prints. London engravers rushed to produce portraits of Sacheverell, icon or target, depending which side one took. Portraits were stuck on walls and revered; others were stuck inside chamber pots and pissed upon. With them came a blast of satirical prints and, although most of these supported Sacheverell, even High Tories quailed at their power. One author went so far as to blame these democratic 'Dutch talismans' for demolishing the magic status of kings such as Louis XIV and Charles II:

Swifter than heretofore the Print effac'd
The pomp of mightiest Monarchs, and dethron'd
The dread idea of royal majesty;
Dwindling the prince below the pigmy size
Witness the once great Louis in youthful pride,
And Charles of happy days, who both confess'd
The magic power of mezzotinto shade . . .[41]

The public will was canvassed through the prints, as it was through ballads, or traditional street theatre.

By the time of the Sacheverell riots Hogarth's life had already been changed by private disaster. When he was ten his family's whole pattern of living collapsed: his father fell into debt. His brother Edmund did not rescue him, and the Gibbons and Helmesley families, suffering their own misfortunes, could not help. For the next four years Richard was confined within the 'Rules' of the Fleet prison, the designated area around the debtors' gaol, with no way to pay his way out. Since credit was a way of life, debt was one of the greatest causes of misery in the early eighteenth century. In 1716, wrote one critic, ''Tis reckoned there are about 60,000 miserable debtors perishing in the prisons of England and Wales.'[42] He exaggerated but, even so, the London prisons were overflowing with debtors, often imprisoned for quite small sums, living in terrible conditions. In the Marshalsea in 1719 a Parliamentary Committee found that three hundred people had died, many of starvation, within three months. Bailiffs acted as middlemen, preying on the indigent, and the original debts grew rapidly, swelled by fees owed to warders and lawyers. The result could be horrifying: with the wage-earner in gaol many families were left destitute and homeless.

The Fleet was the principal prison for debtors in London, a vast place, enclosed by walls the height of three men, surmounted by palisades. New prisoners were crammed into rooms in the 'common side', sleeping on the floor, or even in hammocks tied to the walls, with no sanitation, no fresh air. At every stage, more and more money was extorted from those who had none. When prisoners first arrived, they had to pay for their irons, the chains on their wrists and ankles, to be taken off, and then give fees to the chaplain and gaolers. To get a room of their own, they had to pay again. To leave the prison and live in the cheap lodging houses or inns of the Rules cost five guineas.[43]

By January 1709 Richard Hogarth had paid that fee. He and his family were living in Black and White Court, Old Bailey, next door to the Ship Inn, a few

25

doors from Ludgate Hill. At the same time his brother-in-law, Anne's younger brother, William Gibbons, was confined to Newgate, and his family added to the common burden. To keep them from starvation, the stalwart Anne Hogarth (the silent figure in the background of this story) sold home medicines, while William probably found casual labour. Technically, debtors could not earn until their debts were discharged, but many did. Richard still seems to have taught, as the Old Bailey is where early commentators on Hogarth usually place him as a schoolmaster. He certainly continued with his writing. But he was still a prisoner within the Rules. If he walked down to Ludgate Hill, or up to Fleet Lane, west to the Ditch or east to Cock Lane, he would be arrested again.

The effects of poverty were intensified by the cruel winter of 1709, when many people starved. That of 1710 was little better: Swift told Stella how it snowed all night and was 'vengeance cold', the frost was hard and even the largest fire could not warm them: 'it is very ugly walking; a baker's boy broke his thigh yesterday'.[44] The harsh winters were followed by fiery summers, where Londoners lay without sheets, swam in the river and longed for rain. Illness was everywhere. The words of Anne Hogarth's advertisement for her gripe ointment – 'in the very moment of Application, Cures the GRIPES in Young Children and prevents FITS, one half Crown Pot whereof will bring up a Child past all danger from either' – seem very poignant when we realize that during this time William's two small brothers, Thomas and Edmund, both died.[45] Anne might be stirring her medicines in the same room where her sons gasped for breath.

Richard grew desperate. He saw his plight as representative: at the same time, the country was saddled with a huge National Debt. With manic assurance, as if his self-importance rose while his fortunes sank, in 1710 he sent proposals for increasing the royal revenue to Robert Harley, made Chancellor of the Exchequer that August. Then, in September, he sent Harley a strange, disturbed plea, in effusive Latin. If he could, he said, he would run to Harley through the window, but he cannot, and begs for pity. He hears that others are showing his proposals to solve the debt to people near the Queen, claiming them for their own, but he doubts that anyone will take these 'ignorant butchers and cobblers' seriously: he himself avoids them because they are enemies of the monarch and Harley. Then he turns to his own worth, his 'trustworthiness, diligence, talent and soundness of thought' (which will be guaranteed, he says, by senior clergymen) and to his talent for exploring difficult matters: 'but now I am jailed by perverse misfortune, and my soul wastes away under the weight of twenty-two children, those born to me and

26

those entrusted to me, and still living'. He has no prospect of help. 'Alas,' he cries, 'pity me!'[46]

Those twenty-two children do suggest he was running a school. But his major project, at the mention of which his prose burns with enthusiasm, is 'a most splendid dictionary'. This, says Richard, is compiled from those existing, but fuller than any of them, with lists of Roman antiquities, 'a general phraseology', and other additions.[47] Harley was a known scholar, a collector of antiquarian books and manuscripts (and a close friend of Swift, who was dining with him regularly in October 1710). Surely he would understand? While Richard is struggling on this *magnum opus*, he is nearly perishing. 'I therefore supplicatingly implore your aid.'

The great dictionary was never published. It remained in manuscript, in the possession of the family, and has since disappeared. John Nichols described it as a thick quarto, with bound-in editions of Littleton's dictionary of 1673 and Robertson's Latin phrase book of 1681, annotated with numerous corrections, followed by four hundred pages of manuscript in Richard's hand.[48] Possibly no bookseller was willing to take it. Instead, Richard fell back on school texts: a small grammar book with English and Latin dialogues in 1711 and another book of dialogues two years later. Even here he had to cut his cloth to suit circumstance: the publisher of the first book was a Jacobite, and Richard's index scrupulously lauds Stuart achievements while 'omitting regicides and dissenters'; the second was a Nonconformist, and no such tactics were required.[49]

By 1713, though, Richard Hogarth was free. A petition from insolvent debtors in the Fleet had been placed before Parliament in January 1711, soon supported by pleas from prisons nationwide. By May 1712, the Relief of Insolvent Debtors Bill had passed through Parliament. The Act affected all those who had been in prison since November 1711, obliging creditors claiming debts of under £50 to accept whatever restitution the debtor could make. Debtors had to appear in court and swear an inventory of their estate and income and list of debts owed: notice was published in the *Gazette* for creditors to come forward. Richard Hogarth appeared at the Quarter Sessions on 9 September 1712, taking his family out of the Fleet to live in Long Lane: five days later his brother-in-law William Gibbons was released from Ludgate.[50]

There was something undeniably obsessional about Richard's pleas to Harley from the Fleet, and his fierce devotion to his dictionary. Six years later he died. Hogarth later blamed his death on illness brought on by the usage he had received from grasping booksellers and by 'disappointments from great

27

mens Promises'. He stated baldly that his father's sufferings affected the course of his own life, in making him fight the printsellers' monopoly. And, in the ungrammatical rush of his notes, he suggests that he too might have been drawn to academic pursuits, but turned away, to drawing, because:

'I had before my Eyes the precarious State of authors and men of learning. I saw not only the difficulties my father went through whos dependance was cheifly on his Pen, the cruel treatment he met with from Bookseller and Printers particularly in the affairs of a lattin Dictionary the compiling had been work of some years, which being deposited in confidence the hands of a certain printer, during the time approbation letters on the specimen where obtained from all the great schools in England Scotland and Ireland, [who were] in short pleased.'[51]

Several of these correspondents were, William wrote, 'of the first class'.

By the time Pope wrote of Smithfield muses, the very name threw up a sweat of associations: the muck and clamour of the market, the clustering immigrants, the angry dissenters, the quarrelling, whinging, self-important writers, the farces of the Fair, the misery within the great Hospital, whose colonnades sheltered gamblers, whores and pickpockets. In *The Dunciad* in 1728 Pope turned the Grub Street writers into a mythic force of scurrilous bustle, quarrelling, pedantry and populism. Their varied output – from the Latin dictionaries to the lives of murderers and the obsequious odes – all indicated a culture that had plummeted into a mercenary, self-important skirmish in the mud. Their squalid surroundings merely mirrored their wretched work. But things are different seen from the inside. When Johnson wrote his *London*, in 1737, he wrote from experience, with feeling: 'Slow rises worth, by Poverty depressed.' This was Richard Hogarth's story, a generation earlier. Hard work, fading hopes, greedy booksellers and family hardship wore him down.

While the Tory satirists fostered the image of Grub Street writers as cultural criminals, Hogarth's pictures and Fielding's plays showed them as foolish victims. In the same year as Johnson's poem, in *The Distressed Poet* Hogarth created an enduring image of the benighted writer. His picture was based on details from *The Dunciad* and *The Grub-Street Journal*, and on an earlier print of a poet surrounded by children, dunned by his creditors.[52] Hogarth's writer is scratching his dark hair under his awkward wig, hunting for ideas to fit his subject – 'Poverty'. The cupboard on the wall is bare and a dog is stealing the family chop, left carelessly on a chair. The poet is wearing a shabby dressing-gown while his wife mends his only pair of hose, stopping

28

8 *The Distressed Poet* (1737; 1740 revision)

to look up, startled, at the milkmaid who bursts through the door asking for her money. Lost in his task, the poet takes no notice. Crumpled pages litter the floor by his feet, and in the bed behind him, tucked under the sloping angle of the window, a child rubs its eyes. On a small shelf above the infant stands a pile of books, and above them hangs a print.

In the original painting this tiny picture within a picture showed Alexander Pope, caricatured as an ape; in the second state of the print Pope is a righteous figure, attacking the bookseller Curll. In a third version, of 1740, the little engraving changed completely, to a symbol of fantasy, *The Gold Mines of Peru* and the poem ironically became 'Riches'. Were these revisions a softening of the bitterness against those who attacked Grub Street, an acceptance that the booksellers were the real villains, but also that the dreaming writer brought his

29

own distress? Striving for success, Hogarth made his own compromises with the polite world and its influential figures.

As a youth Hogarth turned his back on Smithfield, and looked west. He returned to work here briefly, to see his family, to catch the shows of the Fair. He came back, too, to decorate the walls of St Bartholomew's Hospital with history-paintings, and to serve on its Board of Governors. His early years pitted strictness and intellectual and domestic discipline against the turmoil and the drama of the district. His art was born, as he was, in this hinterland between the City and the Town, between trade and culture. The energy of these streets, as well as their harshness, infused his pictures and gave them lasting life.

2

Mapping the Town

Be sure observe the Signs, for Signs remain,
Like faithful Landmarks to the walking Train.
Seek not from Prentices to learn the Way,
Those fabling Boys will turn thy Steps astray.
JOHN GAY, *Trivia* (1716)

'HIS FATHER'S PEN', Hogarth wrote at the end of his life, in a terse third person, 'like that of many other authors was incapable of more than putting him in a way to shift for himself' and so 'he serv'd a prentiship to a silver plate engraver'.[1] At sixteen, with the family fortunes partly restored, Hogarth began to look after his own interests. In February 1714 he was bound as apprentice to Ellis Gamble, engraver, who kept a shop under the sign of the 'Golden Angel' in Blue Cross Street, near Leicester Fields. He would work for Gamble for nearly five years out of the formal seven-year term, before setting up on his own.

The opening came through family connections, since his aunt Sarah (wife of his uncle Edmund) was related to his new master.[2] The son of a Plymouth engraver, Gamble was in his late twenties. The year before, he had bought his freedom to trade, not as a member of the Goldsmiths' Company but of the more prestigious Merchant Taylors' Company. He had already taken on one apprentice, the son of a London waterman, charging a premium of £30, about the standard sum, but in Hogarth's case he waived the fee, perhaps sweetened by the family links.

Goldsmiths and silversmiths had once also been bankers to the rich, but the growth of the new banking sector thrust them back into being straight-forward craftsmen – still a lucrative business. The old City links stayed strong (Hogarth's indenture was sworn in the Merchant Taylors' great hall in Threadneedle Street and recorded in the guild book), but the market, and the craft, were changing. Shopping and style, and all that went with it, dictated Hogarth's new life.

The London and the landed rich spent fortunes on damask and rosewood,

31

Turkish carpets and French furniture, and for their Mediterranean fruits and China tea, they bought silver plate. It was sensible for a young man like Hogarth to apprentice himself to a luxury trade. Sometimes there were elaborate commissions, trays, salvers or jewellery, while the vogue for tea and coffee drinking led to extravagant purchases, such as the engraved silver coffee pot delivered a few years earlier to the young Duke of Bedford by the Huguenot goldsmith David Willaume.[3]

Monsieur Gillhomme's bill
Livre par D. Willaume, Orfèvre
27 avril, 1707

	£.	s.	d.
Un pot à thé	14	19	7
Façon	4	2	6
Gravure		7	6

Huguenot immigrants like Willaume, or Paul de Lamerie, with whom Gamble later collaborated, were enormously influential. Under their sway the solid shapes and heavy old embossing gave way to the cleaner lines and delicate engraving of the 'Queen Anne' style, and then to the ovals and scrolls, swags and masks, of early Georgian design. In the early decades of the century, as families such as the Bedfords acquired more and more silver pots, silver tea tables and tea kettles with stands and lamps, the bills mounted up.

In Willaume's bill, engraving is a mere fraction of the cost. Normally the goldsmith cast the plate and added any embossed ornaments, while the silversmith (commissioned by the goldsmith) merely undertook the engraved decoration. Sometimes the engraver was an outworker for the silversmith who kept the shop, and sometimes, as with Ellis Gamble, shop and workshop were combined. Soho and St Martin's Lane were areas of artisans, craftsmen and retailers, forming an axis between the new and the old cities. Many of them were foreign; by 1711 there were six hundred French householders in Soho, plus their children and servants, and over three thousand 'Lodgers who are chiefly French'.[4] They worked in luxury goods, jewellery and watch-making, wig-making and glove-making, gilding and framing. A century later Augustus Sala still remembered the area, before Victorian redevelopment, as full of silversmiths' shops, such as 'Hamlet's' (in Cranbourn Street, where Gamble moved in the 1720s), a 'long, low shop whose windows seemed to have no end, and not to have been dusted for centuries', with 'dim vistas of dish-covers, coffee biggins, and centre-pieces'.[5]

*

As he learned his trade, Hogarth also explored his city. When he walked west to Gamble's workshop from visits to his family in Long Lane, he could take different routes, weaving the mile and a half from Smithfield to Blue Cross Street. He could cross the Fleet Ditch at the bottom of Ludgate Hill, then head along Fleet Street with its printers and toy shops – not the children's shops of today, but gilded emporia selling elaborate clockwork fantasies and catering for other diversions of the rich, providing dice and dominoes, masks and disguises or acting as intermediaries for assignations and affairs. From there he might turn down the Strand, the great shopping street of the day, dotted with coffee houses. On the river side, the foundations of old Tudor palaces and their gardens running down to the Thames now lay buried beneath strings of houses; opposite, narrow streets wound up to Covent Garden.

In the previous generation Covent Garden was a fashionable area, developed during the reign of Charles I by Francis Russell, Earl of Bedford, on the land behind his house on the Strand. By now the long rectangle of Inigo Jones's Piazza, with its elegant Tuscan church of St Paul's and tall sundial topped with a golden ball, was declining in status. The square had long been leased to market traders, whose stalls formed a new rectangle in the centre, their wooden structures with leaning roofs and arched fronts piled round about with willow baskets, handcarts and trestle tables. Country folk arrived as early as two or three in the morning, and in the centre was a special ring called 'Primrose Hill' where the 'simplers' arranged their herbs and dandelions and nettles for infusions. As the early sun slanted over the high houses, servants waking and stretching looked down from high dormer windows on to clusters of flower-, fruit- and vegetable-sellers in wide straw hats and hessian aprons, mingling with the rakes lolling home after a night in the bagnios and gaming dens of Drury Lane and Long Acre.

The Italianate colonnades of the Piazza were home to bawds and actors' booths and puppet shows. Here, at the 'Seven Stars', stood the famous puppet theatre of Martin Powell, whose shows included *Dick Whittington* (with scenes in the style of Italian opera), *Orpheus' Journey to Hell* and *The Vertuous Wife; or Innocence in Danger*. His speciality was Punch and Judy, and he 'made Punch utter many things, that would not have been endured in any other way of communication'[6] and fixed him in his scabrous, scurrilous, aggressive, self-interested role. (A perfect metaphor for politicians, Punch and his wife are still there, offering bribes, in Hogarth's *Election* series in the mid-1750s.)

There were always diversions along the way. Another route, a bit further north, could take Hogarth past Bloomsbury, planned in the 1660s by the Earl

9 Detail from *Canvassing for Votes* (1754)

of Southampton; 'a little town' John Evelyn called it, with its fine square, its market and church, and its open views north towards Highgate.[7] Or he could loop along the city's wavering edge, past the new squares of Gray's Inn Fields, and Red Lion Square, built by the wily entrepreneur Nicholas Barbon. The quickest way, though, would be to dodge down Chancery Lane and through Lincoln's Inn, where the lawyers clustered in their black and white robes, along Great Queen Street, where the painter Sir Godfrey Kneller lived, and down Long Acre, crossing St Martin's Lane to Gamble's shop.

Any route between Smithfield and Soho would take him through a landscape of speculation and energy, where amateur developers – soldiers, officials and courtiers lured by entrepreneurial adventure – had acted hand in glove with high finance. The area where Hogarth himself worked was dense with tall brick dwellings. In 1660, said a 1729 guidebook, there were only a few houses 'scattered up and down between Temple Bar and St James's, which was then but a Field or Pasture Ground'.[8] As soon as the War of the Spanish Succession ended with the Treaty of Utrecht in 1713, signed just a month after Hogarth began his apprenticeship, the builders and speculators moved in again. Further west and further north, the meadows and hedges, marshes and woods were giving way to London brick.

34

Sixteen years later, the guidebook writer marvelled at this western expansion, 'consisting of many thousand Houses, large and beautiful Streets, Squares, &c, where most of the Nobility and Gentry now live, for the Benefit of the Good Air'. The wide new streets had raised pavements, and the clean lines of the squares affirmed their occupiers' rational superiority. In 1724, Defoe's laconic prose was tinged with awe at how the whole area had risen 'not only within our memory, but even within a few years':

'The increase of the buildings here, is really a kind of prodigy; all the buildings north of Long Acre, up to Seven Dials, all the streets, from Leicester Fields and St Martin's Lane, both north and west, to the Hay-Market and Soho, and from the Haymarket to St James's Street inclusive, and to the park wall; then all the buildings on the north side of the street, called Piccadilly, and the road to Knight's-Bridge, and between that and the south side of Tyburn Road, called Cavendish-Square, and all the streets about it.'[9]

Sometimes it seemed that London was like a great mouth, sucking in the lifeblood of the country. Looking back from 1757, Laurence Sterne chose 1718, towards the end of Hogarth's Gamble days, as the birth date of Tristram Shandy, and expressed the 'Squirality's' alarm through Tristram's father Walter, who fears England may catch a sort of 'capital-disease':

'a *distemper* was here his favourite metaphor, and he would run it down into a perfect allegory, by maintaining it was exactly the same in the body national as in the body natural, where the blood and spirits were driven up into the head faster than they could find their ways down; – a stoppage of circulation must ensue, which was death in both cases.

'There was little danger, he would say, of losing our liberties by French politics or French invasions; – nor was he in so much pain of a consumption from the mass of corrupted matters and ulcerated humours in our constitution – which he hoped was not as bad as it was imagined; – but he verily feared, that in some violent push, we should go off, all at once, in a state apoplexy; – and then he would say, *The Lord have mercy upon us all.*'[10]

The city drew people like a rush of blood to the head. The smelly hackney cabs, whose drivers, charging a shilling for anywhere in the city, did a thriving trade. The sedan-chair bearers took up their station at street corners, crowding around Covent Garden and clustering as many as three hundred a time near St James's Palace. Once they had a fare they barged their way through, crying, 'By your leave, sir,' to make pedestrians scuttle, and knocking them down if they did not. (Swift saw one fat man, pinned against the wall, strike back by jamming his elbow through a side window, shattering it 'into a thousand pieces'.)[11] The pavements were crowded with men in buff coats and blue waistcoats, with powdered wigs and polished shoes, and women equally proud of their neatly shod feet, dressed in silk or Indian cotton, according to the season, blocking the way with the enormous hoops of their gowns, and tossing little mantles of scarlet or black velvet round their shoulders. Foreigners were amazed at the openness of English women, the way they laughed and bantered, and kissed men on the lips in greeting, and walked so fast, 'more in order to show their clothes than for the pleasure of the exercise'.[12]

As they walked, the rising streets around them rang to the paviour's hammer, the tiler's clatter, the rumbling of carts and the cries of the thronging crowds. Straws hanging on strings across the road warned the pedestrian of building work in progress. Walking was full of hazards: brewers' barrels rolling across pavements, sedan chairs knocking your shins, fish stalls leaving smelly scales, plaster falling on your head, fresh paint smearing your coat-tails, fops' amber-tipped canes (tucked daintily under their arms) poking your cravat, ungrateful beggars spitting and assaulting you with crutches, boy chimney-sweeps daubing you with black. On fine days, small boys carried on men's shoulders snatched expensive wigs from men's heads; in winter, the same boys piled snow over the deep gutters of the kennels running down the street and hooted as well-shod matrons plunged in the muck beneath.

The impulse to describe this bursting, swarming city was irresistible: its imaginative identity was being shaped as fast as its physical streets were being built. A few years before Hogarth started at Gamble's, one of his heroes, Jonathan Swift, drew the town at dawn in terms of its people, squalid and sexy, guilty and innocent, just as Hogarth later showed it in *Morning*:

> Now here and there a hackney coach
> Appearing shows the ruddy morn's approach.
> Now Betty from her master's bed had flown,
> And softly stole to discompose her own.
> The slipshod prentice from his master's door
> Had pared the dirt, and sprinkled round the floor.
> Now Moll had whirled her mop with dext'rous airs,
> Prepared to scrub the entry and the stairs.
> The youth with broomy stumps began to trace
> The kennel-edge, where wheels had worn the place.
> The small-coal man was heard with cadence deep,

Till drowned in shriller notes of chimney-sweep.
Duns at his lordship's gate began to meet,
And Brickdust Moll had screamed through half the street.
The turnkey now his flock returning sees,
Duly let out a-night to steal for fees.
The watchful bailiffs take their silent stands,
And schoolboys lag with satchels in their hands.[13]

Both Swift and Hogarth saw the city through classical as well as contemporary spectacles. Indeed all the commentators – Swift and Pope, Addison and Steele, Fielding and Sterne – were making use of references taken for granted at the time, but lost to us today. John Gay's 'Trivia', for example, published in the middle of Hogarth's apprenticeship in 1716, was a witty updating of Virgil and Juvenal, framed as a guide to the hazards of walking its squares, streets and alleys, and 'long perplexing Lanes untrod before'.[14] Twelve years older than Hogarth, the son of a Devon Nonconformist family, Gay came to town at the start of the century as apprentice to a silk mercer in the New Exchange: if Hogarth engraved the plate of the rich, Gay measured their clothes. But Gay was soon scrambling on to the first rungs of the literary ladder, working on Aaron Hill's journal, *The British Apollo*, meeting Pope, becoming secretary to the Duchess of Monmouth and having his first play, *The Wife of Bath*, performed at Drury Lane in May 1713. Although it ran for only three nights to lukewarm audiences, Gay had begun his climb.

So Gay's situation was very different from Hogarth's. But he still saw the city from the viewpoint of an outsider wanting to be an insider. In 'Trivia' the rural innocent of Roman satires appears as a bewildered peasant lost in the maze of streets round Seven Dials like Theseus in the labyrinth, or as a Devon yeoman, his fortune filched by a Drury lane whore. Yet Gay saw London, despite its pitfalls, as a proud, Protestant, prosperous city. Its filth was an indicator of its industry and wealth: where there's muck there's brass. And, like Hogarth, in this world of extremes where shivering boot-boys pursued the rich with cries of 'Clean your Honour's Shoes', Gay's narrator knew that west was best. Holding his nose in the stinking lanes of Smithfield, 'where huge Hogsheads sweat with trainy Oil', he cries:

O bear me to the paths of fair *Pell-Mell*,
Safe are thy Pavements, grateful is thy Smell!
At distance, rolls along the gilded Coach,
Nor sturdy Carmen on thy Walks encroach;
No Lets would bar thy ways, were Chairs deny'd

37

The soft Supports of Laziness and Pride;
Shops breathe Perfumes, thro' Sashes Ribbons glow,
The mutual Arms of Ladies, and the Beau.[15]

In his prints, Hogarth would follow the lead of 'Trivia' in linking incidents with specific places in the city, and in creating sharp, personalized portraits in dark corners. Gay's walker, eschewing the decadence of the beaux in their carriages, was poised between rich and poor, observing both, and Hogarth took the same stance.

Another voice also influenced Hogarth greatly in his apprentice days – that of the wry, urbane *Spectator*. The successor to Steele's *Tatler*, appearing daily in 1711–12, and revived (more tamely) for eighty issues in 1714, *The Spectator* shaped the views of men and women for its own and the next generation. It surfaces many times in Hogarth's work, in *The Analysis of Beauty*, in odd recorded comments, and in his prints. Many an awkward young man must have sat in the coffee house, imagining himself as suave as Addison, *au fait* with the ways of the world. The *Spectator*'s social ease was enticing for a Smithfield boy who aspired to Pall Mall: a short cut to 'polite' opinions and the world of Taste. The tone was comic, Whiggish, sceptical; not just that of the plain man but the plain-man-of-power, confident in his judgements, accepted in all company, male and female, servant and lord. The editors, Richard Steele and Joseph Addison, now in their mid-forties, were nearer to Hogarth's father's generation, but their stars belonged to a different constellation: Charterhouse and Oxford, the London stage and the House of Commons. Even Steele, reckless, volatile and always in debt, was knighted in 1715 and made supervisor of Drury Lane Theatre. By then Addison was Chief Secretary for Ireland: in 1716 he was made a Lord Commissioner of Trade and married the Countess of Warwick.

At eighteen, though, Hogarth had no purchase on these circles of influence. His world stayed distinctly un-polite, rooted in the streets, sharing Gay's vertiginous sense of the city's perpetual movement, the crush of bodies, the collision of ranks. London was still an intimate city. In 1724, when Daniel Defoe, now in his seventies, traced its borders, he could walk the thirty-six miles and chart the parish boundaries by such small local details that it sounds like a village: 'from Mr Evelin's garden gate, the line goes north West, taking in all the new docks and yards'.[16] It was also a sensual city, where the traveller was guided by sight and smell rather than number and name. Since there were virtually no street numbers, people identified houses by their setting, like Hogarth's birthplace 'on the corner next to Mr Downinge's the printers'.

Shops, coffee houses and inns hung signs in the street, swinging and clattering in the wind. 'Some of these signs', wrote the French visitor César de Saussure, 'are really magnificent, and have cost as much as one hundred pounds sterling; they hang on big iron branches, and sometimes on gilt ones.'[17] The boards were so big, and jutted out so far, that in some narrow streets they touched one another, running almost from one side to the other. *The Tatler* lamented that many a man had lost his way, and his dinner, because the painting and spelling were so dreadful 'that you cannot know the Animal under whose Sign you are to live that Day'.[18] Tom Brown made the whole city with its 'contradictory Language' sound like an emblematic zoo:

'Here we saw *Joseph's* Dream, the *Bull* and *Mouth*, the *Hen* and *Razor*, the *Ax* and *Bottle*, the *Whale* and *Crow*, the *Shovel* and *Boot*, the *Leg* and *Star*, the *Bible* and *Swan*, the *Frying-Pan* and *Drum*, the *Lute* and *Tun*, the *Hog* in *Armour*, and a thousand others, that the wise Men that put them there can give no Reason for.'[19]

Tradesmen sometimes chose simple signs to indicate their calling – a boot, a fan, a book – or their name – Mr Fox, Mrs Diamond, Mr Thrush. But often they just picked any design they fancied, be it animal, vegetable, mineral or mythical. One of the *Spectator*'s spoof letters comes from an alleged 'projector', a flashy modern schemer who plans to clear up this mess and make money in the process. (Addison says he includes it as 'a Satyr upon Projectors in general, and a lively Picture of the whole Art of Modern Criticism'.) The projector has his eye on a lucrative office, 'Superintendent of all such Figures and Devices', his job being to rectify or expunge all signs that fail his rules. He will ban the monsters: 'our streets are filled with Blue Boars, black Swans and red Lions; not to mention flying Pigs'. He will correct the crazy couplings: the Dog and Gridiron, the Fox and Seven Stars. He will sweep away all signs that jar with the signified: 'What can be more inconsistent than to see a Bawd at the sign of the Angel, or a Taylor at the Lion?' And he will deal with offending mixtures, such as the 'Nun and a Hare', which come, he thinks, from the habit of young traders adding their former master's sign to their own. Some of these, though, spell out long-forgotten stories, like 'The Bell and Dragon' (from the Old English tale of Bel), or the 'Bell-Savage', a large bell with a savage man beside it, which baffles him until he reads an old French romance, 'which gives an Account of a very beautiful Woman who was found in a Wilderness . . . *la belle Sauvage*'.[20]

Hogarth enjoyed the jokes such signs offered. *Noon* shows the Baptist's Head ('Good Eating') with its two mutton chops, and behind it the tavern

10 Detail from *Noon* (1736)

board of a headless woman, known as 'The Silent Woman': as well as being comic, both are almost cannibalistic in their greed, anti-religious, misogynistic, loaded. Londoners learned to read their city visually, skating over an iconographic language as rich and ancient and endlessly reworked as the foundations beneath their feet. The cluttered and fantastic detail of Hogarth's prints was no odder than the streets they walked through, or the shows they watched.[21]

The guidebooks described the streets and sights; the poets evoked the mood in mock-classical verse; the signs both guided and misled the wanderer. But there were other invisible maps of this city, charts of power and allegiances, money and class.

Around the Court, and around Whitehall and Westminster, spun circles of satellites. Within Parliament, power was applied through the Cabinet, through 'boards' and committees and cabals rather than through the old system of individual ministers responsible only to the Crown. Money for the wars was raised through taxes on land, through customs and excise, through the National Debt, through state lotteries and loans, a spreading net of state finance. To administer the many new departments – the Office of Trade and

40

Plantations, the Salt Office, Ship Office, Leather Office and more – a new executive had formed: between 1688 and 1714 the number of professional civil servants trebled.[22] 'Every sort of creature,' concludes the historian John Brewer, 'drones, parasites, sharks and harpies – could be found concealed in the labyrinths of the eighteenth-century English state.'[23] The city swam with bureaucrats, dedicated professionals and cool opportunists, who saw their offices as 'property', to be bought and sold like copses and orchards.

The old aristocratic leaders were still very much in place, and many had profited by the wars. The land taxes struck the country gentry hard and, in some areas, as small estates went under, great ones swallowed them up: the Duke of Newcastle during the war and the Duke of Marlborough after it bought between them thousands of acres of England. For such grandees the pickings were rich: they could scoop heiresses in the marriage market and lavish money on parks and private orchestras, on cabinets of porcelain, galleries of pictures. Yet it was not this aristocratic piracy, but the new *non-landed* wealth, born of the great public-credit revolution, that really galled the squires. The National Debt, swollen by more and more loans as the wars rolled on, offered an annuity, to be funded by the yield of excise duties, for 99 years. By the time of Utrecht, this 'funded debt' stood at £35 million: a whole generation would draw happily on the income. Easy money was also dangled before the people by the state lotteries, which reached their peak between 1711 and 1714. And, at the same time, the great corporations grew in power as the government borrowed heavily from the Bank of England, the East India Companies and the new South Sea Company.[24]

Private as well as public speculation boomed: the jargon of brokers and jobbers seemed like magic incantations, turning paper to gold. Their insidious terms, Defoe proclaimed, could be crueller than bombs and swords, 'a sort of impenetrable Artifice, like Poison that works at a distance, can wheedle men to ruin themselves, and *Fiddle them out of their Money*, by the strange and unheard of Engines of *Interests, Discounts, Transfers, Tallies, Debentures, Shares, Projects*, and the *Devil and All* of Figures and Hard Names'.[25] Defoe also thought the stocks were one reason for the 'prodigious conflux of the nobility and gentry from all parts of England', since thousands of families were deeply involved, and 'find it so absolutely necessary to be at hand to take the advantage of buying and selling, as the sudden rise or fall of the price dictates.[26]

The Tory outcry that forced the peace in 1713 played on the gentry's grudges against these new monied men, pointing out how many directors were foreign – French, Dutch, Jewish – or, even worse, Whigs and Dissenters.

41

One of the most eloquent players on this theme was Swift in *The Examiner*, complaining that those who now made a 'Figure', in town were 'a species of Men quite different from any that were ever known before the Revolution; consisting either of Generals and Colonels, or of such whose whole Fortunes lie in Funds and Stocks: so that Power, which, according to the old Maxim, was used to follow *Land*, is now gone over to *Money*'.[27] By 1715, Gay's lament at the rise of the ostentatious *nouveau riche* was commonplace:

> Now gaudy Pride corrupts the lavish Age
> And the Streets flame with glaring Equipage;
> The tricking Gamester insolently rides,
> With *Loves* and *Graces* on his Chariot's sides;
> In sawcy State the griping Broker sits
> And laughs at Honesty, and trudging Wits.[28]

Few people defended speculation, but many profited by it (among Swift's friends, Pope, Gay and Arbuthnot all had shares in the South Sea Company). And a distinction was made between 'stock-jobbery' and straightforward trade. As traders bought land and squires bought stock, worlds began to merge. Defoe, so suspicious of brokers, welcomed pure 'trade' in sonorous tones:

'the Blood of Trade is mixed and blended with the Blood of Gallantry, so that Trade is the Lifeblood of the Nation, the Soul of Felicity, the Spring of its Wealth, the Support of its Greatness, and the Staff on which both King and People lean.'[29]

Mercantile wealth could be seen as patriotic, the basis of world power. In *The Spectator*, Addison made the Royal Exchange sound like Aladdin's cave. It gratified his vanity as an Englishman, he said, to 'see so rich an Assembly of Country-men and Foreigners consulting together upon the private Business of Mankind, and making this Metropolis a kind of *Emporium* for the whole Earth'.[30] With its covered walkways above, packed with two hundred shops, the Exchange already seemed a global market: on the south side of the great paved court, Spanish, French, Portuguese, Italian and Jewish merchants and American plantation owners traded; on the north worked the Irish, Scots and Germans, and, in the middle, packing the open space, crowded the London brokers. The British merchants seemed like ambassadors, concluding treaties, making alliances, distributing the gifts of nature – and profiting in the process. 'Our *English* Merchant', wrote Addison, 'converts the Tin of his own Country into Gold, and exchanges his Wooll for Rubies. The *Mahometans* are cloathed in our *British* Manufacture, and the Inhabitants of the Frozen Zone warmed with the Fleeces of our Sheep'.

He makes it sound altruistic, but when he illustrates this world exchange of blessings, it is not exactly the needy who benefit:

'The Food often grows in one Country, and the Sauce in another. The Fruits of *Portugal* are corrected by the Products of *Barbadoes*: The infusion of a *China* plant sweetened with the Pith of an *Indian* Cane: The *Phillippick* Islands give a Flavour to our *European* Bowls. The single Dress of a Woman of Quality is often the Product of an hundred Climates. The Muff and Fan come together from the different Ends of the Earth. The Scarf is sent from the Torrid Zone, and the Tippet from beneath the Pole. The Brocade Petticoat rises out of the Mines of *Peru*, and the Diamond Necklace out of the Bowels of *Indostan*.'

The riches of the world rise up from their hiding places, to fling themselves voluntarily, gratefully, lavishly, at Britannia's feet.

The changing balance between land and trade was subtly charted on the contemporary stage. In the drama, many plots still centred on marriages between city and gentry, but the old stereotype of the avaricious businessman cheating the principled aristocrat began to give way to pictures of dignified merchants with principles of their own. In Steele's *The Conscious Lovers* (written about 1714 and published in 1722), Mr Sealand the merchant bluntly dismissed the old snobbery of 'honour' and land:

'Sir, as much a Cit as you take me for – I know the Town, and the World – and give me leave to say, that we Merchants are a species of Gentry, that have grown into the World in this last Century, and are as honourable, and almost as useful, as you landed Folks, that have always thought yourself so much above us; For your trading, forsooth! is extended no farther than a Load of Hay, or a fat Ox – You are pleasant People, indeed; because you are generally bred up to be lazy, therefore I warrant you, industry is dishonourable.'[31]

The border tension between money and land, merchants and aristocrats was complicated by the political map, with its wavering boundaries of Whig and Tory, Hanoverian and Jacobite territory. Hogarth began his apprenticeship in heady times. In the spring of 1714, Queen Anne was dying, aged forty-nine, swollen with dropsy, heavy and frail – the body natural like the body national. Her Tory ministry was bedevilled by rivalry between Harley,

43

Earl of Oxford, Lord Treasurer, and Henry St John, Viscount Bolingbroke, Secretary of State. When Anne sacked Harley, infuriated by their quarrels, hysterical Whigs spread alarms about a Jacobite succession, knowing that Bolingbroke (in fact like all the leaders) had made overtures to the Stuarts. At her death, however, Anne turned to the Whig Lord Shrewsbury, and the Protestant succession was safe. On 29 September, in a fog of appropriate density, George, Elector of Hanover, sailed up the Thames to claim his throne. He landed at Greenwich in a dim glow of candles and torches glancing off the ribbons and jewels of an anxious aristocracy. Next day he rode into London in the sunshine, preceded by two hundred coaches, greeting the City corporation and proceeding to St James's through cheering crowds, past balconies hung with tapestries and packed with fashionable beauties.

Not all Londoners welcomed George, especially as he at once (believing Tory equalled Jacobite) installed a purely Whig government, purged Tories of their seats as MPs and excluded Tory merchants from loans and contracts. Across the country, especially in London, where the Tories had long been the party of the people, there were riots at the Coronation in October. In April 1715 Bolingbroke fled to France and joined the Pretender, James, as his Secretary of State. Popular unrest continued during the elections and on the King's birthday. Since juries often sympathized with the rioters and refused to convict them, a stringent Riot Act was passed.

At the end of the summer, Jacobite rebellion replaced Tory riot: the Pretender's standard was raised in the Highlands in early September. The Jacobite forces were disorganized – a planned uprising in the West Country had already been thwarted – and by the time the Pretender eventually landed in Scotland in late December, his army was in disarray. For five months, however, the nation was tense and alert. Even the winter weather seemed threatening – many poor Londoners starved or froze to death, and even the Thames froze, hampering the sending of heavy guns to the north.

All through these months, while Hogarth was working in Blue Cross Street, the mood in London was uneasy. Troops were stationed in Hyde Park, and army mutineers who had sided with the Pretender were hung, drawn and quartered. Fearing more rebellion the Whigs raised mobs of their own; the Duke of Newcastle spent a fortune organizing 'Loyal Societies', based on the cheap taverns or 'mug-houses', from where they sallied out to do battle with the 'Jacks'. One mug-house was in Long Acre, a stone's throw from Gamble's workshop. From the summer of 1715 until the following July there were pitched battles with crowds of up to five hundred on each side: several men died and many were injured.[32]

44

In the aftermath of the rebellion the riots lessened, but the hostility simmered on. There was discord, too, in Westminster and at Court. The alliance of monarch and Whigs had been forged so soundly on the accession of George I that it would last over forty years, until the reign of his grandson, George III. But the Whigs themselves were divided, and in the coming decades the vital opposition movements, cutting across party interests, came from men seeking power *within* this dominant group. A new wave of leaders was already hustling for influence: the Earls of Sunderland and Stanhope; the Duke of Argyll, the shifty, quarrelsome soldier who squashed the Scottish rebellion; the forceful Viscount Townshend and his young brother-in-law, Robert Walpole. By 1716 the disgruntled Townshend and Walpole had left the ministry and were orchestrating a vitriolic opposition. London pulsated with rumours, cliques and slippery alliances. The very river that ran through its heart seemed troubled: on 14 September 1716, strong westerly winds stopped the tide flowing in 'and drove forward the Water with such Fury that there was only a narrow Channel in the Middle, ten yards wide, and so shallow, that Thousands of people passed over on Foot'.[33]

To the gossip of politics and portents was added a juicy set of court stories: about George I's earlier divorce from his wife and the sinister disappearance of her lover; about his comically contrasting German mistresses with their English titles – the immensely tall, skinny, avaricious Duchess of Kendal and the plumply overflowing Countess of Darlington. (In fact, the latter was not his mistress, but his half-sister.) Most gripping of all were the King's furious rows with his son George, who was banished from St James's in 1717 and set up a separate (much livelier) court with his wife Caroline at Leicester House. Duchesses' carriages, as well as dustcarts and brewers' drays, rolled into Leicester Square through the streets round Gamble's workshop, where a young apprentice from Smithfield worked, and made plans of his own.

45

3

Pleasures and Studies

*Be where I could with my Eyes open I could have been at my
studys so that even my Pleasures became a part of them, and
sweetnd the pursuit.*

WILLIAM HOGARTH (1753)[1]

UNDAUNTED BY RIOT or rebellion, affluent citizens continued to squander the
profits of their trade, their colonies, their speculations. And everyone, it
seemed, from great courtiers to small gentry, wanted their plate engraved,
every goblet and coffee pot, every fork and salt-cellar.

William Hogarth, stolidly engraving this new silver plate, was finding his
apprenticeship irksome. Silver tea services stand proudly on spindly-legged
tables in the portrait groups that he later painted, but as an apprentice he
would work on humbler objects, forks and spoons, dozen by dozen, all
ornamented with the same, endlessly repeated, tiny designs. He began with
initials on tea spoons, then with the elaborate ciphers of interwoven letters,
moving on to the shields and arms on goblets, tankards, plates. Day after day,
he would settle to his bench, watching spiral after spiral after spiral of metal
curl relentlessly away from the groove. As a variation he might engrave a watch
case, or a bookplate or snuffbox,[2] but the opportunity for such invention was
small. Once he had acquired the skill to guide the engraver's tool through the
intricate swirls and lozenges of heraldic design, the quality most required was
patience – something Hogarth never possessed.

The rules for apprenticeships, dating from the sixteenth century, were a
means of protecting trades as much as passing on skills. Theoretically only full
guild members could trade, and men (and sometimes women) had to serve
seven years as apprentices. The length of time was judged in relation to
learning and repayment; for the first couple of years an unskilled apprentice
was unlikely to add to profit; only in the last two or three years could he be
useful to his master, and then, too, he could learn the art of business, running
a shop and accounting. But when Hogarth learned his trade competition and
market demand were replacing medieval regulation; in this new climate it

46

began to be claimed that 'liberty of trade was a natural and common law right'.[3]

The old patterns were changing. It is often said that Hogarth began his apprenticeship late, perhaps because of his father's debts, but in London most apprentices now often took their indentures at eighteen or nineteen, working out their time in their early twenties, and leaving – as Hogarth did – before their term was finished.[4] But some things still held good. By statute, an apprentice lived in his master's family, being paid no wages but receiving board, food and clothing. The hours were also laid down: seven in the morning to seven or eight in the evening in winter, and 'from the spring of the day until night' in summer, with set breaks for meals. (London tailors in 1721 had one and a half hours for breakfast and one for dinner – plenty of time to play dice.) The master had to swear to look after his apprentice, and the latter had to promise to be of 'good moral conduct'. The ideal of care on the one side and obedience on the other is suggested by an exchange between a master and a boy's father in Defoe's *The Family Instructor*, published in 1715, when Hogarth was in his second year:

MASTER: Why, what would you make of me? Must I be a father and a master too?

FATHER: No question of it; he is under your family care. As to his body, he is your servant; and as to his soul, I think he is as much your son as any you could have.[5]

There was bound to be friction when young men were made to live as dependants, in the position of a child. Under these outdated rules rebellion was as common as conformity. In the early eighteenth century about thirty thousand apprentices thronged the city, many of them street children forced into service by the parish, and they were always to the forefront in protests. Rhymes and chapbook stories promoted the idea of the bold apprentice, while streams of regulations, changing with the decades, suggest what they really got up to. After an early indictment of 1609, against playing 'giddye yaddye or catts callett or ffoote ball', came wider rules against dice, cards, taverns and extravagant dress, gradually blossoming into expanded lists of misdemeanours, forbidding apprentices to go to 'fencing or dancing schools, nor to dramatic houses, lectures or playhouses, neither to keep any sort of horse, dogs for honting, or fighting cocks'.[6] Among the hazards of Covent Garden, Gay wrote of the apprentices' wild winter football wars, with the ball gathering snow at every kick, skimming the street and rebounding off the highest windows. The jingling sashes also suffered from 'Nickers' who were, Gay added in a note, 'Gentlemen, who delighted to break Windows with Half-pence'.[7] Hogarth knew this rough world of copper-throwing youths. In *Industry and Idleness* the idle apprentice and his mates play dice in the churchyard with no thought for the future, on earth or beyond.

There was plenty of low-life entertainment near Blue Cross Street. Spectacles, freaks, auctions and bear gardens were advertised daily; there were cockfights where bet topped bet in a fever of shouting and 'gladiators' shows, where men with scarred faces wrestled each other down, and women in bodices and short petticoats, stout and strong or fiery and agile, fought until the blood flowed, having their wounds stitched on stage in front of the crowd. Young men could learn boxing from James Figg 'the Master of Defence' at his famous 'Amphitheatre', where Soho met the Oxford Road.

Literate apprentices kept abreast of the shows and the news, reading papers and journals keenly. 'All Englishmen are great newsmongers,' wrote Saussure. 'Workmen habitually begin the day by going to coffee-rooms in order to read the latest news. I have seen shoe-blacks and other persons of that class club together to purchase a farthing paper.'[8] (In a revised plate of *A Rake's Progress*, Hogarth showed those shoe-blacks avidly gambling in the street, with newspapers thrust in their pockets.) The apprentices met in the coffee houses, or in taverns and alehouses where beer was still twopence a quart. Years later Francis Place described how as a young apprentice he went out with the 'other lads' and 'spent many evenings at the dirty public houses' in a mass of activities all 'immediately connected with drinking' such as 'games of chance or dexterity, skittles, dutch pins, bumble-puppy, drafts, dominoes etc., all provided by the publicans'.[9] (Two of Hogarth's quick sketches, of which very few survive, show games of draughts.)[10] The taverns were rough, with sanded floors, full of men drinking fast in a damp, muggy atmosphere. They often ate here as well as drank, especially their main meal at midday if they did not pick up a pie from a bakery or pie shop, or buy sausages or shrimps from a stall.

In the evenings, tavern sessions usually ended in song, when ballad-singers and musicians came in from the street and the tavern-keeper pinned up new song sheets by the door. Everyone knew the tunes, if not the words, since old songs were constantly turned into new ones, fitting the times. This was another way the common people of the city recorded their feelings, as Macaulay said in his *History*, 'No newspaper pleaded their cause. It was in rude rhyme that their love and hatred, their exultation and their distress, found utterance. A great part of their history is to be found only in their

48

ballads.'[11] The rhyme was indeed often rude, with lame lines and lumpy scansion, but it suited all tastes: there were ballads for boys and apprentices, lovers and matrons, songs of war and adventure, highwaymen and dying confessions, history, politics and sex. After every political row, victory or scandal, the ballad-sellers went to the printing house and bought sheets, taking up their places in the market or alley and bawling out the tune, often dancing to mime the actions:

> The People soon
> Gather about, to hear the Tune.
> One stretches out his Hand, and cries,
> Come, let me have it, what's the Price?
> But one poor Half-penny, says I,
> And sure you cannot that deny.
> Here, take it then says he and throws
> The Money. Then away he goes,
> Humming it as he walks along,
> Endeavouring to learn the Song.[12]

Hogarth loved singing all his life, and his prints are full of musicians and ballad-sellers and singers, living on the fringes, haunting the streets and the brothels and the Tyburn executions, cupping a hand to an ear to hear themselves truly, so that they hit the right note when they launch into their song. His young weavers both have ballads pinned up behind their looms, a practice one Derbyshire weaver remembered continuing at the start of this century (Hogarth's Tom Idle has 'Moll Flanders' and Goodchild has 'Dick Whittington').[13] Music is so prevalent in Hogarth's pictures that one can almost imagine him humming as he worked; his own art, like the ballads, also made old tunes into new to comment on the times.

In the late hours, apprentices swayed out of coffee houses and inns towards gambling dens and brothels. (Sometimes there was no need to move: coffee-house signs showing a woman's arm holding the pot were a sure guide, it was said.) As well as the bagnios (bath-houses, usually synonymous with brothels) there were 'molly houses' with boys and transvestites, dancing and sex. In May 1726 the *London Journal* professed horror at finding twenty 'Sodomitical Clubs', from the Royal Exchange to 'Lincoln's Inn Bog-Houses', St James's Park and Covent Garden, 'where they make their execrable Bargains, and then withdraw into some dark Corners to perpetrate their odious Wickedness'.[14] Sodomy was a capital offence and with vicious self-righteousness, the Society for the Reformation of Manners organized raids, one leading to the execution of three working men, a milkman, an upholsterer and a woolcomber in 1726.[15]

The heat soon went out of this particular moral campaign and anyway public pronouncements differed from private opinions. Judges and juries were reluctant to send a man to his death for his sex life – though happy to hang him for stealing a sheep. Apart from a few trials for lesser offences, and several peltings in the pillory, London's gay community was tacitly accepted by all classes. Meanwhile the female brothels flourished ostentatiously. There were as many prostitutes as ballads, and the sex varied from a quick dive down an alley to a plush session fixed in 'those eating houses in Covent Garden where female flesh is deliciously dressed and served up to the greedy appetites of young gentlemen'.[16] Again and again Hogarth would draw these women of the streets, and often with sympathy.

Some apprentices aped fine gentlemen, keeping a girl in Covent Garden and paying a fortune for her clothes. Some went in for fashion binges, like John Cogg, the printer's apprentice who poured out £7 (a great sum) in one day in 1703 on a silk handkerchief, wig, silk cap, pair of silver buckles, a head for his cane, a sharp knife with tortoiseshell handle, and six pairs of shoes.[17] Competition was fierce and Hogarth might have envied Cogg – in later life he was teased about his flash clothes.

The area between Covent Garden and St James's was also the home of London's theatres, and for a young man in town the theatre was the place to be seen. It had long been a favourite haunt of students from the Inns of Court, whose raucous criticism was a standing joke. The young 'Templar' in *The Spectator* spends all his time in the coffee house, tavern and theatre:

'the Time of the Play, is his Hour of Business; exactly at five he passes through New-Inn, crosses through Russel-Court, and takes a turn at Will's till the Play begins; he has his shoes rubb'd and his Perriwig powder'd at the Barber's as you go into the Rose.'[18]

Theatre managers, wooing the polite, were touchy about appearance – hence the Templar's polished shoes – but apprentices in their best clothes could get in cheaply at the last minute, especially if they saw only the second half, the farce, 'afterpiece' or pantomime that followed the regular drama.

Only a few years earlier the theatre had seemed in decline. The patronage that the stage (and its actresses) had enjoyed under Charles II gave way to Court indifference and then to positive disapproval from the more prudish William and Mary, and Anne. The old theatres were all east of Covent Garden, in Blackfriars, Drury Lane and Lincoln's Inn Fields, and when the

Queen's (later King's) Theatre in the Haymarket opened in 1705 under the aegis of Congreve and Vanbrugh, it was ridiculed as being at the 'Fagg-End of the Town', an expensive coach ride from the City. But by 1715 it found itself in the very heart of society: as the wealthy moved west, the city's centre of gravity, and levity, shifted.

Competition was intense. The play changed every day, and up to forty, sometimes even seventy, plays were staged each season, often running only for a few nights. Rival managers courted customers with more and more variety: plays were introduced by overtures or sonatas and a prologue, while each interval had songs and sketches (between the second and third acts of *Hamlet*, 'Francis Nivelon might offer one of his specialities, the "Running Footman's Dance"').[19] After the main play came 'irregular dramas' and pantomimes. Spectacle ruled supreme: real fountains and flying birds; thunder and lightning and fireworks; orange groves complete with fruit; tapestries that turned to men and women. In 1716, after the riotous reception of *The Three Hours after Marriage*, a satire written with Pope and Arbuthnot, Gay regretted the actors' absurd disguises, writing ruefully,

'Dear Pope,
'Too late I see, and confess myself mistaken in Relation to the Comedy, yet I do not think had I follow'd your advice, and only introduced the *Mummy*, that the absence of the *Crocodile* had sav'd it.'[20]

The audience was part of this spectacle, chattering and preening, the men bewigged and silver-buckled, the women patched and powdered. James Macky described the scene in 1714: the pit with 'the Gentlemen on benches', the front row of boxes holding 'Ladies of Quality, the second the Citizens' Wives and Daughters', and the third the 'common People and Footmen'.[21] Between the acts, he added, 'you are as much diverted by viewing the Beauties of the Audience' as by the play. But in these years, as the 'polite world' increasingly included merchants and financiers, the citizens' wives began almost to outdo the ladies of quality.

The gallery, as Macky said, was the purlieu of working people, artisans, apprentices and footmen (who had a special place, to wait for their employers). These rougher audiences, as well as the gentlemen and students in the pit, embodied the new, thrusting, pleasure-loving capital. They hooted, jeered or cheered as the mood took them, demanding encores, throwing fruit, stamping and hissing. The theatres were already associated with disorder and sexual licence and now became seen as politically and socially dangerous too. They were places where old divisions were on the verge of collapse, and just as the new audiences now ruled the show so, it was feared, 'the people' might wish to run public affairs.

Hogarth's delight in 'shews' was always intense, and his work reflected this. In *Marriage A-la-Mode*, for example, both the decadent aristocrat and greedy merchant are pilloried in the style of an old Restoration drama. But if, like Macky, he watched the audience as much as the stage, he could also size up pretty shrewdly the markets for the artist: the aristocratic and mercantile patrons who might order portraits and expensive engravings – and the 'middling folk' who would go for the cheaper prints.

As his apprenticeship dragged on, Hogarth was impatient to create, and to make money. Silver engraving irked him increasingly, and he soon 'found that business too limited in every respect'. It may be that he had always wanted to be an artist, a painter, and that his family could not afford the necessary apprenticeship. Whatever the case, 'engraving on copper' was, Hogarth said, 'at twenty years of age, my utmost ambition'. Unable to bear the narrowness of silver engraving, he decided it should be followed no longer 'than necessity obliged me to it. Copper plates was the next step.'[22]

All his life, Hogarth had an astonishing gift for catching trends. Although an enthusiasm for collecting prints was evident in London from the early years of the century, up to 1710 the local engraving trade – in fine-art terms – was at a low ebb.[23] Then the French engraver Claude du Bosc opened his own print shop in Covent Garden in 1711 and other foreign engravers followed, selling prints from the Continent, of battle scenes and old masters as well as portraits, and soon copper engraving was flourishing again with a new generation of craftsmen, both English and French.[24]

All the time, however, overlooked by the connoisseurs (and often by art historians) there had been a thriving, dynamic *popular* print trade. This was largely controlled by English booksellers, in particular the Bowles and Overton family businesses, selling maps, topical prints, portraits, expensive illustrated books and chapbooks.[25] Prints appeared on ballads, on playing cards, on broadsheets. The print shops and auctioneers also sold the work of well-known foreign engravers such as Jacques Callot, Wenceslaus Hollar and Sebastien le Clerc, and in the early eighteenth century London engravers such as John Sturt and George Bickham (whose son, also George, later moved in the same milieu as Hogarth) began to construct elaborate satirical designs, witty medleys of images that mimicked the revered Continental engravers.[26]

There was already a lively tradition, stemming from men such as Francis Barlow in the late seventeenth century, who produced vivid political satires and story sequences, as well as playing cards and frontispieces.[27] Paintings and prints extended, too, to scenes of everyday life. The Flemish Francis le Piper made prints like 'Reading the News';[28] Dutch artists such as Egbert van Heemskerk, who died in London when Hogarth was seven, painted taverns, Quaker meetings, magistrates, soldiers and whores. And among the favourite prints were the *Cryes of the City of London*. The 'street cries' was an old European genre, and in 1697 Marcellus Laroon the elder had drawn seventy-four studies of hucksters, street sellers and local characters, with humour and tenderness. Prints of these were published by John Overton, whose son Henry issued two new editions in Hogarth's youth, in 1711 and 1713. Some of Hogarth's most haunting characters – the drummer girl in *Southwark Fair*; the milk-seller in *The Enraged Musician*; *The Shrimp Girl* – look back to these figures, part of the legible story of the city.

When he thought of engraving on copper Hogarth might well have thought first of simply moving into conventional printwork, perhaps making a bit of cash from satire on the side. But in his image-building late writings, he down-played this and stressed that his ambitions had always been 'high'. Describing his youthful restlessness, he wrote that the great paintings at St Paul's Cathedral and Greenwich 'were during this time running in my head'. These paintings were by James Thornhill; the Great Hall at Greenwich could be seen by 1714, and the cupola of St Paul's (for which he was chosen in preference to two Italian and three French painters), three years later. Thornhill was born into a family of Dorset gentry of limited means and came to London as an apprentice with the Painters–Stainers' Company. Politically astute as well as talented, he first won the favour of the Tory minister Harley, and then, when that regime fell, of the Whig Earl of Sunderland. Through their influence he established himself as the only serious British history-painter. In March 1720 he became Serjeant-Painter to the King. That May he was knighted (the first native British painter to receive such an honour), and gave a set of the St Paul's prints to the King. Two years later, he was able to buy back the family estates; he became MP for Weymouth and in 1723 was elected to the Royal Society. Thornhill had succeeded; why should Hogarth not follow his example?

A first step was to study work on the grand scale, and this too could now be seen in the print shops. During Hogarth's apprenticeship two great series of paintings had been engraved: the Raphael cartoons, which hung in Wren's fine gallery at Hampton Court and *The Battles of Marlborough*, painted by Louis Laguerre on the staircase of Marlborough House. Finally, in May 1720, a third series would appear: Thornhill's own paintings from St Paul's. The engravers, however, were all French: du Bosc, Dorigny and Baron. More significant still,

53

printsellers found they could exploit a broad market for such works; Dorigny's original engravings sold to subscribers for five guineas, but Bowles sold copies for one guinea, and the cheapest set of all went for 1/6d a piece.[29]

If these grand baroque images filled Hogarth's mind, so did the markedly un-grand life around him. His urge to take up copper engraving encouraged him to sketch from life: 'drawing objects something like nature instead of the monsters of Heraldry became necessary,' he wrote. He needed to practise but serious study was 'much too tedious for one who loved his pleasure and that came so late to it'.[30] From his apprenticeship onwards, Hogarth said, his studies were always mixed up with his pleasures and his pleasures with his studies. 'If I have acquired anything in my way,' he wrote, 'it has been wholly obtained by Observation.'[31]

Like Gay, Hogarth walked and watched. He drew thumbnail sketches, literally, if we are to believe one friend who noticed him 'draw something with a pencil on his nail. Enquiring what had been his employment, he was shewn the countenance (a whimsical one) of a person who was then at a small distance.'[32] Nichols told a longer story, passed on by another apprentice. One hot day Hogarth and two or three friends set off for Highgate, escaping the city sweat for the cool hills. In a local pub a fight broke out, and one man gashed another's head, cracking it open with a quart pot:

'The blood running down the man's face, together with the agony of the wound, which had distorted his features into a most hideous grin, presented Hogarth, who shewed himself thus early apprised of the mode Nature had intended he should pursue, with too laughable a subject to be overlooked. He drew out his pencil, and produced on the spot one of the most ludicrous figures that ever was seen. What rendered this piece the more valuable was that it exhibited an exact likeness of the man, with the portrait of his antagonist, and figures in caricature of the principal persons round him.'[33]

'Shews of all kinds', violent or comic or both, still enthralled him, with action and audience as equal parts of the spectacle.

Gradually he turned his habit of quick mental sketches into a system that he would later use as a painter and printmaker. Looking back from his sixties, he explained that his frustration in losing so much time on silver-plate engraving had led him to seek 'a nearer way' of learning, 'a Method more suitable to my disposition which was to make my studies and my Pleasures go hand in hand by retaining my mind *lineally* such objects as fitted my purpose best'.[34] Puzzling over how, and to what ends the 'Memory might be managed and addapted', he at last found a method that suited his 'situation and Idle disposition',

'Laying it down first, that he who by any means could come at as perfect Ideas of such objects as [he] might want to draw by memory with facility, as anyone who can write frely hath of the twenty-four letters and their infinite combination . . . must consequently be an able designer.'[35]

Lines – the abstract notation of movement, the geometrical patterns of the instant – became the letters of his alphabet. Combining them to form the 'grammar' of his art, he found a drawing technique that would capture the world around him, the live present. He then repeated in his mind the 'parts' of which objects were composed so that he 'could by degrees put them down with my pencil'.[36] He used lines as a shorthand to catch the bold, expressive turn of the body in relation to the surrounding world: he could combine fixity with immediacy – the sweeping gesture, the slow wink, the water cascading from a jug. John Nichols later gave a lovely illustration of this (based on an earlier caricature by the Carracci brothers), made more graphic by the fact that the figure Hogarth illustrated isn't even there – the serjeant going through the door is evoked solely by the line of the door, his disappearing pike and the swish of his dog's tail.[37]

Since this kind of looking fused with Hogarth's childhood fascination

Hogarth boafted that he could draw a Serjeant with his pike, going into an alehoufe, and his Dog following him, with only three ftrokes ;—which he executed thus :

A. The perfpective line of the door.
B. The end of the Serjeant's pike, who is gone in.
C. The end of the Dog's tail, who is following him.
There are fimilar whims of the *Caracci.*

11 Hogarth's 'Serjeant' going through the door

55

with strong expressions and dramatic action, 'comical or tragical', it also defined the content of his art. In rapidly flowing notes, defying grammar, he explained:

'the most striking incidents that presented themselves to my view ever made the strongest impressions on my memory in their whole for Subjects and in there parts for Execution, and which often were such kinds of subjects as seldom or ever were done in the manner they seemd capable of being represented in. Which Ideas occationally were to be call'd to mind when and composition was required. Hence hath arisen the different kind of subjects I have attempted.'[38]

Technical inadequacy and impatience were the paradoxical mothers of Hogarth's invention: precision born of haste. The anecdotes that describe him sketching on his nail, or calling for paper when a scene struck him, suggest that he was, as he said, 'too keenly interested in human nature to interpose a sketch-book between himself and life'.[39] Life was his commonplace book, memory his pen. He had a storehouse of images to draw on, 'a redundancy of matter'. Armed with his own technique, he could use it to tell a story, to stage a drama, to preach a sermon, to transcribe the world.

Hogarth's graphic 'catching' – one of his favourite words – was like the trick used by his contemporary Samuel Richardson of 'writing for the moment'. In *Pamela* in 1742, Richardson used letters to describe events as they happened, using an artful mock-spontaneity to capture the movement of consciousness as well as the external action. In visual terms, Hogarth's portrayal of action suggests both the frozen instant of the modern photograph and the essentialism of caricature: impression and judgement in one. It reminds one, too, of the popular fear of being 'caught' (or 'arrested') in this way: the refusal to be photographed because you lose something of your soul, the fear of caricature as a form of witchcraft.

Hogarth showed full well that he understood this old superstitious magic: in *The Harlot's Progress* a stick-drawing in Bridewell shows the harlot-hunting magistrate Gonson on the gallows; in *The Invasion* a grenadier scrawls a sketch of the French King on the wall, clutching the emblems of gallows and sword; in *The Four Stages of Cruelty* a boy foretells Tom Nero's fate by drawing a gibbet on the wall.[40] And according to one story, when Hogarth himself was 'one day arrested for so trifling a sum as twenty shillings', and was bailed by one of his friends, 'in order to be revenged on the woman who arrested him (for it was his landlady,) he drew her picture as ugly as possible,

56

12 Detail from 'England', *The Invasion* (1756)

or, as Painters express it, *caricatura*'.[41] Later, Hogarth made a sharp distinction between caricature and character, yet the two constantly operate together in his work: in that sketch of the Highgate pub fight his friends were already struck by the juxtaposition of the 'exact likeness' of the main figure and the 'caricature' of those around him.

Caricature, reducing faces to exaggerated lines, had been a strand in European art since Leonardo da Vinci's drawing of grotesque faces and the well-known line sketches of the Caracci. But Hogarth's early work drew more on Flemish and Dutch sources, both the comic genre paintings of daily life, and political satires like those of Barlow, or Romain de Hooghe, whose cartoon-like sequences spread propaganda for William III. To educated collectors, these satirical sketches were the dangerous art of traders and 'mechanics'. They still kept their aura of popular magic – they were *weapons* as well as portrayals.

Some popular strands were older and deeper than the caricature or political print. The artistic low culture (like the drolls of Bartholomew Fair) had long overlapped with the dominant high culture: in the comic portraits that stole into the borders of illuminated manuscripts, the misericords hidden under choir stalls, the gargoyles leering from dark corners and high columns,

57

the chapbook illustrations and broadsheet woodcuts. In all these forms, tough, realistic studies of men and women making shoes, stirring pots, ploughing fields, dancing and playing music, coexisted with fantasy and symbol, a combination that flowered in the art of Bosch or Brueghel. England had its own tradition of comic ugliness,[42] and Hogarth's adaptation of the grotesque was yet another example of medieval blurring into modern. Misericord meets newspaper cartoon, as it were.

Another old tradition was also at work here, that of the emblem, where a single image stands for a complex idea, more condensed than allegory. Much used on the Continent, in both Catholic and Protestant teaching, such images – springing from the belief that the whole natural world was itself a code compiled by God – were also standard mnemonic tools in English dissenting texts, fables and children's stories. This 'low' iconographic mode was very much alive (although scathingly derided by theorists of high culture), and old works such as Withers's *Collection of Emblems* of 1634 were reprinted and collected throughout the eighteenth century. They were popular partly *because* they were a link with the past, but also because the succinct, cryptic forms were, like the ballads, the language of the common people.[43]

Nearly all contemporary satire used emblems, partly because they were safe, not obviously personal, slanderous or treasonable. The habit of 'deciphering' was deeply engrained – everyone could recognize the tendency so brilliantly lampooned by Swift, when he lets Gulliver explain how government informers unravel 'the mysterious meanings of words' in suspect papers:

'For instance, they can discover a close stool to signify a privy council; a flock of geese, a senate; a lame dog, an invader; the plague, a standing army; a buzzard, a prime-minister; the gout, a high priest; a gibbet, a secretary of state; a chamber-pot, a committee of grandees; a sieve, a court lady; a broom, a revolution; a mousetrap, an empty tun; a bottomless pit, a treasury; a sink, a court; a cap and bells, a favourite; a broken reed, a court of justice; an empty tun, a general; a running sore, the administration.'[44]

Hogarth rarely produced either a wholly political or a wholly emblematic work. One example was the weird *Royalty, Episcopacy and Law* of 1724, advertised as 'A very rare Hieroglyphic Print, composed of emblematic attributes and no human features of limbs; with attendants of similar ingredients'. Here the King has a guinea for a head, a royal chain of bubbles, and an orb and sceptre with changeable moons; his soldiers are fire screens, his courtiers mirrors; the Bishop has a Jew's-harp head which becomes a

58

Some of the Principal Inhabitants of y^c MOON, as they Were Perfectly Discover'd by a Telescope brought to y^e Greatest Perfection since y^e last Eclipse; Exactly Engraved from the Objects, whereby y^e Curious may Guess at their Religion, Manners, &c.

1725. Price Six Pence

13 *Royalty, Episcopacy and Law* (1724)

church-steeple pump, spouting out coins; Law's head is a gavel, and the scales of justice seem to be an over clumsy sword and a sieve.

Hogarth also called this print 'The Inhabitants of the Moon', referring to a recent eclipse, but suggesting, too, how the highly formalized emblems edge towards nonsense and surrealism. His vital contribution was his ability to move easily *between* the symbolic and the realistic.[45] In most of his work, he restricted his emblems to details, a familar buried language like the London street signs or the heraldic devices on silver plate. In *Canvassing for Voters*, for example, which has Punch at its centre hurling coins, the hostess counts her money (from bribes or drink?) while leaning against an emblematic British lion munching a French lily. But the lion is realistic too, since many figure-heads taken down from ship's prows, like this one, were proudly bought up by pubs.

Like many people of his day, Hogarth enjoyed the wit of startling juxta-positions. His desire to record 'striking incidents' went side by side with an enjoyment of variety and intricacy. He felt that pleasure was always intensified by complexity and puzzles:

'allegories and riddles, trifling as they are, afford the mind amusement: and with what delight does it follow the well-connected thread of a play, or novel, which ever increases as the plot thickens, and ends most pleas'd, when that is most distinctly unravell'd?'[46]

And despite his boredom Hogarth's apprenticeship itself encouraged this belief and added to his stock of images. Silver-plate engravers, like printmakers, would study books of emblems, and even the books of ornaments compiled by the engraver Simon Gribelin could be codes of entry into magic, allegorical worlds; monsters and cherubs, griffins and lions, angels and fiery swords.[47]

As an independent engraver, Hogarth would have more control over his work than he had while engraving plate at the behest of others. But the technique itself took long to learn and he could not afford the time for a second apprenticeship; he had to teach himself. By contrast, Hogarth's contemporary, George Vertue, had studied for seven years under the respected engraver Michiel Vandergucht until he set up on his own as a book illustrator and then a specialist in portraits. Many years later Vertue glumly bemoaned his art's low status, far below history-painting, sculpture, portraits, enamels or crayons; even below goldsmiths, coach painters, engravers of coins or government seals:

'all these are fully paid honoured and rewarded for their skill & their works. –

but the only unregarded – unpittyed is the poor copper Engraver . . . who must generally expect his reward for his labours. to be collected, from sharp avaricious persons, whose fortune is rais'd by trading – and gripeing and impositions in every way possible.'[48]

Still, Vertue cherished his craft, explaining how the name of the 'burin', the engravers' special tool with its triangular head was derived from Greek, meaning 'a plowing – or plow share – which cutts lines – like furrowing'. Hogarth would have to learn how to prepare and polish the copper plates, first with water and grinding stone, then a smooth pumice stone, then with charcoal and finally with chalk, or even old bread: at the end he should be able to see his face reflected in the shining surface, without distortion. Then he had to learn how to make the sides and point of his burin absolutely sharp and fine. Next, holding the wooden knob-handle in the palm of his hand, and laying his finger along the burin's side towards the point, he had to master the art of giving it just the right weight and turn as he pushed it through the metal, clearing the twisting wire slivers away, so that when the lines were filled with ink they would leave a clean, clear impression. He had to get the ink mixture right, taking Frankfurt black or heavy French black, and mixing it with pellets of French umber, crushed on a slab, then pouring it into burnt oil, getting rid of all the grit, and dabbing it carefully on the plate. The ink could get everywhere – on hands, on sweating brows, on clothes and hair. Finally he had to learn to pull a proof, turning the wheel slowly and smoothly, experimenting until all muddiness was gone.

In the different technique of mezzotint, recently introduced into England, the craftsman pitted the surface of the plate with a 'rocker', then polished the highlighted areas, achieving a velvety tone. Hogarth never lost his sense of the poetry of this particular craft, with its slowly emerging image. In his mid-fifties he wrote that he had often thought a landscape, 'in the process of this way of representing it, doth a little resemble the first coming on of day':

'The copper-plate it is done upon, when the artist first takes it into hand, is wrought all over with an edg'd-tool, so as to make it print one even black, like night: and his whole work after this, is merely introducing the lights into it; which he does by scraping off the rough grain according to his design, artfully smoothing it where most light is required: but as he proceeds in burnishing the lights, and clearing up the shades, he is obliged to take off frequent impressions to prove the progress of his work, so that each proof appears like the different times of a foggy morning, till one becomes so finish'd as to be distinct and clear enough to imitate a day-light piece.'[49]

He himself never aspired to such skill. To begin with he concentrated on etching. This demanded less precision, since the etchers cut their design with a needle through an acid-resistant coating and then 'bit' the exposed lines out by immersing it in a bath of acid – at this point, the only problem for a beginner was to avoid being nearly suffocated by the fumes.

Many artists used a double techniques, beginning with etching, then engraving the deeper lines and detail. Hogarth was learning all the time, looking at prints by Rembrandt, Van Dyck, Wenceslaus Hollar. In particular, he studied the realistic work of the early seventeenth-century French etcher Jacques Callot. Intended for the Church, Callot ran away with the gypsies to study art in Italy; his small plates, of *Italian Vagabonds* and the *Miseries of War*, are crowded with figures in motion, in striking costume and poses, and Hogarth copied several of his designs. He also copied the method Callot invented to gain the more refined 'swelling and diminishing line' of engraving, either by making the acid bite deeper, or by using a special tool, the *échoppe*, to deepen the etched lines.

This technique was described ten years after Callot's death, in the treatise of another French etcher–engraver, Abraham Bosse, *Traicte des manières de graver*, in 1645, translated by yet another engraver, William Faithorne, as *The Art of Graveing and Etching* in 1662. Through this and other handbooks, like the anonymous *History and Art of Engraving* (which reached a fourth edition in 1770), Bosse remained a standard authority throughout the eighteenth century. Over the generations, craftsmen taught each other. Bosse, for example, hands on Callot's recipe for the acid 'mordant', a recipe repeated – for information as well as interest – as late as 1924. It goes like this:

> White-wine vinegar (distilled is better) .... 3 parts.
> Clear white salt armoniack .... 6 ozs.
> Bay salt (*sel commun*) .... 6 ozs.
> Vert de Griz .... 4 ozs.

'Put them into a covered pot over a quick fire, and let the mixture boil up two or three times. Let it stand stopped a day or too before use. If too strong, pour into it a glass of the same vinegar.'[50]

Hogarth did not need much capital, or space, to set up a workshop. An engraver could work in quite a small room, even in the old houses of Long Lane, among the taverns and tenements, with the carts rolling by to the market and the cries of the hawkers echoing in from the street. In the middle of the room, the light from outside diffused by a thin paper screen across the window, stood the engraver's press, with the moving flatbed, with rollers above and below, and a 'star wheel' at the side to turn it. The inked plate was placed on the bed, and the damp paper stretched over it, cushioned by blankets from the roller above. Long shelves might run round the room, reaching nearly to the ceiling, holding spare plates and parcels of good rag paper (carefully kept off the floor to avoid mildew). Another high shelf held bottles of oil, spirits and solvents, tallow candles, bundles of clean rags for cleaning plates, even duck feathers or squirrel tails for delicately smoothing the ground.

Against one wall, on a workbench, stood the plate, resting on a leather cushion to steady it: sometimes a board was propped over it to act as an arm-rest for the engraver to lean his hand on to keep his line firm. Near by were the the ink slab, etching tools, ground and 'dabber'. In the corner was a stove, with pans for warming the copper plates, and others for the varnish. The scents of resin and oil, mixed with the sharp tang of acid and vinegar and ink, wafted through the house.

Hogarth was ambitious to make his own designs, but often his spirits sank:

'For want of beginning early with the Burin on copper Plates as well as that care and patience I dispaired of at so late as twenty of having the full command of the graver, for on these two virtues the Beauty and delicacy of the stroke of graving cheifly depends. it was much more unlikely if I pursued the common methods of copying and drawing I should ever be able to make my own designs.'[51]

This was one reason, then, why he concentrated on his own quick methods of memorizing the lines he needed to compose a drawing: one thing an engraver *must* do is to have an absolutely clear idea of the whole design before he starts. Errors and changes of heart are fatal – it is simpler to abandon the messed up plate and start all over again. At twenty, impatient and hasty by nature, Hogarth could not bear to waste time.

Nor could he afford to. He had to strike out on his own. Independence became imperative when Hogarth's father, Richard, died in May 1718, worn out, Hogarth believed, by the disappointment of his dictionary. The next year, his uncle Edmund Hogarth died, his will making it clear that Richard's widow and children must fend for themselves. Well before his apprenticeship to Gamble was due to end, Hogarth was back, 'Near the Black Bull, Long Lane',[52] living with his mother and sisters, Mary and Anne. Although his sisters soon opened a draper's shop near St Bartholomew's, his earnings were vital to the household.

Within two years of his father's death Hogarth set up on his own, making trade cards, letterheads and designs for plate. At the end of April 1720 he printed his own shop card, 'W. HOGARTH – Engraver'. Above his name hung swags of fruit and flowers, with two dangling-legged putti holding a vase and a drawing. On the left, Art raised her eyes to this drawing and gestured at Hogarth's name; on the right a benignly shaggy History scribbled with his long quill pen. In the centre, an oval cartouche bore the date: the one now in the British Museum reads 23 April – St George's Day, Shakespeare's birthday. For a beginner, this was not a modest card.

14 Hogarth's Shop Card (1720)

64

4

Meeting the Artists

In London, the poor Painter and Designer is left to die of hunger.

FRANÇOIS BOITARD, engraver, *c.*1670–1717

Drawing in an academy, though it should be after the life, will not make a student an artist.

WILLIAM HOGARTH, 1763

JUST BEFORE HIS TWENTY-THIRD BIRTHDAY, Hogarth took another step to forward his career. In October 1720 he became one of the first members of a new artists' academy in St Martin's Lane, paying a subscription of two guineas for the season. Although at first he may just have wanted to improve his engraving, it was a bold and expensive move that showed he had ambitions. And at the academy he would meet a range of artists, and plunge headlong into the competing ideas and allegiances that governed their lives.

Despite his adolescent admiration for James Thornhill, Hogarth had few illusions about the artist's life and prospects. In Soho, as an apprentice, he had been surrounded by artists, working in the studios round Covent Garden, crowding the coffee shops and taverns. And apart from the famous, with appointments at Court, or lordly patrons, even the decorative painters whose work paraded up staircases and curved over the doors of the new houses saw themselves as tradesmen. One story tells how the young Joseph Highmore, then a law student, visited the painter Vanderstraeten in Drury Lane in 1714. He found him in 'a long garret', surrounded by cans of paint called 'cloud colour', stacked among reds, browns and greens, while a boy ran backwards and forwards bringing canvases. He was busy painting long lengths of cloth, from one end to the other,

'till the whole was one long landscape. This he cut and sold by parcels as demanded to fit chimnies etc., and those who dealt in this way would go to his house and buy three or four, or any number of feet of landscapes.'

He could turn his hand to religious art too:

'One day when Vanderstraeten's wife called him to dinner he cried out, "I will come presently; I have done our Saviour, I have only the Twelve Apostles to do." '[1]

But painting was still alluring: a year later Highmore left the Inner Temple to take up art, joining Kneller's academy in Great Queen Street. Now he was one of the first to enrol at St Martin's Lane, with William Hogarth.

In 1720 the morale of English artists was low. To succeed they were still dependent on patrons but the old system whereby a wealthy aristocrat kept an artist in his retinue had largely disappeared. George I was uninterested and there was no Catholic Church to commission religious paintings, which were viewed with suspicion by right-thinking Protestants. The old Painter–Stainers' guild, which had looked after artists' interests since the Middle Ages, was virtually reduced to a trade body of house-painters and gilders. To raise their status, artists returned with increasing zeal to the idea of an academy.

The issue of a British academy, and the form it should take, would later be of vital concern to Hogarth, who surveyed the movement's history with a partisan eye, praising the democratic and scorning the hierarchical. The first English academy was founded on 11 October 1711 (the feast of St Luke, patron saint of artists), when sixty artists and patrons met in an empty house in Queen Street, and elected twelve Directors. Sir Godfrey Kneller, then sixty-four, was Governor.[2] For a model, they looked to the Continent, both to the rigid Académie Royale in Paris and the more informal academies in Italy, Germany and Holland, which developed from gatherings in leading studios and workshops.[3] Kneller's academy, said Hogarth, followed French form but operated 'with far less fuss and solemnity'; for a guinea a season painters met in the evening to draw or attend life classes. Even so, there were factions: Kneller resigned in 1716 in the face of opposition from Louis Chéron and Thornhill, who became the new Governor. When the disputes continued, what little formality there was, Hogarth remembered, 'was soon ridiculed'. Jealousies arose and parties were formed, he said, and, in an outburst of artistic graffiti, the 'president with all adherents found themselves comically represented in ridiculous procession round the walls of the room'. The proprietors 'put a padlock upon the door', the subscribers supported them, 'and thus ended this academy'.[4]

The school Hogarth joined in 1720 emerged from this row. While Thornhill ran his own free academy behind his house in Covent Garden, Louis Chéron and John Vanderbank started a new school in an old

Presbyterian meeting house off St Martin's Lane, 'with the addition of a woman figure to make it the more inviting to subscribers'. (An advertisement of 1722 described it as 'The Academy for the Improvement of Painters and Sculptors by drawing from the Naked'.)[5] From now on, Hogarth would always work within, and against, the collective impetus of a group. He could be touchy and quick to argue but he was also 'a good liver' as they called it, who enjoyed convivial drinking, uproarious jokes and songs. The cloud of names that the academy introduces is worth lingering over, since the men he met now would remain in his life as teachers and rivals, fellow workers and firm friends.

The two founders were an odd couple. John Vanderbank was twenty-six, the son of the owner of the Soho Tapestry Manufactory in Great Queen Street, chief tapestry weaver to the Crown.[6] When he died in 1717 he left each of his three children £500, a considerable sum, and John put much of this into the academy. Vanderbank was a stylish figure, on good terms with the Prince and Princess of Wales – who dropped in one day in November 1722 and gave five guineas to the woman model.[7] A portrait painter with ambitions to become a history-painter, he had real talent and his portraits were keenly valued. Had Vanderbank not been so careless and extravagant, with horses and carriages and fine dressing, George Vertue claimed that 'he might have made a greater figure than almost any painter this country had produced; so bold and free was his pencil and so masterly his drawing'.[8]

The spendthrift, prodigal Vanderbank fitted easily into the high-living neighbourhood of Covent Garden and St Martin's Lane. His elderly partner Chéron was a complete contrast, a strict Calvinist, trained in Paris and Rome, who came to England for religious reasons in the entourage of the Duke of Montagu in 1695. Penniless, he was supported at first by his sister, also a painter, as he tried to make a name as a history-painter in great houses such as Burleigh and Chatsworth. In later life he was best known as a distinguished designer of engravings and book illustrations, and in 1720 had just completed the illustrations for Milton's *Poetical Works*. (A useful link for Hogarth with the world of book illustration.) Now aged seventy, he was open, affable and sincere, generous with technical advice and much loved by pupils and friends; his careful drawings of classical nudes and figures from Raphael or the Carraci were copied by all his students, including Hogarth.[9]

The curious collaboration of Vanderbank and Chéron was typical of the academy, which was an assortment of age, race and talent. Some members were old hands in their fifties and sixties, like Louis Laguerre, a huge, genial figure the same age as Hogarth's father, a painter in the grand baroque style, who had been a rival of Thornhill for the decoration of St Paul's as well as for the governorship of Kneller's academy. Laguerre was the son of a Catalan who had been master of the *ménagerie* at Versailles and Louis XIV was his godfather, but he had no air of grandeur: Vertue described him as a 'modest unintriguing man', quoting the comment that 'God had made him a painter, and there left him.'[10] He was easy-going and convivial, and once painted a Bacchanalian scene round a Drury Lane tavern as a present for a club of virtuosi who met there, but by 1720 he was 'dropsical and inactive'. He died the following year, just before the start of the benefit night for his son Jack, a scene-painter and actor, who was singing in *The Island Princess* at Drury Lane. Jack, who became one of Hogarth's close friends, was also a talented painter but 'wanted application, preferring the stage to more laborious studies' and was said to work only 'by fits and starts, when he was sulky with society'.[11]

Other foreigners included the Frenchman Louis Goupy, the Swede Hans Hyssing (both favoured at Court) and the young Italian Grisoni. British members ranged from the engravers Joseph Sympson and his son, also Joseph, to the surgeon William Cheselden, a dissectionist passionately interested in anatomical drawing.[12] There was also a notable group of younger men, among them Joseph Highmore and Bartholomew Dandridge, in their late twenties, George Knapton, aged twenty-two, and three nineteen-year-olds, Samuel Barker, Arthur Pond and John Ellys, a pupil of Thornhill and another of Hogarth's friends.

Already the nucleus of Hogarth's professional world was forming. Soon he met other young artists such as Francis Hayman, now seventeen, who had been apprenticed since 1718 to the history-painter Robert Browne. Hayman was a Devonshire man like John Gay, with a huge appetite for food, drink and pleasure. Horace Walpole called him 'a rough man, with good natural parts and a humourist',[13] and he was remembered as 'the best-hearted fellow . . . a sort of knight-errant', always ready to take up the cudgels if one of his friends was slandered (as often happened). Apparently 'it was on one of these occasions that Hogarth said "Now Frank has put on the barber's basin,"' and the phrase stuck.[14]

In the early 1720s Hayman was painting stage scenery at Goodman's Fields. When he and Hogarth first met, Hayman was lanky and gauche but over the years he grew fat and Falstaffian, *'jocularly satirical* and sometimes *affectedly morose'*.[15] He and Hogarth were very close until they argued in the 1750s, and Hogarth painted him affectionately in *Beer Street* as the big-nosed sign-painter, teetering on his ladder in his torn coat with his shirt-tails hanging out,

68

enthusiastically nodding at his own great achievement. Original and talented, Hayman became a key figure in British art mid-century; one of his patrons said that

'if he had not fooled away many years at the beginning of his life in painting Harlequins, trap-doors etc., for the playhouse, he would certainly by this time be the greatest man of his age, as he is now of his country'.[16]

Another future friend, George Lambert, three years younger than Hogarth, was even more closely linked to the theatre. In 1722, he was just 'a young hopefull Painter in landskape',[17] and was soon earning most of his money painting backdrops for John Rich at Lincoln's Inn Fields. And when he went on to paint landscapes in the next decade – 'the first native painter to apply the rules of art to the English native scene'[18] – these outdoor scenes were nearly as theatrical as his stage sets. Lambert was known as 'a person of great respectability in character and profession'.[19] He had a natural ease, being 'delightfully social' with all-comers regardless of their rank, and became known as the 'king' of the artists' great meeting place, Old Slaughter's coffee house.[20] He was also better bred and better off, coming from a minor branch of an old Surrey family, with aristocratic connections and, perhaps, musical rather than artistic ambitions. Hogarth made a teasing bookplate for him in the mid-1720s: a despondent Music with her flute is stuck for ideas and the pages of her book are blank, while Art leans over to touch up the coat of arms, a possible dig at his genteel connections. The quiet, literary Lambert needed his own bookplate; he had a substantial library of seven or eight hundred volumes and when he died in 1765 (the same year as Hogarth) he left among his effects 'a large book case with folding door, a pediment top and carved ornaments' and another 'raised on a rustic basement, with looking glass doors, and pediment top neatly carved'.[21]

The work and friendships of this group overlapped through the years. Jack Laguerre, John Ellys, George Lambert, Francis Hayman and Hogarth were brought close by their involvement with the theatre; it is quite likely that Hogarth, too, worked as a scene-painter.[22] Hogarth was undoubtedly influenced by Vanderbank's lively style, especially his illustrations for *Don Quixote*. John Ellys later bought the Vanderbank factory and the office of Tapestry Maker to the Crown. Joseph Sympson Jnr later engraved Hogarth's prints. In the 1730s and 1740s different members of the group worked together at the new St Martin's Lane Academy, at Vauxhall Gardens, at the Foundling Hospital. And even in these early days the young artists already formed a close-knit web of support and rivalry, shared debts, commissions and hangovers.

None of these young artists was classically educated or had been on the Grand Tour. But, from the start, Arthur Pond and his circle set a different course from Hogarth and his allies. In 1723, he and George Knapton, both sons of rich City families, started the 'Roman' club to promote the discussion and collecting of Italian art. Inspired by Jonathan Richardson's *An Account of Some of the Statues, Bas-reliefs, Drawings and Pictures in Italy* (1721), which urged young artists to travel, they went to Italy in 1725. Gradually this pro-Italian group shifted into the company of the 'virtuosi'. Knapton was one of the first members of the Society of Dilettanti, founded in Rome in the 1730s, and Pond became a major dealer, collector and distributor of 'classical' prints. (A sardonic note of Vertue's in 1741 records that Pond has become 'the greatest or top Virtuosi in London, followd esteemd and cryd up . . . Mr Pond is all in all!')[23]

By the end of the decade the trend for young artists to travel abroad to study, especially in Italy, was well established. But many of Hogarth's group, including Hayman, did not or could not go. Hogarth had a habit of turning *his* practice into an argument for *good* practice; later he would argue fiercely against assuming that foreign training was all in all. He would also attack other conventions – the virtues of Palladian architecture, the praise of foreign artists, the cult of the old masters. Because he was so important in changing the face of British art and because he himself imposed a pattern when he looked back, he is often presented as if he set out with a mission, with his independent aesthetic firmly in place from the start. But the process was far more *ad hoc*; many later statements were rationalizations or justifications of approaches that began as a result of alliances and feuds, career knocks and opportunities.

In his early twenties, ambition and loyalty to old ideals first drove him to take sides, identifying with Thornhill and the Baroque school – who represented the art he had admired and also seemed favoured at Court. But this group was already under attack from men with new ideas and new tastes, and, in the Vanderbank academy, one English member in particular swam with the fashionable anti-Thornhill tide: William Kent. What Hogarth thought of *him* is suggested by the way he wrote his name, in *The Taste of the Town*, in 1724: 'KNT'.

Kent was now thirty-six, burly and fat-cheeked, complacent and ambitious. He was no more genteel in origins than the others – a Yorkshireman who had started as apprentice to a coach-painter. But, as Horace Walpole put it, 'feeling the emotions of genius, he left his master without leave and repaired to London, where he studied a little, and gave indications enough of abilities to excite a generous patronage in some gentlemen of his own county'.[24] The sum

70

these Yorkshire gentlemen raised sent Kent to Rome in 1709. Four years later he met the nineteen-year-old Richard Boyle, 3rd Earl of Burlington, on his Grand Tour, and acted as his agent in buying pictures; in 1719, after they met again on Burlington's second Tour, Kent returned to London under his patronage and moved into Burlington House. It was the start of a relationship that would last all their lives.

If Kent's easy charm (a quality that Hogarth truculently lacked) won influential friends, it alienated many of his fellow artists. He declared that his 'Italian constitution' was at odds with this hard 'Gothick country', and consoled himself by visits to the Italian opera, lording it over the others at the academy. Kent came to represent everything Hogarth disliked, not least the fashion for foreign training:

'a man (by complying with custom prejudice) gets the opinion that he [is] much the better for studying abroad tho he were the worse which oftener has been the case than the better the late Mr Kent (late kings painter) won the prize of Rome and never was there a more wretched dauber but (such) soonest get into palaces in this country.'[25]

Among the easels in the echoing meeting house, this favoured man with his brocade and lace and wafting scents, his fleshy ease and confidence, would hardly notice a stubbly five-foot engraver. It would be hard for Hogarth, always touchy, not to feel envy, or anger. But his feud with Kent was based on outraged principle as well as personal animosity. Kent was at the heart of the new vogue for the classical, Palladian taste, seizing Burlington's patronage as a chance to end the long reign of solemn English Baroque. He hoped, he wrote in a letter home from Italy, to force through change, 'by this lordship's encorgement [sic] and other gentlemen who may have a better gusto, than that damned gusto that's been for this sixty years past'.[26] It seems appropriate that the Italian gusto should come to mean enthusiastic energy, rather than 'taste', as it did then. Over the next thirty years, Kent shaped the look of the century, designing every detail of the great houses he worked on: bridges, obelisks, temples, triumphal arches and gateways; stuccoes, frames and chimney-pieces; chairs and stools, pier-glasses and pedestals and monumental side tables, in softwood or mahogany, painted, carved and gilded. He even designed stage scenery and silver plate and the state barge for Frederick, Prince of Wales. Nothing, he felt, was beyond him.

Burlington made Kent's rise possible. He had begun remodelling his house in Piccadilly in 1711 and by 1719 Kent could boast securely that here, for the first time in London, 'you could see a true Palladian front'.[27] When Hogarth met him, Kent was busy producing Venetian-style paintings for the new apartments: a *Glorification of Inigo Jones*, and vast *Banquet* and *Assembly* of classical gods. Following the precept that 'Princes and Great Men' should lead through generous patronage of the arts,[28] Burlington gathered around him a coterie of artists and musicians (including Handel, then *Kapellmeister* at Hanover, who came to London in 1710 and stayed at Burlington House from 1713 to 1716) and writers such as Gay and Pope. Gay depicted Burlington and the other great patron, the Duke of Chandos, not as ostentatious self-publicists or destroyers of native English culture but as patriots who gave artists the same support they enjoyed in Europe. Critics, declared Gay (sensing where his bread was buttered), were either envious or ignorant, or both:

> While *Burlington*'s proportioned columns rise,
> Does not he stand the gaze of envious eyes?
> Doors, windows are condemn'd by passing fools,
> Who know not that they damn *Palladio*'s rules.
> If *Chandos* with a liberal hand bestow,
> Censure imputes it all to pomp and show;
> When if the motive right were understood,
> His daily pleasure is in doing good.[29]

One of those passing fools, cursing Palladio, was William Hogarth. Hogarth liked mobile perspectives, light and shade, architecture that unfolded its mysteries as people walked through it – not the flat, austere formality of classical orders.[30] In the course of the Palladian revolution Hogarth's own idols had suffered – like Wren, 'so justly esteemed the Prince of Architects', who lost his post as Surveyor General. Others fell too: Hawksmoor was succeeded as Clerk of the Works by the architect Colen Campbell, whose *Vitruvius Britannicus*, in 1715, had championed Inigo Jones and set the fuse to the neo-classical revival. And in 1720, when Burlington was talking up Kent as the 'best History painter – & the first that was a native to this Kingdom',[31] Thornhill was under threat too. Two years later Kent won the commission for decorating Kensington Palace, bidding £300, and undercutting Thornhill by £500.

The battles of taste took place against intense discussion of the role of art in society, of the duty of a connoisseur and patron, of the values that should be applied. These laid down a series of assumptions and ground rules that Hogarth would alternately adopt and resist, follow and scorn, for the rest of his life.

At a fundamental level, the society Hogarth grew up in accepted the Platonic notion that the eye is the dominant organ of sense. If a baby's mind is blank as white paper, a *tabula rasa*, as Locke had said, then the first things inscribed on it would be not words but images – imprinted by a sort of *camera obscura*:

'methinks the *Understanding* is not much unlike a Closet wholly shut from light, with only some little openings left, to let in external visible resemblances or *Ideas* of things without'.[32]

Right reasoning grew from correct interpretation of the world as perceived by the senses, and visual images were therefore a far more immediate graphic representation of the world than language. 'Painting is another sort of writing,' wrote the painter and critic Jonathan Richardson in 1719, but more powerful, because its ideas

'come not by a slow progression of words, or in a language peculiar to one nation only; but with such a velocity, and in a manner so universally understood, that it is something like intuition, or inspiration'.[33]

Hogarth himself profoundly believed that pictures shadowed forth 'what cannot be conveyed to the mind with such precision and truth by any words whatsoever' and that 'ocular demonstration will convince . . . sooner than ten thousand Vols'.[34]

If images were so powerful, then the visual arts could be a force for good or evil. But what standards should people apply? How should they estimate their 'value'? How should a right taste be inculcated, and who should dictate it? These issues seemed even more crucial in an age when an eager new public for culture was developing so fast, and when luxury and consumption and the desire to possess sometimes felt overwhelming. The choice of subjects for art and the whole notion of taste swiftly came to have moral and political overtones.[35]

In the early eighteenth century, the first and enduringly authoritative voice was that of the Earl of Shaftesbury, who held that appreciation of great art could lead to an understanding of beauty, of Nature, and hence of the Deity. Shaftesbury's version of Nature emphasized not its variety but its underlying *order*, the contemplation of which was a moral spur as well as an aesthetic delight, as he explained in his *Characteristics of Men, Manners, Opinions, Times* in 1711:

'This too is certain, that the admiration and love of order, harmony and

73

proportion, in whatever kind, is naturally improving to the temper, advantageous to social affection, and highly assistant to virtue; which is itself no other than the love of order and beauty in society. In the meanest subjects of the world, the appearance of order gains upon the mind and draws the affection towards it.'[36]

Such aspirations fitted Shaftesbury's deism, his trust in a transcendent God whose design was discernible through reason, rather than 'revealed' by unprovable miracles, and his optimistic belief in the innate goodness of human nature. In social terms, 'order' was translated into the civic–humanist ideal of a polity best governed by enlightened, 'disinterested' men. (Keeping faith with these ideals, around 1701 Shaftesbury had himself painted by John Closterman, wearing classical dress, in the guise of a Greek philosopher.)[37] Such men could be princes and patrons, raising the nation's perception. And the art they would champion must convey essence not individuality, unity not variety, beauty not 'deformity'. It followed that the artist – or rather the connoisseur and patron who hired the artist – must therefore turn his back (it was always assumed to be a male back) on the particular in favour of the ideal.[38] Classical subjects, stirring moments in history and elevated allegories of personal or civic virtue must rank highest among the subjects of paintings. One of Shaftesbury's favoured subjects was the *Choice of Hercules between Pleasure and Virtue*, painted for him by Paolo de Mattheis just before 1713, and engraved by Simon Gribelin. This triangle would be constantly replicated, echoed – and parodied – in later works, including those of Hogarth.

What Shaftesbury advocated so passionately was a form of educated leadership in taste that was, it goes without saying, essentially aristocratic – the élite judgement of the Whig grandee. But almost at the same time, *The Spectator* was widening this patrician base of judgement. Its papers on 'The Pleasures of the Imagination' in numbers 411 to 421 were the most resonant of all contemporary statements on taste, and Addison has been called 'the greatest ideologue of British culture' in this period.[39] The keyword here is 'British', suggesting the deliberate promotion of a style for the precarious new nation formed by the Act of Union in 1707. To weld the edgy, diverse interests, this new national style had to be, in essence, 'not English'. So although Addison, like Shaftesbury, looked to Rome for models of civic virtue and to sixteenth-century Italy for the canons of art, he gave the Whig aesthetic a slightly different political slant.

Addison faced problems: it was hard to carve a path between applauding Renaissance virtues and condemning the absolutist 'excesses' of contemporary

74

Europe; hard, too, to transfer classical and aristocratic ideals to the new commercial world. As a mediating factor Addison stressed the quality of intimacy, of responsive 'sensibility' in the appreciation of art. Part of the *Spectator*'s aim was to foster men of 'Polite Imagination', not confined to the aristocracy, who could 'converse with a picture and find an agreeable comparison in a Sculpture'. Its pages were full of references to Michelangelo, to the Raphael cartoons at Hampton Court, to Titian's 'inimitable sunshine' – but also to the pre-eminence of the English in portrait painting.

One early issue offered a guide to judging art in the form of an allegorical dream of a visit to an art gallery one gloomy day. 'When the Earth swims in Rain,' said Addison, he would withdraw 'into the Visionary Worlds of Art, where I meet with shining Landskips, gilded Triumphs, beautiful Faces, and all those other Objects that fill the Mind with gay *Ideas*.' The beauty of ideas is the desired goal, not mere pleasure of the eye, and it is in this light that Mr Spectator watches the artists in his dream gallery. The first is Vanity, with hair tied back in a Ribbon and dressed like a Frenchman, 'the *Toujours Gai* appeared even in his Judges, Bishops and Privy Counsellors: in a word, all his Men were *Petits Maîtres*, and all his Women *Coquets*'. The other artists are no better: Stupidity is a laborious, Germanic workman; Fantasque is a Venetian scaramouch, dealing 'in Distortions and Grimaces'; Avarice works so fast that his pictures fade before they're finished; Industry is a solid Dutchman, fond of realism and murky night-pieces, and Envy does no work of his own but ruins that of others. By contrast, on the opposite wall stand paintings by Raphael, Titian, Guido Reni, Correggio, Rubens, in which all their figures seem 'real and alive'. On this side, only one old man creeps up and down, removing every 'disagreeable Gloss', and adding a 'beautiful Brown to the Shades'. His name, of course, is Time.

Hogarth was undoubtedly an Addisonian, determined to contribute to the new, polite British culture, but he parted from his mentor at some points. It went against the grain with him to believe that age should rule taste. Years later, he wrote that despite Mr Addison's 'beautiful description', Time does not improve good pictures.[40] In 1761, fifty years after the *Spectator* piece appeared, he satirized the whole idea in *Time Smoking a Picture*. He would not be held back by awe of the past – he was happy to look, and learn, but wanted to use these lessons in creating a *new* art, not copying an old.

When he was starting out, several works trumpeted the orthodoxy that old was best, and classical best of all.[41] All were ruled, at base, by the conventional lore of the French academy. Truth in art must be higher than truth to life: Raphael had rightly painted his Apostles as dignified and berobed, not, as they might have been, weary, short or sunburned. In 1715 Jonathan Richardson developed this line further, rewriting the programme of Shaftesbury and Addison in still more popular and practical terms. Richardson, now aged fifty, was an accomplished, straightforward portrait painter, the teacher of George Knapton and of Thomas Hudson (his son-in-law), who in turn taught Joshua Reynolds. In his influential *Theory of Painting*, he allowed that the artist should sketch what he saw before him, anticipating Hogarth in such words as 'there is no better school than nature for expression. A painter should on all occasions observe how men look and act, when pleased, grieved, angry, etc.'[42] But to Richardson this was mere practice, not 'art':

'Common nature is no more fit for a picture than plain narration is for a poem. A painter must raise his eyes beyond what he sees, and form a model of perfection in his own mind which is not to be found in reality, but yet such a one as is probable and rational.'[43]

Richardson inevitably looked back to the Ancients and the Renaissance, where Grace and Greatness (*grazia* and *grandezza*) found their supreme combination. He too placed history-painting at the pinnacle. He too equated understanding art with acquiring virtue. 'Supposing', he wrote,

'two men perfectly equal in all other respects, only one is conversant with the works of the best masters (well chosen as to their subjects), and the other not; the former shall, necessarily, gain the ascendant. And have nobler ideas, more love to his country, more moral virtue, more faith, more piety and devotion than the other; he shall be a more ingenious, and a better man.'[44]

In 1719, in *The Art of Criticism* and the enticingly titled *Discourse on the Dignity, Certainty, Pleasure and Advantage of The Science of a Connoisseur*, Richardson suggested that anyone with money and leisure, if they followed his advice, could join the virtuosi. Connoisseurship was no mystery; paintings and sculptures could be classified and judged almost like plants and minerals. (You could even measure the 'sublimity' of a work, on a scale from one to twenty.) Furthermore, collecting would fill leisure time fruitfully, raise standards, and improve Britain's wealth and status. Native artists would acquire respectability, so that

'a thing, as yet unheard of, and whose very name, to our dishonour, has at present an uncouth sound, may come to be eminent in the world, I mean the English school of painting, and whenever this happens, who knows to what

76

heights it may rise; for the English nation is not accustomed to doing things by halves.'[45]

Sweet words for a man like Hogarth. Richardson had no time for a party-political Whig school of art: he was friendly with both Whigs and Tories, he was a practising artist, and he was the prime encourager of 'a more broadly based commercial school of English painting, firmly rooted in Protestantism'.[46]

Other voices took up these themes, like Francis Hutcheson, in his Shaftesburian *Inquiry concerning Beauty, Order, etc* in 1725. Other books affected the *way* artists treated their subjects, like Le Brun's 'Character of the Passions', in his *Conférences . . . sur l'expression'*, translated in 1701,[47] or John Elsum's *Art of Painting after the Italian Manner*, 1704. But the triumvirate of Shaftesbury, Addison and Richardson set the parameters of the argument about art and taste within which Hogarth worked. And all three were concerned, as Hogarth would be, not simply with theory, but with a practical programme for the nation.

In practice, of course, the market had more influence on what artists actually did – although the writings helped to form that market's taste. Richardson's books were timely and shrewd, particularly *The Science of a Connoisseur*. Keeping pace with the boom in building, one of the most noticeable features of the conspicuous consumption after the Peace of Utrecht was the collecting of pictures to decorate these new mansions. Now that the Continent was open again, rich young men set out on their Grand Tour, coming back laden with antiquities, paintings and *objets de vertu*. Hogarth scathingly compared them to herb-picking peasants. 'The grand Tour, as its calld', he wrote, taken by wandering connoisseurs

'to see and pick up curiosities in art, which they are taught, to distinguish nicely, from one another, by certain names, and marks, may, with no great impropriety, be call'd going a simpling (with this difference only that a Simpler never picks up a Nettle for a marsh mallow).'[48]

In the 1720s to be smart meant to be Continental and all the print shops were stacked with views of Italy and engravings of old masters. Buying art, then as now, was a way of buying 'Taste', of proving oneself superior. And it had to be *foreign* art. The old masters, 'dark pictures' as Hogarth called them, swamped the market. As early as 1711 scouts had been scouring the Continent, bringing back their booty. Auctions abounded, like that promised in a letter in *The Spectator*, in which one guileful entrepreneur proclaims:

'I have travelled *Europe* to furnish out a Show for you, and have brought with me what has been admired in every Country through which I passed. You have declared in many Papers, that your greatest delights are those of the Eye, which I do not doubt but I shall gratifie with as Beautiful Objects as you ever beheld. If Castles, Forests, Fine Women, and Graceful Men, can please you, I dare promise you much Satisfaction, if you will appear at my Auction on Friday next.'

The accompanying advertisement for the sale, to be held at the Three Chairs Coffee-House in Covent Garden Piazza, appears again in the next three issues. Subsuming Europe under Italy, it launches a magical volley of names, a litany of desire:

'A curious Collection of Italian Paintings (by Giacomo and Leandro Bassan, Schiavone, Tintoret, Spagnolet, Nicol and Gaspar Poussin, Claude Lorain, Salvator Rosa, Fran. Bolognese, Mola, the Borgognon, Luca Jordano, Bourdon and the Maltese; as also by Rubens and Vandyke, the Velvet Breughel, Holben, Brower, Berchem, Schalken, Teniers etc).'[49]

Many of the works sold were not originals but cheap copies and in 1721 an act was passed to control this, judging imports by their value. But the plundering of Europe continued for half a century – between the 1720s and 1770s the toll came to around 50,000 paintings and half-a-million etchings and engravings. The vogue peaked extraordinarily fast: in 1725 more than 760 paintings were imported: 330 from Italy, 200 from France, over 120 from Holland, 33 from Flanders and 47 from the Netherlands; these were supplemented by over 11,000 prints.[50] Auctions became part of London life, a mix of commerce, entertainment and socializing. Men made fortunes by dealing, like Andrew Hay, a former portrait painter who held his first auction in Covent Garden in 1725, and travelled six times to Italy (twice *walking* across Europe) and fourteen times to France, before he retired in the 1740s, a wealthy man. Less reputable was Christopher Cock, who founded the first auction house in London, buying from dealers such as Hay, from estates, from connoisseurs down on their luck. Cock allegedly cut the heads out of some Raphael cartoons he was 'restoring' for the Duke of Chandos and sold them separately to others and Hogarth was not alone in damning his sales as stacked with forgeries and blatant copies.[51]

However shady the commerce, this taste for the old and the foreign affected the practical side of the artist's life. According to the connoisseurs and the dealers the only true artists were dead artists – or foreign artists.

78

Stuccoists from Ticino and painters from Venice arrived to concoct elaborate plaster mouldings and decorations on ceilings and walls. French, German, Dutch and Swedish artists and engravers settled in London, adding to those who had already taken refuge from religious persecution. Many raised their families here, and intermarried, so that one comes across whole dynasties, like the Boitards, Vanderbanks, Regniers or Vanderguchts. In the end, this mingling proved extremely fruitful for British art, but in the 1720s young British artists felt blocked by the preference for foreign works. Some undertook piecework as studio assistants or drapery painters. Some, like Hayman and Lambert, worked as scene-painters in the theatre (although managers sometimes preferred to bring in foreign painters for their huge decorative backdrops).[52] Some turned to book illustration, while still others became dealers, retailers or copyists, producing versions of the old masters that were so sought after at the auctions.

The role of art was to dignify the purchaser, not the producer; the artist was just another purveyor of diversions. Richardson put it bluntly:

'the Mechanick parts of Painting . . . require no more Genius, or Capacity, than is necessary to, and frequently seen in Ordinary workmen, and a Picture, in this respect, is as a Snuff-Box, a Fan, or any other Toy.'[53]

Pictures were part of society's 'Ornamental Furniture'. And in this respect, portraits – an English speciality – were a good line of work, since almost any occasion in a well-to-do family, from birth to death, was celebrated with one. A generation before, Sir Godfrey Kneller had turned his art into a virtual 'manufactory', using packs of assistants. Once he had painted the face and sketched the shoulders, the picture was passed 'to the artist who excelled in painting a hat, and when the hat was fixed upon the head or tucked under the arm, the canvas was consigned to the painter of the periwig', who then turned it over to the man who did the coat, which another man then 'ornamented with curious worked buttons, each wrought up with the laborious accuracy of the German school'. One excelled in lace handkerchiefs, one in gold lace, and so on down the line, 'upon as regular principles as the fabrication of carpets at Kidderminster'.[54]

Such portraits were furniture with a vengeance. As Horace Walpole saw it, they were as subject to taste as carpets or curtains, changed as soon as the children inherited the house:

'Portraits that cost twenty, thirty, sixty guineas, and that proudly take possession of the drawing room, give way in the next generation to those of the new-married couple, descending to the parlour, where they are slightly mentioned as *my father's and mother's pictures*. When they become *my grandfather and grandmother*, they mount to the two pair of stairs; and then, unless despatched to the mansion-house in the country, or crouded into the housekeeper's room, they perish among the lumber of garrets, or flutter into rags before a broker's shop at Seven Dials.'[55]

But even among the 'face-painters', the British met competition from abroad. Choosing John Closterman to paint his portrait, Shaftesbury spoke for his class when he wrote off British artists as 'illiterate, vulgar and scarce sober'.[56]

The art market, with all its issues and personalities, was avidly discussed by Hogarth and his friends. The strongly gregarious (and very male) public culture of coffee houses and taverns provided a kind of horizontal fellowship that crystallized at a slightly more formal level into the clubs, with their unspoken rules and freedoms. As Addison put it, 'Man is a sociable animal and we take all occasions and pretences of forming ourselves into those little nocturnal assemblies which are commonly known as *clubs*.'[57] Supreme among them all, from the early days of the century, was the Whig Kit-Kat Club, to which Addison belonged, but his *Spectator* jokes embrace clubs of all kinds, real and made up – Ugly Clubs, Farters' Clubs, Flirting Clubs and Surly Clubs. There were clubs for politics, clubs for rakes, clubs for earnest free-thinkers – and, of course, clubs for artists.

Club members usually met weekly in a tavern, to eat, argue, get drunk and sing, but clubs were also a way of getting work, making contacts, forming alliances. Pond's Roman Club was only one of several that defined the internal politics of the art world. Some years later Vertue totted up his long years of talking to artists 'in all Parts of the Town' and lamented that

'to get into companyes conversations Clubbs, has been a continual expence . . . besides the Rose & Crown Clubb so many years and also the Tip top Clubbs of all, for men of the highest Character in Arts & Gentlemen Lovers of Art – call'd the Clubb of St Luke.'[58]

Vertue himself belonged to the 'Tip top' St Luke's, which looked back to Van Dyck as its founder, and to Kneller, Wren and Closterman as members. But there were artists' clubs of less grandeur, like the Rose and Crown, and the Clare Market Club (for which Hogarth engraved a design for a tankard).

The clubs created bonds, but the art world was never self-contained. Artists shared tables with doctors, artisans with musicians, builders with

80

natural philosophers. The experimental lecturers in that last group, seemingly so different, had much in common with the artists: a culture of enterprise, a desperate search for patronage, a new relationship with the public. The shops of the instrument-makers crowded along Fleet Street and Ludgate Hill and lecturers spoke in coffee houses from the Royal Exchange to St Martin's Lane. Art and science overlapped, and Hogarth's friendships embraced this world as well as his own.

Working in Smithfield and coming over to St Martin's Lane in the evenings, to the academy, the theatres and the clubs, Hogarth threw himself into new friendships and quarrels. He was frustrated, however, with the actual work he was expected to do at the Vanderbank academy. The routine bored him almost as much as his old apprentice work. Classes were held during the winter every evening except Mondays and Saturdays. They taught only drawing, *'disegno'*, considered essential to raise painting from craft to high art through a knowledge of perspective, proportion, anatomy and the principles of antiquity. When John Gwyn later argued for a Royal Academy, he still put this first:

'I have made use of the word *design* in this essay, to express the supreme inventive art of the painter, sculptor or architect abstractly considered . . . The great organ or instrument of this art is *draught* or *drawing* . . . Without this neither the genius nor learning of the designer, painter or sculptor can be displayed to advantage. It is the *sine qua non*, after all other accomplishments are obtained.'[59]

This was all very well, but before you were allowed to draw a whole body you had to do a perfect head. And before you could move on to heads, you had to draw all other parts of the body. Before you could even look at a life model of *any* of these – hands, feet or heads – you had to draw them, with academic, repeatable accuracy, first from prints and drawings, then from *copies* of classical casts. Everything was codified. The rules of proportion, for example, demanded that the face be divided and measured on these kind of lines:

> Forehead to chin = three noses
> Length of mouth = one nose
> Hollow of eyes = one nose
> Space between ear and eye = one nose[60]

81

No wonder Hogarth brooded. In a very late print, *The Five Orders of Periwigs*, he caustically wrote off such academic rules:

One nodule

3 Nasos

each Naso 34 Minutes.

In his autobiographical notes, Hogarth moved straight from the passage about the limitations of silver engraving into an assault on conventional art education. He had learned 'by practice, to copy with tolerable exactness in the usual way', but he felt there were was something wrong, even in copying 'the best masters'.[61] He was learning only to *copy*, not to *draw*, what he saw, with true perception. Sometimes the originals were faulty, and, even when they were good, 'it was little more than pouring water out of one vessel into another'. Copying gave no sense of the whole: since you took your eye constantly from the original, drawing a bit at a time, you could end knowing as little about the subject as you had at the beginning. If drawing was like writing, being a copyist was like being a lawyer's clerk, who copies every line without remembering it or, if it be in Latin or French, without even understanding it.[62]

George Vertue would later tell how Hogarth put everyone's back up with his 'undaunted spirit'.[63] Even as a student he probably spoke out, and all his life he argued against copying: 'A wagish brother replied at the time yes and the best way to learn to swim was never to go into the water.'[64] It was true, Hogarth's trust in observation and memory could amount to a licence for not going to classes at all. When he was involved in running an academy himself in the 1730s and 1740s, this was still the doctrine he 'preach'd as well as practic'd':

'an arch Brother of the pencil gave it this turn That the only way to learn to draw well was never to draw at all. in short these notions as they clash'd with most of the commonly receiv'd ones of the school drew me into frequent disputes with my brethren in which as the torrent was against me I seldom got the better of the argument.'[65]

'The torrent was against me' – that shows how strong he felt the opposition was. But it also suggests his own strength, that of a sturdy swimmer fighting the stream. Sometimes his lack of conventional education was a positive help; he could cut through the cant, invent his own systems. Circumstances held him back, he said, but he had one material advantage over his competitors, the early habit of 'retaining in my mind's Eye whatever I designed to imitate'.[66] The daring and self-confidence are typical, and so is the keen pleasure of gaining an edge over others.

82

The followers of Shaftesbury and Richardson continued to value the classical, putting general, abstract perfection above realism. The kind of skill Hogarth had in drawing an 'exact likeness' came at the bottom of the scale of worth; no connoisseurship was needed to judge *that*. This was especially true if the subject was itself 'low'. So when Hogarth insisted that he would not slavishly copy classical models or dead old masters but would draw from nature and memory, he was wilfully thumbing his nose at established ideas.

Later, when he stressed his pleasure in strolling the streets and catching 'momentary actions and expressions', he added that

'by this Idle way of proceeding I grew so profane as to admire Nature beyond Pictures and I confess sometimes objected to the devinity of even Raphael Urbin Correggio and Michael angelo for which I have been severly treated.'[67]

That this alleged disrespect is untrue is shown by the many borrowings and allusions in his work which reveal him to be steeped in classical tradition – even the head of the little boy crying in *Noon* is taken from Poussin's *Rape of the Sabines*. Some of his careful academic sketches have also survived. Hogarth was acutely aware of new movements as well as those of the past. Among the foreign artists in London in 1719–20 was Watteau, consulting Dr Richard Mead for his failing health, and Hogarth responded swiftly to the new, flowing, delicate French styles.

His astounding memory retained images from all the paintings and prints he saw and he adapted them with flair. He acquired an avid – if largely second-hand – knowledge of the great art of past and present, fusing his mental notation of daily life with models from the long history of art. But he parodied the classics even while he echoed them. If he took a starting point such as Shaftesbury's *Choice of Hercules* he placed the 'choice' in the *real*, grubby, self-interested world: Moll Hackabout between the clergyman and the bawd; Tom Rakewell between the tailor and woman he abandons; the Grenadier at Finchley between Protestant wife and Catholic hag. He brought the baroque heavens down to earth.

In his twenties Hogarth's life swung backwards and forwards across the arc between Smithfield and Covent Garden. As if seeking a place to situate himself in the flow of city life, he veered between the 'ordinary' worlds of the tradesman and the journeyman engraver and those of the popular satirist and the would-be painter, between the critic and the advocate of the 'polite'. Each track had its own continuum, and as Hogarth jumped from one to the other, they merged in a headlong rush of principle and opportunism.

5

Stocks, Operas and Satires

A public or a private robber
A Statesman or a South Sea jobber.
A prelate who no God believes;
A Parliament or den of thieves.
JONATHAN SWIFT, 'To Mr Gay' (1728)

THE START OF HOGARTH'S CAREER coincided with events that cast a hectic shadow over London and the nation. In April 1720, when he was printing his new engraver's trade card, the South Sea Bill was introduced into the Commons. The idea was that the South Sea Company should help the government by taking over a large part of the National Debt. In return it would receive an annual interest of 5 per cent and be granted a monopoly of trade to the Pacific Islands and West Indies. The Company itself was based on John Law's 'Mississippi Company', currently causing a stockmarket boom in Paris, and introducing a new word into the French language – 'millionaire'.

Hogarth's friends were more likely to be dodging bailiffs than buying stock. He had just engraved a benefit card for the comic actor James Spiller, probably for 'The Entertainment of *Robinson Crusoe*' at Lincoln's Inn Fields on 31 March. Spiller was a popular character actor, specializing in old men – smallpox had left him blind in one eye, and he made great dramatic use of his squint, which can be seen in Hogarth's print. A great drinker, known for his low humour, he was perpetually broke (he said the benefit night was for 'myself and my creditors') and was in the Marshalsea or the Fleet as often as on stage. His favourite haunt was 'the Ball and Butcher', run by an ex-gaoler at the Marshalsea, the home of the 'Clare Market Artists Club'. In the benefit card, poor Spiller is poised between tavern and prison. Fortune's wheel turns above the scales, horribly weighted on the prison side, where 'the Taylor's Bill' floats down to join 'Gin', 'Tripe' and 'Tobacco'. To save him, the bills must be counterbalanced by coins thrown down by the benefit audience, but as Spiller hands out tickets marked 'Box', 'Pit' and 'Gallery', he looks like a man at the stake; an ominous trail of gunpowder is running towards the stack of unsold tickets at his feet.

15 Benefit Ticket for Spiller (*c.*1720)

The fuse was being set for many more than Spiller. In the rush for South Sea stock, kindling for a financial *auto-da-fé* was being piled beneath the feet of thousands. Fortunes changed hands and huge parcels of stock 'on credit' were handed out as sweeteners to MPs, officials and members of the Royal Family. As the summer temperatures rose, so did the South Sea fever. Everyone gambled on prices leaping upwards although some canny individuals sold, rather than bought. Sir Isaac Newton, allegedly declaring that while he could calculate the movement of heavenly bodies there was no way he could measure the madness of people, sold £7000 of stock in April, making a solid 100 per cent. Two days later old Thomas Guy began to sell his huge holding, now tripled in value to £150,000. Over six weeks, sailing on a rising market, he sold parcel after parcel of stock – ending up with £234,000: 'the largest honest fortune made out of the Bubble, and the hospital it built is the best memorial the Bubble has left behind it'.[1]

Few people realized it but by the time the Bill became law in May and the price of stock had quadrupled, the whole of the £2 million raised by subscriptions had already been handed as lures to politicians and brokers. Until the London season ended in July and the fashionable departed for their country estates, the Bubble grew. Vast paper fortunes were made and spent. Rents in London rose forty-five times. Smaller bubbles clustered round the greater: every day, new and more absurd companies were floated – for trading in hair, dealing in woad, importing broomsticks from Germany, mining gold in 'Terra Australis', starting coral fisheries and calico factories. Projects listed in the press ran to several pages, many aiming at raising a million, 2 million, 4 million, 10 million pounds, and each based at a coffee house or tavern. Sometimes not even a hint of realism was needed to lure the punters:

'this day, the 8th instant, at Sam's coffee-house, behind the Royal Exchange, at three in the afternoon, a book will be opened for entering into a co-partnership for carrying a *thing* that will turn to the advantage of the concerned'.[2]

But uneasy rumours began to spread. At the end of August, on the eve of Bartholomew Fair, while the streets around the Hogarths' house in Long Lane were packed with people preparing for carnival, dressed as devils, prelates and freaks, crowds began besieging South Sea House demanding to sell – for cash. The Bubble had burst.

The ballad-singers duly recorded the disaster. To the tune of 'Over the Hills and Far Away', they sang a new song that began very jauntily – 'Jews, Turks and Christians, hear my song/I'll make you rich before it's long' – but ended with an ironic, vengeful chorus:

> A bubble is blown up in air,
> In which fine prospects do appear;
> The Bubble breaks, the prospect's lost,
> Yet must some Bubble pay the cost.
>   Hubble Bubble; all is smoke,
>   Hubble Bubble; all is broke,
>   Farewell your Houses, Lands and Flocks
>   For all you have is now in Stocks.[3]

At Bartholemew Fair, travelling players staged *The Broken-Stockjobbers: Or, Work for the Bailiffs*, in which a bank director, Mr Pluckwell, and his colleague, Mr Transfer, swindle all ranks of society from Lord Equipage downwards, via Sir Frippery Upstart, Dr Sinecure and Headless, before they too go bust.

That autumn the tangle of credit, obligations and ruin was gradually revealed. Deaths and suicides in Britain were matched by news of plague in France and the papers wove together the language of infection, disease and

86

corruption.[4] The Edinburgh poet Allan Ramsay told of speculators treating the whores with

> Gowd frae Banks built in the Air.
> For which their Danaes lift the Lap,
> And compliment them with a Clap,
> Which by aft jobbing grows a Pox
> Till Brigs of Noses fall with Stocks.[5]

All through these months, satirical prints from the Netherlands had been flooding the town, their castles in the air, whirling windmills and scantily clad allegorical figures sharing the space with real places – Jonathan's and Garraway's coffee houses, the Exchange, Bedlam and the Fleet. Foxes and fools' caps, jugglers and wheels of fate appeared in broadsheets and ballads, on playing cards and fans, in theatres and pamphlets and poems. In this atmosphere, the whirligigs and freaks of the fair became emblems of a greedy world.

By the end of 1720, when Hogarth was enrolling at the Vanderbank academy, top politicians, courtiers, even the Royal Family, were tarred by responsibility for the disaster. A Parliamentary Commission was demanded and people murmured of Jacobite plots. In January 1721, when the Cashier, Robert Knight, fled to France (Sir James Thornhill had been painting his new mansion only a few months before) the government seemed likely to topple. At this point, Robert Walpole stepped in. He had been saved from ruin himself, when he tried to buy more stock, by a lucky delay in the post and a mistake by his banker. Chance was on his side, and now he made it work for him again. Merely by promising rescue schemes and sacrificing a few minor politicians, he restored confidence with a conjuror's speed and sleight of hand. His luck in others' misfortunes continued; early the next year Sunderland dropped dead and in May 1721 Walpole became First Lord of the Treasury and Chancellor of the Exchequer, the most important posts in the government before the establishment of a formal Prime Minister.

While Walpole's star was rising, many men were ruined. In April 1721 the *Daily Post* spoke for these debtors, and perhaps for William Hogarth too – the Bubble had burst over London only two years after his father's death:

'To imprison an undone Gentleman, or a ruin'd Tradesman NOW; or to keep them confin'd that are already shut up, is it not like murdering those that are sick of the Plague? The Distemper has been a Visitation; *South Sea* has been

87

a Judgment from Heaven; Shall we not pity them whom God has smitten? . . .
When shall the cries of the Prisoners be heard?'

The national scandal was the subject of Hogarth's first surviving print, *The
South Sea Scheme*, probably made in 1721 but not published until three years
later. A beginner's work, it shared many images of the Bubble prints – Dutch,
French and English – that had poured out in the past year, but although
Hogarth was using a common language, the energy he gave it was all his
own. His *South Sea Scheme* has the fairground hysteria and cruelty of
St Bartholomew's Eve: the devil carving flesh from blindfolded Fortune and
hurling chunks to the crowd; the nobles and bawds and bankers riding their
merry-go-round, the truncated horses' heads like pricks and balls. Like

16 *The South Sea Scheme* (1724)

contemporary journalists, he linked the crisis to others that had convulsed the city, like the Plague or the Fire of London, whose monument he adapts. 'And is not the City on Fire now?' cried one paper. 'Has not a devouring flame consume'd Families innumerable?'[6]

Hogarth picked up all the common satirical themes, from the gambling clergy (the Director of the Company, Blunt, was a Bible-spouting Baptist) to the orgasmic mix of speculation and sex. Above all, though, Hogarth attacked the loss of principle. In his allegorical figures in the foreground, Self Interest breaks Honesty on the wheel; Villainy flogs Honour, and Trade lies ragged and abandoned – a crumpled woman in the corner of the square. The use of space, of city buildings, the sense of movement, the witty juxtapositions and the strong emotions – all announced the arrival of a new talent.

In the same year Hogarth carefully etched and engraved another emblematic plate, *The Lottery*. For years lotteries had been the butt of satire, aimed both at a state built on gambling and at the general lust for easy money, the magical dream of a life transformed. Almost every printmaker had something on this theme; as with *The South Sea Scheme* Hogarth was cutting his teeth, testing his invention on a hackneyed theme. This print was in a very different style. It is far more stiff and sober, and the raunchy verse of the South Sea print is replaced by a conventional key. Apollo shows Britannia a picture of the earth enriched by herself, but that picture is an illusion: in reality, Fortune draws blanks and prizes; Suspense is whirled round by Hope and Fear, and Good Luck is seized by Pleasure and Folly. Misfortune subsides in grief, Sloth hides his head and Avarice hugs his money, while Fraud beckons at Despair through a little door in the pedestal wall. The allegorical cast shares the space with well-worn emblems – wheels of fortune, a windmill, castles in the air.

Both the cast and the emblems were also standard features of contemporary pantomimes as well as prints. Hogarth's figures, in flamboyant poses beneath a huge, framing curtain, suggest that lotteries too are theatrical tricks. Yet if *The Lottery*'s world is a stage, it is also a prison, with one tiny barred window letting in the light. And perhaps Hogarth also had another target, the art academy with its constraining rules; while his South Sea scene was based on cheap Dutch prints, this design echoes Raphael's *School of Athens*. By linking great art with cheap greed he undermines the whole panoply of classical 'authority' and 'virtu': *his* 'Virtue', leaning heavily on her tomes of poetry, history and divinity, is sinking slowly through the floor, which is cracking beneath her weight.

Hogarth worked on both these plates, making one or two proofs, but choosing not to publish them. By 1721 his *South Sea Scheme* was already late

89

The Explanation. 1. Upon the Pedestal National Credit leaning on a Pillar supported by Justice. 2. Apollo shewing Britannia a Picture representing the Earth receiving enriching Showers drawn from her self (an Emblem of State Lottery's). 3 Fortune Drawing the Blanks and Prizes. 4. Wantonness Drawing of Numb. 5. Before the Pedestal Suspence turn'd to & fro by Hope & Fear.

The LOTTERY

6. On one hand, GoodLuck being Elevated is seized by Pleasur Folly; Fame perswading him to raise sinking Virtue, Arts &c. 7. On other hand Misfortune opprest by Grief, Minerva supporting points to the Sweets of Industry. 8. Sloth hiding his head in Curtain: 9. On y' other side, Avarice hugging his Mony. 10. Fraud tempting Despair n° Mony at a Trap-door in the Pedestal.
Price one Shill.

17 *The Lottery* (1724)

and could be missed among so many others. If he published it, he would also declare himself politically and this might alienate influential men, even Thornhill himself, who was linked to Robert Knight, the Cashier of the Company, and had made £2000 by selling when stock reached its peak. Meanwhile, *The South Sea Scheme* and *The Lottery* lay stacked in his workshop, collecting dust.

After the fiasco of the Bubble, Hogarth watched the corrupt and greedy system he had attacked increasing in power. Walpole had screened the South Sea directors, and the politicians and the Court, from public scrutiny so successfully that he became known as 'Skreen-Master General'. Soon he tightened his grip by giving every possible office to friends and relatives,

90

reframing London's City charter to increase his allies' hold, and seizing the chance of the failed Jacobite 'Atterbury plot' in late 1722 to purge Tory enemies.[7] Habeas corpus was suspended; the Catholic community was punitively fined; pamphleteers and satirists were arrested. The following year the Waltham Black Act was passed. Ostensibly aimed at a particular group of poachers (with alleged Jacobite leanings), the Act decreed that any man in disguise or with his face blackened was guilty of felony. This created a remit so wide that innumerable trivial crimes were turned at one stroke into capital offences for which men, women and children might – and did – hang: 'the most savage English statute of all time, and, probably, the most bloodthirsty piece of legislation promulgated anywhere in Europe'.[8]

Although Walpole and Townshend were faced with a storm of hostile prints in the next few years, Hogarth kept his head low. His prints are critical of *general* corruption, but he was careful to keep his way clear with both the Court and the Opposition.

18 Shop Card for Ellis Gamble (*c.* 1720)

91

As a working craftsman Hogarth wanted the stability that fostered trade. His money came from the cards and shop bills that were part of the staple work for a small, independent engraver. All tradesmen and tradeswomen liked to have their own designs, often with little pictures showing their place of work, or the goods they sold, ephemera that make up a rich jigsaw of eighteenth-century London life. Hogarth made an early card for the goldsmith and jeweller William Hardy,[9] and one for his former master, Ellis Gamble, when Gamble moved to 'the Golden Angel in Cranbourn Street, Leicester Fields' in 1724. This was an elaborate affair, with English and French inscriptions and a buxom angel wafting on clouds in an elegant scrolled frame.

These small commercial works showed Hogarth's inventiveness, if not his perfect technique (Gamble's angel has six fingers). On a funeral ticket made for a Westminster undertaker he drew a shadowed procession of mourners against a sunlit crowd.[10] In the letterhead for a Tiverton school, he included a little maid watering an orange tree while a boy looks on.[11] He drew men

19 Shop Card for Mrs Holt's Italian Warehouse (n.d.)

92

loading bales and jars and boxes on to a ship ready for 'Mrs Holt's Italian Warehouse', where you could buy fans, Leghorn bonnets, lute and violin strings, essences and balms, 'And in a Back Warehouse all Sorts of Italian Wines, Florence Cordials, Oyl, Olives, Anchovies, Capers, Vermicelli, Bolognia Sausidges, Parmesan. Cheeses. Naple Soap etc.' At first glance it seems that Mercury with winged feet – the patron of merchants – is clearly being dispatched by Mrs Holt with a shopping list. In fact the seated woman is 'Florence', waving him off, and the other trading cities, Naples, Venice, Leghorn and Genoa, are inscribed in the corners. Even in this tiny card, Hogarth is playing wittily on a classical image, adapting his Mercury from a figure in Vaga's cycle *The Loves of the Gods*, which he would have seen in the print shops engraved by Caraglio.[12]

Another window opened for Hogarth in 1722 when he began to get work as a book illustrator, joining a small group of English engravers producing plates for La Motraye's *Travels*.[13] The job probably came through personal recommendation, from men like Louis Chéron or the engravers and book-sellers he met in the coffee houses. Two volumes of the *Travels* appeared in 1723: 'the whole embellished with PRINTS and CUTS, curiously engraved on COPPER-PLATES'. The large, leather-bound volumes were typical of current prestige publishing; five City booksellers were involved, selling to subscribers (including Chandos and Burlington).[14] Most of the engravers copied very closely from a contemporary French work.[15] Hogarth, even at this stage, is freer and more original, using the details from the French prints to create lively groups: a woman at the baths; the 'Grand Seignior' surrounded by sycophantic courtiers; the Atmeydan, where the Turks exercise their horses while a bride rides under a canopy towards a bridegroom she has never seen.

Engravings, especially for these grand publishing projects, were often collaborative works, with different people taking responsibility for different stages. If an artist's name appears with 'del.' (for *delineavit*) beside it, he produced the drawing from which the plate was engraved; 'inv.' or 'invent.' (*invenit*) can mean the same, or imply that the print was taken from a painting, not a precise drawing. The actual work of engraving is marked 'sculpt.' (*sculpsit*), or 'fec.' (*fecit*) if a different process was used. Hogarth signed his name to these plates, but although he had freely adapted other scenes the only one he marked 'W Hogarth invent.' as well as 'sculpt.' is *Charles XII at Bender*, a composite of maps with an uncurling scene above. Like many of the illustrations, this is a mixed, 'functional' work. The lack of realism

93

(as in another lovely Lapland scene, which has to get everything into one place – fishing, hunting, milking reindeer, babies in papooses) was like his early prints, which brought together buildings from different parts of London.

20 *A Lapland Hut*, illustration for La Motraye's *Travels* (1724)

Unfolding these plates, tucked into the back of the first two volumes, you can see Hogarth learning, copying, adapting. Technically, he is still a novice who has not quite mastered the difficult art of writing on the plates (this has to be traced, then engraved – effectively mirror writing). Spelling was never his strong point, even in an age where it varied from person to person, and one of Hogarth's maps, where the names are elegantly arranged around the confluence of rivers, has a phonetic 'artillary', a squadron of 'gards' and a place for 'Battilians'. An 'e' is missing from 'recroutes' and from 'Eusberg' – hastily scratched in above.

94

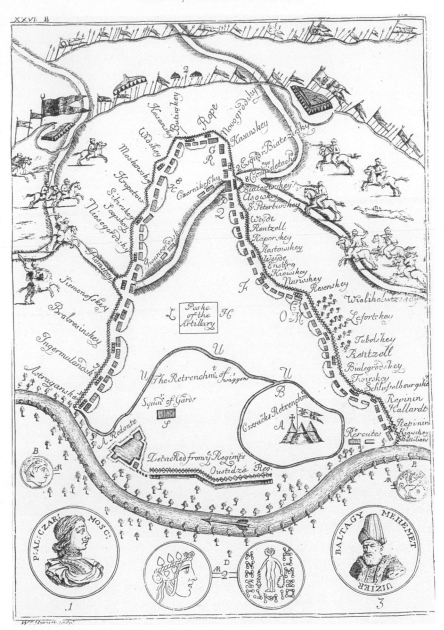

21 *Parke of the Artillary*

95

Book illustration paid, but it also allowed Hogarth to play with the ideal worlds of the imagination and convention, and the real world of nature and city life. As he undertook more work after the *Travels*, each project demanded a different style. Some were commissioned, and some he seems to have undertaken on his own, either for his own satisfaction, or to offer to a bookseller later. He experimented, and varied his style, producing theatrical caves and curtained bedchambers for La Calpranède's *Cassandra*, a high-flown French romance; baroque grandeur for *Paradise Lost*, a Hell teeming with fallen angels, Heaven ablaze with rainbows (never published); gruesome, Callot-like realism for fourteen tiny prints for John Beaver's *Roman Military Punishments*.[16] Callot was still his master: his Roman prints copied Callot's *Misères et Malheurs de la Guerre* in size and subject, and the *South Sea Scheme*'s whirligig also refers back ironically to *La Pendaison*, in the same series, where the central tree bears a dangling crop of hanged men, victims of the Thirty Years War.

By the time the La Motraye *Travels* was published, Hogarth had moved back to his old apprentice district, taking lodgings at the Golden Ball on the corner of Cranbourne Alley and Little Newport Street, just north east of Leicester Fields. From this address in February 1724, aged twenty-six, he felt confident enough to issue his first independent print, *Masquerades and Operas* or *The Taste of the Town*, priced at one shilling. This time, he hit straight at the Burlington–Kent group, at luxury, newness, the foreign and the classical.

Italian opera had been the most derided of all cultural imports ever since it first came to the Haymarket nearly twenty years before. John Dennis had railed against it in 1706; Thomas Betterton had bewailed the loss of serious English drama in the face of 'prodigal subscriptions for Squeaking Italians and capering Monsieurs';[17] Steele and Addison had waged a hilarious battle against it in *The Spectator*. (Addison's view was undoubtedly embittered by the humiliating three-night run of his competing vernacular opera, *Rosamund*, in 1707.) Although Handel, on his first visit to London, had scored a hit with *Rinaldo* in 1710, after the Jacobite rebellion the Italian opera's popularity flagged, and it disappeared from the Haymarket stage in 1717. Two years later, its supporters founded the Royal Academy of Music, specifically for its promotion. It, too, would be run on the lines of a joint-stock company, with each subscriber funding at least £200 of stock. The Lord Chamberlain, the Duke of Newcastle, led the drive for subscriptions with £1000; Chandos and Burlington gave the same amount; sixty other subscribers offered an average of £200, and George I – a lifelong enthusiast for music, despite his reputation

96

for philistinism – promised an annual royal grant of another £1000. Although some merchants and professional men were involved (Pope's friend Arbuthnot was a director), this was very much a Court initiative: the subscribers included seven dukes, a marquis, twelve earls and four viscounts.[18]

The plan was to ensure that operas would continue at the Haymarket, with the Swiss impresario Heidegger as general manager. Handel, as 'Master of Music', was sent abroad to bring back star Italian singers. In the second season, the famous castrato Francesco Bernard, known as Senesino, arrived and signed a contract for an astounding £2000; the next great signing, in December 1722, was the famous soprano, the tiny Francesca Cuzzoni. With Handel's wonderful new music, opera was all the rage again and the tantrums and intrigues of its stars provided Londoners with endless amusement. As an extra diversion Heidegger also introduced lavish masquerades, where as many as seven hundred people would gather at the Haymarket in disguise, in the glow of hundreds of wax lights. Here the art of deception was practised *by* the people as well as on them. Needless to say, to these disguises the Waltham Black Act did not apply.

Inevitably, people compared the craze for opera to the South Sea Bubble. The Academy's drive had begun in early 1720, at the same time as the South Sea Bill was introduced into the Commons. Both company and opera traded in shares, their notices appearing side by side in the press, and they became inextricably linked in the public mind. In March 1720, Steele attacked the 'No sense or Nonsense' of the opera in his journal *The Theatre*. Greed for profit, he declared, was swamping reason and conscience:

'there is a Stock laid in to impose upon the Stupidity of their Admirers; and it is expected that there will be a nightly Succession of Bubbles in Numbers large enough, who will part with their Cash, as well as their Understanding, to support a mechanick and mean Profit rais'd by Gentlemen of Honour and Quality upon ingenuous Arts.'[19]

At the end he quipped: 'Yesterday South Sea was 174. Opera Company 83 and a half. No transfer.' In 1721 Swift extended the analogy, including masquerades as well as the operas:

'I have been concerned for several years past, upon account of the publick as well as of myself, to see how ill a taste for wit and sense prevails in the world, which politicks and South-sea, and party and Opera's and Masquerades have introduced.'[20]

97

Bishop Berkeley raged against all such symptoms of 'luxury' as a spiritual version of the plague:

'Our Gaming, our operas, our Maskerades, are, in spite of our Debts and Poverty, become the Wonders of our Neighbours . . . The Plague dreadful as it is, is an Evil of short duration; Cities have often recovered and flourished after it; but when was it known that a People broken and corrupted by Luxury recovered themselves?'[21]

The issue inevitably became politicized. If operas and masquerades were public wonders, representative of general corruption, then Walpole was the impresario of the state, just as Heidegger was of the Haymarket. In the rush for novelty – as in the scramble for money and power – it seemed that people were being manipulated into losing their traditions, their sense of themselves, their inheritance. In February 1723 Gay told Swift:

'There's nobody allowed to say I sing but an Eunuch or an Italian Woman. Every body is grown now as great a judge of Music as they were in your time of Poetry, and folks that could not distinguish one tune from another now daily dispute about the different Styles of Hendel, Bonocini and Attillio. People have now forgot Homer, and Virgil & Caesar, or at least they have lost their ranks, for in London and Westminster in all polite conversations, Senesino is daily voted to be the greatest man that ever liv'd.'[22]

At the same time, critics also complained that cultural standards were being attacked from below, as well as corrupted from above. The popular success of 1723 was a lavish pantomime staged by John Rich at Lincoln's Inn Fields, *The Necromancer, or Harlequin Dr Faustus* (which immediately prompted a rival at Drury Lane). The 'Contrivance and Deception' of Rich's effects,[23] reached an almost devilish pitch:

'You will see strange alterations, Cloaks flying upon Men's shoulders, Harlequin, Scaramouch, Punch and Pierrot riding upon spirits in the Air; Dancing Wheat Sheaves, flaming Barns, barking Dogs, flying Flasks and Oranges, and Fellows, to escape a Scouring, venture their Necks down a Chimney.'[24]

Horror gave an added thrill when the fiery dragon carried off Faustus. One night the fiery dragon actually took fire, but the 'Dragon Maker' provided another 'which is so well lined and cased, as to be proof against the like Casualty in the future'.

Satire was implicit: the leaders of state could easily be seen as well-cased dragons, proof against 'casualties' like the Bubble. And they could also be seen as Mephistopheles – a figure to whom Heidegger was also often compared. He too effected transformations. At his masquerades, fancy dress or enveloping black dominoes blurred all individual identity, crossing lines of race, class and sex. Masqueraders chirped in high-pitched tones, like birds, to disguise their voices; they were transformed into creatures other than themselves. To many onlookers it seemed as though people were living in a dream world which afflicted them like a sickness.

A stream of satires attacked the 'Taste of the Town', bringing together disguise, luxury and lack of spiritual leadership. The moan was so conventional that even the Haymarket audience had to listen to this prologue in February 1724:

> New Artists, new Machines, new Dances rise
> ('Tis Pity Novelty can't make ye wise,)
> Now shrill Cutzoni reigns, and Harlequin
> And Faustus thunders thro' the magick Scene.
> His Spells, this mighty Necromancer forms,
> How strangely does the subtle Witchcraft spread?

It seemed that this madness was almost built into the stones of the new city rising around the people. London was flowering and collapsing at the same time. Its prosperity, like many of its new houses, was jerry-built, insubstantial, scary. When La Motraye looked back on the great building works of London since 1713, he drew on the imagery of wild inflation:

'It is almost incredible, how much this City has been embellished since that Year. The *Londoners* and the *Parisians* seem to have been possessed with the same Spirit of building on Earth as well as in the Air. Witness *Mississippi* and the *South Sea Bubble.*'25

Hogarth loved spectacle as much as anyone but he knew a rich vein of satire, and a ready market, when he saw them. He did more than join the conventional outcry. As he was to prove so often in the years ahead, his success lay in a brilliant dramatization of contemporary themes, not in original ideas. His own principles were involved here: he did feel that current 'taste' was false, mercenary and harmful and, with his own *métier* in mind, he made a special point of applying this to British art.

In *Masquerades and Operas* he brought key London buildings together in a telling triangle, like the painted flats of a huge stage set, just as he had with the Guildhall, the Monument and St Paul's in the *South Sea Scheme*. This time,

99

Could new dumb Faustus, to reform the Age,
Conjure up Shakespear's or Ben Johnson's Ghost,
They'd blush for shame, to see the English Stage
Debauch'd by fool'ries, at so great a cost.

What would their Manes say? should they behold
Monsters and Masquerades, where usefull Plays
Adorn'd the fruitfull Theatre of old.
And Rival Wits contended for the Bays.

Price 1 Shilling. 1724

22 *Masquerades and Operas* (1724)

though, they were all connected with culture. In the print, the Haymarket Opera House is on the left. Heidegger grins from the window, while the signs mock both high and low culture, the Italian opera and 'Faux', the conjuror Fawkes, who performed here for statesmen and royalty. The signboard for the opera is based on a contemporary print (probably by John Vanderbank) of Berendstadt, Cuzzoni and Senesino perfoming Handel's *Flavio* in May 1723, but here it shows a nobleman flinging coins at Cuzzoni's feet crying, 'Pray accept £8000.' Stories often overlap in these prints, and the kneeling figure is

100

usually taken to be the eccentric hero of the Siege of Barcelona, Charles Mordaunt, 3rd Earl of Peterborough. (He had carried off another leading singer, Anastasia Robinson, to 'a love nest in Parson's Green', eventually making an honest woman of her after 'a wasting illness and the triumph of her devout Christian principles brought him to his senses'.)[26] When this print appeared, Cuzzoni was starring as Cleopatra in a new opera, *Giulio Cesare*, and while London crowds laughed at Hogarth's satire she was ravishing the cognoscenti with her beautiful arias.

Hogarth's grouping links the worlds of opera, Court and money: the devil leading the masqueraders waves £1000, the donation that the King gave to Heidegger. 'Dexterity' – the art of Fawkes – was the hallmark of politics as well as of conjurors and pantomimes. On the opposite side of the print is the theatre at Lincoln's Inn Fields with its banner announcing 'Dr Faustus is here.' And in the background, presiding over the whole scene, is the new Palladian gateway to Burlington House, its gates tightly shut to the common passers-by. On top of the pedestal, with the supporting stone figures of Michelangelo and Raphael bending in reverence, Kent wields his palette like an emperor (but waves his paintbrush, tellingly, towards a badly painted sign). The suggestion is that any 'Academy of Arts' would be as as dubious as the operatic 'Academy of Music', promoted by shady entrepreneurs.[27]

In the square below, Hogarth shows a fool and a satyr (the same figures who seduced 'Good Luck' in *The Lottery*) shepherding men and women disguised as Bishops, Quakers and Turks into the masquerade, while nobles wearing Stars and Garters join the common people flocking to the panto-mime. In the open space between them, an old woman trundles a wheel-barrow full of 'Waste-paper for Shops' – the works of Congreve, Dryden, Shakespeare, Addison and Jonson.[28]

The normal practice was for an engraver to work for a printseller-publisher, who sold the work through his own shop, or in batches to other outlets, and kept the plate, reprinting when needed, with no further income to the artist. Hoping to reap the full rewards of his work, Hogarth published *Masquerades and Operas* from his own workshop, a revolutionary step. The printsellers would not let him get away with this dangerous precedent. Immediately piracies appeared, undercutting Hogarth's original. And immediately Hogarth thought of his father, destroyed by the booksellers and 'great men's promises'. When he himself was providing plates for the book-sellers, he said, 'I found this Tribe as my father left them when he died' –

'So that I doubly felt their usage which put me on publishing on my own

101

account but here again I [met] a monopoly of Printsellers equally distructeve to the Ingenious for the first plate I Published called the Tast of the Town in which the then reigning follies were lashd, had no sooner begun to take run but I found copies of it in the print[shops] selling for half the price whilst the originals return'd [to] me again in which I [was] obliged to sell my plate [for what] these pyrates pleasd to give me, as there was no place of sale but at their Shops.'[29]

With characteristic stubbornness, he refused to give in easily. Before he admitted himself beaten by the pirates, he leapt to the attack, placing an advertisement in the *Daily Courant*. He had obviously arranged his own distribution, from the City to Pall Mall, Burlington's very doorstep. Genuine prints were to be found, he said, at

'Mr Hennekin's, the Corner of Hemming's Row; Mr Regnier's, in Great Newport Street; Mr Bolle's [Bowles], in St Paul's church-yard; Mr Gautier's, in the Piazza at Covent-Garden; Mr Overton's at the Market; at the corner of Pall Mall.'[30]

He ended with heavy irony, giving the final legitimate source,

'at Wm Hogarth's, the Engraver therof, at the Golden Ball in Little Newport-street, and no where else. Price 1s. Copies as well done as the present Copies sold at other petty Print Shops, will be sold for a penny a piece in three Days Time.'

When another 'sham advertisment' appeared, he protested again.

The fuss made Hogarth known, and, ironically, also helped his reputation with the booksellers. In February, his print was praised in the journal *Pasquin*, bringing a useful new connection with its young editor, Nicholas Amhurst. In March, a new edition of Gildon's *Metamorphosis* (a modern version of Apuleius, first published in 1708) was specifically advertised as carrying 'Cutts engraved by Mr Hogarth'.[31] The frontispiece showed his developing skill, with a brisk vignette of the modern story framed in an arch and a curtain pulled aside by two satyrs; above, seated on the curve of the arch, the author swings his feet over the scene, flanked by statues of Apuleius and Lucian.

Hogarth was launching himself upon the town. Three months later, in May, there was a solar eclipse, and in the weeks before Londoners rushed to buy special glasses to view it. Already a shrewd opportunist, Hogarth now published *Royalty, Episcopacy and Law*, at 6d, half the price of his first work. Its inscription: 'Some of the Principal Inhabitants of ye Moon, as they were perfectly Discover'd by a Telescope brought to ye Greatest Perfection since ye last Eclipse', suggested that if people look closely, they see their rulers have no real bodies, no souls, no brains – they are *entirely* made up of clothes, objects, material gains, guineas, keys and candlesticks.

This print's hostility to the ruling cabal of State, Church and Law could not be clearer. Now that his name was known, he had nothing to lose and everything to gain by speaking out. This summer he finally decided to issue *The South Sea Scheme* and *The Lottery*, at a shilling apiece.

1724 was a proving an extraordinary year. Hogarth had won a secure place among the commercial engravers and book illustrators; he had announced himself as an independent satirist; he had battled with piratical printsellers.

In *Masquerades and Operas* he had also introduced what would be a characteristic motif, playing high culture against low, and suggesting that, at base, there was little to choose between them. In his print of *Royalty*, full of 'low' emblems, he made glancing references to the grouping of Thornhill's latest royal paintings at Greenwich. And in this year Thornhill himself made a leap from 'high' to 'low' that suggested a slightly cynical feeling about the kinship between the two. At Greenwich he had to make his modern subjects – George I, his family and Court – recognizable and realistic, while situating them in the cloudy heavens and classical allegories that would command the viewers' awe. The self-portrait in his painting of the Royal Family had a slightly harassed, ironic expression. Grand though he was, Thornhill still drank in the Covent Garden taverns, drew mock-Dutch scenes of revelry, and mixed with a fairly raffish crowd. And in November 1724 he stepped sideways, as it were, into this world, when he painted a portrait of the twenty-two-year-old criminal Jack Sheppard before his execution, in Newgate gaol.

Sheppard, a cockney apprentice, was a popular hero, not because of his crimes (standard housebreaking exploits) but because of his bravery, his daring escapes and his feud with the hated Jonathan Wild, an arch crook who operated through well-organized gangs but never risked taking part himself. Wild was a *modern*, entrepreneurial criminal, who made money by selling property back to its owners and, most significantly, by setting himself up as a 'thieftaker' and claiming official bounty money (thus terrorizing gang members and wiping out rivals). In February 1724 Sheppard was imprisoned in St Giles Roundhouse. He escaped, but in May Wild had him arrested and sent to the New Prison. In a week, he escaped once more. In July Wild caught him again and he was locked in Newgate's condemned cell. On the night before his execution, he vanished. By this time he was famous, and his quips and adventures were circulating through London. After Wild tracked him down again, Sheppard was chained to the floor of the strongest room in Newgate, the 'Castle', but a few days later London erupted with delight when he escaped again – through chains, padlocks and six iron-barred doors. Jack Sheppard seemed a magic figure, a hero of ballads. For three months he was free, protected by the populace, until Wild cornered him in a Drury Lane gin shop. In Newgate, weighed down by three hundred pounds of iron fetters, he was visited by crowds of curious socialites, including Sir James Thornhill. (The Newgate gaolers did well, charging 1s 6d each.) On 16 November he was hanged.

Sheppard was immediately incorporated into London legend, and Defoe wrote a vivid, sympathetic *Narrative of All the Robberies, escapes, etc of Jack Sheppard*. There was already a long tradition of a 'Rogue's Gallery', lives and prints that held up a counter-mirror to the biographies and icons of the great. It was out of this that Gay's mock-heroic *Beggar's Opera* and Fielding's *Jonathan Wild* would spring. Great rogues, like Caesar and Alexander, had their portraits painted – was this any different? But, in a way, the very act of memorializing criminals turned these anti-heroes into heroes: when engraved, Thornhill's portrait made Sheppard look like an artist or a poet, a 'martyr in mezzotint'.[32] And, inevitably, satirists had already begun to connect Jonathan Wild and that other efficient and intimidating 'Great Man', Robert Walpole. Sheppard, as a man who could baffle Wild, could easily become a silent icon for the opposition.

Yet Thornhill had no satirical intent; he was a supporter of Walpole, dependent on the Court, and all his other portraits are conventional studies of eminent men. Why should a royal history-painter turn to such a subject? Could it be simply an affirmation that there *were* two markets for art, the patron and the public, and that even an established painter had the right to move between the two? In this way, too, Sir James Thornhill may have provided a model for his young admirer.

Hogarth managed to weave Jack Sheppard into his own argument about taste at the end of this year, when Drury Lane cashed in on the story with a new pantomime, *Harlequin Sheppard*. In another sixpenny print, *A Just State of the British Stage, or, Three Heads are Better than One*, published on 10 December, Hogarth attacked the hypocrisy of the theatre, which held out for 'high art' while producing pantomimes about a thief's life. Earlier in the year, the caption to the first state of *Masquerades* had imagined the ghosts of Shakespeare and Ben Jonson blushing with shame. This time Jonson's spectre

104

23 *A Just View of the British Stage* (1724)

is not just passively blushing, but rising through a trapdoor and actively pissing on the 'fooleries' produced by the three joint managers: Colley Cibber, the tragic actor Barton Booth, and Robert Wilks. Jonson's anger sprays over the fallen statue of a Roman soldier; other props – dragons, flying flasks, barking dogs – recall *Harlequin Doctor Faustus*, and John Devoto's lavish sets. Flushed with triumph over their rivals at Lincoln's Inn, Wilks gloats 'Poor R—ch Faith I Pitty him.' But to suggest that Drury Lane really *was* descending to the gutter, Hogarth showed Booth dangling a little figure down a hole – a puppet of John Hall the 'Chimney Sweeper', hanged in 1707 and

105

famous for escaping from Newgate by squeezing into the sewers through the privies. 'Ha this will do G—d D—me,' grins Booth. Hall, Hogarth implied, might be their next hero.

He enjoyed drawing this scurrilous rehearsal scene, adding a scornful inscription describing the proposed Jack Hall farce:

'*Concluding wth the Hay-Dance Perform'd in ye air by ye Figures* A, B, C, *Assisted by Ropes from y^e* Muses. *Note there are no Conjurors concern'd in it as ye ignorant imagine.*[Pointing hand] *The Bricks, Rubbish &c. will be real, but the Excrements upon* Jack Hall *will be made of Chew'd Gingerbread to prevent Offence.* Vivat Rex.'

While Hogarth was holding forth about the value and principles of contemporary culture, he was, of course, happily making money from this cheap, crude and topical print. Was he so different from the entrepreneurs of Drury Lane?

6

Great Men and Fools

Let Dogs delight to bark and bite
For God hath made them so;
Let Bears and Lions growl and fight,
For 'tis their Nature too.

But, Children, you should never let
Such angry Passions rise;
Your little Hands were never made
To Tear each other's Eyes.

ISAAC WATTS, 'Against Quarreling and Fighting' (1720)

PIOUS WRITERS MIGHT PREACH fellowship and harmony but Hogarth's satires of the mid-1720s showed a world governed by competition, greed, passions and faction. With a swift comic scepticism he attacked the self-delusion and hypocrisy of *all* who claimed special powers, whether in religion, politics, finance, theatre or art. Like other satirists he followed the market, quick to exploit current scandals and hot news.

Hogarth, however, was ambitious to be more than a satirist. He aimed at the smart life, at social acceptance, at money and status. Even when strapped for cash, he hankered after style, and said later,

'I remember the time when I have gone moping into the City, with scarce a shilling in my pocket, but as soon as I had received ten guineas there for a plate, I have returned home, put on my sword, and sallied out again with all the confidence of a man who had ten thousand pounds in his pocket.'[1]

The way to make that money was not through prints, but through painting: Sir Godfrey Kneller, the esteemed assembly-line portraitist, lost £20,000 in the South Sea Bubble ('this shokt him much,' wrote Vertue) but still ended up with an income of £2000 a year.[2] Sir James Thornhill was now almost the last representative of that grand generation: Laguerre had died in 1721 and Kneller in 1723, carrying stories of his legendary vanity even to the tomb. Louis

Chéron followed in May 1725. And before then, in late 1724, the Chéron–Vanderbank academy was in trouble. It lasted a few years, said Hogarth, 'but the treasurer sinking the subscription money the lamp stove etc were seized for rent and the whole affair put a stop to'.[3]

Vanderbank, deep in debt, left for France, as Vertue reported disapprovingly:

'Mr J. Vanderbanck, having lived very extravagantly. keeping. a chariot horses a mistres drinking & country house a purpose for her . . . run so far into debt that he was forc'd to go out of England to France. & took with him his *lemon* or wife which he could not be prevaild with to part from.'[4]

In October he was back, married, still in debt and driven to living in the Liberties of the Fleet. That November, Thornhill started up another 'free academy', at his house in the corner of Covent Garden Piazza, which Hogarth almost certainly attended.[5] It's hard not to conclude that Hogarth *went* for Thornhill, attaching himself to his hero as if the magic of his success would rub off simply by proximity. He stayed loyal all his life, and yet in terms of advancement it was a misguided choice; the coming men were of the Burlington camp, while Thornhill's star was fading.

Thornhill was a leading Freemason, Master of the Greenwich lodge, but in the early 1720s the London Masons were deeply divided – and in late 1724 Hogarth adroitly turned his satire against the faction that Thornhill opposed. The Masonic movement had flowered in London during the building boom after the Great Fire: at the end of the seventeenth century, when the trade guilds were losing their power, the working stonemasons took in prosperous tradesmen and gentry to swell their funds and boost their influence.[6] Outsiders were attracted both by the Masons' architectural and mathematical skills and by their ancient rituals and 'mysteries'. Soon Freemasonry was the height of fashion; in 1717 the first London Grand Lodge was founded, bringing together Masonic drinking clubs from three taverns, the Apple Tree, the Rummer and Grapes and the Gridiron. By 1721 they were bold enough to hold a formal procession through the streets, dressed in full regalia.

During the early 1720s, the London Masons, who were always suspected of Jacobite leanings (and many City merchants did have such sympathies), acquired a new, strongly Whig, leadership. The government hold on the movement grew: Walpole was himself a Mason, using the network as a spy ring. In 1723 a controversial set of *Constitutions* appeared, written by a Scots cleric, James Anderson, and published under the aegis of the Duke of Montagu and the Huguenot mathematician John Theophilus Desaguliers.

The *Constitutions* radically shifted the old mysteries into line with the rational, Whig, civic–humanist philosophy (the Emperor Augustus himself was co-opted as a Masonic forebear) and also demanded that a Mason should 'obey the Moral Law; and if he rightly understands the Art, he will never be a stupid Atheist, nor an irreligious Libertine'. Almost more important, he should be 'a peacable subject to the Civil Powers'.[7]

The old conservative core, whose Lodge meetings had often been no more than solidly jovial feasts and drinking sessions, took umbrage at this imposition by the serious, 'speculative', Whig faction. Instead of re-electing Montagu as Grand Master they chose the dissolute and eccentric Duke of Wharton, despite his Jacobite links. (Wharton was also a well-known rake, leader of the 'Hell-Fire' club, which caused havoc in London streets in 1721, and a frequenter of the Clare Market club, where Hogarth supposedly drew him in 1724 starting yet another club, the 'Schemers', dedicated to the advancement of flirtation.)[8] A compromise was reached, by which Wharton became Grand Master with Desaguliers as his Deputy, but the next year Wharton was defeated by a single vote. It was now hinted that his camp would withdraw altogether and at this point one of the Montagu clique came up with an elaborate hoax. A press notice suddenly appeared, announcing that the 'truly ANCIENT NOBLE ORDER OF THE GORMAGONS', founded by the first Emperor of China, had recently come to England and admitted 'several Gentlemen of Honour'. They would hold a chapter at the Castle Tavern in Fleet Street, and the notice was to inform the public that 'there will be no drawn sword at the door, nor Ladder in a dark Room, nor will any Mason be receiv'd as a member till he has renounced his Novel Order and been properly degraded'. A note added that a deposed Afghan prince, and the Czar who currently sheltered him (an obvious reference to the Pretender and France) were already members.

This ludicrous mix of mumbo-jumbo and pointed innuendo immediately caught the pamphleteers' attention. Snapping up the subject like a modern newspaper cartoonist, Hogarth promptly produced *The Mystery of Masonry Brought to Light by the Gormagons*. His print, showing a ridiculous 'Gormagon' procession, would please the Whig speculatives, to which Thornhill belonged. But Hogarth was also making some points of his own. He deliberately echoed a print published in Paris that spring, very popular in London print shops, Coypel's *Don Quixote attacking a puppet show*.[9] The procession gave him the chance to show he was abreast of all the styles, and to hit the familiar targets derided in his attacks on the Bubble, the opera and the pantomime – mystification, vanity, self-importance, exaggerated 'feminine'

24 *The Mystery of Masonry Brought to Light by the Gormagons* (1724)

display, exotic foreign habits. The troop is led by four grandees who look like mock magi, despite being labelled in the key as the Chinese Emperor, mandarins and 'the sage Confucius'. But the poor novice with his head stuck in the ladder has his nose almost stuffed up the bare backside of the grotesque old woman on the ass, and in front of him prances a monkey decked out in apron and gloves.

Hogarth would later make a point of looking up the skirts of 'Nature' uncluttered by artistic rules – and his point is satiric as much as aesthetic. The figures who invite the viewer into this particular print are Sancho Panza and the fat butcher (wearing a working, not a Masonic, apron), hooting at the procession's garb and poses. As the inscription suggests, the 'great men' are as daft as the dressed-up monkey:

> What Honour! Wisdom! Truth! & Social Love!
> Sure such an Order had its Birth above.
> But Mark *Free Masons*! what a Farce is this?

110

How wild their Myst'ry! what a *Bum* they kiss.
Who would not Laugh when such Occasion's had?
Who would not Weep, to think ye World so Mad.

Although these particular Masons made such good copy, Hogarth did not disdain the movement as a whole. By November 1725 he himself had joined a lodge, at the Hand and Appletree in Little Queen Street.[10] As he walked across in the evening, he could look forward first of all simply to another men's heavy night out. The food and drink, speeches and songs, appealed to his sensual and sociable appetites; the dressing up would tickle his sartorial pride; the coded stories and secret handshakes and ornate rituals would suit his love of emblems, puns and 'difficulty'.

Masonry, even then, was also a good way for an aspiring man to make contacts. The London Masons had recently come under fire for mixing gentlemen with rude artisans, but, as in the early coffee houses, inside the lodge all bias was (theoretically) left at the door. At meetings Hogarth raised his glass with lawyers and wine merchants, surgeons and bankers, and aristocrats such as the Duke of Montagu. With its degrees of apprentice, fellow craft, warden, master and grand master, Masonry had an internal structure that fitted his upward strivings. All preferment was 'grounded upon real worth and personal merit only'.[11] Even better, the warmth of equality was balanced by the glow of belonging to an élite club. Here Hogarth was not an outsider: he was one of 'us'.

His membership of the Masons, like his cultivation of Thornhill, provided a route into the Whig establishment. But Hogarth, cannily, looked in all directions for advancement. Many Masons were City Tories, and in his private work, in the long hours in his workshop at Smithfield, among the butchers and the tradesmen of the market, Hogarth was absorbed in a project that would appeal to them too – and provide a showcase for his skills.

Over the previous three years he had been etching small illustrations to *Hudibras*, Samuel Butler's satire of the Civil Wars, published in the 1660s. Butler's poem, like Bunyan's *Pilgrim's Progress*, would have been known to Hogarth from childhood. Although modelled on Quixote, Hudibras is no would-be chivalric hero but a pedantic Presbyterian of the Commonwealth who sets out for the wars on his scrawny horse with his 'squire' Ralpho, a member of a different sect, the Independent Baptists. Fiery, absurd, theological debates are interwoven with his 'adventures'. Hudibras is finally exposed as a coward, but to the reader he is ridiculous throughout, distorting the world through the dim spectacles of scholarship and prejudice.

Hudibras – admired by Swift and Voltaire – was constantly quoted in *The Spectator*, but was a special favourite of Tory pamphleteers in Queen Anne's reign. This 'anti-puritan, royalist classic', attacking bigotry and fanaticism, was a standby of the staunch Tory merchants – the wealthy printer John Baker had recently arranged for a memorial to Butler in Westminster Abbey.[12] It was a clever subject to choose and by mid-1725 Hogarth and the printseller Philip Overton were planning a set of *Hudibras* illustrations, to be issued on their own, not with a text. These were to be much larger than the little woodcut-like prints Hogarth had been creating on his own and, over the summer, he did careful drawings. Overton invited subscriptions for 'twelve Historical and most Diverting Prints, taken from the Celebrated poem of HUDIBRAS (the Don Quixot of this Nation) describing in a Pleasant Manner the Humor of those Times'.[13] Promised for Christmas, they eventually appeared in February 1726, with a sterner title page than the advertisment: 'Exposing the *Villany* and *Hypocrisy* of those TIMES'. They proved such a sucess that Hogarth's smaller prints were also published as illustrations to a new edition of *Hudibras* that May.

One can see why Hogarth liked this poem. Sceptical and pessimistic though it is, it bursts with oddity, eccentricity, farce, caricature, and emblem – the exuberant energy and the hidden 'difficulty' that mark Hogarth's own art. The ordinary and everyday become transformed, like the household implements in the Civil Wars; which, argues Hudibras, were not only melted down to become weapons, but sprang up as whole armed men, like the dragon's teeth of legend:

> Did they coyn Piss-pots, Bouls and Flaggons,
> Int' Officers of Horse and Dragoons;
> And into Pikes and Musketiers
> Stamp beakers, Cups and Porringers?
> A Thimble, Bodkin, and a Spoon
> Did Start up living men, as soon
> As in the Furnace they were thrown.[14]

Underneath this phantasmagoria is a keen morality very like Hogarth's own. Butler judges from the viewpoint of common sense, valuing the reasonable and practical – qualities patently missing from the England of the Commonwealth, with its self-righteous Puritan zeal, and of the licentious Restoration. He is staggered on one hand by men's capacity for self-delusion and on the other by their breezy hypocrisy, their ability to cite religion or the public good to cloak their own interest, and he uses the real to deflate the heroic, and the low to expose the great. A bloodthirsty general may ride in triumph, but a common murderer will swing. Is Talgol the butcher, gleaming with oil, a mighty fighter, very different from those demi-gods and heroes? The work they share is simply:

> Slaughter, and knocking on the head,
> The Trade to which they all were bred;
> And is, like others, glorious when
> 'Tis great and large, but base if mean.
> The former rides in Triumph for it;
> The later in a two-wheeled Chariot,
> For daring to profane a thing
> So sacred, with vile bungling.[15]

Butler's language is the most powerful weapon in demolishing his hypocritical heroes – a racy, basic vernacular undercutting Latinate pretension. When Hudibras sees the villagers pouring out in a 'Skimmington' (the rough music that mocked cuckolds, hen-pecked husbands and shrewish wives), he insists it is a 'heathenish' procession, whose creator has 'observ'd all fit Decorums/We find describ'd by old Historians'. When he assaults them with long words, he gets quite different missiles back.

> At that an *Egg*, let fly,
> Hit him directly o're the eye,
> And running down his Cheek, besmear'd
> With Orange-Tawny slime, his Beard . . .
> And streight another with his Flambeaux
> Gave Ralpho's, o're the eys, a damn'd blow.[16]

The terrible rhyme makes the point. Epics and romances are relics of the past; to handle the material of the present in such a style could only produce excruciating comedy. This was pretty much how Hogarth saw the idolizing of the classical forms of art: in designing this scene, he makes the same point in his own medium, borrowing the arrangement of these tough men and women from Annibale Caracci's *Procession of Bacchus and Ariadne*.[17] Such pungent visual wit is typical, although it can be argued that Hogarth's intention was more serious – that he was working his way towards modern 'history'-painting, adapting the composition of Raphael or Caracci to suit his ironic vision.[18]

The passages he chooses are not always visual scenes – sometimes, as in

25 'Burning the Rumps at Temple Bar', *Hudibras* (1726)

'Hudibras Sallying Forth', he invents a scene to fit an abstract image – but all the pictures are packed with figures, faces and comic details, the little boy pissing on Ralpho's shoes in the stocks, the crocodiles and skeletons suspended in Sidrophel's cell. The most vivid of all are the crowd scenes: the encounter with the bear-baiters, the Skimmington, the Saturnalia of 'Burning the Rumps at Temple Bar', where the London crowds, protesting at the Rump Parliament after Cromwell's death, take rumps of beef from the butchers' and roast them on bonfires, shouting 'No more Rump'. With its street signs and effigies this carries us into Hogarth's own London, to Temple Bar, just down the road at the end of the Strand, and to

> That beastly Rabble, – that came down
> From all the Garretts – in the Town,
> And Stalls, and Shop-boards – in vast swarms,
> With new-chalk'd Bills – and rusty Arms,
> To cry the Cause – [19]

This is a street festival, a ritual of the people, not an élite masquerade. No one is disguised here.

Working on *Hudibras*, Hogarth was feeling his way towards telling a story in pictures, while finding a mode that mimicked the pronouncements of critics on the highest genre of all, history-painting. Richardson had demanded

114

that, 'to paint a History, a Man ought to have the main qualities of a good Historian, and something more; he must yet go higher, and have the Talents requisite to a good Poet; the rules for the Conduct of a picture being much the same with those to be observed in writing a Poem'.[20] Hogarth had 'borrowed' a poem, *Hudibras*, that could also be read as the work of a historian, of a highly satirical and also metaphysical kind. Seen in this light his own work begins to seem like a tongue-in-cheek satire on the rules, fulfilling Richardson's demand that a history-painter should know 'the Habits, Customs, Buildings, &c of the Age, and Countrey, in which the thing was transacted'.[21] While it was hard to know the customs of ancient Rome, Hogarth certainly knew modern England – so he *was* illustrating 'history', almost as it happened. At the end of his life he cited this faithful transcription as one reason why his prints might remain of interest, especially with a commentary that 'may be instructive and amusing in future times, when the customs manners fasheons Characters and humours of the present age in this country may be alter'd and perhaps in some respects . . . be otherwise unknown to posterity, both at home and abroad'.[22]

When the complete set of *Hudibras* prints was issued to the 192 sub-scribers, the title page carried a dedication, 'to WILLIAM WARD Esq; of Great Houghton in Northamptonshire; And to Mr ALLAN RAMSAY of Edinburgh'. Dedications were usually a grateful acknowledgement of patronage and in this case William Ward, a barrister, had apparently commissioned Hogarth to do a set of *Hudibras* paintings (never undertaken) while Allan Ramsay, the Edinburgh bookseller, had taken thirty sets of the prints. But Ramsay was far more than a bookseller, and Hogarth's dedication is a mark of respect and admiration.

Now just turned forty, Ramsay had been a wigmaker whose real passion was poetry, and who began publishing his own work (as Hogarth had tried to) in 1718. Like Hogarth, he fought off pirate printers; his 'Bubble' poems ran parallel to Hogarth's satires; his 'low life' comic poems, like Hogarth's prints, had a racy realism, a broad humour and mimicry. Ramsay's verse and his pastoral comedy, *The Gentle Shepherd*, won him the admiration of Pope and Gay, while his collections of Scottish poems and songs, the first great ballad collections of the century, were not the result of mere antiquarianism but an impassioned cultural nationalism. All this made Hogarth feel, perhaps, that Ramsay was a fellow spirit, who might understand his art. They were curiously alike in other ways. Small, dark and forthright, with an earthy humour and kindliness, Ramsay, like Hogarth, was exuberantly vain about his 'natural' abilities, sure that he was 'ane of the warld's wonders'. His painter son, also Allan, called his father 'one of the extraordinary instances of the power of uncultivated genius'.[23] He was, apparently, touchingly proud of Hogarth's dedication.[24]

As the dedication to Ramsay implies, the *Hudibras* prints were 'literary' pictures which used story to cast light on history, and the same would be true of his Progresses of the Harlot and the Rake. These drew on story structures familiar to all, setting the brutal reality of the everyday against delusory dreams and ambitions. Around this time, Hogarth also returned to the story of that still more famous dreamer, Don Quixote, a figure that had a lasting fascination for him, and for many of his contemporaries. He and John Vanderbank were both involved in discussions for plates to accompany a lavish new Spanish-language edition commissioned by Jacob Tonson and sponsored by Lord Carteret: Hogarth did six designs and left his plates with Tonson, but the prints were not issued until after his death.[25]

While he worked on *Hudibras* Hogarth was still publishing the odd topical print. He had to juggle loyalties, and in politics it was hard for an artist to know which horse to back. If he was looking for patrons, then Thornhill had connections with Walpole and the Court – yet the public wanted anti-Walpole prints, and in the mid-1720s a powerful, if not coherent, opposition was emerging, which might also provide patrons. Bolingbroke had returned from France in 1723, his Jacobite leanings abandoned. The charm of his elegant French wife and his own dextrous promises appeased the Court and won back his property but not his seat in the House of Lords. With William Pulteney (who followed Walpole and Townshend when they were dismissed in 1717 and was now smarting at being insufficiently rewarded), Bolingbroke wooed the Prince of Wales at Leicester House. Around them they gathered disaffected MPs, City merchants and disgruntled courtiers such as Lord Chesterfield.

Pulteney was an eloquent speaker and incisive satirist. Bolingbroke was a dazzling polemicist, his dry irony lit by a flying imagination. In December 1726 they founded the *The Craftsman*, which was soon being devoured in city coffee houses and country mansions and in all the courts and embassies of Europe. It would bedevil Walpole's life for the next decade. The *Craftsman*'s editor was Nicholas Amhurst, who had been sent down from Oxford in 1719, officially for his wild living, although he himself claimed that his satirical verse, supporting the Whig latitudinarians (some said 'deists') had offended Oxford's High Church Tories.[26] Hogarth and Amhurst were exact contemporaries, lived near each other, and thought on much the same lines. Amhurst criticized Palladianism and praised Hogarth in his previous paper,

Pasquin; Hogarth engraved a frontispiece for Amhurst's *Terrae Filius: Or, the Secret History of The University of Oxford*, when it was published in book form.[27] Despite his Thornhill links, Hogarth too may have hoped for patronage from the opposition group around the Prince of Wales, at least judging from his print *His Royal Highness George, Prince of Wales*. Here Hogarth depicted Peace and Hercules (leaning on his club above the slain hydra, a reference to young George's military victories) displaying the Prince's portrait to three Graces: industry, arts and authority.[28]

On 3 December 1726, two days before the first issue of *The Craftsman*, Hogarth announced a print based on *Gulliver's Travels*, which had been published anonymously at the end of October, setting the town on fire. 'The whole impression sold in a week,' Gay told Swift. 'From the highest to the lowest it is universally read, from the Cabinet Council to the Nursery.'[29] Hogarth, who was a great admirer of Swift, used Gulliver to make a general anti-government point. His *The Punishment Inflicted on Lemuel Gulliver*, eventually published at the end of December, showed Gulliver being given an enema through an enormous syringe ('a Lilipucian Fire Engine' – which takes ten men to carry it). This was Hogarth's own invention, not Swift's, for Gulliver's punishment for extinguishing the fire in the Royal Palace by pissing on it.

Hogarth's Gulliver is gullible, like the 'common man' of England. He has

26 *The Punishment Inflicted on Lemuel Gulliver* (1726)

saved Lilliput (the Walpole–Hanover interest), yet now he kneels behind a curtain, his great bum showing, being stuffed up the backside without using his great strength to resist. A tiny Prime Minister supervises and a tiny priest sermonizes (from what looks like a chamber pot): both of them ignore the rats pouncing on children, and the people worshipping Priapus at a makeshift altar. Yet Hogarth's Lilliputians aren't quite presented as a swarm of tiny adults. They are dwarfishly or childishly rounded, with big hands, so the scene looks like a malevolent nursery rhyme. Hogarth's real subject was credulity itself. He was bemused, angered and fascinated by people's willingness to let themselves be deceived and abused; Gulliver and his tormentors are as foolish as each other.

This autumn Britain was given a truly bizarre demonstration of public gullibility. In late November, Mary Tofts, a woman from Godalming, claimed to have given birth to rabbits. Part of the excitement was 'scientific', as the births were seized on as living proof of the effects of the imagination during pregnancy – Mary had reported that she and a friend, weeding in a field, had seen two rabbits and chased them. The failure to catch them created 'such a longing' that she miscarried, and from then on could think only of rabbits.[30] Soon she began to produce parts of animals: a rabbit's liver, the legs of a cat, and then, in a rush, nine baby rabbits, one a day. Reporting this, the Guildford male-midwife, John Howard, challenged sceptics to see for themselves. Fashionable medical men descended, including Nathanael St André, the Swiss Anatomist to the Royal Household (a teacher of fencing, dancing, French, German, before turning to surgery), and Cyriacus Ahlers, another royal surgeon. Both men 'delivered' rabbits and Ahlers took the skin to show the King. Prompted by Caroline, George I then sent the distinguished male-midwife Richard Manningham, who kept a scrupulous diary.[31]

By now the story was everywhere. John Howard lectured to the Royal Society and Mary Tofts was brought to London where she stayed in Mr Lacy's bagnio in Leicester Fields, being examined by more prestigious doctors and ogled and pummelled by fashionable visitors. Lord Hervey, who came with Dr Arbuthnot, told Henry Fox that

'every creature in town, both men and women have been to see and feel her: the perpetual emotions, noises and rumblings in her Belly are something prodigious; all the eminent physicians, surgeons and man-midwives in London are there Day and Night to watch her next production.'[32]

Hervey, like Hogarth, recognized that this was a fight between reason and inexplicable 'evidence': 'between the downright affirmation on the one hand

118

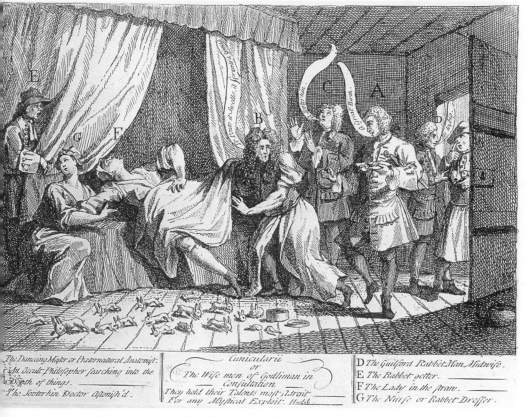

27 *The Cunicularii, or the Wise Men of Godliman in Consultation* (1726)

for the reality of the fact, and the philosophical proofs of the impossibility of it on the other'. Lord Onslow told Sir Hans Sloane that it had 'almost alarmed England'.[33] The general public, indeed, was so moved that 'until the imposture was exposed rabbit stew and jugged hare disappeared from the dinner table'.[34] Sooner or later, the 'reality of the fact' had to triumph: by the seventeenth 'birth' Manningham's faith had wavered. The hoax was finally rumbled when one of the bagnio's porters admitted smuggling in a rabbit. On 7 December Mary confessed that the original rabbit (and subsequent bits) had been roughly inserted into her vagina. The next day, St André, who had written a forty-page pamphlet, *A Short Narrative of an Extraordinary Delivery of Rabbets*, publicly apologized. Four days later William Hogarth published *The Cunicularii* ('The Rabbit Warren') *or the Wise Men of Godliman in Consultation*.

The story, of course, was irresistible to Hogarth. His print shows St André,

119

marked 'A', with the fiddle under his arm, and Manningham, 'B', with a bubble coming from his mouth, 'It Pouts it Swells, it Spreads it Comes'. A third man, 'C', defined as 'The Sooterkin Doctor Astonished', could be Ahlers but is more likely to be John Maubray, who only two years before had described monstrous human–animal births in the Netherlands, which he thought were called 'sooterkins' (mishearing the Dutch endearment *sooter-kinds* - 'sweet children').[35] By the door skulks John Howard, 'D', turning down a proffered rabbit with the words 'It's too big.' All these 'doctors' are rendered ridiculous. The room is cluttered with the paraphernalia of medicine and magic and the whole effect is as rich as Sterne's wonderful debunking of the male-midwife in *Tristram Shandy*:

'Truce! – truce, good Dr Slop! – stay thy obstetric hand; – return it safe into thy bosom to keep it warm; – little dost thou know what obstacles; . . . Besides, great son of Pilumnus! what canst thou do? – Thou hast come forth unarmed; thou hast left thy *tire-tête*, – thy new-invented forceps, – thy crotchet, – thy squirt, and all thy instruments of salvation and deliverance behind thee.[36]

Hogarth enjoyed the comedy. His rabbits (or parts of them) look as though they are scampering on the floor and St André stands on one foot with delight. And he added a touch of bawdy, with Mary spreading her legs for the groping male-midwife. But this is also a very graphic *birth* scene, as Mary clutches her belly with brawny hand, her mouth agape in pain. The key calls Manningham 'An Occult Philosopher searching into the Depth of things' and Maubray raises his hands to heaven like one of the three Wise Men at the Nativity. This is the work of a realist who scorns fantasy, medical or religious. Blasphemously, Hogarth was satirizing *any* miraculous birth, comparing the way his age blurred the boundaries between human and monstrous to the equally dubious fusing of human and divine. From now on, in his most powerful work, he would show how the politics of sex, power and class could be drawn in terms of the human body.

It is noticeable, too, that the gullible, self-important men in this print look far more absurd than the strong, supine woman. For once the 'lower' groups – the women and the poor – have hoodwinked the rich and the experts: the Court of George I and Walpole; the foreigners and dancing masters and fraudulent doctors. But to Hogarth the ultimate absurdity was that so many people had been ready to believe in this 'conjuror', as in others: but then, if you could whisk rabbits out of a hat, why not out of a womb? Mary Toft spawned rabbits as profusely as projectors did 'bubble' projects and impresarios did operas. Indeed, within a week or so of Mary's exposure,

Lincoln's Inn Fields had a new 'Rabbit' scene in their *Harlequin the Sorcerer*. In this respect, *The Cunicularii* was another blow against cultural idiocy and mystification.

Several other cartoons appeared, including a comic strip with verse, *The Doctors in Labour: or the New Whim Wham from Guildford*.[37] Hogarth was just one among many satirists. But the prints of the mid-1720s show how he took the pulse of the times, feeling not just the tempo of current affairs but the underlying beat, the lust for the 'wonderful'. His diagnosis of this fever was instant and accurate. Mary Tofts was a prime example. After brief celebrity in Bridewell (where Jack Laguerre painted her portrait with a rabbit on her knee) she lapsed into obscurity, surfacing to face charges for handling stolen goods in 1740 and dying in 1763, noted by a brief paragraph in the press. Years later, Horace Walpole mockingly compared the 1720s to the early 1740s:

'I don't know how it is, but *the wonderful* seems worn out. In this our day, we have no rabbit women, no elopements, no epic poems finer than Milton, no contests about Harlequins and Polly Peachums . . .'[38]

By that time even the annual satirical parades of 'Scald Miserable Masons' born of the Gormagon squabble had finally vanished from the streets.

Hogarth was profitably topical, but he also used his satirical skills to continue his aesthetic battles, especially with Thornhill's rival, Kent. As an architect, Kent could shrug off Hogarth's barbs, but not as a painter. In 1725 he had produced an altarpiece for St Clement Danes, complete with celestial choir, floating cherubs and the Holy Spirit as a dove. It was not only appallingly painted, but was also read as showing Catholic, Jacobite leanings. The solid citizens, disdaining Kent's aristocratic success, petitioned the Bishop of London and had it removed to the vestry. (The story goes that it stayed in the vestry, 'being occasionally borrowed to decorate the music room of a nearby tavern'.)[39] Quick as a flash, Hogarth published a caricature, with a barbed (and misspelt) inscription:

'exactly Engraved after ye Celebrated Altar-Piece in St Clement's Church . . . taken down by Order of ye Bishop of London (as tis thought) to prevent Disputs and laying of Wagers among ye Parrshioners about ye Artists meaning'.

He offers his own 'explanation', which he suggests could be hung below the original so that the parish's £60 'may not be Entirely lost'. By bringing in the readings circulating through the town, he slurs both Kent's politics and his

28 *A Burlesque on Kent's Altar-piece at St Clement Danes* (1725)

aesthetics: this is not, he says, 'the Pretender's Wife and Children as our weak brethren imagin. Nor yet St Cecilia as the *Connoisseurs* think but a Choir of Angells playing in Consort'. A key sorts out the 'meaning' of the angelic arms and legs: 'F', for example is a harpist's leg 'but whether right or Left is yet undiscover'd', while 'H' is 'the other leg judiciously Omitted to make room for the harp'. Both sides could be sharp in their ridicule. It was at the end of this summer, while London laughed at Hogarth's burlesque, that Gay wrote to the Countess of Burlington about Bartholomew Fair and the need for a 'guide' to Thornhill's Greenwich paintings.

As Thornhill's pupil, Hogarth was also beginning to paint. He began with subjects at the opposite end of the spectrum to grand history-painting, such as *A Paviour's Sign*,[40] a scene tied to the world of work and the growing city. But when Thornhill's style of life became more gentlemanly in the mid-1720s, Hogarth was among the assistants who helped him, allegedly touching in a satyr on a ceiling painting in the Hampshire house of John Huggins, the Warden of the Fleet Prison, and working on the staircase paintings in a Dean Street house.[41]

Thornhill's example pushed Hogarth towards the world of the rich patron, but in some ways he was not the best of models, being renowned for chasing commissions and demanding high fees.[42] As well as trying to enter Thornhill's line of work, Hogarth rashly imitated his aggressive business style. In 1727, maybe on Thornhill's recommendation, he was asked by Joshua Morris, a Soho tapestry weaver, to paint a design for 'The Element of Earth'. This was probably for one of a series of tapestries of the Four Elements – Fire, Earth, Air and Water – destined for Cannons, the country mansion of the Duke of Chandos, where Thornhill had been working. It was a real chance to move into the lucrative world of decorators, much in demand for work on luxurious new houses, and it was an astounding break for such an inexperienced painter, showing that Hogarth aimed from the start at the sublime, the high allegorical subjects of the history-painters. Bluffing his way into the job, he claimed that he was 'well skilled in painting that way', promised 'to perform it in a workmanlike manner' and asked a sizeable fee of twenty guineas.

When Morris heard Hogarth was a young engraver, he was, not unnaturally, 'very uneasy about the work' but the servant he sent to check received a typically direct rebuff: '"that it was a bold undertaking, for that he never did anything of that kind before; and that if his master did not like it, he should not pay for it"'.[43] Time passed, and no cartoon appeared. Eventually, rather than facing the incensed Morris, Hogarth delivered it straight to his workshop rather than to his house, as he had promised, but Morris quickly retrieved it and asked his skilled workmen if they could work tapestry from it. The answer was a unanimous no. (Hogarth was not only a beginner; as a painter he always worked naturally in bold strokes and blocks, nowhere near precise enough for a design to be traced and made.) With surprising patience,

Morris sent the cartoon back, saying that it would not do, but if it was properly finished, he would take it. Hogarth promised it in a month, and finally delivered it in three. It was still judged impossible. Morris had to hire a new painter for 'The Element of Earth' and, while he was waiting, had to put his men to work on another piece. Since this was uncommissioned, and did not sell, Morris was another £200 out of pocket.

It sounds very much as though Morris was the loser. Yet it was Hogarth who went to court, demanding his fee plus payment for materials, amounting to £30. When the case was heard in May 1728 at Westminster Hall, Morris's witnesses, experienced weavers and craftsmen, faced Hogarth's fellow painters, including Thomas King, Vanderbank, Laguerre, a certain 'Cullompton' and Thornhill himself. Somehow, they convinced the court that the painting was 'competent', even if not usable for a tapestry. Hogarth won his case, and got his money.

Artistic feuds also got entangled in these legal fights. A month after the Morris case was settled, Thornhill was embroiled in another case. He had demanded a staggering £3,500 for decorations at Moor Park, and when Benjamin Hesketh Styles, the owner, rejected his work on grounds of poor finish, Thornhill sued him, appearing at court in July 1728 with a train of expert witnesses, including Jonathan Richardson. Styles dropped the proceedings, giving Thornhill his fee and a 'handsom present' in addition. But the case was not just about money. George Vertue was convinced that the rejection of Thornhill's pictures was fomented by Kent's friends at Court 'to slurr the reputation of Sr James'. It was widely agreed, he said, that Thornhill had excelled at Moor Park: 'But what is Merit when envy joynd with power. to oppose it.' When Thornhill argued the price of his paintings of '8 heroic Virtues' for Styles, he demanded the same fee per picture as Kent had received for the St Clement Danes altarpiece: 'Sr James is resolvd to take no less.'[44]

By siding with Thornhill, Hogarth made some enemies himself, Kent among them. Although eager for patronage, he found it hard to stifle his pride and dampen his sarcasm. Again and again, he would sabotage his own best interests. Furthermore, he was not a Court painter who could name his price, and his battle with Morris meant that patrons might be chary of employing him to paint their walls and ceilings, the starting point for a man determined to be a history-painter. The close-knit crowd of designers, tapestry-makers and wall-painters had now all heard of his lateness, his inadequate design and his belligerent lawsuit. Probably he did not much care. He saw recourse to law as part of the artist's struggle to assert his rights.

*

124

If Hogarth had hoped for more work through Thornhill's Walpole connections, it soon began to look as if that chance too, might disappear. On 11 June 1727, George I suffered a severe stroke in his carriage on the road to Hanover; he was carried to the house of his brother, the Duke of York, Prince Bishop of Osnabruck, to die there a few hours later, so Lord Hervey reported, 'in the very same room where he was born'.[45] Three days later a road-weary messenger broke the news to Walpole as he sat at dinner in Chelsea. It was the last news that he, or anyone, expected, since apart from occasional 'fits' George had left England an apparently healthy man of sixty-seven. Walpole's power had depended largely on his influence with the King; by contrast, George, Prince of Wales, had railed against him in recent years. But Walpole now had to dash – in so far as a fifty-one-year-old man of twenty stone could dash – to inform the Prince at Richmond. Ushered in by the Duchess of Dorset, he found the Prince in bed with his wife Caroline. Flustered and half dressed, George answered Walpole's pressing queries by muttering curtly that he should take his directions from Sir Spencer Compton, his Treasurer and Speaker of the House of Commons.

George II's reaction made good gossip: 'The King seemed extremely surprised,' Lord Hervey wrote sardonically,

'but not enough to forget his resentment to Sir Robert one moment; neither his confusion, nor his joy at this great change, nor the benevolence so naturally felt by almost everybody towards the messenger of such good news, softened his voice or countenance in one word or look.'[46]

It seemed that Walpole's end had come. Euphoria spread through the opposition, while courtiers of all ranks were swept by panic at the thought of losing their places. At Leicester Fields, the square was full of cheering crowds and every room in the house was packed with nobles anxious to kiss the hands of the new King and Queen and 'knocking their heads together to whisper compliments' as Spencer Compton passed.[47]

Walpole, however, was already working behind the scenes. Within a day, he had gained the ear of Caroline; the orders to Compton were revoked and for the time being, at least, he was still Lord Treasurer. Within a fortnight he made his position safe by drawing up a generous new Civil List for the King's funds, far exceeding that of George I, and doubling the allowance to the Queen. The royal couple knew perfectly well that only Walpole could steer this extravagance through the Commons. His chief ally was Caroline, with whom he often talked of theology and philosophy. The quick-tempered, pedantic yet insecure King was besotted with his blonde and heavy-bosomed wife, depending on her sexually and emotionally far more than on his mistresses. She was content to be cruelly snubbed in public (and often was) if she could rule in private. Courtiers believed her adept at putting her own ideas into George's head while pretending they were his. If George II thought he ruled the country, the populace knew better:

> You may strut, dapper George, but 'twill all be in vain;
> We know 'tis Queen Caroline, not you, that reign –
> You govern no more than Don Philip of Spain.
> Then if you would have us fall down and adore you,
> Lock up your fat spouse, as your dad did before you.[48]

But Walpole was even more subtle at managing people than Caroline and many of the ideas she complacently took credit for were probably his. Thirteen years later, he calmly advised his successor, Henry Pelham, on how to deal with George II:

'Address and management are the weapons you must fight and defend with: plain truths will not be relished at first, in opposition to prejudices, conceived and infused in favour of his own partialities; and you must dress up all you offer with the appearance of no other view or tendency but to promote his service in his own way, to the utmost of your power. And the more you can make anything appear to be his own . . . the better you will be heard.'[49]

By the end of his first year on the throne George II was Walpole's firmest supporter. The art of politics, even at the highest level, was the art of disguise and manipulation. As Hogarth had suggested in his prints, 'Dexterity', the sleight of hand of Dr Faux (or Dr Faustus) was the requisite skill.

In flattering Caroline, Walpole had, as he famously said, 'taken the right sow by the ear'. The opposition had relied on the other sow, Henrietta Howard, George's mistress for the past ten years. It was easy to believe she had the greater influence, since George, with his mania for time-keeping, visited her so regularly every evening at nine o'clock that he was even seen pacing restlessly up and down in front of Caroline looking at his watch. Henrietta Howard, charming, funny and sensible, was a friend of Swift and Gay. Four years later Swift wrote sourly, 'I always told you that Mrs Howard was good for nothing but to be a rank Courtier . . . she has Cheated us all, and may go hang her Self, and so may her – '.[50] In October 1727 Gay was piqued that she had not won him a good appointment. When the list was published he found himself Gentleman Usher to two-year-old Princess Louisa: 'which', he told Swift huffily, 'upon account that I am so far advanc'd in life, I have declin'd accepting'.[51]

Many others were even more disappointed. In June 1727, when the opposition's brief opportunity came and went so fast, anti-Walpole feeling had erupted in a blistering attack of lampoons, squibs and pamphlets and a year later, when Prince Frederick arrived from Hanover, a rival Court clustered around him. Hervey described how Pulteney tried to woo him from the King to the Prince of Wales. He offered money laced with threats, picturing a people 'ripe for insurrection', appalled at Walpole's foreign policy and the losses of merchantmen in the West Indies, left open to Spanish attack. All this, roared Pulteney, would shake Parliament and

'the minds of all England . . . as stout as our shitten monarch pretends to be, you will find we shall force him to truckle and make his great fat-arsed wife stink with fear before we have done with her. We shall make her give up his minion and him his myrmidon or I am much mistaken.'[52]

This speech, of course, is cleverly quoted by Hervey to blacken Pulteney's name, displaying a coarseness calculated to repel. But its exaggeration and rhetorical anthitheses tremble on the edge of absurdity just as Hogarth's realism teeters on the brink of caricature. More than that, physical excess itself – too fat, too female, too skinny, too smelly – affords a vocabulary of disdain. In the mid-eighteenth century, the visual was a moral language, falling swiftly into types, as in these contrasting clerics in Hervey's memoirs: 'Dr Hare had the cruel, sharp, dark-lanthorn stiletto countenance of an Italian assassin, whereas Sherlock had the bloated, swelled, heavy look of an indolent church glutton.'[53] Or his picture of Caroline at the Coronation, which slides from catty personal description into slick satirical judgements:

'The dress of the Queen on this occasion was as fine as the accumulated riches of the City and suburbs could make it; for besides her own jewels (which were a great number and very valuable) she had on her head and on her shoulders all the pearls she could borrow of the ladies of quality at one end of the town, and on her petticoat all the diamonds she could hire of the Jews and jewellers at the other; so that the appearance and the truth of her finery was a mixture of magnificence and meanness not unlike the éclat of royalty in many other particulars when it comes to be nicely examined and its sources traced to what money hires or flattery lends.'[54]

Mary Wortley Montagu showed the same taste for physical exaggeration when she described the Coronation to her sister, Lady Mar. But in her eyes it was not the Queen, but the old Countess of Orkney, who drew the most eyes, since she

127

'exposed behind a mixture of fat and Wrinkles, and before a considerable pair of Bubbys a good deal withered, a great Belly that preceded her; add to this the inimitable roll of her Eyes, and her Grey Hair which by good Fortune stood directly upright, and 'tis impossible to imagine a more delightful Spectacle. She had embellish'd all this with a great deal of Magnificence which made her as big again as usual.'[55]

The scent of sex, excess and corruption beneath finery clung to the Court's furnishings, almost as part of its tradition. The Countess of Orkney, for example, had been mistress of William III: once, on meeting Lady Dorchester (mistress of James II) and the Duchess of Portsmouth (mistress of Charles II) in the royal drawing room, she had allegedly chortled, 'Who should have thought we three whores should have met here?'[56] This is the cast of mind behind the broad sexiness and pointed sketches of Fielding's novels –

A. a sacrifice to Priapus. B. a pair of Lecherometers shewing yᵉ Companys Inclinations as they approach 'em. Invented for the use of Ladys & Gentlemen by yᵉ Ingenious. Mᵣ H———r price one shill.

29 *Masquerade Ticket* (1727)

128

Thwackum and Square, or Lady Bellaston, or Squire Western – and the overflowing physical detail of Hogarth's prints.

Since the accession of George II made little difference to the *status quo*, Hogarth continued to blast merrily at his old targets. The *Masquerade Ticket* of 1727, another dig at Heidegger (and Walpole), showed the fashionable throng swarming beneath statues of Venus and Priapus. Signs for 'Supper below' take on double meaning. Matching 'Letcherometers' measure levels of expectation, hope and desire, and a drunk or satiated Lion and Unicorn loll on their backs, playing with their tails, against a clock which marks the hours with 'Wit' and the minutes with 'Impertinence'. In 1728 Hogarth's print caught the eye of the twenty-one-year-old Henry Fielding, newly come to town. In his first published work, 'The Masquerade', he too described this world turned upside down:

> As in a madman's frantic skull,
> When pale-fac'd Luna is at ful
> In wild confusion huddled lies
> A heap of incoherencies:
> So here in one confusion hurl'd,
> Seem all the nations of the world;
> Cardinals, Quakers, judges dance;
> Grim Turks are coy, and nuns advance.
> Grave churchmen here at hazard play;
> Cinque-ace ten pound – done, quater-tray.
> Known prudes there, libertines we find,
> Who masque the face, t'unmasque the mind.[57]

To these foolish folk, the only true fools were those who stood out against the flow, as Fielding later concluded:

'while the crafty and designing Part of Mankind, consulting only their own separate Advantage, endeavour to maintain one constant Imposition on others, the whole World becomes a vast Masquerade, where the greatest Part appear disguised under false Vizors and Habits; a very few only shewing their own Faces, who become, by so doing, the Astonishment and Ridicule of all the rest.'[58]

Fielding's Parson Adams would be one of those whose ideals of charity and honour, like Quixote's outdated chivalric delusions, set him at odds with those around him. But Hogarth was harsher than Fielding – few of his characters have Adams's innocent dignity. With compassion, but cruel accuracy, he depicted great men and fools, perpetrators and victims, dancing together, in the world's long masquerade.

7

Imitation Games

Through the whole Piece you may observe such a Similitude of Manners in high and low Life, that it is difficult to determine whether (in the fashionable Vices) the fine Gentlemen imitate the Gentlemen of the Road, or the Gentlemen of the Road the fine Gentlemen.

JOHN GAY, *The Beggar's Opera* (1728)

HOGARTH SAW HIS ART in terms of the stage, of imitation, of human actors engaged not only in comedy and tragedy, but in the muddled morality play of daily life. He was fascinated by the seductive pull of power and the theatre of deception that maintained it, and when he really started to paint, at the end of the 1720s, it was to the theatre itself that he turned: to the great hit of the day, John Gay's *Beggar's Opera*, and to Britain's greatest playwright, William Shakespeare.

His Shakespearean painting was *Falstaff Examining His Recruits*, completed in 1730. There is no evidence that this was based on an actual production, but the popularity of the fat knight was clear from Thomas Betterton's adaptation of *Henry IV, Part II*, which cut many non-Falstaffian scenes, running as *King Henry IV or the Humours of Sir John Falstaff*.[1] In his picture Hogarth concertinaed the long scene at Shallow's house (Act III, scene iii) where Falstaff and Bardolph recruit men to fight the rebels, combining the grilling of the villagers with the later moment where Bardolph slips bribes from Bullcalf and Mouldy into Falstaff's palm, so that he impresses the decrepit Feeble and Shadow instead. On the walls of Shallow's house, he placed a picture of a local giant and an archery target, reminders of yeoman strength and proud English bowmen.

This scene had a topical edge. At the time London was full of rumours of war. Plots and counter-plots in Europe had sent spies and double spies scuttling between nations, and while many MPs fumed against paying for Hessian mercenaries to defend the King's Hanoverian interests, others accused Walpole of wanting peace at any cost. To hint at this farrago, all

130

30 *Falstaff Examining His Recruits* (1727–8)

Hogarth had to do was to show a fat, arrogant, jumped-up man, feathering his nest while neglecting his patriotic duty.

In 1728 Hogarth made an engraving of *Henry VIII and Anne Boleyn*, which also commented on current state events. This certainly was based on a recent production, Colley Cibber's staging of *Henry VIII*, the Drury Lane hit of the previous year. When it opened, on 26 October 1727, the audience was ravished by an extravagant interlude depicting the procession at Anne Boleyn's coronation. The parade effectively restaged that of George II's Coronation, only a fortnight before. 'Performed with greater Order and Magnificence, by the Richest and Largest Figures that have ever been seen on the English Stage',[2] Cibber's procession cost £1000, an astronomical sum, and 'rivalled in mock splendour the ceremonial at the Abbey'.[3] It proved so popular that it was soon given separately as an afterpiece to totally unrelated plays; everyone had to see it, and the King and Queen themselves came several times. Its success, in turn, prompted a burlesque by John Rich at Lincoln's Inn Fields, called *Harlequin Anna Bullen*.

As always, Hogarth was catching the tide, and his engraving, like the stage

31 *Henry the Eighth and Anne Boleyn* (c. 1728–30)

procession, cleverly dramatized the present in terms of the past. In *Henry the Eighth and Anne Boleyn* he pointedly showed their marriage as setting the scheming Wolsey on one side, and in the first state of the print, beneath the bulky shape of the glowering Cardinal, ran the following lines:

> Whilst *Woolsey* leaning on his Throne of State,
> Through this unhappy Change foresees his Fate,
> Contemplates wisely upon worldly Things,
> The Cheat of Grandeur, & the faith of Kings.[4]

Indeed, the implied hope of both Hogarth's Shakespearean pictures (as *The Craftsman* noticed) was that such men must eventually get their come-uppance.[5] Henry had shed Wolsey, and Prince Hal had dispensed with Falstaff. Might not George II finally see through his vast, bluff, epicurean adviser?

Walpole's 'grandeur' had been forced down the throats of the populace and the rivalrous aristocracy by his sumptuous Palladian pile at Houghton, in

Norfolk. Designed by Colen Campbell and James Gibbs, Houghton took seven years to build. Before it was finally finished in 1729 the existing village was pulled down, removed from the park and rebuilt outside the gates. In the house itself no costs were spared: there were marble fireplaces, gilded mirrors, mahogany doors and elaborate plasterwork; Kent designed lavish suites of furniture, scrolled, polished, inlaid; paintings by old masters were gathered from all corners of Europe – Poussin and Rubens, Murillo and Holbein, Titians, Rembrandts and Raphaels. Stories spread about Walpole's feasts and footmen, hunting parties and champagne, and gossip reached a peak when he bought the office of Ranger of Richmond Park for his son and then installed his mistress, the plain and sensible Maria Skerrett, in the hunting lodge.

Such extravagance, nepotism and adultery made Walpole an easy target and the satirists enjoyed themselves all the more because he took their taunts so badly, sulking and scowling, and trying to arrest the perpetrators if he could not buy them off. Although the satires cast him as different characters, from Punch to a masquerade impresario, from a juggler to a fiddler, the stress was always on his bold-faced duplicity and 'Brass' became a constant nickname as well as 'Screen'. There was no need to court danger with his real name: everyone knew who the coachman 'Brazen Face' was, sought in a mock advertisement, who had 'plunged, bewilder'd and overset his present Master, imposed upon and decieved his Mistress, and plundere'd, robb'd and stript the whole Family'.[6] As Walpole flourished and became 'The Great Man' besieged by supplicants, it was a short step from seeing him as this crooked footman to painting him as a highwayman, 'king of the road', or to linking him with Jonathan Wild, the master criminal posing as a government servant, who had been finally caught and hanged, to the jeers of hostile crowds, in 1725.

In February 1728 a new production at Lincoln's Inn Fields was set entirely in the world of the gaoler, 'thief-taker', highwayman and whore: John Gay's *The Beggar's Opera*. Nothing like it had been seen before. As Gay's friends watched the first-night audience take their places, none of them was sure whether it would succeed or be booed off the stage. Pope reported that he and others were 'much encouraged' by hearing the Duke of Argyll, in the next box, declare roundly: 'It will do – it *must* do! I see it in the eyes of them!'[7] It became fixed in story as a turning point of theatrical history:

'The first Act was received with silent Attention, not a Hand moved; at the End of which they rose, and every man seemed to compare Notes with his neighbour and the general Opinion was in its Favour. In the second Act they broke their Silence by Marks of their Approbation, to the great Joy of the frighted Performers, as well as the Author; and the last Act was received with universal Applause.'[8]

The key moment (so theatrical legend went by the time of Boswell) came in the tenth scene, when the nineteen-year-old Lavinia Fenton wrung the audience's hearts with Polly's ballad of despairing love:[9]

> Oh, ponder well! be not severe;
> So save a wretched Wife!
> For on the Rope that hangs my Dear
> Depends poor *Polly's* Life.[10]

Outdoing any known precedent, the opera played for sixty-two nights. John Rich made a fortune by crowding his theatre to its limits – on one night in March over thirteen hundred people squeezed into Lincoln's Inn Fields, with nearly a hundred seated on the stage itself. While the smart set met for dinner and then proceeded to their boxes, shopkeepers, servants and apprentices packed the galleries, hummed the familiar street tunes and cheered the age-old gags about plaguey wives and mistresses. There were quips for all classes, like the thief who, to Peachum's horror, has become a tailor 'because he deems it an honest profession' (rousing double laughs at the tailors' expense), or the outraged whore Suky Tawdry, bursting with indignant virtue because her 'last friend' accused her of taking five guineas ('Now I never suspected he had counted them.').[11]

On a different level, delighted audiences pounced on every conceivable political innuendo. There was no need for Gay, still smarting from his treatment at the hands of Walpole and the Court, to make his satire specific: his references could be broad, combining safety for the author with hilarity for the public. You could, for example, see Walpole as Macheath, the dashing highwayman preying on innocent travellers, and then squandering the profits in gambling; or as Peachum, a Jonathan Wild figure, weighing the gains from his gang of thieves against the rewards from betraying them; or as Lockit, the lumbering Newgate gaoler who extorts fees for the very chains he puts on. Macheath juggling his two 'wives', Polly Peachum and Lucy Lockit, could be Walpole between his wife and Maria Skerrett. Even a passing mention of a minor gang-member could add to the layers of enjoyable identification: '*Robin of Bagshot*, alias *Gorgon*, alias *Bluff Bob*, alias *Carbuncle*, alias *Bob Booty*'.[12]

Gay played safe by attacking the general culture of politics and the Court, claiming to hold an inverted mirror to the world, leaving the audience to decide whether 'the gentlemen of the road' imitate the 'fine gentlemen' or the other way round. *The Beggar's Opera* appealed to the courtiers as well as to the crowd – they could laugh at the jokes made at their expense, without feeling that they themselves, as individuals, were targets. By applauding the rotten apples, they showed themselves to be the sweet and uncorrupted ones (even Walpole was said to have attended one perfomance, teeth gritted, and shrewdly demanded an encore). But the language of the play, from beginning to end, made it clear that Gay saw mercantilism as the real poison. Like Fielding in *Jonathan Wild*, he hit the bourgeois merchants at the same time as the Court. A Hobbesian view of man, a vision of society devouring itself, lay beneath his wise-cracking, genial humour. As Lockit says,

'Lions, Wolves and Vultures don't live together in Herds, Droves or Flocks. – Of all Animals of Prey, Man is the only sociable one. Every one of us preys upon his Neighbour, and yet we herd together.'[13]

The gamblers work together to catch their dupes:

> But if by mishap
> They fail of a Chap,
> To keep in their Hands, they each other entrap.
> Like Pikes, lank with Hunger, who miss of their Ends,
> They bite their Companions, and prey on their Friends.

This feral, cannibalistic world – the world of Hogarth's *Progresses* – was kitted out in an imitation of culture and civility. Gay's masterstroke was to dress his own 'Newgate Pastoral' in the mock finery of Italian opera, replacing arias with affectionate burlesques of Handel or Bononcini, and with English airs, catches, folksongs and ballads. By the late 1720s the opera and the Academy of Music were in financial trouble – the initial subscriptions, supposed to last twenty-one years, had run out in seven. 'I doubt operas will not survive longer than the winter,' wrote Mrs Pendarves to her sister, 'they are now at their last gasp.'[14] There were quarrels among directors, disputes among subscribers, disorder among footmen and squabbles between stars: this fashionable, aristocratic form was uncannily like the money-grubbing, brawling street world and Gay's knowing audience could catch every musical allusion. In the song fights of Lucy and Polly, they instantly saw reflected not only Walpole and his wife and mistress, but the great opera gossip of 1727, the fierce rivalry between the two prima donnas Cuzzoni and Faustina. Both singers were paid huge salaries (reputedly £2,500) and both had passionate admirers: 'No Cuzzonist will go to a tavern with a Faustinian,' wrote Hervey, 'and the ladies of one party have scratched those of the other out of their list

135

of visits.'[15] While the singers fought – onstage as well as off – their supporters fomented near-riots, which climaxed on 6 June at a performance attended by royalty: 'the Contention at first was only carried on by Hissing on one Side and Clapping on the other; but proceeded at length to Catcalls and other great Indecencies'.[16]

The Beggar's Opera was a wonderful mix of slang and quickfire jokes, satire and symbolism, ballad and burlesque. From now on, it would be a constant reference point in Hogarth's work. He loved its zest, its barbed politics, its low-life toughness and sexy sentiment. He liked it, too, because it made Italian opera seem absurd rather than chic, and thus hit at the Burlington–Kent clique. (Burlington, once Gay's patron, refused to speak to him thereafter.) Yet there is a frisson of horror beneath Gay's fun and Hogarth, who had grown up next to Newgate and had seen the cart set forth in the misty mornings, could feel the pang of Polly's lament and Macheath's dismay.

It would have been quite in line with Hogarth's practice to publish a quick print to cash in on the vogue – by the summer of 1728 The Beggar's Opera was everywhere, pictured on snuffboxes and fans, praised and attacked in pamphlets and verses, castigated in sermons and celebrated in songs. But instead of producing a print for the public, he chose, instead, to paint Gay's opera for particular patrons. This was both commercially clever and conceptually apt. Painting, as the form collected by the gentry, 'upgraded' the subject in the same way that Gay had upgraded his thieves through his parody of opera. Hogarth turned Gay's allusions into the language of his own art – the statuesque poses of history-paintings with kings and queens surrounded by 'inferior' courtiers became those of actors playing thieves and whores, encircled by a 'superior', but admiring, audience.

One night Hogarth took his sketching things, using large sheets of dark-blue paper which would not glare in the middle of the audience, and roughed out a scene being played on stage.[17] The Falstaff scene is sketched on similar paper, and he may have seen them as companion pieces: both show private rapacity masquerading as public interest, exposed by a British play-wright. Both were also true originals: Falstaff is the first English painting of any dramatic scene, while The Beggar's Opera is the first to show a scene actually in production, in a particular theatre. The scene he chose comes towards the end of the play (Act II, scene xi) and contained all the main characters, which made it a useful souvenir piece for theatre-goers, with portraits of Mrs Egleton (Lucy), John Hall (Lockit), Tom Walker (Macheath), Lavinia Fenton (Polly) and John Hippisley (Peachum).

The scene was also significant in other terms. Hogarth froze the play at the moment where Lucy and Polly both sink to their knees before their respective fathers, suing for Macheath's life; immediately before, they have been pleading with Macheath himself, both claiming him as their 'husband'. Although Macheath's dilemma has been likened to a parody of the Choice of Hercules, between Virtue (Polly) and Pleasure (Lucy), his actual song renounces any choice at all, in a jovially misogynistic air:

> Which way shall I turn me? – How can I decide?
> Wives, the Day of our Death, are as fond as a Bride.
> One Wife is too much for most Husbands to hear,
> But two at a time there's no Mortal can bear.[18]

Peachum and Lockit are just as dismissive of female pleading: 'We know our own Affairs, therefore let us have no more Whimpering or Whining.' The poses of the painting, even more forcibly than Gay's play, stress the clash between male individualism and 'law', and the strength of female feeling, even when shot through with rivalry.

Over the next eighteen months Hogarth painted at least five versions of Gay's hit, less, perhaps, because the subject so intrigued him than because these repeat performances had a ready market. In 1729 John Rich commissioned a large version to hang in the new Covent Garden theatre which he built on the proceeds of this unexpected hit (prompting the undying quip that *The Beggar's Opera* 'made Gay rich, and Rich gay'). Other copies were ordered, one, in November 1729, by Sir Archibald Grant, an MP who could well have been one of Gay's subjects: as a member of the 'Charitable Commission for the Relief of the Industrious Poor' he embezzled the funds, was declared bankrupt and expelled from the House of Commons in May 1732.

The paintings fall into two groups, three relatively simple works and two more sophisticated later versions. (One small painting, taken to be the first, is now accepted as a copy, made for John Rich by another artist, different from his large version.)[19] Looking at the changes, from the first sketch to the later paintings, one seems to see Hogarth bursting into life as a true painter, in an astonishingly short time. He found his own lively style and technique as if he conjured it up from nowhere, with flickering brushwork, vivid blocking of colour, and a lovely, delicate – almost French – use of highlights. And as he reworked the scene, his presentation of it changed. None of his versions is a direct copy or a repetition, and he played in particular with the position of the artists and spectators, as he would do so successfully in his later prints.

In the first paintings, about 20 by 24 inches, we are close up to the

32 *The Beggar's Opera*, II (1729)

characters, almost on the broad boards of the stage. Macheath's leg irons stand out as a stark triangle of fetters, emphasized by the lines of his coat and his tricorn hat, a bold shape that seems to comment on the bonds of the emotional triangles, the central group of Polly, Lucy and Macheath folding outwards into the matched trios of lover/woman/father. Behind the upright figures of the men and the softening silk and lace of the pleading women, is a dim stage-set dungeon, with the light falling murkily from barred windows, glinting on the heavy irons hanging on the wall. The spectators in the side boxes are not emphasized at all, and (apart from a wide-eyed black page-boy, another marginal outsider who appears only in Hogarth's third version) they seem hardly interested in the action. Were it not for the heavy fringed curtain framing the action, they could be tourists chatting and gawping at the intimate scene, like visitors to Bedlam or Newgate. However stagy their postures, it is the actors who carry the 'real' emotional tension.

In the final two versions, however, the spectators became increasingly important. Hogarth's painting, which had been a 'stage' scene, became a 'theatrical' scene, a comment on plays and playgoers and the wider world.[20] By the last paintings, from late 1729, the prison walls have receded and lost their power to chill. There are more windows and doors, flanking steps and an arching roof, and the brickwork is delicately shaded in contrast to the brute strokes of the early version. Even the stage seems a warmer place, crowded with actors waiting for their scene. Attention is focused less on the whole group than on Polly, picked out as if by a spotlight. Instead of bare boards she now kneels on a carpet, with Macheath's foot on one side and her father's on the other, and the line from her head to Peachum's slanted hat directs our eyes up the stairs, out of the barred door – out of the prison and off the stage completely. Her arm is no longer outstretched towards the highwayman but curved towards the audience, and her gaze meets the eyes of a nervously upright figure, wearing the Star of the Garter, who is following the text in a little book. This is the middle-aged Duke of Bolton, so passionately enamoured of Lavinia Fenton on the first night that he returned every night to see her and swept her off the stage at the end of the season to make her his mistress. 'The D of Bolton', Gay pronounced zestfully in July, 'I hear hath run away with Polly Peachum, having settled £400 a year upon her during pleasure, and upon disagreement £200 a year.'[21] It was not as great a salary as Cuzzoni's, but it was

33 *The Beggar's Opera*, IV (1729)

139

a start: the Duke remained devoted and when his wife died twenty-two years later, Lavinia became his Duchess, having borne him three stout sons.

This was a drama of society, not of the stage. Lavinia's father was a naval lieutenant and her mother kept a coffee house near Charing Cross, and from the beginning of the play's run she was both adored and slandered. While she was fêted in her modest costume in a thousand prints, she was also alleged to be a whore, brought up in the Mint, who had now 'raised her price from one guinea to 100'.[22] By highlighting her romance Hogarth added the piquancy of sex, class and topicality. The satyr gazing down on the couple suggested that in life, as in this satire, dukes and players really are on the same level. The last paintings have the air of a chain of partners linking actors to spectators, like guests waiting for a partner at a ball. But here the grace and lightness of the dance flashes out against prison walls. Macheath's feet are chained: his next dance may be when he dangles from the gallows. Gay's wit already spun on the brink of darkness, the businesslike diction cloaking the men's greed, the women's smooth talk masking a literally poisonous rivalry. Both playwright and painter, in their different modes, queried the gloss of politeness, the social philosophy of the Town.

By the end of this series, Hogarth's painting had widened – from the play, to the theatre, to life. In the final versions the great curtain bears two mottoes, 'Utile dulce' ('useful and sweet'), signifying the artist's duty to instruct through entertainment, and 'Veluti in speculum' ('even as in a mirror'). His satire struck ever further and further outwards, towards the people who viewed his pictures as well as those they showed.

The Beggar's Opera linked three worlds, about all of which Hogarth felt strongly. The first was that of the prison, a reminder of a past he was keen to shake off yet which stirred in him a profound, angry sympathy. The second was that of the theatre, at once the centre of his own social, and sociable, milieu, and a target of satire with its profiteers and projectors. The third circle was that of 'polite society', Parliament and the Court, upon whose fringes he hung and upon whose commissions he depended.

While Hogarth was working on his *Beggar's Opera* paintings in the close, hot summer of 1728, the denizens of the Town scattered to their shady parks and fishing lakes, taking with them their favoured writers, musicians and painters. While Lavinia was running off with her duke, Gay himself was heading for Lady Scudamore's estate in Herefordshire: 'The weather is extreamly hot,' he told Swift, 'the place is very empty, I have an inclination to Study but the heat makes it impossible.'[23] Walpole too escaped to Richmond and Houghton, but he rarely rested. He had long been confirmed in office, and on 15 August 1728 he received the new Great Seal from George II – custom held that the old one was melted down to be made into a salver, traditionally given to the previous minister, which in this instance, of course, was Walpole himself. Certainly the retiring minister received plate of roughly the weight of the seal. The unusual square salver was made by Paul de Lamerie, and – although the piece is unsigned – it is generally held that Hogarth was chosen to engrave it. The design for this prestigious commission adapted the fashionable theme of Hercules destroying Calumny and Envy. The hero supports two circles, the two sides of the Great Seal itself, against a panoramic background of London, like Atlas holding up the world (and Walpole supporting the monarchy).[24]

It is very likely that Walpole chose Hogarth; he had a way of winning over

34 *The Great Seal of England* (1728–9)

141

potential critics. He could do it by charm – the bluff, apple-munching Norfolk squire in the Commons, the generous host at Houghton. He could do it by threats. And he could do it by bribes. In the next decade Henry Fielding, Hogarth's friend, found himself the recipient of both threats and bribes, and left a vivid coded description. In October 1740 he wrote a satire featuring a quack doctor who offers golden pills to a hostile writer: a hundred to 'stay at Home and be quiet and neuter', two hundred to 'say a *single word* in my favour', and, if he will 'declaim handsomely upon my Nostrums', three hundred, 'besides something very good to take twice a Year'.[25] By then Fielding had already suppressed one book (probably the draft of *Jonathan Wild*). Did Hogarth, likewise, sell out? Neither he nor Fielding was averse to taking favours from those they disapproved of. In their circles profit often outweighed principle and no one thought the worse of a man for using what 'interest' he could get: Hogarth's friend John Ellys, for example, helped Walpole acquire his great collection of paintings for Houghton, for which he was rewarded, rather oddly, by the sinecure of 'master-keeper of the lions in the Tower'.[26] Hogarth himself grasped any useful connections; when Thornhill was commissioned by the Speaker, Sir Arthur Onslow, to paint *The House of Commons*, with a flattering portrait of Walpole in the foreground, Hogarth painted Onslow's head, and Thornhill's own, and one or two others.

The Walpole salver could have been a brief nod from the great man: a small sop, a gesture of largesse and, perhaps, of warning. Almost at the same time came a demonstration of what might happen if an artist or writer did incur Walpole's wrath. In December 1728, when Gay finished *Polly*, the sequel to *The Beggar's Opera*, John Rich received notice forbidding rehearsals of 'any new play whatever' until it was shown to the Lord Chamberlain. The court, said *The Craftsman*:

'spread a report through every part of town that the sequel to the *Beggar's Opera* was a most insolent and seditious libel; that the character of Macheath was drawn for one of the greatest and most virtuous men in the kingdom; that this was too plain in the former part; but that in the second, he is transported; turns pirate; becomes Treasurer in a certain island abroad; proves corrupt; and is sacrificed to the resentment of a certain people.'[27]

Polly became the talk of the Town. To the delight of gossips, the Duchess of Queensberry was thrown out of Court when she touted for subscriptions to the published playscript and the subscription list eventually read like a roll-call of Walpole's opponents: the Duchess of Marlborough, the Earls of Bathurst and Oxford, Bolingbroke, Pulteney, William Wyndham. The publication of *Polly*, on 25 March 1729, coincided with that of the *Dunciad Variorum*. But Pope was a cannier operator; he had his text carefully checked and his book was presented to the King and Queen by Walpole himself. Soon, while Gay was outcast, Pope was a virtual favourite.[28] Outside the Court, however, Gay's popularity soared. As Arbuthnot told Swift, 'he is the darling of the City; if he should travel to the country, he would have hecatombs of Roasted oxen sacrificed to him'.[29] There were two lessons here for a potential satirist. One was to keep his head down and tread carefully if wanted patrons at court; the other was that the market for anti-Walpole satire was insatiable.

Hogarth took notice. But as a printmaker with an eye on the market he also registered Gay's images of Walpole, both as Macheath and as the plantation owner Ducat in *Polly*: 'I build, I buy plate, jewels, pictures, or anything that is valuable and curious, as your great men do, merely out of ostentation.'[30] Ducat's other acquisitive lust is served by the procuress Mrs Trapes who confesses that while she can't rival London, 'where we can have fresh goods every week by the waggon', she can still offer 'a fresh cargo of ladies just arriv'd'.[31] When Polly Peachum lands in this new world, searching for her highwayman lover, she is met by Mrs Trapes and displayed to the old lecher like market produce: 'Do but cast your eye upon her, Sir; the door stands half ajar.'[32] This image, and many others from Gay's work, would carry forward into the *Harlot's Progress*.

From now on Hogarth played his cards very carefully, painting in broad strokes rather than identifying individuals in his satire. Yet he still attacked the pyramid of greed of which Walpole was the apex, and kept in mind Gay's message:

> In Pimps and Politicians
> The Genius is the same;
> Both raise their own Conditions
> On others' Guilt and Shame.[33]

*

In 1729 Hogarth next turned directly to the real-life background of Gay's criminal dramas, when he painted a group portrait of the Inquiry into the state of London prisons. *A Committee of the House of Commons* is a curious and powerful study, which, like *The Beggar's Opera*, was at once a topical 'conversation piece' (he may have hoped to sell copies to those who were there) and an expression of his own preoccupations.[34]

The Parliamentary Inquiry was prompted by outrage at conditions in the Fleet prison, which Hogarth knew well. His decision to paint the Committee –

rather than produce an anonymous satirical print on the subject – is another example of the way he juggled risks and opportunities. In this case, he had to weigh the possibility of patronage from the Committee members against the possibility of offending Thornhill, to whom he was now so close. For fifteen years, the Warden of the Fleet had been John Huggins, the man for whose house Thornhill and Hogarth had recently provided paintings. It was rumoured that Thornhill owed both his royal post and his knighthood to Huggins, whose shady skills at underhand deals in the corners of the Court and Westminster had won him many powerful friends. Hogarth's project could, therefore, have offended the Serjeant-Painter since it was bound to show Huggins as unscrupulous and cruel.

For the office of Wardenship of the Fleet, Huggins had paid Lord Clarendon £5000, covering the lifetime of himself and his son William, and to recoup this outlay he charged extortionate fees on the one hand and cut costs on the other – the prison's drains stayed blocked, the roofs leaked and the bedding stank. Even the corpses of prisoners who died there rotted until relatives or friends paid for their release.[35] Rumours of maltreatment and murder mounted, resulting in numerous petitions and inquiries in the 1720s. One case in particular brought damning evidence, the fate of a poor man, Edward Arne, who was thrown naked into a rough shed by Huggins's assistant, James Barnes. One Sunday morning, starving and shivering, Arne escaped and rushed into the parlour next to the chapel where the service was being held. Wrapped in an old mattress which had been thrown in to him by a fellow prisoner, he looked like a grotesque fowl: 'the feathers stuck and were clotted upon him by his own excrements, and the dirt, which covered his skin'.[36] After he was hurled back into his dungeon, still naked and now unable even to speak, appeals were made to the Warden who peered in at the pathetic prisoner, 'lifting up his eyes to Mr Huggins. The said Huggins had no compassion on him, but caused the door to be close locked upon him.'[37] Through cold, hunger and pain, he died. Huggins's answer was that he was not responsible; he had merely relied on Barnes.

His deputy was Thomas Bambridge, a lawyer, and in August 1728, perhaps feeling the heat of criticism, Huggins sold the wardenship to Bambridge and another colleague, Dougal Cuthbert. Very soon two scandals broke. The first concerned a scholarly debtor and architect, Robert Castell, father of 'numerous small children'. Unable to pay Bambridge's vast fees, Castell was locked in a nearby sponging house where smallpox was raging, yet, despite his pleas, Bambridge went ahead.[38] Castell died: the world of Palladian gentility (he had just published his *The Villas of the Ancients Illustrated*) had fallen into

144

the clutches of a Lockit-like gaoler. Six months later came a second incident. In January 1729, after months of harassment, a baronet, Sir William Rich, was threatened with a red-hot poker pushed against his chest, to make him pay the fees; next day, surrounded by the warden's armed ruffians, he struck back and wounded Bambridge.[39] As a punishment, Bambridge loaded Rich with shackles and flung him into the Strong Room, a dark pit beneath the Fleet, used for obstreperous prisoners but also for the unburied dead; only a thin floor of boards separated it from the common sewer beneath.

Bambridge's error was to extend his cruelty from the poor, like Arne, to the well connected. The MP Sir James Oglethorpe, an energetic philanthropist (who later founded the colony of Georgia in 1733, in part for released debtors), had already raised questions in the Commons about the death of Castell. Now Rich's friends had Bambridge brought to court. On 25 February Oglethorpe was appointed head of a Commons Committee to inquire not only into the Fleet, but into the King's Bench and the Marshalsea and the state of English gaols in general. Two days later, with representatives from the Lords, the Committee visited the Fleet. Holding their noses against the stench they found prisoners huddled in dungeons without light or heat, or packed thirty to forty in a room. Moved by their cries of 'God bless you', the MPs questioned the debtors and ordered Rich's irons removed.[40] Next morning they found him loaded with irons of three times the weight, fixed so tightly that his arms were horribly swollen.

The story filled the press. The Committee included several opponents of Walpole, including Pulteney and Wyndham, and their findings provided another stick for *The Craftsman* to batter the Ministry. In late March Bambridge, Huggins and four accomplices were arrested; all the efforts of Huggins's powerful cronies could not stem the torrent of public disapproval. On 26 April the Committee published its horrifying report and soon legislation was passed to 'disable' Bambridge from keeping the wardenship. (Thornhill was a member of the Joint Committee of Commons and Lords who discussed Bambridge's disablement.) In June, when Bambridge's reign formally ended, the Fleet prisoners carried his effigy in a triumphal chair, decking it with fetters and packing its paunch with gunpowder for explosive celebrations.[41] It was a piece of popular theatre equalling Hogarth's 'Burning of the Rumps' in *Hudibras*, or Pope's *Dunciad* processions. Meanwhile the elderly Huggins, ill and weak and loaded with manacles in Newgate, was tried for the murder of Arne, but in late 1730 powerful lobbying behind the scenes set him free, the court accepting that the man responsible was his then deputy, James Barnes.

145

In practical terms, *The Committee of the House of Commons* was extremely useful in bringing Hogarth into contact with parliamentary circles. But it also demonstrated his concern with imprisonment and injustice. When he obtained official permission to paint the Committee in action, he decided to show a confrontation between the keeper and an abused prisoner. The figure of the 'inhuman gaoler' impressed Horace Walpole, who owned this first oil sketch, as a supreme example of Hogarth's ability to capture expression:

'It is the very figure that *Salvator Rosa* would have drawn for *Iago* in the moment of detection. Villainy, fear, and conscience are mixed in yellow and livid on his countenance; his lips are contracted by tremor, his face advances as eager to lie, his legs step back as thinking to make his escape; one hand is thrust precipitately into his bosom, the fingers of the other are catching uncertainly at his button-holes. If this was a portrait, it is the most striking that was ever drawn; if it was not, it is still finer.'[42]

The prisoner was believed to be a Portuguese Jew, Mendes de Sola, who had been kept shackled for two months in the foul Fleet Strong Room. On seeing Bambridge, 'he fainted, and the blood started out of his mouth and his nose'.[43] To make the point more dramatic, Hogarth set this scene not in the panelled

35 *A Committee of the House of Commons* (1729)

146

Commons Committee Room but in a dripping stone cell, almost resembling his *Beggar's Opera* background. Against this background he implicitly probed the status of those concerned. Who are the true 'criminals'?

As with *The Beggar's Opera*, Hogarth painted several versions for different patrons (including the seedy Sir Archibald Grant), and once again the intimate, energetic tension of the first sketch gradually gave way to a more generalized comment. Instead of the dramatic stand-off between gaoler and prisoner, glaring across the heads of the other men, the final version is like an official group portrait, bland and corporate. The bewigged Committee stares soberly out, and the prisoner is a minor figure, kneeling with his back towards us like a helpless supplicant or a noble savage before colonial conquerors; in his respectful painting Hogarth's questioning of authority is still visible. And to those who knew Hogarth's work the picture's composition might recall the discredited Rump Parliament in *Hudibras*, with its members' hats ranged neatly round the walls, or the disreputable 'committee' of Falstaff, Shallow and Silence. The small, murky painting hangs today in the National Portrait Gallery, a memorial of officials of the past. Its presence there celebrates too, of course, the national status of the painter from Smithfield and the Fleet, an irony Hogarth might have relished.

There were already several ironies, not least the friendship between Thornhill and John Huggins. In Hogarth's early sketch the leering gaoler is clearly labelled, in a later hand, 'Huggins the Keeper', but in the painting the portrait is obviously of Bambridge. Some equivocation, some compromise began here. In one of those unnerving blurrings of sides, Hogarth later painted fine portraits of the callous old Huggins and his son William, who became a close friend. (In another twist, after Archibald Grant's bankruptcy, William Huggins bought Grant's copies of *The Beggar's Opera* and *The Committee*.)

The other complication was that by the time he began work on *The Committee* Hogarth's relations with Thornhill were already strained. He was himself caught up in an imitation game of some complexity. Hogarth was not a man ever to give up something he had set his heart on, and by 1728 it was set on two goals – Thornhill's enviable eminence, and Thornhill's daughter Jane. The two, perhaps, went hand in hand. He was already a friend and drinking companion of Thornhill's son John and he had known Jane since he first came to the academy behind their house in 1724. Then she had been fifteen, a girl in a house of art filled with enviable possessions, from Titians and Raphaels to classical casts. Jane was now nearly twenty, and Hogarth was thirty-two. Like Dick Whittington in the old story (and like the good apprentice in his

147

own later engravings of *Industry and Idleness*) he could leap up the ladder by marrying his master's daughter. One can't help remembering his search for 'short cuts' and his urgent desire to combine his 'pleasures and his studies'.

On 20 March 1729, at a time when Thornhill's attention was distracted by Commons business concerning the Huggins–Bambridge trial, and by the newly granted permission for him to copy the Raphael cartoons at Hampton Court, Hogarth obtained a marriage licence. Three days later the wedding took place just out of town, in the parish church of Paddington village – a curious location, given that the licence placed them both as members of the parish of St Paul's, Covent Garden. Afterwards, so the story goes, Hogarth and Jane crossed the river, possibly to South Lambeth, where Hogarth had lodgings.[44] But within a week the news was broadcast to the town by *The Craftsman*: 'Mr Hogarth, an ingenious Designer and Engraver, was lately married to the Daughter of Sir James Thornhill, Kt. Serjeant-Painter, and History-Painter to his Majesty.'[45]

In *The Beggar's Opera*, Lucy and Polly plead for their lover with their fathers against the background of Newgate. Did Jane's intercession for Hogarth begin as early as 1728, and was it frustration at Thornhill's intransigence that led to the secret wedding? We can only speculate. Even if they did not technically elope, Jane's marriage to this mere engraver, however 'ingenious', was undertaken without Thornhill's consent. Nichols put it more forcibly:

'This union, indeed, was a stolen one, and consequently without the approbation of Sir James, who, considering the youth of his daughter, and the slender finances of her husband, as yet an obscure artist, was not easily reconciled to the match.'[46]

Hogarth gambled the inevitable rift against later reconciliation. But perhaps he was risking all for love and not for status, imitating the passionate drama and not the bourgeois fable. He was said to love Jane, and he remained a stout defender of Thornhill. When he painted his wife a few years later, he posed her facing calmly forward, handsome and direct, proudly holding a miniature of her father. Yet he knew it was a double betrayal. Thornhill had made the plebeian engraver his protégé, trusted him and worked with him: Hogarth may have staked as much on Thornhill's feelings for him, as for his daughter. But there was a risk: at the very end of his life Hogarth painted an emotionally charged picture of Boccaccio's heroine Sigismunda, mourning her husband Guiscardo, her father's squire, killed by him after their secret marriage. The model he used was Jane.

Jane was another escape route. There is no way of knowing if his childhood

148

36 *Jane Hogarth* (*c.*1738)

haunted him, if he shrugged it off, or if it made him more determined. Yet it cannot be ignored that repeatedly, from the age of twenty to thirty-five, more than any other contemporary artist, Hogarth drew prisons: the barred window in Spiller's benefit ticket; the stage set where Polly and Lucy plead for Macheath's life; the dank bricks of the Fleet behind the Committee Room; the draughty sheds of Bridewell, the Fleet and Bedlam. He reworked the image, as if trying to divest himself of its feel, like a dog shaking off rain. But he also clung to it like a criminal returning to the place of the crime, as if working to control it and fix it in brushstrokes and ink.

When he thought back to these years in his old age he thought of his father – but as an image from which he must distance himself. He could never quite bring himself to trust the 'great men' and he simultaneously courted them and exposed them. He had to prove himself independent; even of Thornhill, whose teaching, patronage and family now offered a way forward.

8

Painting the Polite

Envy, to which th'ignoble mind's a slave
Is emulation in the learn'd or brave:
Nor Virtue, male or female, can we name,
But what will grow on Pride, or grow on Shame.
ALEXANDER POPE, *An Essay on Man*

HOGARTH AND JANE started their married life in lodgings, virtually on her parents' doorstep. Shortly before, Hogarth had moved from Little Newport Street to Covent Garden, where a friend of his, William Tothall, was working for a woollen merchant on the corner of Tavistock Court in the Little Piazza, on the south-eastern side of the square. Hogarth rented rooms above the warehouse. It was a good place to show off his wares. Covent Garden was still the centre of the artists' territory, 'inhabbited by Painters (a Credit to live there)', wrote Vertue in 1726, counting eleven artists of different kinds who had studios there.

By the beginning of 1730 then, Hogarth and Jane were settled above the 'Broad Cloth Warehouse' in the Little Piazza. Their rooms had one other inhabitant, Hogarth's dog 'Pugg' (one of several pugs he owned in his life), who was lost, much to his master's distress in December 1731, prompting an advertisement offering half a guinea's reward.[1] In front stretched Covent Garden, clamorous and colourful, holding all the rough contradictions of the London Hogarth painted, with its great porticoed church, market stalls, brothels and coffee houses.

Near by were two of Hogarth's favourite haunts, the Bedford Arms Tavern on the southern side, close to the various bagnios run by John Rigg and the beautiful Betty Careless, and the Bedford coffee house, under the more salubrious eastern arches of the Great Piazza.[2] The Bedford coffee house was the stamping ground of wits, critics, playwrights and actors; John Rich's house was almost next door. And after Addison's death in 1719, it had also taken over from own his coffee house, Buttons, as a centre for Whig politicians, poets, pamphleteers and natural philosophers. In addition, it later

151

became the lecture theatre – and home – of the innovative mathematician, engineer and prominent Mason, J. T. Desaguliers; by 1734 Desaguliers was on his hundred and twenty-first course of lectures. The culture of enterprise was as strong and problematic for scientists as it was for the artists, both groups hunting for aristocratic patrons on the one hand and appealing to a new, wider public on the other. The Covent Garden circles thus extended from artists, theatre people and writers to scientists, doctors, tradesmen and lawyers – and schoolteachers such as Vincent Bourne, of Westminster School, who devoted a Latin poem to 'Gulielmus Hogarth' in 1734. French and Italians, Dutch and Germans, mixed with the English, from painters, musicians and silversmiths to refugees such as Voltaire, who lived in Maiden Lane, off the market, for three years from 1726, rubbing up his English by going to Drury Lane and following the play in spare prompter's copies.

This robust, gregarious, cosmopolitan crowd was familiar to Jane, but the Thornhill circle was definitely wealthier and grander than Hogarth's. Although her husband was moving away from their old Smithfield life, he never turned his back on his family, and painted tender portraits of his sisters a

37 Mary Hogarth (c.1738) 38 Anne Hogarth (c.1738)

few years later. One of the last trade cards he made, in 1728, was for his sisters, when they moved from 'the old frockshop' by St Bartholemew's Hospital, on the corner of Long Walk, across the road to the King's Arms by Little Britain gate. He gave them classical busts, urns overflowing with flowers, royal arms and leafy swags but showed practical-looking bales leaning against the formal frame. Against a background of high-stacked shelves, a smart gentleman holds

39 Shop Card for Mary and Anne Hogarth (1730)

his daughter patiently by the hand while a plump, rather woeful boy is being eased into his new coat (the choice is difficult – another coat lies on the counter, and yet another hangs ready by the door behind). The sisters stand by, eager to help. Their shop, they claim in the proud, straightforward inscription: 'Sells the best & most fashionable Ready Made Frocks, sutes of Fustian, Ticken & Holland, script Dimmity & Flannel, Wastcoats, blue & canvas Frocks'. They sold suits for the 'Bluecoat boys' at Charterhouse near by, and plain materials in the piece, 'Wholesale or Retale at Reasonable Rates'.

By 1729 Hogarth was on the threshold of a new direction as an artist. With the Thornhill connection fixed, if still distinctly sticky, and with Jane by his side – tall, calm, determined, with a definite (and much needed) glint of humour – his fortunes looked set, if he worked hard. But if he had his feet under the table of prosperity, sometimes he might have doubted if the feast in

153

40 Detail from *Sancho's Feast* (date unknown)

front of him was too good to be true. After Hogarth's death, Jane Hogarth told the etcher Richard Livesay that he had included a self-portrait in his engraving of *Sancho's Feast*, dating from around this time.[3] It shows how poor Sancho, thinking himself King of Barataria and attending a magnificent banquet, 'is Starved in the midst of Plenty. Pedro Rezzio, his Phisician out of great Care for his health ordering every dish from the Table before the Governor tasts it'. Sancho stares in dismay, his fork stayed halfway to his mouth, his snub-nosed, stubbly face a sharp contrast to his lacy bib. By his side, as the delicious dishes are whisked away, two elegant ladies point in unsurprised disdain, while opposite the kind of people whom Sancho resembles – the busty, toothless whore, the black servant, the rough peasant – roar with laughter. This episode from *Don Quixote* seems to have been an accepted cipher for social-climbing; in March 1729, regretting his health would not allow him to come to London, Swift told Pope, 'and I did design to live like a gentleman, and, as Sancho's wife said, to go in my coach to court'.[4]

It was Hogarth's marriage that first catapulted him into the notebooks kept by George Vertue, who recorded every rise and fall of London's artistic life. Finding the entry in these crowded pages is like seeing someone entering a party, rather late, but with plenty of credentials to make an introduction worthwhile.

'Mr William Hogarth first learnt to grave armes on Silver plate. &c. from thence study'd in the Accademy St. Martin's lane. some time having a quick lively genius made several Charicatures. prints etch'd afterwards the designs & plates of Hudibras. but finding it more agreable to his mind, took up the pincill & applyd his studyes to painting in small conversations. or fancyes. wherein he now has much reputation. & lately married to ye daughter of Sr James Thornhill. without his consent – '5

These scribbled lines fall in Vertue's notebook after a note of March 1729 reporting that Thornhill had obtained permission from the King to copy the Raphael cartoons at Hampton Court, and a similar entry stating that Hogarth's friend John Ellys had been copying the portraits in the royal palaces. After the Hogarth note, come accounts of three engravers: the Anglo-Dutch John Faber, who has just made some good mezzotint portraits; Henry Fletcher, whose first public print, *The Story of Bathsheba*, has just been published; and the Dutch Henry Hulsberg, who died after two years' illness and 'was buried in the Savoy by the Lutheran Church, of which he had been Warden – & was supported by them & the brethren of a Dutch Box-Club'. Then comes a longer entry on the portrait painter Bartholomew Dandridge, 'a near neighbour to Highmore in Lincolns Inn fields & corrival – seems to have as much merit with less modish assurance'.[6] In this busy, rivalrous world, which embraced all ranks from royal painters to indigent engravers, Mr Hogarth had finally arrived.

Hogarth himself wrote that

'engraving in the first part of my life till near thirty did little more than maintain myself in the usual gaieties of life, but in all a punctual paymaster. Then maried and turned Painter of Portraits in small conversation Peices and great success.'[7]

But as Vertue noted, Hogarth already had a reputation as a painter: marriage did not drive him to it (nor did it turn him entirely from 'the usual gaities of life') although he now needed more money and had to hunt commissions more eagerly. His new connections might have helped him come into his own, but he wanted to paint for other reasons too. Painting gave him greater control, free from the reliance on printsellers. It was also more lucrative, so long as he could get the work, and was a move into the more refined circles of 'fine art', away from the mechanic trade of the printseller, away from the streets and the theatre to the salons of the West End and St James's.

In the late 1720s he largely left aside engraving, apart from a few frontis-pieces, and while he worked on his theatrical paintings and the Fleet Committee, he also collected individual commissions. Between 1728 and 1732

155

he painted over two dozen pictures, single portraits and groups. Once he began, the commissions flowed in, one recommendation leading to another: as for all freelance workers it was hard for him to say no in case he was not asked again. In the log jam of work – not being prosperous enough to employ assistants (although he later made this a matter of principle) – he left several paintings unfinished. When he listed these in 1731 as 'half payment received' he unwittingly left a map of his ladder of patrons. Among his first commissions, in 1728, was one from the auctioneer Christopher Cock (he of the fashionable clientele and shady reputation), a near neighbour in Covent Garden. Another came from John Rich, who ordered a family group as well as buying one version of *The Beggar's Opera*. A third early purchaser was Thomas Wood, who apparently drank with Hogarth in the Bedford Arms and wanted a picture of his family, never finished, and did eventually receive portraits of his daughter and his dog Vulcan, who was famous for arriving with a lantern in his mouth to guide his master home from the pub.

These were hardly upper-crust clients but, still, they provided useful links. Cock, for example, was not only an influential auctioneer but was the son-in-law of the art collector Sir Andrew Fountaine, and Hogarth soon painted a work for Fountaine that included Cock showing him a picture. But this commission could have come by another route, as Fountaine was also a Mason, as was another early client, the lawyer Stephen Beckingham. Or it could have come through the Commons Committee, of which Fountaine was a great promoter; or simply through the artists' grapevine – Fountaine had been a patron of the Vanderbank academy in the early 1720s, and it was he who brought the future George II to see the artists there at work in 1722. The networks interwove and overlapped. Hogarth's membership of the clubs and the Masonic lodges, his work in the theatre and the Committee of the House of Commons was beginning to pay off.

The Committee, in 1729, seems to have been especially fruitful. Soon the unsavoury Sir Archibald Grant ordered a copy of that painting, along with *The Beggar's Opera*, and within a short while John Thomson, Grant's associate on the dubious Charitable Corporation, also placed an order. More distinguished members of the Fleet Inquiry Committee appear on Hogarth's list: John Conduitt, Master of the Mint, and Viscount Malpas, Walpole's son-in-law. Through Malpas, a key member of Prince Frederick's entourage, Hogarth had a chance of reaching the Prince of Wales's circle at Leicester House. Through Conduitt's connections, and through Fountaine (who was the Prince of Cumberland's tutor), Hogarth could just see the glimmer of a route towards the Court of St James. For the moment, the sky was the limit.

To set up as a portrait painter required a certain style, and the artist had to foster an image of a man much in demand. The studio was a shop, and an advertisement, as well as a workplace. When he was explaining to French readers how the London system worked, Hogarth's friend Jean André Rouquet, who came to London in the early 1720s, wrote that every portrait painter had 'a room to show his pictures, separate from that in which he works. People who have nothing to do, make it their morning amusement, to go and see these collections'. A footman lets them in, and the artist 'does not stir out of his closet' unless called: if he is, he pretends to be very busy on a portrait – a good way of showing how requested he is:

'The footman knows by heart all the names, real and imaginary, of all the persons whose portraits, finished or unfinished, decorate the picture room: after they have stared a good deal, they applaud loudly, or condemn softly, and giving some money to the footman, they go about their business. An argument, if it follows, is a good thing, as it makes the visitors who are *for* the painter commission him to do their portraits, to prove themselves right.'[8]

As a beginner in Covent Garden, Hogarth probably did not have a separate room – his visitors simply wandered about his studio, while he worked. And from the start he was more informal than most painters. He would not, for example, let his sitters run the gauntlet of servants with their hands out, as the Reverend William Cole, who was included in the painting of the Western family in the mid-1730s, remembered long afterwards:

'When I sat to him, near fifty years ago, the custom of giving vails to servants was not discontinued. On my taking leave of our Painter at the door, and his servant's opening it or the coachdoor, I cannot tell which, I offered him a small gratuity; but the man very politely refused it, telling me it would be as much as the loss of his place if his master knew it. This was so uncommon, and so liberal in a man of Mr. Hogarth's profession at that time of day, that it much struck me, as nothing of the sort had happened to me before.'[9]

Hogarth's servants did not lose out: he was a punctual paymaster, and those who worked for him stayed for many years.

It was important for an artist to impress his sitters so that they brought others to see his work. Hogarth made an impact, fast, because of the talent he revealed for painting small groups, 'conversation pieces', linking the formal and the intimate. His canvases grew rapidly in size, as did his reputation; starting with little pictures of twelve to fifteen inches, by 1732 he was working on large pictures of over four feet square. By January 1730, Vertue was noting 'the daily success of Mr Hogarth in painting small family peices & Conversations with so much Air and agreeableness'. Commenting that he now had a growing following and a great deal of work, Vertue filled in the outlines of Hogarth's brief biography again, astonished that a silver-plate engraver should have risen so far and so fast. After the academy, Vertue wrote:

'he by a fluent genius designed and Invented freely several things which he etchd particularly some Caricatures. of several persons or affairs of the times. & lastly drew & gravd the set of Prints from Butlers Hudibras. afterwards got some little insight & instructions in Oyl Colours. without Coppying other Paintings or Masters immediately by the force of Judgment a quick & ready Conception. & an exact immitation of Natural likeness became surprizingly forward to be the Master he now is.'[10]

Could he have seen these private notes, Hogarth would have been pleased, as they emphasize all his own points – his 'free' invention, his refusal to copy, his independent judgement and speed of conception, his gift for a likeness. All that Vertue misses is his theatrical slant, his placing of characters and suggestion that their polite pose is an 'act'.

Politeness had its origins in the ideal gentleman of Shaftesbury's writings, and of *The Spectator*.[11] Culture, taste and refined manners would, it was held, enable society to bridge, or at least mask, disparate elements and interests: Court, City, professions, trade. Such cultivation involved an ease of social address, reflected in physical grace. In part, this could be learned, and the dancing master was the most important teacher: although it was important to be a bit casual, not to be *too* like a common dancing master oneself. Manuals abounded, giving details of how a proper gentleman or lady should stand (feet at an elegant angle, toes pointed out), sit, present a gift, smell a flower, dress, hold a glass, open a door.

Painters followed these conventions, in order to present their subjects as people of quality. Richardson had insisted, for example, that a painter should not strive to give a true likeness, but 'to raise the Character: to divest the unbred Person of his Rusticity, and give him something at least of a Gentleman'.[12] In turn, people then copied the paintings. One dancing-master's book, in 1735, made this explicit:

'Let us imagine ourselves, as so many living Pictures drawn by the most excellent Masters. Indeed, we ought to set our Bodies in such a Disposition, when we stand in Conversation, that, were our Actions & Postures delineated, they might bear the strictest Examination of the most critical judges.'[13]

Conversation, in the sense used here, did not mean simply talking to another person, but politeness in action, the art of behaving in company. Art that resembled conversation was thus both intimate and public; the new genre of the 'conversation piece' derived from the Italian *conversazione*, an informal group. Hogarth however, often ruffled the polished surface of ease and good breeding to suggest an underlying *un*-ease in those he painted. The problem was, as he knew, that if politeness was the deliberate acquisition of a veneer, then the veneer was all. Where was 'nature'? Where was the self? Was character itself something created, a mere 'imitation'? Or was there an essence below the surface for the artist to catch?

There was a real confusion about how much the face could give away. Some writers believed, as Addison put it,

'Every Passion gives a particular Cast to the Countenance, and is apt to discover itself in some Feature or other. I have seen an Eye curse for half an Hour together and an Eye-brow call a man Scoundrel.'[14]

But Hobbes had long ago noted that the word 'person' derived from the Latin *persona*, a mask worn by an actor, and that appearances themselves were a second mask. In his paintings Hogarth examined these visors and masks. His pictures took to a literal degree Richardson's advice that subjects should be 'good actors' and that artists should give a sitter the air one might wish to put on 'when one comes into Company, or into any Publick Assembly, or at the first sight of any Particular Person'.[15] But he went further, painting people in social situations, at a wedding, playing cards, at tea, examining a picture, while still subtly suggesting they were *acting*.

Hogarth was not the first to paint conversation pieces in England. The term had been in use since 1706, particularly for 'merry company' paintings by artists such as Marcellus Laroon the elder and Van Heemskerk.[16] A more aristocratic form appeared when the Huguenot artist Philip Mercier arrived in London in 1725, to paint groups and couples against the landscape of their private estates in a style echoing Watteau's *fêtes galantes*.[17] Mercier, a restless, lively personality, had previously worked in Hanover, and when Frederick, Prince of Wales, arrived in 1728, he became his official painter. The genre had a fashionable gloss, and was taken up fast. Wit and emblem were introduced in background details in the mid-1720s by the Flemish painter Joseph van Aken, who painted his landed sportsmen between two paths (a clear Choice-of-Hercules allusion), or slyly suggested that social activities were not so polite by placing a cast of Bacchus behind a family tea table.[18]

The conversation piece was civilized but informal, fanciful and new, and,

159

despite van Aken's Netherlandish idioms, predominantly French in style. It was radically different to baroque decoration, classical solemnity or even to the sympathetically straightforward portraits of Thornhill and Richardson. Hogarth, with his keen eye for the new, took to it straight away. His *Beggar's Opera* pictures already showed a deftness that suggested he had been devouring French prints, perhaps original paintings as well, and memorizing their approach and techniques. Some of his early pictures are particularly French in their graceful composition, like the portrait of *Ashley Cowper with his Wife and Daughter* (now in the Tate Gallery) with the greyhound, pastoral background and classical urn bearing an Arcadian inscription from Virgil's Tenth Eclogue,[19] or the lovely *Fishing Party* at Dulwich, where the child holds a rod arching over a shining lake. In the late 1720s and early 1730s other British artists, including Bartholomew Dandridge, Charles Phillips and Gawen Hamilton, took up this form with speed and skill, but Hogarth made it so much his own that he has understandably, if falsely, been called its inventor. The conversation piece was perfect for him, with his gift for a telling likeness, his fanciful imagination and humour. He could show off, and flatter and tease his patrons at the same time.

41 *An Assembly at Wanstead House* (1730–31)

These paintings usually paid a graceful tribute to family life, its domestic feeling, its happy occasions and social standing. Often (like traditional portraits) they marked rites of passage: marriages and anniversaries, appointments as MPs or Governors, people leaving home, even the memory of someone who had died. By showing families 'at home', they also showed their importance in the public sphere. But by making details comment on the scene, Hogarth could also make his works 'intimate' in another sense, in that only those in the know could read the subtext; the vulgar were excluded. And even within that circle he could address different audiences; however much he approved of the drive for refinement his background was as a satirist, and he could not altogether leave it behind. In the crowded canvas of *An Assembly at Wanstead House* which Sir Richard Child, Viscount Castlemaine, had ordered to commemorate his silver wedding, most people would catch the obvious symbols: the ace of spades (a card to trump all others) or the paired whippets (a famously monogamous breed).[20] But Child, the son of Sir Josiah Child, Chairman of the East India Company, was a great financier and supporter of Palladianism. The scene is the ballroom of his lavish new house at Wanstead in Essex, designed by Colen Campbell. By bringing together details from elsewhere in the house, like the ceiling from the great hall, painted by Kent, and the heavily scrolled furniture, also designed by Kent, Hogarth casually draws attention to the ostentatious artifice and autocratic power – over people as well as possessions.

The group portraits, praised for their truth to life, thus go beyond 'realism'. In *The Wedding of Stephen Beckingham and Mary Cox* it looks as though Hogarth is painting the actual ceremony: the groom has the ring ready, the vicar holds up his book, marked 'Of Matrimony', the bride's father leans on his stick and other relatives look expectantly on. We seem to see it as it happens. Not so. The wedding actually took place in St Benet's, St Paul's Wharf, but Hogarth moved it to the new, grander, St Martin-in-the-Fields. Time, as well as place, is at the artist's command. To the side of the main group, her blue dress half in shadow, is a melancholy figure with a funerary tablet behind her: probably the mother of the bride, who died in 1727. And the wedding group has an audience. While they stand stagy and frozen, lit sharply from the front, a different source of light slants from the side behind them, softening the soaring columns and ornate ceiling and picking out two urchins, leaning curiously over the balcony above, painted in a far livelier, sketchy style, as if style itself is a comment. Another reminder of the 'real' life of a church, when the picture was first painted, was a kneeling figure arranging the hassocks in the left corner. This verger with his hassocks reappears in *The*

161

42 *The Wedding of Stephen Beckingham and Mary Cox* (1729)

Rake's Progress, and certainly Nichols, in the 1780s, thought Hogarth was tactless to include such details: 'an artist who, representing the marriage ceremony in a chapel, renders the clerk, who lays the hassocks, the principal figure in it, may at least be taxed with want of judgement'.[21]

Hogarth often reworked his pictures. Here the clerk was painted over, and at some stage the flamboyant carpet, and the putti with their cornucopia were painted in, perhaps to add more richness or to link the subjects better with the rather overwhelming background. Did the Beckinghams think Hogarth had been insufficiently respectful? Most patrons were delighted with their likeness and with the backgrounds that showed off their wealth and prestige. But some were discomforted. Hogarth was not afraid to show that there were other ways of life – those of childhood, of the streets – which were more 'natural' than society manners. And he suggested too the effort that supported this apparently effortless ease, the work of the footmen and vergers, farm labourers and servants.

The Beckinghams were substantial country gentry and lawyers. Stephen, owner of a Kent estate, had been admitted into Lincoln's Inn ten years before, while the bride's father, Joseph Cox, was a Kidderminster attorney. They were typical of Hogarth's first patrons, but as his reputation spread, his subjects moved up in infinite, important gradations. Ashley Cowper was a barrister, the Clerk of Parliaments from 1740 to his death; *The Ashley and Popple Families*, of 1730, featured Alured Popple, Secretary to the Board of Trade, and a future Governor of Bermuda;[22] *Captain Woodes Rogers and his Family* showed another colonial Governor, a famous Bristol seaman.[23] Woodes Rogers had commanded a privateering fleet in the Pacific in the War of the Spanish Succession, sailed round the world and tackled Caribbean piracy. Out of favour for some time, in 1728 he was reinstated as Governor of the Bahamas. Hogarth's picture celebrated his return to the Bahamas in 1729 with his son William and daughter Sarah. The background was emblematic, like an old Dutch portrait, with its ship and globe and the map William holds – but Hogarth still let real life intrude, painting a stoutly plebeian maidservant peering over Sarah's silk-clad shoulder.

He kept up the raillery in the larger groups such as *The Wollaston Family*, where a little pug stands on its hind legs imitating the host. This painting was probably commissioned when William Wollaston, MP for Ipswich, succeeded to the family estates in 1730. William was the son of a famous rationalist divine, author of an influential treatise, *The Religion of Nature Delineated*, in 1724; his wife Elizabeth was the daughter of Dr John Francis Fauquier, a Director of the Bank of England. Their relations, gathered here, include wealthy merchants and City figures such as Sir Robert Godshall, a future Lord Mayor, and Elizabeth's brother Francis Fauquier, later Governor of Virginia.[24]

So while the picture celebrated prosperous, congenial, extended family life, Hogarth was also painting a polite study of networks of power, showing that commerce need not be hard and ruthless but could be easy and agreeable, the basis for a refined culture.[25] On a large canvas, over three feet by four feet, he divided the company into two groups, at a tea table and card table, and linked them by the standing figure of Wollaston, who gestures towards a

163

43 *The Wollaston Family* (1730)

servant, asking him to arrange a chair for a gentleman to join the card players. The natural movement snaps up a passing moment. But the faces here are rather wooden, like early Victorian photographs held in a long pose. Through the central 'V' shape between the groups, Hogarth drew the eye backwards, into the depths. We look past Wollaston, through the gap between the tables, past the footman and the liveried black servant, down a corridor towards a lighted window. This perspective, plus the way the whole scene is framed by a huge, theatrical curtain, makes the family seem like a cast of actors and, in the end, despite the pictured ease, we may feel that 'real' life takes place offstage. From the pug in front to the exit behind, Hogarth makes his point without detracting at all from the scene's genuine sociability.

Vertue, with his keen eye for coming men, spotted *The Wollaston Family*, 'really a most excellent work containing the true likeness of the persons, shape aire & dress – well disposd. genteel, agreable – & freely painted & the composition great variety & Nature'.[26] It was a virtuoso piece, too, in showing Hogarth's ability to handle a crowd – and typical of Hogarth to cram more people in than any of his rivals. There are seventeen figures here, all recognizable portraits, and an astounding twenty-four are crammed into *The Assembly at Wanstead House*. Such pictures were themselves talking points. Hogarth's name was spreading: soon Mrs Pendarves picked him as the artist she wanted to do a portrait of Lady Sunderland in preference to the miniaturist Zincke, explaining, 'I think he takes a much better likeness, and that is what I shall value my friend's picture for, more than for the excellence of the painting.'[27]

As he worked on these paintings, Hogarth became more and more experimental. The woodenness disappeared, the finishing became more delicate, the poses more fluent, the composition far more daring. He dealt more confidently, for example, with problems of setting. Some patrons wanted to be painted in their town houses and others in their own country seats. Both posed challenges. The difficulty of the large indoor groups was creating a 'natural' arrangement from individual portraits taken at different times; some painters sketched the face and then arranged the group using lay figures, little dolls, with beautifully made miniature clothes. (This is one reason why Arthur Devis's figures do look, literally, doll-like). But Hogarth invented as he went, adjusting the arrangement of figures as he worked, as later cleaning has shown. With country-house settings he faced another problem: sittings took place in London but he had to build up background from sketches, or imagination.

The Jones Family (plate 1) was commissioned by the twenty-four-year-old Robert Jones in March 1730, a year before he left on his Grand Tour. Robert's father had been an MP and his mother came from a powerful City family, so the Joneses lived for most of the time in London, in Bruton Street near the new Berkeley Square. Yet Robert chose to have them portrayed on their estate in Wales, perhaps because the painting was intended not only as a memento for his family while he was away, but also as a tribute to his native landscape before he set out for the olive groves of the South.[28] Robert stands between his widowed mother, in dignified dark blue, and his older sister Mary, facing his younger brother and sister, Oliver and Elizabeth. In the deep 'V' between the two groups, a vista stretches back to a crenellated house with a mountain beyond, representing the family seat, Fonmon Castle in the Vale of Glamorgan.

The details sparkle with a wonderful gaiety and luminescence, making Hogarth's composition even more dramatic. The confidence that came as his work was admired seems to have given him greater freedom, reflected in his treatment of 'freedom' itself. In such rural pictures, informality and pastoral ease were intended to join hands with dignity and decorum, but Hogarth, typically, often let indecorum enter too. A conventional pastoral – very French in its details – is suggested by a basket of flowers, balanced awkwardly between Oliver and Elizabeth, and by Mary's straw hat, held against her fine satin dress. But a *real* pastoral, oddly disconcerting, and hard to make out, invades the central space. Here a rough, barefoot boy wearing a servant's livery (looking like one of the Beckingham urchins), is trying to wrest what looks like a bun from a pet monkey, an old symbol of licentiousness and natural appetite. And while Mary Jones points languidly towards the castle, her hand guides us first to a lazy shepherdess, and then to two tiny figures unmistakably cavorting on top of a hayrick. Hogarth's sexy hints and sophisticated undercutting, like Gay's mock-pastoral or mock-heroic, were part of his appeal. After Robert Jones's early death in 1742, his mother noted against the inventory of his paintings, that 'ye family peice cost about 23 guineas' and she 'does not care to dispose' of it.[29]

Increasingly, Hogarth now began to show the energy of the uncontrolled pressing forcibly against the artifice of decorum. One picture, *The Cholmondely Family*, indeed is almost broken in two by its startling change in mood. On one side, beneath the familiar swathed curtain, sit the adults. The weight of history, property, responsibility and even death lies upon them – the stiff lady with the baby and the putti above is a memorial portrait of Mary,

44 *The Cholmondely Family* (1732)

166

Lady Malpas, the daughter of Sir Robert Walpole, who died of consumption in France in 1731 and whose body was lost in a shipwreck on the way home for burial. The living greet the dead: George Cholmondely, Viscount Malpas, looks tenderly down on his lost wife, holding their youngest child, Frederick. The Viscount's brother James, in red colonel's uniform, stands behind him, but *his* gaze swings out of this solemn space, past the heavy bookcase and the edges of the carpet, ominously ruffled, towards the Malpases' two sons, George and Robert, aged about eight and five. Robert, balancing on a chair, is on the point of kicking over a pile of books: one is in mid-air, and any second it will crash to the ground, shattering the polite grown-up poses. George is running towards his brother – to join him or to stop him? That question is underlined by the way that one of his feet remains on the carpet, in the 'adult room'. Hogarth suggested a story in a single scene, swinging the eye out beyond the frame into a realm where people do not pose, and dogs and children can rush free – until the leash or the chains of adulthood rein them in.

A painting like this suggests a society whose manners are built up, stage by stage, over the spontaneous, fluid responsiveness of childhood – very much as Hogarth himself applied the fine details of lace, silk and eyelashes over the bold, free blocking of his paintings. The child is moulded into the desired adult. He suggests something similar in the companion pieces, *The House of Cards* and *A Children's Tea Party*.[30] Playing in a park, a dreamlike realm of nature tamed, these look like the same children in each painting, but are not, quite: obvious portraits (never identified) blend into types. The children's future roles are laid out like their little formal dresses. They mimic marriage and build a card house, a delicate construction, already teetering dangerously; a small boy plays soldier and a girl gazes in a mirror. Their play is fun, yet precarious – it takes only a bounding dog to set their tea table flying, in front of the stiff-faced doll. And as the girl holds up the mirror it is directed not towards her but outwards, at the adults who see themselves, the child within, in a time left for ever.

Hogarth saw nothing cruel in learning by emulation but he did show that the process was inexorable; a good performance won applause. There was a fashion at this time for child actors playing adult roles in the theatre (including a child performance of *The Beggar's Opera*). This became a whim of high society and, after a revival of *The Indian Emperor*, Dryden's heroic drama of the Spanish conquistadores, at Drury Lane in 1731, the theatre's manager, Theophilus Cibber, directed a private performance at the house of John Conduitt, Master of the Mint. Conduitt's daughter Catherine (Kitty) was

45 *The House of Cards* (1730)

among the cast, which also included Lord Lempster and Lady Sophia Fermor, children of the Earl of Pomfret, and Lady Caroline Lennox, daughter of the Duke of Richmond. So successful was this that they were invited to appear before the King and Queen at St James's Palace in April 1732. By then, Conduitt had commissioned Hogarth to record it.

In *A Performance of 'The Indian Emperor or The Conquest of Mexico by the Spaniards'* (plate II), a number of 'conversations' take place: within the audience, within the play, between stage and spectators, between adults and children, past and future. Beneath the high mantel, in a little royal box, sit the ten-year-old William Duke of Cumberland and the Princesses Mary and Louisa (the little princess Gay had refused to nanny in 1727). At the back, the Duke of Montagu and the Earl of Pomfret are talking to Thomas Hill, Secretary of the Board of Trade, while the Duke of Richmond leans on his wife's chair. Almost all the 'audience' have their backs turned and our gaze too is directed to the stage. In the foreground, at the front of this cleverly raked audience, is the graceful triangle of the royal governess Lady Deloraine and her two daughters. One little girl, plump, restless, innocent, incorrigible, is

46 *A Children's Tea Party* (1730)

being kept quiet by being asked to pick up her mother's fan. While she turns her back on the play, her sister, pink-cheeked and wide-eyed, propping her chin on her fan, is wholly entranced, rigid with fascination at the action on stage.

This beautiful painting, with its shimmering surfaces of cream, gold and red, with the flash of blue sashes against the umber walls, speaks of power and of Britain's greatness – of royalty, aristocracy, money and science. But Hogarth does some curious things with it. The Conduitts themselves are absent, simply represented by two portraits on the wall, looking down at their guests, pictures within the picture. Above the royal box stands another portrait, whose authority hangs over all, a bust of Newton: below it is Rysbrack's relief of his achievements, designed by Conduitt, now being placed on Newton's Westminster Abbey tomb. Conduitt had married Newton's favourite niece, Catherine Barton, and had served and succeeded him at the Mint. The true aristocracy, one is led to think, is that of the 'scientific, philosophical intellect'. And beside the diminutive stage beneath its crown of candles, stands the distinguished mathematician and leading Mason, Dr Desaguliers, also a loyal follower of Newton, now acting as prompter to children.

169

The Newton bust, while adding dignity and status, allows Hogarth a pun on 'gravity', in all senses. It is counterpoised against a statue of the muse and of Pan with his pipes, a symbol of art – and of disorder. And the scene he chose links this polite performance with the *The Beggar's Opera*, in which the 'gentlemen of the road' mimic the 'fine gentleman' and vice versa. As Desaguliers peers through his spectacles, his book shows 'Act IV, Scene IV', the point in Dryden's play where the two Indian princesses, rivals for Cortez's love, find him a captive of Cydaira's father, Montezuma. The swing back to Gay's emotional triangles is emphasized by the prison background and the little boy standing between the two girls, complete with red coat and leg irons, a miniature Macheath. The unheard lines speak of betrayal, conquest and revenge:

CORTEZ: What words, dear saint, are these I hear you use?
            What faith, what vows, are those which you accuse?
CYDAIRA: More cruel than the tiger o'er his spoil;
            And falser than the weeping crocodil:
            Can you add vanity to guilt, and take
            A pride to conquests, which you make? . . .
CORTEZ: . . . With what injustice is my faith accused!
            Life, freedom, empire, I at once refused;
            And would again ten thousand times for you.
ALMERIA: She'll have too great content to find him true;
            And therefore, since his love is not for me,
            I'll help to make my rival's misery.
[*Aside*]   Spaniard, I never thought you false before:
            Can you at once two mistresses adore?[31]

These children may one day be princes, ministers and fine ladies. While the picture remains informal, Hogarth suggests the tangle of passion, conquest and deception that they will encounter in adult politics and politeness; a maze that can perhaps be escaped by Newtonian reason. In his brilliant rendering of the drama of the stage reflecting the world, of children emulating the ambition and heartache of adults, the satire of his masquerade prints flows into a deeper critique. Here are enacted all the difficulties, as well as the delights, of the highest polite conversation.

9

Impolite Conversations and Probing Ideas

The main design of the Fable . . . is to show the Impossibility of enjoying all the most elegant Comforts of Life that are to be met with in an industrious, wealthy and powerful nation, and at the same time be bless'd with all the Virtue and Innocence that can be wish'd for in a Golden Age.

BERNARD DE MANDEVILLE, *The Fable of the Bees* (1723)

IN MARCH 1731 Hogarth provided a drawing for the frontispiece to a ballad opera, *The Highland Fair* by Joseph Mitchell, a Scots poet living in London.[1] Mitchell had puffed Hogarth the year before in one of three 'Poetical Epistles' to painters, the others being Dandridge and Lambert. His poem was conventional enough, but picked out traits that from now on Hogarth's contemporaries would always highlight: his independence, his capturing of emotion, and his probing beneath surfaces.

> You have the Skill to catch the Grace,
> And secret Meanings of a face;
> From the quick Eyes to snatch the Fire,
> And limn th'Ideas they Inspire;
> To picture Passions, and, thro Skin,
> Call forth the living Soul within.[2]

Mitchell elevated Hogarth through classical and biblical comparisons (from the prophets to Pygmalion) but we can hear the artist's own sturdy claims in the appeals to nature and to the theatre, to the blending of high and low, and to a stubborn originality:

> Shakespeare in Painting, still improve
> And more the World's Attention move.
> Self taught, in your great Art excell,
> And from your Rivals bear the Bell.
> But, Rivals – you have none to fear –

171

Who dares, in such a Style, appear
Dutch and Italian, wide Extreams
Unite in you their diff'rent Names!
Still be esteem'd the First and Last,
Orig'nal in your Way and Taste.

This hyperbolic verse suggested Hogarth might even outdo his father-in-law, but it is the comparison with Shakespeare, not with Thornhill, that catches the attention. It was not yet the automatic, extravagant accolade that hindsight makes it seem. Shakespeare broke all the rules of dramatic unity and was far from the model of classical, generalized decorum. And yet, as Addison had written in *The Spectator*, his variety was the source of his power,

'Our inimitable *Shakespear* is a Stumbling-block to the whole tribe of these rigid Criticks. Who would not rather read one of his Plays, where there is not a single Rule of the Stage observed, than any Production of a modern Critick, where there is not one of them violated?'[3]

Hogarth wanted to extend these dramatic freedoms to the rule-bound world of art. Shakespeare gave him a precedent for making a virtue of rule-breaking and also for making 'liberty' an expression of nationalism, a tribute to the self-governing, near-anarchic spirit of 'the Free-Born Englishman'.

In a remarkably short time, Hogarth had made himself a master of painting. In person as well as on the canvas he was quick, pungent and spirited, and Mary Granville Pendarves, who liked his style, caught his tone of voice well. 'I have grown passionately fond of Hogarth's painting, there is more *sense* in it than any I have seen,' she told her sister in 1731. He had been painting the Wesley (or Wellesley) family, including Lord Mornington and his sister Mrs Donellan: 'I have had the pleasure of seeing him paint the greatest part of it; he has altered his manner of painting since you saw his picture; he finishes more a good deal.' Then she added, 'Hogarth has promised to give me some instructions about drawing that will be of great use, – some rules of his own that he says will improve me more in a day than a year's learning in the common way.'[4] That sounds like Hogarth: he never shed his swagger of self-importance, his air of being above the rules. If he had tried harder to charm he could probably have done even better – society women liked taking drawing lessons, and with plenty of purchasing power and influence they could even provide an entrée to Court. (Mrs Pendarves was a lady of the bedchamber to Queen Caroline.) But Hogarth was never much good at smooth talk and, unlike his rival Arthur Pond, he let such opportunities slip.[5]

172

He was also, it has to be said, getting bored. Every few years he seems to have needed a new stimulus, a new challenge. Around this time he decided to move in a different direction – back to the wider market. His painting of conversation pieces, he said, had some novelty and succeeded for a while, but although it 'gave more scope to fancy' than common portraits it was still 'a kind of drudgery', especially as he could not employ assistants and so turn this genre into a kind of 'manufacture'.[6] 'That manner of painting', he wrote elsewhere, 'was not sufficiently paid to do everything my family requird.' He was painting several portraits for the price of one. Instead he decided to send future clients to other painters, and 'turn my thoughts to a still more new way of proceeding, viz painting and Engraving modern moral Subject, a Field unbroke up in any Country or any age'.[7]

This 'modern moral subject' was indeed Hogarth's great invention. But his laconic boast, made thirty years later, glosses the fact that some of his first modern subjects were hardly intended as moral; they were meant to entertain, to startle and stir. They lay in the realm of his impolite, not polite, conversations. Hogarth in his twenties and early thirties was a slippery soul. If you look *only* at his conversation pieces, he supports an Addisonian ideal, applauding a good and graceful British society, built on land and trade. He was no fool – this was, after all, what his patrons *wanted* to see – and he did believe in these ideals, but his prints and his comic genre paintings suggest that he had reservations.

London politeness was a precarious thing, threatened from without and from within. The Quality could tell themselves that excessive consumption or 'luxury' was almost a civic duty, bringing prosperity to all ('Yet hence the Poor are clothed, the Hungry fed,' as Pope assured Burlington). But as they rolled round street corners protected by swinging footmen, in coaches padded with velvet and leather, with shining crests on the door, they might well feel that their bright edifice of refinement perched on the edge of a cliff, its base eroded by a relentless sea of poor, of limbless beggars, rickety children, shouting hucksters, resentful labourers, pickpockets and thieves. And that glossy refinement was itself often only skin deep, or not even that; baths were taken rarely and even the best wigs held lice. At society dinners, as in Covent Garden brothels, chamber pots lay handy so that men did not need to leave the room in their after-dinner stupor. And even the most polite were prey, as Hogarth suggested, to ambition and pride, their 'natural' innocence lost, their equally natural rapaciousness disguised beneath fine manners.

The digs Hogarth made in his conversation pieces were mild, incorporating and making safe the wildness that might subvert politeness.

Lord Malpas, for example, must have liked the picture of his irrepressible young sons since it was probably through his influence that Hogarth was asked to paint the heads of the Prince of Wales and others, including Malpas himself, in a large sporting picture by Wootton for the Prince's collection.[8] Other patrons, however, found his increasingly forthright likenesses hard to take. Horace Walpole, much as he admired Hogarth, felt that painting portraits was 'the most ill-suited employment imaginable to a man whose turn certainly was not flattery, nor his talent adapted to look on vanity without a sneer'.[9]

47   *The Christening, or Orator Henley Christening a Child* (*c.*1729)

Hogarth saw the seamy side of polite life, its seductions and brawls, its broken families and gambling debts, as well as the satin and lace. His group portraits were not confined to the polite; he followed the low-life conversation tradition too, and sometimes let one comment on the other. Two paintings of 1729, *The Christening* and *The Denunciation, or A Woman Swearing a Child to a Grave Citizen*, were conversation pieces with a difference. In *The Christening*, set in a richly decorated bedchamber, a plump, pompous clergyman almost drops the doll-like baby in his eagerness to peer down the

174

48 *The Denunciation (c.1729)*

low-cut dress of a buxom woman; a fop preens in a mirror and the baby's sister tips the holy water on the floor. In *The Denunciation* a po-faced merchant raises his hands in woeful innocence while his wife scowls, shouts and raises her fist. The row is caused by a pregnant, and pretty, young woman, supported by her fresh-faced lover as she swears to the magistrate that the merchant is the father of her child. Two beaux, sniffing flowers, laugh in the corner and some intrigue may indeed be going on since the young woman is being egged on by a male friend behind her back. Next to the magistrate's desk sits a little girl, teaching her dog to beg. Everyone is being coached in the ways of the world.

These two pictures, with their lascivious aura, mocked the official sacredness of family, status and ceremony. This, suggested Hogarth, was life beneath the gloss. But he was also making a sound comment about attitudes to women and children. In an age of severe infant mortality baptisms could be casual and drunken midwives were even known to get the sex wrong – one girl in 1730 was christened 'Robert'.[10] How, then, could children like the over-looked baby in *The Christening* have identity, or dignity? *The Denunciation* made a similar point. The parish was supposed to look after the children of

175

the poor, legitimate or not, and unmarried mothers had to name the father before a justice, who would then either make him marry her or ask the parish officials to pay for the baby's keep. A current scandal, raised in *The Gentleman's Magazine* in 1731, was the way many alleged fathers in this tricky corner made straight bargains with officials to take the child off their hands 'which is commonly done for a treat and ten or twelve pounds'.[11]

Londoners of the day also enjoyed these two pictures for their personal as their moral piquancy. They quickly named the fat cleric in *The Christening* as Dr John 'Orator' Henley, the famously eccentric preacher who ran his independent chapel as a business near the butchers' stalls in Clare Market, wrote for Walpole's propaganda sheets and preached effusively on secular as well as religious subjects. Henley held notorious views on baptism and was widely mocked for his 'monstrous jumble of divinity and buffooncry'.[12] Similarly, the magistrate in *The Denunciation* was said to be Thomas de Veil, of Bow Street, whose strictness on the bench was balanced by the laxity of his life away from it. So at the same time as he was harvesting commissions from the great and good Hogarth was ridiculing them openly in other pictures standing on his easel in Covent Garden. Friends and patrons spread the word and others came to see.

He began to be known as a caricaturist of London dignitaries as well as a coming society portraitist. In 1730, when he admired Hogarth's conversation pieces, Vertue also noticed that 'a small piece of several figures representing a Christening being lately sold at a public sale for a good price got him much reputation'. Hogarth's works, he added, 'gain every day so many admirers that happy are they that can get a picture of his painting'.[13] That bold step of selling at a public auction, where everyone could peer and point and whisper and laugh and speculate, was an open bid for attention. Even in 1730 he might have had a hunch that he could make more money from selling conversations of this kind to the public, as prints, than he could from painting politer versions for individual patrons.

A year later came a story that Vertue really relished. Hogarth, he said, had lately painted a 'singular representation of Justice'.[14] A notice in the press announced that 'a certain ingenious painter' (identity an open secret) was working on a piece that, when finished, would be hung in the Hall of the Old Bailey. Crowds flocked to Hogarth's studio, to find a picture of the Whig Sheriff, Sir Isaac Shard, a City magistrate and 'prodigious penurious K[nigh]t', sitting in a great chair as if in judgment. The criminal was a 'great Hungry dog' who had stolen a scraggy shoulder of mutton from Shard's kitchen: 'Mrs Cook being highly enrag'd appears to be his accuser and a

176

certain old fellow a neighbouring Cobler the executioner who holds the dog in a String.' Many other details made the picture 'an entertainment for all who saw it'. No one laughed more than the new Lord Mayor, Humphrey Parsons, a Tory and known Jacobite, who was generally believed to have commissioned the attack: Cits had their feuds, as well as Courtiers. Shard did not demean himself to come and see it, but his son did and was so furious that he drew his sword in a rage, then took a knife and cut the head right out of the canvas. Not long afterwards, so the story goes, one very ugly nobleman, smarting under Hogarth's truthfulness to life, refused to accept his portrait. At once, Hogarth capitalized on the public exposure of Shard, threatening the nobleman that if the picture were not collected in three days he would add a tail and 'some other little Appendages' and sell it to 'Mr Hare, the Famous Wild-Beast-man' for exhibition.[15] The money came, the picture was collected, taken home, and burned.

Hogarth found he could trade on the sting in his painting. This practice of ridiculing the very classes who should provide his patrons – magistrates and merchants, gentry and clerics – reads like a deliberate act of defiance by someone who is dependent yet wants to feel he has power, like a cook who displays arsenic in the store cupboard. And if he was committed to the politeness, he was also keen to show the 'uncivil' elements that undermined it.

There had always been another, rougher side to Hogarth's work, the vigorous demotic politics of his satires, creeping into paintings such as *The Christening* and *The Denunciation*. While Jane kept house with Thornhill-

49 *A Midnight Modern Conversation* (1730/31)

177

like composure, her husband's studio was sure to have something pungent, even shocking, with a sexy, political edge.[16] Men about town delighted in caricature and cat-calling, in seeing eminent people at a disadvantage, in rows such as that over the portrait of Isaac Shard. The same appeal attached to scenes like the drinking club in *A Midnight Modern Conversation.* In this painting, which Hogarth later turned into one of his most successful prints, the clock shows that it is well past midnight but the befuddled topers are too far gone to care, collapsing in a dizzying circle. These are middle-aged men, dignified folk, whose varied wigs (all slightly old-fashioned) are now, like their owners, in fairly wild disarray.[17] The painting's swirling composition makes one drunk just to look at it. Commentators, of course, hunted at once for the personal and local. Deciding the setting was St John's Coffee-House near Temple Bar, they argued whether the clergyman was Orator Henley or Parson Cornelius Ford, a debauched cousin of Samuel Johnson; insisted that the man thrusting his wig on the cleric's head was John Harrison, a tobacconist known for his comic songs; that the lawyer was Kettleby, famous for his full-bottomed wigs and dreadful squint; that the nightcap belonged to a deaf bookbinder, Chandler; that the man lighting his necktie instead of his pipe was a politician – and so on.[18]

'Reading' such pictures was entertaining, but Hogarth's works also had a moral bite. Like his stage scenes or polite conversations, these paintings too froze moments in the flow of time. They implied a story, a before and after. During 1730 Hogarth was actually painting scenes of *Before* and *After*, in a specific sexual sense. Treading the narrow line between art and pornography he worked on 'two little pictures' for the Duke of Montagu, a leading Freemason and courtier, but also a buffoon with a taste for cruel, infantile jokes, and two for the crooked MP John Thomson.

Thomson's erotica were set outdoors, in a leafy grove. Glossing the crude, Hogarth made them fashionably French, very close to *risqué* versions of *fêtes galantes* of the mid-1720s.[19] In the first picture a demure, bonneted maid is pressed by a sweet-faced youth, thrusting his leg into the folds of her skirt. In the second her bonnet is gone, hair messed up, petticoats bunched round her waist to show her creamy thighs and rumpled stockings; the sweet youth is no longer *galant* and his face as red as his prick, which lies limp between linen shirt and open breeches. He looks bothered, as if he'd like to leave as soon as possible. Hogarth's version is less comfortable than the dreamily seductive 'after' of the French pictures, and his picture of very human, semi-comic disarray is made even sharper by the pastoral background which smiles on unaffected by the 'natural' act.

178

50 *Before* (1730/31)   51 *After* (1730/31)

The Duke of Montagu's pictures took the scene inside, into a London boudoir. Rustic romance gave way to urban manners, and the graceful French air was replaced by a more brutal, ribald, emblematical Dutch treatment. Because of that, this was the obvious set to turn into popular prints. In those prints, made in 1736, the heat of 'before' is shown by the urgency of the man on the bed clutching the resisting woman, by the excited lapdog barking round their feet, by the painting on the wall showing Cupid lighting a rocket. As the woman pulls away she grabs at her unstable dressing-table, but we know that she, like the table, mirror and powder box, must fall. *After* displays a second picture on the wall, with Cupid's rocket falling flaccidly to earth; the dog sleeps, panting among the shards of mirror and chamber pot; the man hoists his trousers and is keen to be off; now it is the woman who clutches and pleads.

A tremor of disquiet unnerves Hogarth's worldly jokes. The classical tag in the indoor *After*, in a book on the floor marked '*Aristotle*', is 'Omne Animal Post Coitum Triste Est', and this post-coital sadness seems genuine, a true regret as well as a physical deflation. A sharp ambivalence about sex, its lure and muddled aftermath, pervades these scenes: whether pastoral or citified, the lovers seem uneasy. This applies to the men as well as the women, although in the orthodox thinking of the day, it was the women who took the blame – and suffered the consequences. As virtuous, obedient wives, women commanded respect and protection but once they 'conversed unlawfully' with men they fitted Johnson's later dictionary definition:

'WHORE: 1. A woman who converses unlawfully with men; a fornicatress; an adultress; a strumpet.
2. A prostitute; a woman who receives men for money.'[20]

Men's sexual misdemeanours were peccadilloes, women's were grave sins. No laws forbade men to consort with prostitutes, but the prostitute herself was a criminal. A double standard prevailed, in law and in life. In biblical–moral terms, especially those of the dissenters among whom Hogarth grew up, sex had been the chief lure of the devil since the serpent tempted Eve and she offered Adam the apple: 'a Strumpet is the Highway to the Devil', bellowed Captain Alexander Smith in 1715, 'and he that looks upon her with Desire, begins his Voyage'.[21]

Hogarth nods to these ideas. In the rural *Before* the young girl has been gathering apples in her apron, and in the Montagu prints the elegant towns-woman's corrupt imagination is revealed by an open drawer where 'Novels' and 'Rochester's Poems' nestle alongside 'The Practice of Piety'. These were familiar references: in 1700 Tom Brown had explained that

180

52 *Before* (1736)

53 *After* (1736)

'the bawd, like the hangman and the physician, lives by the sins of the people. Though she has generally The Practice of Piety in her window, yet she knows of no religion but short quarterns and easy bubbles; and as she thinks of heaven, so she dreads no hell like the justice, the beadle, the informer.'[22]

Yet in the way he paints them, Hogarth seems to feel sympathy for the women who are used and left, and if he condemns anyone, it is the men. When he engraved the indoor scenes he turned the young male lover of the painting into an older, bewigged man, heightening the air of squalid exploitation.

Both sets of *Before* and *After* were still unfinished when Hogarth made his list of current commissions in early 1731. In time the Duke of Montagu collected his, but Thomson never did: that October, clutching his fraudulently gained profits from the Charitable Corporation, he decamped for France. His *Before* and *After* now hang in a niche behind the grand gallery doors of the Fitzwilliam Museum, Cambridge. Smoked by time, as Hogarth would say, erotica become art. The boundary between Eros and Art was already blurred. These were cabinet pictures, to be savoured by a close group of friends, hung in a private (men-only) room with other pornographic pictures, or with portraits of fellow rakes and scenes of excess. Connoisseurs

181

were happy to see themselves as libertines; the brothels of Paris, Rome and Athens were accepted stops on the Grand Tour, as much as the art galleries. The nudes and rapes of classical art were not savoured for their formal lines alone.

54 *The Fountaine Family* (1730)

The link between the lust of the collector and of the rake was an open joke. Hogarth played with it, one suspects, in *The Fountaine Family*, where the art collector Sir Andrew appraises a Renaissance canvas of semi-nude women sprawled before a spurting fountain (a double play on his name). While this painted nubility is offered to him by a dealer – his son-in-law, Christopher Cock – his wife and her friend chat innocently opposite, one handling a ripe fruit, the other commanding her spaniel to 'sit'. The women ignore, yet see. They too are bought like pictures, selected like a sweet pear. They too are expected to be docile and playfully loving, like the lapdogs they love.

In the 1750s, Hogarth painted Sir Francis Dashwood, one of the founders of the Dilettanti Society in 1734. Linked with paganism and freethinking, Dashwood later created his own parodic 'Order of St Francis at Medmenham Abbey', whose anti-clerical satire was often entwined with obscenity. A typical

182

Medmenham product is Thomas Potter's limp parody of Pope's 'Dying Christian to his Soul', retitled 'The Dying Lover to his Prick':

> Now you recede, now disappear!
> My eye looks round in vain, my ear,
> Fanny, your murmur rings:
> Lend, lend your hand! I mount! I die!
> O Prick, how great thy Victory!
> O Pleasure, sweet thy stings![23]

Hogarth painted Dashwood dressed as St Francis, reworking a painting by Dashwood's fellow Dilettanti George Knapton, who had depicted several members of the society in historical dress, and had shown Dashwood as St Francis paying his devotions not to Christ on the cross but to a statue. Hogarth took the joke further: the object of adoration was a real, miniature woman laid naked in Dashwood's palm, as subject to the connoisseur's gaze and appetite as the tumbled fruit on the ground.

Hogarth did not moralize, but a quick-witted painter might well feel a wry sympathy for the ogled, submissive women in *The Fountaine Family* or the Dashwood portrait. He too sold his talent to the highest bidder.

Obedience and submissiveness were never Hogarth's virtues. Despite his adherence to ideals of politeness, he belonged at heart to Covent Garden, Drury Lane and Grub Street, the territory of needy actors, small traders, hard-working painters and engravers. He straddled the divide between entertainment and refinement, rather like Christopher Cock, John Rich at Drury Lane, or young Jonathan Tyers, the owner of Vauxhall Pleasure Gardens. He had high aims for his art and he *wanted* to win plaudits, to be seen as a great painter, to be part of the drive that united culture with commerce and nationalism. Yet he was also an instinctive iconoclast, suspicious of models, rules, accepted forms, pushing against the boundaries of what was decreed acceptable. These tensions ripple through his work.

Others were pushing against old forms too, and Hogarth was closer in this respect to experiments on the stage and in literature than in painting. (He often called himself the 'author' instead of the 'inventor' of his prints.) In the early 1730s he found a natural ally in a new rule-breaker, Henry Fielding. Ten years younger, Fielding came from an entirely different background: his mother's family were Somerset gentry and lawyers; his father (with Irish, aristocratic connections) was a feckless military man, gambler and womanizer. After Eton, Fielding surged briefly into London in 1728 and then spent eighteen months at the University of Leyden, reappearing abruptly in 1730, leaving books, belongings and bad debts behind him on the Continent, and facing no choice, he said, except between being 'a Hackney writer or a Hackney Coachman'.[24] Within months he had a startling success with *The Author's Farce*, followed by a string of satirical dramas that made him, by the age of twenty-four, the most talked-about playwright in London.

They must have made an odd couple, strolling through Covent Garden. Hogarth was under five feet tall, square in build and flashy in dress; Fielding a good foot taller, long-limbed and large-nosed, untidy and charming with a casual well-born 'ease'. Hogarth was better off, with a home and a steady income; Fielding staggered from tavern to seedy lodgings, to scribble his plays in the early hours. He spent money as fast as he earned it, rescuing his snuff-stained velvet coat from the pawnshop for first nights. Recklessness and debt were common to most of the actors and writers Hogarth knew (Joseph Mitchell was hopelessly extravagant and had opened his paean of praise to Hogarth with equivocal words, 'Accept the Praise a Friend bestows/A Friend who pays but what he owes'), but Fielding beat them all. In his first really successful season in 1732, he earned and lost over a thousand pounds in weeks: 'His Elbows have destroy'd the Off-spring of his Brain; and in Spight of all his good Sense he has been Stript at Play by Sharpers.'[25]

The two men shared more than a love of drink and plays and wit. Both were ambitious to forge new forms, combining realism, allusion and comedy to 'expose the follies of the age'. Both were great debunkers and both were also extremely knowing about the *mode* of their art, expecting their audience to be so too. This let them play exuberantly with conventions: in the dashingly crazy final scene of Fielding's farce *Tom Thumb* (launched on 24 April 1730) the human characters find themselves literally related to Punch and a cast of puppets. When this was revised as *The Tragedy of Tragedies*, with a cornu-copia of mock-learned notes, Hogarth drew the frontispiece, graphically sharpening Fielding's wit: in his squat Princess Huncamunca, with her pop eyes and sideboard bust, many saw a less than flattering image of Caroline, their Queen.[26]

Fielding's novels, a decade later, were extravagantly visual and he often cited Hogarth as his ideal. He sometimes drew on Hogarth's narratives too, recasting the experience of his own early years in London. The history of Mr Wilson in *Joseph Andrews* is a schematic 'rake's progress' of a young man fresh from university adrift among tailor's bills and theatre tickets, doses of clap and discarded women. His first mistress is an innocent young girl, gradually corrupted by the company of rakes and kept women until she is 'rapacious of Money, extravagant to Excess, loose in her conversation; and, if I ever demurred to any of her Demands, Oaths, Tears and Fits, were the immediate Consequences'.[27] Cast off, she becomes a common prostitute, ending her miserable life in Newgate. By contrast, his second mistress is a fashionable married woman, a *'coquette achevée'*, whose wily husband prosecutes him for £3000. The first story looks back to Hogarth's *Harlot's Progress*; the second glances forward to *Marriage A-la-Mode*.

When Wilson turns to male company, he also describes a London Fielding and Hogarth knew. On one hand there were the 'jolly companions' who slept all day and drank all night and whose 'best Conversation was nothing but Noise: Singing, Hollowing, Wrangling, Drinking, Toasting, Sp—wing, Smoking'.[28] On the other were the clubs of earnest deists fired by the *'Rule of Right'*, who searched for truth over the bottle late into the night: Wilson's faith in these 'philosophers' is shaken when one man disappears with another's wife, a second skips bail, and a third borrows money and then denies it. Despite Fielding's comic rejection, in the 1730s he certainly flirted with freethinking and deism. So, no doubt, did Hogarth.

It would be almost impossible for such an alert and thoughtful observer *not* to be influenced by deism. The term covered a multitude of attitudes, and for forty years it had raised arguments reaching sporadic peaks of high-pitched controversy: by 1733 one dissenting divine could thunder that deism was 'the greatest controversy of the present age, and which ever was in the Christian world, when the whole revelation is placed at the bar'.[29] The theological baselines had been set in the 1690s, with the uproar over John Toland's *Christianity not Mysterious*, and Locke's more conciliatory *The Reasonable-ness of Christianity*. Discussion spread outwards from the denial of miraculous revelation and the nature of the Trinity, to the divine authority of the clergy, who could be seen as promoting a deliberate mystification, a cunning 'priestcraft' boosting their own power. Under Queen Anne, rational Anglican arguments were developed by men such as Samuel Clarke, rector of St James's, Westminster, who spoke powerfully for a Low Church, almost Unitarian, belief that Christ was 'more than man but less than God'.[30] Among Clarke's followers was Benjamin Hoadly, a pre-eminent Whig churchman, loud in the defence of 'civil and religious liberty', who sailed into fame in Anne's reign, combating both the High Church party and the Dissenters. As a reward, after the arrival of George I he was made Royal Chaplain, then Bishop of Bangor: the 'Bangorian Controversy' of 1717 arose from his controversial (but politically useful) sermon claiming that the jurisdiction of the State, not the Church, was supreme. With his knife-keen intellect Hoadly became a valued polemicist, a constant thorn in the side of the more orthodox Edmund Gibson, 'Walpole's Pope', Bishop of London.

These 'broad-church' moves offended many, but in the 1720s the pious were shocked by a resurgence of more extreme views in Anthony Collins's *The Grounds and Reasons of the Christian Religion* in 1724, and then in the *Discourses* of Thomas Woolston.[31] A sincere, clear-thinking man, Woolston interpreted miracles as allegories or even conjuring tricks (as Hogarth seemed to). In addition, he accused the clergy of greed, corruption and abuse of their position and used ridicule – as Hogarth and Fielding would do – because, he said, it could dent thick clerical skulls better than plain reasoning.[32] Woolston's books sold 30,000 copies. In 1730 even more intense passions were roused by Matthew Tindal's *Christianity as Old as Creation*, and a furious counter-attack came from Gibson, whose 'Pastoral Letters against the Deists' flooded the town.

Hogarth himself had plenty of deist friends.[33] His Masonic connections, too, might have fostered an interest in the more radical deism of Toland and Anthony Collins. The figurehead of the progressive speculative Masons was Isaac Newton, whose theories, as developed in the *Principia* in 1687, were generally employed (as they were by Newton himself) to argue for a universe governed from above by divine providence and thus to sanction a similar hierarchical model on earth below. But some Masons, merging Newton's mechanical laws with strands drawn from Renaissance humanism, argued that what Newton really showed was that the universe was a self-contained, self-governing system. If the 'divine spirit' was not above but inherent in nature, a 'natural' society would be democratic, even republican. These arguments, spinning through the London lodges, added another dimension to Hogarth's appeal to 'Nature'.

These disputes were canvassed in journals, argued in tracts and blasted in sermons. Men wrangled over them in their clubs, as the candles guttered and smoked and glasses were emptied and refilled. They plumbed current anxieties about the society and its beliefs. They certainly entered Hogarth's work, and it has even been argued that his whole aesthetic is built on the deist replacement of a male 'God' by female 'Nature'.[34] But the prints can be read differently. In some versions of *A Harlot's Progress*, for example, Hogarth labelled two small portraits on the rich Jew's wall 'Woolston' and 'Clarke', and in another scene Moll wraps her butter in one of Gibson's *Pastoral Letters* (it was a common joke that all 'great literature' ended up wrapping food or lining trunks). These might not demonstrate allegiances, but rather Hogarth's shrewd awareness that Tory Londoners would be happy to identify Woolston

186

55 *The Sleeping Congregation* (1736)

and Clarke with 'enemies of Christ'. (Woolston took the persona of a rabbi in his *Discourses*.) Similarly, Hogarth often removed the name and symbols of God from his prints, as in *The Sleeping Congregation* of 1736.[35] Yet this might not be a deist, or Masonic denial of divinity, but a conventional nod of respect, or even a pointer to a 'godless', empty world.

He did, most definitely, abhor phoney mystification employed to dignify *any* professional group: clergy, doctors, lawyers – and art critics. And he saw the Church, like the Law, as part of a monolithic system that often rolled over the lives of the people instead of helping them. But much of his anti-clericalism was rough, down-to-earth comic observation – like the slipshod priest in *The Christening*, or *The Sleeping Congregation*, where the clerk leers at a dozing woman's breasts, and the parson drones on from the text 'Come unto me all ye who labour and I shall give ye rest', while exhausted working men snore in the pews before him. Although he later painted religious paintings – for St Bartholomew's, for the Foundling Hospital, for St Mary

187

Redcliffe in Bristol – there is no sign that Hogarth followed any faith. But his prints do have a Christian message, in a lopsided way, through their humanization of suffering. And by criticizing a deluded, selfish individualism, he advocates its opposite, an ethic of *active*, down-to-earth communal love.

There is nothing unconventional here – like hosts of others, Hogarth was promoting the practical Christianity championed by Latitudinarian clerics like Hoadly, Bishop of Salisbury by 1730, who preached that sincere belief of any colour was what counted, not a particular sectarian stance.[36] Hogarth came to know this powerful man (whose first wife, Sarah Curtis, was a portrait painter) through his sons, Benjamin and John, who both swam in the shallows of London's literary, artistic and theatrical life. Benjamin was a doctor, fat, jolly and scholarly; he was elected to the Royal Society in 1726, aged only twenty. His brother John, five years younger, was also a fine scholar and an easy-going, energetic man. He wrote the verses for *A Rake's Progress* and became one of Hogarth's lasting friends. In 1731 the brothers collaborated in a successful play, *The Contrast*, which was staged in Lincoln's Inn Fields, but was suppressed and never published, at the urgent request of the Bishop. This did not stop them trying, and John's later play, *The Suspicious Husband*, provided one of Garrick's favourite and most famous roles.

Hogarth could easily have satirized their father: Hoadly was known for his love of good living, especially after 1734 when he became Bishop of Winchester, the second richest post in the Church, with an income of £5000. Hogarth could have attacked him, too, for staying in London instead of his diocese, but the portraits he later painted of the Bishop suggest that he admired the strength with which he overcame his disability – he was so crippled that he had to preach on his knees – and his balance of worldliness, conviction and tolerance.

The whole issue of 'worldliness' was the subject of another tough debate, stirred up by the brusque (and often very funny) analysis of Bernard de Mandeville, which stripped the wraps off social 'virtue' and politeness. In *The Fable of the Bees*, published in successive editions in 1714, 1723 and 1729, Mandeville declared with uncompromising bluntness that no trading state, as Britain now was, could honestly claim its aim was altruism rather than profit. He set out to show,

'the Unreasonableness and Folly of those, that desirous of being an opulent and flourishing People, and wonderfully greedy after all the Benefits they can receive as such, are yet always murmuring and exclaiming against those Vices and Inconveniences, that from the Beginning of the World to the Present Day,

188

have been Inseparable from all the Kingdoms and States that ever were fam'd for Strength, Riches and Politeness, at the same time.'[37]

The moral language of politics and culture, so beloved of Shaftesbury and Addison, was hypocritical and should be dropped. (And the word 'disinterested' hardly sprang to mind when one thought of the great Whig magnates.) People should recognize that 'luxury', so loudly condemned as a vice, effectively powered the economy, while religion and politeness oiled the wheels. Fielding rephrased this later in his journal *The Champion*:

'Virtue is a sort of Cash unknown to the Butcher, the Baker, the Draper, the Tailor. If a Man carries nothing but Virtue to Market, he will, I am afraid, carry nothing else from it.'[38]

Fielding, clinging as long as he could to his generous belief in the innate goodness of human nature, argued with Mandeville for years. Hogarth, recording what he saw (or chose to see), created a universe that was partly Mandevillean and partly old-fashionedly moral. Commerce, he felt, could bring great good, but the excesses that often accompanied it could do matching harm. His characters are not compelled to be hypocritical, emulative and luxury-obsessed but *choose* to be so; their fall stems both from outer pressure and inner weakness. Once down, though, they are relentlessly crushed beneath the wheels of the system, and the weight of their own guilt.

Hogarth was not entirely a cynic. Underlying his 'low' paintings and prints there is always the sense that things *could* be different, if people did not treat money as a god, did not sell their souls for status and fashion, did not get a kick from cruelty and power. His sympathies are conveyed in the intimate detail of his portraits of children, servants and luckless women, which blend clear-sighted realism with compassion. His values are defined by their sad or comic negatives.

The passionate arguments of the time – theological, economic, political and artistic – all fed into Hogarth's work. Seasoned by such questioning, his novel mix of high and low could appeal to the quarrelling philosophers as well as the 'jolly company' of boozers, seducers and swearers. But to convey the 'humours' of his age in a form that would also *sell*, stunning the town as *The Beggar's Opera* had, he needed to find a compelling story. It must combine the ingredients that drew men to his studio: caricatures of well-known people, buried anti-Walpole satire, sex and 'morality'. And it had to be treated in a new way, one that would satisfy the popular market as well as the connoisseurs yet would not prostitute his art and reduce him again to low printmaker status. As much by luck as judgement, he hit upon the answer almost at once. Instead of illustrating a given story, like *Hudibras*, he would create his own, something no one had done before. In 1730 Hogarth began a series of six paintings, to be called *A Harlot's Progress*.

10

A Harlot's Progress

All Crimes are judg'd like fornication;
While rich we are honest no doubt.
Fine ladies can keep reputation
Poor lasses alone are found out.
If justice had piercing eyes,
Like ourselves to look within,
She'd find power and wealth a disguise
That shelter the worst of our kin.

JOHN GAY, *Polly* (1729)

IT WAS A STROKE of genius on Hogarth's part to choose a harlot as the heroine of his first graphic series – a figure so familiar yet so fluid. The idea seems to have come almost by accident. In 1730 he painted a 'trifling subject', a Drury Lane whore and her servant. And a chalk sketch does survive showing such a pair, amid washing strung on the line, curling prints, piles of clothes, a crumpled novel and mangy cat. Quack medicines, dirty sheaths and a syringe lie on the table, for protection and rough cure for venereal disease. Hogarth's sexily realistic painting caused a great stir, as Vertue remembered:

'he began a small picture of a common harlot, supposd to dwell in drewry lane. just riseing about noon out of bed. and at breakfast. a bunter waiting on her. – this whore's deshabille careless and a pretty Countenance & air. – this thought pleasd many. some advised him to make another. to it as a pair. which he did. then other thoughts encreas'd, & multiplyd by his fruitfull invention. till he made six. different subjects which he painted so naturally. the thoughts, & strikeing the expressions that it drew every body to see them – which he proposing to Engrave in six plates to print at, one guinea each sett. he had daily Subscriptions came in, in fifty or a hundred pounds in a Week – there being no days but persons of fashion and Artists came to see these pictures.'[1]

Hogarth, so often an illustrator of the news, had now, at thirty-four, become news himself.

191

56 *A Scene in a Garret* (*c.* 1731)

Vertue's analysis of his ever multiplying ideas and 'fruitful invention' rings absolutely true. He responded to demand, 'this thought ples'd many', and to the suggestion of a pair, an even lower, 'Before' and 'After'. As the possibilities dawned, it was clear that the subject would attract a wide audience. He could make a name, and a lot of money and could still build his satirical reputation, attacking 'imitation' as well as the hypocrisy of justice, the selling of bodies and souls. What was more, it could be seen as moral – a voyeuristic tease for men, clothed as an attack on their vices and as a dire warning for innocent girls.

Rakish virtuosi liked sexual subjects, and there was also a huge popular market for the scandalous lives of harlots, the female equivalent of highwaymen – like the *Authentick Memoirs of the Intrigues and Adventures of the Celebrated Sally Salisbury* (1723), or the *Courtezan, and Posture Mistress, Eliz Mann* (1724), or *Mrs Mary Parmans, The Tall Milliner of Change Alley* (1729).[2] These books had a distinctly *anti*-aristocratic tinge, especially in the case of Sally Salusbury, valued for her 'tell-all' stories of noble clients. Here

192

the whore was both seductress and victim, the toy of a decadent, diseased upper class.

The harlot also had an almost mythic, archetypal power, going back to the Bible and beyond. Her role was always ambivalent; she was at once the object of desire and of disgust, of power and subjection, a creature of evil ambition or heart of gold. Although the reality might be sharply different (London swam with successful courtesans) in literary terms the curve of her moral and poetic tale was long established – even if she began as innocent, once seduced she was lost and all her triumphs were just a glittering preface to a long slide into ignominy, sickness and death. In Britain the pattern was enshrined in the late fifteenth century in Robert Henryson's moving *Testament of Cresseid*. This tale of 'The fatefull destinie/of fair Cresseid that endit wretchitlie' took up Chaucer's story to show Cresseid as a prostitute, rejected and smitten with leprosy, then thought both a punishment of God and a venereal disease; when the passing Troilus tosses coins at a disfigured beggar he does not recognize the woman he once loved, although strange memories flood into his mind.[3] Britain had no pictorial tradition of whores' lives, but in Italy whole picture stories appeared. One such was the seventeenth-century Venetian *Mirror of a Whore's Fate*, where a young girl is won over by a bawd behind her mother's back and spirals downward to disease and death after betraying a rich lover. The tale has obvious links to Hogarth's series, and one or two of the illustrations are so similar that it is hard to think he did not see a copy.[4]

All that Hogarth needed to turn the ancient tale of the harlot into an eye-catching modern story was a strong current scandal. And in the spring of 1730 Colonel Charteris – rake, connoisseur and ally of Walpole – helpfully provided one.

That February the papers were full of the trial of Colonel Charteris for the rape of his servant Anne Bond, having frightened her 'into Compliance with his filthy Desires' by holding a pistol to her head. The gentry, including Charteris's influential friends, packed the court to hear the riper details. They heard how Anne, out of work, was sitting at the door of her lodgings when 'a woman who was a stranger to her, came to her, and ask'd her, if she wanted a Place'.[5] Anne came to Charteris as a servant to find herself under a sexual barrage. When she resisted his bribes the house doors were locked to prevent her from leaving, and at seven one morning the inevitable happened: 'On the 10th of November, the Colonel Rang a Bell and bid the Clerk of the Kitchen call the Lancashire Bitch into the Dining Room.'[6] Telling her to stir the fire, he locked the door, threw her on the couch, 'shove what she could, and cry'd out as loud as she could', then gagged her with his nightcap and raped her. When she threatened to tell her friends, he brought out his horsewhip, beat her and took all her clothes and money.

Despite bringing witnesses to claim Anne's story was a cover for the theft of £20, the Colonel was convicted: 'After a very short stay (of about a Quarter of an Hour) the Jury found the prisoner Guilty, DEATH.'[7] But Charteris never faced the gallows, and was in Newgate for less than a month. On 10 April he received a royal pardon, negotiated by an aristocratic friend. That autumn, people noted, he was seen giving generous gifts to Walpole. It was a bitter rebuff to popular notions of justice.

The common people had long hated Charteris. In 1711 the Colonel was accused (but discharged with a warning) for collecting money from desperate debtors by fraudulently placing their names on the register of his company, since they could be freed by enlisting in the army. He had also made a huge fortune from South Sea stock, and possessed vast acres in Lancashire. The 'Rape-Master of Britain', he boasted of seducing well over a hundred women, sending his servants out, it was reported, with orders to find

'none but such as were strong, lusty and fresh Country Wenches, of the first size, their B—tt—cks as hard as Cheshire Cheeses, that should make a Dint in a Wooden Chair, and work like a parish Engine at a Conflagration'.[8]

His many crimes and misdemeanours – gambling, using loaded dice, bearing false witness, sexual assaults and denial of his bastard children – were detailed in a host of mock-solemn pamphlets, poems and broadsheets. In one incident a girl had been rescued by her sister, who called all the neighbours until 'an infinite Mob was immediately raised', storming Charteris's house with 'Stones, Brickbats, and other Such Vulgar Ammunition'.[9] When he was released from Newgate after the Anne Bond case, he was set upon by a London crowd.

As a fraudster, speculator, rapist *and* an associate of Walpole, Charteris was a ready-made emblem. Pamphlets such as *The History of Colonel Francis Ch—rtr—s* are blatant political satire, written in mock-defence of the 'Great man', slandered by 'a pack of Scribblers, who write themselves into a Dinner at any Cost, without Regard to Truth or even common Decency'.[10] Well-known key phrases make their point: Charteris, like Walpole, is 'an admirable Proficient in the Art of Legerdemain'. The subtitle of this *History* is 'The Birth, Parentage, Education, Rise, *Progres* [my italics], and most memorable Exploits of that Great Man, down to his present Catastrophe in Newgate'. In

A Harlot's Progress Hogarth could show the progress not of the criminal but of his victim, and, by analogy, of the British people in the hands of such 'Great Men'. And beyond the inverted language of political satire he drew on the familiar Bunyanesque spiritual 'Progress', turning this upside-down too, depicting not the journey from sin to grace but the slide from innocence to damnation.

Popular theological language had already crept into the Charteris press. One oft-cited case was that of Sarah Selleto, 'a raw country Girl' who was 'inveigled into his Service by one of the Devil's Purveyors, whom the Colonel kept in constant Pay'.[11] If his servants were not instruments of the devil, Charteris did indeed employ them as pimps, like John Gourlay, his 'Lieutenant', and he did retain bawds to scout for him, the most notorious being Mrs Elizabeth Needham. The great London bawds (always called 'Mrs' or 'Mother') were powers in the city, from the elegant Mrs Gould to Mrs 'Hell Fire' Stanhope. Each had their territory – Covent Garden, Soho, Bloomsbury – but Mother Needham, in Park Place, St James's, had particularly high-class clients and she was closely identified with the Court. When she was arrested in the spring of 1731 by Sir John Gonson (the Westminster magistrate, and known scourge of prostitutes), and placed in the pillory, the crowd filled St James's Street:

'at first she received little Resentment from the Populace, by reason of the great Guard of Constables that surrounded her; but near the latter End of her Time she was pelted in an unmerciful manner'.[12]

Bruised and battered, she died three days later in the old prison of the Westminster Gatehouse. Charteris was rich and flourished; Needham was poor and died.

Lesser criminals were also in the news in 1730 and some of *them*, unlike the colonel and the bawd, were popular heroes whose stories provided Hogarth with another ready-made ironic balance. Within a month of Charteris's release, two highwaymen were executed. One was James Dalton, who died on 12 May. Dalton was a special favourite of the people, like Jack Sheppard, loved for his boldness, said as a boy to have ridden in the cart to his father's execution sitting between his legs, to have locked the watch into their own watch-house, to have captured a ship which was transporting him, and even to have tried to rob the Queen – he got the wrong coach.[13] (Hogarth would make him Moll's lover, and draw his labelled hat-box above her bed.)

The other highwayman to hang was Francis Hackabout, three weeks before Dalton, on 17 April. Two months later (just as Charteris was making up with his wife), Kate Hackabout, the highwayman's sister, was arrested in one of Gonson's brothel raids.[14] Newspapers revelled in Gonson's harlot-hunting and sometimes seemed to cheer when the prostitutes gave as good as they got, like the brothel-keeper and gang-leader Moll Hervey, who was rescued by her men armed with clubs and staves but recaptured later, in bed with her 'pretended Husband': 'She was (as usual) very outrageous in her Behaviour, and not only beat the Constables, but the Justices too, before whom she was carry'd.' In the raid that caught Kate, small fry were scooped up as well as large:

'Eleven men and Women were at the same Time brought before the Justices; but seven of them being young Sinners, and never in Bridewell before, were discharged, upon their seeming Penitence and Promise of Amendment; and the remaining four were committed to Bridewell in Tothill Fields to hard Labour. Three of them were taken at Twelve and One o'clock, exposing their Nakedness in the open Street to all Passengers, and using the most abominable filthy Expressions; the fourth was the famous Kate Hackabout (whose brother was lately hang'd at Tyburn), a woman noted in and about the Hundreds of Drury, for being a very termagant, and a Terror not only to the Civil Part of the Neighbourhood by her frequent Fighting, Noise, and Swearing in the Streets in the Night-Time, but also to other Women of her own Profession, who presume to ply or pick up Men in her District, which is half one side of the Way in Bridges Street.'[15]

In *A Harlot's Progress* Hogarth took Kate's famous surname (doubly apt as 'hack' was also slang for a whore, a hackney carriage for hire to all) and gave it to one of the 'young sinners'. His story looks like a straightforward moral fable of a girl who is entrapped by a bawd when she gets off the coach from the country, becomes a classy courtesan and mistress of a rich Jew, and then declines into shabby prostitution, imprisonment, disease and death. But at each point the 'blame' for Moll's predicament is hard to fix. Moll is an ambiguous figure: at the start her expression is hard to read – she could be an innocent dupe, or she could be an opportunist, determined to snap up the opportunity the bawd offers.[16] At times she looks triumphant, casually erotic and confident; at others she is an icon of female suffering. Towards the end her individuality, her face, disappears altogether, lost beneath the folds of blankets in her illness and hidden in her coffin at her death.

This clever complexity reflects the difficulty that Hogarth's contemporaries found when they discussed prostitution. The topic was endlessly debated: since the beginning of the century the rigorous citizens of the Society for the

Reformation of Manners had set about 'cleaning up' the streets; more sympathetic observers such as Defoe resignedly recommended the encouragement of marriage – or flogging and transportation; satirical analysts like Mandeville ironically welcomed prostitution as a means of safeguarding respectable women and suggested state brothels with resident doctors (he thought two hundred houses with around two thousand women should do for London).[17]

Thoughtful writers were troubled by their own ambivalence. In 1712, as 'Mr Spectator', Steele had described being in a city inn-yard to collect some goods, when he overheard a conversation conducted in questions and answers like a 'Church catechism', only to peer round the corner and see 'the most artful Procuress in Town, examining a most beautiful Country-Girl, who had just come up in the same Waggon with my Things'. He went on to admit his own troubled mixture of desire and compassion when accosted in Covent Garden:

'we stood under one of the Arches by twilight; and there I could observe as exact Features as I had ever seen, the most agreeable Shape, the finest Neck and Bosom, in a Word, the whole Person of a Woman exquisitely beautiful. She affected to allure me with a forced Wantonness in her Look and Air; but I saw it checked with Hunger and Cold: Her Eyes were wan and eager, her Dress thin and tawdry, her Mien genteel and childish. This strange Figure gave me much Anguish of Heart, and to avoid being seen with her I went away, but could not forebear giving her a Crown. The poor thing sighed, curtsied, and with a Blessing, expressed with the utmost Vehemence, turned from me.'[18]

It could be said that such breast-beating and self-congratulatory charity allowed writers and readers to indulge sentimental pity, moral disapproval and prurience all at the same time. But Steele's confusion is genuine, and Hogarth's first scene may look back to his picture of the inn-yard (which already has a recognizable 'literary' shape) in more than one way. Moll's trunk is simply labelled 'M. Hackabout' – 'M' was the initial used in the Prayer Book catechism to stand in for the first name, so the alarming implication is that Hogarth's 'M' can be any woman, any girl, any country innocent.

In keeping with this open identity, Hogarth played on the fact that the story of the country girl turned whore could be read in different ways. On one hand it could signal the corruption of rural simplicity by city luxury, the ruin of the innocent by the guilty and the weak by the powerful. On the other it could be seen as a tale of mercantile self-interest, of the harlot as a businesslike predator who lures men off the streets and robs them of wealth and health.

The question of who is exploiting whom is far from clear, as is shown by the leaps from lust to self-righteous disdain on almost any page of Boswell's diary:

'At night I took a streetwalker into Privy Garden and indulged sensuality. The wretch picked my pocket of my handkerchief and then swore that she had not. When I got home I was shocked to think I had been intimately united with a low, abandoned, perjured, pilfering creature.'[19]

In the city, values, as well as bodies, were 'intimately united'. In the South Sea Bubble poems and prints the whore was shown as just another entrepreneur, speculating on greed and gullibility. She could even be a mocking female counterpart of the successful bourgeois, like Daniel Defoe's Moll Flanders who constantly professes her respectable desire to be a 'lady', while £ signs punctuate her tale. But there is a difference between legal merchant and criminal woman: Moll is branded by her initial seduction, and haunted by the constant threat of the beadle and the justice. Defoe, with his robust Nonconformist conscience, never lets us forget this.

Defoe's Moll is a resilient survivor; Hogarth's is not. But Hogarth matches Defoe in his underlying dissenting voice as well as his swift moments of action, skilful illusion of realism and precise topography. Hogarth's realism and awareness came from experience. The streets he walked through from Covent Garden down to the Strand, or across to Bow Street and Drury Lane, were packed with prostitutes of all ages. Brydges Street, Kate Hackabout's patch, lay just across the way, with Drury Lane Theatre at its north-east corner. Its reputation for assignations stretched back forty years. In the Epilogue to *King Arthur*, Dryden gave these lines to Mrs Bracegirdle as she reads a sheaf of billets-doux:

> Here one desires my ladyship to meet
> At the kind couch above in Bridges Street,
> Oh sharping knave! that would have – you know what,
> For a poor sneaking treat of chocolate.[20]

By now the area was almost synonymous with prostitution. Decent people objected that you could not walk that way without women flashing their breasts at passing men in broad daylight. Covent Garden Piazza was described as 'the greatest square of Venus', with enough 'lewd women' to found a colony. In the mid-eighteenth century an annual guide, *Harris's List of Covent Garden Ladies*, listed their fleshly attractions like job-lots at an auction or quarry on the hunting field.[21] Drury Lane was cheaper and more dangerous, since thieves and con men, as well as women, hung around the theatre doors:

in 1725 one shocked commentator counted 107 brothels in and around the street.[22] The most notorious was the Rose Tavern, which Hogarth later drew in *A Rake's Progress*, where crooks and gentlemen gathered to watch the 'posture dancers', and where the porter, known as Leathercoats, was a giant of strength who would lie down in the street and let a carriage roll over him for the price of a drink.

This area, where Hogarth's first sketch was set and where Moll soon ends up, is the scene of Swift's cruel mock-pastoral 'A Beautiful Young Nymph Going to Bed':

> Corinna, pride of Drury Lane,
> For whom no shepherd sighs in vain;
> Never did Covent Garden boast
> So bright a battered, strolling toast . . .[23]

This is the final fate, as it were, of Addison's young girl. As the old whore takes off her wig, removes her false eye, eyebrows, teeth and corset, Swift's picture of her abused body conveys a disgust for the whole 'gentle', 'fair' sex:

> With gentlest touch, she next explores
> Her shankers, issues, running sores;
> Effects of many a sad disaster,
> And then to each, applies a plaster.

But even here, as in her dreams of Bridewell, the lash and transportation and in the appalling scene of her attempts to reassemble herself next day, Swift lets a note of pity sound before his final recoil and loathing:

> But how shall I describe her arts
> To recollect her scattered parts?
> Or show the anguish, toil, and pain,
> Of gathering up herself again?
> The bashful muse will never bear
> In such a scene to interfere
> Corinna in the morning dizened
> Who sees, will spew, who smells, be poisoned.

A host of models can be found behind *A Harlot's Progress* – political, social, literary, dramatic and artistic. But all these would have been as nothing without Hogarth's own vivid response to the daily life around him and his extraordinary memory for 'remarkable and striking subjects', by which

199

means, he said, 'what ever [I] saw, became more truly to me a picture than one that was drawn by a camera obscura'.[24]

Hogarth had already illustrated a story in prints with *Hudibras*, but he had not *told* a story without a text. In the event, *A Harlot's Progress* works less like a poem or a tale than a play, with short dramatic scenes, each focusing on the heroine but seeming to flow into one another by the way characters enter and exit. In conception, he started right in the middle of his story. The original sketch was the scene developed in the third plate of *A Harlot's Progress*; a true mock-classical beginning '*in medias res*'. This is the only print in which Moll Hackabout looks directly at the artist and at us, sexy and slanty-eyed, poised on the edge of her shabby, curtained bed like a sitter for a portrait of a sexy

57 *A Harlot's Progress*, Plate 1 (1732)

200

Court beauty by Lely. The stolen watch she dangles shows a quarter to twelve – approaching the hour of reckoning. In the full series of paintings, and the prints that followed them, Hogarth traced the 'before' and 'after' of this moment. And since the paintings were destroyed by fire in 1755, the prints alone remain to tell Moll's tale.

The cycle starts with a sweet country girl with a rose in her bosom and her little purse and scissors hanging by her side, arriving off the York wagon at the Bell Inn (the women still inside the wagon, ranged tightly behind the bar, also look like sheep bound for market). Hogarth told the French commentator Jean André Rouquet that the clergyman so deep in his letter to Edmund Gibson that he ignores the girl's plight (as ambitious clerics ignored their flock) was Moll's father. Rouquet had to explain this to his Catholic readers:

'The clergy in England are not bound to celibacy, and make great use of their privilege. They all marry, and as the revenue of their benefices is not enough for the establishment of several children in the world, these children and above all the daughters, are reduced to strange ways of providing for their own subsistence.'[25]

This, too, was an old line: Tom Brown's huge, greasy bawd who collects 'whole wagon-loads' of country lasses, explains that one of her girls 'had been a celebrated beauty, a parson's daughter'.[26]

In Hogarth's print, the confident bawd is the most dramatic figure, with her finery and patches, immediately recognizable as Mother Needham. (Moll stands, in effect, between 'father' and 'mother', both grotesque parodies of the parental role.) Behind the bawd, with his hand suspiciously deep in his pocket, is Colonel Charteris, attended by a cringing Jack Gourlay. Gourlay's supplicating crossed hands mirror Moll's – both are 'bound' as servants to satisfy Charteris's needs. Ordinary life goes on behind them as a woman hangs her washing out against a cloudy sky, but the tokens are ominous. The neck of the goose, neatly labelled for 'my lofing Cosen in Tems Street', droops over the edge of the basket; the panniers pushed by the munching horse are about to tumble to the ground.

Even when she is at the height of her career, Moll (like the townswoman in *After*) is surrounded by objects falling, crashing, scattering. By Plate 2 she has become the mistress of a rich Jew, a sure sign of success: 'I madam', boasts Gay's whore Slammekin in *The Beggar's Opera*, 'was once kept by a Jew; and bating their religion, to women they are a good sort of people.'[27] But Moll snaps her fingers at good luck, and is already deceiving him. As he takes tea, a young lover creeps out, trousers undone, the startled maid clutching his

58 Plate 2, 'The Quarrel with her Jew Protector'

shoes. Moll provides a distraction, flashing her eyes and baring a nipple, flicking her fingers and kicking her tea table, much to the alarm of the scalded Jew, the pet monkey trailing her bonnet and the little black slave bringing the tea kettle. She seems in control, but she too is a slave and a pet, ministering to a rich man's desires.

Too greedy, too flighty – as her masquerade mask shows – Moll slips to Drury Lane status, with a fat noseless bunter instead of a chic black slave, a stray cat raising its neat hindquarters instead of an exotic monkey, a cracked punchbowl and vials of ointment instead of a silver tray of tea. This is the point of her second fall, from whoring to crime, as she swings the stolen watch from her fingers. And this, too, is the moment of her legal fall – it is not a bold young lover, but the unmistakably creepy Justice Gonson who steps

59 Plate 3, 'Apprehended by a Magistrate'

thoughtfully through the door, finger to lips, followed by the watchmen with their wooden staves.

The tale is sharp, the actors strong. Each picture has its own 'before' and 'after', its open, angled doors in the corner. As a story, *A Harlot's Progress* invites our collaboration, asking us to fill in the gaps, to imagine the people, to guess about cause and consequence, to dwell on the graphic detail of place, clothes, atmosphere. Hogarth's prints deepen and echo in the imagination; like a playwright offering images as well as action, he lays a trail of clues. Some are familiar symbols: the goose, the falling buckets, the slave and the monkey, the mirrors and broken china. Others are inscribed on the walls, hidden in corners, repaying a close, leisurely reading. Time inevitably dims the clarity of Hogarth's allusions. To appreciate his layered images and to see how he appealed to all markets, from the illiterate to the scholar, we need the help of the historian and art critic.

In each plate, Hogarth placed messages to entertain the social, political and religious critic of his day and the connoisseur. The coffee-house gossips could spot celebrities: Mother Needham, Charteris and Gonson or the two notorious quacks Richard Rock and Jean Misaubin. Playing to prejudice, Hogarth also invited his viewers to argue about the identity of the Jew and indulge the common anti-Semitic complaints about Jewish speculators, friends to Walpole and the Court. Beyond that, poring over the prints, they could decipher the pictures on the wall. Some were emblematic, like the sign for the Bell Inn (which links the notion of *belle* with a more universal theme, Donne's 'Ask not for whom the bell tolls') or the mock escutcheon at the end, Moll's own 'trade sign'. Some were taken from the art world, from portraits to smoky old masters. The Jew's room, for example, is decorated not only with those portraits of Woolston and Clarke, attacked as enemies of Christianity, but with two pictures of Old Testament history. Appropriate, of course, but their content is mocking. In one, entitled 'Jonah, why art thou angry?', a weeping Jonah rages because God has not destroyed Nineveh (the Gentiles) as he promised. In the other David dances with his harp, while Uzzah steadies the Ark, toppled by the oxen: for this sacrilegious act, God, through his priest, stabs him in the back. In the 'real' scene, where the Jew who has 'sacrilegiously' touched a Christian girl is balancing the tilting table with his hand as Uzzah does the ark, the lover's sword also seems to 'stab him in the back'.

Both pictures undermine the Jew, presenting him as vengeful and tainted, but both also criticize the harshness of Old Testament justice and the cruelty of religious zeal. The Jew (like Moll) is an outsider and a victim of prejudice. In the next scene of Moll's Drury Lane garret, the critiques of justice reach into the present. Moll has an Old Testament print of Abraham striking Isaac, but there will be no divine hand to stay her fate. She is a witch, her masquerade hat suggests, who will be hunted and burned. The whippings she gave to men with her little broom will now be turned on her. Her other decorations show that she is hopelessly romantic, a Polly Peachum with High Church, Jacobite airs. She has John Dalton's wig-box above her bed and a pin-up of Macheath on the wall but she also has a portrait of Dr Sacheverell, whose inflammatory sermons had caused riots, and a little oval icon of the Virgin – and she wraps her butter in one of Gibson's 'Pastoral Letters'.

Beyond these visual quotations, the formal composition of some scenes exploited analogies with great religious art – with the Visitation in the first

204

plate or the Annunciation in the third, with Gonson as a dark anti-archangel. The references are there; indeed Hogarth made them as obvious as possible, but (as with the parodic nativity of the rabbits in the *Cunicularii*), he suggested that life itself, in all its absurdity and pathos, can be as powerful as any hallowed religious mystery. Moll is no Virgin Mary – although her initial is the undeciphered 'M'. She is a flesh-and-blood woman, who suffers not from the will of God but from her own ambition, men's appetites and the cruelty of the Law.

From the key third scene, where Gonson treads heavily across the boards, his finger to his lips, the curve of Moll's life moves inexorably down. In the fourth plate, she is beating hemp in Bridewell among other petty thieves and prostitutes. The warder will sell the product of their labour, spending just

60 Plate 4, 'Scene in Bridewell'

205

enough on food to keep them standing at their work from six in the morning until six at night. Moll's fine dreams are mocked, just as her fine dress is tweaked by the leering, half-blind, syphilitic crone behind her, perhaps the gaoler's wife. She is hardly able to lift the heavy hammer and her sexiness is grotesquely transferred to the over-ripe body of her bunter, pulling up the ragged stocking with its fashionable silk clocks, probably handed down from her mistress.

When the prints came out, Moll was identified with Mary Muffet, a well-known Drury Lane character committed to hard labour in Tothill Fields Bridewell in 1730, where she was reported as 'now beating hemp in a gown very richly laced with silver'.[28] This kind of contrast had a dark allure; in 1725 young Saussure was agog to see a woman in fine linen and lace, committed for stealing a gold watch from her lover. A queenly figure covered in sweat from beating with her heavy mallet, she was wearing 'a magnificent silk dress brocaded with flowers. The captain took great heed of her; he had made her arm quite red with the little raps he gave her with his cane.'[29] The hint of titillation here, and in Hogarth's print, flowered unashamed in one verse commentary:

> When Moll I view'd at Hempen Block
> Brocaded Gown and laced Smock . . .
> I could have ventured Plague and pox
> And all that fill's Pandora's Box,
> To've had a silly snotty Pleasure
> But she, poor Girl, was not at leisure.[30]

The women's prison, however, was more than an image of a prostitute's decline or a sadist's delight. It was the incarnation of domination, the body subdued and beaten for punishment and profit, not enjoyed for pleasure. In particular, the pregnant black whore in the background stung the imagination of later eighteenth-century commentators, like the irrepressibly responsive Lichtenberg:

'a negress poor devil! And as I gather from her rotundity, a double one besides. What a nest of prisons for the embryo! Imprisoned in a mother who herself sits in the Penitentiary, in a world which again is a Penitentiary for her whole family. Oh let us be thankful that we were born with the colour of innocence and the livery of freedom.'[31]

Only a torn playing card, a caricature of Gonson on the gallows and inscriptions on the pillory and whipping post – 'Better to work than stand

61 Plate 5, 'She expires, while the Doctors are quarrelling'

here' and 'The Wages of Idleness' – adorn Bridewell's stark, uncompromising shed. The next room, Moll's sick room, is even barer. Both Justice and Nature have punished her. The law sent her to Bridewell, and disease sentences her to death. The rich bed-hangings of the second plate are replaced by a pathetic line of washing, the pictures on the walls by obscure obscenities on the ceiling and crude objects, diagram-like parodies of female and male: the round cake of 'Jew's bread' – a perforated Passover biscuit, used as a flytrap – and two limp sheaths. In the middle of the scene two quacks argue violently, sending chair and table crashing to the ground, one being the fat Dr Rock, inventor of the 'famous, Anti-Venereal, Grand, Specifick Pill' and the other the thin Dr Jean Misaubin, creator of a rival cure. Ignoring them, a tough-faced woman rifles the little trunk that once stood by the hopeful girl in Bell's Inn Yard and

207

Moll's small son scratches his head over the meat as the pot boils over. On the floor, among smashed pottery and spilt ink, a paper advertises the 'Practical Scheme Anodyne Necklace', which was both a universal panacea for everything from croup to syphilis and a slang name for the noose. Amid this turbulence and noise, the crashing and shouting, the hissing water and raging fire, Moll's life is seeping from her. She has no strength, no bite. She has been suffering the cure of 'salivation', wrapped in blankets to make her sweat the disease away, dosed with mercury that makes her gums swell and her teeth fall out – they lie to one side on a crumpled paper marked 'Dr Rock'. She looks like a huge silent insect in a chrysalis, a shapeless bundle supported by her horrified old maid in a grim burlesque of the death of the Virgin.

Some commentators felt that the series should end here, with Moll's death,

62 Plate 6, 'The Funeral'

208

the wages of her sin. But Hogarth's bitter comedy insists that life goes on. Like a satirical afterpiece following a tragedy, his last print shows the mourners before Moll's funeral. Scene by scene, from the open air of the coachyard Hogarth tracked his heroine's increasing confinement down to her last tight space, her coffin. One young woman looks at her face, hidden from us. Around this gesture of pity and, perhaps, identification, women stand in extravagant stage poses of grief. Hogarth mocks the pompous rites of death favoured by his age, and by baroque art, by showing the indifferent callousness of life. The erotic play continues to the end, and viewers (or voyeurs) might laugh more than weep. The clergyman, spilling his brandy, has his hand up the skirt of a demure-looking woman who coyly hides his gropings with her hat. The smooching undertaker helps a whore with her funeral gloves, while she steals his handkerchief. The little boy, in full adult gear, with lace around his black felt hat, examines his spinning-top oblivious to the fuss, a study in absorbed concentration from his open mouth to his feet, dangling down in their buckled shoes. On the far wall hangs his mother's old country hat, next to a satirical–obscene coat of arms made up of three faucets, plugged with spigots. On the floor in front of them all lies a dish with sprigs of rosemary – for remembrance.

Throughout 1730 Hogarth painted his pictures, weaving in the stories of Charteris and Dalton, Gonson and others. As Vertue said, the way that these 'drew everybody to see them' led naturally to the idea of engraving. In March 1731 he launched his subscription, selling tickets from his house at Covent Garden, half a guinea on subscription, half on completion of the set when subscribers would present their receipt. The subscription ticket itself was at once a joke, a promise of salaciousness and a claim to seriousness.

Called *Boys Peeping at Nature*, the ticket showed a faun, or miniature satyr, peering up the skirts of the many-breasted Diana of Ephesus. The faun is held back by a putto, while another is painting Nature at an easel (tactfully reducing the number of breasts): we can only 'unveil' nature through art, yet art itself is censuring and artificial. Numerous allusions crowd the allegory, itself a reference to Rubens's *Nature Adorned by the Graces* – a picture Thornhill owned. This ticket was aimed squarely at the 'fashionable people' and the artists.

At first he planned to find someone to engrave his paintings for him: Vertue reported at the time that he 'proposd to get them gravd. by the best gravers in Lond. but none that he employd pleasing him he has set about them himself'.[32] This sounds all too likely – Hogarth was often impatient with

63 *Boys Peeping at Nature* (1731)

others who engraved his work – but with the benefit of hindsight, he conveniently misremembered these events, presenting the sequence as part of a strategic master plan. At the same time as he established himself as a moral satirist and visual dramatist, he would gain control of his own production, and assert his independence. Rather than selling one picture to one patron, he wrote, 'dealing with the public in general I found was the most likely to do provided I could strike the passions'. Prints would bring in 'small sums from many', and by engraving his own pictures, 'I could secure my Property to myself'.[33]

Hogarth had luck on his side too. In the summer of 1731, while the public was waiting for his prints, the mutable figure of the harlot was given new power by George Lillo's bourgeois tragi-comedy *The London Merchant* at Drury Lane. Lillo, a Rotherhithe goldsmith, came from a dissenting background, like Defoe and Hogarth. His play, based on a seventeenth-century ballad, tells of the seduction of the young apprentice George Barnwell by Sara

Milwood, who persuades him to kill his rich uncle; both are tried and hanged. Without Gay's irony, Lillo made the fate of an ordinary apprentice as tragic as that of the heroes of high drama; the first-night audience who came to sneer, wrote Cibber, stayed 'to drop their ballads and pull out their handkerchiefs'.[34] But, like Hogarth, Lillo gave a fierce twist to the drama when Milwood answered her accusers' charge that she abused her 'uncommon perfections of Mind and Body':

'If such I had, well may I curse your barbarous Sex, who robb'd me of 'em, ere I knew their Worth, then left me, too late, to count their Value by their Loss. Another and another Spoiler came, and all my gain was Poverty and Reproach. My Soul disdain'd and yet disdains, Dependance and Contempt. Riches, no matter by what Means obtain'd, I saw secur'd the want of Men from both; I found it therefore necessary to be rich; and to that End, I summon'd all my Arts. You call 'em wicked, be it so, they were such as my Conversation with your sex had furnish'd me withal.'

The particular objects of her rage are the clergymen and magistrates, no different from those they condemn, who use the laws to screen their own villanies: 'The Judge who condemns the poor Man for being a Thief, had been a Thief himself had he been poor.' This play, and Hogarth's prints, remained favourites of the British people, carrying a critique that spreads outwards from the dilemma of women to the inequities of the whole society. Fielding too helped the cause when he referred slyly to Hogarth's paintings (which many of his audience must have seen in his painting room), by referring to the bawd, the stagecoach and the colonel in his play *The Lottery*, in January 1732. That month *The Craftsman* carried a notice from the '*Author of the Six Copper Plates* representing a Harlot's Progress', promising delivery in two months and explaining the delay as 'being disappointed of the Assistance he proposed, he is obliged to engrave them all himself'.[35] The subscribers were waiting eagerly, and at the beginning of March Hogarth announced that his series was nearly ready. With ironic timeliness, his notice followed hard on the heels of the much discussed death of Colonel Charteris, on 24 February; the Colonel had left a vast fortune and at his funeral there were unseemly riots, with people hurling rubbish, sodden vegetables, dead cats and dogs into his open grave and trying to rip his body from its coffin. Throughout this month Hogarth ran notices advising that the prints could be collected on 10 April. The repeated announcements, catching latecomers and building up tension, gave the project the aura of something new, important and newsworthy.

A Harlot's Progress fulfilled all the promises: 'it captivated the Minds of most People persons of all ranks & conditions from the greatest quality to the Meanest'.[36] All 1,240 subscription sets were sold. Moral tale or not, much of the excitement was spurred by the sexy subject and by eagerness to see key names pilloried. Everyone soon found Charteris and Gourlay and 'pious Needham', Rock and Misaubin and Gonson. Hogarth's friend William Huggins claimed that at the Board of Treasury, a day or two after the series appeared,

'a copy of it was shewn by one of the lords, as containing among other excellencies, a striking likeness of Sir John Gonson. It gave universal satisfaction; from the Treasury each lord repaired to the print-shop for a copy of it, and Hogarth rose completely into fame.'[37]

At Moll's funeral, folk spotted a portrait of the prostitute Eizabeth Adams (later executed for robbery) in the woman flirting with the clergyman, and of the bawd Mother Bentley lamenting by the large brandy bottle.

Hogarth's prints sold fast, but his advertisements had always insisted on a limited number of impressions. He kept his word, but little over a week went by before Giles King 'at the Golden Head in Brownlow Street Drury lane' was advertising copies authorized by the artist, with explanatory captions.[38] By the end of the month these were out, selling at four or five shillings – a canny way of increasing Hogarth's profits by selling to the lower classes and not offending the subscribers. Then came the piracies. As Vertue put it, 'no Sooner were these publisht but several Copies were made by other. hands & dispersd all over the Countries'.[39] The leading printsellers Thomas and John Bowles were quick off the mark, but the most effective set was a softened, green-tinted mezzotint version by the engraver Elisha Kirkall which was published by a group of booksellers, including the Bowleses' rivals, the Overtons, in November.

As soon as she appeared Hogarth's Moll had a life of her own. Within a week came the first pamphlet, a standard whore's life with an adapted ending. Three days later, a second pamphlet told Moll's story in crude verse, identifying all the characters and amplifying all the suggestive details, as when she refuses Charteris's bribes:

> This said, the Tarquin flew at Hackabout,
> Who scream'd, and from him turn'd her Back-about.
> But he, as void of Grace as Fear,
> Began to charge her in the Rear.[40]

212

And so on. By June, like Gay's Polly Peachum, Moll was adorning the mounts of fans. By the next spring (Polly Peachum in reverse) she had her own show, *The Harlot's Progress; or the Ridotto Al Fresco: A Grotesque Pantomime Entertainment* by Theophilus Cibber. This was staged at Drury Lane, and Moll was also featured in pantomimes at Goodman's Fields and Sadler's Wells. Another ballad opera, *The Jew Decoy'd; or the Progress of a Harlot*, was published but not performed. All these emphasized the playfully pornographic satire, but the moral readings – equally implicit in Hogarth's treatment – soon followed, beginning with yet another verse pamphlet, with versions of the prints, *The Lure of Venus: or A Harlot's Progress* by 'Joseph Gay' (John Durant Breval).

With the pantomimes and operas the cycle partly inspired by *The Beggar's Opera* and *Polly* came full circle, back to the stage. Hogarth himself always thought of his art as theatrical and in this series his old love of the drama fused with a tongue-in-cheek adaptation of current art theory. He gave a nod to all the received wisdom: of portrait sitters as actors; of history-paintings as showing powerful actions, carried by a few grand characters; of the great episodic cycles, painted and engraved. Just as Gay mocked the opera, as Butler and Pope adapted the epic and as Fielding undercut bombastic tragedy, so Hogarth merged the formal values of high art with the 'low' comic tradition. In the process he created a new genre.

Hogarth's underworld history-painting could comment effortlessly on the 'lust' corroding national life. His female, anti-heroic cycle was both a commercial success and a bold experiment, a challenge flung at the snobs who preferred dead old masters. Yet *A Harlot's Progress* also dignified its subject, opening up a new territory to serious art. Social satire such as this, built on duality, ambivalent about the exploitation inherent in the very act of *looking*, could be humane and profound as well as popular.

NOON

1732–1748

64 The Parish of St Martin-in-the-Fields (1756)

11

Nobody and Somebody

NOBODY. *All the People in Great Britain, except about 1200.*

. . .

WORTH. *Power. Rank. Wealth.*
WISDOM. *The Art of acquiring All three.*
WORLD. *Your own Acquaintance.*

HENRY FIELDING, 'A Modern Glossary', 1752

A HARLOT'S PROGRESS, so the story goes, brought Hogarth back into favour in the Thornhill household. In late 1730 the shrewd Lady Thornhill allegedly advised her daughter to 'place in her father's way' some of the scenes Hogarth was then painting. Early one morning Jane carried several canvases into the dining room at Covent Garden, appealing to Sir James as both father and artist. 'When he arose,' says Nichols, 'he enquired whence they came; and being told by whom they were introduced, he cried out, "Very well; the man who can furnish representations like these, can maintain a wife without a portion!"' This grudging praise does sound like an excuse for 'keeping his purse strings close', as Nichols says, but the ice was broken. Thornhill was soon 'reconciled and generous to the young couple'.[1]

Hogarth and Jane moved back into the house and Thornhill included them in a pencil sketch, perhaps an early drawing for a planned conversation piece of domestic harmony and artistic status. Thornhill's family and friends are grouped in front of the grand marble chimney-piece in the gallery, admiring a grand classical canvas, and underneath a couple on the left is scribbled roughly 'Mr Hogarth &c'.[2] This was his address when the orders for *A Harlot's Progress* were pouring in, '& all this without Courting or soliciting subscriptions', as Vertue noted, 'all comeing to his dwelling in common Garden – where he livd with his father in Law Sr James Thornhill'.[3]

If in 1729 Hogarth saw himself as Sancho, the out-of-place plebeian, three years later he was beginning to be a name in the land. In June 1732, Fielding's friend James Ralph, a tireless writer for the political opposition, picked Hogarth out by name in an essay in his journal *The Weekly Register*. Complaining that

217

British painters were by and large conventional, unimaginative and timid, rarely daring to treat a new or uncommon subject, he went on:

'fewer still have commenc'd Authors themselves, that is to say, invented both the story and the Execution; tho' certainly 'tis as much in their Power as the Poet's, and would redound as much to their Reputation, as the late *Progress of a Harlot* by the ingenious Mr. *Hogarth* will sufficiently testify'.[4]

This is the first recognition of Hogarth as a modern 'history-painter', but at the moment he was still experimenting, caught in a hinterland, dodging between the tracks of public story-teller and private portraitist. His juggling was risky as well as full of promise, since the very success of his prints was a potential drawback to his chances of winning influential patrons. Would a polite gentleman really want himself, his wife, his daughter and his house to be painted by the satirist of magistrates, the chronicler of Drury Lane?

This was the world with which Hogarth was increasingly identified. In May, when Fielding produced his play *The Old Debauchees*, based on the recent French trial of a Jesuit and his lover, he added a deliberately Hogarthian afterpiece, a political–sexual burlesque, *The Covent-Garden Tragedy*, featuring the bawd Mother Punchbowl and full of little echoes of Hogarth's series. The prologue makes the general satirical application (of the prints as well as of this very funny play) abundantly clear:

> Our poet, from unknown, untasted springs
> A curious draft of tragic nectar brings,
> From Covent Garden culls delicious stores
> Of bullies, bawds, and sots, and rakes, and whores.
> Examples of the great can serve but few;
> For what are kings' and heroes' faults to you?
> But these examples are of general use.
> What rake is ignorant of King's Coffee-house?[5]

Covent Garden was now Hogarth's base, his workroom and his home – and often his subject. In the steamy summer months, however, he and Jane, like other Londoners who could afford to, moved out of the sweating city to avoid the stench that drifted up from the gutters. Some people went north to the clear hill air of Highgate and Hampstead and others moved up-river, to Thames-side villas in Chiswick, Twickenham and Richmond. In the early years of their marriage the Hogarths themselves turned in the other direction, favouring the small hamlets on the south bank of the Thames. Crossing the river had long spelled pleasure to Londoners. Right opposite Somerset House were the slightly seedy Cupers Gardens, fondly known as Cupid's Gardens, and moored near by was a converted barge called *The Folly* where an apprentice could safely take his girl for the evening in the 1720s, although in later years furious gambling took over. Further downstream were St George's Fields in Southwark, with racing and sports and cockfighting, and the little spa of the Restoration Tavern. This was said to equal that of a rival inn near by, the famous Dog and Duck, which had started selling the water from its mineral spring in 1731, and two years later was doing a booming trade, offering a dozen bottles for a shilling. All these venues prospered in the commercially minded 1730s, and none more so than Vauxhall Gardens, owned by young Jonathan Tyers.

In the spring of 1732, Hogarth and four friends, in a burst of collective madness, went on an outing that took them further afield than an evening's entertainment at Vauxhall. One Friday night at the end of May, six weeks after the *Harlot*'s triumphant appearance, Hogarth was at the Bedford Arms Tavern with his brother-in-law John, who lived behind his parents' house in Red Lion Court. Also drinking in the Bedford Arms that night were William Tothall, the lawyer Ebenezer Forrest and the seascape painter Samuel Scott, who had just finished a series of paintings of East India Company settlements, in collaboration with George Lambert. (Scott, like Hogarth, was under five feet tall: when Vertue included them both in a note about flourishing British art he added, 'but one little remark, I observe the most elevated Men in Art here now, are the lowest in stature'.)[6]

Here were five interesting, idiosyncratic men. John Thornhill had just succeeded his father as Serjeant-Painter to the King, but although he climbed the ranks of the Painter–Stainers' Company he never actually painted much; he moved to York Buildings off the Strand the following year and left London altogether in 1745 to settle on the Thornhill estates in Dorset, returning only occasionally to town. William Tothall also later left London to live in Dover, where Hogarth went to stay with him, but at the moment he was running a successful business in Covent Garden, trading on a colourful past. His widowed mother, a midwife, had placed him as a boy as apprentice to a fish-monger uncle but he ran away to sea, sailing the globe from Newfoundland to the West Indies, where he was captured by the Spaniards. In the late 1720s, aged thirty, he had settled to work for a London draper who helped him to start two sidelines, selling trimmings to tailors and running a rum and brandy business from the cellar, beginning with a puncheon of rum sent by West Indies friends.[7]

Forrest was a writer as well as a lawyer; his satirical ballad opera on modern marriage had been staged by Rich at Lincoln's Inn Fields in 1729.[8] All were close friends and near neighbours. Scott and his attractive, clever wife Anne lived across Covent Garden, in 'Bedford Ground' at the south-east corner of the square, and during this year Tothall took a house next door but one from them. Forrest and his wife lodged close by: in 1740 they would move next door to John Thornhill in York Buildings, to a house that became a centre for artists, musicians, actors and antiquarians.

As midnight passed and the bottles emptied, inspiration arrived: they decided to set off at once, on an impromptu 'Grand Tour' – of North Kent. They ran home, left messages and grabbed spare shirts.[9] Scott, whose anxieties and testiness made him mercilessly teased (he was later described as 'extremely passionate and impatient')[10] also took his greatcoat to guard against the cold. Through the narrow streets they weaved across the city singing popular songs such as 'Why should we quarrel for Riches' until they reached Billingsgate dock, where, wrote Forrest, they 'dropped anchor' at a quayside inn known as the Dark House. Here Hogarth drew a caricature of a porter who called himself the Duke of Puddle Dock, and 'his Grace' stuck the sketch on the cellar door. Then they settled down to tell broad stories, being 'agreably entertain'd with the Humours of the Place, Particularly an Explanation of a Gaffer and Gammer a Litle Obscene tho[h.] in presence of Two of the Fair Sex'.

Here they stayed till 'the Clock Struck One' when they took to the water in a hired boat, huddling on straw under a loose canvas roof, or 'tilt', in a strong south-easterly and driving rain. At four they gave up hope of sleep and took to singing (and drinking) again, 'at Cuckolds Point Wee Sung S[r.] John, at Deptford Pishoken and in Blackwall Reach Eat Hung Beef and Biscuit and Drank Right Hollands'. Passing Purfleet they could make out the men-of-war at anchor in the dawn and they gave a lift downstream to one of their pilots, who sent Hogarth to sleep with his stories of Spanish insults and 'other Affairs of Consequence'. Suddenly Hogarth woke, determined to tell his dream, fell asleep again and forgot he had dreamed at all. By six they had reached Gravesend and after dealing summarily with a boy who had wedged his boat between them and the landing place and refused to let them cross it, 'wee happily accomplish'd this Adventure and Arriv'd at Mrs Bramble's at six.

'Then we Wash'd our Faces and hands', wrote Forrest, '& had our Wiggs powder'd, then Drank Coffee Eat Toast and butter; paid our Reckoning and Sett out at Eight.' For the next five days Hogarth and his friends marched energetically, if haphazardly, from the Thames to the Medway. On the first morning they made a brisk survey of Gravesend – its new church, 'the unknown person's Tomb and Epitaph' and the market place – and then set out across Gads Hill to Rochester. This was a long, tiring walk on which 'nothing remarkable happened' except the drinking of three pots of beer and the first indication of a recurring refrain: 'Some Small Distress Scott Suffer'd in Travelling through some Clay Ground Moistoned by the Rain, But the Country being Extreamely pleasant alleviated his Distress, and made him Jocund.'

Scott was their comic anti-hero. He enjoyed himself well enough, playing hopscotch with Hogarth under the colonnades of Rochester Town Hall or sketching on the bridge, but he was a natural, accident-prone victim who took setbacks badly. By the Medway he sheltered from a shower under a hedge, emerged covered 'with an Ordural Moisture of a verdant Hue' and lost the white cambrick handkerchief that Anne had lent him: 'he soon found it, yet was his Joy at that Succes again abated by his Fear that it was Torn, But being soon Convinc'd that he was More afraid then Hurt, Wee all proceeded Merrily'. In a mock fight, he and Tothall daubed each other with soft cow-dung; in one village he had to share a bed with Forrest amid burlesque marriage rites in which 'they threw the Stocking, Fought perukes and did a Great many pretty things in a Horn'. When he proffered profound thoughts about the impossibility of passing through, as opposed to over, the earth, his friends weighted his pockets with stones. He flounced indignantly when asked to sleep in a garret on a 'flock bed with no curtains', and then reeled with fright when he got a good bed in the inn but saw something 'Stir under the Bed-clothes'. (It turned out to be 'a Litle Boy of the House who had Mistook ye Bed'.) 'This relation', writes Forrest, 'according to Custom made us very Merry.'

The characterization continues to the end. It has to be Scott who leaves his penknife 'Value Five Shillings' at an alehouse; who is badly seasick; who finds that his precious greatcoat, left at Gravesend for safety, has been lost; whose shirt gets so soaked by a sudden swell that he has to hold it like a banner in the wind, but 'the Sun Shining Warm, he was soon Dry and recovering his Surprize Joyn'd with us in Laughing at y^e Accid$^{t.}$'.

Scott's plunges into misery and returns to jollity provided a subplot to picaresque adventures and scholarly sojourns. The friends carefully noted Rochester's fine bridge, cathedral and castle: as they peered down the bottom-less well at Rochester castle, they watched a small boy climb down into its depths and bring up a jackdaw. They took in the old hospital and a town house whose front had 'four Figures in Basso relievo after the Antique Done by some Modern hand representing the Seasons': but then fell asleep on chairs in the inn dining room. Culture, curiosity and appetite took equal shares. At Chatham, they bought shrimps to eat while they walked round and admired the great naval vessels and 'the Kings Storehouses and Dock yard which are Very Noble':

'Wee went on Board the Marlbro^h; and the Royall Soveraign which last is reckoned One of the Finest Shipps in the Navy, Wee saw the London the Royall George and Royall Anne, all First Rate Men of Warr, at Six Wee return'd to our Quarters at Rochester and pass'd the time agreably till Nine, and then Quite Fatigue'd with Pleasure, Went to Bed.'

It was a good, if exhausting, trip. On their second day they followed the north coast of the Medway to Upnor (where Forrest got cockles from a blind man and a half-blind woman in a little boat on the river) and on to Hoo and the Isle of Grain. On the next day, the Monday, they persuaded a boatman to take them across to Sheerness on the Isle of Sheppey. Here they stayed in the one-street town of Queensborough, and at a nearby well they met some sailors who had been attending a young midshipman, a general's son, the day before. They had run their boat ashore in the mud and had been left without money, food or drink, while the genteel midshipman went to Sheerness. With the good will common towards sailors (but not soldiers) Hogarth's party gave them sixpence to buy cockles; when the sailors came back to offer them some, they were so touched that they gave sixpence more. This was not the end of the encounter: later they found the tars in an aggrieved huddle in the street. Their midshipman, they said, had met a sailor with a woman

'whom the Midshipman wanted to be free with and the Sailor opposed Insisting She was his Wife, & hindred him from being Rude, which ye Midshipman resenting was gone to ye Mayor to redress his Greivances. Wee tho^t this a Very odd affair. But Did not Stay to see the Result of it.'

Such tangles of class and conditions, like knots of awkward, ordinary life, often intruded. Feeling came in waves, reaching back in time as the five men contemplated castles, churches and graves, or climbed up to the great abbey of Minster, gazing out across the saltmarshes and sandbars. The politics of their own day pressed in when they inspected gun batteries and men-of-war. Sudden glimpses took them far across the globe, like the epitaph to a harpooneer buried in Queensborough churchyard who had made twenty-four Arctic voyages:

In Greenland I whales Seahorse Bears did Slay
Though Now my body is Intombe in Clay.

Hogarth and his friends pondered on these things, and discussed their dreams as they lay in bed in the morning, 'and left off, no Wiser than we begun'. But their concerns were often more basic: salt-pork, black bread, butter and buns and good malt liquor, beer ('severall Cans of Good Flip') and suppers of lobster and eggs and bacon. The grand eating began at Rochester, when they woke from their hard chairs to face a two-hour dinner:

'a Dish of Soles & Flounders with Crab Sauce, a Calves heart Stuff'd and Roasted ye Liver fry'd and the other appurtenances Minc'd, a Leg of Mutton Roasted, and some Green pease, all Very Good and well Dress'd, with Good Small beer and excellent Port'.

Heroic meals were matched by un-heroic fooling, with more than one 'Batle Royall with Sticks pebbles and Hog's dung', and water fights to cool them down. Forrest's favourite words are 'Pleasure' and 'Adventures' and 'Laughter': Scott is laughed at for smelling the newly discharged gun carriages at Sheerness, and Hogarth is too, for cutting his toenails in the garrison.

Hogarth flouted propriety most. Recounting their visit to the churchyard at Hoo, Forrest solemnly transcribed a servant girl's bitter epitaph to her master (in true antiquarian style) and then immediately and straight-facedly reported:

'Hogarth having a Motion; untruss'd upon a Grave Rail in an Unseemly Manner which Tothall Perceiving administred pennance to ye part offending with a bunch of Netles, this occasion'd an Engagement which Ended happily without Bloodshed and Hogarth Finish'd his Business against the Church Door.'

The juxtaposition may not be accidental. Hogarth would have taken the girl's side against the ungrateful master who left her nothing: his shitting on a grave, and then against the church, was characteristic (even emblematic) of his anti-clerical, anti-authority stance. His wit often had such crude bravado, a metaphorical determination to crap where he would, even on the holy of holies. By the end of the century, a new climate of refinement made such acts, like Swift's scatological poems, quite unmentionable. Nichols's collaborator Steevens profoundly disdained Hogarth's crudeness.

'Having rarely been admitted into polite circles, none of his sharp corners had been rubbed off, so that he continued to the last a gross uncultivated man . . .

223

To be a member of a club of mechanics, or those not many removes above them, seems to have been the utmost of his social ambition; but even in these assemblies he was oftener sent to *Coventry* for misbehaviour than any other man who frequented them.'[11]

But Tothall and Scott, Forrest and Thornhill did not send Hogarth to Coventry. They pretended outrage – like Tothall with his nettles – but they laughed at his rudeness. Horseplay was not 'ungentlemanly', but common to men of all classes. Indeed it is quite clear that the five saw themselves as gentlemen, a cut above the rustics of Sheppey. We hear a note of complacency when Forrest reports how the sailors sprinkled their address 'with yor. worship at every word' and throughout the trip, between the dung fights, they were scrupulous about their shirts and wigs. In their regard for titles, and for cleanliness, they shared the concerns that marked the new, anxious 'middling orders'. (By the end of George II's reign, the novelist Richard Graves would claim that 'Sir' and 'Your Honour' were bestowed on anyone 'that appears in a clean shirt and powdered wig'.)[12] In this circle where the cultured and the crude overlapped, Hogarth was valued and accepted.

On the Tuesday evening, in strong winds and heavy rain, they sailed back to Gravesend. The choppy crossing brought back Tothall's seafaring days, and he insisted on going aboard one of the custom-house sloops to meet his friend Captain Robinson. Scott and Hogarth, one 'Very Sea Sick' and the other extremely queasy, were dismayed at the delay, but forgave Tothall when he came back 'with some Milk punch and some Fire to Light pipes which was greatly Wanted'. In the dusk they watched porpoises gambol around their boat, and swapped songs with the cockswain's sea-shanties, but 'our Notes were soon Chang'd' by running aground on Blye Sands at the start of an ebb tide. Tothall's old skill helped the crew push them off, saving them from hours amid the 'Beating of the Winds and Tides'. Their adventures were nearly over. On Wednesday, 31 May, with a favourable wind and a 'Mackrell Gale', sitting on trusses of fresh straw with a bottle of good wine and pipes of tobacco, they breezed up the Thames back to Billingsgate. There they took a wherry to Somerset House, 'from whence Wee walk'd all together and arrived about Two at the Bedford Arms Covent Garden, in the same Good Humour we left it to Set out on this very Pleasant Expedition'.

This is one of the few moments in Hogarth's life that is recorded in any detail, because the outing was conceived from the start as a mock-antiquarian tour and was enthusiastically recorded by Forrest as *AN ACCOUNT of what Seem'd most Remarkable in the Five Days Peregrination of the Five Following*

Persons Viz. Messieurs Tothall, Scott, Hogarth, Thornhill & Forrest.* The record was read aloud in the Bedford Arms, signed by the five and bound in brown leather with a motto pinched from Dulwich College porch on the title page, *Abi tu et fac Similiter* ('Go thou and do likewise'). The finishing touch was a gilt label, which read TRAVELS. 1732. VOL. I. This was a dig both at the multi-volume memoirs of Continental travellers and at the numerous antiquarian surveys, especially the *History of Kent, Vol I* by John Harris – who had promised four more volumes but died in poverty before he could write them. Despite the rain and wind of an early British summer, the whole trip was undertaken in this spirit, and it shows how deeply ingrained the parodic cast of mind was, that they could *live* their burlesques as well as write them and engrave them.

The 'Account' was a collaborative venture. Forrest wrote the text in his flowing round script; Thornhill drew a map tracing their route in neat dotted lines; Tothall kept the accounts, scrupulously listing each item in the total expenditure of £6; and Scott and Hogarth contributed the drawings. Forrest tells us how they put a chair in the street at Queensborough, where Hogarth sketched, gathering a 'great Many Men Women and Children ab.* him to see his performance'. To make the pictures a true record of the group, if not the

65 'Breakfast', from the *Peregrination* (1732)

225

scene, Hogarth included himself. In this scene, he is talking to the sailors in the street; in another, he showed himself sketching the morning at the Nagg's Head, where, Forrest reports, they had been grievously bitten by gnats all night, but 'had our Shoes Clean'd, were Shav'd and had our Wigg's Flower'd by a Fisherman in his Boots and Shock Hair without Coat or waistcoat'. Hogarth also appears in Scott's drawings, a diminutive figure balancing on oars to get into a boat, or gesturing towards a castle.

The two artists both drew tombs in Minster church, Scott choosing 'the Spanish Embassador' and Hogarth a hero of local legend, Lord Shorland. This Elizabethan noble had ordered a priest who had refused to bury a man without fees to be buried alive himself. Panicking at his act, Shorland wrote a petition and made his horse swim across the channel to the Nore, where the Queen was inspecting the Armada fleet. After receiving her pardon he was carried back to Sheppey by his brave horse through heavy seas, but when he landed an old crone prophesied that though 'the Horse had then saved his Life, he would be the cause of his Death'. Shorland promptly slew his steed. Much later, walking on the beach, he kicked the skull – and died of a 'mortified toe'.

Hogarth's relish for this tale of priestly *and* aristocratic comeuppance is felt in his sketch of the noseless knight, his feet resting on a human skull beside a grinning horse-head. But his iconoclasm shows most clearly in the emblematic head and tail pieces he drew for the book: Mr Somebody and Mr Nobody. 'Somebody' is a torso clutching a boat's mast, with a ruined keep and fallen column, emblems of the empty antiquarian quest. 'Nobody' is a Cheshire-Cat head, perched on crossed oars. He grins broadly above his little legs, from which hang the essential equipment for the good life – knife, fork, spoon, bottle and glass. Odd as they look, these drawings would have been well understood in Hogarth's day when Somebody and Nobody were staples of folk myth.[13] The cunning Nobody was as ancient as Homer and could change his shape from saint and mythic hero ('Nobody' lives for ever, slays the dragon, sees God) to sinner and scapegoat (Who did it? – Nobody). In English chapbooks, plays, woodcuts and satires, this tattered figure was also the common people, put upon by the fat-bellied Somebody. Hogarth gave him the last laugh.

What did Jane say when Hogarth reappeared late that Saturday afternoon at the end of May in 1732, with his shirts to wash and boots to clean? No one knows. She is the invisible woman in the house, glimpsed only through her husband's portraits, silent until after his death. This is not to say that they

226

66 Frontispiece, 'Somebody'

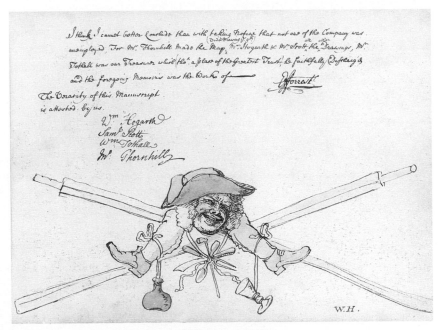

67 Tailpiece, 'Nobody'

weren't happy, just that Hogarth, like many men of his day and his milieu, spent more of his leisure time out of the house than in it – at the coffee house, the tavern, the club. And these gatherings were chiefly male; if women were present they were not considered to be on the same level as the wives and daughters left at home. They were serving girls, stall-holders, actresses, prostitutes, viewed with affection as well as ribaldry. The public worlds of men and women were not rigidly separated; women conducted trades and the sexes mixed and mingled in shop and street, church and theatre, pleasure-garden and salon. Yet there were separate spheres just the same, and within these spheres the 'somebodies' – at least in official eyes – were usually the men.

As autumn drew in, the (male) nobodies were out on the London streets. The previous year, congratulating himself on deals with Spain and Austria which left France isolated, Walpole had reduced the land tax so hated by the independent 'country' members. To recoup the lost revenue he increased excise tax instead. In February 1732 he brought back the tax on salt (removed only two years before), an action attacked as an assault on the poor and on the merchants. Tempers calmed when summer came, bringing the parliamentary recess, but by autumn it was clear that the salt tax was just a first step. It provided only a third of the income Walpole needed and now he announced a new plan, to make the tax on wine and tobacco into a general 'inland' excise, charging duties at the point of sale rather than on import. In response, the city and the country erupted with plots, petitions and marching mobs, and Walpole was pilloried in ballads and broadsheets, pamphlets and prints.

The issue was not so much wine and tobacco themselves as the vaunted liberty of the free-born Englishman. Smuggling was almost an Englishman's right (Walpole himself had brought dark cargoes of wine up the Thames) and the excise-man was a feared bogeyman. Since the seventeenth century, excise duties had been hated because they gave the officers wide powers of search and increased the jurisdiction and summary power of magistrates and commissioners. They were seen as threatening a man's freedom in his own home, and diluting the right to trial by jury. Excise was thus damned as a 'foreign' tax, halfway to the absolutism, standing armies and popish slavery imposed on clog-wearing Continental peasants.

A new print and pamphlet war started, on now accepted lines, as *The Craftsman* pointed out:

'When the People find themselves generally aggreived, They are apt to manifest their Resentment in satyrical Ballads, Allegories, and ironical Points of low Wit. They sometimes go farther, and break out in hieroglyphical

228

Expressions of their Anger against the *Person*, who they consider to be the Projector of any Injury done, or intended to be done them'.[14]

The print the writer referred to showed a many-headed dragon driving a chariot in which sat 'a very portly Person, receiving prodigious sums of gold' spewed into his lap by the dragon. The song beneath the woodcut hurled a defiant warning:

> See this Dragon, EXCISE,
> Has Ten Thousand Eyes,
> And Five Thousand Mouths to devour us,
> A Sting and sharp Claws,
> With wide-gaping Jaws,
> And a Belly as big as a Store-house.
> *Horse, Foote and Dragoons,*
> *Battalions, Platoons,*
> *Excise, Wooden Shoes and no Jury*
> *Then Taxes increasing,*
> *While Traffick is ceasing,*
> *Would put all this Land in a Fury.*[15]

One enterprising trader imported a shipload of clogs (claiming they were French, not Dutch) and handed them to the mob to carry through the streets on staves. In an 'epidemic madness', excise was painted in ever more hideous colours. People began to believe:

'that food, and raiment, and all the necessaries of life were to be taxed; that armies of excise officers were to come into any house at any time they pleased; that our liberties were at an end, trade going to be ruined, Magna Carta over-turned, all property destroyed, the Crown made absolute, and Parliaments themselves no longer to be called'.[16]

In London the guilds of the vintners, brewers, grocers and tobacconists of London were united in their opposition. On 22 December 1732, tradesmen gathered in force at the Swan Tavern in Cornhill, and passed a forthright resolution 'That the Merchants, Traders, and Citizens here present will act with utmost unanaimity, and by all dutiful and lawful means, strenuously oppose any new excise'.[17]

In the week leading up to this declaration Hogarth, very cleverly, did not produce a 'hieroglyphical Expression' of the people's anger, as he would have done a decade ago. Instead he launched a subscription for the print of

229

Think not to find one meant Resemblance there
He lash the Vices but the Persons spare

A MIDNIGHT MODDERN CONVERSATION
W.m Hogarth Inv.t Pinx.t & Sculp.t

Prints should be prizd as Authors should be read
Who sharply smile prevailing Folly dead

68 *A Midnight Modern Conversation* (1733)

A Midnight Modern Conversation, with its scene of lusty English 'freedom', its twenty-three empty wine bottles and plentiful pipes. He turned his social satire into double-edged political satire, laughing at both sides, consumer and controller, showing his 'politician' with both the pro-Walpole *London Journal* and the opposition *Craftsman* tucked into his coat pocket. His caption, too, made the satire general, not personal:

> Think not to find one *meant Resemblance* there
> We lash the *Vices* but the *Persons* spare –
> *Prints* should be *prizd* as *Authors* should be *read*
> Who sharply smile prevailing Folly dead.

With as much luck as judgement Hogarth promised his subscribers that this print would be ready for 1 March 1733. This turned out to be the month when the Excise Bill finally came before the Commons: in front of a packed house, Walpole's long, determined speech met with furious ripostes. On

230

10 April, when he spurned a petition from the City of London, apprentices rioted, bonfires blazed through the night and Walpole and the Queen were burned in effigy. Next day, on the second reading, Walpole proposed a tactical retreat, postponing the Bill for two months. Refusing to leave the Commons by a back way, he dived into the crowd through a lane of special constables and in the flurry,

'there was such a jostling and struggling, that had anybody fallen down they must inevitably have been trampled to death. The oaken sticks and constables' staffs were so flippant over the heads of friends and enemies, without any possibility of distinction, that many blows were given and received at random.'[18]

The battles continued until June on the streets, in the press, in the Commons and Lords. And all the time, among the mass of overtly anti-Walpole prints, Hogarth's booze- and smoke-filled conversation sold on, with a train of piracies and copies on fan mounts, snuffboxes and mugs.

In the Excise riots of April 1733 another person was burned in effigy alongside Walpole and the Queen, the figure of a twenty-five-year-old murderess, Sarah Malcolm.[19] This was typical of the eclectic iconography of protest, the fusing of different current scandals, and also of the obsession with the 'unnatural' – the supposed protectors of the nation becoming its dragon-like 'devourers', the beautiful maiden becoming a cold killer. Women, like men, could rise out of the anonymous mass, and make themselves visible, through spectacle, scandal and crime. And just before the issue of *A Modern Midnight Conversation*, Hogarth and Thornhill were linked in a highly commercial venture involving Sarah Malcolm.

The facts were not in doubt. In Mitre Court, Fleet Street, on 4 February, Sarah Malcolm had strangled an eighty-year old widow, Mrs Lydia Duncombe, and her companion, Elizabeth Harrison, and had cut the throat of their seventeen-year-old maid, Anne Price. Sarah's master, or neighbour (accounts vary), informed on her when he uncovered a silver tankard and a blood-stained apron and shift, and the matter was settled when she was found with 45 guineas hidden beneath her cap. At first she tried to save herself by blaming three accomplices, but her story was not believed and she was sent to await execution in Newgate, where she received the full attention of the press and pamphleteers.

Sarah was only twenty-two, and her brutality and youth fascinated the public as if she were the villainess of a popular tragedy. At her trial she had scandalized the court by asking witnesses to speak up and by loudly declaring that the blood on her shift came from menstruation, not murder. After her conviction she caused further sensation by suddenly declaring herself a Roman Catholic, and ordering a shroud (and a pair of drawers) for her hanging. On 7 March, denying her guilt to the end, Sarah Malcolm walked to a gibbet that had been specially built facing Mitre Court, the scene of her crime. She appeared in style, made up for her final exit, 'neatly dressed in a crape mourning hood, holding up her head in the cart with an air, and looking as if she was painted, which some did not scruple to affirm'.[20] Fleet Street was packed, scaffolds for spectators collapsed, arms and legs were broken. A Mrs Strangways, who lived in the street, was allegedly swept over to a neighbour opposite across the heads of the crowd without once touching the ground, so great was the crush. When Sarah's body was taken down and laid out at the undertakers, crowds paid to see it, 'among the rest a gentleman in deep mourning, who kissed her, and gave the people half a crown'. From a nobody, a young woman who made beds for the lawyers in the Temple, Sarah swung into history. Her body was dissected, and her skeleton, in a glass case, was given to the Cambridge Botanic Gardens.[21]

Two days before Sarah's death, Thornhill and Hogarth paid her a visit. From his sketches, Hogarth produced both a portrait and a print. After his pictures of the harlot, a portrait of a woman-murderer by 'the ingenious Mr Hogarth' was news in itself. A day after Sarah's hanging, his visit was reported in *The Craftsman* and *Daily Advertiser* and he then placed his own advertisements, saying the prints would be ready in two days, by Saturday, 10 March. This was an extremely quick turnaround, showing a ruthless eagerness to strike while the iron was hot – or the corpse still warm.

Sarah had received the two artists with cheeks red-rouged for her portrait and the story that comes down has Hogarth turning to Thornhill: 'this woman (he said) by her features is capable of anything'. The face, to him, still expressed the inner soul. His painting showed a heavy, sharp-faced woman leaning on the table, resting on those arms that had been strong enough to strangle two, with her rosary in front of her. In the print the beads have gone, and the air of imitation, of dignity and sinister politeness is stronger. It is a remarkable image, the dangerous thin-lipped face above the powerful frame: 'A Lady Macbeth in low-life', John Ireland called her.[22]

Hogarth's alliance with his father-in-law in this venture shows how closely they were working together again, but with a rather different balance of roles from the old days, when Sir James made his sketch of Jack Sheppard and Hogarth followed in his wake. Hogarth was still, however, very much his

69 *Sarah Malcolm* (1732)

father-in-law's supporter and admirer – Thornhill's feud with the Palladians was also his own – and once they were reconciled he was drawn firmly back into the old fights and factions of Thornhill v. Kent, the drinking and dinners and late-night plots. One salvo against Kent and Burlington had been fired in 1731, with a print called *Burlington Gate*, showing Kent directing the work while a small figure splattered whitewash on other rival patrons passing by, the Dukes of Chandos and Buckingham. (The whitewasher was recognizably a caricature of Pope, who had just praised Burlington in his *Moral Essay: On the Use of Riches*.) Many people, including Vertue, were convinced that this print was by Hogarth and in 1732 Kent had him in his sights.

The Thornhill camp was determined not to give in easily. Thornhill's own star had long been in decline and he was reduced to pottering at Hampton Court over his Raphael copies. But his son John was now Serjeant-Painter and in 1733 it looked as if his son-in-law Hogarth was also on the brink of becoming a painter to the Royals. He was still working on the *Scene from the Indian Emperor*, which included the Royal children. This led first to a separate portrait of the young Duke of Cumberland and then to the suggestion that he might paint a picture of the Royal Family as a group. As a start, he made two small oil sketches for conversation pictures, with the same

233

composition set against indoor and outdoor backgrounds.[23] But all the time, his heart was set on something grander and more prestigious. He wanted to paint the wedding of the Princess Royal and the Prince of Orange, which was announced in May 1733 and planned for the autumn.

Hogarth may well have seen a good possibility here for a popular print as well as a prestigious painting, since this marriage fascinated the Town even more than most royal weddings. For one thing, the Prince himself was known to be deformed – he was extremely small, with a humped back and notoriously foul breath – so the prospect had a certain freak-show allure. And although the alliance was greeted with public cheers as a noble sacrifice on the part of the Princess Royal, giving herself to this unprepossessing frog-prince to strengthen the certainty of a Protestant succession, privately it was rumoured to be a desperate last resort. Europe held no other possible suitors so the Princess had to choose 'between a husband and no husband . . . and whether she would go to bed to this piece of deformity in Holland, or die an ancient maid immured in her royal convent at St James's'.[24] The wedding was also known to be a bone of contention between Walpole and the King, who was suspicious of the ambitions of the House of Orange and who behaved with chilling rudeness when the bridegroom arrived in November. When the Prince fell dangerously ill and the wedding was postponed, none of the Royal Family went to see him. The King thought it beneath his dignity, 'and the rest, whatever they thought, were not allowed to do it'.[25]

The Prince's open friendliness, meanwhile, had won the hearts of Londoners, who could not care less about his looks. If Hogarth could make a print of the wedding it would certainly sell fast on the back of curiosity, scandal-mongering and partisanship. In October, before the Prince's illness caused the wedding to be postponed, Hogarth made his move. He made a careful, considered approach to Caroline, either through a lady-in-waiting (as Vertue suggests) or (as later critics have thought) through Lord Hervey, who was Master of Ceremonies for the wedding. First, Hogarth said, he needed to sketch the inside of the French Chapel next to St James's Palace, now packed with carpenters and craftsmen erecting the decorations and the scaffolding for guests. The Queen agreed to this and to the subsequent painting of the marriage. But when Hogarth reached the chapel and settled himself to draw, he was immediately asked to stop, on the instructions of the Master Carpenter – none other than William Kent. Indignantly, he stood his ground and quoted the Queen's permission but his protest was fruitless. He was ordered out by the Lord Chamberlain himself, the Duke of Grafton – Burlington's son-in-law and Kent's patron.

Vertue tells the story with zest, as one might expect, explaining that the Queen slid out of responsibility by agreeing that she had given permission,

'but not reflecting it might be of use or advantage to Mr Kent, which she would^{nt} interfear with, or anything to his profitt. So that M^r. Hogarth complains heavily. not only of this usage but of another, he had some time ago begun a picture of all the Royal family in one peice by order the Sketch being made. & the P. William the Duke had sat to him for one. this also has been stopt. so that he can't proceed.^{26}

Kent had won. The doors of opportunity were slammed in Hogarth's face. These were 'sad Mortifications to an Ingenious Man', said Vertue, but Hogarth was paying for those earlier caricatures which had annoyed Kent, diverted the Town, and rebounded on him 'when he least thought on it'. He was paying, too, for his ties with Thornhill, who was identified with 'interest & spirit of opposition'. It was a double blow, Vertue added, since Hogarth had by now 'lost the advantage in portraiture and owned he had no employment that way'. Instead he had to draw encouragement from his subscriptions for his prints, 'those designs of inventions he does. – this prodigious genious of invention characters likenes. so ready is beyond all others'.

When Hervey eventually led the stately procession to the wedding of the Prince and Princess in March 1734, there were great public celebrations. Bonfires flared, church bells rang and guns were fired. The great Somebodies of the land gathered in the chapel, which was decorated with velvets, gold and silver tissue, fringes, tassels, gilt lustres and sconces. All this was the creation and the preserve of William Kent, while William Hogarth remained shut out, grinding his teeth. From now on the little drawings he had placed at the head and tail of the *Peregrination* became emblems of his choice as an artist. In part he had chosen, and in part he was pushed, but by 1734 it was clear that for the time being, at least, it was with the Nobodies, the public not the patron, that his best chances lay.

12

The Fair and the Rake

Blasted! Blasted! so many hopes of gain:
Hundreds of sober merchants are insane;
Widows have sold their mourning clothes to eat;
Herds of pale orphans forage in the street;
Many a Duchess, divested of gems,
Has crossed the dread Styx by way of the Thames.
O stricken, take heart in placing the blame –
Rakewell. Rakewell. Ruin. Disaster. Shame.

W. H. AUDEN, Libretto for *The Rake's Progress*

ONCE HE DECIDED to gamble on the wider public, Hogarth worked hard to ensure that the odds were in his favour. By 1733 he was engraving his own work as standard policy, partly, as he said in connnection with *A Midnight Modern Conversation*, to 'preserve his Property therein and prevent the Printsellers from graving base Copies to his Prejudice',[1] but also to get the maximum revenue, cutting out the engraver's costs and keeping the plate for future impressions. All that was left for him to gain complete control was to bypass the middleman. One way of doing this was to sell wholly by subscription, as he did with the *Harlot* and intended to do at first with the *A Midnight's Modern Conversation*, announcing that the painting and print could both be seen 'next Door to the New Play-house in Covent Garden Piazza, where Subscriptions are taken in'.[2] But subscription was frustratingly limited when there was such a large potential market, so in January 1733 he added another stage, announcing that after the five-shilling subscription was fulfilled, the print could be bought directly, for 'three Half-crowns'.[3]

By March, when he published *Sarah Malcolm*, he seems to have made that print quickly from the original sketch, turning immediately to the broadest, cheapest audience possible. The sixpenny prints were sold at Regnier's in Newport Street and other print shops. But though this was wide-scale trading, purchasers still had to go to the printseller to buy their copies, and the printseller's margin still cut into Hogarth's own profits. The answer was to sell

236

them himself. Yet he could hardly sell prints from his father-in-law's back door, lowering the tone of the former painter to the Royal Family. It was clear that he needed a shop of his own, and that summer he established one.

On May Day 1733 Jonathan Tyers wrote to Hogarth from Vauxhall, addressing his letter to 'Leicester Fields'.[4] By the previous autumn, while Excise riots were convulsing the town, Hogarth and Jane had moved into a house in this wide city space which more refined residents were beginning to call 'Leicester Square'. It certainly looked dignified, a long rectangle with a garden of grass and trees and gravelled walks in the centre and with Leicester House, refuge of the Hanoverian princes, stretching across its northern side. But although there were some fine houses, it never quite achieved the height of smartness of the new squares to the west. Leicester House itself had a meagre garden at the back, and was fronted not by fine walls and gates, but by four ramshackle wooden lock-up shops. Although the square was quiet it remained, like so much Hogarth territory, uneasily balanced between two worlds.

The occupants were always trying to improve it and, in 1737, *The Craftsman* announced that the square was going to be 'fitted up in a very elegant Manner', with a new wall and rails, and a 'Bason' in the middle, like

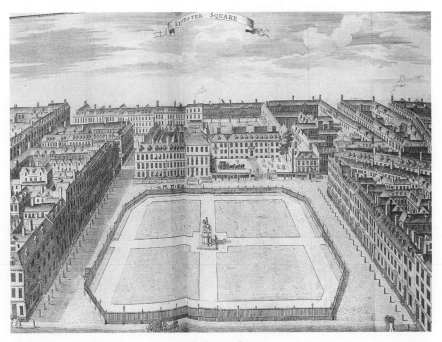

70 Leicester Square

237

Lincoln's Inn Fields. A decade later the gardens acquired the statue of George I on horseback, saved from the Duke of Chandos's gardens, when his house, Canons, was pulled down. But the square's stylishness was still marred by the busy trading streets around it, the ruffians round the livery stables and the horse-dealers drawn by the Royal Mews to the south. On its western side lay the inns and theatres and puppet shows of the dusty Haymarket. Ragged boys used the open space to play at 'chuck' and, ironically for such a bull-headed patriot as Hogarth, it had a slightly foreign air. French Camisards, German music teachers and Italian opera-singers lived here. This aura lingered on into the nineteenth century, when local residents complained that the long terraces where Newton, Hogarth and later Reynolds had lived were now rows of hotels with foreign names, where notices proclaimed 'table d'hôte à cinq heures' and moustachioed loungers breathed garlic and tobacco.[5]

Hogarth himself had probably played chuck in the square when he was an apprentice, working in Blue Cross Street. He had come a long way since those days, and he meant to show it, but he intended to assert that he was still a trader as well. His tall terraced house, which he took over from a Lady Howard, was the third from the end in the south-east corner, and over the door he hung a shop sign, flouting the residential calm. His sign was a bust of Van Dyck, the great adopted English artist, who, Hogarth wrote later, turned aside from the potential 'grossness' of Rubens, his master, and 'imitated Nature just as it chanced to present itself'.[6] Van Dyck's shadow lay long over English painting and Hogarth's use of his image was both a mark of admiration and a flamboyant claim. He carved the head himself out of 'several thicknesses of cork compacted together' and gilded it lavishly, blazoning the shop's importance as a source of *English* art.[7] From now on the Golden Head would be his sign.

Soon he built a painting room behind the house to get the best northern light. He now had a smarter place to display his work, which would hang in the rooms downstairs, facing the square, with a curved bow window at the back. Here prospective purchasers could come and look at the new paintings and clients could wait for sittings and even choose a 'posture', feeling suitably grand. If he wanted to progress, an artist had to have a genteel establishment, even though, as one portrait painter later complained, the rent was 'a burthen, under which the demands of our profession compel us, quarterly, to groan'.[8] Jane and William lived on the floor above, their cook scurrying up from the basement with dishes, and retreating at night, with the manservant and maid, to rooms under the sloping roof.

The Hogarths' house was smart enough for Sir James and Lady Thornhill to visit but Hogarth had no intention of leaving his own relatively humble family entirely behind. Soon after he settled in, his mother and sisters came to live near him, renting lodgings in Cranbourn Street just north of Leicester Fields. Anne and Mary Hogarth were now in their forties and looked unlikely to marry. They might have carried on their business here, as there was a big cloth warehouse in the street, selling all the materials they had advertised in Long Lane, cambrics and muslins, Irish linen and striped hollands.[9] The alley near by was later known as the 'great bonnet mart' of London, where a pretty young woman was posted at every door, enticing customers into the shop – an unfashionable bonnet would be spotted from one end of the court to the other, and the girls would swoop on the derided victim with cries of ridicule.[10]

Cranbourn Street was where Ellis Gamble had run his shop, and in St Martin's Court, which joined crookedly between here and St Martin's Lane, a certain 'M. Gamble' was in business at the Golden Fan. Among the wares he was advertising at the beginning of the year when the Hogarths moved into the Fields were 'The Church of England Fan', price 2s., and 'a new edition of the Harlot's Progress in Fans, or singly to frame'.[11] By the autumn, his stock also included the

'new EXCISE FAVORS, proper for all gentleman and Ladies to wear upon my Lord Mayors Day, with this present Lord Mayor's picture upon them, and this motto:
'Barber behold, congratulate his Fate,
Who trimm'd the City, and who shave'd the State.'

*

In early October 1733 when he was still angling for Court patronage and the chance to paint the royal wedding, Hogarth also announced his next major commercial project. 'Mr Hogarth', stated the *Daily Advertiser*, was 'now engraving nine Copper Plates from Pictures of his own Painting, one of which represents the humours of a Fair; the other eight the Progress of a Rake.' Subscriptions would be taken at 'the Golden Head in Leicester Fields, where the Pictures are to be seen'.[12]

The Rake was a natural sequel to the Harlot. The two were often paired in plays and broadsheets, criminal lives and cartoons, and in the original Italian pictorial story cycles. In 1732 the versifier of *The Harlot's Progress or, The Humours of Drury Lane* had followed it up almost automatically with *The Rake's Progress; or The Humours of St James's*. Rakes, like harlots, gave an easy opportunity to link the glitter of the fashionable salons with the sleazy underworld, their story a modern version of the prodigal son with a bitter

239

ending. But by adding a separate print to his series – the world of the fair – Hogarth enlarged and complicated his message.

Writers on Hogarth tend to place *The Fair* (later called *Southwark Fair*) and *A Rake's Progress* in separate groups, classifying the former among Hogarth's 'city scenes', unrelated to the modern moral histories. And at first, as the eye moves from the holiday crowd in the open air to the intense private story of Tom Rakewell, the two do seem completely opposed. Yet the drama of Hogarth's first progress had already been adopted by the London fairs. In 1732, Lee and Harper's booth at the lower end of Mermaid Court in Southwark was showing Theophilus Cibber's pantomime *The Harlot's Progress*, while, not far away, Yeates's booth was staging a ballad opera of the Harlot.[13] The individual story grew from a face in the crowd, and returned to it again.

Hogarth advertised his prints of the fairground and the Rake together for a reason, transposing the same themes in public and private spheres: dress and show; representation and reality; money and love; the dangerous blurring of fantasy and life. The single scene and the series both play on the dangers of acting and imitation, showing nobodies dressed up to be somebodies – the strolling players with their grand tragedies and high-flown fantasies, and the sad young man aspiring to be a Man of the Town. They are complementary, in form and in substance; one being a single scene with several stories, and the other a single story with several scenes. The overlapping narratives of *Southwark Fair* show the world of the common people, the bustle of crowds and the glow of shared excitement; the single story-line of *A Rake's Progress* explores the doomed loneliness of affectation, the hollow shell of the polite. The juxtaposition of the two makes a statement about politics and values, popular and artistic, and the fate of the individual in the throng.

When he announced his new proposal Hogarth used *The Laughing Audience* for his subscription ticket, with its divisions between the fashionable beaux on the top level ignoring the stage and turning their attention to the orange-seller, the bored connoisseur in the centre looking down his nose, and the ordinary folk 'below' them roaring with enjoyment at the play. *The Fair* belongs to those ordinary people. Far larger than the paintings, or the prints of the *Progresses*, *The Fair* represented a considerable technical achievement, both in painting and engraving. (Although, with so much detail, Hogarth occasionally gave up redrawing individual figures for the reversal needed for the print: clothes button up the wrong way and the mounted prize-fighter is a left-handed swordsman.)

The fair bursts with movement and incident. But although it looks like a documentary of chaos it is brought together formally by its flow of curving lines, and conceptually by its numerous variations on choice and the 'fall'. In every corner we find wild ambitions and sudden reversals. This, as W. H. Auden and Chester Kallman recognized in their libretto for Stravinsky's opera, is also the story of the Rake, and of every speculator who believes he can dodge reality because the wheel of fate will spin for him:

'Here I stand, my constitution sound, my frame not ill-favoured, my wit ready, my heart light. *I* play the industrious apprentice in the copybook? *I* submit to the drudge's yoke? *I* slave through a lifetime to enrich others, and then be thrown away like a gnawed bone? Not *I*! Have not grave doctors assured us that good works are of no avail for Heaven predestines all? In my fashion, I may profess myself of their party and herewith entrust myself to Fortune.'[14]

In painting his Southwark scene, Hogarth staged a modern morality play, a Vanity Fair, a more genial acting out of the fantasies of the South Sea Bubble

71 *Southwark Fair* (1732)

241

but one that could be fatal none the less. Men cannot fly. In October 1732 a 'flying man' had actually died when his rope went slack while he was swinging down from Greenwich Church.[15] Here he dangles precariously from his rope, attached to the steeple of St George's in The Borough, Southwark. Will he fall – or be saved? Either way, he belongs to a fallen universe. One booth has a showcloth for *The Old Creation of the World*, with a picture of the Fall above the favourite 'Punch's Opera': on stage Punch's horse picks Harlequin's pocket. The church is almost blocked out by the sign for Settle's *Fall of Troy*, with actors and actresses sitting on the scaffold below it (including a Priest and Scaramouch).[16] Another rope-dancer is swinging across to more booths, where the eight-foot German giant Maximilian Muller will appear.[17] To one side, a lantern promises *The Fall of Bajazet*, and here the whole raised stage is toppling over, tumbling its richly costumed actors on to a china stall below while a monkey clings desperately to the scaffolding, like a drowning sailor to a spar.

This is the topical focus of the print. The showcloth above the collapsing stage is a reverse copy of a print made in early July by Jack Laguerre, depicting *The Stage Mutiny* that had provided rich London gossip all summer. In 1732 Robert Wilks, one of the managers of Drury Lane, had died, and the following spring Colley Cibber sold his share of the patent for a princely sum to the unpopular new manager John Highmore. In protest, a rebel group of actors defected to the Haymarket, led by Cibber's son Theophilus, who felt deprived of his 'birthright' – thus putting an abrupt stop, incidentally, to Henry Fielding's most successful season yet, when six of his comedies were running in London theatres. Laguerre could mock both sides with the freedom of one who painted scenes for the rival Rich, at Covent Garden. And Rich milked the quarrel with a ballad opera, *The Stage-Mutineers: or, a Play-House to be Lett*, in which Fielding was satirized as the confident, opinionated Crambo, complaining that the dispute 'has ended very unhappily for the Town and me, for now Igad the Town will lose its Entertainment and I my Benefit'.[18]

Hogarth's London audience, avid playgoers and gossips, could 'read' the showcloth even in miniature. They could recognize the actors Theophilus Cibber as Pistol and Harper as Falstaff, chuckle at the banner for 'Liberty and Property', and recognize the setting as the Rose Tavern. Those in the know could even identify the figure with the paint pot as John Ellys, who acted for Wilks's widow in managing the theatre. This print within a print highlighted suggestions of other mutinies spread through Hogarth's scene. The kingly theme of Bajazet might remind people of Prince Frederick's defiance of his father. Punch's opera might hint at operatic rebellions – at Frederick's sponsorship of a new company at Lincoln's Inn Fields, which had left the troupe of the King's favourite, Handel, playing to an empty Haymarket. The fire-eating quack in the centre might warn of false cures in the state, as of the body. The grim figure of James Figg sitting on his blind horse could suggest that old political prize-fighters too should be wary of challengers. The rickety platform and slithering actors could recall Walpole's trouble with bishops and Dissenters over toleration, or with merchants and mobs over Excise. Would this conjuror, this quack, this bruiser, this over-reaching rope-dancer finally misjudge his balance? Would he crash to the ground like the flying man in the elections of 1734?

People could pore over and argue about every corner of the picture, but its lasting appeal lay in the way Hogarth brought all the worlds of the Fair together. He overturned time, setting the squabbling Drury Lane actors next to the showmen of his childhood, like Fawkes, who had died in 1731, but who appears here with the waxworks of the 'whole Court of France' advertised in 1733. He defied space, including shows like *Bajazet* from that summer's Bartholomew Fair. He put stage high-life next to street low-life and blended realism with allegory, setting the fate of Troy and the expulsion from Eden against the little falls of daily life like picked pockets and arrests for debt. Yet in the middle of this tumbling press of humanity with its fire-eaters, bagpipe-players and battered broad-sword fighters, there is a moment of magic. The little black trumpeter sounds his horn and the drummer girl, caught in a shaft of light, steps gracefully forward and touches her drum.

After he painted *Southwark Fair*, there were stories that the drummeress advertising the troupe of players stepped out of Hogarth's own life. Giving her husband a heroic role, Jane told Samuel Ireland that 'passing through the fair, on seeing the master of the company strike her and otherwise use her ill, he took her part and gave the fellow a violent drubbing'.[19] Whether 'this chastisement arose from a liking to her person or respect for her sex we know not', continued Ireland, 'but it is certain that she was the kind of woman for which he entertained a strong partiality'. It is true that the drummeress embodied an ideal type for Hogarth, the common woman of the people made beautiful by art, her own and his. He drew variations on this woman, still centres of unexpected power, throughout the 1730s, tantalizing like Moll Hackabout or murderous like Sarah Malcolm, beautiful and talented or plain and stoical – like loyal Sarah Young, hovering in the background of *A Rake's Progress*.

Turning to the first small painting of *A Rake's Progress* from the large, packed canvas of *Southwark Fair* (nearly 4 by 5 feet) is like putting a telescope to one

243

of the figures in the crowd, focusing in, further and further, to pick out one particular fall from grace. Contemporary moralists held rakes up as examples of egotism, of pleasure bought at the expense of responsibility, and of danger to others, especially women. In common understanding a rake was an aristo-crat, a cold hedonist, whose cult of pleasure was equalled by a chilly disdain, a brutal sensualist rather than a man of passion. But Hogarth's Tom Rakewell is no Lovelace, no dashing blade, conquering fashion, decoying women and terrorizing the town with nonchalant, demonic arrogance. He is a young bourgeois, first seen as a trembling youth with a fresh face haloed in curls, attractive, open, innocent – and weak. Like Moll, Tom is less a seducer than an outsider who is himself seduced, ruined and killed by the city. He imitates the rakes but can never be one of them, not because his money runs out but because at every stage he is also shown as a man of feeling, who rails against fate and descends into madness. In the fiery dark of the city, aspiring to beauty but sinking into filth, Tom Rakewell could even be seen as a fallen 'flying man', a prototype of the Romantic hero.

Although he follows a man's path, buying art, fighting, gambling and whoring, to a large extent Tom is a curiously passive, feminine figure. In Hogarth's hands, the situation of his Harlot and Rake have shadowy similarities; most of all, they are dangers to themselves. The higher Tom aims and the more he spends, the faster and deeper he falls, spiralling inexorably from debt to the desperate remedies of loveless marriage and hopeless gambling, down to the prison and the madhouse floor. This reads like another brusque moral tale of the wages of sin, the hardworking bourgeois taking puritan revenge on the idle rich. But Hogarth's morality is more intricate, questioning how far people are responsible for their fate and how far they are the victims of others. In the first scene, the father's notebook, lying open on the floor, notes, '1721 May 1 my son Tom came down from Oxford', but beneath this news old Rakewell has also written '5th, Put of my bad shilling'. The miser may have foisted his dud coins on others, but now his own 'bad penny' has turned up. This follows an old convention of procedure by contraries – the mean father followed by the spendthrift heir – and yet we also see Tom as a newcomer to the city being measured by others for their use (like Moll in the inn-yard being eyed by the bawd and Charteris). In this first scene, the lawyer scoops up loose change behind his back. By his side, the tailor holds a tape-measure to his thigh: the scissors Moll carried, as if to snip vainly at the Gordian knot of fate, are in the tailor's hands.

Tom has inherited a fortune but he is also the impoverished heir of a parent's neglect. The portrait above shows Tom's father 'raking' it in; and as

72 *A Rake's Progress* (1735), plate 1, 'The Young Heir Takes Possession'

the workman tacks the mourning drapes to the rotten woodwork, hoarded coins tumble from the ceiling, on to a floor littered with mortgages, leases and 'India bonds'. There is no warmth here. The empty grate and hold-all for candle-ends show how the old man scrimps on heat and light, shivering in the dark in his old coat, which hangs behind the door, and his fur hat, still on the mantelpiece. (When he revised the plate Hogarth drove the point home, including a Bible with its leather binding hacked out to sole the old man's shoes.) His deformity was deeper than the lameness for which he needed the crutches now leaning against the wall. He was also an emotional cripple who gave his son no nourishment but gold, a hard and fatal metal, leaving

245

him like the starving cat, sniffing vainly for food at a chest stuffed with coins.

Yet Tom is a predator as well as a victim. Whereas, in the first *Progress*, Colonel Charteris filled the inn-yard doorway (Moll's route 'in' to society and its vices), here Tom is already the insider – *his* doorway frames a weeping country girl holding a wedding ring, while her angry mother carries an apronful of letters and false promises. But Sarah Young, the seduced girl, is far from an insignificant nobody. Out of mind and sight while Tom is surrounded by sycophants or passing out in a brothel, she appears again as soon as he is down on his luck, finding money when he is arrested, trying to stop his marriage, collapsing at his suffering in the Fleet and comforting him in Bedlam. Indeed in the paintings, as compared to the reversed images of the prints, Sarah seems to frame the whole story. Her weeping figure on the left of the first painting is the first form we see, and the same figure, with her handkerchief to her eyes, is also the last, as she kneels beside Tom's collapsed body on the right of the final picture. At the beginning she weeps for herself; at the end she weeps for him.

Sarah may be a fool to stick so loyally to this heartless loser, but she is also a nobody who gains dignity by suffering selflessly for love. Tom, by contrast, like his father before him, makes the mistake of thinking that cash can replace love. From the moment he tries to buy off the pregnant Sarah we know that he is doomed. Hogarth believed that individual natures were formed by upbringing, and their expectations by society, but he never accepted that this deprived them of freedom altogether. Moll is shown poised between the dark-walled world of the bawd and the open sky above the city washerwoman; Tom is poised between his money chests and Sarah Young, carrying his child. Both make their choice.

Tom's life is as full of fantasy as Southwark fairground. That, too, is a highly theatrical work, but at the fair the actors can take their costumes off at the end of the day, the jugglers and conjurors pack their bags, and the fairgoers go back to their homes. Tom cannot stop his act. His desires are horrifyingly woven in to the furniture and fabric of his life. The expectations of the Town mould his fortunes just as his new clothes 'refashion' his form. In the next two plates, spending his money, he tries to fill the lonely vacuum of his childhood with the false friends of fashion and the diseased charms of whores. Yet (unlike Moll with her first lover), Tom *never* looks happy. Even when he thinks himself rich and free, he is somehow deprived and enslaved.

The second scene shows him, still in his nightcap, receiving a host of hangers-on at his morning levee. John Hoadly's verses for the print stressed the way that the spiritual poverty and loss of mental freedom illustrated here must lead to Tom's final fetters. His own wealth provides the chains:

73 Plate 2, 'Surrounded by Artists and Professors'

Prosperity, (with Harlot's smiles,
Most pleasing when she most beguiles,)
How soon, Sweet foe, can all thy Train
Of false, gay, frantick, loud & vain,
Enter the unprovided Mind,
And Memory in fetters bind;
Load faith and Love with golden chain,
And sprinkle Lethe o're the Brain!

This scene is the one in which Hogarth catered most to his gossipy, portrait-

247

hunting readers; he delayed finishing his paintings so that he could add more well-known figures in 1734. The outer room is crowded with tailors and milliners and poets with their offerings, while Tom holds court beneath a *Judgement of Paris* (another omen of false choice) foisted on him by the picture-dealers. The men clustered around him represent two different sides of the Rake's life, one being that of smart London salons and the other that of the 'bloods' who enjoy the old squierarchical pleasures of gaming cocks, racing, quarter-staff fighting and hunting. Tom is dabbling in all these, and winning at first, to judge by the rose bowl his jockey holds, but the solid English prize-fighter James Figg is being pushed into the background by a French fencing teacher. This was a portrait of Dubois, who died in May 1734 after a duel (oddly, with an Irishman of the same name), and Tom holds a note from 'a man-of-honour', a mercenary who will stand in if he has to fight a duel himself. Strains of violence underlie the outer show.

The fine (and expensive) taste of the Palladians is now shaping Tom's world: the man holding a plan is Charles Bridgeman, a landscape gardener beloved by the Burlingtonians, gardener to the Royal Family, adviser to Alexander Pope at Twickenham and famous for his introduction of the 'ha-ha', that hidden ditch between the smooth park and the wild country. The scene is the epitome of 'politeness', invisibly shielding culture from chaos. In the centre stands a smirking dancing master, pointing his well-shod toe, while a musician sits at a harpsichord marked 'I. Mahoan', (Joseph Mahoon, the maker of instruments for royalty). Tom is aiming high. In the painting, the music book bears the initials 'F.H.', for Frederic Handel, and the title makes it clear that this is the score of a new opera, *The Rape of the Sabines*. Discord is implied, not harmony, for Handel was currently engaged in a losing battle with the rival impresario and composer Nicola Antonio Porpora, who had just brought over the charismatic castrato Carlo Broschi, 'Farinelli'. And all aficionados would get the joke against opera in general when they saw that in the long roll of the cast list, flung over the musician's shoulder in the third and fourth states of the print, the parts of the 'pure' virgins were given to scandal-laden sopranos, while the four 'ravishers' were played by the rapacious Cuzzoni and the three castrati, Senesino, Carestino, and Farinelli.

Fashionable women collected Farinelli's portraits and busts, sent him love letters, screamed and fainted at his performances. Most famously, at one performance a rich patroness screamed the blasphemous tribute 'One God, One Farinelli' – and this is inscribed on the engraved title page of the poem that lies on the floor, 'dedicated to T. Rakewell Esq.', showing a portrait of the singer on his pedestal. There was something strange and powerful about the

248

sway Farinelli held over women by the sheer force of his art, and yet he was emasculated. He might look like an exploiter and a ravisher but his virility, like Tom's, had been sacrificed to the fashionable taste.

Tom, too, is a victim on the altar of fashion. He wins an illusory popularity among his parasites but he loses his integrity – and his money. And what of the people *not* in this picture, the Sarah Youngs, the poor creditors and the artists and builders and caterers and musicians who furnish these gilded amusements? In 1737 'Hercules MacSturdy', in a satire on Vauxhall pleasure-goers, was only one of those who pointed out that the indulgences of the rich (while in theory they fuelled the general economy) were all too often enjoyed at the expense of the poor, of the tradesmen with their bills unpaid, whose children starved in consequence. His indictment of aristocratic carelessness has echoes both of Tom and of Moll's rich benefactor:

> Here sits my Lord, with Vest of Gold emboss'd,
> And there his Taylor sighing for the Cost.
> One month will see him to the Prison sent
> Where, six months past, his Lordship's Butcher went . . .
> . . . No matter – tho he's in the Butchers Books,
> His Bills unpaid, not so his new French Cooks.
> Besides, my Lord, when he was to be paid,
> Had lost six hundred pounds at the Masquerade,
> Had given Farinelli fifty more
> And laid out twenty on a Monkey for his Whore![20]

Tom's bills, however, are catching up with him. In the scene in the Rose Tavern, he seems as impotent as the great castrato himself. He may have beaten some poor old watchman, whose lantern lies at his feet, but his sword hangs limply out of his scabbard. Even in this state he clings to marks of gentility, holding his glass just as the manuals of politeness decreed (the genteel held it by the stem, the uncouth by the bowl).[21] In this polite world turned upside-down the dancing master of the salon is replaced by the brisk, preoccupied posture woman, stripping to pose and gyrate on the huge platter that the porter Leathercoat is bringing through the door, with the candle she snuffs out obscenely in her dance, a mockery of sex. Here, too, there was a joke for up-to-date art lovers – in Tom's incapacitated, sprawling pose, with his legs at that curious angle, Hogarth took over a pose used by Watteau in his painting of *Antoine de la Roque*, an old soldier 'disabled' by a wound at Malplaquet, resting on a bank with a satyr and a group of curious wood nymphs peering from the background.[22] The print of this was engraved only

249

74 Plate 3, 'The Tavern Scene'

in 1734, while Hogarth was already working on his paintings. It was very new, very French, very clever. And the jest was taken further by Hogarth's placing of the posture woman's corset, lying on the floor, notably similar in shape to Watteau's soldier's discarded breastplate.

In this libertine underside of the connoisseur's world, all the 'art' around Tom is debased – the portraits of Roman emperors are defaced (except for Nero), the mirror is smashed, the map of the world is set on fire by a careless girl's candle. The music is no longer offered by Handel, but by a heavily pregnant street woman singing the lewd ballad 'Black Jake' and by a trumpeter and harpist in the corner. The latter might remind Hogarth's viewers of the

75 Plate 4, 'Arrested for Debt'

moment in *The Beggar's Opera* where Macheath, among his 'free-hearted wenches', not knowing that he is about to be betrayed with a kiss by Jenny Diver, calls for a song:

'But hark! I hear music. The harper is at the door. If music be the food of love, play on. Ere you seat yourselves ladies, what think you of a dance? Come in. [*Enter Harper*.] Play the French tune, that Mrs Slammekin was so fond of . . .

'Let us drink and sport today,
    Ours is not tomorrow.
Love with youth flies swift away,

251

76 Plate 5, 'Married to an Old Maid'

Age is nought but sorrow.
Dance and sing,
Time's on the wing.
Life never knows the return of spring.'[23]

The scene, with its *carpe diem* air, is lively and noisy – by far the most vital in the whole story – and the energy of the women, even the quarrelling pair spitting gin, has a wonderful gutsy life. But there is a sinister undertone. Tom's watch has been pinched by the girl behind (who looks suspiciously like Moll). Time is being snatched from him. The women's patches spell

77 Plate 6, 'Scene in a Gambling House'

disease, and the box of pills on the floor hints that Tom is already infected.

The drama spins from the brothel scene to the next tableau, the arrest in Pall Mall, where Sarah offers her pittance to help. By now it is too late; Tom is gambling his way to hell. When he revised the print of the arrest, Hogarth made this new theme still stronger, replacing a small crop-headed boy stealing Tom's silver-topped cane by a group of street boys playing cards. Of all the scenes, this is the one Hogarth returned to most, darkening and deepening it, as if the sudden shock of his father's own arrest had never left him – and making it seem like a judgement on the whole fashionable world. In the painting, the sky above St James's where the coaches crush together to attend

78 Plate 7, 'The Prison Scene'

the royal levee is a startling eggshell blue; in the first state of the print, the storm clouds are gathering; by the third state, the sky is black, split by a jagged fork of lightning.

Tom buys his way out with a furtive wedding to a rich, leering old woman among the cobwebs and cracked Commandments of Marylebone Church, while Sarah, with his baby in her arms, struggles vainly to stop the banns. His second fortune vanishes as fast as the first and we next see him in a gambling den where smoke billows through the wainscoting, an emblematic hint of the flames to come (and a realistic reminder of the fire at White's in May 1733). Wigless and grimacing, Tom shakes his fist at heaven. Beside him sits a disconsolate highwayman, brooding on his losses while a little pot-boy tugs his sleeve. When Tom himself sits helpless in the Fleet with all his money gone, he wears that same fierce inner gaze, and another small boy reminds *him* of his drink and holds out his hands for coins.

Hogarth's drawing always recalls the theatre; a stage gesture of rape, an actor's broad presentation of misery and madness. But in the Fleet scene Tom's pose is a startling physical contrast of introspective despair, in the stillness of his head and shoulders, and the jerking agitation of his restless hands and feet. Opposite him Sarah has fainted, while their child tugs her skirt. And beside her stands a wry reminder of men like Hogarth's own father, a puzzled, dishevelled figure with a cheap wig aslant on his dark hair, his blunt, stubbly face gawping in distress; from the pocket of his dressing-gown, full of holes, a paper floats to the ground, 'A New Scheme for solving the Debts of the Nation'. Once again, we are in the stage set of nightmare, the locked room of bricks and barred windows. Looking back, the bars and chains have always been there – the padlock on the miser's wall, the fire grille in the gambler's den – even the wedding ring is a fetter. But Tom has always dreamed of escape, of grand solutions and bottomless wealth. Here those dreams come to haunt him in the fantasies of the other debtors: the old man's schemes to solve the national debt; the harness of feathers that might let a man soar free like Icarus, only to fall in the heat of the sun and drown in the sea of despair; the crazy alchemist trying to make gold. These are the dreamers. The realists are the sturdy turnkey, the eyeless old wife whispering like an angry sybil in Tom's ear, the stout and stalwart women slapping Sarah's hands and offering smelling salts.

The final plates of *A Rake's Progress* outreach any moralizing. In the Fleet Hogarth shows a fearful borderland, a man lost in an inner desert more terrible than the jarring, grasping, elbowing crowd around him. He has become locked into himself and can only plunge deeper, into madness itself. In Bedlam, the most awful thing is that this private horror is also a public spectacle. The actors of Southwark Fair who tumbled off the platform in their lavish clothes, the gods and kings and fiddlers of the stage, have become *real* men acting out their madness to an audience of sightseers. On a hot Saturday in September a smart woman might yawn and wonder how to fill an empty afternoon – which would she choose? A visit to Southwark to see flying men fall – or a visit to the madhouse to peer through her fan at a mock king on a throne of straw, pissing in a corner? Bedlam, after all, was quite safe – the 'dangerous maniacs, most of them being chained and terrible to behold' were firmly manacled on the second floor, and the tourists could saunter

79 Plate 8, 'Scene in a Madhouse'

confidently along the wide gallery among 'inoffensive madmen', peering at colourful lunatics in little side cells.[24] These piquant visits could always be justified, as Steele said:

'I took Three Lads who are under my Guardianship a rambling in a Hackney-Coach, to show 'em the Town, as the Lions, the Tombs, *Bedlam*, and the other Places which are Entertainment to raw Minds, because they strike forcibly on the Fancy.'[25]

Hogarth's scene was not a documentary but a symbolic presentation of the follies of the age; it cannot be used as literal evidence of what Bedlam was like.

256

Yet it does have an imaginative reality, because Tom's story is so powerfully dramatized. And Hogarth, too, was perfectly aware that although the verses below his print spoke of 'Death grappling with Despair', his picture was designed to 'entertain', to draw upon the avid shudder that made apprentices and flower-sellers look forward to Tyburn holidays or pulled crowds to see Sarah Malcolm in her coffin.

Bedlam, like the fairground, was often described as a theatre of delusions of grandeur (on one visit Steele spotted 'five Duchesses, three Earls, two heathen Gods, an Emperor and a Prophet'). Hogarth constructed his scene on the lines of conventional satire by including a bevy of well-known madmen. Some believe they have great power: the straw-crowned king; the religious maniac with his medallions of saints and wooden cross; the man who thinks he is the Pope. Some claim profound knowledge: a blind astronomer plays with a paper telescope and another man scrawls on the wall, by a diagram of the world from the 'North Pole' to the 'Antarctic Circle'. He is calculating on the lines of William Whiston, the renegade Newtonian and Whig philosopher whose attempt to assess longitude at sea by firing mortars made him a choice butt of satire.[26] Others think they are masters of art and fashion, like the mad musician, or the lord who fancies himself a tailor (an ironic reminder of the first scene, where the tailor made the man). Some are victims of love, like the brooding man who has scribbled 'Charming Betty Careless' on the stair rails. This is William Ellis, unhinged by his passion for Betty Careless, a prostitute whose innocent-looking sweetness was famously at odds with her promiscuity, drinking, smoking and trooper-like swearing.[27]

In all these cases, the gulfs between illusion and reality have driven men mad. If *A Rake's Progress* is about the ruin of the prodigal, or about the curse on a father who starves his child of love, it is also about making life into a work of art, a lesson in the fearful lure of the imagination:

> Madness Thou Chaos of ye Brain
> What art? That Pleasure giv'st and Pain?
> Tyranny of Fancy's Reign!
> Mechanic Fancy; that can build
> Vast Labyrinths, & Mazes wild,
> With Rule disjointed, Shapeless measure
> Fill'd with Horror, fill'd with Pleasure!
> Shapes of Horror, that wou'd even
> Cast Doubt of Mercy upon Heaven.

In real life, all these men had been somebody. Now they are nobody. But all

257

except Tom are still great in their own mad minds – gods, kings, mighty lovers. Tom has no role. He lies naked on the floor, stripped of clothes and reason, echoing Cibber's huge statue of Melancholy Madness on the hospital's gatepost. The patch on his breast hints he has tried to stab himself, an event so common in Britain that French used *se suicider* as a conscious Anglicism. Foreigners were aghast at the national epidemic of 'self-murder':

'all the Reflections they make, before their coming to that frantic extremity, are purely the Consequence of a black, gloomy, troubled humour, and a savage Disposition, unable bravely to support the Reverses of Fortune'.[28]

Tom's statuesque madness embodies the despair of his country, 'the Englishman's disease'. It displays the wages of sin, suggesting the dark violence of advanced syphilis. It illustrates the vicissitudes of fate, 'the Reverses of Fortune'. Yet he remains a man, rousing human emotions: Sarah still loves him; the surgeon looks down with pity; even the turnkey shows compassion as he loosens the manacle on his bony leg. And in his extremity, Tom the piteous individual is almost a type of Christ, suffering for all. In the painting, where he wears a loincloth rather than breeches and Sarah mourns him like a Magdalen, the composition resembles a Deposition from the Cross. Such agony, as Hoadly's verses say, makes one doubt the mercy of Heaven; in *A Rake's Progress*, Hogarth puts the mystery of sacrifice firmly back on earth, among grubby, failed people who buy clothes, catch fleas, drink gruel.

The story is presented as moral teaching, but in the 1740s, explaining these prints to his French readers, Rouquet doubted the effect, if not the force of Hogarth's lesson. 'Do you think that it is possible to reform men?' he asked wryly:

'for me, I know no example of it. It seems to me that they are born what they are, and that both their vices and virtues are part of their temperament. I imagine it is almost as reasonable to hope to cure a blind man by laughing at him as to flatter oneself of reforming a miser or a gambler by turning them into ridicule. It is none the less praiseworthy to labour to do so, and to try and inspire aversion or contempt for all that is evil. Besides, the folly of mankind is incontestably the patrimony of satire.'[29]

Tom Rakewell is both a dreaming miser's son and a version of Everyman, embodying the follies (and genuine madness) of mankind. The final image of Bedlam prompted Swift, in Ireland, to imagine Hogarth as his ally in 'The Legion Club', when he railed against the 'insanity' of the Irish parliament:

How I want thee, humorous Hogart!
Thou I hear, a pleasant Rogue art;
Were but you and I acquainted,
Every Monster should be painted;
You should try your graving Tools
On this odious Group of Fools;
Draw the Beasts as I describe 'em,
Form their Features, while I gibe 'em,
Draw them like, for I assure you,
You will need no Caricatura;
Draw them so that we may trace
All the Soul in every Face.[30]

Such recognition from his hero – one of the three writers always included in his pantheon, with Shakespeare and Milton – validated Hogarth's aim. But it was the way he drew 'all the soul' in the face of Tom Rakewell that raised his art above caricature. There was beauty as well as bitterness. The six paintings in the small gallery of the Sir John Soane's Museum, filling a single wall, are almost shockingly lovely. Hogarth painted fast, in rough blocks and sudden details, the texture thin and sketchy, with sudden disconcerting flashes of colour and complementary tones – like the glowing pink dress of the fashionable woman in Bedlam, cruelly mirroring the naked flesh of Tom's body. Visitors lingering by these pictures comment not on the morals, but on the emotions: 'She must have really loved him, don't you think?' asks one man, nodding at Sarah Young with her handkerchief.

In the end it is not the bourgeois moral but the unblinking realism and poetic power that makes Hogarth's series great. In Auden's view, the story of a man destroyed by the temptations offered by good fortune is timeless: 'it is a myth; it represents, that is, a situation in which all men, at least potentially, find themselves, in so far as they are human beings'.[31] In Hogarth's day the *Harlot* was more successful. In the twentieth century, when the lure of materialism, success and fashion are so strong, the *Rake*'s themes of ambition and glamour, ruin and disaster have been constantly reworked in art, literature, music, opera and ballet. Allied to a lonely, existential sense that fate is a matter of individual will, Hogarth's Rake has invaded our psyche and made his home there, in a different and more powerful way.

259

13

Liberty and Property, Clubs and Cabals

Though the earth and all inferior creatures be common to all men, yet every man has a 'property' in his own 'person'. This nobody has any right to but himself. The 'labour' of his body and the 'work' of his hands, we may say, are properly his.
JOHN LOCKE, *Of Civil Government* (1690)

ALTHOUGH THE PRINTS of *A Rake's Progress* were delayed, *The Fair* was ready on 1 January 1734. Gossip helped Hogarth's sales, as the Drury Lane mutiny ran on through the winter. Highmore threw public sympathy to the winds when he had the actor John Harper committed to Bridewell on a vagrancy charge, and by February Theophilus Cibber had won. On 9 March the rebels returned in triumph. Their victory showed how determined men could win, first if they banded together and then if they used the law – lessons Hogarth took to heart.

'Liberty and Property', the slogans on the banner in the print, were watchwords for artists as well as actors. Their talent was their property, but the use it was put to and the price it was valued at were dictated by others – patrons, auctioneers and printsellers. Hogarth aimed to change this if he could. In a sparkling self-portrait of 1735, he showed himself wearing his wig, brandishing his brush and looking out from the canvas with a quizzical smile. From now on he emerged as a leader among the artists, organizing his fellows, making them get the law on their side, raise their status, find public places for display, free themselves from dependence on patrons.

The artists got together in their clubs and coffee houses. Most of Hogarth's close friends, like George Lambert and Jack Laguerre, were long-time *habitués* of Old Slaughter's Coffee-House in St Martin's Lane, 'a rendezvous of persons of all languages & Nations Gentry artists and others'.[1] Run by Thomas Slaughter since the 1690s, this coffee house was the true centre of gossip, power-broking and friendship for London artists, writers and actors for almost half a century, a place where hacks, cranks and connoisseurs met and argued into the small hours.

This was no club of 'rude mechanics'. In the mid-1730s, these artists were

80 *Self-portrait with Palette* (*c.*1735)

mostly young, high-spirited and fired by a common rebellion against rigid Palladianism, with its straight lines and formal rules. They held out against the 'gentlemanly' theories of art propounded by Pond's Roman Club, and the new Society of Dilettanti. They looked to the public as well as to patrons, and appealed to nature instead of rules, to informality and curving lines. Indeed,

261

Old Slaughter's has been called a key centre for men with new ideas and a strong reaction against traditional academic values, 'who all contributed to an anarchic, destructive and unbalanced movement in all the arts, almost an early form of Dada; they were intent on the destruction of the old dogmas and taboos, of stylization and intellectualism, and on bringing in a new freedom and tolerance'.[2]

'Destructive' is strong, but the mood was certainly one of innovation and irreverence. There were many stories illustrating this – of Fielding's mockery, or of Hogarth caricaturing the solemn, respectable types who monopolized the seats by the coffee-house bar, and, not surprisingly, the place had a daunting reputation for scurrility.[3] In 1741, Baron Bielfeld described it as 'the centre for all the wits and the greatest part of the men of letters in town'.[4] The regulars made fun of the older generation and their cherished theories. Joseph Highmore's grandson told John Nichols that one evening Jonathan Richardson was at Old Slaughter's, declaiming proudly (as he often did) about the classical knowledge of his son, 'and as constantly regretting his own inferiority in the attainment of literature'. Bringing out a draft of his forthcoming work on Milton, he said,

'I know well enough my eye is no eye at all. I must apply to my Telescope; my Son is my Telescope; tis by his help I read the learned languages.'[5]

(This anecdote reworks the words of Richardson's preface, where he uses the telescope image in connection with his son and continues, ''Tis by the help of This I have seen that in Milton which to me otherwise had been invisible.')[6] Hogarth, delighted, allegedly took out a letter and made a sketch; the likeness of Richardson was so strong that the old man was mortified. Hogarth repented – he was fond of Richardson – and burned the drawing, but an etching survived (supposedly by Joseph Sympson), showing Richardson peering up a telescope wedged into the cleft of the bare buttocks of his son, who is standing on a desk eyeing a copy of 'Virgil' on a shelf above. (Samuel Ireland included this print but, by 1817, when the *General Works* appeared, the public was more decorous; here Jonathan Junior is clothed, and the telescope modestly shortened.)[7]

While some of the group, like Lambert, were gentlemanly and quiet, most of them enjoyed such jokes. London artists (when not greeting polite clients) were often crude and argued with considerable violence. Marcellus Laroon could spit fire at connoisseurs quite as lustily as Hogarth. In 1729, when several 'painters Judges, &c' questioned the authenticity of a Van Dyck he had recommended to Walpole, he retaliated furiously:

262

'he was so much offended at them. & on purpose came to a Tavern club where he said much. in praise of himself, & at last this following

'*An Extempore*

'I Challange any or all of your Tip Top Top-most Conoisseurs, Proffessors & Judges in the Art of Painting (besides all pretenders)

'From the Highest to the Lowest, of every degree whatsoever

'Chafferers bidders and buyers of pictures. their Bullies Baudes & Panders.

'From the Great great Sr Hu (Mr Howard) Director & Privy Councellor to Noblemen & Gentlemen that purchase Pictures – Down to the lowest scrubb even to Nunis the Jew (a little ugly fellow a picture jobber) all

'I do solemnly Challenge & every one of them defy to compare with me in Judgment & Art –

'wittness. *my hand*, with sword and Pencil'.[8]

The interpolations are Vertue's but the salty, brutal blend of pride and prejudice was typical of Laroon and his fellow artists.

Although the Old Slaughter's group would always be associated with the revitalization of 'English' art, the prejudice was more often levelled against the London connoisseurs than against foreigners themselves. For one thing, too many families from abroad had grown up in the square mile around St Martin's Lane and, in addition, stimulating new styles were now entering the world of crafts and art from France. Goldsmiths and silversmiths in nearby workshops had already begun to borrow details from the graceful French rococo, a blend of the relaxed *style régence*, and the *genre pittoresque* with its serpentine scrolls, its love of asymmetry, of flowing watery forms such as rocks and shells, cascades and waves, and its fondness for whimsy.[9] The lighter style was also found in the lively drawings of John Vanderbank, and in recent book illustrations.[10]

In the early 1730s the clientele at Old Slaughter's included two particularly influential Frenchmen: the sculptor Louis-François Roubiliac and the Parisian engraver Hubert-François Gravelot. Both lived in these crowded streets of bookshops and studios, printsellers and theatres, weavers and cabinetmakers; Roubiliac had a studio in St Martin's Lane, and Gravelot (who arrived in England in 1732, aged thirty-three) lived first at the Golden Cup in King Street and then at the sign of the Pestle and Mortar in Covent Garden. In the late 1730s Roubiliac's vigorous, informal sculpture noticeably affected the poses in portraits by Hayman, Hogarth and others.[11] Gravelot, a student of Boucher, had, Vertue noted, 'a fruitfull genius for desseins inventions of history and ornaments'.[12] He brought a new, easy, decorative style to

263

illustration, and his delicate and intimate painting and carefully finished engravings (lighter and more fluid than the stiff English work) transmitted the spirit of Watteau and Gillot to a responsive generation of painters and engravers – including Hogarth.

Gravelot knew he was good, and made it clear, with touchy Gallic sarcasm. At Old Slaughter's, according to Vertue, he too often held forth 'with much vehemence & Freedom. for or against whom he pleases speaking often very slightly of others and extolling his own merit'. He once abused Sir Andrew Fountaine for never employing persons of merit, 'only stupid silly blockheads or bunglers in Art'.[13] This nettled Andien de Clermont, the decorative painter whom Fountaine had employed. Taking it as a direct affront he demanded an apology,

'upon which Gravelot not doing – nor endeavouring to do, this Sig^r Clermont gave him a stout box on the face, telling he deserv'd that justly. and should have more if he liked it. the other took it. and passd it off. but came no more as he usd to do every evening.'

Grignion remembered this too, saying that Roubiliac and others urged Gravelot to go back and return the blow, 'but his spirit was too timid'.[14]

William Blake, commenting that the English always met contempt on the Continent, remembered his master, the engraver James Basire, imitating Gravelot's heavily accented views: 'De English may be very clever in deir own opinions, but dey do not draw de draw.'[15] The opinionated English did learn drawing from Gravelot, whom they appealed to, Rouquet said, 'as a kind of oracle',[16] but the Frenchmen all had to put up with taunts; Fielding, apparently, used to imitate Roubiliac's accent cruelly. Roubiliac was teased, too, for being wrapped up in his work, or his cards, to the obliteration of all else. After one late tipsy evening, he offered to put up a friend who had forgotten the key to his lodgings, and showed him the spare room, 'but just as he was nearly undressed, he was horror-stricken at the sight of the corpse of a black woman laid out upon the bed'. He called frantically for Roubiliac, who exclaimed,

'Oh dear! my good fren', I beg your pardon! I did not remember poor Mary vas dare: poor Mary! She die yesterday vid de small-poc! Come, come, and you must take part vid my bed – come – poor Mary vas my hos-maid for five six year – more!'[17]

Can this be true, one wonders? Perhaps the story got muddled up with one from a few years later, when Hogarth and some friends fixed up the boastful womanizer John Highmore (of Drury Lane mutiny fame), with a pretty woman whose place in bed was taken by a black prostitute – when Highmore drew back the bed curtains they pounced, and Hogarth circulated a crowing print, *The Discovery*, among their friends.[18]

Hogarth's vehement arguments and hoaxes were in tune with the common mood, not, as often appears, the outbursts of a wild individual. The loose associations of the coffee house were reinforced by more formal links. The Masonic web was still important to Hogarth, and by the early 1730s he and Ebenezer Forrest, with John Ellys and Jack Laguerre, and the actors James Quin, Theophilus Cibber and William Milward all belonged to a lodge that met in the east of the City.[19] The Lodge Master was the Earl of Strathmore, and senior members included the Duke of Montagu and Dr Desaguliers. In 1734 Hogarth was chosen as one of the twelve Stewards of the Grand Lodge (representing all the London lodges) for the following year. On the evening of 30 March 1734 a dinner was held at the Earl of Crauford's house, where the Masons' white aprons and silver buckles were reflected in a glitter of plate and crystal, and afterwards the outgoing Stewards handed over their white rods in a solemn procession. In this intimate society Hogarth had proved his worth; the Stewards had a lodge of their own, which met quarterly on his own doorstep, at the Shakespeare's Head, Covent Garden. Hogarth designed a 'grand Jewel' for them, which would be used in the Stewards' ceremonies for a century to come.

Hogarth was a clubbable man, to use Dr Johnson's phrase, and marriage did not change this. A story used to illustrate his graphic memory (and to suggest the 'realism' of *A Rake's Progress*), placed him in a brothel with Francis Hayman, watching two quarrelling prostitutes,

'one of them, who had taken a mouthful of wine or gin, squirted it in the other's face, which so delighted the artist that he exclaimed, "Frank, mind the b—'s mouth."'[20]

This may be turning art back into life, but Hogarth certainly enjoyed the freedoms – and the rules – of the man's world. *A Midnight Modern Conversation* includes some of his own drinking acquaintances and several of his other pictures also show men enjoying themselves among their friends.

For Hogarth, the club world was one of shared aims and politics as well as pleasures. The subscription ticket for *A Midnight Modern Conversation* was another all-male group, the energetic *Chorus of Singers*. He almost certainly based this on a sketch made in late 1732 of an actual rehearsal for the oratorio

81 *A Chorus of Singers* (1732)

Judith, whose libretto was written by his friend William Huggins, to music by William Defesch. Each figure has a distinct personality and the man in the corner peering over his score is said to be another old friend, William Tothall. Sadly, the enthusiasm that has so infected Hogarth's singers – the conductor's wig has flown right off his head – was largely wasted. *Judith* was first postponed, due to the 'Misconduct and pretended Sickness of Cecilia Young, who had ingaged for the part of Judith', and then hissed off the stage at the critical moment when the heroine strikes Holofernes:

As to sever,
His head from his great trunk for ever, and for ever.[21]

Despite this débâcle, the libretto was published, and Hogarth designed a frontispiece, showing Judith about to perform the fatal act.

Hogarth loved singing (as the *Peregrination* shows), and must have been interested, too, in the arguments raging in London's music clubs. Musicians had their own clubs, in taverns such as the Castle in Paternoster Row or the Swan in Exchange Alley, and these were concerned with professional matters

266

as well as enjoyment. They, like the artists, bridled at Continental competition:

'Are not our *English* Singers shut out, with our *Mother-Tongue?* So engrossing are the *Italians*, and so prejudiced against their own Country, that our Singers are excluded from our very Concerts; *Bertolli* singing at the Castle, and *Senesino* at the Swan, to both their Shames be it spoken; who, not content with monstrous salaries at the Operas, stoop so low as to be hired to sing at Clubs! thereby eating some *English* singer's Bread.'[22]

Hogarth and Huggins both belonged to the Academy of Ancient Music,[23] a concert club based at the Crown and Anchor in the Strand, which gave fine recitals and collected a superb music library but also acted as a body to represent the British musicians. This was just the kind of lobby group Hogarth wanted for the London artists, and he now poured more and more energy into banding them together.

That spring he seems suddenly to have decided to take control, perhaps spurred by the death of Sir James Thornhill on 4 May. Thornhill had been ill on and off for the past year, much afflicted with gout (the ubiquitous eighteenth-century ailment). For some time, Vertue said, his legs had been swollen with dropsy (the second favourite complaint) but he remained 'alwayes a man of High Spirit'. In late April he fell violently ill, losing his voice and retreating to the quiet of his Dorset estate. Worn out by the journey, he died there a few days later, peacefully sitting in his chair. Tributes came in showers. The great English history-painter, who had wrestled with the foreigners for the painting of St Paul's and Greenwich, had gone. No one looked ready to step into his place.

Hogarth was keen to lay claim to Thornhill's role, as well as to the painting apparatus that he inherited. Thornhill's pictures at Greenwich had been a prime example to him of the decoration of public spaces, a topic much canvassed in the early eighteenth century. In 1734 the Governors of St Bartholomew's Hospital were choosing an artist to decorate the grand staircase in their new wing, designed by James Gibbs, and in February, just before Thornhill's illness, Hogarth had been horrified to hear that the commission would probably go to a foreigner, the Venetian Jacopo Amigoni. This was a peculiarly irritating threat – not only was Bart's next door to Hogarth's birthplace but Amigoni had been the man chosen to replace Thornhill's wall panels at Moor Park after his legal battle in 1728. Amigoni seemed to be everywhere. He had recently covered Rich's ceiling at Covent Garden with his picture of the Muses presenting Shakespeare to Apollo, was painting the royal princesses, and was also the inseparable friend of Farinelli.

Infuriated, Hogarth immediately offered to paint the whole staircase free of charge. His offer was accepted by the hospital's 'Renter', John Lloyd, and almost instantly (as if Hogarth had at once roped in his supporters) James Ralph announced the fact in *The Weekly Register*, even naming the subjects as 'histories of the Pool of Bethesda and the Good Samaritan'. Such publicity would make it hard for the Hospital Governors to go back on their agreement.

The affair became a focus of London art politics. James Ralph, although in general a supporter of Palladianism, had been waging a long-running campaign in his *Weekly Register* since October 1733, criticizing the style and decoration of London's public buildings. This spring he kept Hogarth's name in the foreground, and specifically attacked Amigoni.[24] In June *The Grub-Street Journal* associated Ralph and Ellys with 'an eminent painter' in the assault on Amigoni, and the accusation that interested parties were at work was repeated in September.[25] Such opposition, of course, only fired Hogarth's determination the more. In July he had been elected a Governor of the Hospital, his gift of his paintings standing in lieu of a donation. Now, for the first time, he could try grand decorative painting himself, without feeling as if he was stepping on his father-in-law's toes or trying to rival him.

Hogarth's mission to defend the rights and property of British artists carried over into his work as an engraver. The prints of *A Rake's Progress* had not been issued to subscribers with *Southwark Fair* that January for two reasons. First, Hogarth had been working on his pictures, adding new characters thrown up by the news. Second, he had plans to beat the printsellers and the pirates and did not want to release the prints too soon. He had decided to petition Parliament for an Act that would give designers and engravers the same statutory copyright that authors had won in 1709. Working out the details with his friends, Hogarth proposed a Bill that would give them an exclusive right to their work for fourteen years from the time of publication. This would not only mean that they retained the financial rewards now creamed off by the printsellers, but it would also establish a different meaning of 'ownership' of works of art: at last, the engraver could legally 'own' the property produced by his labour. Furthermore, it enhanced the dignity of the work itself, giving the multiple print a similar status to that of the single painting. And it meant that fine prints could retain their integrity and no longer be debased, 'cheapened' by poor copies.

Hogarth put forward his argument in an open letter to a Member of Parliament. He could never write a dry document, and the little pamphlet storms off the page. He blasts at the printsellers, who have fattened on the labour of the poor engravers, working day and night at 'miserable prices'. The tyrants he fights are not rich patrons, or rich artists, but the 'overgrown shopkeepers' who band together in a vicious monopoly: if a printmaker dares ask a reasonable price, the printseller immediately has copies made and sold dirt cheap, to squash his rebellion. Hogarth was not thinking merely of himself but of the problems facing all engravers: the poorer workers who have no shop or studio to show their prints and *have* to be reliant on the printsellers; and those who are successful but are forced to use their time to act as shopkeepers (if they don't want to be at the mercy of the publishers), rather than work on their art. Many of these complaints were echoed by Vertue in his later note lamenting that engraving was the least profitable of all arts. This was partly, he thought, because of the mass production, 'the necessity of such works being printed on paper. a sheet being of small value – subject to be multiplyed. and consequently more in number so each of less value'. Prints were also often 'marr'd or ill printed' by ignorant workmen.[26] But the worst feature was the way 'the print sellers squeeze and screw. trick and abuse the reputations of such engravers – to raise their own fortune by devouring that of the Sculpture-Engravers'.

Hogarth's open letter, *The Case of Designers, Engravers, Etchers etc.*, made a case for the importance of copyright as a general good, not just an individual benefit. Good-quality prints would raise the artists' reputations, and higher standards of reproduction, he argued, would improve the status of British art in general. Secure in the knowledge that they would reap and keep the rewards of their work, more people would enter the engraving trade; the public would have a wider choice and – in the end – even the printseller would profit.

At the end of 1734 the engravers' petition was drawn up. William Huggins, as a lawyer, tried (not wholly successfully) to ensure that the legal technicalities were correct and in the following February it was presented to Parliament. It bears the signatures of engravers whom Hogarth had known, worked with and drunk with since the 1720s: George Lambert, anxious to protect the new engravings of his East India scenes; Gerard Vandergucht, who had engraved many of Hogarth's book designs; John Pine, whose work had brought a new vigour into the British trade; the architect and engraver Isaac Ware; George Vertue, and Joseph Goupy, now drawing teacher to Frederick, Prince of Wales.

In 1735, under a combination of commercial pressure and Hogarth's urging, old rivals were acting as one. Other engravers came forward to give their evidence to the Commons Committee, and the Bill went smoothly

269

through the Commons and Lords. Finally a date was set for the Act to receive the Royal Assent: 25 June 1735. The assent was given, with nice irony, in a flourish of legal French. At the end of April, as soon as the Bill had the essential approval of the Lords, Hogarth rushed his advertisements for *A Rake's Progress* into the press. On 3, 5 and 7 May, he announced in the *Daily Advertiser* that the prints would be delayed until 25 June 'in order to secure his Property' by the new Act, which would prevent prints

'being copied without Consent of the proprietor, and therby preventing a scandalous and unjust Custom (hitherto practised with Impunity) of making and vending base Copies of original Prints, to the manifest Injury of the Author and the great Discouragement of the Arts of Painting and Engraving'.

He could not win, of course. Such a blazon of defiance roused the print-sellers into action. Quickly, they sent scouts round to Hogarth's studio to spy out the paintings of the Rake. They then rushed back to put as much as they remembered on paper. Working from their sketches and muddled descriptions, hired engravers created a sub-*Rake* before Hogarth's true one appeared. Major printsellers (Henry Overton, the Bowles brothers and John King) placed their own notices in the *Daily Advertiser* – for 'The Adventures of Ramble Gripe, Esq, Son and Heir of Sir Positive Gripe'. As well as making Hogarth quickly change his hero's name from Gripe to Rakewell, the print-sellers' actions made him lash out. On the day of their advertisement he appealed vehemently for support against men 'who are capable of a Practice so repugnant to Honesty and destructive of Property'. All prints that appeared before 24 June, he added, would be 'an Imposition on the Publick'.[27] In mid-June, he announced that to protect that public he would have authorized copies made, to be sold at 2s 6d a set through Thomas Bakewell in Fleet Street. Eventually, the subscribers' prints were issued on 25 June, followed by new impressions, sold at 2 guineas a set by Hogarth and Bakewell, and finally by Bakewell's cheap, smaller copies in mid-August.

So 'Hogarth's Act' did not solve all his problems. And when it was finally tested in court in 1753, it proved to have certain weaknesses due to technical problems with the drafting with regard to assignees: it was typical of Hogarth, who liked to do everything himself, not to think of the problems that might arise if someone else was doing the engraving for you.[28] Nor did his Act protect those who *copied* old-master drawings or engravings. Nevertheless, he could write defiantly in his autobiographical notes that it had not only scotched piracies but improved British engraving, 'there being more business of that kind done in this Town than in Paris or any where else and as well. Such inovations in these arts gave great offence to dealers both in pictures and Prints.'

The printsellers' habit of living off the ingenuity of the industrious had suffered, and 'if the detecting the Rogurys of these opressers of the rising artists and imposers on the public is a crime I confess myself most guilty'.[29] The significance of the Act had, perhaps, been greater than even he realized. The idea of the original, unique canvas as containing all worth was diluted; mass production was not seen as a slippage, a stigma, but as another legitimate route for an artist to take.

Hogarth was no maverick, thinking up this campaign in an isolated moment of genius. Similar arguments about intellectual and artistic property were going on in several fields in the 1730s. Musicians were worried about pirated scores and plagiarized performances; writers were seeking to extend the copyright through the 'Society for the Encouragement of Learning'; playwrights and theatre managers were arguing against censorship. The theatre, too, faced problems of internal politics and external pressures, of a slightly different nature. While Hogarth was galvanizing the engravers into concerted action, Fielding was also forging a new platform, forming his own company, 'The Great Mogul's Company of English Comedians' (adding ironically, *Newly Imported*). In February 1735, with James Ralph as partner and a group of young actors, he took over the Little Theatre in the Haymarket and launched a volley of irregular plays, beginning with *Pasquin*, a staggeringly successful political farce. Fielding, too, was challenging the Establishment; and the playwrights also laid claim to free expression and the ownership of their talent. When Walpole eventually introduced a Bill to license theatrical performances, Lord Chesterfield declared that the Bill

'is not only an encroachment on liberty, but is likewise an encroachment on property. Wit, my lords, is a sort of property: the property of those who have it, and too often the only property they have to depend on. It is indeed a precarious dependence.'[30]

*

Determined to protect his 'precarious dependence' – although by now he was earning good money, and could even be styled well-off – Hogarth emerged in 1735 as a galvanizing spirit among the clubs and cabals. His professional and social life came together in two more groups that he helped to found this year, the St Martin's Lane Academy – and the Sublime Society of Beefsteaks.

The Academy was work but the Beefsteak Club was play, drawing in all the loose confraternity of Covent Garden: artists, musicians and theatre people, professional men and dilettanti. Stories about its origin differ. In one version, it was said that because John Rich had no time to go out during a packed day at Covent Garden, he used to grill a steak over the fire in the painting room. Visitors would drop in, to partake 'at two o'clock, of the hot steak dressed by Rich himself, accompanied by "a bottle of port from the tavern hard by"'.[31] As it was the painting room, it seems more likely that the picnicker was Lambert (as in a common second version),[32] but certainly he and Rich worked together, and as their friends began making this makeshift meal a habit, by early December 1735 they decided to make it a club.

Membership was always kept to twenty-four. In the first list, topped by Lambert, Hogarth and Rich, several familiar names appear: William Huggins, Ebenezer Forrest, John Thornhill, William Tothall and Gabriel Hunt (whom Hogarth sketched snoring, with his knife stuck in his pocket, to defend him from street robbers).[33] These were joined by actors and other old friends, like John Ellys, who joined in the late 1730s. To begin with the club had no great pretensions, rather like the earlier witty, Whiggish, Beefsteak Club of the early 1700s, which was also linked to Covent Garden and whose secretary was the charming comic actor Dick Estcourt, much loved by Richard Steele.[34]

Apart from the long summer break from July to September, the new Beefsteaks met on Saturdays in the painting room, and later in a more comfortable room in the theatre. With their beef they ate baked potatoes, onions and beets and toasted cheese, and drank port and punch, porter and whisky toddy. The mood was easy and formal wigs gave way to velvet caps, but from the beginning, with the love of mock-formality that marked so many clubs (as it did the *Peregrination*), they also evolved elaborate rituals and rules. At one stage they even wore a uniform – a blue coat, and blue waistcoat with brass buttons impressed with the club motto, 'Beef and Liberty'. This motto also appeared on rings, and on the badge of the society, a silver gridiron worn from a red ribbon round their necks. They had mock 'officers', who took their places in rotation: a President, Bishop, Recorder and 'Boots'. The unhappy President was the common target: he not only had to pay for the beef but he had to sing, whether he wanted to or not, 'THE SONG OF THE DAY', invariably Fielding's appropriate 'The Roast Beef of Old England' in Leveridge's new setting.[35] Before announcing each toast, he had to slam on his hat, and as soon as he finished he had to whip it off again: if he forgot the company booed and hissed and roared. The Bishop, wearing a mitre and accompanied by 'halberdiers' in absurd costumes, probably ransacked from

272

the theatre, had to bring in new members, blindfold, and make them swear and kiss a book – for which a bone of beef was substituted. The Recorder drew up (or invented) a list of offences, charged members and handed out 'punishments' and forfeits. The ignominious Boots, the newest member, had to decant the wine and dish out the steaks.

The rigmarole seems at once ludicrously childish and eerily significant – a mirror image of civil forms and controls which both mocked and endorsed them. But the Beefsteaks' rituals also parodied those of the smarter, richer Dilettanti Club, which had been active in London for a year now. They too dressed up. Their President of the Day wore a scarlet Roman toga, and – since they favoured booze more than beef – their badge was no gridiron but 'a small Bacchus bestriding a Tun with a silver chain', while their toasts, as opposed to 'Beef and Liberty' were to 'Viva la Virtu' and 'Grecian Tast and Roman Spirit'.[36]

Hogarth was a member of the Beefsteaks for only a few years, from 1735 to 1740, and from 1742 to 1744; afterwards he went as a guest only. But during his membership years most Saturdays he would roll up for a couple of hours with his friends – the broiling began at two and the tablecloths were taken off at half-past three. Verses were read, songs were sung, drawings passed round. The first members set a tone that carried through the decades, jovial but tough. If anyone had a weak point, remembered one later member, 'his faulty armour was speedily pierced'. If he winced under a sarcasm, or was nettled by the bantering and chaffing, the Beefsteak Club was not for him.[37] The real advantage was talking in confidence: one of the strictest rules emphasized that nothing said there would be repeated.

The conspiratorial air and sub-Masonic goings-on were part of the attraction, and indeed the 'Sublime Society' may have been partly provoked by a sensational news flurry of 1735. On 30 January, a group of young rakes, seven of them members of the Dilettanti, had celebrated noisily at a tavern, even starting a bonfire in the street, without (so they said) remembering that this was the anniversary of Charles I's execution. Quickly a rumour spread that the virulently Republican, free-thinking 'Calves-Head Club' of the Restoration had met again, with their treasonous king-killing oaths. A furious crowd, some carrying calves' heads on stakes, hurled stones and stormed the inn for two hours until those inside were rescued by the guard. Epigrams and broadsides flooded the town, as one of those involved noted, when he drily explained the reality to a friend:

'This is the whole story from which so many Calves-heads, Bloody napkins,

273

and Lord knows what has been made, it has been the talk of the Town and the Country, and Small Beer and Bread and Cheese to my friends the Garretters in Grub Street for these few days past.'[38]

Rich, Hogarth, Lambert and their friends – upholders of King and Country to the hilt – had exactly the satirical humour to set up a real club as a counter-image, bullocks against calves, flaunting their patriotism. Their plebeian-but-polite gathering was also an answer to 'the Liberty or Rumpsteak Club, founded in 1734 by a group of Whig peers to whom George II had shown his backside at levees'[39] (another – this time regal – expression of manly 'Liberty'). Then the addition of 'Sublime' to the down-to-earth 'Beefsteaks' dug at the high theorists of art, whose attempts to define 'sublimity' had echoed on since Boileau's *Longinus on the Sublime* was translated nearly forty years before.[40]

The symbolic politics of names was amusing, but almost irrelevant. The whole ethos of eating, drinking, bingeing and singing was linked to their 'Englishness'. Beefsteak was a 'natural emblem for Englishmen whose manhood seemingly hinged upon being three bottle fellows'.[41] The oozing red meat, the feasts and freedoms – like the wearing of leather shoes instead of wooden clogs – set the English against the feeble, starving peasants of the Continent, as their song made abundantly clear:

> When mighty Roast Beef was the *Englishman's* Food
> It enobled our Hearts, and enriched our Blood;
> Our Soldiers were brave, and our Courtiers were good.
>   Oh the Roast Beef of Old *England*
>   And old *England's* Roast Beef!
>
> Then, *Britons*, from all nice Dainties refrain
> Which effeminate Italy, *France* and *Spain*;
> And mighty Roast Beef shall command on the Main.
>   Oh the Roast Beef of Old *England*
>   And Old *England's* Roast Beef.[42]

A generation later the Club's menu was praised as the bastion of Englishness facing an invasion of Continental foppishness. In *The Connoisseur*, a letter bewailed the low status of English beef, declaring that, 'Our only hopes are in the clergy and in the Beef-steak Club . . . composed of the most ingenious artists in the kingdom', who 'never suffer any dish except Beef-steaks to appear.' These indeed, the writer continued, 'are most glorious examples: but what alas! are the weak endeavours of a few to oppose the daily inroads of fricassees and soup-maigres?'[43]

274

In late 1735 many of the early discussions at the Club must have been about the artists' new plans to oppose the fricassees of foreign taste. At the same time as the engravers were fighting for copyright, the artists were reiterating the need for an academy to raise their status. Around 1760, when Hogarth recalled this period, his writing was spiked by a current battle against those who wanted a Royal Academy on formal lines and remembering the impetus behind the 1735 school, he proudly laid claim to a founding role. Since the Vanderbank and Chéron academy folded in the 1720s there had been *nothing*, he wrote, apart from Thornhill's own school behind his house. So when he inherited Thornhill's painting equipment in 1734 he suggested that the artists should join together to hire 'a room big enough for a naked figure to be drawn after by thirty or forty people', and proposed a subscription to rent one in St Martin's Lane. In his own words, since

'the expenses attending in this was soon agreed to by sufficient number of artists he presented them with a proper table for the figure to stand on a large lamp iron stove and benches in a circular form'.[44]

By the winter the school was under way, almost certainly in the old meeting house in St Peter's Court that the former Vanderbank academy had used, and Vertue noted that 'Mr Hogarth principally promotes or undertakes it.'[45]

Hogarth's ideas, far more than his equipment, shaped the Academy's form. They were fundamentally democratic, reflecting his own dislike of anybody lording it over him. Since the failure of previous academies, he thought, could be attributed to the leading members assuming a superiority that their fellow students could not brook, he 'became an equal subscriber with the rest signifying at the same time that superior and inferior among artists should be avoided especially in this country'.[46] *This* academy would have no 'leaders'.

In practice, there was some rough hierarchy; Hogarth and Ellys were the official proprietors, and in the 1740s there were individual teachers for specific subjects, among them Gravelot, who taught drawing, and Hayman, who taught painting. But the animating principles were those that Hogarth later came back to in the *Analysis*, in effect a set of questions about proportion, colour, line, harmony and perspective – all answered either from observation of the real – details of stance, of clothes, of dance and movement – or from close appreciation and criticism of works of the masters. Here, Hogarth hoped, the dead hand of the copyist would give way to free enquiry. For the next thirty years this would be the leading school in Britain for painting and the graphic arts. Young artists were drawn into its orbit, including Allan Ramsay, son of the Edinburgh poet, who had lodged for a few months in

275

Orange Court, Leicester Fields, as a pupil of Hans Hysing in 1732, and was briefly in London four years later before leaving for Italy. It was a site of education, a means of mutual protection like the old trade guilds, and another, better, club. After the early 1740s Vertue does not mention the old tip-top St Luke's Club; St Martin's Lane took over the St Luke's Day Feasts celebrating the artists' patron.

Over the next twenty years the roll-call of artists linked with Old Slaughter's and St Martin's Lane included many painters, from Hayman, Highmore and Scott to Ramsay and Gainsborough; engravers like Gravelot and Pine; book illustrators like Samuel Wale; specialists like George Michael Moser, the German-Swiss silver chaser, and Richard Yeo the medallist; architects like Isaac Ware (although he was a loyal Burlingtonian) and the occasional craftsman like John Linnell, a woodcarver, furniture-maker and superb designer. The closeness of the art world meant that they collaborated in innumerable ventures. Hogarth drew figures for Lambert's landscapes and Scott's seascapes; Scott and Lambert worked together on commissions for the Earl of Pembroke. Hayman and Gravelot joined forces at Vauxhall Gardens, and on the illustrations for *Pamela* and the Hanmer *Shakespeare*. The touchy, conspiratorial Moser also later designed plasterwork for Vauxhall, while Ravenet and Hayman engraved Moser's vignettes for books. Roubiliac made busts of other members of the group, including Hogarth and Isaac Ware. Henry Cheere, the sculptor, for whom Roubiliac worked when he first came to England, and whose son Charles and assistant Richard Hayward were also part of the set, made statues and tombs, and chimney-pieces joyous with shells and garlands. St Martin's Lane was also the hub of the furniture-making industry and from there John Linnell took the rococo style across town to his thriving workshop in Berkeley Square.[47]

The links between these artists were as entwined and elaborate as one of Gravelot's leaf-fringed festoons. From their collective energy – although there were quarrels and factions as well as alliances – a distinctive style spread through London and the country. In painting, an 'English school' would slowly emerge, as Hogarth pushed the painters towards new public exhibition spaces in Vauxhall Gardens and then the Foundling Hospital. In the 1730s, in the studio, the coffee house, the club and the academy, Hogarth was active and vigorous. His trader's concern for his property fused with a creative desire for liberty; for the freedom of the artists to choose subject and style, and to decree, finally, the meaning of their work.

276

14

Allegories of Healing

*The infinite Number of Fires . . . the clouds of Stinking
Breaths and Perspirations, not to mention the ordure of so
many diseas'd, both intelligent and unintelligent animals,
the crowded Churches, Church Yards and Burying Places,
with the putrefying Bodies, the Sinks, Butchers Houses,
Stables, Dunghills etc. . . . more than sufficient to putrefy,
poison and infect the Air for Twenty Miles around it, and
which in Time must alter, weaken and destroy the healthiest
of constitutions.*

GEORGE CHEYNE, *The English Malady* (1733)

IN THE SUMMER OF 1735, suddenly, in the middle of his campaign for the
Engravers' Act, Hogarth was hit by tragedy. Between eleven and twelve at
night, on Monday, 9 June, a fire broke out at a 'Brandy-Shop in Cecil Court,
St Martin's Lane': three days later the Irishwoman who lived there was
sentenced to Newgate for starting the fire deliberately. It flared and spread
fast, catching St Martin's Court, one exit of which led into Cranbourn Street
where Hogarth's mother and sisters lived, and raged unchecked for two
hours, while the local people struggled to get water to the fire engines. Foot-
guards were called in and the leaping flames and crashing timbers drew great
crowds. At that date the control of fire, involving troops, often brought royalty
to the scene, and in this case the Prince of Wales climbed to the top of a house
in St Martin's Court to survey the scene, then hurried down 'to direct the
Engines, and animate the Firemen'. The Prince, and local landowners like old
John Huggins, who owned property in St Martin's Lane, handed out money
to encourage men to help (and to discourage the thieves who were already
looting the buildings, or rather 'saving' things from the fire) but not until three
o'clock did the flames finally die down. By the time they were extinguished
about fifteen houses had been gutted and many others damaged. By then,
amid the acrid smell of smoke and damp ashes, Hogarth's mother Anne
had died.

Anne Hogarth was in good health when the fire started, but seems to have collapsed with shock as the flames raged near by. All that was publicly stated was that she died 'of a Fright' occasioned by the fire, at her house in Cranbourn Street. She was buried at St Anne's Church, Soho, on the evening of Thursday, 12 June. She was seventy-four, had borne eight children and lost five, and had held the family together in the hardest times, selling pills and ointments when Richard Hogarth was in the Fleet and running the home in Long Lane after his death, providing a base for Anne and Mary to start their millinery business and for William to open the engraving workshop that would eventually bring them security. Now William and his sisters, Mary and Anne, all childless, were all that remained of the household that had been through so much in those early years in Smithfield.[1]

Hogarth's childhood had also been darkened by the deaths of his brothers, Richard and Thomas, and by family memories of earlier Hogarth children who died even before he was born. The streets around him had been full of sickness and want, with the ancient hospital of St Bartholomew's standing like a refuge in their midst. Now the Hospital became the focus of his own energies. In one of his jumbled, third-person notes, he later wrote that before he concentrated on his modern moral subjects:

'the puffing in books about the grand stile of history painting put him upon trying how that might take, so without haveing a stroke of this grand business before immediatly from family pictures in smal he painted a great stair case at Bartholomews Hospital with two scripture-stories, the Pool of Bethesday and the good Samaritan figures 7 foot high this present to the charity he by the pother made about the grand stile thought might serve as a specimen to shew that were there any inclination in England for Historical painting such a first essay whould Proove it more easily attainable than is imagined.'[2]

Hogarth wanted to show that English history-painters could outshine the Italians. He also wanted to try history-painting 'to see how that would take' and make his reputation in a new field; there were lamentably few opportunities for grand public schemes, and by snatching the St Bartholomew's commission he hoped to make a bravura show, leaping in one mighty stride from small conversation pictures to seven-foot figures. An additional motive (in which self-interest and disinterest are also hard to disentangle) was his desire to be an active participant in the great philanthropic movements so central to his age.

Involvement with charities was a sign of status as well as of benevolence. Hogarth had made good money from the prints of the *Harlot* and the *Rake*, of

Sarah Malcolm and the *Midnight Modern Conversation*, and he still had a small but steady revenue from his portraits, ranging from £8 for a head and shoulders to £60 for a large group work. He had no assistants to pay and, allowing for the expenditure on canvas, colours, oils and frames, from 1733 to 1735 he could probably count on an income of between £1,500 and £1,700 a year, equivalent to the earnings of a substantial merchant. From a platform of financial security he could afford to donate his work – which set him free both to paint as he liked and to make a statement about his own prosperity.

There was a long tradition of public charity in Britain: from Tudor times it had been the done thing for a well-off citizen to leave something to the community in his will, such as the endowment of an almshouse or a school. In the late seventeenth and early eighteenth centuries more emphasis was put on collective activities than individual bequests, applying to charity the method of the new joint-stock companies of the 1690s, which raised capital by finding small sums from many people. (Just as Hogarth, too, in his role as a trader, was turning from the single patron to the mass of lesser purchasers.) But although charitable giving was a matter of national pride and established custom, it was also a matter of conscience. It was the duty of the rich to give, almost as compensation for their own good fortune, 'a Sort of Restoring that Proportion of Wealth which doth not belong to You', wrote Robert Nelson in 1715. If 'you do not do Good with Your Riches, You use them contrary to the Intention of GOD, who is the absolute Master of them.'[3]

In secular terms, distress at the suffering of a fellow was seen as a demonstration of the powerful sympathy that bound one man to another, and proponents of 'benevolence' emphasized the benefit to the giver as well as to the receiver of charity; alleviating suffering brought not only status but feelings of intense pleasure, akin to the appreciation of beauty. Fielding's Tom Jones, for example, finds real pleasure – an almost sensual expansion of spirit – in charity, even, or especially, to the undeserving. What are worldly goods, he asks, 'compared to the warm, solid Content, the swelling Satisfaction, the thrilling Transports, which a good Mind enjoys in the Contemplation of a generous, virtuous, noble, benevolent Action'?[4]

Medical causes benefited from this ethos. The sick and maimed of London were an open, visible sore on the face of the capital, an affront to national pride and an appeal to personal pity. Children roamed the streets with rickety limbs and legs so bandy they were called 'cheese cutters', their 'scald heads' covered in scabs.[5] The terrible lack of sanitation brought ague and fever to the poor, whose long-worn clothes often rotted on their bodies, crawling with lice. The hospital movement, of which the refurbishment of St Bartholomew's was a prime example, was prompted by distress at such sights, but also by the new optimism about disease. In earlier centuries religious foundations such as St Bartholomew's and St Thomas's, which developed from the medieval hospices, were principally seen as last resorts for the needy. But as diseases became 'secularized', thought of as curable ills rather than as visitations from God, great new buildings arose in London: the Westminster in 1720, Guy's in 1724 and St George's, formed by a group of doctors who split from the Westminster, in 1733. The London and the Middlesex followed in the 1740s. Building alone, of course, did not solve the problems or offer solace for chronic sufferers: patients with cancer, consumption or smallpox were still turned away. The hospitals' façades were imposing but the great open wards were sites of chaos and pain. Amputations and minor operations were carried out fast, without anaesthetic, while hefty attendants held the patient down: skill and speed were vital – Cheselden could whip out gallstones in under a minute – but infection was rampant and the death rate was desperately high.

The doctors pushed reform for professional as well as humanitarian interests. In medicine, although the picture is not straightforward, there was still a pyramid of prestige. The Oxford- and Cambridge-educated College of Physicians clustered at the top, looking down on the surgeons, who learned

82 *An Operation Scene in a Hospital* (*c.* 1745)

280

through apprenticeships and were part of the Barber–Surgeons Company until 1745, and on the apothecaries, who had won the right to advise as well as to dispense drugs in 1703, but whose practice still smacked hopelessly of 'trade'. The surgeons had to fight deep unpopularity – the knife roused more fear than pill or potion – and both branches of medicine were linked with the cruelties of the State: for almost two hundred years Royal Charters had granted them the right to take the bodies of hanged men and women for public dissection in the cause of anatomical research and teaching. Often there were riots, and after 'numbers of disorderly persons' gathered at Tyburn in 1729, molesting the body-collectors from Surgeons' Hall, the sheriff was given special powers to arrest offenders. But even these hated anatomies were not enough. To achieve progress, doctors were eager to study and experiment on the living, and hospitals were the only places where they could get their hands on clinical material.

Hospitals brought them other benefits. Medicine and law were well-proven routes from humble beginnings to high status: successful practitioners mixed with the élite and, like the painters, had to prove themselves 'gentlemen' to win rich patients and clients. Appointments to the hospitals, on an honorary basis, brought status, publicity and contact with potential patrons among wealthy Governors. And although no doctor in the free hospitals was allowed to charge for treatment, he could take paying students, and give private courses of lectures, providing a fat addition to his income. When Hogarth painted the grand staircase, Bart's had two physicians in their early sixties, Richard Tyson, who was more interested in rebuilding the hospital than in curing patients, and the ambitious Pierce Dod,[6] and two surgeons, William Green and the pious and quarrelsome John Freke, a general surgeon and an expert in 'couching' for cataracts.

The great hospital movement thus served the growing professions as well as the sick and, more generally, allowed rich men to show disinterested benevolence. All the new hospitals were civic rather than State projects, paid for by subscription, and each had its own specific style of donor: the Westminster, for example, was founded by a group led by the banker Sir Henry Hoare, while the patrons of St George's were grander, including the Prince of Wales, the Royal Family and a clutch of Bishops and Lords (Chesterfield, Burlington, Bathurst) as well as Sir Robert Walpole himself. Bart's had always turned to the City and since Queen Anne's days had been linked with the High Church Tory interest so that it was hard for a non-Tory to get a post there. The fundraising involved annual tub-thumping sermons followed by a procession to a hall or a tavern, and a great dinner where purses opened while the wine flowed.

This philanthropic boom was changing the city for the better, and at forty, famous, ambitious and still idealistic, Hogarth was keen to be part of it. But he was also, true to his nature, somewhat sceptical about the self-congratulatory nature of the enterprise. He could detect that the hospital movement reflected an uneasy panic on behalf of the better-off – it was safer to 'warehouse' the unsightly urban sick than leave them to spread their diseases through the streets. Charity was not all pure in heart; the poor were supposed to be duly grateful, and sermons were as frequent as surgery.

When Hogarth was growing up near by, St Bartholomew's Hospital was almost bankrupt, its revenues diminished by the loss of rents and the cost of rebuilding after the Fire. A new gateway was built in 1702, but the old medieval lath-and-plaster buildings inside were crumbling. Slowly the income was recouped, and James Gibbs, then the most prestigious city architect, was commissioned to design new buildings. His great classical square would eventually be built over thirty years, wing by wing, and plans for the first wing, on the northern side of the courtyard, were approved in 1728. Clay dug in Kent was fired into bricks at the kilns on the city outskirts; slates were brought from Wales for the roof; ships from Norway and the Baltic brought deal for floor and roof timbers; seasoned oak from British woods came by the cartload for polished floorboards and staircases; honey-gold stone was sent from Ralph Allen's quarries at Bath to face the front of the building. For four years glaziers and plasterers, masons and painters flocked to Smithfield to work on the hospital. This 'grand Part of the Hospital' including the apartments where 'the Governors, the President and the Physicians would meet together' was finished by 1732, and by the time Hogarth began work the ceiling of the Great Hall had already been decorated with coloured stucco, and its huge oak fireplace carved with shields, festoons, roses, 'Oak leaves, ribbons and Herons'.[7]

After he won the contract in 1734, Hogarth worked slowly on his vast canvas, so large that he probably painted it in the scene-painting room at Covent Garden Theatre, where George Lambert (still the theatre's principal painter) helped him with the landscape background. Finally, in March 1736, the first painting, *The Pool of Bethesda*, was finished. The canvas was carried carefully across London, over the Fleet and across the dusty space of Smithfield, through the archway and into the inner courtyard, then up the steps and through the door to the new wing. The carpenters were called in, the scaffolding went up and the painting, in its decorative oval cartouche, was raised for all to see. On 12 April the Hospital announced proudly, through the *London Evening Post*, that:

'The ingenious Mr Hogarth, one of the Governors of St Bartholomew's Hospital, has presented to the said Hospital a very fine Piece of Painting, representing the miracle wrought by our Saviour at the Pool of Bethesda, which was hung up in their great stair-case last Wednesday.'

This was almost as much of an advertisement for Hogarth as for the picture and the Hospital. Vertue certainly thought Hogarth had put it in the paper himself, typical of the man, 'a good Front and a Scheemist', who had so skilfully supplanted Amigoni. But he admitted that Hogarth possessed an 'extraordinary Genius' and versatility, having succceeded in designing and engraving, in conversations and caricatures,

'& now history painting –, joyn'd to a happy – natural talent à la mode . . . but as to this great work of painting it is by everyone judged to be more that coud be expected of him'.[8]

The staircase did take the art world by surprise. Perhaps deliberately, since Hogarth had so much control over Thornhill's effects, its completion was announced just as the print was issued of Thornhill's altarpiece of the Last Supper, in Weymouth Church, and it was unveiled only a fortnight after the death of Nicholas Hawksmoor, the last of the old Wren school and a Governor of the hospital. With both these forebears in mind, Hogarth's work could be seen as a fitting display of English history-painting designed for English architecture, showing that a native artist could tackle a religious subject successfully.[9]

The Pool of Bethesda glows at the head of the grand staircase, celebrating, as the hospital minute book says, the 'Charity extended to the Poor Sick and Lame of this Hospital'.[10] In St John's Gospel, Jesus goes to the pool at the sheep market of Bethesda in Jerusalem, where a crowd of sick people lies under the five porches: 'a multitude of them that were sick, blind, halt, withered' (v. 6). At certain times an angel descends and troubles the water, after which the first to plunge in will be cured. When Christ hears that a man has lain there crippled for thirty-eight years, he asks him 'Wilt thou be made whole?':

'[7] The sick man answered him, Sir, I have no man, when the water is troubled to put me into the pool: but while I am coming another steppeth down before me. [8] Jesus saith unto him, Arise, take up thy bed, and walk. [9] And straightway the man was made whole, and took up his bed and walked.'

In Hogarth's *Pool of Bethesda*, however, the miracle of healing, and the

283

83 *The Pool of Bethesda* (1736)

vision of the body, sick or sound, is almost undermined by the politics. Like the people who step past the cripple in the parable, the courtesan's servant pushes roughly through, determined to get his mistress to the pool first, and another man is taking bribes to upset the queue. To Horace Walpole, this was typical of Hogarth's cynical humour, appropriate to the *Progresses* but not to divine history-painting. 'The genius that had entered so feelingly into the calamities and crimes of familiar life, deserted him,' Walpole wrote, 'in a walk that called for dignity and grace. The burlesque turn of his mind mixed itself with the most serious subjects. In *The Pool of Bethesda*, a servant of a rich ulcerated lady beats back a poor man that sought the same celestial remedy.' Such a touch was 'justly thought, but rather too ludicrous'.[11] But the harshness Walpole felt as an aesthetic affront stemmed from Hogarth's perception of a social outrage. While the hospital beds were full to overcrowding (one perk of being a Governor was having tickets to get your 'charges' in, useful when faced with sick servants), the poor swallowed poisonous patent medicines hawked at fairs and grander folk called in smart quacks. Hogarth shows Christ curing whoever comes to him, rich or poor; it is the very uncelestial attendants who take the bribes and corrupt the process.

He was also making a further point, that charity must override law, precedence and dogma. The real crux of the Bethesda story in St John's Gospel was that Christ's act of healing offended the Jewish authorities

284

84 The Good Samaritan (1736)

because it took place on the Sabbath. Ignoring the miraculous cures, they were outraged by the breaking of their rules. Hogarth's second painting for St Bartholomew's, *The Good Samaritan*, focuses on the same issue. Finally completed on the side wall of the staircase in May 1737, it again exalts charity as the foremost virtue, above faith or adherence to religious laws and rules: the Samaritan stops to help, while the righteous Levite and the Pharisee walk past the wounded man in case his blood makes them unclean.

This call to active philanthropy is also found in Fielding's witty, heart-felt readings of the Good Samaritan. Both he and Hogarth emphasize that appearances are not all; it is often the most outwardly unworthy who are the true Samaritans. Just as the old bunter helps the dying Moll, or Sarah Young and the turnkey lean tenderly over Tom's body in Bedlam, so in *Joseph Andrews*, when Joseph is found beaten up and naked in a ditch and the occupants of the coach refuse to take him in – the lady out of prudery, the lawyer out of fear – the Postilion, a youth later transported 'for robbing a Hen-roost', gives up his greatcoat.[12] Fielding repeatedly returns to this, notably in the Lucianic satire *A Journey from this World to the Next*, where Minos has to decide who is let into Elysium. Minos answers the lawyer's question that prompted the parable of the Good Samaritan, 'What shall I do to inherit eternal life?', by replacing the rigid 'justice' of law and religion with judgment based on feeling. The prude, the false patriot, the upright citizen

285

who disinherits his son for getting a bastard are all turned back: the man hanged for robbery of eighteen pence who has been a tender son and father is admitted. But there is, of course, a perpetual tension. While praise is meted out to movements of the heart that melt rules or warm the cold codes of law, both Fielding and Hogarth saw that their society was never going to *shed* its rules, and indeed, that it needed its laws – Fielding was, in the end, a magistrate.

Hogarth asks for clear vision, for feeling that discriminates but does not overturn authority. And he also suggests that unlikely people can be great benefactors. As if to bring home his point, at St Bartholomew's he added small panels in a red tint, below the carved frame of the stories, showing the story of Rahere, the minstrel who entertained Henry II, made a pilgrimage to Rome and founded the hospital. No one, walking up the staircase at St Bartholomew's, should ignore the local artist. Hogarth determinedly brought London history and London streets into the New Testament story. Even the dogs who roamed the alleys find a place here; the cur licking his wounds in *The Good Samaritan*, the eager pointed-nosed mongrel leaping down the gilded scrolls of the frame in *The Pool of Bethesda*, the dog barking to rouse Rahere from his dream.

Such details had no place in 'high art': Hogarth's appeal to nature wrenched the tradition. The *Pool* in particular, whose curving arches and grouped figures refer back to Raphael's *Healing of the Lame Man in the Temple*, departs from the generalized dignity of classical history-painting. Here Hogarth's artistic influences seem as mixed as the stuff dresses and shawls mingling with the biblical robes, his graceful nude recalling Rubens or Titian, his crowd of poor looking grotesquely Dutch. Rather to the discomfort of critics then and since, many of the sick who crowd to the pool are recognizably real – indeed they could almost be current inmates of St Bartholomew's. These cases could all be seen in London: an old man leaning on crutches holding his tumour-swollen belly; a girl with an inflamed breast, a woman with jaundice and another with the thin frame and greeny pallor of TB; an obese 'cretin-faced' girl, a blind man with his stick and a man cradling his painful gouty arm. Even the rich naked woman was rumoured to be a portrait of Nell Robinson, a celebrated courtesan with whom Hogarth had been 'very intimately acquainted' in early life, here seeking a cure for her inflamed arthritic knee, a symptom of gonorrhea or early syphilis.[13]

This medical inclusiveness reflects Hogarth's artistic interests, as well as his social politics. He was deeply intrigued by the infinite variety of human forms and faces seen in a crowd, by their deformity as well as beauty. One

286

long-time medical friend was James Parsons, who shared his interest in physical oddity and facial expression; he published a book on hermaphrodites in 1741 and one on physiognomy in 1747. All artists knew the principles of Le Brun, whose classic work, or 'common-drawing book' as Hogarth called it, followed the ancient theory that the passions, lodged in the soul, were transmitted through animal spirits rising from the brain 'from tranquillity to extreme despair', and creating specific facial and bodily expressions for hope, anger, fear, love, delight and misery.[14] But Hogarth – a man of his age – blended these old theories of 'passions' and 'humours' with empirical observation.[15] He sought *physical* causes for expressions – the effect of habitual muscle movement in frowning or smiling, the creeping impact of old age, the stress of pain and disease, even the way that temperature and weather made such a difference to the look of 'the same beauty in a winter morning in the park and a sommers evening'.[16]

He was fascinated by anatomy, which he wove into his discussion of the curving line in the *Analysis of Beauty*.[17] You can almost hear him talking this over with anatomist friends. Almost every muscle and bone, he wrote, has a kind of twist:

'there is scarce a straight bone in the whole body . . . and the muscles annex'd to them, tho' they are of various shapes, appropriated to their particular uses, generally have their component fibres running in these serpentine lines, surrounding and conforming themselves to the varied shape of the bones they belong to: more especially in the limbs. Anatomists are so satisfied of this, that they take a pleasure in distinguishing their several beauties.'[18]

Translating into layman's language, he goes on to talk about the thigh bone and the hips, with 'the beautiful bones adjoining, call'd the ossa innominata', and the muscles which wind round them:

'as to the running of their fibres, some anatomists have compared them to skains of thread, loose in the middle, and tight at each end, when they are thus consider'd as twisted contrary ways around the bone'.

The writing is as vivid as if he has just attended a dissection himself, but his emphasis is *aesthetic*, not medical. He used physical observation to help him paint, reinforcing assumptions, for example, about the different approach to portraiture of men, women and children. He noted the joints of fingers, down to the lines in the wrinkles of the knuckles or the 'taper dimpled' fingers of fine ladies. He had firm ideas about gender and body shape, insisting that 'there is an elegant degree of plumpness peculiar to the skin of the softer sex, that

287

occasions these delicate dimplings in all their other joints, as well as these of the fingers', a sweetness and simplicity 'as will always give the turn of the female frame' a preference to that of the finest man, as Venus to Apollo.[19]

This peculiarly excited sensual–aesthetic response is found even where he writes of the concealing, rounding role of the skin, which 'tenderly embraces' the angles of muscle and bone, admiring the way

'nature most judiciously softens these hardnesses, and plumps up these vacancies with a proper supply of fat, and covers the whole with the soft, smooth, springy, and in delicate life, almost transparent skin'.

Nature herself is a sculptor, a painter; the language of anatomist and artist merge. Elswhere, talking of colouring, he writes that,

'nature hath contrived a transparent skin, called the cuticula, with a lining to it of an extraordinary kind, called the cutis; both which are so thin any little scald will make them blister and peel off . . . the cuticula alone is like gold-beaters-skin, a little wet, but somewhat thinner, especially in fair young people, which would show the fat, lean, and all the blood-vessels, just as they lie under it, as through Isinglass, were it not for its lining the cutis.'[20]

In the cutis, 'composed of tender threads like network', the 'different coloured juices' determine the complexion; the pigments of nature must be transferred into those of the painter's palette.

Hogarth could be unnervingly direct in his detached, visual appreciation of the physical. The hugely successful surgeon and midwife William Hunter, who performed public anatomies in the 1740s and 1750s and also lectured to the artists, later wrote:

'You cannot conceive anything lying snugger than the foetus in utero. This puts me in mind of Hogarth. He came to me when I had a gravid uterus to open and was amazingly pleased. Good God, cries he, how snug and compleat the Child lies. I defy all our painters in St Martins Lane to put a child in such a situation. He had a good eye, took it off and in drawing afterwards very well expressed it.'[21]

This passionate, detailed vision of the body feeds Hogarth's work, whether it be the naked body of Tom Rakewell in Bedlam or the robust, shining faces of solid burgers and dancing children.

The harsh subjects of Hogarth's paintings are often strangely softened by his sheer beauty of detail and vivid colouring. This is true of *The Pool of Bethesda* and *The Good Samaritan*, as it is of the paintings of *A Rake's Progress*. But as soon as he turns to engraving, the ideas leap out, and the sensual grace of his brushstroke gives way to the intellectual bite of the acid or the burin. It is as if disgust at the gulf between ideal and real is suddenly released in the acid of his black-and-white prints. Thus he could paint glowing conversation pieces while meditating sharp satires of the same set of people, or moving parables of healing while etching caricatures of would-be healers.

In March and April 1737, for example, while he was putting the finishing touches to the *The Good Samaritan*, Hogarth advertised a print of a mock coat of arms called *The Company of Undertakers*. This was originally to have been called just 'A Consultation of Quacks'. John Ireland later said that three things marked out the doctor of the day, 'his gravity, his cane and his periwig': the canes, like the wigs, marked the doctors' gentlemanly status, their silver

85 *The Company of Undertakers* (1737)

289

tops often pomanders carrying salt and scents to offset infections. Hogarth had already showed the cane-carrying quacks in *A Harlot's Progress*. In this funeral escutcheon, a grim cloud of medics appears above the motto 'Et Plurima Mortis Imago' ('everywhere the image of death').[22] A dozen 'proper doctors' cluster at the bottom, nine sniff or nod on their canes while two examine a urine glass and a third dips in his finger to taste its contents, an ancient diagnostic method. The portrait spotters identified one as Pierce Dod, a fierce opponent of smallpox inoculation, and another as Dr Bamber, 'a celebrated anatomist, physician and man-midwife', who had also worked at Bart's. (Much later, in *The Stages of Cruelty*, Hogarth also drew the Bart's surgeon John Freke.) In the top rank of this coat of arms, complete with formal heraldic explanation, were three characters so famous they could not be mistaken: 'two 'demi-doctors' on left and right ('dexter' and 'sinister' in punning heraldic terms) and a 'complete doctor' in the centre, a trio of notorious quacks.

On the left, with 'an eye couchant' decorating his cane, is the insufferably self-publicizing John Taylor, who trained under William Cheselden before becoming a wandering oculist, fêted in the Royal Courts of Europe, exposed for his fraudulent 'wonder cures' and now oculist to the King.[23] On the right is Joshua Ward, called Spot Ward for the birthmark shading his face, the inventor of 'Ward's Drop', whose mixture of arsenic and antimony could bring paralysis, blindness and death. His devotees included Princess Emily and the King, but his medicine, said Hervey, 'vomits, purges and sweats in a great degree'.[24]

In the centre, queening it over the self-important men below, is Sarah Mapp, a famous bone-setter. The daughter of a Wiltshire farrier, she had travelled the country as 'Crazy Sally' before coming into vogue with the élite. 'In most cases,' wrote Nichols bluntly, 'her success was rather owing to the strength of her arms, and the boldness of her undertakings than to any knowledge of anatomy or skill in chirurgical operations.' In August 1736 she was in the news: her new husband ran off with 100 guineas (she said gaily that she was better off without him) and a week later a satiric paean appeared in *The Grub-Street Journal*. The poem invokes Ward and Taylor, but Mapp reigns supreme:

> Let these, O Mapp! thou wonder of the age!
> With dubious arts endeavour to engage:
> While you, irregularly strict to rules,
> Teach dull collegiate pedants they are fools.[25]

She attended the Queen and was the star of a special evening at Lincoln's Inn Fields in October, where 'The Wife's Relief: or the Husband's Cure' and 'The Worm Doctor' were put on at her request. The latter included 'A Harlequin Female Bone-Setter' (Hogarth dresses her thus) and a 'Doctor Pestle' and included a new ballad, which also lies behind his print:

> While Mapp to th'actors shew'd regard,
> On one side Taylor sat, on t'other Ward
> When their mock persons of the drama came
> Both Ward and Taylor thought it hurt their fame:
> Wonder'd how Mapp cou'd in good humour be –
> Zounds! cries the dame, it hurts not me,
> Quacks without art may either blind or kill,
> But demonstrations shew that mine is skill . . .
>
> You surgeons of London, who puzzle your pates
> To ride in your coaches, and purchase estates,
> Give over for shame, for pride has a fall
> And the Doctress of Epsom has out-done you all.[26]

Hogarth might have felt some sympathy for Mapp as an 'irregular' expert besting pomposity, but this is topped by his sheer relish for her as the Quackest Quack of all, and female to boot. In Hogarth's print the dark goddess rules over her court of fools, men who have taken over the ancient realm of women's healing, and now profit from the people's ills and credulity. This too, is one of Hogarth's all-too-human allegories of healing.

This was only one of a flurry of prints that Hogarth brought out in the winter of 1736–7, working on them hard, as soon as *The Pool of Bethesda* was installed. He followed up the success of the *Harlot* and the *Rake* by engraving earlier works with risqué themes, like the indoor *Before* and *After*. But his eye was now definitely on the self-serving professionals. In many prints he implicitly links the priests, doctors and teachers with intellectuals and artists, criticizing them all for being out of touch with the needs of those around them. *The Sleeping Congregation* was published in October 1736; the *Scholars at a Lecture* in January 1737; and *The Distressed Poet* in March. In the same month, he bunched together *A Chorus of Singers* and *The Laughing Audience*, with the *Scholars* and *The Company of Undertakers*, selling them as 'Four Etchings of different Characters of Heads in Groups'. This was partly a response to Arthur Pond's series, begun in 1736, of prints based on Italian caricatures –

86 *Scholars at a Lecture* (1737)

sophisticated linear reductions of faces and expressions. Hogarth would always insist he drew characters, not 'caricatures', and his work at St Bartholomew's, despite its grand style, was a further demonstration of the power of the face and physique to reveal the inner life.

The large scale of his hospital paintings seems to have been a spur. In the mid-1730s Hogarth moved with exuberance and brio from one mode to another, from small, sharp prints to huge canvases, as if confident that he could do anything, and do it well. His spirit and ambition seemed to soar. Working in the painting room behind his house, inspired to experiment in the 'grand manner', he produced a classical painting of *Danae* (now lost, but listed among those sold in 1745) and a rich Shakespearean scene from *The Tempest*.[27] One of the most startling pictures he ever painted stems from these years, *Satan, Sin and Death*. Perhaps prompted by Jonathan Richardson's book on Milton, which he had mocked so unkindly, he took up a scene of terror from *Paradise Lost*. History-painters, Richardson suggested, might visualize the confrontation at the Gates of Hell when Satan encounters Death and the awful figure of Sin:

87 *Satan, Sin and Death* (c. 1738)

Before the Gates there sat
on either side a formidable shape:
the one seem'd Woman to the waste, and fair,
But ended foul in many a scaly fould
Voluminous and vast, a Serpent arm'd
With mortal sting . . .[28]

This is an exercise in the Sublime, celebrating Britain's epic poet as Italian painters had done the works of Tasso or Ariosto. Satan and Death, 'Fierce as ten furies, terrible as Hell', are on the verge of combat when Sin surges between them, explaining that she is Satan's daughter and Death their incest-born son.[29] Hogarth follows Milton's description, from the hell-hounds round Sin's waist, to Death's 'dreadful Dart', kingly crown and 'horrid stride'. Amid the sulphurous clouds, the red of blood and the black of death, points of light flash from Satan's dart and eyes. In the centre, above the mass of snakes, Sin flows forward, arms outstretched, vulnerable yet immune.

Probably commissioned by Jonathan Rich, the painting is a work of such

293

theatrical originality that it seems to be quite out of its era, leaping forward like a bridge between the Baroque and the Romantics at the end of the century: Fuseli, John Martin and Blake.[30] This was the inner vision of madness, sublime or demonic, whose outer shell he had showed in Tom Rakewell. This darkness, too, sprang from Hogarth's mind, as vividly as the realism of the sick at Bethesda or the scenes of Bedlam. Where, he asks – like a man who shuns revelation and redemption yet is haunted by Puritan visions of struggle and faith – is the parable of healing that can salve this overwhelming human ill, the sickness of Sin and the bony stride of Death?

15

City Spaces

Houses, churches, mixed together,
Streets unpleasant in all weather;
Prisons, palaces contiguous,
Gates, a bridge, the Thames irriguous.

Gaudy things enough to tempt ye,
Showy outsides, insides empty;
Bubbles, trades, mechanic arts,
Coaches, wheelbarrows and carts.

Warrants, bailiffs, bills unpaid,
Lords of laundresses afraid:
Rogues that nightly rob and shoot men,
Hangmen, aldermen and footmen.

Lawyers, poets, priests, physicians,
Noble, simple, all conditions:
Worth beneath a threadbare cover,
Villainy bedaubed all over.

Women black, fair, red and grey,
Prudes and such as never pray,
Handsome, ugly, noisy, still,
Some that will not, some that will.

Many a beau without a shilling,
Many a widow not unwilling;
Many a bargain, if you strike it:
This is London! How d'ye like it?

JOHN BANCKS, 'A Description of London' (1738)

HOGARTH WAS BUSY in 1736, painting for St Bartholomew's, organizing the new Academy, publishing prints under the new Engravers' Act. He still

295

undertook portraits, but the main thrust of his work was towards the public, from the mass production of prints to the use of the Hospital as a place of display. And all his arguments about the subject, style and status of his work were linked to deep-held views about the city and the people, and the function of art.

In Leicester Fields he lived in the heart of the city, a patch of art and commerce like the central panel of a triptych, between the old bourgeois City and the smart West End. Winding through the middle, from Charing Cross to St Giles, like a marker of the district's character, ran St Martin's Lane. Obliterate the map of modern London – no Trafalgar Square, no Shaftesbury Avenue, and a different view emerges. Imagine Hogarth, on a summer day in 1733, visiting a bookseller in Round Court at the southern end of the Lane. In this crowded, angular space, amid the perfumers and milliners, hang a forest of classical signs – 'Cicero's Head', 'Horace's Head', 'Plato's Head'. But the bookseller's fare is mixed: Addison and Boyle share shelves with treatises on midwifery and texts of recent plays, and the 'Camden's Head' has Newton's works and Thomson's *Four Seasons* with 'Curious copper-plates' designed by Kent. Across the way, where Pinchbeck trades at the 'Fan and Crown', one can snap up 'The Ladies Historical and Political Fan; or, the European Race'.[1]

Walking home from here, in September 1736, Hogarth might duck back into the Strand. Turning right, past the King's Head and the Checkers Inn, he would walk down towards the curving triangle of Charing Cross. On his left, Whitehall ran down to Westminster. In front were the Great Mews where the royal horses were kept, with the Green Mews behind them; another reminder of his rival, for in 1732 the old mews had been knocked down and replaced with Kent's new buildings, following Burlington's designs. Past their dignified, ostentatious façade, Cockspur Street swung up towards St James's and the Court.

Curiosities could make passers-by linger at Charing Cross; in November 1732, for example, the German giant, Maximilian Muller, whom Hogarth included in *Southwark Fair*, was displaying himself for money to all-comers. But just as the Strand funnelled into the open space, Hogarth might swing right, into the narrow, muddy opening to the Lane by the Checkers Inn. Opposite the crossing to Spring Gardens was swept by a one-legged beggar, Ambrose Gwinnett, who had been hanged at Deal for murder, but was cut down by his family and fled to sea.[2] Every corner had a story. In this part of the Lane, with the Star Inn on the east and Woodstock Court, Dukes Court, Ellis Court and Red Lion Court crammed up against the Mews walls on the west, lived more booksellers and bookbinders. The houses were old, built over fields

296

and hop gardens a century ago; one or two, like the leaning Italian warehouse, still had their rich Jacobean carvings and projecting windows. Hogarth would pick his way through the mud and dung spattering the roadway from the White Horse Livery stables, and the spray thrown up by children playing in the horseponds on each side of the lane. The horseponds were sites of rough justice, where the mob ducked offenders. A woman who picked a man's pocket in August 1734 (while bystanders gawped at the ruins of a fire) was flung into the pond behind the mews near Leicester Fields, and a gin-informer was 'horseponded' in the one in Moor's Yard, next to St Martin-in-the-Fields.[3]

Hogarth walked past scenes of city punishment, sin and repentance, prayer and play. Facing the church stood the stocks and the old round-house prison, where the prostitutes and petty thieves were herded nightly. Just by the stocks was 'the Barn' where the chess and draughts players met, and where a legendary match took place after a bet at Old Slaughter's, when Roubiliac persuaded Smith to play Blind Parry, one of the best draughts players in England.[4] On the south side of the church was the King's Arms Tavern, with its rough, horse-dealing clientele. And near by, close to the Rainbow Coffee House, in Lancaster Court, was the shop of John Williams, bug destroyer, who advertised in *The Craftsman* of 1733 with a plate showing six of the 'buggs' he destroyed; ten years later he claimed he 'had the Honour to be employ'd by the greatest Nobility, Gentry and others in Town to destroy Bugs out of Palaces and other ancient Buildings', promising that his 'infallible liquid (not to be paralleled in England)' was 'not offensive to the nose, or dangerous to fine furniture'.[5]

Once past the church, if Hogarth wanted to turn quickly into Leicester Fields, he could veer left into Hemmings Rents, the first throughway for carriages in the Lane, where coaches swung past, crushing walkers against the wall as they scurried into Dennis Pere, the jeweller, at the sign of the Ring and Pearl.[6] If he kept straight on up the Lane, however, Hogarth would pass Johnson's glass shop, with its 'curious lustres, new fashion Salts, Diamond cut and scallop'd Candlesticks, Decanters, Plates, Dishes, Bowls, Basons, Cups, Saucers, Middle-Stands, Desart Glasses, all cut, scallop'd and flower'd Glasses'.[7] China shops and furniture warehouses spilled on to the pavement, which was itself a thing of wonder, with broad flagstones replacing the old cobbles. There were few fully paved streets in London, and in other parts of the city each house and shop-owner cared for the patch outside the door; fops in high red heels would stumble and sway between gleaming slabs and dusty ruts, stepping delicately past the piles of rubbish, ashes and oyster shells.

The pavement was always crowded, with beggars in doorways, burly shopmen, footmen on errands, women out shopping. Hogarth's route wound past Tom's Coffee House, where prints and rare books were auctioned; past Dawson's buildings (where the London Coliseum now stands); past Charles Court, where the Palladian architect Isaac Ware had worked as a chimney-sweep in his youth; past the shop of Mrs Lewis who held the monopoly for condoms, clumsy affairs made of sheep-gut, tied round the balls with red ribbon.[8] On he would go, past the houses where Chippendale later established his workshop at 'The Covered Chair'; past Roubiliac's studio; past the old Camisard's Coffee-House. Beyond Long Acre, he entered 'Little St Martin's Lane' with its inns and coffee houses, shops and workshops: the Cross Keys Inn, the chandler's shop, the coachmakers at the Golden Boy and the Golden Lion. Here, on the west side, three doors from Newport Street, was Old Slaughter's, and a few doors on was the St Martin's Lane Academy.

As he walked through the city, Hogarth noticed tricks of light and shade, perspective and distance – how a church tower, exactly the same colour as a cloud behind it, seemed to disappear completely, so that the lead-coloured spire 'seemd suspended in the air'; how the steeple of Bloomsbury Church, when you walked down from Hampstead, 'seems to stand upon Montague-House, tho' it is several hundred yards distant from it'.[9] He scanned the people, their dress, their way of walking and the way their trades affected their bodies, turning them into recognizable types. The great weight that the chairmen carried made their calves stout, so they became '*characters* as to figure'. Watermen, by contrast, had thin legs, because their whole strength was needed in their shoulders and arms. All this bolstered his belief that daily life, not antiquity, should be the artist's model:

'There is scarcely a waterman that rows upon the Thames whose figure doth not confirm this observation. Therefore were I to paint the character of a Charon, I would thus distinguish his make from that of a common man's; and in spite of the word *low*, venture to give him a broad pair of shoulders, and spindle shanks, whether I had the authority of an antique statue, or basso-relievo, for it or not.'[10]

'Low' people, he found, were as good critics of proportion as any artist. Women could always 'speak skilfully of necks hands and arms', outdoing many a man of science. As soon as men stripped for boxing, even a butcher could judge their physique and give you odds on the winner; he had heard a blacksmith harangue like an anatomist or a sculptor on the beauty of a boxer's figure, 'tho' perhaps not in the same terms'.

Hogarth was not only beautifying London's public buildings when he

298

painted the St Bartholomew's staircase, he was painting the Londoners he saw – the sick and the well, the benefactors and the hypocrites. At the height of allegory he was still depicting the city. Hogarth's prints still hang dustily in corners of the city's bars and cafés and theatre foyers; he built a London of the mind, matching the rising bricks and the spreading net of streets and squares. He painted the chandeliers of St James's, the dark corners of Bridewell, Bedlam and the Fleet, the raucous pleasures of Southwark Fair or the Rose Tavern.

Hogarth's London was also a moral map, which its inhabitants could follow as they traced the progress of his Harlot westwards from the Bell Inn in Cheapside, to the house of the Jew in the City, or, perhaps, in Covent Garden, and then to the slums of Drury Lane and St Giles. The Rake's progress reached further west, into the purlieus of luxury, as he moved from his father's crumbling City house to his smart salon in the West End; his arrest took place on the corner of Piccadilly and St James's Street, with St James's Palace in the background, right outside the doors of White's. Inexorably, as in a terrible game, Tom swings around this central hinge between the polite world and the city, before falling back eastwards to the Fleet, and to Bedlam on the corner of the stinking Moorfield marshes.

While Hogarth's topography had an allegorical value as clear as Bunyan's hills and valleys and sloughs and cities it was also vividly accurate; in many cases still recognizable today. For the scene of Tom's marriage Hogarth drew the dilapidated walls of Marylebone Old Church. The setting was symbolic: the Creed ruined by damp, the Ninth Commandment cracked, the poor box covered by a cobweb. But the inscription on the pews, announcing that the Forset family vault lies beneath, was genuine enough; so was the mural monument to the Taylors, seen under the window. And so was the inscription on the wall announcing the church 'was beautifyed in the year 1725, Tho. Sice, Tho. Horn *Church Wardens*'. These men really were the churchwardens when the 'repairs' were done, and Hogarth need show no more to suggest they had cheated the parish. The crumbling church was pulled down six years later.

Just as Londoners rushed to identify Hogarth's individual portraits, so they enjoyed finding real streets and alleys and inns and churches and characters. Hogarth, too, enjoyed the detail, sometimes elaborating it in later revisions. Thus in the picture of Tom's arrest, when he replaced the ragged boy stealing the cane with seven urchins, each had his own identity. A chimney-sweep, peering over a post-boy's cards, raises two fingers, showing he has two honours, and another child is deep in the *Farthing Post*, a piratical newspaper (avoiding the stamp duty) publishing news and gossip. 'The chief

299

of these', wrote Nichols, 'who wears something that seems to have been a tie-wig, was painted from a French boy who cleaned shoes at the corner of Hog Lane.'[11]

In this scene, even the smells of London seem present: the dung of the horses, the mixed odours of shoe-blacking, fresh paint and lamp oil, the perfume of the fops, trailing clouds of scented powder from their newly dusted wigs, the sweat of the chair carriers, soaking their cambric shirts and heavy coats. And the sounds are there too: Tom's cry of distress and Sarah's pleading, and the threatening rumble of the bailiff demanding his money. Many of Hogarth's paintings and prints echo with silent sound – from the solemnly repeated verses and the whispering of the governess in *The Conquest of Mexico*, to the cries and trumpets and yells and sounding drum of *Southwark Fair*.

The most sonorous print is *The Enraged Musician*, a companion to *The Distressed Poet*. Everything that can make a noise seems to be here, while the desperate musician looks out of his window, helpless against the barrage of the street's wild music. The noise in London's streets astonished foreigners, and seemed like an epitome of English licence, anarchy or – as Englishmen preferred – their freedom. This could well be the noise of St Martin's Lane, or perhaps further over, near Drury Lane, since a playbill advertises *The Beggar's Opera* which was playing there when the print was first advertised in 1740. But the songs of Gay's show – itself an assault on the pretensions of Italian opera – echoed through every city street in these years.

Music was everywhere: the wandering oboe, or 'hautboy', player was a well-known character and so was the ballad-singer with her baby, crooning the tragic song of 'The Ladies Fall'. But how could these compete with the bashing of the pavior in his Irish cap, the clattering of the dustman heaving his basket to his head, the tinny beating of the pewterer at his shop in the background, the knifegrinder sharpening his screeching blades, the pealing bells ringing from the steeple, celebrating the public holiday marked by its hoisted flag? Small boys join in, beating a drum and trapping squawking birds. The little girl holds a rattle, and even the city wildlife adds its chorus, from the screeching parrot to the rooftop cats howling at the emerging chimney-sweep. The poor professional has as much chance of making sweet music as the girl does of planting her garden in the cobbles, prompting a boy to piss loudly all over it.

The hunt for the musician's name was irresistible and three were soon suggested. First he was said to be a bass-player, Cervetto; then Castrucci, the leader of Handel's orchestra, who had invented an instrument called 'the

88 *The Enraged Musician* (1741)

violetta marina'; then John Festin, 'the first hautboy and German flute of his time'.[12] It could even be the composer Thomas Arne, about thirty at the time, whose father lived near by in King Street. But Festin used to teach fashionable pupils every morning, and made a huge fortune in this way. One morning at nine o'clock, so a clergyman told Nichols, he went to one pupil, the future Lord Vernon. Since he was not yet up, Festin went into his room, opened the shutter and sat down by the window. A man was playing an hautboy outside.

'A man with a barrow of onions came up to the player and sat on the edge of his barrow, and said to the man, "if you will play the Black Joke, I will give you this onion". The man played it. When he had done so, the man again desired

301

him to play some other tune, and then he would give him another onion. "This", said Festin, "highly angered me; I cried out, Z—ds, Sir, stop here. This fellow is ridiculing my profession: he is playing on the hautboy for onions".'[13]

Being a friend of Hogarth, Festin told him the story – hence *The Enraged Musician*.

It's a good story, true or not, typical of the way people liked to link these living pictures to real life. The print itself, like many of Hogarth's works, is curiously ambivalent. On the one hand, Hogarth seems to sympathize with the bedevilled musician trying to hear his own music; yet he also makes him comic, as if criticizing his pretension and asserting the right of those outside to make what noise they will. The street has its grace as well as its chaos, and amid the rabid noise the milkmaid crying her wares is as haunting as his drummer in *Southwark Fair*; far more beautiful, for example, than the milk-seller dunning the worried wife in *The Distressed Poet*. Hogarth shows her pacing her 'milk-walk', a territory that was bought and sold. As she went, she would chalk up the tally on each customer's doorpost, probably working for her father, a milk-carrier who had fetched the milk early that morning from one of the cow-keepers in the parks or outside the city. Her creamy milk was a small city luxury, a taste of nature amid the bricks and mortar, as precious and life-giving in its way as music itself.

In 1736 Hogarth portrayed London in a different way, in four paintings of *The Four Times of the Day*: *Morning*, *Noon*, *Evening* and *Night*. Later, the paintings were sold to private buyers, but not before Hogarth had them engraved, with the help of the veteran French engraver Bernard Baron. As in the case of the *Rake*, the mood of the paintings is interestingly different from the prints, the shift from colour into black and white reinforcing the disconcerting mirror-image reversal of the engraving. While the prints are satirical, the paintings are lyrical, their sweeping brushwork and flowing colours suggesting a tolerance of oddity, even a profound attraction to the elements the 'refined' viewer is asked ostensibly to disapprove.

The four paintings look at first like a comic documentary of London and they have often been celebrated, from the late eighteenth century onwards, as illustrating Hogarth's originality, translating the tropes of pastoral poetry into city life. In fact they are yet another instance of his buoyant adaptation of artistic, rather than literary, conventions.[14] The classical 'Times of Day' tradition of Greece and Rome, celebrating the gods while registering the transience of human life, had been humanized in Michelangelo's four great sculptures for the Medici Chapel; in the sixteenth and seventeenth centuries this theme was a favourite of Dutch and German engravers and it crept into French engraving too, in the early eighteenth century, in charming allegorical *fêtes galantes*.

In the early Dutch prints, the allegorical figures of Dawn or Night lounge in classical poses on scrolling clouds above emblematic scenes, accompanied by verses reminding us of the brief spell of light between enveloping shades, the inevitable progression from youth to weary age, spring to snowy winter. Within these scenes, complex patterns of symbols refer to other traditions, drawn from astrology, religion or classical poetry. Gradually, in one line of artistic descent, the deities disappeared and their resonance became embedded in the landscape itself, a pastoral heavy with meaning. In another tradition, the mythological figures alone remained, separated from their scenes and descending like hieroglyphs into the conventional poses of the emblem books.[15] These foreign treatments of what became known as the *points du jour* were standard furnishings of English stately homes; prints of them were pinned up in the printsellers', sold at auctions, used in weavers' pattern books and tucked into the copy books of students and artists.

In *The Four Times of the Day* Hogarth was therefore reworking a cliché, or rather restating it in an entirely new way, implicitly criticizing the tired imitations that had gone before. In *Morning*, Aurora, the goddess of dawn, steps out as a prudish English spinster heading to the temple-like front of St Paul's, Covent Garden, with a shivering footboy instead of chubby putti. In *Noon*, the pagan Venus, Cupid and Apollo lounge among the midday crowds, in the guise of an English maid with her son and African 'sunburnt' lover, 'outfacing the churchgoers'. In *Evening*, a fierce (but unchaste) Diana, carrying a fan which tells her mythic story, drags her hen-pecked, cuckolded husband back from a day out in the 'groves' of Sadler's Wells. In the city lanes of *Night*, Proserpina becomes a gawping woman tumbled from her chariot, and Pluto a drunken Freemason, a tyrannical magistrate who holds the London underworld in thrall, but defies sobriety and justice in his own private life.[16]

The clever references would be quickly spotted by everyone familiar with the *point-du-jour* prints, who could follow the allusions in all the details of signs and clothes, houses and food. For people without this knowledge, who pressed their noses to the print-shop windows, the prints told a simpler story, painting the contrasts of their own city in heat and cold, youth and age, festival and fast. Adjusting his stage set of buildings and streets very slightly, Hogarth showed them a London they knew. Here is Covent Garden on a snowy

MORNING

89 *Morning, The Four Times of the Day* (1738)

morning, its tall roofs soft with snow against a lowering sky, icicles hanging like lace from Tom King's coffee house. The church clock of St Paul's, surmounted by the grim reaper with his scythe, shows five minutes to eight. The market woman still needs her lantern as she carries her huge basket to her stall and children in stout coats, with bags on their back, sniff fresh-baked bread. Dr Rock is already up selling his pills and in Tom King's coffee house, a fight is going on, staves are waving in the shadowy entrance and a wig is flying through the air. (Perhaps the woman pleading is Moll King, who took over after her husband's death in 1737. She made it a rule to open the door after the taverns closed, from midnight to dawn; the beaux went there straight from Court, in full dress with their swords, mingling in their rich brocaded coats with porters and soldiers and sweeps.) Hogarth shows the drooping-eyed rakes fondling their girls, their inner heat warding off the cold, while the scrawny older women crouch over the kindling, or raise a hand to beg.

If the scene were only this, then it might be called a documentary. But at the centre of the picture – and in the painting she focuses the light in her acid-lemon dress – stands a thin middle-aged woman on her way to church, touching her fan to her lips in apparent distaste at the display of young lust. As she judges them, she herself is implicitly condemned by her bony shape and her pursed lips, and by the young page who follows her, shivering in the cold, carrying her prayer book under his arm: with a hint back to *The Good Samaritan*, the page, not the rich woman, is the one who has his hand in his pocket, directly in line with the beggar woman's outstretched palm. A hidden suggestion is that this prudish spinster in her finery who disdains charity and expresses dismay at amorous display may herself, secretly, be on the look-out for a lover. (Fielding took the measure of Hogarth's judgement when he cited her in connection with Bridget Allworthy in *Tom Jones*. Bridget, as the reader later discovers, is far from frigid, indeed she is full of desire, but she will not admit to it openly and her 'prudence' and desperate care for appearances almost ruins the life of her unacknowledged son, as well as her own.)

At this stage, Hogarth did not wholly damn the loud life of the streets. Instead he judges those who judge, exposes the hypocrites, ridicules those who put form over feeling. In *Noon*, anarchy erupts beneath the signs of good eating and the tavern flagons. Appetites of all kinds are pounding, and are often frustrated. An angry houswife hurls her husband's lunch, a leg of lamb, straight through the window. A black servant, a 'natural' part of this overly physical crowd, nuzzles the maid's cheek and squeezes her breasts; she throws her head back dreamily, 'her pye-dish tottering like her virtue, and with the most precious parts of its contents running over'.[17] Stunned by the sudden

305

stream from the pie's nipple, the baker boy breaks his plate, bangs his head, screws up his face and explodes with absurd, howling distress, leaving the quick neat-fingered girl to snap up his fallen food. Chaotic it may be, but this side of the road is certainly lusty, hungry and alive. Opposite, where the congregation leave the French Church, daintily avoiding a dead cat in the gutter, that is not the case.

The Huguenots had done well in London, and Hogarth suggests that although the righteous elders stick to their old ways, appearing in dark clothes with downturned mouths, the next generation, flourishing their simpering smiles, have become mannered and affected. Their faith, we are asked to think, is as limp as the heaven-bound kite, drooping sadly from the rooftop. Their children are overstuffed dolls who mimic their elders: indeed they may even outreach them, for one has the air of a lord, and the other the wig of a judge. In this kind of company the kiss of 'politeness' – directly opposite, and thus burlesquing the real kiss of the young couple – is the embrace of two ugly old crones. There is no need to ask where the artist's sympathies lie.

After the vitality of *Noon*, *Evening* has all the genuine exhaustion and edgy nerves of the end of a summer outing. This too is a variation on the theme of affectation. Hogarth shows a family trailing crossly back from their trip to the mill and the inn and the milk-rich cow at Sadler's Wells, the wife imitating the excursions and airs of her betters. The theatre is behind them, and the tavern on the left, its sign bearing the portrait of the philanthropic Sir Hugh Middleton, who brought fresh water to London through conduits from the reservoir at Islington. Hogarth's wit embraces the 'middling folk', the shopkeepers and carpenters who traipse out to the country on a boiling day, only to crowd inside a pub and blow smoke from their pipes into each other's faces, while the women in the garden eagerly eavesdrop on their conversation. But for his principal subjects the pastoral excursion has been far from refreshing. Even the dog looks as if he has had enough. The heat has made the stout woman's face as red as sunset (in the print Hogarth used a red ink to make his point) and if she is Diana, she is not a virgin goddess but the lusty deity of procreation, as her pregnancy and the cow's horns, peeping over her husband's head, suggest. Her daughter, with a fan to match her mother's, seems to follow her lead, pointing forcefully at the king-shaped gingerbread man held by her little brother, who howls, almost tripped up by the knob-headed cane that his father has lent him for a hobby-horse.

There are plenty of old jokes here about masterful women and emasculated men, and perhaps some topical allusions too, since there was much talk of the Queen's influence over her strutting little husband. But there is a sweet

90 *Noon* (1738)

91 *Evening* (1738)

realism and tenderness too in Hogarth's image – look at the accuracy with which he paints the tired father carrying his small daughter, his hands clasped around her ruched-up skirt, as she rests her head on his shoulder and clutches his cravat in a tiny fist, letting her feet loll free.

Days end; seasons pass. In *Night*, darkness and danger envelop the city. The lust of the people that seemed innocently warm at noon turns to dangerous flame at dusk. The scene is full of pain, fire and misrule: the street signs for bagnios and drinking houses point into the sky like spears. The poor sleep huddled in the shadow of a stall, beneath a row of bleeding-dishes and above them the barber draws blood while he shaves his client, squeezing his nose; the alarming sign reads 'Shaving, Bleeding and Teeth Drawn w$^{th.}$ a Touch'. The body here is sore and foul. Instead of sweet rain, or country milk, a chamber-pot showers urine which bounces off the lintel straight on the reeling Mason beneath, still in his apron, being guided home by his steward. So drunk is he, that he hardly seems to notice the chaos behind, where a bonfire flares, the Canterbury flying coach is overturned, and men stand by ready to throw firebrands at the wreckage. Fireworks, torches and candles add to the flaring light, for this particular night, judging by the oak leaves, is 29 May, anniversary of the restoration of Charles II – the 'patron of brothels'.

In this final print, the anti-French jokes of *Noon* and the broad misogyny of *Evening* turn to political satire; the narrow street leads down to Charing Cross, where the statue of Charles II by Le Suer rears on it plinth, and the oak-leaf wreaths are not a call for restoration of the Stuarts, but an emblem of bad leadership. The boss-eyed Mason, a lurching king of misrule, was at once recognized as the Bow Street magistrate Sir Thomas de Veil, renowned for the gulf between his severity on the bench and his wayward private life. In 1736 he was loathed by the London mob for implementing the recent Gin Act, an attempt to control the sale of spirit (since 1720 the sale of gin had risen rapidly, with over seven thousand gin shops in London and up to thirty thousand people in the trade). Londoners took to the streets with mock funeral processions for 'Queen Gin' and black drapes over the gin shops. In September 1736, the bookseller at the Camden's Head in Round Court was advertising 'The Deposing and Death of Queen Gin, with the Ruin of the Duke of Rum, Marquis of Nantz, Lord Sugar Cane, &c. Price 6d. As it was acted on Monday last at the New Theatre in the Haymarket'. One revenge story told of de Veil sampling a particular tot of gin, only to find out it had been replaced with piss – hence the flowing chamber pot in Hogarth's print. So violent was the feeling against him that in January 1738 a crowd surrounded his house in Frith Street, threatening to raze it to the ground and kill his

92 *Night* (1738)

'informers'. A local man, Roger Allen, known to be backward, was made a scapegoat and tried for inciting the mob: Westminster Hall was packed with cheering crowds on his acquittal.

Violence often exploded on public holidays. Hogarth's print, with its fiery uproar, its bonfires and oak leaves – reminders of the Civil Wars and the fragility of 'civilized' national life – spoke to Londoners not only of the unrest that dogged de Veil, but of the far worse riots against Irish labourers in Spitalfields that year. And the picture of de Veil in his cups made it clear that double standards still prevailed with a vengeance for rich and poor. A few years later, in July 1742, three young aristocrats, including the brother of the Duke of Marlborough, and Lord George Graham (whose portrait Hogarth later painted), were caught in a raid on a Covent Garden bagnio, ordered by de Veil. They were released but the women with them, and others picked up in the street, were taken to St Martin's Lane Roundhouse. Twenty-eight women were thrust into a hole six feet square and kept there all night:

'The poor creatures who could not stir or breathe, screamed as long as they had any breath left, begging at least for water: one poor wretch said she was worth at least eighteenpence and would gladly give it for a draught of water – but in vain! So well did they keep them there, that in the morning four were found stifled to death, two died soon after, and a dozen more are in a shocking way . . . several of them were beggars, who from having no lodging were necessarily found in the street, and others honest labouring women: one of the dead was a poor washerwoman, big with child who was returning home late from washing.[18]

No one swung for these murders: Londoners had good reason to hate their strict and hypocritical magistrates.

Hogarth began *The Four Times of the Day* in 1736, while he was working on the religious scenes for St Bartholomew's. In the two very different kinds of painting, he mixed biblical or classical myths with harsh realism. When the *Times of the Day* were engraved in 1738, Hogarth acknowledged their double reference, by adapting *Boys Peeping at Nature* as his subscription ticket. He also added a fifth picture, *Strolling Actresses Dressing in a Barn*, and just as the communal drama in *Southwark Fair* commented ironically on *A Rake's Progress*, so the packed scene of *Strolling Actresses* added a new dimension here, stressing both the fusion and the *difference* between illusion and reality.

This exuberant, dishevelled troupe is preparing to put on a play at the George Inn, aptly called *The Devil to Pay in Heaven*. Their playbill lies on the

93 *Strolling Actresses Dressing in a Barn* (1738)

bed, with the cooking grill leaning against it, next to some broken eggs and Ganymede's empty trousers; the dramatis personae includes Jupiter, Juno, Diana, Flora, the Night, a Siren, Aurora, an Eagle, Cupid, two Devils, a Ghost and attendants – the cast list of deities behind *The Four Times of the Day*. At first Hogarth's glimpse behind the scenes into the dusty and smelly barn seems 'straightforwardly' mock-heroic, stripping off the glamour of performance, like Swift's poems, or like Fielding's farce *Tumble Down Dick*, where props and dirty linen and inadequate costumes cause no end of trouble for would-be gods and goddesses.

Hogarth's print too brings divinities brutally down to earth – crowns mixed with chamber pots, kittens playing with orbs and lyres, a monkey peeing in a helmet. Instead of crystal chandeliers, their stage will be lit by the (very phallic-looking) tallow candles stuck in clay, now toppling on the floor. Next

312

to Hymen's flower-wreathed arch, chickens perch on the great rollers used to show the motion of the waves. Diana is in disarray, practising poses with her hoop round her feet and a quart pot and pipe on her stage altar. The children dressed as devils are stealing Diana's drink, while their mother shrieks at them – her hands are tied, holding a scrabbling cat while 'the Ghost', a devilish-looking crone draws blood from its tail, a nasty business in which real magic and stage magic are interwined.

The cat adds a dark note but most of the inset scenes are intimate and domestic, all the stranger for the 'characters' of those involved. A winged Cupid is balancing on a ladder to reach Apollo's stockings (complete with fancy shooting-star 'clocks') hung out to dry on the dragon's wings; Apollo, in sun-god hat, directs and holds the ladder. Flora, in her hoop petticoat, is dressing her hair with a flour shaker and a candle. In another corner Juno is rehearsing, stretching out her leg on a wheelbarrow, so that the dark-faced Goddess of Night in a starry stole can darn her stocking. Her book is propped against a big salt-cellar with a rolling-pin in it – not a domestic touch this time, but a primitive theatrical noise-making, 'thump-and-rattle' machine, stacked here with a tinder box and Jupiter's 'thunderbolt'.[19] Energy and excess leap out of the stench and disorder; all is smoky and swirling and strange. Through his curling, intricate lines, Hogarth turns the mock-heroic upside-down, and gives the ordinary and the shabby an air of stature, mystery and grace. Like the Peeping Tom gaping through the hole in the roof, or Acteon gazing on Diana in the myth, we *are* privileged to see the players in their intimate undress.

There is something admirable and strong about the *real* lives of these players, helping each other, living together, braving out the ups and downs of their profession. And there is something oddly dangerous about them too. These really are 'actors', women on the verge of turning into something else: one of the plays Hogarth was alluding to was Charles Coffey's ballad opera, also illustrated in the supper-box paintings at Vauxhall – *The Devil to Pay, or the Wives Metamorphos'd.*[20] In this play a shrewish wife is magically swapped for sweet, submissive Nell, the cobbler's wife, by a travelling 'doctor'. In the end, all is resolved, and the independent wife vows eternal obedience. But in Hogarth's 'topsy-turvy' world, magic is stronger than misogyny. A girl dressed as Jove's eagle feeds her yelling baby, balancing the bowl of gruel upon a crown. A black Aurora picks lice off the collar of a kneeling actress, whose flouncing skirt flows up into a siren-mermaid's tail. The siren in turn is pressing a tot of gin to ease the toothache of the slim actress playing Ganymede, who is dressed as a man but with flowing hair and rounded thighs which proclaim her firmly a woman. The urgent sense of power comes from this imminent transformation, the tipping over from one world to another, the mixing and melding and miscegenation of grotesquerie and beauty, foul and fair, human and divine and demonic.

The danger for the viewer, the artist, the man on the roof, is the old Hogarthian threat of credulity, of being seduced by what you see. There's a kind of wonder about it too – the lure of *wanting* to believe. It speaks of Hogarth's love affair with the inventive fantasy of the stage and those who followed its unstable fortunes. The original painting, destroyed by fire in 1874, must have been amazing. No wonder that Horace Walpole said that 'For wit and imagination without any other end', this was 'the best of all his works'.[21] It is a celebration of the subversive festival spirit in all people, and the pagan divinity of the ordinary, which cannot be put down.

By the time the print was published, that festival spirit was threatened. In the playhouses old British 'freedoms' and polite restraint coexisted in uneasy balance. In the spring of 1737, Drury Lane was embroiled in a row with disruptive footmen, who used to wait for their employers in a separate gallery, hurling witty abuse at the players and audience. On 19 February, the pit rose in a body to drive the footmen out, refusing to let the main piece, Addison's *Cato*, be performed until Theophilus Cibber promised to close their gallery. In retaliation the footmen stormed the theatre, hacking their way into the gallery, huzzaing and bellowing after each act, until the High Constable was called; the afterpiece, Fielding's new farce, *Eurydice*, was hissed to a standstill.[22] Two days later an even more serious riot had to be quelled by de Veil, as chief magistrate for Westminster.

Such disturbances helped to make the theatre a government target, but the chief irritants were Fielding's farces themselves, especially *Pasquin*, *The Historical Register for 1736*, and the self-mocking *Eurydice Hiss'd* which combined a comic account of the February fiasco with an attack on Walpole, delivered with dashing bravura. Fielding's popularity was so great, however, and his allusions so cleverly veiled, that Walpole needed a more blatant excuse. He found one – or perhaps commissioned one – in a scurrilous, pro-Jacobite farce called *The Golden Rump*, due to be staged at Lincoln's Inn Fields; when this was read to a shocked House of Commons, his carefully drafted Theatre Licensing Act found a smooth passage. From now on, it was illegal to stage a play without a licence from the Lord Chamberlain, and all performances outside the royal patent theatres (Drury Lane, Covent Garden and the Royal Opera House in the Haymarket) were banned. Fielding's theatrical career was over.

In Hogarth's print the 'Act against Strolling Players' (a section of the

314

Licensing Act) lies on the crown in the foreground, under the baby's bowl of gruel. Since the Act applied to male actors, Hogarth's troupe of women and children could have found a loophole, but the playbill on the bed announces that this 'Company of Comedians from the Theatres at London' is embarking on 'the last time of Acting before ye Act commences'. The freedom of the people – and the artist – to criticize through fantasy, allegory, pantomime and festival is at an end; in this make-believe heaven there really is the devil to pay.

Hogarth first announced the prints of *The Four Times of the Day* in May 1737. As usual, he was late, so he put in another notice. He announced the series again in January 1738, cleverly choosing the day of Roger Allen's trial for inciting the riot against de Veil. But in reality the plates were still unfinished; at the end of February he announced that they would be ready for collection on 1 May, the great public May Day of carnival. Placed beside *The Four Times of the Day* in a portfolio, or hung in line with them on the wall, *Strolling Actresses* made *Morning, Noon, Evening* and *Night* seem like topical tableaux, tiny mythic farces, silent dramas of city life. It seems absolutely right that the paintings should later be copied to decorate Jonathan Tyers's supper pavilions at Vauxhall.

Vauxhall Gardens, across the river in Lambeth, was originally a private estate, twelve acres of gardens opened to the public by Sir Samuel Morland in the Restoration; Pepys went there to eat lobster and syllabub, listening to the nightingales, the Jew's harp and the fiddles. The Vauxhall groves had been popular ever since and the dusky walks acquired an appropriately shady reputation which lasted until 1728 when the lease of this 'rural brothel' was taken by the twenty-six-year-old Jonathan Tyers. It was a bold move, to take the lease for thirty years at £250 a year, but one that proved so successful that Tyers eventually bought Vauxhall outright in the late 1750s. To begin with, though, the prospect was daunting. One morning around 1730 Hogarth was allegedly passing when he saw the young entrepreneur looking low. Mary Lewis, Jane Hogarth's companion, told the story like this:

'"How now, master Tyers, why so sad this morning?" "Sad times, master Hogarth, and my reflections were on a subject not likely to brighten a man's countenance," said Tyers. "I was thinking, do you know, which would be likeliest to prove the easiest death – hanging or drowning." "Oh!" said Hogarth, "is it come to that", "very nearly, I assure you," said Tyers; "then", replied Hogarth, "the remedy you think of applying is not calculated to mend the matter – don't hang or drown today. I have a thought that may save

315

the necessity of either, and will communicate it to you tomorrow morning."'

Tyers came, and the result, according to Mary, was the concocting of the first *ridotto al fresco* – an outdoor entertainment – and the start of the Gardens' success. She added that 'Hogarth was then in prosperity, and assisted Tyers, more essentially than by a few pieces for the decorations.' There are muddles here; Hogarth never painted personally for Tyers, although his pictures were later copied for Vauxhall – but the story gives a vivid glimpse of the *impression* Hogarth made: quick off the mark, taking set-backs as a spur; fertile in ideas which he immediately, impatiently, wanted put into action, a pushy organizer but a generous supporter of friends. Tyers did indeed reopen the Gardens in 1732 with a grand *ridotto*: 'We hear that several painters, and Artificers are employed to finish the Temples, Obelisks, Triumphal Arches, Grotto Rooms etc. for the Ridotto Al'Fresco, commanded for the 7th of June', announced the press.[23] The Prince of Wales came, and a select four hundred of the *crème de la crème*. Paying a guinea for the privilege, they arrived between nine and eleven, wearing dominoes and masks. The lights blazed out, the music played, and Vauxhall's reputation was saved. Whether Hogarth prompted this or not, Tyers was certainly grateful for something: as a 'testimony of regard' for

94 Vauxhall Gardens

316

past favours, in 1733 Hogarth received a gold medal engraved with Tyers's portrait, which gave him free admittance for life with 'a coachful' of six friends. The medal was still in Jane's possession when she died.

In the season, from April or May until late August, the Gardens were open three times a week. Part of the charm of Vauxhall (which made Horace Walpole prefer it to Ranelagh, whose vast rotunda opened in Chelsea in the 1740s) was the trip by water. On summer evenings, Jane and Hogarth might head for Westminster or Whitehall stairs, where wherries were always waiting, and glide across to join the scramble on the other bank a short way upstream (almost opposite where the Tate Gallery now stands). At the narrow landing stage the boats shoved and nosed their way in and there was always confusion, quarrelling and swearing, but after the short walk up the lane the revellers entered a magic world. Over the years Tyers added pavilions, supper boxes, statues, porticoes and colonnades and elaborate *trompe-l'oeil* effects, and thousands remembered the shock of delight as they walked through the gates and saw the hundreds of lights glimmering through the trees. The orchestra played from seven until nine ('new songs from Vauxhall' were always in vogue) and then broke for supper; chicken and beef and ham of legendary thinness, cheesecakes and tarts, strawberries and sweet custard, port for the men and hock and sherry for the ladies. As dusk turned to dark and couples began to wander off into the groves, flirtation began in earnest.

Vauxhall brought down on Tyers's head exactly the same sort of criticism that Heidegger had endured for his masquerades – accusations of sexual licence, assignations and, worst of all, an indiscriminate mixing of classes, allowing footmen to dally with countesses and clergymen with parlourmaids. One anonymous critic of 1732 thought this false, erotic, Arcadian blurring of levels brought nothing but harm, simply transporting the dissolute Covent Garden world to the other bank of the Thames:

> From *Drury*'s bounds see shining Throngs repair
> With borrow'd Charms to breath in sweeter Air;
> From stinking Rags and lofty Garret free'd,
> Lo! *Oyster Betty* shines in stift *Brocade*,
> See *Fops* and *Haggs* dress out, a Glitt'ring Show!
> Each *Barber*'s Prentice makes a powder'd *Beau* . . .
>
> . . . The Reck'ning call'd appears a tedious Score,
> The *Belles*, the *Shades*, the *Birds* delight no more;
> Home they retire to mourn their threat'ning Ills
> And learn to live on Gruel, Broth and Pills.[24]

But while Hogarth had damned Heidegger, he and the artists he was linked to played a major role at Vauxhall, not only helping Tyers with his embellishments but making real use of his much visited Gardens as the first public exhibition space for paintings and sculpture, available to all classes. Indeed, Tyers's long campaign to make his Gardens 'refined', as well as profitable, paralleled Hogarth's own project to find a middle way between art and commerce, high society and common citizens.[25]

Tyers tried hard to oblige 'the Polite and Worthy Part of the Town, by doing everything in his Power that may contribute to their Ease and Pleasure' and keeping the riff-raff out, 'such as are not fit to intermix with these Persons of Quality'.[26] He worked to exclude prostitutes and pimps, and was constantly praised in puffs from supporters such as John Lockman for reforming its morals. But, as at the masquerade, the crossing of boundaries was part of the charm. The Vauxhall crowd on a soft June night brought all London's worlds together, and the satire of 1737 by 'Hercules MacSturdy' makes no bones about the Gardens' sexual aura, their charms bestowed as openly – and as expensively – as those of the women he takes there, 'two Punks, who freely share their Bounties,/Mercantile one, and one a rampant Countess':

> The motley Croud we next with Care survey,
> The Young, the Old, the Splenetic and Gay:
> The Fop emasculate, the rugged Brave,
> All jumbled here, as in the common Grave.
> Here sat a group of Prentices, and there
> The awkward Daughter of a late Lord Mayor;
> Next to them a Country Bumpkin and his Cousin,
> And stuck about, Red-Ribbon'd Knights a Dozen;
> Like ruddy Pinks, or Gilly-flowers in Pots;
> 'Mongst Bawds, and Rakes, and Sempstresses and Sots.[27]

Vauxhall was just the place for the likes of Moll Hackabout on an outing with her rich protector, and for all the Londoners, gentry and citizens, who bought Hogarth's prints of her story.

To improve the tone, in 1736 Tyers changed from subscription tickets, which were often exchanged, or sold surreptitiously by his own servants, to charging a shilling at the gate. The next year Gravelot designed an elegant head piece for 'Adieu to Spring Gardens', a song with words by Lockman and music by Boyce, but even his charming design had an air of intrigue which was quickly picked up by bawdy copies.[28] However much Tyers tried for decorum, the sexy and the popular could not be kept out. This undercurrent ran through the paintings he now put in the supper boxes, perhaps at Hogarth's suggestion. At first these boxes were flimsy, canopied structures, and according to the *Scots Magazine* of 1739, paintings on rollers were 'put up last Spring to protect the Ladies, while sitting in the Arbours, from catching cold in their necks by the inclemency of the weather'.[29] Unrolled like stage backdrops behind the diners' heads, the decorative canvases shut out the rural background and offered instead

'a very entertaining view, especially when the Ladies, as ought ever to be contrived, sit with their heads against them. And what adds not a little to the pleasure of these pictures, they give an unexceptionable opportunity of gazing on any pleasing fair one, without any other pretence than the credit of a fine taste for any piece behind her.'

The women, works of art themselves, could be gazed at with licensed enjoyment, against scenes of stage comedies, dancers, children's games. All these, and

'other whims that are well enough liked by most people at a time they are *disposed to smile*, and every thing of a light kind, and tending to *unbend the thoughts*, has an effect *desired*, before it is *felt!*'[30]

In the early 1740s the supper boxes were rebuilt and a new set of approximately fifty pictures was commissioned, most of them by Hayman. These paintings too allowed into the Gardens (metaphorically) many of the elements Tyers wanted (practically) to keep out. Here were sex, gambling and danger; dancing milkmaids, Wapping landladies and saucy tars; tumbling embraces on a see-saw, risky games, cards and slides on thin ice.[31] Through these delightful rococo pictures, low pleasures were embraced in Vauxhall's 'high' diversions – although a decorous touch was added by their warnings against vanity and frivolity.[32] Hogarth's *Times of the Day*, copied for this set, were perfectly in line with this subtle mood, letting the supper-box set feel superior to 'ordinary Londoners', but also conveying hints of desire, glimpses of riot.

Music was as important as art in Tyers's campaign of refinement. In 1735 he opened his orchestra building, later installing musical entertainments such as 'a symphony of singing birds' and a set of musical bells. Handel's concertos were a favourite part of the band's staple repertoire, and two years later Tyers commissioned Roubiliac to make a statue of the great composer, London's idol. The sculpture was installed with great publicity in April 1738 and the *Daily Post* puffed Tyers, and the *expense*, quite as much as the sculptor and the maestro. The statue, it said, was carved:

319

'out of one entire Block of white Marble, which is to be placed in a grand Nich, erected on purpose in the Great Grove at Vauxhall-Gardens, at the sole expense of Mr Tyers, Undertaker of the Entertainment there, who in Consideration of the real Merit of that inimitable Master, thought it proper, that his Effigies should preside there where his Harmony has so often charm'd even the greated Crouds into the profoundest Calm and most decent Behaviour; it is believed that the Expence of the Statue and Nich cannot cost less than Three Hundred Pounds.'[33]

Roubiliac's relaxed and informal statue was a sensation, a work of genius entirely appropriate to the cultured, leisured aura of Vauxhall, with a winning touch of humour.[34] His Handel, like Orpheus, fingers a lyre while a cherub takes down the notes at his feet. But as he charms the wild souls, he wears a velvet cap, not even Handel's usual flowing wig; his indoor coat, like a dressing-gown, drapes loosely round him, his shirt is open and his breeches unbuttoned at the knees, while a slipper dangles from his toe. Roubiliac's bold experiment caught Handel's likeness perfectly, down to his slightly flat nose, protruding underlip and famously bushy eyebrows, and it added charm without loss of dignity, embodying exactly 'those qualities of mingled grandeur and intimacy' that marked Handel's music.[35] His sculpture exerted a great influence on the portrait painters of the Old Slaughter's group, so much so that the cross-legged pose almost became a hallmark of Hayman's portraits.[36]

The composer himself, as well as the statue, fired the artists' imaginations. Foreign opera might have irritated Hogarth but he never denied Handel's greatness. Although Hogarth was an obstinate patriot, he put nationalism second to quality – unlike some. A letter in *Common Sense* in this year, 1738, had suggested that the British composer Maurice Greene should be called on to compose a national tune, a suggestion made not, the writer awkwardly added, out of disrespect to Handel, but fearing that his German birth, 'might give a German tendency to the mind and therefore greatly lesson the National Benefit'.[37] This might well be the incident behind the story of Hogarth, at a dinner with some doctors, where someone mentioned that 'a few evenings before, at Dick's coffee-house', the Bart's surgeon John Freke:

'had asserted that Greene was as eminent in composition as Handel. "That fellow Freke", replied Hogarth, "is always shooting his bolt absurdly one way or another! Handel is a giant in music; Greene only a light Florimel kind of a composer." – "Ay," says our artist's informant, "but at the same time Mr Freke declared you were as good a Portrait-painter as Vandyck" – "There he was in

320

the right," adds Hogarth; and so by G—d I am, give me my time, and let me choose my subject." '38

A remark like Freke's would provoke as well as please. Hogarth's art now stretched from satirical prints to huge religious paintings; he had drawn the harlot, the fair and the rake, the musician and the poet, the poor and the polite. But he still had to prove himself as good as Van Dyck, whose gilded head hung above his door. He made sure that his next ambitious work would be a portrait – and a work in which patriotism and quality *could* be combined. He turned from the city spaces to the individual man, and true to his word, he chose his subject carefully.

16

Country, Coram and Children

Britons where's your Magnanimity,
Where's your boasted Courage flown?
STREET BALLAD (1739)

'I don't know what is worse,' cries Deborah, 'than for such
wicked strumpets to lay their sins at honest men's doors . . .
For my own part, it goes against me to touch these mis-
begotten wretches, whom I don't look upon as my fellow
creatures. Faugh, how it stinks! It doth not smell like a
Christian.'

HENRY FIELDING, *Tom Jones* (1745)

ON 2 JUNE 1737 the *Daily Post* reported the suicide of François Lemoyne, painter to the French King, implying that Lemoyne had been driven mad by the criticism of a 'vast Work, which he had been four Years about'. The sting came at the end, in a comparison of Lemoyne with the painter of the Great Hall at Greenwich, who, the writer said, showed 'much more Resolution; notwithstanding there are as many Faults as Figures in that Work he died a natural death, tho' an Englishman'. It was not the suggestion that Thornhill was melancholic (typically British in foreign eyes) that maddened Hogarth, but the casual way in which any British art with pretensions was automatically dismissed. He wrote a bristling essay, printed a week later in the *St James's Evening Post*, in the same issue that announced the prints of *The Four Times of the Day*.

Hogarth opened with the words,

'Every Good-natur'd Man, and every Well-wisher to Arts in England, must feel a kind of Resentment, at a very indecent Paragraph in the Daily Post of Thursday last, relating to the Death of Mons. le Moine.'[1]

He took exception to the 'very unjust, as well as cruel' reflections on Thornhill and launched into an attack on 'narrow, little Genius's' and 'peddling

322

Demi-Criticks' who think they can make a quick reputation by quibbling at the works of great men. But then he leapt ahead to his real *bêtes noires*, the European dealers, those '*Picture-Jobbers from abroad*', whose direct interest it was to depreciate English work, since praising it might hurt their trade,

'of continually importing Ship Loads of dead *Christs*, *Holy Families*, *Madona's* and other dismal Dark Subjects, neither entertaining nor Ornamental; on which they scrawl the terrible cramp Names of some *Italian* Masters and fix on us poor *Englishmen*, the Character of *Universal Dupes*'.[2]

Hogarth was now flying. What if, he asked, a commonsensical man were faced with one of these 'sham Virtuoso-pieces':

'he wou'd be very apt to say, "Mr. *Bubbleman*, That Grand *Venus* (as you are pleased to call it) has not Beauty enough for the Character of an *English* Cook-Maid" – Upon which the Quack answers with a Confident Air, "O L—d Sir, I find you are no *Connoisseur* – That Picture, I assure you, is in *Alesso Baldovinetto's* second and best Manner, boldly painted, and truly sublime, the *Contour* gracious; the Air of the Head in the high Greek Taste, and a most divine Idea it is". Then spitting on an obscure Place, and rubbing it with a dirty Handkerchief, takes a Skip to t'other End of the Room, and screams out in Raptures, – "There's an amazing Touch! A man *shou'd* have this picture a Twelve-month in his Collection, before he can discover half its Beauties". The Gentleman, (tho' naturally a Judge of what is beautiful, yet ashamed to be out of the Fashion in judging for himself) with this Cant is struck dumb, gives a vast Sum for the Picture, very modestly confesses he is indeed quite ignorant of Painting, and bestows a Frame worth Fifty pounds on a frightful Thing, without the hard Name on it not worth as many Farthings.'

Hogarth's plea was for the public to see with their own eyes, not through the lens of connoisseurship, to use nature as their guide and trust their own taste. Even Thornhill, he admitted, in compliance with the so-called experts of his day, had called in Andrea to help with Greenwich Hall, yet his ceiling, he added with defensive pride, stands out for its harmony and play of colours, its grand composition and 'the great Fire and Judgment' of the main figures. 'Thus much, is in Justice due to that great *English Artist* from an *Englishman*.'

The essay was signed 'BRITOPHIL' and in a short postscript, Hogarth pointed out that the money from visitors to Greenwich went to support sixty Charity Children. As at St Bartholomew's, in Britain art and philanthropy could work hand in hand.

*

Hogarth's nationalism was not just the jealous self-interest of the artist, although it always had a tinge of that. His was one voice in a swelling chorus of patriotism, orchestrated by the opposition to Walpole that rallied round Frederick, Prince of Wales. In December 1736, when the Prince was made a Freeman of the City and gave a great dinner for the Lord Mayor and Aldermen, the rafters rang to all the old slogans. Hervey told the Queen that Frederick's speech was 'the most ingratiating piece of popularity',

'and neither the "Prosperity of the City of London" – "the Trade of this Country" – "the Naval Strength of England" – "Liberty and Property" – nor any popular toasts of that kind were omitted. "My God," says the Queen, "popularity always makes me sick; but Fretz's popularity makes me vomit".'3

Caroline would not be appeased – her son was 'a nauseous beast', she hoped daily that he would die of an apoplexy, that the ground would open and sink him to 'the lowest hole in hell'.4 Even so, as Walpole's staunch ally, she was his last hope of healing the rift between the King and his son and her death in 1737 ended the possibility of even a staged reconciliation.

That year, a new opposition journal was founded called *Common Sense* after a character in Fielding's *Pasquin*, with the Prince's friend Lord Chesterfield as a director. Since 1735, this particular branch of the opposition had been collecting young politicians, including Fielding's Eton school-fellows, George Lyttleton and William Pitt, who spoke so vehemently against Walpole that he was dismissed from his army cornetcy. Lyttleton's uncle was Richard Temple, Viscount Cobham, a kindly, coarse-mouthed man connected by marriage to the powerful Grenville family, and under Temple's wing these young opposition recruits became known as 'Cobham's cubs' or 'the Boy Patriots'. Joining forces with the *Craftsman* group, they promoted Frederick as a constitutional prince who would return to 'true' English principles. As rewritten by Bolingbroke, British history was a continuous battle between the spirit of Liberty (represented by the Patriots) and Faction (as embodied by Walpole); he looked back to ancient Britons and Saxon freemen as models, invoking the brave struggle against Norman despots and tyrannical Tudors.5 This vague, nostalgic and hypocritical rhetoric – no one manipulated 'faction' like Bolingbroke – had a wide appeal, reflected in James Thomson's 'Rule Britannia' of 1740, with its hallowed refrain, 'Britons never shall be Slaves.'

By now, Walpole was on the defensive. Outside Parliament, he lost his majority in the Court of Aldermen and thus his grip on the City. The London riots over the Gin Acts and the Irish workers and the theatres were beacons in a chain lit in the name of 'liberty' which flamed across the land. In Edinburgh, in September 1736, Captain Porteous, supervising the execution of a local smuggler, was lynched by the mob, and the government's determination to fine the city alienated Walpole's powerful Scottish allies such as the Duke of Argyll. At the end of 1737, the King's Speech which closed the parliamentary session thundered against all popular demonstrations:

'You cannot be insensible, what just scandal and offence the Licentiousness of the present times, under the colour and disguise of Liberty, gives to all honest and sober men; . . . defiance of all authority, contempt of magistracy, and even resistance of laws, are become too general.'[6]

The following year, the preachers George Whitefield and the newly 'converted' John Wesley gathered vast crowds in their open-air field sermons in the West Country. There was a sense that the ordinary people had been betrayed by their leaders, both in the State and in the Church.

In this unsettled climate, Walpole finally bowed to the militant clamour for action in the Caribbean, where British buccaneers, flouting the trade regulations, had met a draconian response from the Spanish authorities. A frenetic campaign was stirred up, enlivened by Pitt's brilliant speeches, feeding off old stories of sailors rotting in Spanish gaols, of crews being tortured and of Captain Robert Jenkins whose ear had been cut off by a Spanish coastguard. The public prints flowered with lurid nationalism. One showed the mutilation of Jenkins's famous ear in a scene accompanied by a song:

> Britons where is your great Magnanimity, where's
> your boasted Courage flown,
> Quite perverted to Pu-si-la-ni-mi-ty, Scarce
> to call your Souls your own.[7]

To Walpole's despair and the opposition's delight, war against Spain was declared in October 1739.

The widespread popular unrest and the demands of the war for manpower both drew attention to the poor. Paupers were seen in sharply differing ways, either as neglected victims or as a dangerous, threatening underclass, but all agreed that there was a terrible 'waste' of lives that could be 'used' more profitably for the nation. George II's reign had also seen a decline in population so large that it effectively wiped out the entire gain since the Restoration. Meanwhile the populations of France and Spain were known, fearfully, to be growing. So in 1739 the mood was propitious for one small initiative, a scheme that had been canvassed unsuccessfully for over twenty years, the opening of

325

a hospital for London's foundlings. This immediately seized Hogarth's full attention, as a patriot, as a man who believed in public benevolence, and as an artist.

95 Detail from *Night*

In one corner of Hogarth's *Night* a snub-nosed boy is blowing on a lighted torch. He is probably a link-boy, making his money by lighting strangers home at night through the dark streets. He is poor and rough, but like the shoe-boys and sweeps he is lucky to be scraping a meagre living. The children of the poor, like the children of the rich, were little adults: in 1724 Defoe thought that all children were able to earn their living by the age of five. The link-boy is lucky, most of all, to be alive at all. All through the 1720s and 1730s the rate of infant mortality stayed high in London parishes. One sign of Hogarth's respect and compassion towards Moll in a *A Harlot's Progress* was in showing that she kept her child alive, and even when she herself was dying in squalor her boy was fed and stoutly clothed. Many were not treated so, especially the illegitimate. An aristocratic bastard might be given titles and jewels, attend Court and gamble away a fortune, but the very poor, the prostitutes and sempstresses, the milliners and market women, hardly had enough to live on themselves, let alone to bring up a child. To the 'middling orders' illegitimacy was a stain that could not be washed clean, and the child would always carry the sins of its parents. Fielding's Deborah in *Tom Jones*, holding her nose at the foundling baby, believes thus. 'If I might be so bold to give my advice', she declares,

' "I would have it put in a basket, and sent out and laid at the church-warden's door. It is a good night, only a little rainy and windy; and if it was well wrapt up, and put in a warm basket, it is two to one but it lives till it is found in the

326

morning. But if it should not, we have discharged our duty in taking proper care of it; and it is, perhaps, better for such creatures to die in a state of innocence, than to grow up and imitate their mothers; for nothing better can be expected of them." [8]

Many felt this way. When a baby was laid at the door of Buckingham House one night in 1734, the servants would have put it in the park if the Duchess of Gloucester had not heard about it. She ordered it to be clothed and fed, and put a notice in the paper asking the mother to let her know, anonymously, by penny post, if it had been baptized. But her notice also carried a disclaimer: 'Her Grace doth not propose that this instance of her tenderness should encourage any further presents of this nature, because such future attempts will be found fruitless.' [9]

Single instances of charity were not enough. Hence the bundles laid nightly with tears in church doorways, squalling or silent, swaddled in a gin-doped stupor. Hence the cold forms found by the sides of city roads, their tiny limbs rigid and icy, their destiny the city dung heaps. It was easy to pass by on the other side. The old Poor Law had rendered each parish responsible only for its own, and the burden of cost fell heavily on the grumbling, prosperous citizens who paid the poor rate. To keep the rates down vagrants were ejected and pregnant women, who presaged more mouths to feed, were turned back at the parish boundaries. 'Parish-nurses' (or 'killing nurses') were hired to care for foundlings and their role was tacitly accepted: they simply let their charges die. In 1715, a Parliamentary Committee investigating the poor rates of St Martin-in-the-Fields had reported that three-quarters of these children perished in the care of nurses

'hired by the Churchwardens to take off a Burthen from the Parish at the cheapest and easiest rates they can; and these know the Manner of doing it effectually, as by the Burial Books may easily appear.' [10]

Pauper children who did survive had to beg on the streets, or be apprenticed by the parish in appalling conditions. Increasingly, poverty was seen not as a result of ill-luck, or a bad environment, but as the fruit of indolence and profligacy; the new, more punitive Poor Law of 1722 decreed that instead of dispensing out-door relief, parishes could now erect workhouses and deny aid to all who would not enter them, thus forcing the 'idle' poor to labour. In these overcrowded, urinous, pest-ridden buildings, babies under two years old died at a rate of almost 99 per cent: they were Britain's dying rooms.

327

In 1738, a year after Hogarth's *Good Samaritan* was raised on the walls of St Bartholomew's Hospital, a first glimpse of practical hope glimmered for the city foundlings, the fruit of many years untiring work on the part of one man, Captain Thomas Coram.

Thomas Coram was stroppy and pugnacious as well as open and good-hearted, a man of the people who had reached eminence through his own initiative, refusing to be deterred by set-backs. His friend Dr Brocklesby described him in words that apply equally to Hogarth:

'What he thought, he spoke; what he wished, he declared without hesitation, pursued without relaxation or disguise, and never considered obstacles any further than to discover means to surmount them.' [11]

Like Hogarth, too, he was chippily proud of his roughness: 'I could never speak good English,' he wrote; 'how is it possible I should Write good Grammar?'

The son of a master mariner, Coram was born in 1668 in Lyme Regis in Dorset (a few miles from Sir James Thornhill's home), went to sea at eleven and at sixteen was apprenticed to a shipbuilder. During the wars, in 1697, commissioned to buy oak for the Navy, he set sail for Boston and established a shipbuilding business. Over the next ten years in Massachusetts he made his fortune, cannily lobbying the government to pass an Act to encourage the import of 'naval stores' from America, thus opening up the lucrative trade in pitch from Carolina's pinewoods and breaking the Swedish monopoly. He was a tough man of commerce, and a tough man of principle, drawn into fierce litigation and outright brawls with his Puritan neighbours and flaunting his unpopular Anglicanism by giving land for a church and building an Anglican school.

He was very much a man of his time, combining Patriotism and Protestantism with an expansionist view of trade and a colonialist zeal. In 1715, returning to England, he proposed that the discharged soldiers roaming the land after Marlborough's wars should be sent to settle Massachusetts. Nothing came of this, but in 1730, acting as trustee for a group set up by Dr Thomas Bray, founder of the Society for the Propagation of Christian Knowledge, he was working on a scheme for debtors and paupers to found a new colony in Savannah. By now Coram was recognized as an authority on the colonies. He was one of the Trustees when George II signed the Charter for the Colony of Georgia, with Oglethorpe as its first Governor, and in November 1732, he stood at Gravesend watching the first boats sail. But he never felt the task was finished: after fighting the Trustees when women were excluded from inheriting land in Georgia, by 1735 he had withdrawn from active involvement. That same year, however, he was already petitioning George II to found a colony of 'industrious protestant families' in Nova Scotia, to solve the problem of unemployed artisans and workmen flocking to the capital; he thought Britain could get a better return on their existence.

Since 1722, when the new Poor Law came in, Coram had been fighting a long-running campaign for London's foundlings. In the 1720s, living at Rotherhithe and walking into the city, day after day, at dawn and dusk, he saw the corpses of abandoned babies by the road. There were foundling hospitals supported by Church and State in Paris and Lisbon, Amsterdam and Rome, but virtually nothing in London, although Addison had argued strongly for provision for foundlings on European lines in the *Guardian* as early as 1713. Coram followed him in taking a humane view of infanticide, believing, as Addison had put it, that what overcame the mothers' natural tenderness was simply 'the fear of shame, or their inability to support those whom they give life to'.[12] Despairing of State help, he proposed to found a hospital by establishing a non-profit-making joint-stock company, with capital from public subscriptions; as a collective entity it would be free from reliance on single benefactors, and as a legally chartered body it could receive legacies and endowments.

This method had been successfully used by Thomas Bray, whose charity-school movement had managed to open over fourteen hundred schools by the mid-1720s. But in 1722 joint-stock ventures had a bad name after the Bubble crisis and Coram found it hard to enrol distinguished allies. He could no more prevail on any bishop or noble to press his cause, he said, than he could persuade them to 'putt doun their breeches and present their Backsides to the King and Queen in a full Drawing room such was the unchristian Shyness of all about the Court'.[13] Over the next fifteen years he courted influential groups in turn, first the grand ladies of London, persuading eight duchesses, eight countesses and five baronesses to sign his petition, then the men – dukes and earls, doctors and merchants – and finally the Justices of the Peace and 'persons of distinction'. Along the way, he faced storms of criticism, including the argument that a shelter for bastards would encourage licentiousness. His own petition to the King in 1737 put the issue bluntly: far from weakening morals, it would protect the polite from the depredations of the poor. The high-born ladies supported his appeal, he said, because they were deeply touched by 'the frequent Murders committed on poor Miserable Infant Children at the Birth by their Cruel Parents to hide their Shame and for the inhuman Custom of Exposing New-born Children to Perish in the streets or the putting out of such unhappy Foundlings to wicked and barbarous Nurses who undertaking to bring them up for a small and trifling sum of money do often suffer them to starve for want of due sustenance and care.'

If allowed to live, he continued, many were hired out to thieves' gangs or professional beggars, being 'Blinded or Maimed or Distorted in the Limbs in order to move Pity and Compassion and therby become the fitter instruments of gain to those Vile, Mercyless Wretches'.[14]

When the petitions reached him, George II was moved. He was well disposed towards the plan, which seems to have been dear to Caroline; before her death she had already asked for an account of the running of the Paris hospital, published in 1739. More cynically, the Spanish war had made those in power think seriously about the need to conserve population, to provide soldiers and sailors for the future. In this context the King gave his approval and Coram drew up a list of 375 potential Governors. Of these, nearly two hundred agreed to be active, rather than honorary, Governors, among them William Hogarth. On 14 August, George II signed the Charter, and the Great Seal was affixed on 17 October. Hogarth was present at the meeting for the incorporation of the Charter. And he was there a month later, on 20 November, when the carriages rolled up to Somerset House and the nobility and gentry filed in under the chandeliers to watch Coram hand the Charter to the Duke of Bedford, the Hospital's first President.

That was a solemn, symbolic occasion, with 170 Governors including fifteen dukes and earls. Just over a week later, a more down-to-earth General Committee of fifty met in 'Mr Manaton's Great Room' at the Crown and Anchor in the Strand, to get down to the real work. This body, which included dignitaries such as Arthur Onslow, Speaker of the House of Commons, and eminent doctors such as Richard Mead and Sir Hans Sloane, had three main tasks: to find out how such hospitals were run abroad and draw up their own plans, to raise money from legacies and gifts, and to find a building as soon as possible. Towards the end of the year the Committee approved a design for a seal, given by Coram, to be used on authorized business. Its design was suggested to him, Coram said, by

'the affair Mentioned in the 2nd of Exodus of Pharoah's daughter and her maids finding Moses in the ark of Bulrushes which I thought would be very apropos for an hospital of foundlings Moses being the first foundling we read of'.[15]

330

96 Letterhead for the Foundling Hospital

Hogarth did not design the seal, but he made a drawing in late 1739 which was engraved as a headpiece for the official fund-raising letter for the 'Hospital for the Maintenance and Education of Exposed Young Children'. In a rural scene overlooked by a church the white-haired figure of Coram takes centre place, immediately recognizable although he is clad in biblical robes, with the Charter and its seal under his arm. He looks compassionately down at a weeping woman, who has crossed a bridge (from misery to hope) and dropped a dagger, her last cruel resort. Behind her another woman finds a bundled-up baby by a hedge, and in front a naked infant sprawls in a ditch. As Coram gestures towards his new hospital, he reassures the kneeling woman about her child's future. Boys wave at the ships out at sea – they will be sailors or soldiers; two who hold a sickle and a rake will work on the land; others emerging from the house with a trowel and plumb rule will go into the building trade. The girls, with their brushes and spinning wheel, will doubtless be servants. It is all immensely practical, assuring potential donors that the hospital will be no hotbed of religious fervour, or forcing-house where paupers are taught to read and get ideas above their station. But the children receive kindness as well as training; the little boy balancing on the steps, flourishing a comb for carding wool, is being given a hearty hug.

That winter the street children suffered more than ever. On Christmas Day, it was suddenly cruelly cold. Ice patches formed near the banks of the Thames, around the stairs and landing stages and the piers of the bridge, gradually spreading until a complete sheet of ice covered the dark current. People remembered the Great Frost of 1564 when archery and dancing took

331

place on the ice, and that of 1684 when Charles II visited the Frost Fair and the city streets were full of a deathly fog of frozen smoke. This time, too, there were festivals and fairs, and traders from the Strand roasted a whole ox on the ice. But there was also great hardship. Tramps froze to death; families died of pneumonia and influenza; processions of watermen and fishermen, carpenters and bricklayers wound past Charing Cross, dressed in mourning, carrying a boat and the tools of their trade, begging for relief. Birds dropped stiff from the sky, bread hardened into rocks on market stalls. The leaden skies and piercing chill hung on well into February. Indoors, maids scurried to lay fires in the draughty rooms, their breath crystallizing in the clammy air. Even the theatres were closed. At Lincoln's Inn Fields, Handel's *Acis and Galatea* was put off week after week, despite the promise that

'Particular Care has been taken to have the House survey'd and secure'd against the Cold, by having Curtains plac'd before every Door, and constant Fires will be kept in the House 'till the time of Performance'.[16]

Through these icy weeks, Hogarth worked in Leicester Fields, his mind on the Foundling Hospital. The canvas before him was huge, almost eight feet high and five feet wide, much larger than any he had used before, apart from his paintings for St Bartholomew's. The picture he built up, layer by layer, stroke by stroke, was a great 'state portrait' of Captain Coram.

Captain Thomas Coram (plate III) was a bold, brilliant tribute to an individual, and to British public benevolence, to ordinary people undertaking what the State would not do. It was also a patriotic artistic statement, painted in the spirit of Hogarth's Britophil essay, demanding that men judge with their own eyes, insisting that the foreign and the old were not supreme. And it was a personal act of bravado, to demonstrate his loud claim that he could equal Van Dyck.

National and the personal motives overlap in his own account. Infuriated by the way portrait painting was swayed by fashion and always monopolized by a few artists, and aggravated in particular by the great vogue for the newly arrived French painter, Van Loo, he tried to stir his fellow painters to compete: 'I exorted the painters to bear up against this torrents and to oppose him with spirit, my studies being in another way.' The answer came back, 'you talk, why done do it yourself[?] provoked at this I set about this mighty portrait, and found it no difficult than I thought it.'[17] That kind of bragging both maddened and entertained his colleagues at the Academy, like young Allan Ramsay, and in turn their teasing barbs pushed him on:

'upon one day at the academy in St martin's lane I put this question, if any at this time was to paint a portrait as wel as Vandike would it be seen and the person enjoy the benefit – they knew I had said I believ'd I could. the answer was made by Mr Ramsey and confirmed by the Rest possitivly No. and confirmed by about twenty who were present, the reason then given very frankly by Mr R . . . our opinions must be consulted and we will never allow it. Upon which I Resoved if I did do the thing, I would Affirm I done it.'[18]

Having boasted, Hogarth had to succeed. And he did. *Captain Thomas Coram* was extraordinary, a landmark. It had *éclat, bravura, panache* – foreign virtues, foreign terms – and downright English humour and directness. In his first 'full-length' painting, to the scale of life, Hogarth took the size of canvas usually reserved for royal, noble or heroic subjects and used it to paint a commoner, without making any pretence about his bluff bourgeois origins. He domesticated the grandeur of the royal style, transferring dignity from remote functionaries of State, Church and Court to an elderly merchant, suggesting that trade and colonial expansion can be the basis for benevolence. Coram had adapted mechanisms of law, of aristocratic patronage, of company organization to new charitable ends: in painting him Hogarth too adapted conventions (as he had done with *The Four Times of the Day*) and filled them with new substance.

It is hard to reconstruct how daring, and even shocking, this would appear to Hogarth's peers. His painting echoed grand baroque works, like Verrio's painting of Sir Christopher Wren, finished by Kneller and Thornhill, in the Sheldonian Theatre, Oxford, and particularly Hyacinth Rigaud's portrait of the powerful French financier Samuel Bernard, known through a 1729 print by Drevet.[19] These already followed rules for portraying heroes, great men leaning back in dignified ease, gesturing elegantly to the symbols of their achievements: Rigaud has a globe and a glimpse of sea behind, and Wren has a vista of the river and St Paul's. Hogarth pinched all the standard baroque trappings: the steps with their symbolic objects explaining the sitter's status and history; the column and the vista; the curtain and shadowy painting, an image of Charity; the heavy folds of the coat, as stiff as the drapery of a bronze statue. By using such devices he both parodied the postures of grand portraiture and dignified his own plebeian subject.

His huge canvas is replete not with grandeur, but with strength, colour and vigour, the humour and warmth of feeling of the sunburned, stubborn old man. Captain Coram looks justifiably proud, clutching the seal of the hospital in one hand, and clasping his gloves in the other. But he also looks slightly awkward, as if he were not used to being posed like a courtier, as indeed he was not. Both his glowing pride and his discomfort are touching, and every point is intensified by the contrast between the courtly convention and the real man. Instead of flowing robes or court velvet, Coram wears a striking red greatcoat of stiff broadcloth, over a black suit, stockings and shoes. The coat seems a bit too big, for Coram (like Hogarth) was a 'little man': his feet hardly touch the floor, and his swinging left leg conveys his restlessness. Books of manners and manuals of portraiture decreed that a gentleman must turn his feet elegantly outwards at a right-angle; Captain Coram's plain buckled shoes are clumsily parallel. There is no Richardsonian improvement of nature here; for Hogarth, Coram's own nature is quite good enough.

It was Coram's moral, not physical or social stature that interested Hogarth. He made the Captain look as if he had just sat down, leaning his black three-cornered hat against the table leg. The hat itself added meaning, since another of Coram's philanthropic projects was his support of the hatters against unfair competition from the colonies; he refused to accept any payment except a hat, which was specially made for him and whose size, as his friend Dr Brocklesby wrote, 'spoke the good wishes of the makers in a very legible way'.[20] Like the hat, all the details speak in this 'legible way'. The globe on the floor is turned to show the Atlantic, scene of Coram's voyages, with the faint reflection of a window between Carolina and Georgia and the home coasts of Britain. Even the cross of the reflected window bars can be 'read' as a reference to the mission to West Indian Negroes run by Bray's SPCK, of which Coram was a Governor.[21]

Coram is the rough but kindly seaman long celebrated in British literature and drama. He looks out from beneath his untidy sweep of white hair – his own, not the curling wig of a grandee – alert and determined, proud but unpretentious. There is wit in Hogarth's handling but this old man is still a model, painted in the spirit of Richardson's aim for a portrait, that men should be 'excited to imitate the Good Actions . . . of those whose Examples are thus set before them'.[22]

In May 1740, the Foundling Hospital's Committee voted that sixty children be given places as soon as possible. At the same meeting Hogarth gave the hospital, free of all charge, his great full-length portrait of its founder. The ironic echoes of paintings of the French Court in this work remind us that the Foundling Hospital was London's answer to Paris's much-lauded *Hôpital des Enfants-Trouvés*, founded by Louis XIV. The difference was that in London the King and the Court followed the lead of the people, marshalled by an elderly mariner. When Rouquet later described the decoration of the hospital, this was the point he made:

'They have lately built an hospital in London for exposed and deserted children; a noble institution, which this famous metropolis greatly wanted. We may say that in England everything is done by the people. This hospital is now a very large building, and was raised by the subscription of a few private persons, who were desirous of seeing such an establishment. The King subscribed to it like others, and the public benefactions are every day increasing.'[29]

The appeals were successful. In June Lord Abercorn gave £100 and William Hogarth, not to be outdone, gave £120. In October, the Daily Committee produced a detailed report, outlining their plans, and even considering questions such as 'How long a Child ought to continue to Suck?' and was it right, or 'pernicious' to follow the 'Universal Custom among Nurses, to give Opiates to the Children, when restless?' While such issues were being disputed, after several false starts, the Governors found a temporary site in Hatton Garden, on the heights looking down towards the Fleet Ditch. For the long term, they bought fifty-six acres half a mile further west in Lamb's Conduit Fields. In Hatton Garden, nurses and cooks and watchmen were hired, clothes and cutlery were ordered, blankets were stacked up. On the evening of 25 March 1741, all was ready for the first child. Hogarth painted a shield, which was ceremoniously hung over the door, and he was one of the four Governors who volunteered to be present on this historic night, with Captain Coram, Martin Folkes and Theodore Jacobsen, the architect for the new hospital. Hogarth eventually painted the portraits of all three of his fellow Governors.

The Committee's minutes make a moving narrative. When Hogarth and the other Committee members arrived, at seven in the evening, a great crowd of women was already hovering about the door, with babies in their arms. Many had already been begging for their children to be taken in and had been turned away; no preference should be given before the due time came. For a hour the crowd waited. Then, at eight, as if to shroud the women's passage from despair to hope as much as to hide their identity, suddenly the lights in the entry were put out. The porter opened the outer door, the bell rang, and a woman brought in a child. A servant led her in to a room on the right of the door, where Dr Nesbitt and others inspected the baby, to make sure it was healthy and not over two years old, as the plan required. On that first night two were refused, one being too old, the other 'appearing to have the Itch'.

The child received a number – one, two, three – and three people confirmed the ticket of entry, the 'Billet of its Description'. Then the woman was sent away, without being 'asked any questions whatosoever'. As she disappeared into the darkness she often left behind some message, some token, some ring, to give the baby a link with its shadowy origin. Many of these sad little tokens are still there today, held under glass. As soon as one child was admitted another was brought in. For four hours the trail of women continued until thirty babies were admitted, eighteen boys and twelve girls.

At midnight the porter was sent to tell the crowd that the house was full. When trouble threatened, one of the Governors stepped forward to explain that all the places were taken but as soon as there was a place free, a public advertisement would be issued. Seeing seven or eight women with children pressing towards the door, and still more in the crowd behind, they begged them not to drop their babies in the street to die, but to keep them until the hospital could take them in. Calmed, the crowd melted into the darkness. Although the evening was a triumph it was a pitiable occasion, for the tears of the women who left their children were as grievous as those who were turned away. Nearly all the new babies were 'dressed very clean, from whence', declared the minutes tartly, 'they appeared not to have been under the care of the Parish officers'. But many seemed stupefied, and some starved, too weak even to suck; two died within three days.

The day after the first admissions, according to the minutes,

'many Charitable Persons of Fashion visited the Hospital, and whatever Share Curiosity might have in inducing any of them to Come, none went away without shewing most sensible Marks of Compassion for the helpless Objects of this Charity and few (if any) without contributing something for their Relief'.

In came the nobles and gentry in their velvet coats and long waistcoats crackling with gold embroidery, flashing lace at wrists and neck. With them came their wives, swishing their hooped skirts. Everyone was part of the spectacle, although the tone was different to the cruel visiting of Bedlam. The babies, washed and brushed, were on display to be pitied, but the fashionable visitors, also washed and brushed, were equally on display. They were here to be seen and admired for their generosity, which bespoke their easy wealth, and their tears, which bespoke their feeling hearts. Hogarth stayed away from this grand visitation, returning the next day, when, to the distress of all, it was discovered that the first of the sick babies had died, and arrangements were made for Dr Mead to advise about their care.

An even greater display of fashionable benevolence took place four days later, on 29 March, when the first group of children was baptized before

'Persons of Quality and Distinction; His Grace the Duke of Bedford, our President, their Graces the Duke and Dutchess of Richmond, the Countess of Pembroke and Several other honouring the children with their Names and being their Sponsors'.

This time they were giving not only their money and their compassionate glances, but their very names. When the sick infants lay in their cradles in Hatton Garden, or the healthy ones lay sucking at the breasts of wet-nurses in Surrey and Yorkshire, their nurses called them by names heavy with history, the gift of Dukes and Duchesses and Members of Parliament, little Russells and Finches and Lennoxes. But not all the names carried the glitter of diamonds. The first two babies carried up to the Reverend Samuel Smith of All Hallows, London Wall, who conducted the service, were baptized Thomas and Eunice Coram. And among the newly christened infants were a diminutive William and Jane Hogarth.

The giving of names was repeated with each batch of new receptions, and over the years there was always a pair of surrogate Hogarth children. (The naming could, however, prove an embarrassment when foundlings turned up to claim a relationship, or demanded to be treated like proper godchildren.) By a curious but typical integration of charity with culture, when the benefactors' names ran out children were named after heroes and heroines of novels, or famous artists and writers – so the William and Jane Hogarths of future years might play alongside Clarissa Harlowe and Tom Jones, John Milton and William Shakespeare, and even a Peter Paul Rubens and a Michelangelo. More ideas came from crafts and trades, birds and beasts, before invention failed and the hospital finally drew up a list of ordinary, serviceable names.

The hospital grew and flourished, and the death rate, which seems high to us, was low for the time: in the first year 56 children died, out of 136 admitted. The children were placed with country foster-mothers until they were three, or even five, when they were brought back to London, where they learned to read (but not to write, which might foster subversion) and to ply useful crafts, boys making nets and picking oakum, girls sewing and spinning. Around the age of nine boys were enrolled as apprentices or cabinboys, and girls went into service. Their apprenticeships were unusually long, the boys' lasting until twenty-four, the girls' until twenty-one, to prevent them drifting back on to the streets.

Coram himself was a frequent visitor, although he was impatient at the

Trustees' slowness to build, and he left the Committee in 1742 after an argument caused by his spreading angry rumours about dissolute nurses. All his wealth went to the foundlings, and he lived out his days as Hogarth's neighbour in lodgings in Leicester Fields on an annuity sponsored by friends. He died in his early eighties in 1751, receiving a ceremonial burial in the vaults of the new hospital's chapel, and honoured for posterity by Hogarth's portrait, which still hangs at the top of the stairs at the Thomas Coram Foundation in London.

Although Hogarth was only a sporadic attender at Governors' meetings after the first two years, he remained a dedicated supporter. He designed the children's uniform in 1745, supervised wet-nurses in Chiswick in the 1750s and had children to visit his house. In the 1740s he continued, too, to use the hospital to display his work and that of other artists from St Martin's Lane. A dual interest in exposing the harsh rules of society and expanding the rigid rules of art had run side by side in his career ever since his early prints of *The South Sea Scheme* and *The Lottery*. He never saw criticism and commerce as incompatible, or felt a conflict between altruism and self-advertisement. His portrait of Captain Coram doubled up with equal lack of qualms, celebrating British philanthropy while also striking a new, aggressive note in British portraiture. The 'Charitable Persons of Fashion' who came to view the babies at the Foundling Hospital were also the patrons of artists, particularly portrait painters, and Hogarth made sure that when they visited they would also see and admire *his* work. On 1 April 1741, at the Governors' meeting where he received the treasurer's receipt for his pledged donation, he was also 'pleased to give the Corporation the Gold Frame in which Mr Coram's portrait is put'.[24]

17

The Index of the Mind

It has ever been allow'd that, when a Character is strongly mark'd in the living face, it may be consider'd as an Index of the mind, to express which with any degree of justness in painting, requires the utmost Efforts of a great Master.
WILLIAM HOGARTH, inscription to 'The Bench' (1758)

CAPTAIN CORAM was the most significant of a flurry of portraits Hogarth painted at the end of the 1730s – a constellation of men, women and children, among them his sisters, Anne and Mary, and his wife, Jane. This intense activity was prompted by professional and patriotic pride. Just as he had leapt to offer his services to Bart's when he thought the plum commission was going to Amigoni, so his sudden burst of portraiture was pricked on by foreign competition – and by one artist in particular – a Frenchman, Jean-Baptiste Van Loo.

Van Loo had been a successful history- and portrait painter in Paris and Turin before coming to London in December 1737. He was in his fifties but looked younger, and Vertue recorded his arrival with beady curiosity:

'Lately he came to England. (a man aged about 35 or rather more.) tall well shaped and of good aspect. – as far as I can find he had no importunate invitations from any Nobleman or Grandee of Court. to come hither.'[1]

To show his skill Van Loo first painted the actors Colley Cibber and Owen Swiney, and within three or four months 'a most surprising number of people of the first Quality sat to him for their pictures'. His cosmopolitan gossip of the Courts of Rome, France, Sardinia – his chatter of how he and the King of Poland had smoked a pipe together while he painted his portrait – gave him a fashionable glamour and he swiftly embarked on the portrait 'manufactory' Hogarth detested. By the spring of 1738 he was the favourite of the Town, with up to five sittings every day at his studio in Henrietta Street off Covent Garden.[2] When Roubiliac's statue of Handel was being unveiled at Vauxhall, Van Loo was painting the Prince of Wales and the Princess Amelia, having already made portraits of Walpole, the Duke of Grafton and other dignitaries. His rapid success exceeded 'any other painter that is come to England in the memory of any one living –'.[3]

London portrait buyers were notoriously fickle. Many artists basked in a few sunny months only to tumble into a wintry dearth. There were other more talented foreign artists, such as the Italian Andrea Soldi (whose lively poses and strong colours – and his high-living and debts – shared the St Martin's Lane spirit) but Van Loo was the name of the moment. His reception, remembered Rouquet,

'was flattering to a very high degree. Scarce had he finished the pictures of two of his friends, when all London wanted to see them, and have theirs drawn. It is impossible to conceive what a rout they make about a new painter in that great town, if he has but any share of abilities. Crowds of coaches flock'd to Mr Vanloo's door, for several weeks after his arrival, just as they crowd to the playhouse.'[4]

He could reckon his commissions in hundreds, his waiting list was six weeks long, and the man who kept his sitting book accepted handsome bribes to help eager patrons jump the queue.

Van Loo had a gift for creating a convincing likeness, adapting his urbane French style to staid British taste. As his star rose, the English painters suffered, feeling 'great uneasines it has much blemished their reputation – and business'.[5] Watching Van Loo's triumph, Hogarth's gorge rose. Van Loo, he said later, having been told of the British craze for portraits – 'the English are to run away with' – was so skilled at puffing that he won over all the people of fashion so that even artists then in vogue plunged 'even into the utmost distress and poverty'.[6] John Vanderbank, who had been much in fashion with his easy, elegant poses, lost trade and relapsed into debt. His financial state was even worse than it had been in the 1720s and at the end of 1739 he died penniless. In his years of success he had moved westward, to Cavendish Square; his landlord, who was a friend, took no money but accepted his paintings of Don Quixote instead and 'at his death laid hands on all'. Vertue, full of praise for Vanderbank's talent but disapproving of his morals and his careless exploitation of friends, put his death down to

'Consumption – or complication – of ailments perhaps occasioned by his irregular living (of women and wine) – for his age was not above 45 – or thereabouts but had livd galantly or freely according to the custom of the age'.[7]

340

There were other casualties but in the end Van Loo's reign did not last long. He was driven back across the Channel, defeated by the cold, not the competition. In 1741 Vertue reported that he was troubled by gout and rheumatism and often talked of retiring home to Provence, the golden land of wine and olives and lavender, 'and complains this winter of the Climate and the air don't agree with him'.[8] He took on no new work but finished his commissions, including portraits of the Prince and Princess of Wales, while his illness kept 'increasing ebbing and flowing', despite drastic recourse to Dr Ward's pills. On 16 October 1742, doubtless with a sigh of relief, he returned to Aix-en-Provence.

A gleeful Hogarth behaved atrociously, at least in the eyes of Vertue, who found a notice in the paper, 'with a sting in the tail'. The spoof announcement began by declaring that the King had just knighted the painter Stephen Slaughter for a portrait of the Prince of Wales, judged 'to be an uncommon Imitation of nature' (in other words, given George II's opinion of his son, completely hideous). The notice continued that this 'may justly be said to excel the Famous *French Painter* (lately gone abroad for the Recovery of his Health) as far as he did the English Painters in general'. It ended with a final jibe at *all* the London painters by asserting that Slaughter finished the whole work himself '– not common'. Recoiling, Vertue's always erratic syntax spluttered like a firework:

'this peece of Witt or sarcasm. being stuffed with falseity. is sd to be the
       of Ho . . . a man whose high conceit of himself & of all his operations, puts all the painters at defiance not excepting the late famous Sr Godf. Kneller – & Vandyke amongst them.'[9]

Hogarth soared on, oblivious and uncaring.

Hogarth's irritation with current taste cannot have been assuaged in 1739 when his old enemy William Kent was made the 'Kings Face Painter'. Vertue, who scribbled this news straight after that of Vanderbank's death, thought it enough comment, both on Kent and on the taste of George II, merely to add a coffee-house jingle:

> As to Apelles, Ammons son
> would only deign to sit,
> so to thy pencil Kent alone
> shall Brunswick's Form submit.
>
> Equal your envied Honors, save
> this difference, still we see:

341

one would no other Painter have
none other would have thee.[10]

There was a dearth, it seemed, of inspired British portraitists: Richardson and Michael Dahl were old now, and their work was routine. Yet Joseph Highmore could be expressive and vigorous or polished and elegant as occasion required, always with a natural ease; Bartholomew Dandridge had an airy lyricism and George Knapton a cultured sophistication. William Hoare, like Knapton, was doing fine work in pastels; Frank Hayman could produce fine relaxed portraits and Arthur Devis, though decried by contemporaries, was beginning to paint strange, quiet portraits and groups of great originality. Thomas Hudson, though, was the man who would later scoop the prize. He could be dull, but patrons liked his solid flattery; as Horace Walpole cuttingly explained, the loyal country gentlemen 'were content with his honest similitudes, and with the fair tied wigs, blue velvet coats, and white satin waistcoats, which he bestowed liberally on his customers, and which with complacency they beheld multiplied in Faber's mezzotintos'.[11]

In 1740, as a portraitist, Hogarth was undoubtedly ahead of all the field. But although he was less bothered by his countrymen than by the foreigners, his competitive spirit was certainly stirred by the arrival of a new, young painter, Allan Ramsay. The son of the Scots poet to whom Hogarth had dedicated *Hudibras*, Ramsay trained in Edinburgh and briefly in London under Hans Hysing, before spending eighteen months in Italy. He studied in Rome under the history-painter Francesco Imperiali (where his fellow pupil was Pompeo Batoni, who painted so many British travellers in Italy) and then in Naples with the revered Francesco Solimena, where he also painted many English residents, coming back with a clutch of useful introductions. On his return to London in 1738 he set up his studio in the Great Piazza, Covent Garden, and enrolled in the St Martin's Lane Academy.

Ramsay astounded Vertue at first by his Italian underpainting of faces 'all red – of lake or vermilion', which gave a delicate, luminous freshness to his flesh tints.[12] Hogarth scoffed at such tricks, typical of painters from abroad, who claim to have discovered 'some new stratagem of painting a face all red or all blue or all purple at the first sitting'.[13] But he had to take Ramsay seriously; they would be friends, colleagues and competitors. Ramsay never forgot his awe as a boy, when he pored over Hogarth's prints in father's shop, and despite his bristling and jibes at 'the Ram's eye', Hogarth was fond of, and respected, the younger artist. From the start, though, they moved in different circles. Dark and handsome, clever and open-hearted, the charming

342

'blackbeard Allan' moved easily among the aristocrats and connoisseurs and soon found patrons among influential Scottish circles in London. He was also taken up by Richard Mead, doctor to the Court, famed for his great private library and art collection, and in 1739 he joined Mead's exclusive Dining Club of scholars and antiquarians – a far cry from the Beefsteaks in their theatre painting room.

Vertue recalled that Ramsay made

'small appearance at first but soon after Dr Mead & the Scotch interest and favour, appearing in his behalf – and the Duke of Argyle at the head of many others so far promoted his interest than in less than a years time he became one of the most employed in ye portrait way of any. notwithstanding Vanlo was still in great business'.[14]

He satisfied all the requirements cynically laid down by Robert Campbell, advising on the choice of careers and trades in 1747:

'The good Face Painter must have the Name of having travelled to Rome; and when he comes Home, he must be so happy as to please some great personage, who is reputed a Conoisseur, or he remains in Continual Obscurity. If he should paint a Cobbler, with all the Beauties of Art, and the most glaring Likeness, he must paint only Cobblers, and be satisfied with their Price; but if he draws a Duke, or some Dignified Person, though his features should prove so strong that the mere Signpost Dauber could not fail to hit the likeness, he becomes immediately famous and fixes what Price he pleases on his Work.'[15]

The fact that Hogarth had not 'been to Rome' made him appeal ever more loudly to an *English* tradition. *Captain Coram* was the only portrait Hogarth mentioned specifically in his autobiographical notes, and Van Loo and Ramsay – and Van Dyck – met in his memory of its conception. It was a deliberately confrontational portrait, conjuring the spirit of Van Dyck in a way that was almost as nostalgic as Bolingbroke's 'Patriot' rhetoric. Hogarth knew that no one would wish to return to the State baroque style, although his influence showed strongly in Ramsay's ferociously regal portrait of Dr Mead, which was hung like a challenge next to *Captain Coram* at the Foundling Hospital in 1747.

The witty combination of grandeur and simplicity made Hogarth's work stand out. His portraits still have a lively, uncompromising directness. His 'frankly plebeian and highly personal' style[16] and his preference for the round, energetic and open face as opposed to the long, dignified Kneller oval could create a startling vitality, unlike the work of any other artist, which reflected his own thrusting energy as much as the sitter's. In 1740 Roubiliac sculpted a bust of him, wearing the velvet or silk cap that gentlemen donned when they took off their wigs, and authors like Pope wore in their studies. Roubiliac caught the truculence in Hogarth's crooked jaw and cleft chin, the sensuality in his wide mouth, the humorous shrewdness of his appraising eyes with their late-night, slightly rakish bags beneath; the cool aggressiveness in the fighting angle of the short neck, and the pride in the high forehead with its flaunted scar – it was said that Hogarth deliberately wore his hat pushed back to let this show. However pugnacious Hogarth could be in public, friends like Roubiliac loved this acute, intelligent man, this terrier snapping at the heels of the great, just as Hogarth himself loved his irreverent pug, Trump, who crept into so many pictures and was now immortalized by a sculpture to accompany his master's.

Roubiliac's bust was an informal, perceptive view of a friend by a friend, not a public tribute like his statue of Handel. Hogarth doubtless thought he was almost as great as the composer, but after Kent turned him out of the Chapel Royal he never got near the Court, the true, if increasingly less important, fount of patronage. His chief aristocratic patron was William Cavendish, Marquess of Hartington, who later become Lord Lieutenant of Ireland and as 4th Duke of Devonshire would be a useful friend in the 1750s. Yet when Hogarth painted him in 1741 in his soft green coat with its heavy gold frogging, it was not the expected aristocratic portrait; Hogarth's fondness for quickness of expression, with bright eyes and full mouth, brought out Cavendish's mischievous humour but definitely shaved his lordly dignity.

It was Hogarth's reputation for wit rather than for elegance that attracted the rakish dilettante. Another member of the Cavendish Irish circle, and a great collector, was Gustavus Hamilton, Viscount Boyne. After Hogarth painted his portrait in the mid-1730s, Boyne asked for two 'modern moral conversations' of himself and his friends, who included Horace Walpole's older brother Edward, whom Boyne had met on the Grand Tour. One painting, *A Night Encounter*, showed the cronies out on the town, very much the worse for wear. A later handwritten note explains that it

'represents his lordship and Sir E. Walpole coming late from a Tavern. Sir E. Walpole is defended by Lord Boyne from the assault of a watchman: at the same instant, but for the timely check of the coachman, he was in more danger from the horses of Lord Peterborough's coach.'[17]

344

97 Louis-François Roubiliac, *Bust of William Hogarth*

98 *Pug* (c. 1740)

99 *William Cavendish, Duke of Devonshire* (1741)

The other picture is *Charity in the Cellar*, a dissipated group portrait with a statue of Charity in the background, parodied by the pose of Sir Philip Hoby, whose friends lean on each side, holding up globular claret bottles against his coat to mimic Charity's flowing breasts. On a bench behind them the stupefied Lord Galway opens his mouth to the wine dripping from a barrel on the shelf above.[18] As far as Boyne's circle was concerned, these scenes did not illustrate decadence; their antics were another version of English 'liberty'.

With lighter humour, Hogarth also painted *Lord Hervey and his Friends* in 1738. In this intimate view of an in-group, the homo-erotic closeness slyly

346

100 *Lord Hervey and his Friends* (1738)

mirrors a domestic conversation piece.[19] Against the background of a summery garden, with a boat tied up on the lake and a statue of Britannia behind (or perhaps Minerva, goddess of wisdom), Hogarth showed five aristocratic Whigs grouped round a table. All were members of the Walpole circle, and all were currently in favour at Court. Hogarth's details make this clear: Hervey is now Vice-Chamberlain, and his gilt key flashes prominently against his lilac silk coat; Charles, 3rd Duke of Marlborough, has just shifted allegiance from Prince Frederick to the King and been promoted to Colonel (hence his red officer's uniform); the portly Henry Fox, womanizer and gambler, has recently been made Surveyor-General (so Hogarth makes him hold up the architectural plan to which the limp-wristed Hervey gestures to so airily). The other two friends are Lord Winnington, on the right, a Lord of the Treasury, and Stephen Fox, on the left, Henry's brother and Hervey's long-standing *amour*.[20]

Hervey was married, with children, and Stephen Fox too had recently taken a bride, but gossip refused to die: 'There are three sexes,' sniped Mary Wortley Montagu, 'men and women and Herveys.' Pope had written a vividly bitchy caricature of Hervey as Sporus, 'this bug with gilded wings,/This painted child of dirt, that stinks and stings':

347

Amphibious thing! that acting either part,
The trifling head, or the corrupted heart,
Fop at the toilet, flatt'rer at the board,
Now trips a Lady, and now struts a Lord.
Eve's tempter thus the Rabbins have exprest,
A Cherub's face, a reptile all the rest,
Beauty that shocks you, parts that none will trust,
Wit that can creep, and pride that licks the dust.[21]

Hogarth, who so cruelly depicted the fop and the rake in his prints, makes no such judgement. Instead, his painting is full of gaiety, evoking a mysterious moment. At first glance, Stephen Fox looks as if he is merely enjoying the feast, but on closer inspection his cane is quietly upending the chair on which stands a black-robed clergyman, gazing at a church through a telescope and now destined to splash into the lake.

Here lies a puzzle, still unresolved, its answer known only to those long-dead friends. The teetering clergyman has often been said to be the Reverend Peter Willemin, gazing at the living of Eisey which Henry Fox had just granted him. Willemin won this living by officiating at the secret wedding of Stephen Fox and the thirteen-year-old heiress Elizabeth Strangways in 1736, a double scandal, since not only was Stephen blatantly involved with Hervey but the marriage (which outraged Elizabeth's father) was abetted by her mother – who was Henry Fox's mistress. So a joke at Willemin's expense seems likely. Horace Walpole, however, said the minister was J. T. Desaguliers, known for his interest in optics and telescopes. Since Desaguliers was such a prominent Mason, some Masonic reference could underlie his imminent fall; Stephen Fox and the Duke of Marlborough had been Masons since 1729, and in the original painting the plan that Henry Fox holds up was a little piece of paper stuck on to the canvas. This too may have held Masonic designs. If so, it was a reference Hogarth could share and his lodge connections would put him on a special plane with these worldly men.[22]

Hervey and his friends, so insouciant in 1738, were soon to be sharply disconcerted. By 1740 the ups and downs of the war against Spain led to a new onslaught against Walpole. In February 1741 motions were put forward asking the King to sack his Minister and Parliament was dismissed in a mood of high tension. Someone, soon, would kill Cock Robin. In a fevered general election Walpole's bitter critic Admiral Vernon, the hero of Porto Bello – the only victory in the Spanish war – was nominated (and elected) in several constituencies at once. By now Walpole was not sleeping and was staring into

348

space at meals: 'the politics of the age are entirely suspended, nothing is mentioned,' wrote his son Horace, 'but this bottling them up, will make them fly out with the greater violence the moment Parliament meets'.[23]

When Parliament did meet, the streets of London were uneasy. On the night of Admiral Vernon's birthday Hogarth's haunt, the Bedford Arms, was taken over by masked men, trying to beat up a mob.[24] At every division in Parliament, great tavern dinners were given for the faithful in each faction: every vote counted: 'it was a most shocking sight, to see the sick and dead brought in on both sides!', wrote Horace Walpole, continuing in terms that anticipate Hogarth's painting of electors, not politicians, in *The Polling*: 'Men on crutches! and Sir William Gordon from his bed, with a blister on his head, and flannel hanging out from under his wig.'[25] By January Walpole faced the Commons like a cornered bear. Although George II wept and pleaded, the 'Great Man' – Britain's first, if untitled Prime Minister – finally resigned as First Lord of the Treasury and took his seat in the House of Lords, as Lord Orford, on 11 February 1742.

During and after the crisis, parliamentary news was punctuated by the usual gossip of affairs and duels, opera stars, auctions and masquerades, where duchesses glittered in jewel-encrusted masks. And although it was rumoured that Walpole would be sent to the Tower (people rushed to hire rooms overlooking his route), it soon seemed that little had changed at Westminster either. As one print observed, although the actor had left centre stage, the puppet master still worked behind the screen:

> He was the Punch at first you saw;
> He gives the other Puppets Law,
> And by his secret strings he still
> Governs the others as he will.[26]

The town was flooded with all the motifs of the Screen, of Punch, of Wolsey and the sleight-of-hand juggler that Hogarth and his fellow satirists used in the 1720s. For the time being, however, Hogarth had left satire behind. He was too deep in his bid to be a leading portrait painter.

During Walpole's slide from power Hogarth was focusing on individuals, not public platforms. He thought hard about technique, colour, the representation of skin tones, the contours of limbs. He was keenly interested, as he always had been, in the way the face and body *physically* displayed emotion and character, setting the lessons from textbooks such as Le Brun against his own experience. His forceful voice echoes in his writing, as if he were teaching

349

pupils at St Martin's Lane or arguing about exactly *how* the face was the index of the mind:

'Some features are formed so as to make this or that expression of a passion more or less legible; for example, the little narrow chinese eye suits a loving or laughing expression best, as a large full eye doth those of fierceness and astonishment; and round-rising muscles will appear with some degree of chearfulness even in sorrow; the features thus suiting with the expressions that have been often repeated in the face, at length mark it with such lines as sufficiently distinguish the character of the mind.'[27]

When he painted groups, he had to think further, to see how the lines of his composition mirrored the collective psychology and relationships, just as the individual faces showed the nature of each sitter. He was still painting conversation pieces and had gained in dramatic skill after the *Progresses* and *The Four Times of the Day*. He now grouped his figures more intimately, making the sense of imminent motion, hovering gesture or unheard word more immediate. In these private pictures for the walls of family homes, each

101 *The Western Family* (1738)

350

102 *The Strode Family* (*c.* 1738)

touch contained references decipherable only by those involved. In *The Western Family*, what is the clergyman saying to the servant at the door with a letter? Why does the lady of the house reach out to grasp his black robes, while with the other she reaches towards her husband, holding a shot bird? And what is the servant in the background up to?

One reason why Hogarth found conversation pieces unprofitable was that he was so slow. He fussed and altered, painting out backgrounds and recasting details, keeping pictures back (sometimes even recalling them) and working from different sittings over months, even years. This seems to have been the case with *The Strode Family*, one of his most elegant – and most worked over – groups.[28] The Strodes lived at Ponsbourne in Hertfordshire where William Strode's father, a rich South Sea broker, had bought an estate. In 1736, William's marriage to Lady Anne Cecil, daughter of James, 4th Marquess of Salisbury, was certainly an event to mark with a portrait, but Hogarth's canvas was not delivered until the early 1740s, by which time William was MP for Reading.

351

Hogarth still poked fun at his patron's affluence – as the butler, Jonathan Powell, carefully pours from the well-used silver kettle into the china tea-pot, Lady Anne holds her delicate cup very carefully, high above the folds of her pink silk dress and white apron. At her feet stands the black strongbox where she keeps her valuable tea-caddies safe under lock and key. Influence, as well as possession, is seen and felt. William Strode reaches to touch the hand of the Reverend Arthur Smyth, a son of the Bishop of Limerick, now a tutor with his book on his knee. (Smyth, eventually Archbishop of Dublin, had also been the tutor, on the Grand Tour, of Lord William Cavendish, who ensured his preferment in the Irish Church.) Art is admired – and criticized. On the walls, the old masters that allude to Strode's recent visit to Italy are undercut by Hogarth's notable inclusion of a dead tree in the foreground of the largest painting, implying his own view of the Venetian school. And Colonel Samuel Strode (in polite dancing-master pose) has left his chair to point his cane firmly down at his plebeian pug, who is staring out the patrician poodle, bristling over a titbit on his plate.

Hogarth did snatch the occasional bone from the aristocracy, but mostly, like Frank Hayman, he painted men and women and families from the middle rank and the professions. And if he painted worldly vice for Boyne, courtly jokes for Hervey, and affluent ease for the Strodes and the Westerns, he could also paint innocence, transience, hope and loss. All these moods were present in his touching portraits of children.

When the first foundlings took their names at the font at the Foundling Hospital, William and Jane had been married for ten years, yet they had no children of their own. In 1740, Hogarth would be forty-three, and Jane nearing forty. Her years of safe child-bearing were over; the house in Leicester Fields would need no nursery. The tenderness of a childless man stole into Hogarth's painting. He had always been fascinated by children, by their capacity for imitation, their borderline swerves between order and anarchy, charm and cruelty. He painted street children and aristocratic heirs, noting their curiosity and their keen eyes, their wobbly stance and unselfconscious sureness. He looked at them all intently, observing that their faces showed personality only when they were in motion, and that 'Children in infancy have movements in the muscles of their faces peculiar to their age, as an informed and unmeaning stare, an open mouth and simple grin.'[29]

His paintings of children were superb – yet not everyone liked them. When she was an old woman, Harriet Cowper, whose sister Theodora had been included in the early group *Ashley Cowper and his Wife*, wrote that

352

'Hogarth, who excell'd so much and whose fame will never dye, made all his children Frightful! He had none of his own, and my dear Father, who knew him well, has often said he believ'd his friend Hogarth had an aversion to the whole Infantine Race, as he always contriv'd to make them hideous.'[30]

He was sensitive, but not he was not sentimental in the style Harriet admired. In 1740 he painted *The Grey Children*, the baby bouncing upright with biscuit in hand and coral rattle hanging near, the older child dangling a squirming puppy by one leg.[31] The charm was double-edged – were these little angels, or devils?

Two years later he began one of the most spectacular of his portraits of children, the family of the apothecary Daniel Graham, two years older than Hogarth. In *The Graham Children* (plate IV), the tall girl in blue, holding the wrist of the baby, Thomas (clad according to custom in feminine dress), is the eldest daughter, Henrietta. Next to her, proudly displaying her fine skirt of flowered silk, is seven-year-old Anna Maria, and beyond her sits the eight-year-old Richard, playing his 'bird-organ' and gazing up at the singing bird in the cage.[32]

This was a rich and successful family, at the opposite end of the scale from the weeping mothers who queued in darkness at the Foundling Hospital. The Grahams and their relations the Malthuses had been apothecaries to royalty since the days of Queen Anne, concocting the special oils for anointing the King at the Coronations of George I and George II. In 1739 Daniel Graham was also appointed apothecary to Chelsea Hospital; he had a shop in Pall Mall, and was rebuilding it as a grander establishment. Hogarth's painting, with its rich draperies and marble floors, acknowledges this heightened affluence. The dynasty would continue: young Richard succeeded to his father's post in Chelsea Hospital, and Henrietta grew up to marry her cousin Daniel and to be the mother of the famous economist Thomas Robert Malthus.

Even in this intimate, juvenile group Hogarth was determined to equal Van Dyck, deliberately introducing echoes of the *Five Eldest Children of Charles I*. Again this is an unusually large canvas, a rare full-length portrait on the scale of life. Just as he set Coram amid the trappings of a State portrait, so here he endowed the bourgeois children with the grace and symbolism of a royal group yet let them lose nothing of their sweetness and determined small identities. The care he lavished on this canvas is immaculate, from the silver bowl of fruit (proving he could do a Dutch still life) to the crisp frills of lace on caps and aprons and the solid, smooth sheen of the little Thomas's gold dress. Each nail glows on the baby's stubby fingers curling around the

353

biscuit; points of light glint in Richard's eyes as he gazes at the goldfinch; bold stripes, flickering whiskers, parted jaws and extended claws make the watching cat alarmingly alive. In the centre, Anna Maria is a miniature rococo beauty, dancing and dimpling in a shimmering light.

Our awareness of time is never more acute than when we look back at pictures of children. Hogarth, with his stated delight in catching the moment, knew – or certainly intended – that this picture would hang on the walls of Graham descendants. His composition caught, yet tamed, the natural zest of childhood; on the bird-organ he sketched an oval frieze of Orpheus taming the beasts. On the opposite side of the picture, on top of the clock, he made Cupid hold the scythe and hour-glass of Father Time. Love steals Time, but only for a while. The goldfinch is safe only because it is in a cage. And maybe it is not singing to the music? Maybe it is cheeping and fluttering in panic at the tabby, which Richard cannot see. Did Hogarth want to suggest that the boy's happy sense of control was a delusion? Or even that the boy is *like* the cat, and will in time find his prey?

The children too are in a gilded cage, the protected Eden of childhood. The youngest three are completely engrossed within the world of the picture: Anna Maria glances sideways as if asking for parental admiration, Richard is entranced by the bird and Thomas is torn between his biscuit and the cherries. Henrietta is rather different. In madonna blue, caring for the baby, she holds the double cherries, the symbolic 'fruit of Paradise' and childhood, but she is already on the threshold, looking out with steady eyes. Her gaze, like that of the milkmaid in the street and of the central actress in the barn, is a repeated gesture in Hogarth's work, one that both snags the viewer's eye to the *display* and insists on an implicating common knowledge.

There was a distinctively realistic Hogarthian humour in the way he made this group tremble on some verge, as if their semi-spontaneous poses are about to collapse as the baby topples over in reaching for the cherries, or the cat leaps suddenly at the bird. If it does, Anna Maria will drop her apron and squeal, Richard will stamp, Henrietta will scoop up a crying baby. Such a painting licenses the imagination of the viewer, primarily the parents. It becomes even more poignant when we know that Hogarth's painting was not, as was long thought, a hymn to sunny family happiness. Like Eden, it contained its own sadness. By 1742, when the picture was finished, the infant Thomas had died – living for his grieving parents only in paint. This is a fine, elaborately finished painting, yet all Hogarth's portraits of childhood, large and small, convey a similar deep feeling.[33]

*

354

Portraits of children, as of women, were a special sub-genre; the staple works were paintings of distinguished men, often later sold as engravings, open statements of status. Hogarth painted doctors and scientists, writers and merchants, naval captains and actors, many of whom were personal friends and liked his bold directness. Some portraits were formal tributes, like the fine picture of Theodore Jacobsen, the rich merchant and amateur architect who was Hogarth's fellow Governor at the Foundling Hospital. Jacobsen gave his plans for the hospital free, and Hogarth stressed his architectural talent rather than his business acumen, showing him holding a stylus and a plan of a house to an original triangular design (of which Jacobsen was very proud).[34] He gave a similar occupational pose to Joseph Porter, a great Hamburg trader, seated at his desk about to seal an important letter. He too was a close friend, and Nichols (who thought this one of Hogarth's best works) described him as 'a gentleman with whom he was very intimate, and at whose houses in Mortlake and in Ironmonger's-Lane he spent much of his time'.[35]

He also still spent much of his time in the theatre, and always felt most at his ease breathing an atmosphere of greasepaint. Among his many theatrical friends, he painted a characterful oval of James Quin, his head tilted challengingly upward. Quin was jovial but vain and peppery, said to have killed two actors in duels, and the painting vividly evokes his ebullient physical presence. Richard Cumberland, who saw Quin as a schoolboy, remembered him dominating the stage, 'in a green velvet coat embroidered down the seams, an enormous full-bottomed periwig, rolled stockings and high-heeled square shoes', delivering his speeches 'in a deep full tone, accompanied by a sawing kind of action . . . he rolled out his heroics with an air of dignified indifference'.[36] Hogarth caught exactly the quality of ineffaceable ego that Charles Churchill noted later:

> In what'er cast his character was laid,
> Self still, like oil, upon the surface play'd.
> Nature, in spite of all his skill, crept in:
> Horatio, Dorax, Falstaff, – still 'twas Q[UI]N.[37]

Hogarth's contacts, however, were wide and a particularly interesting group among his sitters are the scientists and surgeons: Thomas Pellett, wearing the robes of President of the Royal College of Physicians; Sir Caesar Hawkins the surgeon; Edwin Sandys, a noted biologist.[38] These men, too, were part of Britain's burgeoning polite culture.

Two of Hogarth's grandest portraits, almost approaching the dignity of *Captain Coram*, were commissioned by the astronomer and mathematician

George Parker, 2nd Earl of Macclesfield; a likeness of himself and of his now elderly tutor William Jones, a great mathematician who had collaborated with both Newton and Halley.[39] Both sitters were Fellows of the Royal Society; Jones had become Vice-President in 1737, and Macclesfield himself would be President in 1752. The Earl was Hogarth's exact contemporary. He had a London house in Soho Square and was Vice-President of the Foundling Governors and would have known Hogarth through the Hospital, through the Masons, and through their mutual scientific friends. In 1740 his patronage set the seal on Hogarth's distinction as the favourite painter of the Newtonian set. Several suggestive connections with Newton wind through Hogarth's life and work, from Sir James Thornhill's portrait of Newton to Hogarth's painting of the Conduitt family, and on to his echo of Kneller's bust of Newton in the portrait of Thomas Pellett, and the Macclesfield portraits.

At his Oxfordshire estate, Shirburn Castle, Macclesfield had built a chemical laboratory and a finely equipped observatory, and in 1740 he had just begun his first observations with his protégé James Bradley (soon Astronomer Royal at Greenwich). It was a moment to celebrate and to share with William Jones, the tutor who had inspired him. Hogarth's paintings of them would hang in the Shirburn library, its shelves laden with scientific works, its walls hung with portraits of philosophers and friends. As 'host', the Earl's own portrait would doubtless hang above the fireplace, placed slightly higher than the others, which may be why he sits 'lower' than Jones in the portrait – tactfully refraining from looking down on his friends.[40] Finely dressed in his brocaded silk waistcoat, Macclesfield's head is turned, his eyes are alert and his hand outstretched as if caught in the midst of a discussion. By contrast Jones, in his wonderful mole-brown velvet and loose white necktie, looks restrained and unassuming, but Hogarth's portrait is a sensitive tribute to this quiet but brilliant man, subtly adapting the colours and pose of John Vanderbank's 1725 portrait of Newton at the Royal Society.[41]

Macclesfield's predecessor as President of the Royal Society was a very different character. Martin Folkes, who took on the Presidency in 1741 after Sir Hans Sloane retired, was a Norfolk landowner and a thorough-going dilettante: President of the Society of Antiquaries, a keen theatre-goer, a frequenter of Old Slaughter's, a Mason, and a Foundling Hospital Governor. Neither a scientist nor a scholar, he was blamed for his irreligious attitudes and for making the Royal Society a laughing stock by allowing 'trifling and puerile papers', many on antiquarian topics.[42] Hogarth later complained how difficult it was to get real depth of character into a plain portrait, yet he managed to convey a great deal – this particular portrait (which Folkes presented to the

356

103 *James Quin* (1738)

104 *Martin Folkes* (1738)

105 *George Parker, 2nd Earl of Macclesfield* (*c.* 1740)

106 *William Jones* (1740)

107 *Benjamin Hoadly* (1738)

Society in 1742) acknowledged the sitter's public eminence, but the thick-set, slightly seedy face also hinted at a bullying streak and an unruly private life.

In a head-and-shoulders piece like that, hints were all Hogarth could manage – through expression, or background details or emblems. Three-quarter or full-length portraits gave him more leeway, like the study he painted in 1738 of his good friend Benjamin Hoadly, sitting at his desk. Although the portrait may have celebrated Benjamin's distinction in delivering the Galstonian lectures at the Royal College of Physicians the year before, the likeness is affectionately accurate (including squashed nose and pointy eyebrows) rather than respectful. In 1741, Hogarth painted Benjamin's brother, John Hoadly, now a round-faced cleric of thirty drawing a solid income from several fat livings. John was a trained lawyer before he turned, very sensibly, to the Church and benefited hugely from his father's influence; as a lawyer, he was made Chancellor of Winchester in 1735, at only twenty-six, and after his ordination that December he immediately became a chaplain to the Prince of Wales. He looks very satisfied in Hogarth's portrait.

358

108 *John Hoadly* (1741)

Both sons bear a clear resemblance to their father, Bishop Hoadly, whom Hogarth painted more than once. In one small painting, thought to date from around 1738 (though this is disputed) he showed Hoadly sitting in state against a background of columns and drapery, with a glimpse of Windsor Castle beyound the balustrade (the pose adapted for *Captain Coram*). The castle, and the star on his shoulder, refer to his membership of the Order of the Garter, the highest civil order. In 1745 this smaller painting was made into a matched pair, when Hogarth painted Hoadly's second wife, Mary Newey, daughter of the Dean of Chichester.[43]

A couple of years later, however, Hogarth painted a far larger portrait of Bishop Hoadly.[44] In this three-quarter study, Hoadly completely fills the frame in his enormously puffed-out clerical white lawn sleeves and rich black velvet robes, whose rich gold ropes and tassels compete for glory with the worldly red star of the Garter. The face is that of a smallish man, conscious of strain and pain, worldly and knowing but without malice; the contrast between the imposing pyramid of drapery and gold and the slight human frame

359

109 *Bishop Benjamin Hoadly* (1741)

beneath it is moving and imposing. Behind Hoadly and his Bible a stained-glass window glows in the darkness, showing a crowned angel with the Winchester diocesan arms and St Paul with his book and his sword, alluding to Hoadly's low-church Pauline theology.[45] Packed with references, rich and brilliant, with a twist of the grotesque, Hogarth's affectionate portrait manages to illuminate Hoadly's physical frailty and intellectual and spiritual strength, without denying his hearty enjoyment of the worldly life.

360

This was a strong, disturbing portrait. Yet Hogarth had also had a simpler, bourgeois style – *Coram* without the grandiloquence – that struck contemporaries even more sharply. Around 1740 he painted a marvellously blunt portrait of the merchant George Arnold (plate v).[46] He placed this strong-featured man facing straight out at the viewer, almost filling the canvas, a solid bulk against the grey background that brings out the sheen of his silver-blue suit. His head is slightly cocked, his button eyes alert and shrewd, his mouth turned down in a determined line. His hands grasp his good black hat. It is an assertive pose: the old merchant meets the viewer's eye, and Hogarth made no attempt to hide the warts and the double chin, or the lines that give such force to his expression. The completeness of the image, and the pliant brushwork, proclaim Arnold as a man Hogarth admired.

He painted this while staying at Ashby Lodge, the house Arnold built on his estate in Northamptonshire, a county where Hogarth had several acquaintances and sitters. The picture was matched by the portrait of Arnold's daughter Frances, and perhaps a third, of his son Lumley.[47] Together, as the portraits hung in the dining room, another unspoken narrative brushed the room, of parents and children, father and daughter, demands and expectations. Similar echoes, beyond inherited likenesses, run through the paintings of Bishop Hoadly and his sons, or of William and John Huggins. Were these strong fathers, one wonders, disappointed in the softer, smoother, next generation – as the grand, earnest Victorians were in their languorous Edwardian sons?

Frances Arnold is no mere shadow of her father, though. In her silk dress with wide lacy cuffs she is handsomely plain and benign, a character in her own right. Hogarth's strong portraits of women, as of men, spread across the range of his friends and acquaintances and gave him even more opportunity to play with styles and poses. For many female portraits he revived the tradition of posing his subjects like sculpted busts within an oval. Richardson had noted that 'it has been much disputed, which is the most excellent of the two arts, painting or sculpture', and the argument had been recently revived by the popularity of Roubiliac's new, informal busts.[48] In 1747, *The London Tradesman* reported that the current taste for sculpture 'in some measure interferes with Portrait painting. The nobility now affect to have their Busts done in that Way rather than sit for their Pictures'.[49] Sculpture offered three dimensions, while painting offered colour – and the *illusion* of volume. Hogarth was never one to pass up a challenge; he used the bust in an oval format for men, too, including James Quin, and sometimes for whole families, like the four portraits of members of the Jones family, around 1744, but it was particularly effective in his paintings of women.

110 *Frances Arnold* (c. 1740)

His approach was simple but decorative, always adjusted to the sitter. When he painted a wedding portrait of Catherine Vaslet, the daughter of a Frenchman, he transformed her undistinguished features by stressing her fashionable French gown and the haze of rococo ornament, jewels and flowers and furs.[50] He gave a quite different mood to the plump, settled beauty in a fashionable cap, said to be Lavinia Fenton, Gay's 'Polly', richly dressed and sedately charming after ten years of the Duke of Bolton's protection and the birth of three fine sons.[51] Hogarth subtly altered the tone again when he painted Mary Blackwood, Mrs Desaguliers, shimmering and lustrous with her chestnut curls and pearls, in shining ochre silk with orange bow and blue sash.[52] This is quite a 'grand' picture: in 1745 Mary, the daughter of an eminent art dealer and collector, had married Major-General Thomas Desaguliers, the son of J. T. Desaguliers and the godson of the Earl of Macclesfield. (She was said to have run away with her future husband from Ranelagh.)[53] As Chief Firemaster of the Royal Artillery, Thomas was the first scientific maker of

111 *Mrs Desaguliers* (1741)

cannon. In painting her, Hogarth seems deliberately, but delicately, to evoke the court portraits of Van Dyck and Lely.

In contrast again, as the colour illustration (plate VI) shows, he could make a solid, plain woman into a vibrant and vital subject without any trickery, as he did in 1741 when he painted Elizabeth Salter, the wife of the Reverend Samuel Salter, Prebendary of Norwich Cathedral and later Master of Charterhouse.[54] Elizabeth was a Lincolnshire woman from Grantham in her early twenties, round-faced, snub-nosed, full-lipped and big-breasted, with eyes as round and bright as a robin's. In her oval frame she is not transformed into a beauty but made radiant by Hogarth's delicate painting of her clear skin and steady gaze, and by the picture's warmth, the orange dress, pink flower and apple-green shawl (classic 'rococo colours') offset by a tumble of white lace.

The finest of all his female portraits is also enriched by colour – a striking, blossoming study of Mary Edwards (plate VII), painted in 1742. Hogarth had known Mary for ten years, and his portrait catches the boldness of this striking, unconventional woman. In 1728, aged twenty-four, Mary had inherited all the great wealth of her father, Francis Edwards of Welham, and was rumoured to be the greatest heiress in England, with spreading estates and an annual income of between fifty and sixty thousand pounds.[55] She had always had an independent streak, found the country dull, and as a girl wrote to her mother about one society marriage, 'The Duke of Bedford is justly to be pity'd, 'tis exceeding cruel to marry Children and I wonder he who was at his own disposal wou'd consent.'[56] As far as she was concerned, she would choose for herself; but she chose badly. Among many suitors she fell in love with a Scots guardsman, Lord Anne Hamilton, godson of Queen Anne and son of the 4th Duke of Hamilton, who had been killed in a famous duel with Lord Mohun in 1713. In 1731, before anyone could intervene, they were married in a clandestine 'Fleet wedding', one of the rushed ceremonies performed for money by the Chaplains of the Fleet, not restricted by ecclesiastical by-laws – until the Marriage Act of 1753 many women were trapped in this way, wedded hastily in a tavern or even in the street, before they could change their minds. It did not take Mary long to change hers. Within months Lord Anne was squandering her funds at London's gaming tables, taking her coat of arms and her name; by late 1733, as 'Lord Anne Edwards Hamilton' he was transferring stock by the thousand from his wife's holdings to his own.

During that summer Hogarth painted their son, Gerard Anne, in his well-lined cradle, a bothered baby holding a toy soldier, with the corners of his mouth turned down, while the family whippet looks up at him, startled.[57] In a group portrait of the same year showing the family on the terrace of their Kensington house, little Gerard is just able to walk, still clutching his toy. Lord Anne looks casually preoccupied, but Mary is gesturing towards the child and displaying *The Spectator*, open at an essay which tells of the omnipresence of God, and the virtuous upbringing of children.[58] By now she must have realized that she had to protect herself and her son. To do so she literally wiped out her marriage. In March 1734, she removed the records from the Fleet Chaplain's registers and replaced the note of Gerard Anne's baptism with a notice in the church register describing herself as a spinster. From thenceforward – in the public eye – she was a woman who had engaged in 'criminal conversation' and her son was a bastard, but the money and property were hers. By defying convention, she had won. Women rarely bought pictures on their own account, but in late 1734, Mary bought Hogarth's *Southwark Fair*. Like the drummeress who walks on as the plumed actor is arrested, she stepped out alone.

Mary Edwards's act was extraordinary: to win back control over her life, she deliberately became a nobody, a 'harlot'. By 1740, she was being described as an unmarried woman of fortune, who had openly kept the dashing Lord Anne until she tired of him and threw him out.[59] Gossips described her as 'cantankerous', 'idiosyncratic', 'eccentric' yet she had sailed over the crisis; she had good lawyers, and ruled her estates well; 'She, moreover, understood the mysteries of property owning, a talent not widely distributed.'[60] Two years later, Hogarth painted her portrait, sparkling and resplendent and free. He gave her a rich, bejewelled magnificence rare in English portraits. Her red damask sack, worn over a large bell-shaped hoop, shimmers with lustre; the wide lappets of her mob cap frame her bright face; fine Flemish lace – an essential and expensive asset of the fashionable wardrobe – edges her kerchief and forms the ruffles of her chemise. Around her neck hang pearls and diamonds in the popular design of ribbon bows with a pendant cross. Diamonds flash on her bodice buckle and in her drop ear-rings, and the sheen of gold burns from her watch in its ornamental case.[61] Her expression is powerfully enigmatic and yet open: knowing, sexy, proud, reserved *and* sweet.

The busts behind Mary are of Alfred the Great and Elizabeth I and the paper beside her is Elizabeth's speech to the English troops at Tilbury as they embarked to meet the Armada. It is inscribed with these lines; 'Do thou great Liberty inspire their Souls', and 'make their lives in their possession happy, or their deaths glorious in thy just defence'. If Hogarth's Captain Coram was shown as a great courtier, his Mary Edwards is a Patriot princess. Leaning on the table with its globe, she commands her own world.

18

Marriage A-la-Mode

Pictures like these, dear Madam, to design,
Asks no firm hand, and no unerring line;
Some wand'ring touches, some reflected light,
Some flying stroke alone can hit 'em right:
For how should equal Colours do the knack?
Chameleons who can paint in white and black?
ALEXANDER POPE, 'Epistle to a Lady' (1735)

HOGARTH COULD SEE – although he never abandoned the fight – that at present he was going to miss the highest honours and fattest fees in both history-painting and portrait painting. No further commissions followed his work at St Bartholomew's: 'I found no Effects and the reason upon consideration was so plaine that I dropt all the old Ideas of that,' he wrote twenty years later.[1] As a portrait painter, however fine, he had about ten commissions a year, which was nothing compared to his rivals – in 1738 Soldi was working on thirty portraits between April and August alone. He recalled how although *Captain Coram* stood supreme, the current view ran that 'it was not my tallent':

'and I was forced to drop the going on, the only way by which a fortune is to be got, as the whole nest of Phizmongers were upon my back every one of whom has his friends and all were taught to run em down, my women harlots, and my men charicatures'.[2]

There was only one recourse: 'my graveing and new compositions were calld in again for employ, that being alway in my power'.

When he wrote those notes his mind was black, but at the time, in his mid-forties, he was high-spirited and combative. In the previous few years he had been the prime force behind artistic initiative in London. His schemes crackled outwards in sharp lines of energy, from Old Slaughter's to St Bartholomew's and the Foundling Hospital, from St Martin's Lane to Vauxhall, from Leicester Fields to the House of Commons and the Engravers' Act. He turned back to his engraving less as a last resort than because this was the area in

366

which he reigned unchallenged. His prints won him money and fame in Britain and abroad. He was inventor and master of the 'modern moral Subject'.

By this time Hogarth was selling his work in folios as well as separately, binding his prints in order, like an author's collected works. And it was authors, not artists, who most appreciated him. Fielding was now editing *The Champion* (a journal founded with James Ralph) and setting out, in the guise of 'Captain Hercules Vinegar of Hockley in the Hole', to attack all hypocrites, slanderers, false scholars and ambitious politicians. In June 1740, to explain the teaching power of satire, he used the same motto that Hogarth had placed above his final version of *The Beggar's Opera*, '*tamquam in speculum*' – 'even as in a mirror'. Visual examples beat verbal argument hollow, declared Fielding – 'our eyes convey the idea more briskly to our understanding than our ears' – but a guide was still needed, and who better than 'the ingenious Mr Hogarth . . . one of the most useful satirists any age hath produced':

'In his excellent works you see the delusive scene exposed with all the force of humour, and on casting your eyes on another picture you behold the dreadful and fatal conseqence. I almost dare affirm that those two works of his, which he calls the Rake's and the Harlot's Progress, are calculated more to serve the cause of virtue, and for the preservation of mankind, than all the folios of morality which were ever written; and a sober family should no more be without them, than without the Whole Duty of Man in their house.'[3]

'Hogarth as Moralist' would be stressed by solemn commentators in just this way in the late eighteenth century. But critics who cite Fielding as the instigator of this view always quote out of context; he never wrote without irony and it is fatal to read him straight – this is 'Captain Hercules Vinegar' speaking and Captain Vinegar likes extremes. Immediately before his accolade to Hogarth, he gives a 'personal' example:

'I have heard of an old gentleman, who, to preserve his son from conversing with prostitutes, took him, when very young, to the most abandoned brothels in this town, and to so good purpose, that the young man carried a sound body into his wife's arms at eight and twenty . . .'

Perhaps, he admits drily, such scenes may not always have the same effect: *this* is why a man needs a 'monitor'. With the ludicrous example in mind, conjuring up Hogarth's rowdy brothel scenes, few people could read the line about 'a sober family' needing his prints as much as the *Whole Duty of Man* without a chuckle.

367

What Fielding admired was Hogarth's ability to weave a poignant human story through scenes of exuberance, excess, vitality and energy – as he would do himself in the brawls and romps and chases of *Joseph Andrews* and *Tom Jones*. Any fool could tell a pious tale but true 'morals' were inseparable from *mores*, the way people lived, in all their wild and glorious and dirty detail. Hogarth had sympathy as well as wit and this saved his 'moral' comedy from stark denunciation, although some of his friends, like the satirist Paul Whitehead, a Leicester Fields neighbour since 1739, saw this as a limitation – he could expose folly but not kill vice:

> 'Load, load the Pallet, Boy!' hark, Hogarth cries,
> 'Fast as I paint, fresh swarms of Fools arise!
> Groups rise on groups, and mock the Pencil's pow'r.
> To catch each new-blown folly of the hour.'
>   While hum'rous Hogarth paints each Folly dead,
> Shall Vice triumphant rear its hydra head?[4]

Yet Hogarth's prints came to life because he created recognizable beings, *not* mere diagrams of vice and virtue. Both he and Fielding drew types who were also individuals, taking traits of character to the cliff-edge of caricature without losing the richness of absurd reality.

Hogarth was deeply insulted, to the end of his life, when people called his work 'caricatures'. He admired the Italian caricatures and thought them clever, but compared to true portraiture, which showed the mind in the face, they were merely the 'Scrawlings of a Child'. Once again, it was Fielding who put into words the *kind* of comic truth to nature Hogarth aimed at. In his Preface to *Joseph Andrews* in 1742, he declared his conviction that people were far more likely to show benevolence after two or three hours at a farce 'than when soured by a Tragedy or a grave Lecture'. He himself was now attempting a new form, 'a comic Epic-Poem in Prose', which would steer a middle way between overblown romance and crude burlesque.[5] To illustrate the difference between his type of comedy and burlesque he compared 'the Works of a Comic History-Painter, with those Performances which the Italians call Caricatura'. The comic history-painter, he said, copies *Nature*, so that the viewer automatically rejects any false exaggeration, whereas the caricaturist exhibits monsters, not men. Anyone, therefore, 'who should call the Ingenious *Hogarth* a Burlesque Painter, would, in my Opinion, do him very little Honour'. It was much easier

'to paint a man with a Nose, or any other Feature of a preposterous Size, or to expose him in some absurd or monstrous Attitude, than to express the Affections of Men on Canvas. It hath been thought a vast Commendation of a Painter, to say his Figures *seem to breathe*; but surely, it is a much greater and nobler Applause, *that they appear to think.*'[6]

Fielding achieved two things for his friend. First, he separated him from the caricaturists. Secondly, by calling his own novel a comic epic and Hogarth's satires comic *history-painting* he demanded that their work be put on the highest footing in the hierarchy of the arts: a daring, even outrageous claim.

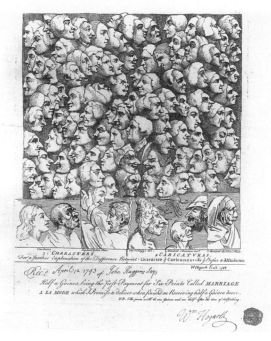

112 *Characters and Caricaturas* (1743)

The next year Hogarth responded with *Characters and Caricaturas*, a cloud of heads of every kind, long-nosed and snub-nosed, toothless and heavy-jawed, bewigged and bald, round and skinny, pensive and scowling. Beneath his strange abstract pattern of profiles, where each is both a real face and a mask, he placed three dramatic heads from the Raphael cartoons opposite a quartet of grotesques. And underneath the labels of 'Characters' and 'Caricaturas' he added one line: 'For a farther Explanation of the Difference betwixt Character and Caricature see ye Preface to Jos. Andrews.' In the middle, in the second row above the grotesques, two heads grin broadly, one

369

with beaky nose and arched brows, the other plebeian, snub-nosed and squat. Are these Fielding and Hogarth, sharing their joke?[7]

Hogarth's next work also shared the spirit of Fielding, whose *Shamela* and *Joseph Andrews* (where an innocent footman fights off his rapacious mistress) were both ripostes to the hit of the moment, Samuel Richardson's long epistolary novel *Pamela*. Pamela's trials, as she parries the assaults of her master Mr B— (including kidnapping, near rape and imprisonment) until their final happy marriage, made gentlewomen weep and clergymen preach with passion. Fielding, however, saw the novel as hypocrisy taken to new heights, promoting self-interest under the cloak of virtue, made all the more dangerous by its hypnotic realism and by the immediacy of the letter form. In March 1741 he tossed off a wild and sexy satire, *An Apology for the Life of Mrs Shamela Andrews*, unmasking Pamela as 'Shamela', a Covent Garden wench sent by her mother, a bawd, to win a husband. The joke is double-edged, since by the mercantile standards of her day Shamela is actually operating in the 'right' way, a neat little capitalist out for contracts not promises:

'nothing under a regular Keeping, a settled Settlement, for me, and all my Heirs, all my whole Life-Time, shall do the Business – or else cross-legged is the Word, faith, with *Sham*, and then I snapt my fingers.'[8]

In 1740 Richardson asked Hogarth to provide illustrations for *Pamela*. But although he admired Richardson, shared his tradesman's background and respected his views, Hogarth was a realist to the bone, quite unable to manage the decorous reflectiveness required. His views on many marriages in high society were more like Fielding's: Tom Rakewell, marrying the old woman in Marylebone Church to pay his debts, is not very different from the scheming Shamela. In an earlier oil sketch, *The Marriage Contract*, he implied even more clearly that marriage was often less a matter of the heart than of 'the Business', as Shamela put it.[9] In addition, by surrounding the young couple in this painting with pictures, busts and sycophants, he linked the worldly, contractual view of matrimony with the passion for acquisition. The latter could be intoxicating, as Mrs Delaney implied when she admired Sir Charles Cotterel's amazing new library at Rousham in November 1743, and his

'prints that cost between two and three thousand pounds – I mean the prints only. The house abounds with valuable antiques of all kinds such as bustos, statues, bronzes, basso relievos that are enough to make one wild'.[10]

370

In this world, houses and objects and cash were the ruling trinity, a point ironically suggested by the paintings of the Virgin and Child and the Holy Family in the background of Hogarth's painting.

Hogarth always had an eye for the success of the moment, and while he pondered on returning to engraving and on 'new compositions' the furore over *Pamela* filled the coffee houses. Even more interesting was the way *Shamela* attacked not only Richardson's book, but the whole cultural ambience surrounding it: the puffing by friends, the dedications, the admiring letters and sanctimonious sermons, all the layers that created literary fashion, a 'book-*à-la-mode*'.[11] Fielding's wrath was exactly in tune with Hogarth's irritation when the beau monde puffed new portrait painters and the dealers dictated taste.

Artistic taste and polite behaviour had come together in two manuals translated in 1737 and 1738. The first was *The Art of Painting in All its Branches*, by Gérard de Lairesse, a lengthy volume intended, among a host of other things, to ensure that artists made no *faux pas* when depicting genteel patrons, and the second was François Nivelon's *Rudiments of Genteel Behaviour*. Both works – guides for social emulators as well as for artists – cried out to be satirized. And in 1740 other matters also made Hogarth look closely at fashion and style. Mary Edwards, supposedly furious because her smart acquaintances sneered at her 'old-fashioned' clothes, asked Hogarth to lampoon the current modes in a painting, *Taste in High Life*. Extravagant as always, Mary paid him sixty guineas, but insisted she tell him exactly what to paint. It wasn't only clothes that she specified. Everything is here: food, dress, paintings, French frivolities, Chinese porcelain and an exotically dressed black page. At Vauxhall, in keeping in with this fashionable eclecticism, Jonathan Tyers would soon build a Turkish Tent, a classical Temple of Neptune and Chinese pavilions to add to his Gothic orchestra.

Taste in High Life is packed with verbal and visual puns, its realistic detail turned into formal patterns almost abstract in their strangeness.[12] An old lady, whose dress spreads out in an amazingly exaggerated pyramid, swaps raptures over a tiny cup with a skinny beau, complete with cane and outsized muff. Mocking the humans, a monkey in fashionable rig is perusing a fantastical menu of 'cocks combs [coxcombs], ducks tongues, rabbits ears, fricassey of snails, grande beurre d'oeufs'. A young woman, with hoops so wide she has to hold them up, sexily tickles a young Negro's chin (the bill reads 'Lady Basto Dr to John Pip for cards – £300'.) The pictures on the wall are equally mad and modish. One shows the Venus de Medici in stays, high heels and hooped

371

113 *Taste in High Life* (1746)

petticoat standing on a pedestal; behind her, one Cupid carves a fat woman into chic slimness, while another burns last year's fashions. Another picture, labelled *Insects*, shows an admired dancer, Desnoyer, amid swirling butter-flies. A third, *Exoticks*, displays a heap of solitaires, petticoats, French shoes, queue-wigs, bag-wigs and muffs.

Hogarth was smartly accurate; among the fashionable purchases young Horace Walpole made in Italy in 1741 were 'a trifling fairing' of 'six chocolate cups and a muff and tippet' for his friend Fernando Pandolfini.[13] In 1740 Charles Hanbury Williams entertained his close circle with a comic rhapsody on the intense competition for 'the newest thing', whether it be a cuttlefish or a tea-pot:

> The monkey, lap-dog, parrot, and her Grace
> Had each retired from breakfast to their place,
> When, hark, a knock! 'See Betty, see who's there.'
> ''Tis Mr. Bateman, ma'am in his new chair.'
> 'Dicky's new chair! the charming'st thing in town,
> Whose poles are lacquered, and whose lining's brown!'
> But see, he enters with his shuffling gait:

372

'Lord,' says her Grace, 'how could you be so late?'
'I'm sorry, madam, I have made you wait,'
Bateman replied: 'I only stayed to bring
The newest, charming'st, most delightful thing!'[14]

The commonest target of satire was not taste in general but female fashion. The prints were always full of scorn – showing fat ladies wedged in doorways or on narrow stairs, their hoops revealing all – and they did reflect a real absurdity, which crystallized in telling moments. In 1744 when Handel's *Messiah* was being rehearsed in Dublin, Faulkner's 'Dublin Journal' wrote that 'as the Audience will be very numerous, we hear, the Ladies have resolved to come without Hoops'. But as few could bear to appear hoopless, they still came in their full width, 'otherwise there would have been space for one hundred more seats' – those extra seats would have been sold to help debtors, by the 'Charitable Musical Society for the Relief of poor Prisoners'.[15]

Such satires, of course, were directed not just against fashion but against the whole perceived issue of women's 'affectation'. By the 1740s it seemed to some commentators (usually men) that women had come to dominate the world of leisure – they had no clubs, but they were all too visible at assemblies and routs, card parties and concerts, masquerades and operas. 'Superfluous' women rushed to cities and spas, unable to bear the *ennui* of the country, and young girls were paraded in a sexual market. Marriage was their chance of moving up in society, gaining a title, a carriage and a new town house. While men could marry below them for love (as Mr B— married Pamela) that was unthinkable for a woman. Lugubrious contemporaries blamed the collapse of marriages on upbringing as well as infidelity, on the way 'our young Misses of Rank and Quality, and even some Shopkeepers Daughters' were taught to aspire to 'a Life of revelling, visiting and gadding about'.[16] Yet, as Edward Moore implied in *Fables for the Female Sex* of 1744, angling for a husband meant treading a difficult line between appearing a vivacious beauty and a manipulating coquette. Women had to put on the character required, just as they put on their petticoats and lace. 'Most Women have no Characters at all,' scoffed Pope. All that distinguished them was the way they chose to present themselves, and all were salacious beneath their decorous disguise:

How many pictures of one Nymph we view,
All how unlike each other, all how true!
Arcadia's countess, here, in ermin'd pride,
Is there, Pastora, by a fountain side.
Here Fannia, leering on her own good man,

373

And there, a naked Leda with a Swan.
Let then the Fair one beautifully cry,
In Magdalen's loose hair and lifted eye,
Or drest in smiles of sweet Cecilia shine,
With simp'ring Angels, Palms and Harps divine;
Whether the Charmer sinner it, or saint it,
If Folly grow romantic, I must paint it? [17]

*

Noting the current vogues and snapping satires, and keen to upgrade his earlier *Progresses*, Hogarth could see that the private misery locked behind the superior smiles of a smart conversation piece could provide as powerful a story as the public spectacles of Bridewell, Bedlam, or the Fleet. The 'middling sort' who sobbed over *Pamela* and laughed and tutted through Congreve-like comedies, would go for such a tale. And if he handled it right and produced an elegant work – 'polite' in itself – he could sell it to the Quality as well. Now was the time to follow Pope's command:

Come then, the colours and the ground prepare!
Dip in the Rainbow, trick her off in Air;
Chuse a firm Cloud before it fall, and in it
Catch, e'er she change, the Cynthia of this minute. [18]

Back in his painting room at Leicester Fields, Hogarth began painting *Marriage A-la-Mode*.

This series shares Pope's fascination with a woman playing a part. Hogarth's countess, casting off her 'ermin'd pride' appears as a nymph, as 'Fannia leering at her man' and as a Magdalen, while the art works that surround her include the poses of Pope's poem: angels and palms, a prostitute dressed as a shepherdess, and Leda and the swan. But Hogarth's work had a dramatic warmth quite at odds with Pope's cold sneering and like all his series, it was more like a play than a poem. It was cast in separate scenes, with subplots and intervening events suggested by background incident and detail; the actors were ranged against elaborate wings and backdrops, and the plot line, as well as the staging, came from the theatre.

'*Marriage A-la-Mode*' even sounds like a comedy of manners: indeed it was the title of a Dryden play, revived by Cibber, which appeared in Tonson's collected edition of Dryden's *Dramatick Works* in 1735, with a frontispiece by Gravelot engraved by Gerard Vandergucht. [19] The evasions and intrigues of worldly marriages had long been standard playhouse fare. [20] And although

374

Marriage A-la-Mode, (Plate I)

114 *Marriage A-la-Mode* (1745), plate 1, 'The Marriage Contract'

Hogarth took up the barter of money and title, his young couple do not even choose for themselves. In the first scene they are about to be yoked with as little say in the matter as the dogs chained together on the floor. Seated back to back, they are entirely uninterested in each other. The simpering, snuff-taking groom, Viscount Squanderfield, tosses back his head and perks himself up on his high-heels to gaze lovingly at his own reflection; the bride droops listlessly in white satin embroidered with gold, threading her muslin scarf through the constricting hoop of her gold ring. Her very show of feeling, compared to his worldly cool, betrays her lower class. In more ways than marriage, their fate is decided. His black beauty patch may shield a syphilitic sore; her dismay is soothed by the whispering barrister, Silvertongue.

The actual deal is being done between their fathers. The Alderman, in red

375

broadcloth with a sheriff's gold chain, peers through half-raised spectacles and clutches the marriage settlement. The arrogant Earl is as desperate for cash as the merchant for status, having spent all his money on French paintings and grandiose building schemes, like the half-built Palladian mansion outside his window. He will recoup a lot from this marriage; in front of him notes and coins are piled high and a lean usurer is proffering him the mortgage, now redeemed; in return he offers his lineage, the great scroll of his family tree descending straight from 'William, Duke of Nomandye'. He can afford to lean back grandly in his brocade and fine lace, resting his gouty foot on the coroneted stool.

Among the Quality, parents had long assumed control over their children's marriages, their objective being financial or social aggrandizement. Critics had attacked this for years, stressing the feelings of the prospective partners, but cynics like Lord Lyttleton could still say quite straightforwardly that

'after all that sentimental talkers and sentimental writers may produce on the subject, marriage must be considered as a species of traffic, and as much a matter of commerce as any commodity that fills the warehouse of a merchant . . . One marries for connections, another for wealth, a third from lust, a fourth to have an heir, to oblige his parents, and so on'.[21]

For high-spending aristocrats the motive was usually money. Hervey put it pungently, explaining the advice he gave a friend in 1735, that the first thing to be considered was fortune:

'I never said, if one knew anything very bad of any woman's temper or morals, that money on one scale ought to be looked upon as a balance to any qualities you could put into the other (nor was that the case). But I did say, and continue to say, that the fortune may be a *certainty*; and that for the rest you must take your chance, for there is no getting a wife bespoke – you must take her ready made.'[22]

Money was the surer bet:

'in the fortune you may know to a farthing what your wife will be worth: and in the merit, as there is no touchstone for that ore but experience, you may marry pinchbeck for gold'.[23]

In 1742 London society gulped at the *The Irish Register*, published for the use of 'The Brave and Heroic Society of Adventurers of Dublin', a bachelor's guide to all eligible English heiresses, from dowager duchesses to 'Widow Ladies, Maiden Ladies and Misses of large Fortunes'.[24]

376

115 Plate 2, 'Early in the Morning'

In *Marriage A-la-Mode*, the aftermath of such a contract is inevitable. The newlyweds have nothing in common and live their lives quite separately. In the second picture, called variously 'After the Marriage' or 'Early in the Morning' the clock stands at twenty past twelve but the blinds are still drawn, and, as Rouquet put it, 'this encroachment of night on day, tells strongly of the disorder which governs the house'. The Viscount has come back shattered by a night's debauch. His broken-tipped sword speaks of a battle with the watch and the cap stuffed into his pocket, eagerly sniffed by the dog, smells of a session with his mistress. The Viscountess stretches, sensual and sly, noting her husband's pallid, hung-over disarray and thinking her own thoughts – her masquerade mask, the scattered cards in the salon and the copy of 'Hoyle on

377

Whist' (newly published in 1742), suggest what she has been doing. And someone else has been here, and has disappeared fast, leaving his violin uncased, his music book open and his chair overturned . . . Horrified, the prudish steward gestures to heaven as he tiptoes out with a copy of *Regeneration* stuck in his pocket. Only one receipt, marked '1743', is stuck on his spike, but he grasps a sheaf of unpaid bills.

Few would be surprised by this scene. Six years later, Horace Walpole noted:

'Lord Coke has demolished himself very fast; I mean his character; you know he was married but last spring; he is always drunk, he lost immense sums at play, and seldom goes home to his wife till eight in the morning . . . she married him extremely against her will.'[25]

The society that accepted contractual marriages also accepted their consequences. Since the Restoration, aristocratic husbands had assumed a natural right to have mistresses, making no secret either of their *amours* or their bastards. And although female chastity – for reasons of property, not propriety – was considered imperative until an heir was born, after that highborn women soon claimed equal rights. Succeeding generations of earnest bourgeoisie were shocked to think this élite culture of adultery might spread downwards, becoming the fashion of the town for *women* as much as for men. However much Pope might say that 'every woman is at heart a rake', nothing could be further from the ideal of the middle classes, as expressed by the *Letter of Genteel and Moral Advice*, which went through eight editions between 1740 and 1766:

'There is great discretion required, to keep love alive after marriage; and the conversation of a married couple cannot be agreeable for years together, without an earnest endeavour to please on both sides. If the love of a wife be tempered with a tolerable share of good sense, she will be sure never to have any private views of her own; nor do anything of consequence, which her husband may possibly dislike, without consulting him.'[26]

One witness to the Viscountess's social-climbing is her willingness to drop such bourgeois submissiveness. Neither party here will make 'an earnest endeavour to please'. At first the husband's pleasures seem the more sinister. In the third plate he wears a rich red, gold-laced suit, like his father's, but instead of attending at Court, he is winsomely holding out a box of pills to a vile-looking quack. An angry bawd, huge in her black hooped skirt, glares down on him, and a weeping young girl dabs her handkerchief to a sore. Here

116 Plate 3, 'The Scene with the Quack'

Hogarth weaves his medical satire into the social. No matter who has infected whom, he implies that the pills will be as useless as the narwhal horn and the stuffed crocodile that hang from the ceiling: the Viscount's phallic cane, so gaily raised, points straight at a skeleton, dangling his bony wrist over the genitals of an embalmed man. The dingy room is full of horrors – a wolf's head, a skull, a two-headed hermaphrodite, a collection of mummies. Around the doomed aristocrat and the sick child, pulleys, chains and gallows-like models condemn antiquarian and apothecary alike, and the monsters from 'darkest Africa' hint at the white man's savagery as well as his primitive science.[27]

The magic that his wife succumbs to is more frivolous. Hogarth paints her in her bedchamber receiving guests at her toilette – a much derided habit

379

Marriage-A-la-Mode. (Plate IV)

117 Plate 4, 'The Countess's Levee'

imported from France. The coronets over her pink-canopied bed (its open curtains a salacious female invitation), and over her gilt mirror, declare that her husband is now an Earl; the little coral rattle hanging from her chair tells us that she has a child, making the disease of the previous scene more ominous still. Neither change in status, to mother or to Countess, has had a sobering effect. She tosses a cloth across her shoulders to protect her yellow satin while the French valet curls her hair. A lolling Italian castrato flashes his presents of diamond rings and ear-rings as he sings to the music of a German flautist. A fop in curl-papers points his toe and sips his chocolate, an exaggeratedly over-perfect illustration from Lairesse, who specified that it was correct to hold things lightly and 'in appropriate instances to extend

380

one's little finger elegantly'.[28] A rapturous woman spreads out her arms – an acceptable display of aesthetic 'sensibility', not vulgar personal feeling. Behind her the handsome black servant, smiling, hovers with her cup, while her country-squire husband yawns in the corner next to a fan-holding man-about-town. The scene looks silly but harmless – yet it will prove just as fatal as the quack's chicanery. The music and the fallen cards on one side of the room are balanced on the other by the little slave in Moorish dress, who grins and points at the antler horns of Actaeon, changed into a stag for watching Diana bathe naked. Behind him the Countess's lover, the lawyer Silvertongue, gestures eagerly towards the screen with its picture of a masquerade: the tickets are already in his hands.

Hogarth's wit had never been so assured. Each scene had a different kind of humour. The marriage contract, like the opening of a comedy of manners, introduced formal contrasts of class; the bourgeois and the aristocrat conform to convention – the Alderman stooping, feet wide apart, the Earl lying back with a pseudo-Watteauesque grace. The morning scene, so acute and penetrating in its psychological study of the young couple, damned both the idle rich and the doom-demanding Methodist servant. The consulting room wove the darkness of Jonson's *Alchemist* into a satire on modern doctors. The brilliant, billowing lines of the morning levee blended the comedy of intrigue with a stab at 'effeminate' artifice of culture.

In these early scenes the dance of the eye is lilting, but now the tempo changes. All along, the harmonies of Hogarth's painting have included a sombre note, a hum of warning. Despite Fielding's praise of his 'force of humour' Hogarth often tips towards tragedy. In stage comedy, characters often overcome obstacles and find happiness; even in the plays of Jonson or Molière, which end with the exposure and punishment of frauds, the world is returned to some promise of order. But there is no happy resolution for Moll Hackabout or Tom Rakewell, or for the new Earl and his Countess. Instead, after an illusory whirl of excitement, they slide down a bleak declining curve.

In the fifth scene the shimmer turns to darkness and blood. Silvertongue and the Countess have retreated to the Turk's Head bagnio – the flames of the fire shine on a mask, a set of stays and a hooped petticoat, and the masquerade costumes of a nun and friar lie crumpled on the floor. The pursuing Earl has burst in upon them and in a fast, chaotic duel Silvertongue has stabbed him to the heart. Now the lawyer, bare-legged, is clambering from the window, lit by a guttering candle, and the watch thrusts through the door, their horror caught in a lantern's glare. The fiercely lit

Marriage-A-la-Mode, (Plate V)

118 Plate 5, 'The Death of the Earl'

triangle at the heart of the picture is framed in the angle of two swords, one quivering, piercing the floor, the other covered in blood.

Suddenly, the poses of religious martyrdom, so far confined to the pictures on their walls, are given to the main characters themselves. The dying husband with blood staining his shirt strains back against the table, his body curved like Christ's in a Renaissance deposition, but with no one to support him; his young wife kneels like a Magdalen, clasping her hands in penitence. Part of the shock comes from the sense of blasphemous travesty, yet this too is 'à la mode' – from the Restoration onwards grand ladies of the Court had, as Pope said, enjoyed being painted as Magdalens. Yet beneath the double irony there is that familiar, ironic Hogarthian insistence that real life can be a crucifixion, without a mythic promise of redemption.

The crisis is followed by a second tragedy. Distraught at the account of the execution of Silvertongue which she has seen in the broadside dropped at her feet, the Countess has drained a phial of laudanum. Her head is thrown back. Her feet, in their elegant buckled shoes with modish up-turned toes, stick out like a stiff, pathetic reminder of the vivacious, yawning, saucily alive woman who smiled over tea and toast. A maid brings her child to kiss the mother's corpse, but the patch and the leg irons show that the infant is already riddled with syphilis. Shockingly, the grim comedy of life goes on. The apothecary, stomach pump in his pocket, shakes the dimwitted servant who bought the poison. And even while the doctor is disappearing through the door, the merchant glumly eases off the wedding ring to save the gold before his daughter's fingers stiffen.

119 Plate 6, 'The Death of the Countess'

383

While the Earl's death is almost Romantic in its extreme poses and intense expressions, the final scene has a horrifying realism. Hogarth put aside the Italianate grandeur mockingly appropriate to the aristocrat and the duel, and turned to the Dutch tradition, where comedy and pathos meet. He closed the circle in the Alderman's house with its view of London Bridge, balancing the opening scene in the Earl's house, with its glimpse of the Italianate mansion. The French lavishness of the aristocrat's world is countered by the merchant's bare boards, miserly meal and scrawny dog. The price of the contract the two men made was the death of their children, the squandering of fortune and the loss of inheritance – the diseased child will be the last entry on that branching family tree.

Hogarth reworked these paintings obsessively, adding and changing until the last possible minute. He added details, changed positions, subtly altered the narrative. In *Marriage A-la-Mode*, as in the earlier *Progresses*, he made use of every inch; the snaking line of the action divides the pictures in three, the decorated walls and ceilings above, and the cluttered floor below. As he blocked out his paintings, it wasn't only the contractual marriage, but the *way* a fashionable couple lived, that he planned to expose. He could make the pictures on their walls, the carpets beneath their feet, even the cups they drank from, tell of their empty, dangerous lives.

Sometimes he chose old emblems – the chained dogs in the first picture, or the quack's skeleton. More often the emblematic role is played by 'realistic' detail, like the mishmash of objects on the mantelpiece in the early-morning scene – oriental vases and figures in *blanc de chine*, shoved next to a broken-nosed Roman bust – which reflect the cult of mindless eclecticism that passes for 'taste', as well as the disharmony of the marriage, the defying of authority, the hint of disease. The note of jarring weirdness continues in the rococo picture of Cupid playing 'O Happy Groves' above the fireplace, and the crazy girandole that is both clock and candle-holder, where a fat buddha smirks among foliage, with fishes leaping through the leaves and a cat grinning above. The rococo style was the newest of the new and Hogarth himself was one of its great promoters, but he could certainly mock its excesses; here too he was ahead of his time.[29]

Many details carry sexual innuendoes. In the gallery behind the couple, where the yawning servant snuffs the candles, among the paintings of saints hangs one canvas so shocking it has to be covered by a curtain with only a naked foot peeping out. At the levee, a copy of Crebillon's *La Sopha*, a shockingly licentious novel (in which a sofa describes what happens on it)

384

lies next to Silvertongue; this was translated into English in 1742 and is just the sort of book the Countess *would* have read. French modishness here goes hand in hand with *freedom* from 'polite' restraint and makes one look afresh at the black servant; Crebillon's heroines enjoy liaisons with 'Negroes', who 'are capable of giving way to all the Fury of Vigorous Desire', and know 'the most hidden mysteries of love'.[30] An even cleverer pointer to the Countess's adulterous giddiness is the image of Leda and the Swan on the dish in the page-boy's basket, a motif from the pornographic prints of Giulio Romano. On the walls hang three 'Correggios' – a *Rape of Ganymede* very obviously positioned above the head of the fop, a sexy *Jupiter and Io* and *Lot and his Daughters* – and a portrait of her lover. The clutter of objects from the auction, still with their tickets on, leads our eye to the figurine of Actaeon, while a strong diagonal runs across from the fop's curl-papers to the antlers. Two jokes are made at once, the page-boy's grin implicating the cuckolding couple and his pointed finger suggesting that the fop is as ridiculous, and 'unnatural', as the statue.

Poring over the tiny mock pictures, carefully outlining their rich gilt frames, adding more and more objects, Hogarth continually deepened his story's meaning. He took his argument outwards, fusing the satire on mercenary marriage with his assault on connoisseurship; the fact that the Countess's wanton bedroom pictures are all supposed 'old masters' hints at the lubricious decadence of collecting itself. 'You can't think what a closet I have fitted up!' Horace Walpole exclaimed gleefully in 1741, 'Such a Mixture of French gaiety and Roman virtu!' Walpole turned the collector's clutter into a virtual mantra as he listed the contents of his Italian 'box':

'a small Diana of Ephesus; an Etruscan *patera*; an Apis; a harpy; an Etruscan Mars; several vows and lamps; an Egyptian hand with hieroglyphics; a Fortune; a talisman . . . a Ceres with silver eyes and a cow in her lap . . .'[31]

Hogarth had used objects and pictures within pictures before, but never so lavishly. In every scene the walls are hung with canvases, from the Earl of Squander's mansion with its Italian old masters and grandiose military portrait of himself to the Alderman's sordid room with its Dutch scenes of boys pissing and smokers puffing. And beneath the modern drama the pictorial references suggest the strand of mock-religious wrath peculiar to Hogarth. All the paintings in the first scene, apart from the Earl's portrait, are of violent biblical deaths and martyrdoms, mostly based on Titian; Prometheus being gnawed by the vulture; Judith and Holofernes, St Sebastian, David and Goliath, the Slaughter of the Innocents, Cain and Abel, St Lawrence on his gridiron. This is doubtless how the Earl feels as his creditors descend, but it is a gloomy chorus for a wedding contract. Even in the bagnio there is a tapestry of the Judgment of Solomon, obscured by a portrait of a huge-breasted prostitute dressed as a shepherdess. Above the door where the watch bursts in hangs a portrait of St Luke with his ox – patron of doctors (too late) and also of the artist, recording and freezing the action – like the appalled Medusa in the opening scene.

Every picture, statue, plate, mask, pill-box and book has a point to make. The long, careful deciphering they demand recalls Hogarth's belief that the mind delights in riddles. Walpole saw it more concretely. 'It was reserved to Hogarth', he said,

'to write a scene of furniture. The rake's levee-room, the nobleman's dining-room, the apartments of husband and wife in Marriage Alamode, the alder-man's parlour, the poet's bedchamber, and many others, are the history of the manners of the age.'[32]

'The dumb rhetoric of the scenery', as Lamb called it, played a speaking role, 'for tables and chairs and joint-stools in Hogarth are living and signi-ficant things.'[33] Hogarth knew that trappings and manners made man. He showed a marriage destroyed on one hand by pride and honour and on the other by vanity and affectation. Dynastic and financial greed undermined society instead of underpinning it, while the Countess was seduced by fashion (like Tom Rakewell) as much as by Silvertongue. This so-called polite society castrated men for the pleasure of a pure voice, owned black slaves, traded women like horses and offered up its children as a sacrifice of blood to the idols of houses and furniture, titles and foreign toys.

Marriage A-la-Mode was a stylistic *tour de force*, a rococo drama whose elaborate detail and intertwined forms have a unique complexity and richness. In each scene, flowing lines lead the eye through the curve and angle of arms and gestures, of bending bodies and exchanged glances, drapery and detail. The triangular compositions that Hogarth loved embody the narrative tension, sometimes through an inverted 'V' of space between the characters, as in the first scene, sometimes through a dramatic central pyramid, like the kneeling Countess and her dying husband, framed in the two swords. But a rippling line always plays horizontally across the action, uniting the parts, and leading on to the next picture. Against delicate back-grounds of dull green and ochre, russet and brown, the light plays on brilliant colours, reds and pinks, blues, acid yellows and shimmering olive green. All the tones of his palette were brought to bear on their shifting surfaces and sombre depths.

Hogarth painted his six pictures to be bought as *paintings*, not just as sketches for the engravers. But the big money, he knew, would come from the prints. To get the delicate French tone that would attract the very circles he was mocking, he decided – despite his vaunted nationalism – that he must have French engravers. On 2 April 1743, he announced his intention in the *London Daily Post*. His advertisements were getting even longer, amounting to little manifestos. This time, before specifying the price (a guinea), he took a defensive stance:

'MR. HOGARTH intends to publish by Subscription, SIX PRINTS from Copper-Plates, engrav'd by the best Masters in Paris, after his own Paintings; representing a Variety of *Modern Occurrences* in *High-Life*, and call'd MARRIAGE A-LA-MODE.

'Particular care will be taken, that there may not be the least Objection to the Decency or Elegancy of the whole Work, and that none of the Characters represented shall be personal.'

The last clause was a reassurance to patrons. And the prints would be delivered 'with all possible Speed, the Author being determined to engage in no other Work till this is compleated'.

The subscription ticket was *Characters and Caricaturas*. And being determined to refute the name of caricaturist, in his next advertisement he said he would engrave the heads himself, 'for the better Preservation of the Characters and Expressions'. A month later, George Vertue, tired of Hogarth's claims, noted that 'Mr Hogarth is set out for Paris – to cultivate knowledge or improve his Stock of Ass . . .'. It wasn't assurance that Hogarth wanted, but skill and a delicate touch. This was his first trip abroad, but he was single-minded, no tourist. The Dover coach left from Spring Gardens, jolting through the streets and then along the dusty white Kent roads. From Dover the cross-Channel packet tacked with the winds in the tricky Channel tides between the North Foreland and Calais, a long haul for a man who felt queasy just crossing from the Isle of Sheppey to Gravesend. Then the post-coach, following the printed timetables, swept him over the dull plains of northern France to Paris, which entranced most English visitors with its paved streets, shady gardens and formal gravel walks. But while the British quality took tea with Ducs and Vicomtes in the *grands hôtels*, gossiped in the salons with *savants* and *beaux-esprits* and shopped furiously for clocks and lace, bronzes and vases, necklaces and new gowns, Hogarth headed for the workshops and studios of the best engravers. In his view, he had to pay well over the odds for this foreign talent; in the view of the French he showed typical English meanness. One engraver who eventually agreed was Simon François Ravenet, who felt that he got a hard bargain. (If this was so, he later got his own back, refusing indignantly when Hogarth asked him to engrave *Sigismunda* in the 1760s.)[34] Vertue noted his disdain for English talent morosely:

'Mr Hogarth I am told has got over a young Engraver from Paris to assist him in his plates or to work for him – this according to custom was told to me – not to comfort me – so much as shew (their malicious) envy.'[35]

In the end Hogarth found six engravers, two of whom, Scotin and Baron, worked and lived in London: Scotin had helped with *A Rake's Progress*, and Baron had engraved *Evening* in *The Four Times of the Day*. The idea was to ship at least some of the paintings over to Paris, so that the engraving could be done there, but it was a bad time for Anglo-French ventures. In May, while Hogarth was criss-crossing the Seine and admiring the pastels of Quentin de la Tour, George II was already contemplating war. Theoretically the two countries were allies, but in the Continental skirmishes of the previous three years between Habsburgs and Bourbons, English troops often faced French soldiers on the battlefield. War was a reality long before it was formally declared in February 1744. There were threats of an invasion (stopped by bad weather in the Channel rather than the British navy) and on the Continent the fortunes of battle ebbed and flowed.

Hogarth's plans were frustrated. He dared not ship the canvases to Paris; his French engravers dared not come to Britain. He told young Joshua Reynolds, 'I shall very soon be able to gratify the world with such a sight as they have never seen equalled!' – but 'soon' was not the word. At the beginning of November he put another notice in the press. It was almost eighteen months since he promised that *Marriage A-la-Mode* would be delivered 'with all possible speed'. Now, claiming that the plates were 'in great Forwardness' and would be ready, bar accidents, by next Lady Day, 25 March, he explained the delay:

'In the month of June 1743, the following French masters, Mess. Baron, Ravenet, Scotin, Le Bas, Dupré and Suberan, had entered into an Agreement with the Author (who took a Journey to Paris for that Sole Purpose) to engrave the above Work in their best Manner, each of them being to take one Plate for the Sake of Expedition; but War with France breaking out soon after, it was judged neither safe nor proper on any Account, to trust the original Paintings

388

out of England, much less to be engrav'd at Paris: And the three latter gentlemen not being able, on Account of their Families, to come over hither, the Author was necessitated with the three former to finish the Work here, each undertaking two Plates.'[36]

'The Author', he wrote, 'thinks it needless to make any other apology for the Engravings being done in England.' No one would suppose that these engravers, 'who stood in the first Rank of their Profession when at Paris', would perform worse in London. Probably the opposite, he ended robustly, as the work could be done under his inspection – fast, 'the gentlemen having agreed to engage in no other Business till this shall be finished'.

Ravenet did come over to help Baron and Scotin, but although Hogarth tried to recoup some funds by publishing a second edition of *A Harlot's Progress*, it was galling, having acknowledged the superiority of French work, to have to apologize for not getting it. Vertue thought his advertisement ludicrous, noting happily that others did too;

'the Orator Henley – seeing this Puff. proposed at his assembly a Moral Consideration of the little Game Cock of Covent Garden against. 4 Shakebaggs – meaning four print sellers of London – 2. Mr Bowles. & 2 Mr Overtons. who had sold & publisht. coppys always of Hogarths plates – now he defyes them – haveing an Act of Parliament on his side.'

In January 1745, Hogarth was still promising his prints in March; they were finally issued on the last day of May. The fine engraving made the detail even clearer and the book titles and scattered papers legible, from the Countess's discarded invitations to 'Lady Townley's Drum' or 'Miss Harebrain's Rout' to the gibbet drawn on 'Counsellor Silvertongues last Dying Speech'. Despite the ingenuous denial of personal references, the race to identify characters began: the lawyer proffering the mortgage was said to be Peter Walter, the grasping Peter Pounce of Fielding's *Joseph Andrews* who made a fortune by buying up bankrupt estates; the doctor was Misaubin, crouching in his 'museum' in St Martin's Lane. The singer was Senesino or Cerestino; the flute-player was Weidemann; the ecstatic woman was Lady Fox Lane, who had uttered that ultimate cry, 'One God, One Farinelli'.

Protected by his Act, Hogarth feared no piracies, although commentaries soon appeared, like the interminable and vacuous *Marriage A-la-Mode: an Hubrastic Tale, in Six Cantos, in Hudibrastic Verse*, described as 'Very necessary for those that are posses'd of Mr HOGARTH's prints'. The Preface made more claims for Hogarth: if the 'Comic Poet' and satirist are admired, so

389

the artist who conveys 'a pleasing and instructive moral through the history he represents, may claim a rank in the foremost class, and acquire, if the term is allowable, the appellation of the Dramatic Painter'.[37] In 1746 Rouquet's commentary, drawn from long conversations with Hogarth, clarified many background details. Novelists took note too; in their different styles, Fielding in *Tom Jones* and Richardson in *Clarissa* both showed daughters resisting forced marriages. And twenty years later, two years after his death, Hogarth's pictorial drama rooted in the comedy of manners received its due theatrical tribute in Garrick's *The Clandestine Marriage*:

> Poets and painters, who from Nature draw
> Their best and richest stores, have made this law:
> That each should neighbourly assist his brother,
> And steal with decency from one another.
> Tonight your matchless Hogarth gives the thought,
> Which from his canvas to the stage is brought.
> And who so fit to warm the poet's mind
> As he who pictur'd morals and mankind?
> But not the same their characters and scenes;
> Both labour for one end, by different means;
> Each as it suits him, takes a separate road,
> Their one great object Marriage-à-la-mode . . .
> The painter dead, yet still he charms the eye;
> While England lives, his fame can never die.[38]

19

Public Stage, Private Art

. . . he, who struts his hour upon the stage,
Can scarce extend his fame for half an age;
Nor pen nor pencil, can the Actor save,
The art, and artist, share one common grave.
DAVID GARRICK, *The Clandestine Marriage* (1766)

THE BRITISH WERE a nation of shoppers, as much as shopkeepers. Foreigners like Rouquet never ceased to be amazed at London shops, extending back from the street frontage like deep caves, lit from above, with everything 'rubb'd clean and neat', decorated with showy mirrors, painted frames and gilded signs.[1] In the 1740s there was such a fashion for adding classical pilasters, friezes and cornices that the shop door often looked more like the gate to 'a little temple than a warehouse'.

There were also 'extraordinary sales of pictures and curiosities', Rouquet wrote, and no shops were finer than the London auction rooms. These were lofty and spacious, well lit by windows on the higher levels. They were also effectively the only public exhibitions and 'the inhabitants of London amuse themselves with going to see the goods exposed to sale, just as the people amuse themselves at Paris in the great hall, where the performances of the artists of the academy are exposed to public view'.[2] Auctions were still the heart of the art trade, and were a peculiarly, though certainly not exclusively, British phenomenon, with their catalogues, customs and rules. Sales began at twelve noon, and there were usually about seventy items. People sat on benches opposite the rostrum, which was four feet from the ground so that the auctioneer – looking very grave with his ivory hammer – could command attention like a tragic actor on the stage. Passions were intense and nothing could be 'more entertaining' (in a Frenchman's eyes) than the sight of a desperate broker or an ashen woman lamenting the loss of a purchase. The auctions were powerful, too, thought Rouquet shrewdly, because they spread

'a pretty general taste for pictures in London; a taste which they not only

120 *An Auction of Pictures* (n.d.)

excite but form; there you learn to know the different schools and different masters; in a word, it is a kind of gaming, where the knowing ones employ all the rules and artifices imaginable to make dupes of the unwary; and too often they succeed.'[3]

Hogarth, as had long been known, was an enemy of auctions for just such reasons. In the early spring of 1745, while he was waiting for his engravers to finish *Marriage A-la-Mode*, he made an even more dramatic play for attention than usual. In February he sent out special tickets to 'Gentlemen, Noblemen & Lovers of Art'[4] – but not, apparently, to his fellow artists – inscribed with this message, '*The Bearer hereof is Entitled (if he thinks proper), to be a Bidder for* Mr Hogarth's Pictures, *which are to be sold on the last Day of this Month.*' The accompanying engraving was *The Battle of the Pictures*, which showed Hogarth's own works roundly defeating a set of old masters (overturning Swift's satire on the Battle of the Books, where the Ancients put the Moderns to rout). He was in a triumphant, cock-a-hoop mood.

Although people gasped at the idea of an artist holding his own auction, they grudgingly admired his nerve and *cleverness*. An exasperated yet awe-struck Vertue gave vent to his mixed feelings in a note of unusual length, lyricism and lost syntax:

'as all things have their spring from nature. time and cultivation – so Arts have

392

their bloom & Fruite &, as well in other places in this Kingdom. on this observation at present a true English Genius in the Art of Painting – has sprung and by natural strength of himself chiefly, begun with little & low shrubb instructions, rose, to a suprizing hight in the publick esteem & opinion. as this remarkable circumstance is of Mr Hogarth.'[5]

Flicking back, Vertue ran through Hogarth's apprenticeship to 'a mean sort of Engraver of coats of arms', his humorous conversations, portraits and family groups, and his 'attempted History',

'thro' all which with strong and powerfull pursuits & studyes by the boldness of his Genious – in opposition to all other professors of Painting, got into great Reputation & esteem of the Lovers of Art, Nobles of the greatest considera- tion in the Nation. & by his undaunted spirit, dispisd under-valud all other present, & preceedent painters. such as Kneller – Lilly Vandyke – those English painters, of the highest Reputation – such reasonings or envious detractions he not only often or at all times – made the subject of his conversations & Observations to Gentlemen and Lovers of Art But such like invidious reflections he would argue & maintain with all sorts of Artists painters sculptors &c.'[6]

There writes a man who has lost an argument more than once.

Hogarth himself admitted he might have gone too far, and argued too loud, but he had won a reputation for irreverence and bold-faced pugnacity that was hard to shake off, so he shrugged and accepted it. A few years later, when he advised young Hester Salusbury (later Mrs Thrale) to seek out Dr Johnson, 'whose conversation was to the talk of other men, like Titian's painting compared to Hudson's', he said, '"but don't you tell people now, that I say so (continued he), for the conoisseurs and I are at war you know, and because I hate *them*, they think I hate *Titian* – and let them"'.[7]

It was hardly surprising if his hearers thought this way. In *The Battle of the Pictures* a scene from *Marriage A-la-Mode* stands on the easel in an open studio while ranks of identical Italianate copies march past a prison-like auction house. The auction room has cracks in its walls and a weathercock (for Christopher Cock) on top, its compass points replaced by P, V, F, S, for 'Puffs'. The scene on the first of the file of paintings is a sketch of the flaying of Marsyas – as if the thin-skinned Hogarth felt he too was being flayed by the dealers. But all the little squares behind, representing more pictures, are marked 'Do' (for ditto). In other words *all* the canvases bear this scene of classical pain. The endless copies that pretend to be original reduce both the

121 *The Battle of the Pictures* (1745)

value of the art and the terrible, authentic power of the myth. In the swirling winds that assail Hogarth's open room, these copies rise in thermals of rage and join battle with Hogarth's works. A praying St Francis slices into Hogarth's spinster from *Morning*; a magadelen attacks Moll Hackabout in her garret; an Olympian feast is holed by the scene of Tom Rakewell in the Rose Tavern, and a procession of Bacchus is slashed by *A Midnight Modern Conversation*. At the moment the odds are even – Hogarth's auction, which this ticket advertises, will show which side wins.

The breathtaking cheek of the ticket was matched by a hail of press advertisements, appearing every day throughout February. From the middle of the month these carried elaborate and intriguing instructions: every bidder would have a whole page in the sale book, marked with his name, address, and the amount; on the day of the sale a clock would strike every five minutes and, at five past twelve exactly the first picture in the sale book would be sold to the highest bidder. So it would go on until the whole lot had gone. No one, he

394

added, should 'advance less than Gold at each bidding'. The morning came and the carriages rolled into Leicester Fields, from the City and St James's. Shrugging off their greatcoats, the curious crowd filed into the painting room where the clock was set, and the bidding began.

Sarah Malcolm was snapped up for five guineas by Horace Walpole, who remembered seeing 'a poor old cripple', Mr Wood, bidding for the Rake, saying '"I *will* buy my own progress"', though he looked as if he had no more title to it than I have but by limping and sitting up'.[8] In the end William Beckford, a future Tory MP, later Alderman and Lord Mayor of London, bought the eight pictures of the *Rake* at 22 guineas each, and the six of the *Harlot* at 14 guineas apiece. Wood ended up paying 26 guineas for *Strolling Actresses*. The Duke of Ancaster bought *Noon*, *Evening* and the painting of Danae and the golden shower, while the banker Sir William Heathcote took *Morning* and *Night*. The biggest individual sum was 60 guineas for the *Danae*. (For a comparison, a curate's salary could range from £23 to £60 a year.) The total came to nearly £500 for nineteen paintings. This was not bad for modern paintings, when £8 was standard for a portrait, but not good enough for Hogarth. The prices for old masters ranged from £80 to £500 – in the market place they still held the battlefield.

Vertue saw the event as an attempt to beat both critics and auctioneers, a blatant demonstration of Hogarth the showman. We must, he said,

'admitt the Temper of the people loves humorous spritely diverting subjects in painting. yet surely. *the Foxes tale* – was of great use to him. as Hudibrass expresseth

> yet He! that hath but Impudence,
> to all things, has a Fair pretence.'[9]

*

Hogarth's bold pretence extended to his portraits. Over the year he finished four very different works, of Archbishop Herring, of Captain Lord George Graham, of David Garrick – and himself. Each had a touch of theatre and each showed his fascination with the way men wore costumes and took roles, and positioned themselves carefully and deliberately in the public gaze.

This tension between a man and his robes of office, felt in the painting of Bishop Hoadly, emerged in a different way in a formal three-quarter-length portrait of Thomas Herring, commissioned, perhaps on Hoadly's recommendation, to mark his appointment as Archbishop of York in 1743.[10] Although Herring liked his 'burlesques', Hogarth was hardly an obvious choice for an episcopal portraitist and he was determined to exploit the chance.

122 *Thomas Herring, Archbishop of York* (1744/47)

Influenced by the pastels of Quentin de la Tour, he took a simple and bold approach.[11] With strong and certain strokes, he filled the canvas with the swoop of Herring's bishop's robes and sleeves, creating a cascade of black and white against a sombre green curtain. Above this flowing dress of power the rather ineffectual face of the Archbishop gains a strong, eagle-like dignity, while the turn of his hand, not raised in a gesture of blessing but opening to the viewer, suggests that he is just about to intervene, very courteously, in some formal debate.

Hogarth was rightly proud of his work. He signed it 'W. Hogarth pinxit, 1744', and apparently told the Archbishop with confidence:

'Your Grace, perhaps does not know that some of our chief dignitories in the Church have had the best luck in their portraits. The most excellent heads painted by Vandyck and Kneller, were those of Laud and Tillotson. The crown of my works will be the representation of your Grace.'[12]

Alas, only he thought so. In November 1745 Herring wrote peevishly that

396

'none of my friends can bear Hogarth's picture'.[13] It was too extreme, too '*outré*', and did not do justice to his Grace's 'benevolence'. In 1747 an angry Hogarth drastically repainted the figure (the vigorous white strokes on the sleeve have been described as 'an audible scream of rage').[14] But no token of approval came from Herring, by then Archbishop of Canterbury.

The Herring portrait stressed the office, and hinted at the man. The opposite was true of *Lord George Graham in his Cabin*. Graham, younger son of the Duke of Montrose, had worked his way up from midshipman to captain in 1740; in the same year he was made Governor of Newfoundland and in 1741 became MP for the County of Stirling. He was also a senior Mason, but none of this official dignity entered Hogarth's picture, a study in browns and green and startling red. Hogarth painted Graham at ease in his snug panelled cabin, about to share a meal and a bowl of punch with the dark-clad ship's purser. Instead of his naval uniform, he is smoking his pipe in a gold-tasselled cap and fur-lined cloak and to underline his casual pose Hogarth lavished as much attention on the minor figures as on the captain: the Negro servant playing the drum; the round-faced, open-mouthed singer; the grinning cabin-boy bringing in the fowl. As a final touch he introduced his own pug, wearing Graham's discarded wig, toting a roll of paper like a musket and ready to sing his own song.

123 *Lord George Graham in his Cabin* (1745)

397

This group was performing – singing and posing – but its members were also being themselves, in a private room. When Hogarth came to paint David Garrick his challenge was to *find* that 'real self', for the actor was completely subsumed in the role. Indeed Hogarth had great difficulty in all his pictures of Garrick, in painting his face, so mobile and shifting that it dodged the fixity of portraiture altogether. In this case, he made so many attempts and scrubbed out the face so often that in the end he painted it separately, on a piece of canvas that was later stitched into the whole. And was he painting Garrick, or the character that made his name, Richard III?

Garrick had flared into fame like a new comet in the heavens in the autumn of 1741. To get round the Licensing Act which forbade plays outside the Royal patent theatres, the Goodman's Fields management put on concerts of 'Vocal and Instrumental Musick', dividing them into two parts and sneaking in a dramatic entertainment between them, often a full-length play. On 19 October 1741 this was a full scale *Richard III* with the leading part played by 'a gentleman (who never appeared on any stage)': David Garrick. His performance became legend overnight: his natural style, foreshadowed only by Macklin's great Shylock a few months before, was the theatrical equivalent of Hogarth's truth to life, and the inspiration, perhaps, of a new vitality in Hogarth's painting. The *Daily Post* spoke of his 'extraordinary and great reception' and other papers praised the way the passions surged across his face, his grace, his easy delivery, his wholehearted absorption in his role. The style they *usually* saw is implied by the astonished negatives of this report in *The Champion*, which praised Garrick's elocution and continued:

'He is not less happy in his mien and gait, in which he is neither strutting nor mincing, neither stiff nor slouching. When three or four are on the stage with him, he is attentive to whatever is spoke, and never drops his characters when he has finished a speech by either looking contemptuously on an inferior performer, unnecessary spitting, or suffering his eyes to wander through the whole circle of spectators . . .'[15]

Watching him, Quin, master of the old heavy-handed delivery, was said to mutter glumly, 'If he is right, we are all wrong.' Hogarth and Fielding were both entranced and soon became close personal friends.

Since then Garrick had gone from strength to strength. In 1742 Horace Walpole noted the success of Fielding's new farce, *Miss Lucy in Town*, with Kitty Clive and John Beard, adding 'but all the run is now after Garrick, a wine merchant who is turned player at Goodmans Fields. He plays all parts, and is a very good mimic.'[16] Walpole could see nothing special in his acting, 'but it is

I *The Jones Family* (1730–31)

II *A Performance of The Indian Emperor, or The Conquest of Mexico* (1732)

III *Captain Thomas Coram* (1740)

IV *The Graham Children* (1742)

V *George Arnold Esq. of Ashby Lodge* (c. 1740)

VI *Elizabeth Salter* (1744)   VII *Mary Edwards* (1742)

VIII *A Painter and His Pug*

IX *The Country Dance* (*c.*1745)

X *The Shrimp Girl* (?1740s)

XI *David Garrick and his Wife* (1757)
XII *An Election 4: Chairing the Member*

XIII *Picquet, or Virtue in Danger*; or *The Lady's Last Stake* (1759)
XIV *Sigismunda Mourning over the Heart of Guiscardo*

heresy to say so'. Three years later, such heresy would merit excommunication. Garrick had become a figure in the Town, jubilant in his success and his love affair with the actress Peg Woffington, sweeping up Hogarth and his circle in his 'Theatrical revolutions'. In December 1744, for example, Garrick was passing on the gossip to John Hoadly about the sale of the Drury Lane patent to James Lacy. He was also discussing the comedies written by the Hoadly brothers, and asking, 'When shall I see You in Town pray? with yr Funny Head, laughing Face, honest Heart & crammed Pockets – crammed Pockets Sir; remember that.'[17] He was living in rooms above a wigmaker in James Street, Covent Garden, and in the spring of 1745 the actors and artists at Old Slaughter's and the Beefsteak Club watched avidly as his triumphant *King John* at Drury Lane closed down an old-style staging of the same play at Covent Garden, starring Colley Cibber, emerging once again from his 'retirement'.

124 *Garrick in the Character of Richard III* (1745)

Hogarth's *Garrick as Richard III* flagged a turning point in British theatre, just as his *Beggar's Opera* paintings had done twenty years before. It illustrated the moment in Act v, scene iii, of Shakespeare's play, where Richard wakes in his tent on the eve of Bosworth Field, haunted by earlier crimes, crying out:

399

Give me another horse! bind up my wounds!
Have mercy, Jesus, Soft! I did but dream.
O coward conscience, how dost thou afflict me.

Garrick as Richard is frozen by terror, reaching for his sword and fending off the ghosts with his raised hand. Hogarth is interested in the *response* to action, not action itself – the face as mirror of the mind within, worked on by the scene without. Above his taut, elongated body, the great red curtains of the tent, with the crown and a painted Christ resting in their shadows, draw the eye backward to the camp with its flaring bonfires and the dawn beyond, breaking over distant hills.

Hogarth's painting was a roughly accurate picture of the actor on stage – his scattered armour (specially borrowed from the Tower of London), his quasi-Elizabethan costume, his dramatic diagonal pose and powerful expression. But his work also verged on baroque history-painting, presenting a 'sublime' interpretation of Shakespeare's version of British history as well as of Garrick's performance. Although Garrick – like Hogarth – was known for his naturalism, his pose still derived ultimately from stage manuals of gesture and expression, just as Hogarth's painting (influenced perhaps by Roubiliac's dramatic funerary monuments) drew on models such as Le Brun's famous *Family of Darius before Alexander the Great*. Their art sprang from tradition, and their greatness was defined by their leap from the norm.

Both men were known for their versatility and their popular appeal. Garrick too wanted to raise the standard of his art, to revive the 'true' Shakespeare, whose humour mingled tartly with tragedy, and also to show that he, as a performer, could succeed in every genre. Again like Hogarth, he was a great publicist, putting the spotlight on the *actor* as Hogarth did on the artist; two years later, when he eventually accepted Lacy's offer to manage Drury Lane, he swept the audience off the stage and brought in footlights instead of chandeliers, framing the actors in light behind the proscenium arch.

In line with his effervescent self-display, Garrick very much liked being painted. In October 1745 he was chivvying Frank Hayman (who was now working on Shakespearean paintings for the Prince's Pavilion at Vauxhall) about scenes from *Lear* and *Othello*. His headlong bounce shows why he had so many friends:

'I write to you without connection or Correction; I am now in a Room full of Brothers & Sisters, the greater part is female & consequently more noisey & confounding; however if Your Taste is like Mine, You'll chuse a plain Simple Meal with a Hearty Wellcome, before the most regular, ceremonious entertainments: therefore take Pot luck with Me when You please, & I'll do the Same with You, & damn all formality between Us. Have You finished My Picture Yet? Dr Newton has been here & prais'd it extravagantly.'[18]

Hayman's painting was probably the small picture of Garrick and his friend William Windham, although he too painted Garrick as Richard III in a later work exhibited at the Society of Arts in 1760. The more portraits the better as far as Garrick was concerned, and in the next couple of months he was eager to know what Hogarth was doing, writing to his friend Somerset Draper, 'Mr Wyndham sends me a great account of *Hogarth's* Picture; have you seen it lately?', and 'Pray, does *Hogarth* go on with my picture, and does he intend a print from it? Pray, when you see him, give him my services.'[19]

Hogarth did make a print of the portrait, engraved for him by Grignion. When it appeared in July 1746, it sold well; Vertue felt that at last London engravers had shown they could equal the Italians or the Dutch.[20] By then Garrick and Hogarth were firm friends and their closeness was lasting. Both men, as Peter Quennell succinctly put it, were 'short, spirited, vain, gregarious, with a needle-sharp eye for the comedies of everyday existence'.[21] And although Garrick's brilliance and charm won him entry into circles in which Hogarth did not move, this volatile actor would prove his most loyal friend in a crisis.

Hogarth's greatest pleasure, in connection with his portrait of Garrick, was that he sold the original painting to a Mr Duncombe, of Duncombe House, for £200 – finally reaching old-master levels. This price, about which he boasted for years, reaffirmed his claim to be at the centre of England's art trade. Largely through his initiative, paintings were now on display to the public at Vauxhall. Through his influence too, the St Martin's Lane Academy was flourishing. In 1744 thirty-six artists were studying there, and in July 1745 a meeting at the Half-Moon tavern in the Strand took subscriptions for the next winter. Hogarth had no official role, but Hayman taught history-painting, Gravelot drawing, Moser 'chasing', Roubiliac sculpture and Yeo the engraving of seals. An unnamed painter, perhaps Lambert, taught landscape and the Reverend James Wills, the Treasurer, was in charge of portrait painting.[22]

When the light was bad, or the session long, all painters were tempted to stretch and yawn, clean their brushes and abandon shop. At such times Hogarth would walk over to Old Slaughter's or to the Academy, to drink and gossip and argue. In late 1745 Vertue noted that Hogarth (in opposition to the painter Giles Hussey, who thought all proportions could be corrected by triangles or trigonometry) was making much comment 'on the inimitable curve and beauty of the S undulating motion line, admired and imitated in the great Sculptors and painters'.[23] In his Garrick portrait, the pose of the actor's terrified frame had followed a strong 'S' curve, and this serpentine line could be found weaving across all his group compositions for some years past, from *Lord Hervey* to *Marriage A-la-Mode*.

Later, in *The Analysis of Beauty*, Hogarth explained his ideas at length, but this year he made his first cryptic reference to his theory, a deliberate challenge to the curious. That autumn he took down an old self-portrait, with wig, coat, and gold-buttoned waistcoat, perhaps painted to match the portrait of Jane, and carefully painted over it. In its place he created a striking new image of himself, wearing his painter's smock, framed in an oval, posed between his pug and his palette, life and art. The palette, a conventional artist's prop, had been in the original portrait, with brushes poking through it. X-rays reveal that in his first reworking, above the palette 'and much more prominent, is the shiny knob of a large graver that held pride of place on top of the pile of books'.[24] But, by 1745, Hogarth wanted to claim gentlemanly status as a *painter*, and only the palette remained. Suspiciously clean, it was decorated with a simple line curving up, in an implied three dimensions (you can see the shadow below), inscribed 'The LINE of BEAUTY And GRACE, W.H.1745'. In the Preface to the *Analysis*, Hogarth said he painted this to see if his fellow artists had the faintest idea of what really constituted beauty, or could find a better definition for 'grace' than the vague 'je ne sais quoi' of foreign theorists:

'The bait soon took; and no Egyptian hierogliphic ever amused more than it did for a time, painters and sculptors came to me to know the meaning of it, being as much puzzled with it as other people, till it came to have some explanation; then indeed, but not till then, some found it out to be an old acquaintance of theirs, tho' the account they could give of its properties was very near as satisfactory as that which a day-labourer who constantly uses the leaver, could give of that machine as a mechanical power.'[25]

He knew how to make people curious. And how to annoy. His artisan image implied that as far as the artists were concerned, the old slur of 'mere mechanics' was sometimes all too true – except with William Hogarth, who not only knew beauty when he saw it, but understood its rules.

The colours of this self-portrait (plate VIII) are a decorous, conventional dark red and green but Hogarth's red coat is draped across him like a cloak in a late-baroque portrait, flaring against his black waistcoat and white stock. The colours are picked up in the black hat with its red and gold tassel, pushed back as usual to show his scar. His eyes are keen, meeting ours with an alert stare, and his mouth is firm and humorous. Yet this is a painting – imitating a sculpture bust – within a painting. In front sits his dog, ears cocked and tongue hanging out, bored of sitting so long – a 'natural' element, his patient restlessness suggesting an animal life *outside* the formal frame of art.[26] But if Hogarth was claiming he could represent nature, he wanted his intellectual side shown too; his painting resembles the formal portraits in the collected works of authors and when he engraved it in 1749, as the frontispiece for his bound engravings, he asked to be 'read' and placed in a literary line. The oval portrait of the artist, tacked to its stretcher, rests on three leather-bound volumes – Shakespeare, Milton and Swift – comedy and tragedy, sublimity and satire.

This was the public face of his art. But Hogarth's work, unlike Garrick's, took place without an audience. Instead of emerging from the wings into the footlights' glare, he walked down the corridor to the painting room, inhaling the smell of the size and the oils that filled the air, creeping into the house. When he opened the door, checking the light that flooded in through the north-facing windows from the grey London skies above the neighbouring roofs, he took stock of the canvases leaning stacked against the walls. These came in different sizes, nailed to their stretchers – half length, Kit-Cat (the size used by Kneller for his portraits of the club) and three-quarter length – rarely full length for him. The pictures he had finished and not sold, like the brilliant canvases of *Marriage A-la-Mode*, might hang either here or in the large front room, but several half-finished pictures lay waiting for a final touch, and sheafs of prints – his own and others – lay on different surfaces, tipping gently in the draught. The plates and the tools for his engraving had a space of their own.

Rather than buying ready-primed canvas, Hogarth liked to do everything himself. Under the hand raw canvas was rough, and warm. His brushes, the stiff ones of hog's hair and the thin, delicate ones of sable and squirrel, stood cleaned and ready. Here, too was his maulstick (or *mahlstick*) with its knob covered with soft leather, which he could rest against the painting to serve as a support for his wrist when precision was needed, and the palette knives and spatulas and palettes, both the oval ones shown in his portraits and an old shovel-shaped board.[27] In pride of place stood his large 'paint-box' or colour cabinet, a capacious cupboard with fifty-four drawers for pigments and oils, plus vessels for mixing; and after 1750, when mahogany came into use, Hogarth also acquired a fine painted press with glass doors and sliding shelves.[28] Hogarth's colour cabinet was not as elaborate as Richard Wilson's – a six-foot-high model of his home in Covent Garden, with arches made into holders for his brushes and oil bottles[29] – but it held the ingredients of his alchemy with their magical names, including colours as old as Pompeii.

For many years certain tints had been used for the skin – yellow ochre, vermilion, red lead, light red, Indian red, lake, smalt, blue-black, terreverte, brown-pink, umber and bone-black – carmine for cheeks and ultramarine for the shadows of the flesh.[30] In the 1740s new colours came into use. Instead of indigo, Prussian blue was mixed with yellow to make a surer green than verdigris and other old copper greens, while new yellows that did not fade took the place of the ancient vegetable dyes. There were some commercial colour shops, like Mr Powell's in St Martin's Lane, but most painters had their own recipes, their own secrets jealously guarded. They preferred to buy supplies directly from the workshops of the colourmakers in Hoxton and Shoreditch, or south of the river in Southwark.

Hogarth thought hard about colour, writing in detail in the *Analysis* about the physiological basis of complexions, the infinite variations of natural tints and their translation into the 'bloom tints' of the artist.[31] He was intensely interested in the physical properties of pigments, the way that the oils softened and mellowed the shades and the need to find the 'clearest oil', which would not yellow the tints. He watched and noticed how colours changed, according to their material base – metal, stone or vegetable. How could one call age an 'improver' when colours decayed so visibly? Time could not operate

'otherwise than as by daily experience we find it doth, which is, that one changes darker, another lighter, one quite to a different colour, whilst another, as ultramarine, will keep its natural brightness even in the fire'.[32]

How could the theorists hold forth, when they lacked the artist's expertise and observation? If anything, time was a vandal, which 'disunites, untunes, blackens, and by degrees destroys'.

His technical curiosity fed simultaneously into his practice and into his aesthetic battles. His own palette was brighter than that of most of his contemporaries, and his colours stayed fresh. He arranged his pigments on his palette, growing progressively darker as they moved away from the thumb-hole: his self-portrait of 1735 showed a palette of flesh tints from white to vermilion. But in the *Analysis* he worked out an elaborate, eccentric, arrangement, following Leonardo's account of the rainbow, mixing the colours in a bow, numbered from 1 to 7.[33] The most brilliant group, the 'virgin tints' lay at the meridian, at number 4. The lower, darker, tints would gradually sink into black 'either by twilight, or at a moderate distance from the eye', while to the right, he said, they were almost as beautiful as the central tints since they were always gaining in light. He illustrated this with a diagram showing a palette so crammed that there is no room for mixing, and no black or white, placing the five 'bloom tints' – red, yellow, blue, green and purple - in a spectral sequence, graded in seven values from dark to light.

In practice, he used a much simpler palette, and as a painter he was conservative in habit, if not in style and address. He still used linseed oil, which dried quickly, and walnut and poppy oils, which did not yellow, for mixing with white and blues.[34] Each paint made its own demands, and he mixed them carefully, varying the tones to suit his needs. Standing before his big easel, he steadied his new canvas, covering it with size to stop the oils leaking through. Then he prepared his favourite grey ground, mixing the flake-white and chalk with black and umber pigments and binding them with linseed oil. When it was the right consistency, he spread it fast across the naked canvas, working with broad strokes that left fine lines, catching the light like birdtracks in city snow. Another layer of size, another layer of ground, and then he let it dry.

The strong colours would come later, olive greens and flashing scarlet, clear blue and crusted gold, striking the eye the more brilliantly as they sprang out from the cool ground. But the first touch on that ground was like the moment when a conductor raises his baton, provisional yet poised – yet not like, for Hogarth's harmonies built slowly and the grace notes were added only at the end. He worked directly on the canvas, block by block, intricate touch by intricate touch, adding and smoothing, softening and sharpening, working the picture out as he painted and overpainting when he had a second thought.

Many painters worked fast, a legacy from Kneller. Highmore, for instance, often finishing the faces at one sitting, 'never touches them more', as Rouquet said. But Hogarth followed the old style of Van Dyck's era, beginning with a thin layer of the 'dead colours' to provide a foundation. For a portrait, taking the colours from his cabinet, he mixed a range of flesh pinks, adding his sage greens and yellow-ochres, his ultramarine and lake for the greenish and blue half-shadows, and using brown-pink and black for the deepest of all. Taking his brush, he worked in patches and 'sweetened them' while wet, criss-crossing and blurring their joins with a clean brush. Next came the hair, sketched in at first in light and dark tones. Sometimes Hogarth painted a face in only one layer, working quickly in patches of local colour while the base tones were wet. Or he might pause to rub in oil, wiping it off to leave an infinitesimally thin layer to stop the later paints from sinking. And then, pulling up his painting chair, 'a large affair running on wheels', he could settle down to work in fine details, slowly transferring the image from his mind to his easel before him.[35]

Painting was not all solitary labour. The sounds of the house and the distant square would enter his studio – maids running up the stairs, tradesmen calling, children playing, servants opening the door to visitors, carriages rumbling on cobbles. The women of the house might put their heads round the door, but their territory was upstairs, in the sunny drawing room, looking down on the square, where Jane and her mother received callers. Anne Hogarth, too, had moved here in late 1742, a year after her sister died suddenly. With her shopkeeper's training she also took charge of accounts, paid bills and helped her brother keep his books. Patrons arrived for sittings and friends called in to talk.

He was alone among London artists in insisting on painting the whole work himself, without assistants, affirming the integrity of the individual work. The use of drapery painters, even the skilled Van Aken (whose services were shared chiefly between Ramsay and Hudson in the 1740s) always roused his scorn. Smart portraitists would 'strut especially' and cry 'how we apples swim', he snorted, although their 'taylor artists', did nine-tenths of the work.[36] When Van Aken died, in 1749, Hogarth made a satirical drawing of his funeral, showing all London's portrait painters as mourners 'overwhelmed with the deepest distress'.[37] His patrons expected a high finish and Hogarth could often match their expectations, although he never achieved the smoothness of Ramsay's surfaces or the shimmer of Van Aken's silks and satins. In *Marriage A-la-Mode* he had painted each detail precisely, for the engravers, but when he was released from the pressure of commissions and the demands of prints he occasionally let himself go, enjoying the paint for its own sake.

After finishing *Marriage A-la-Mode* he fell into this mood. Influenced perhaps by Highmore's serene paintings of *Pamela*, he planned a series on a happy marriage, born of love not ambition, set in a country manor house not a city mansion. In his painting room, Hogarth worked on six scenes: the first, fourth and fifth are now lost, while the second was reduced to fragments, so only the third and the last are left to suggest his aim. The first scene, 'Courtship', was apparently set in a garden with the young couple bent over a passage in a book. The second followed their procession to church, while the third was 'The Wedding Banquet'.[38] Here the bride's father raises his glass to their health and their friends hold a canopy and break the bridal cake for good luck. Musicians tune up, while the guests wait. This marriage, in contrast to *Marriage A-la-Mode*, would present an ideal of benevolence and harmony, in scenes of visiting the poor and dancing a round in the garden. It was an

English idyll, typified by the assertion that the father of the bride was 'old Roger de Coverley'.[39] Finally, in the last painting, the music bursts out in the joyous *Country Dance* (plate IX), where the tenants and workers join the gentry in another idealized image of Britain, with the bouncing country dance offset by the married couple dancing a swirling minuet, the landowners teaching their people the graces of politeness.[40]

The effect of this picture is hypnotically beautiful, with the vivid dancers framed in an uneven darkness as if the painter is sitting in the next room, looking in aslant across the blaze of light to the half-tones of night outside. The only elements completely finished are the chandelier, whose candles flame against the shadows, and the bald man mopping his head and staring at the moon as it sails across the sleeping countryside. In the hall, wigs fly, coats curl, heads turn, feet step and snap and twist as the music plays. Old and young, straight and squat, slim and fat, dance together. Even in a sketch, each character is distinguished, yet they are all just streaks and dashes of paint, edgings of colour, flicks of the brush. Nowhere else in eighteenth-century art does paint convey such movement and rhythm: 'The greatest grace and life that a picture can have', said Hogarth, quoting Lomazzo, 'is, that it expresse *Motion.*'[41]

Hogarth left *The Happy Marriage* scenes as sketches, never finishing them, nor engraving them, except to adapt 'The Wedding Dance' as an illustration for *The Analysis of Beauty*. No one knows why he stopped. It could have been because the market for happiness was smaller than that for misery and wit, or because Garrick criticized 'The Dance'. But maybe the sketches themselves, with their mazy dance of colour, said all he had to say. 'There are no lines in nature,' Hogarth wrote. For a painter, if not a philosopher, the external world is simply what light communicates to the eye, 'and those things must be considered as appearances only, produced and made out merely by means of *lights, shades* and *colours*'.[42] And those lights and shades and colours are not stable and fixed but for ever in movement, their iridescent glow changing and fading, as evanescent as life itself.

When he hunted for words, music and dance often gave Hogarth the language to convey his ideal:

'There is so strict an analogy between shade and sound, that they may well serve to illustrate each other's qualities: for as sounds gradually decreasing and increasing give the idea of progression from, or to the ear, just so do retiring shades shew progression, by figuring it to the eye . . .'[43]

And if a 'gradating shade' pleased the eye just as a swelling note pleased the

407

ear, so dancing was a communal expression of beauty and grace in visual, physical form; 'the lines which a number of people together form in country or figure dancing, make a delightful play upon the eye'. Milton, he said, when he described the angels dancing on the sacred hill, 'pictures the whole idea in words':

> Mystical dance! –
> – Mazes intricate,
> Eccentric, intervolv'd, yet regular
> Then most, when most irregular they seem.[44]

As well as *The Country Dance*, other sketches stayed in his studio until he died. One was *The Staymaker*, which may have been part of this series, where a tailor measures a woman standing in her petticoat, turning her head to see the mirror; a little girl pours water, naughtily, into the tailor's hat and a nurse, besottedly kissing the baby's bare bottom, holds it up to play with its father, who is lounging happily in his dressing-gown.[45] Only a few rough swirls of paint outline the lace around their heads and the baby's crumpled gown, and the canvas still shows through the thick strokes of the brush. Only half begun, the scene is a ghostly dream of family life.

The greatest of his sketches, *The Shrimp Girl* (plate x), is not spectral at all but radiant with life. As if the girl were moving fast towards us, her wicker platter of shrimps with its carefully balanced measuring jug cuts right across and out of the frame, its lattice-work painted so fast that Hogarth's brush has rushed down on to her green hat beneath. This is a moment caught on the wing, and Hogarth conveyed all the movement in the girl's body as he loaded his brush with pinks, vermilions and greens – the bright colours of the rococo palette – and made fast curving strokes to outline the fall of her shoulders and breasts. Framed by her hat, with its loose white ribbons, her hair curling freely beneath its brim, she glances quickly sideways and grins at a joke, or a compliment no one will hear. The light is caught and reflected in her wide dark eyes and her open smile.

In *The Shrimp Girl*, the act of painting *is* the picture: this very 'real' image tosses in the air all notions of realism. The sketch stresses the physical movement of the brush and the feel of the paint itself as if *they* were as beautiful as the woman they gave life to. Yet the subject is also significant. The picture is a manifesto, spontaneous, confident, subtle and sharp. One page of Hogarth's own notebook, its short lines tumbling over, directs us to his point, with his usual force and irony:

When a subject is trifling or Dull
the execution must be excelent
or the picture is nothing.
If a Subject is good provided
such material parts are taken care of
as may convey the Sens perfect
as for example if the action and
passion may be more truly and destinctly con
veyed by a corse bold stroke or brush
than the most delicate finishing . . .[46]

The contradiction is brilliantly put. The truth and distinctness of the coarse bold stroke, the high art of the low, lies at the heart of much of Hogarth's best work. After his death, Jane would tell visitors who saw *The Market Wench*, as it was known, 'They say he could not paint flesh. There's flesh and blood for you; – them!'[47] But while painting flesh and blood, Hogarth was also painting a myth. He had always drawn street sellers. When he was a boy, longing to paint and admiring Thornhill's swirling baroque heavens, Laroon's *The Cries of London* were selling in every printshop. From these popular images, like Venus from the sea, emerged his own street goddess, glimpsed in a crowd, beating her drum, treading the street with her milk-pail on her head, raising her arm as Diana in a barn while her petticoats fall around her. Domesticated, shorn of her sexiness, she protects the poet in his garret, or rides a cart behind an army with a babe at her breast. His shrimp-seller pretends to be nothing but herself – yet Hogarth, with his brushes and pigments, had shown beauty and grace more erotically alive on a London street than in any classical sculpture:

'Who but a bigot, even to the antiques, will say that he has not seen faces and necks, hands and arms in living women, that even the Grecian Venus doth but coarsely imitate.'

And what sufficient reason, he added, 'can be given why the same may not be said of the rest of the body?'[48]

20

The 'Forty-five

O Lord our God arise,
Scatter his enemies
And make them fall;
Confound their politicks,
Frustrate their knavish tricks.
On him our hopes are fix'd
O save us all.

God Save the King (1745)

'Tush man, mortal men, mortal men.'

Falstaff, *Henry IV, Part I*

WHILE HOGARTH WAS WORKING on his oil sketches, pondering the mysteries of colour and mass and arguing with fellow artists about his serpentine line, the country was in turmoil. By the beginning of 1745, the confusing and expensive War of the Austrian Succession had made George II's ambitions on the Continent extremely unpopular. The previous November, the King had been forced into accepting a new 'Broad-Bottomed' coalition under Henry Pelham, Walpole's protégé, incorporating some Tories and Opposition Whigs. George II's favourite adviser, Carteret – now Lord Granville – was officially ousted, although the King still consulted him in private, and the continuity of Walpole's ideas was assured by a powerful 'Old Corps' triumvirate: the affable and diplomatic Pelham, his incredibly fussy, neurotic but long-serving brother Newcastle, and the stern-minded Philip Yorke, Lord Hardwicke, Lord Chancellor since 1737.

Engineering this Pelhamite 'succession' was Sir Robert Walpole's last act of statesmanship: in March 1745 he died, dosed to death, so people said, by fighting surgeons and physicians – even his death gave rise to a war of pamphlets and prints. With the great man gone, a queasy stability reigned. The war thundered on in Flanders, where the Battle of Fontenoy in May was a crushing defeat. 'Our army is running away, all that is left to run, for half of

410

it is picked up by 3 or 400 at a time,' wrote Horace Walpole a month later, quipping that London society would have to exchange their high-heeled *pantoufles* for wooden shoes.[1] But the day was redeemed by the heroic advance of the British infantry under the young allied commander, the Duke of Cumberland.

Cumberland, still only twenty-five, was to play a notorious role in the coming national drama. After the thwarted invasion two years before, the Young Pretender, Charles Edward Stuart, had stayed on in Paris, urging his father James to try again, without French support. This summer, Charles set out on his own with a small band of Franco-Irish adventurers, landing in the Outer Hebrides on 23 July. When he crossed from Skye to the mainland two days later only a few of the Highland chieftains rallied to his side, but with the King in Hanover and the English army in Flanders, he marched rapidly south, outmanoeuvring General Cope's raw local troops.

The threat was not taken seriously at first, but when George II returned at the end of August and the Pretender then defeated the government forces at Prestonpans in September, lethargy gave way to fear. London flowered with anti-Jacobite and anti-Catholic prints – in which Archbishop Herring, who gave a rousing speech to raise funds for a volunteer association in Yorkshire, was depicted as a hero, a militant in a mitre, leading a procession of armed clerics shouting, 'King George and the Church of England for ever.'[2] Nearly sixty volunteer 'associations' to fight the rebels were mustered in England and Wales, and Handel wrote the music for a special song for the 'Gentlemen Volunteers of the City of London'.[3]

On 28 September, *God Save the King* was sung publicly for the first time, at Drury Lane Theatre. The audience, having absolutely no doubt that a Protestant God must be on the Hanoverian side, cheered and shouted and cried for encores – ironically, considering that the song had been around in popular versions for fifty years or more, sung with special enthusiasm by supporters of the Stuarts in exile. On 30 September, George II's birthday, the 'National Anthem', as it would become, was played at the end of the performance at both Covent Garden and Goodman's Fields.[4] Printed in newspapers, magazines and broadsheets, and carried in the packs of travelling ballad-singers, its words and music spread across the land.

Men, like music, could change their tunes. Henry Fielding, whose Patriot friends were now included in the government, dropped his opposition stance and became a scaremongering propagandist, writing three pamphlets (including a satirical *Dialogue between the Devil, the Pope, and the Pretender*) and editing a strident newspaper, *The True Patriot*, from November 1745 to

411

June the following year.[5] All through the autumn, while Hogarth was touching up his self-portrait, the news was bleak. In October the Young Pretender had crossed the border and the Jacobite forces marched on through Cumberland, Westmorland and Lancashire without a shot fired against them. In Newcastle, John Wesley found frightened gentry rushing headlong to the south.[6] In Preston and Manchester, resistance was nil. By 4 December, the Highland army had taken Derby, only a hundred and thirty miles from London, and when the news hit the capital on 'Black Friday', City merchants packed their bags and confusion reigned. In fact, they should have been celebrating a victory. By then, his resources stretched, finding little support in England and fearing none would come from France, Charles had already decided to retreat and retrench. Unknown to him, that week Louis XV had at last decided to invade, and when this news arrived on a second 'Black Friday', 12 December, London trembled once again. But the winds changed and after Admiral Vernon worsted the French ships in the Channel, the would-be invaders slunk back to port. Events had played into Hanoverian hands.

Turning on their heels, abandoning their arms and supply wagons, bending their heads beneath the terrible icy winds, the exhausted Jacobite troops trudged north through heavy snow. The English they passed, sullenly un-resisting before, were now callously violent, killing all those who fell behind – one drained young Scots recruit had his throat slit by a vagrant woman as he slept by the wayside.[7] In the early spring, despite a victory at Falkirk, the rebels' cause was demolished for ever at Culloden. For four miles the ground was covered with the dead, the bodies of villagers and farmworkers as well as of soldiers. One Hanoverian officer wrote that the moor was covered in blood, 'and our men, what with killing the enemy, dabbling their feet in blood and splashing it about one another looked like so many butchers rather than Christian soldiers'.[8] After Culloden, the name of the Duke of Cumberland, that upright young prince of Hogarth's portrait and *The Conquest of Mexico* a decade before, became synonymous with butchery.

Cumberland alone was not to blame: Westminster was wholeheartedly behind him. In February, when the crushing of the rebels looked certain, Pelham had seized the chance to enforce his parliamentary power: irritated by George's continued reliance on Granville, virtually the whole of his administration resigned *en masse*. After trying vainly to form a new govern-ment the King surrendered, sacked Granville and accepted the Old Corps back on their own terms. Secure in their power, over the next two years this ministry and their Scots allies set about wiping out Highland defiance for ever. Statutes limiting hereditary jurisdictions and seizing estates struck at the power of the old clan chiefs, while the notorious 'Disarming Acts' forbade the speaking of the Gaelic and the wearing of the tartan. A whole way of life was driven underground or overseas. This dark internal colonialism was also part of the forging of 'Britain'.

As early as the spring of 1746 a note of sympathy and romantic nostalgia for reckless bravery in a doomed cause sounded as soon as the real Jacobite threat was removed. Tobias Smollett, a Lowland Scot, 'made every tender-hearted Whig feel himself for moments a Jacobite'[9] with his ballad, 'The Tears of Scotland':

> Mourn, hapless Caledonia mourn
> Thy banished peace, thy laurels torn!
> Thy sons, for valour long renowned,
> Lie slaughtered on their native ground;
> Thy hospitable roofs no more
> Invite the stranger to the door;
> In smoky ruins sunk they lie,
> The monuments of cruelty.[10]

In Scotland the government carried on a policy of slaughter, exterminating Jacobite soldiers as 'wild beasts' and 'vermin'.[11] For weeks the rebels were pursued, their cattle stolen, their houses burned. Hundreds died in prison, a hundred and twenty were executed and a thousand more were transported for life. In London, attention turned to the Jacobite peers – Lords Kilmarnock, Cromarty and Balmerino – brought south to be tried by the House of Lords.[12] The town was packed, as if for a coronation, and carpenters built scaffolds for seating in Westminster Hall, all hung with scarlet. This was public theatre on a grand and gruesome scale.

That month, however, Hogarth was more concerned with private theatre than with national drama. His engraving of Garrick as Richard III had just appeared, with its slanting reference to civil wars, and John Hoadly asked both artist and actor down to stay at one of his livings near Southampton. The idea of a trip to Hampshire was alluring: London was hot and crowded, the inns for miles around packed with sightseers drawn by the trial of the Highland leaders. Garrick's friend, the fat, witty, teasing physician Messenger Monsey (a colleague of Daniel Graham's at Chelsea Hospital) was already staying with Hoadly, and the actor and the artist both jumped at the offer to get away. 'The little-ingenious *Garrick* with the ingenious little *Hogarth*', Garrick wrote, 'will take the opportunity of the *plump Doctor's* being with You, to get upon a Horse-block, mount a pair of Quadruped (or one if it carries double) & hie away to the rev'd Rigdum Funnidos at ye aforesaid Old Alresford, there to be as merry, facetious Mad & Nonsensical, as Liberty, Property & Old Order can make 'Em! Huzza!'

He would settle everything with John's brother Benjamin, he said, and they would all go down together. He had roles ready for everyone:

'I am in raptures at the Party! huzza again Boys! shan't I come with my Doctor? Yes; he gives me the potions and the motions? Shall I lose my Priest? my Sir John? no, he gives me the proverbs & the No verbs. My cares are over, & I must laugh with You: Your French Cook is safe & sound & shall come with Me; but pray let us have no Kickshaws: Nothing but laugh & plumb pudding.'[13]

In a postscript he thanked Hoadly for his good wishes but said he would rather have Beef and pudding than prayers (and presumably some 'Old Order' ale).

The Jacobite Rebellion and trials seemed a lifetime away. The vicarage was new, elegant and roomy, and John Hoadly had filled it with his mother's collection of pictures, many of them painted by herself.[14] But on this holiday the stress was on theatre, not art, and for once Hogarth was made to play his part. In the evenings they put on their own play, *Ragandjaw*, an ebulliently silly spoof, written by Garrick, of the quarrel between Brutus and Cassius in *Julius Caesar* in which he turned Shakespeare's Roman generals mourning Portia's death into a sergeant and corporal in a tent bewailing the loss of their sheep-worrying bitch. John Hoadly played 'Brutarse' and Garrick played 'Cassiarse'. No one knows who played their servant Lucius ('Loosearse') but Hogarth took on Grilliardo the Devil's Cook, standing in for Caesar's Ghost. To stage directions of 'Thunder and Lightning', he entered with this immortal threat:

GRILLIARDO: I am Old Nick's Cook – & hither am I come
              To slice some Steaks from off thy Brawny Bum,
              Make Sausage of thy Guts, & Candles of thy Fat,
              And cut thy Cock off to Regale his Cat.[15]
BRUTARSE: Art thou, in Hell, a Ruler of the Roast?
              I would not care a – (*snaps his Fingers*) – for such a Ghost.

At Brutarse's sneer, Hogarth delivered a hefty speech of Senecan violence *à la*

414

Tom Thumb, turning wife-murder, parent-murder and incest into a recipe book of culinary crimes ('You, Nero-like, rip'd up your Mother's Belly,/And boil'd your father to make Calvesfoot Jelly') and threatening, as a good Beefsteak Clubman should, to get a red-hot Gridiron ready for their torture. In the end, though, Garrick let the satiric painter speak:

GRILLIARDO: But first to Westminster I'll take my Way,
And with a Gang of Lawyers load my Dray;
Next to fam'd Warwick Lane away I'll Whiz,
My Master Satan wants a Household Phiz:
Last to where Convocation sits I'll fly,
For I've a fatars'd Chaplain in my eye.
But ha! I'm call'd – Hell gapes! I'm on the brink!
Brutarse, prepare – for now I feel, I sink.
[*Walks off.*]

The part was perfect but according to his friends Hogarth could never remember his lines. In despair,

'they hit on the following expedient in his favour. The verses he was to deliver were written in such large letters, on the outside of an illuminated paper-lanthorn, that he could read them when he entered with it in his hand on the stage.'[16]

All in all, the sketch was a huge success, at least in the eyes of Garrick, who copied the whole thing out ('Ragandjaw meets with Universal Applause among my Friends,' he told Hoadly) and dedicated it to another friend, William Windham.[17] After staying at Cheltenham in September, he wrote,

'I was never in better spirits or more nonsensical in my life, allways excepting those never to be forgotten or parall[ele]d Days that were spent at O. Alresford in the Reign of *Ragandjaw* in the Month of July Anno Dom 1746; – *It was a Time, take it for all in all &c.*'[18]

The eminent group at Old Alresford was made up, if you document 'official' roles, of London's most famous actor, most newsworthy artist, a prominent vicar, a fashionable doctor and a Fellow of the Royal Society. Yet they took their parody just as seriously as Hogarth and his friends from the Bedford Arms had treated the mock-antiquarian 'Peregrination' thirteen years before. All the details were thought of. Hogarth made a playbill ('with the characteristic ornaments', as Nichols and Steevens wrote laconically) and painted sets to represent 'a sutling booth with the *Duck of Cumberland's* head

415

by way of sign'.[19] The Rebellion was thus not altogether forgotten, but their version of it was scarcely heroic – a sutler was a rough trader who followed the army and sold provisions to the soldiers.

When he returned to London, Hogarth was greeted by a grim spectacle. On 30 July the officers of the rebel Manchester Regiment were hanged, drawn and quartered in front of a gaping mob and their heads were stuck on poles at Temple Bar, where canny tradesmen rented out spyglasses at a halfpenny a look. (Two skulls stayed there, their empty eye sockets catching the wind for thirty years until they finally fell.) Further east, onlookers were pressing round the Tower, trying to spot the Highland Lords at their windows as they waited for the death warrant. Grand ladies treated them like romantic idols: Lady Townshend swooned with passion for my Lord Kilmarnock, 'whom she never saw but at the bar of his trial, and was smit with his falling shoulders'.[20] She sent messages, smuggled in his dog and snuffbox and burst out in 'floods of tears and rage' at mention of his execution. Cromartie was reprieved, through the Prince of Wales's intercession and through sympathy for his wife, pregnant with her tenth child, but, on 18 August, Kilmarnock and Balmerino were executed in front of crowds so great that men hung from the masts of ships in the river to watch the axe fall.

One more trial was to follow, that of Simon, Lord Lovat. The wily old Lord, now seventy, had been taken in July as the navy searched the west coast of Scotland. His capture was a great *coup*, for in the minds of many Lovat was the most powerful and compelling of all the clan leaders. Legends sprang up about his life, how in his youth he had tried to abduct a great heiress, the daughter of his relation, the tenth Lord Lovat; when he failed he had carried off and married her widowed mother instead, 'her screams of protest being drowned by a chorus of pipers stationed outside the bedroom door'.[21] Soft southerners were awed by his rude manner of living, with straw for his retainers, 'which they spread every night, on the floors of the lower rooms, where the whole inferior part of the family, consisting of a very great number of persons took up their abode'.[22] He was said to be immensely ugly, a foul-mouthed despot who burned, plundered and poisoned at will and treated his clansmen like slaves. In 1745 he had professed loyalty to Hanover while sending his son to join the rebels, 'hoping *he* might be rewarded for his son's service, if successful; or his *son* alone be the suffererer for *his* offences, if the undertaking failed: diabolical cunning! monstrous impiety!'[23] Londoners, including Hogarth, could hardly wait to see him.

On his way south, Lovat stayed for three days in St Albans from 12 to 14

Simon, Lord Lovat
Drawn from the Life and Etch'd in Aquafortis by Will.m Hogarth.
Publish'd according to Act of Parliament, August 25.th 1746.

125 *Simon, Lord Lovat* (1746)

August to recover his health and there (as he had done with Sarah Malcolm) Hogarth paid a special visit to see this great 'criminal'. He was invited by Dr Webster, who was looking after Lovat at the White Hart Inn, but he may have known Lovat before, through Scottish connections, since one story describes how when he came into the room, Lovat was being shaved and jumped up and embraced him with a 'kiss fraternal', leaving lather on Hogarth's face.[24]

Hogarth sketched Lovat as he told tales of the Rebellion, counting on his fingers how many clans had joined the Pretender, '"Such a general had so many men, e&c."' On the table by his side lie his pen, and a blank book, headed 'Memoirs'. In Hogarth's drawing the old Lord is a figure of immense force and guile, squatting under the thick, folded skin of his greatcoat like a huge toad, his glistening eyes flickering over his listeners. Lovat later said that he would have to be hanged, not beheaded, 'for that his neck is so short and bended, that he should be struck in the shoulders', but Hogarth noticed that 'the muscles of Lovat's neck appeared of unusual strength, more so than he had ever seen'.[25]

Lord Lovat reached London just before Kilmarnock and Cromartie went to the scaffold. The town was expecting more executions of rebel officers that week and the bloodlust was at its peak. Hogarth had already dashed back to Leicester Fields to make an etching, which he published a week later. No print had ever met with such demand. 'The impressions could not be taken off so fast as they were wanted,' wrote Nichols, 'though the rolling-press was at work all night for a week together. For several weeks afterwards he is said to have received at the rate of 12L. per day.'[26] (When the run was finished a printseller allegedly offered to buy the plate for its weight in gold.) Two pages after praising the engraving of *Garrick as Richard III*, Vertue's pen spluttered in inky indignation at this opportunist scoop:

'in august. the picture of Ld Lovat sketchd drawn by Mr Hogarth & etchd by him from the life in his drole nature & manner. was thought to be surprizingly like. and from his humorous Character, was greatly cryd up & sold every where at pr. 1sh many many hundreds (nay thousands)

'this is according to the old saying of a Man that has the Vilest character. and the hatred of all partyes. & besides that a barefaced rebel. if some persons had Engravd and publisht his picture, it had been highly Criminal – but as some are winkt at that steal a horse, whilst another is hangd for looking over a hedge. – but in this case Art overcomes Malice –'[27]

Altogether, Hogarth's shilling print made him well over £300 – far more than any of the paintings on which he laboured so lovingly and long.

In December, Lovat was impeached before the House of Lords. His trial eventually took place in March and April the following year, when he added to his reputation for callousness by trying to turn the blame on his son. The crowds came out in force again and Hogarth's print, enjoying a new rush of sales, doubtless sharpened their image of the old ruffian. 'The first day, as he was brought to his trial,' wrote Walpole,

'a woman looked into the coach, and said, "You ugly old dog, don't you think you will have that frightful head cut off?" He replied, "You damned ugly old bitch, I believe I shall."'[28]

Lovat was right, although in the last two days of his trial he played the buffoon, joked and laughed and then burst out in fury when his tenants were brought to testify against him. On 11 April, in a cold spring wind, he was beheaded. He behaved with great dignity and made no speech except to say that he had followed his faith and his principles and was glad to suffer for his country, quoting '*dulce est pro patria mori*'. As well as turning patriotism on its head, Lovat did obtain some sort of revenge, increasing the myth of his evil eye. The high scaffold for spectators, specially built at the foot of Tower Hill, was overpacked with people and collapsed, injuring scores of people and killing seven, including a woman found dead with a living baby in her arms.[29]

So babes in arms, it seems, were brought to executions. Babes in arms, too, were carried by the women who followed the troops. They would appear in all corners of Hogarth's other memorial of the ''45' Rebellion, his great scene of *The March to Finchley*, painted a couple of years later in 1749.

During the autumn of 1745 all the regular regiments recalled from Flanders had moved north to support General Wade in Yorkshire, and later to join the Duke of Cumberland, who hoped to cut off the rebel advance at Northampton. The capital was left virtually undefended, and Cumberland suggested that a camp at Finchley 'would prevent any little party of them who might give me the slip . . . from giving any alarm in London'.[30] By 6 December, that 'Black Friday' when news came that the rebels were in Derby, a camp had been marked out between Highgate and Whetstone and regiments from Dartford in Kent (including one Highland regiment) were ordered 'to march to Finchley Common to encamp there'.[31] In the excited city the Spitalfields weavers offered a thousand men, and even the lawyers raised a 'regiment' from the Inns of Court. Their help was politely turned down, but on Saturday, 7 December, everyone turned out to see three regiments of foot-guards, horse-grenadiers and life-guards march up the Tottenham Court Road.

Hogarth showed the soldiers saying their farewells at the Tottenham Court turnpike after their last night in town, before they filed off up the Hampstead Road. His crowded canvas, like *Southwark Fair*, looks like the stage set for a ballad opera. The troopers here are ordinary men, drunk, greedy, lecherous, unshaven and unbuttoned: like Garrick in his summer farce showing the sergeant and the corporal in their makeshift tent, Hogarth plumped for Brutarse, Cassiarse and Loosarse instead of Brutus and Cassius. The cultural forebears of his troops are not heroes but Pistol and Bardolph and Falstaff's scraggy band in *Henry IV, Part I*: 'good enough to toss; food for powder, food for powder; they'll fill a pit as well as better: tush man, mortal men, mortal

126 *The March to Finchley* (1749)

men'. These are just the kind of mortal men that Fielding's Tom Jones also falls in with, quarrelling violently over who will pay the beer bill, 'marching against the rebels, and expected to be commanded by the glorious Duke of Cumberland'.[32] When Tom joins them they are commanded solely by a worthy old lieutenant, a Frenchman and a couple of boys who have won their commissions through interest, 'one of whom had been bred under an attorney, and the other was son to a nobleman's butler'.[33] *En route*, the men take their verbal revenge on these officers:

'Much mirth and festivity passed among the soldiers during their march. In which the many occurrences that had passed at their last quarters were remembered, and everyone, with some freedom, made what jokes he pleased on his officers, some of which were of the coarser kind, and very near

420

bordering on scandal. This brought to our hero's mind the custom which he had read of among the Greeks and Romans, of indulging, on certain festivals and solemn occasions, the liberty to slaves, of using an uncontrolled freedom of speech towards their masters.'[34]

Britons 'never shall be slaves', we remember (although there is still something patrician in Fielding's image of the plebeian troops granted liberty of speech).

Tom Jones hangs on to a naïve idealism, sure that the men will fight like 'Greeks and Romans' when they have to. Hogarth believes this too – his unruly mob *will* turn into the neat marching ranks in the background. At the moment they are saying goodbye, after a last night in the tavern or in the King's Head cat-house, or, in some cases, with their wives and children. Hogarth is tough, his humour stemming from the contrast between the reality and the glamorous uniforms and heroic ideal. He shows a march of disarray, a parade of folly, a detached undercutting of military glory. Yet he is not so much disapproving as comically blunt – simply saying, 'This is how it is.' And he also finds something admirable in the soldiers' frank display of lust and humour and sentiment – if you want to oppose Stuart absolutism and Catholic rigidity, on the French model, you have to accept the near-anarchic freedom of the British crowd; their disorder is more valuable than it is frightening. Rouquet probably expressed Hogarth's own views when he contrasted the orderly file in the rear with the casual groups in the street, telling his French readers that it was well said that 'order and subordination, only refer to slaves, and the quality that we (in France) call license, in England is given the glorious name of liberty'.[35] And like *Tom Jones*, in which Tom's erring, generous heart is infinitely preferable to the hypocritical sanctimoniousness and 'prudence' of Blifil, *The March to Finchley* is exuberant and energetic and full of life, dignified by the exhilarating beauty of Hogarth's brushwork, spreading his reds and browns against the eggshell blue sky, crisped by the white of caps and aprons and clouds.

His treatment recalled realistic Dutch painters such as Adriaan van Ostade and Jan Steen, and also Watteau, who had painted ordinary soldiers and their bivouacs and baggage trains. Engravings of all these were on sale in England.[36] What *The March to Finchley* emphatically was not was a grandiose military painting, celebrating discipline and heroism. Hence the anecdote describing the response of George II, who had asked to see the painting, only to recoil in horror: 'Does this fellow mean to laugh at my guards?' The answer being obviously yes, he exploded, 'What a *bainter* burlesque a soldier? He deserves to be picketed for his insolence! Take his trumpery out of my house.'[37] (Hogarth was said to be irate that his painting had been commanded to St James's and returned without a word; he dedicated the print to the King of Prussia, 'Encourager of ARTS and sciences!'. To objections to an English print 'being inscribed to a foreign potentate', he replied, 'We'll soon remedy that,' and told the printer to make a few impressions 'covering the dedication with fan paper'.)[38]

True, the scene Hogarth created looks more like a public holiday than a national emergency. But he was painting in 1749, when the Rebellion was long past, and the Hanoverian victory assured. He made the requisite point about the patriotic choice very clearly: on the right, the sign of Charles II leads the eye to a dead tree, the moribund Stuart line; the sign on the right, of Adam and Eve, hangs beneath a tree whose leaves wave vividly green against the sky. The central group, posed against the British flag, makes the same point. The handsome grenadier is tugged in two directions, on one side by a pretty, pregnant ballad-singer, with a print of the Duke of Cumberland hanging from her basket and a copy of *God Save the King,* and on the other by a haggard, though equally pregnant, older woman with a Catholic cross round her neck, who threatens to batter him ('give him a remembrance') with rolled-up copies of *The Jacobite Journal* and *The Remembrancer, or a Weekly Slap on the Face for the Ministry.*

As everyone knew which way Britain had chosen, so Hogarth could broaden the reference of the soldier's dilemma into a study of other kinds of choice. He composed his picture like a triptych, the light falling on three groups in the forground, two set against the darkness of the rising buildings, the central grenadier against the panel with the British flag and the open sky. And so finely balanced is his depiction of the crowd that the viewer has to choose as well as the subjects. On the left is a drummer, bashing his drum to give the signal to depart, while his wife and son (who shares his unruly red hair) tug at his clothes. If you think of Hogarth purely as a cynical satirist, the drummer's vehemence can be read, as it was by Bonnell Thornton, as a determined attempt to drown out the wails of his own '*Two Remembrancers,* a woman and a child, the product of their kinder hours'.[39] On the other hand, looked at closely, the drummer's bent head, his watery eyes and the shape of his mouth, sucking in his lower lip, speak vividly of a man torn in two by leaving those he loves behind.

Sometimes, however, Hogarth's ambivalence slides into criticism. On the right of his painting a messenger has slid into a puddle; his friend, a pioneer with a red cap, is offering him water, but the sodden soldier turns away in disgust, reaching out to his wife for another *real* drink. As she pours him a tot

422

of gin, the baby on her back reaches out eagerly for the little bottle on its string round the mother's neck, a heartbreaking gesture clearly observed from the life. While the central grenadier's dilemma is a 'low' version of a classical 'Choice of Hercules', this group parodies *The Good Samaritan*, treated so reverently at St Bartholomew's. The pioneer offering the water has a stolen hen shoved into his pocket, her wings peeping out over his military bag and her two chicks left fluttering their wings on the edge of the puddle. There is compassion as well as wit in Hogarth's rich references – the sprawling man with his attendants mimics the heroic battle deaths that would later culminate in the famous scenes of the death of Nelson, while his pose also echoes the sad Rake in Bedlam, and the many Depositions from the Cross.

These woven lines of suggestion about the strengths and frailties of men, and the choices people make, run across the painting in a mesh of curling lines. Like the grenadier, the picture itself is wrenched in two directions. Hogarth gave the tension of departure an almost physical force by painting the tidy ranks marching *away* – highlighting their neat lines by flashes of sunlight glancing off their bayonets and white cross-bands – but showing the confused crowd moving *forward*, posing his figures with one foot placed towards us. Pinned in by the walls of the houses, the triangular crowd flows towards the viewer, funnelled from the narrow opening with its backdrop of hills and sky, where Highgate and Hampstead glitter on the heights. Country clarity shows up the city chaos.

Even the walls that compress this crowd hum with incident. Behind the inn sign of the King's Head, with its picture of Charles II, patron of brothels and restorer of Stuarts, the whores wave and cheer from the windows, ranked in order with the finest below and the poorest above and topped by the cats on the roof. Recognizable figures enter the scene, made even clearer when it was eventually engraved; in the first window the large-bosomed bawd – Mother Douglas of Covent Garden – prays ostentatiously for the safe return of the troops (and her trade). Opposite, the crowd around the boxing at George Taylor's booth includes the inveterate gambler, the blind Lord Albermarle Bertie, and 'Jockey James' the aproned cobbler beneath the signpost.[40] One sign reads 'Tottenham Court Nursery 1746'. Like Taylor's amphitheatre this was a real nursery garden, and the idea of fruitfulness is picked up by the Adam and Eve inn, run by 'Giles Gardiner'. Realism and allegory meet yet again: you could look at the bare-knuckle fight beneath the sign as human frailty outside Eden, the murderous rivalry of Cain and Abel now translated into civil war. Or you could see it as the 'natural' fighting spirit of the people, cheered on by an excited crowd.

In the inn sign the parents of mankind are shown at the moment of tempta-
tion, and within the busy street chains of comic temptations run like falling
dominoes in a series of rippling stories. Behind the grenadier, a fat sergeant
with his pike watches a young officer kiss the milk-girl and squeeze her breast;
as her pail sinks to the ground a man tips the milk into his hat; a boy sweep is
watching this, and so is a pastrycook, so rapt that he doesn't see a soldier
reaching up to steal his pies. Behind them the snooty lieutenant, his nose in
the air, notices nothing, and behind *him*, a girl fights off a grenadier while a
soldier steals her washing.

On the other side more incidents cluster. A whispering Frenchman passes
a note to a disguised Jacobite (ineptly disguised, as we can see his Highland
plaid beneath his coat). Near them a soldier with the clap pisses painfully
against a wall while he reads Dr Rock's advertisement and the girl above him
hides her face. On a laden cart, where a boy blows a trumpet and two old
gossips puff at pipes, a woman as quiet as a madonna feeds her baby, her calm
beauty haloed by a curve that runs from the sergeant's lily-like pike, over her
head and down the rainbow-shaped mark on the wall. And as at Southwark
Fair, but on the fringe of the scene, stands a single figure of innocence and art,
an intent boy playing his fife with his regimental trumpet at his side.

Hogarth painted this from life, paying the boy piper half a crown.[41] He was
making a topical point, since Cumberland had only recently brought boy
pipers into the army. But it was right that he should hold such a symbolic
position, for Hogarth's interest is as much with women and children as it is
with soldiers and war; the red-haired boy who wants his father, the baby at the
breast in the cart, the round-faced, button-eyed infant on her mother's back,
the little girl stretching for the gin, the unborn child of the dashing grenadier.
Amid this patriotic panic, Hogarth seems to say, those who really care for the
nation's future should care for its children.

When he eventually finished *The March to Finchley* he organized a lottery –
yet another novel way of selling art. All subscribers to the print could enter if
they paid an extra three shillings over the price of 7s 6d, 'so that every person',
as Vertue pointed out, 'rather subscribed half a guinea than three half-
crowns'.[42] This was yet another of Hogarth's smart moves, 'thus cunning &
skill joynd to gether. changes the proverb. (say well is good, do well is better.)'.
Hogarth had valued the painting at £200, a high price, but this way he more
than trebled the sum to £900, 'such fortunate successes are the effect of
cunning artful contrivances, which men of much greater merit, could never get
or expect'. (Hogarth himself said that disposing of it by lot was 'the only way
a living painter has any probability of being tolerably paid for his time'.) But

Vertue ignored another fact, which was that Hogarth had virtually rigged the lottery anyway, or at least heavily fixed the odds. He made out 2000 tickets, sold 1,843 and gave the remaining 157 away – to the Foundling Hospital. On Monday, 30 April 1750, at two o'clock, amid a crowd of men and women of quality, the box of tickets was opened, 'and the fortunate Chance was drawn, no 1941, which belongs to the said Hospital; and the same Night Mr. Hogarth deliver'd the Picture to the Governors'.[43]

EVENING

1748–1762

21

Bible Stories: Foundling and Apprentice

Dark and cheerless is the morn
Unaccompanied by thee,
Joyless is the day's return,
Till thy mercy's beams I see;
Till they inward light impart,
Glad my eyes and fill my heart.
CHARLES WESLEY, 'Morning Hymn' (1740)

HANGING THE MARCH TO FINCHLEY in the Foundling Hospital might seem a touch ironic; the scene could hardly be considered a good example. But it was the dignified Governors who would see the painting, not the children, and to them it might act as a reminder of the realities of London life. A reminder, too, for Hogarth, of how much of his painting time during the months of the Rebellion had been taken up with the hospital. After he finished his portrait of Garrick in October 1745, and throughout the next year, when the rebels were defeated and he published his brilliant satire on Lovat, his plans for decoration of the hospital were always his underlying concern.

At the start of 1745 the west wing, the first stage of the new building designed by Theodore Jacobsen, was almost complete. The carpenters and glaziers and plasterers moved out, and in the spring work began on the furnishings, the ordering of bed linen and beakers, cutlery and pots and pans. Since the day it opened, the hospital had been deluged with demand, so much so that to avoid the pushing and shoving and unruly scenes at the door the Governors brought in admission by ballot. The mothers dipped their hands into a box and pulled out a ball; a white ball spelled entry, a black one denial, and a red meant they had to stand and wait, holding their swaddled bundles, anxiously, selfishly hoping that a place might be free if a 'white' baby failed the doctor's examination. More places were desperately needed, and the new wing could take 192 children, two to a bed. On 25 September, when the Jacobite rebels were setting out for the English border, the Governors held their final meeting in Hatton Garden. A week later, on the first day of October, the

429

removal carts came and the children and nurses, with all their belongings, moved down the road to Lamb's Conduit Fields.

The new hospital was a stately building, plain, useful and austere. All hints of luxury were confined to the Court Room where the Governors met. In contrast to the bare corridors and long wards this room was elaborately elegant, with a fine fireplace, a beautiful plasterwork ceiling, and delicate mouldings on the panelled walls. All the work was given free, the ceiling by the sculptor William Wilton, the mantelpiece by the mason J. Devall and the marble-topped table by John Sanderson, the architect who supervised the building work. The names of the last two donors can still be seen, Devall's carved – at eye level – into the fireplace surround, and Sanderson's cut rough and large into the lively wooden sculpture that forms the table base, carved as an oak tree, with a naked child sitting astride a goat and holding one of its horns as he reaches up to pull a branch from the 'national tree'. The table came complete with a gilded oval pier-glass carved with palm fronds and foliage, an extravagant, opulent piece.[1]

Hogarth may have had a hand in the table's design; he was deeply involved in the decoration of the whole room. Since donating his portrait of Coram five years before, he had come to see the potential of the hospital as an exhibition place, and his fellow Governors were more than willing to listen to his plans to ornament their building, since fine art would add to the gloss of refinement, bringing in visitors and hence more donations. (In the 1750s, when the Chapel was complete, they would also embrace music as another lure, one of their greatest supporters being Handel.)

Smart citizens had made it fashionable to visit the Foundling Hospital. They came to see the children at all times of day, watching them work, eat and even sleep, until this was stopped by a decree that the sightseers must leave by seven o'clock. This hospital, more than any other in London, would be an attractive place to display pictures – children were much more appealing than lunatics or sore-encrusted cripples, and the Quality might well be tempted to dally, basking in an overflow of sensibility. The Foundling Hospital's double aspect, offering rigorous charity to the poor and emotional indulgence to the rich, was built into its fabric as surely as the contrasting Court Room and wards. Contemporary prints reflect this without a trace of irony. One, based on a drawing by Samuel Wale of 1749, shows plainly dressed women waiting with their babies in their arms, coming forward one by one to dip their hands into the bag, trusting their children to the coloured balls of chance, while rich ladies in brocade sigh with feeling behind their fans.[2] Two other designs by Wale, engraved by Grignion, make the contrast even clearer. One is gay, with

430

children gambolling round a fountain as smart visitors arrive on the annual May Day holiday; the other is bleak, drawn at an angle that makes the walls loom high, as mothers queue patiently before the same iron gates.

Hogarth's plan was to provide works of art for the Court Room that would exploit this duality, combining the theme of charity with dignified 'politeness'. As a first step, he brought in the sculptor John Michael Rysbrack. Hogarth did not often go to official meetings, but the minute book shows that he was present in late December 1744 when the Treasurer, Taylor White, put forward Rysbrack's name as a Governor. An old colleague of Thornhill and Gibbs and a member of the prestigious St Luke's Club, Rysbrack was the country's leading sculptor, with many aristocratic connections. Much respected by fellow artists, he was universally liked for his calm, courteous temperament, the opposite of Hogarth's noisy fire. What was more, unlike Hogarth's much closer colleague Roubiliac, Rysbrack could (just) be considered an 'English' sculptor; although born in Antwerp he had worked in London for many years as his artist father had before him.

In March 1745 this useful ally was duly elected a Governor and by October the next year he had finished a fine bas-relief to go above the Court Room fireplace.[3] On similar lines to Hogarth's small drawing of *The Foundlings*, Rysbrack sculpted a classically robed Charity 'tying a floundering ship to an oak tree with Hope's anchor'.[4] Charity holds a baby in her arms and another woman milks a cow to feed the clustering children, all busy in idyllic toil, one holding a sheaf of corn, another carrying a sickle and three more coiling a rope by the anchor, suggesting the placing of foundling boys as sailors.

To fill the walls and complement this Arcadian over-mantel, Hogarth appealed to the painters of the St Martin's Lane Academy. In the middle of 1746, after noting Highmore's success at portraits, Vertue added that he had begun

'one of the History pictures (Hagar & Ishmael) – to be set up in the foundling Hospital it promises much and shews that his Genius is not so confind, but it may extend it self in that branch of painting with due commendation – as painter of History if he coud meet with suteable incouragement'.

Hogarth aimed to get just such encouragement, to show – as he had tried to do at St Bartholomew's – that English artists could be fine history-painters if given the chance.

As well as Highmore, the painters of the biblical pictures were Hogarth himself, Frank Hayman and James Wills. All four worked on texts linked to children and benevolence. Highmore showed the angel of God diving from the heavens to reassure the thirsty and exhausted Hagar in the wilderness, after she left her son Ishmael beneath a bush and moved away, 'for she said, Let me not see the death of my child.' Wills's *Little Children Brought to Christ* restated the words of that angel from Genesis in New Testament terms, as Christ tells his disciples not to stop the children crowding round: 'Suffer the little children to come unto me, and forbid them not.'

While these two artists illustrated the religious sanction of the hospital's merciful errand, Hogarth and Hayman used the Bible to stress the secular side, the well-born, compassionate benefactor. Hayman painted *The Finding of Moses in the Bulrushes* and Hogarth showed the next stage, when the five-year-old Moses was returned to the palace by his nurse – who was, of course, actually his natural mother. The choice of text, recalling Captain Coram's original appeal and the design on the hospital seal, was clever as well as apt. The two pictures showed the benevolence of an aristocratic princess (the Foundling Hospital, perhaps because of the link to sexual impropriety, had few women subscribers and was keen to encourage them), and they also alluded to the two stages of the hospital's programme, the taking in of the baby and the return of the child, at five, from his foster mother in the country.[5]

Both paintings, too, attempted a vague approximation of historical realism – rather like Garrick's neo-Elizabethan stagings of Shakespeare – shifting the emphasis from the universal values of classical history-painting towards the particular response of individuals. But while Hayman produced a conventional, Poussinesque rendering, Hogarth characteristically stretched the rules of decorum. His *Moses Brought before Pharoah's Daughter* is unusually warm and tender for a public work, displaying a real sympathy for the troubled little boy, who clutches his mother's dress of madonna blue, while the jewelled princess in her cream and coral robes calls him towards her. In an acutely observed pose, Moses' hand hangs limply, only half outstretched, as if he knows he ought to take hers but doesn't want to. And as she reaches out, and points her sandalled toe towards his stubby bare foot, the gulf between them, in the centre of the canvas, grows eloquent. Within the deep dip made by the walls of the building on the left and the canopied pillar on the right, a dusky cityscape mingles the shapes of pyramids with the smoke of fires and a shadowy cloud which evokes the ghost of St Paul's. This is modern London as well as ancient Egypt. Even the texture of the paint makes a point, the face and robes of the princess being finished with the smoothness of a society portrait while Moses' curls are picked out in brisk, rough, 'plebeian' brushstrokes.

432

127 *Moses Brought before Pharoah's Daughter* (1746)

Within the conventions he followed, Hogarth was bluntly realistic in his reading of the Bible. He picked up the verse that Hayman illustrated – when Moses is handed to his mother for payment – and linked it with the next:

'[9] And Pharoah's daughter said unto her, Take this child away, and nurse it for me, and I will give thee wages. And the woman took the child, and nursed it. [10] And the child grew, and she brought him unto Pharoah's daughter, and he became her son. And she called his name Moses; and she said, Because I drew him out of the water.'

Behind Moses, his mother looks down, her expression poignantly mixed, sad to lose him but thinking it for the best, loving him but still holding out her hand for the coins. (When the painting was turned into a print, the hoard was made even larger, as if in a recruitment drive for nurses.)

There is a complicated undercurrent about 'nature', here, as the barefoot natural mother effectively sells her child to the gracious, self-regarding bene-factress. And some of Hogarth's 'historical' details were certainly *not* in the Bible. By the feet of Pharoah's daughter lies a crocodile, used in emblem

433

books as the symbol for the continent of Africa, but depicted here too as a kind of royal household pet. An appropriate touch, but one that might make people wonder, uncomfortably, if the foundling child Moses was not also a whim, a 'monstrous pet' like the monkeys that fashionable women of the 1740s favoured. And behind the princess's chair a black servant whispers in the ear of a lady-in-waiting who raises her hand in alarm, perhaps hearing the rumour that this 'foundling' is the princess's son. Scandal is already spreading. Once again, as in *The Pool at Bethesda*, 'low' subjects had invaded Hogarth's high art.

The artists won status as well as praise. On 31 December 1746, New Year's Eve, when the General Court was held, the Treasurer announced that fifteen 'Gentlemen Artists had severally presented and agreed to present Performances in their different Professions for Ornamenting the Hospital'.[6] The fifteen were Hayman, Wills, Highmore, Hudson, Ramsay, Lambert, Samuel Scott, George Moser and John Pine (all friends of Hogarth) and Peter Monamy, Richard Wilson, Samuel Wale, Edward Haytley, Thomas Carter and Robert Taylor. All were at once appointed Governors. Together they formed a committee, with Hogarth, Rysbrack, Jacobsen and the medallist Zincke, to meet every year on 5 November, to consider further 'ornaments', with the careful proviso, 'without any expence to the Charity'.

Three of the biblical paintings were hung in February 1747, but the Hayman was not quite finished. Then at last, on Wednesday, 1 April, the Foundling Hospital held a great public dinner for 170 benefactors, especially to show the four history-paintings, as Vertue noted,

'newly put up, done Gratis by four eminent painters – by Hayman, Hogarth, Hymore. & Wills – & by most people generally approved and commended. as works in history painting in a higher degree of merit than has heretofore been done by English Painters'.[7]

Amid all the commendation, he added, in an inserted note, 'its generally said and allowd that Hogarths peece gives most striking satisfaction – and approbation'.

All the paintings carried a clear inscription saying that they had been done free, and in May Hogarth, typically, got the Governors to agree that the artists had the right to choose their own engravers, limiting the copyright to themselves and the hospital. While the paintings at Vauxhall, of games in the supper-boxes and Shakespeare in the pavilion, had linked art to the effort to 'refine' polite leisure, these works also allied it to the charitable movement,

434

emphasizing the way private social virtues could play a significant part in public affairs.[8] 'A cultivated taste for the polite arts', David Hume had written in an essay of 1741, 'improves our sensibility for all the tender passions.'[9] Art could change hearts as well as impress minds, and Hogarth and his fellow painters had now ensured that their work unequivocally allied art with benevolence.

The four artists who painted the biblical pictures would, however, have been particularly pleased by Vertue's description of their work as history-paintings, which elevated their achievement, as well as their charitable aims. Not everyone was so approving. When John Loveday of Caversham visited the hospital the following year, he liked the 'fancy' in Wills's composition and praised the way that Hayman's faces revealed character but rudely thought the Highmore was 'meanly performed'. As far as Hogarth was concerned, he was disappointed, but acute, 'The child is not so beautiful as the sacred text describes him – the Princess is English all over.'[10]

Despite such dismissals, Vertue's note had marked the beginning of an 'English school', at last given the accolade that it needed. This point was taken up by Rouquet in 1755:

'in short, every kind of painting, and even sculpture itself, has contributed towards this decoration. This exhibition of skill, equally commendable and new, has afforded the public an opportunity of judging whether the English are such indifferent artists, as foreigners, and even the English themselves, pretend.'[11]

By that time the 'exhibition of skill' in the Court Room included the series of small roundels which had been placed between the biblical pictures in 1751. These were painted by a different set of artists, also connected with St Martin's Lane: Samuel Wale, Richard Wilson, Edward Haytley and the twenty-one-year-old Thomas Gainsborough. Each picture, set in a circular oak-leaf frame with a scrolled white plaster decoration in a graceful chinoiserie style, showed a different London hospital. As well as the Foundling Hospital itself they included St George's, peaceful among spreading meadows; Greenwich, by the river; the fine redbrick courtyard of St Thomas's; the neat parterres of Chelsea; the frightening gates of Bedlam; the old buildings of Christ's Hospital and Charterhouse, with their blue-coat boys. Almost every picture, with the exception of Gainsborough's Charterhouse where boys play on the sunlit walk, shows well-dressed people visiting these charitable founda-tions. The effect of the whole room is telling as well as beautiful, setting the paintings of charity in a context of refined civic virtue.

All the artists in the Academy discussed the Foundling project, and many were involved in different ways. Hogarth's initiative in giving *Thomas Coram* was followed by other painters, who donated portraits of benefactors. In 1746 Hudson presented portraits of Theodore Jacobsen and Judge John Milner, the hospital's Vice-President, and Highmore gave an earlier painting of the rich confectioner Thomas Emerson, who had left the hospital £12,000 in his will. The following year Ramsay gave his impressive portrait of Richard Mead; through the halls and up the stairs, more and more imposing men looked down at the poor women who carried in their children. Over the years the collection grew, with paintings by Wilson, Reynolds, Cotes and Shackleton, including seascapes and pastorals as well as portraits – George Lambert gave a landscape in 1757.

Great things grew from this. The establishment of a permanent exhibition space, the organization and self-awareness that went with it, and the annual 5 November dinners, beginning in 1747, cemented the artists as a group. From here and from St Martin's Lane developed the drive that led eventually, after many divides, false starts and heated arguments, to the founding of the Royal Academy.

Hogarth remained committed to the hospital. In 1747 he designed its coat of arms, a shield showing a naked child reaching to heaven, supported on one side by many-breasted Nature and on the other by Britannia. On the crest, in his drawing, stands a lamb, and the motto reads simply HELP. The quick sketch bears the mark of his quick humour – scribbled beneath are the words, 'These arms are to be altered by the desire of the Committee a Wolf in Fleecy Hosiery is to be substituted for the lamb, and the Supporters are to be taken out.'[12] So much for childish innocence, natural love and British virtue.

In their new building on the edge of the open fields, the children were well fed and warmly clad. Here, too, the Governors appealed to Hogarth, who designed them a special uniform. He took this very seriously, making sure the clothes would look distinctive, like those of Christ's Hospital and other foundations, but be easy to move in and simple to take on and off. The colours were a warm brown and red and the material was made to last: coats and skirts of sturdy wool, Lancashire sheeting for shirts and shifts, Irish linen for the caps. At their public May Day 'Breakfasting' in 1747 when Jacobsen laid the cornerstone for the new chapel, attended by a 'great concourse of Nobility and Ladies of Distinction', one visitor drew a sketch of a boy and a girl carrying a basket of flowers 'to present to the Ladies' and added a note on the uniforms' designs:

'The Boys have only one garment which is made jacket fashion, of Yorkshire serge with a slip of red cloth cross their shoulder; the skirts lapping over their collar resembling a cape; their breeches hang loose a great way down their legs, instead of buttons is a red cloth furbelowed. The Girls Petticoats are also of Yorkshire Serge; and their stays are covered with the same, of which a slip turns back over their shoulders, like that of the boys, and is of the same colour. Their buff bib and apron are linen, the shift is gathered and drawn with bobbins, in the manner of a close tucker. The Boys and Girls hats are white, and tied round with red binding.'[13]

A proper children's outfit was needed now, because the first children taken in at Hatton Garden were reaching the age of seven and eight: they had been back at the Foundling Hospital since it moved to Lamb's Conduit Fields, and the Governors had to pay increasing attention to their education, and their future. In two years' time, as young as nine or ten, they might begin the next stage of their lives, their apprenticeships.

The Act that established the hospital had given it the right to apprentice the children under its care up to the age of twenty-four for boys and for girls until they reached 'the age of twenty-one, or shall be married'. This followed the old acts of Tudor times, the Statute of Artificers of 1562 and the Vagrancy Act of 1601, sources of misery for many pauper children since they allowed parish officials to apprentice them at a small fee to masters who then bound them for years of slave labour. The fate of the poor boys in George Crabbe's *Peter Grimes* was not a wild horror story – fishermen's and watermen's boys were notoriously ill-treated. And in many other trades they were often beaten and half starved. Only a few cases reached the courts, and even then justice was not always done. Sarah Meteyard and her daughter were hanged for murdering a thirteen-year-old girl, one of four apprentices who were kept locked up like prisoners to make nets and mittens. James Durant, on the other hand, a ribbon-weaver who beat his apprentice, 'a very little boy', with a mop-stick until he died, was acquitted.[14]

The Foundling Hospital's Governors were determined to protect their charges and when the first application for a girl apprentice arrived in 1749 from Elizabeth Rich, a widow of Fishmongers Alley in Southwark, they made three decisions: that they would never give money with a child (thus discouraging people from taking them just for the fee, and then abandoning them); that they would always get details about the applicant from the parish, and that at present, at least, all the children were too young to be apprenticed, as the oldest was not yet nine. Apprenticeship, however, would eventually be their

437

fate. And it would also be the subject of Hogarth's next major series of prints, *Industry and Idleness*, on which he worked during the summer of 1747, almost as soon as the Foundling Hospital paintings were unveiled.

Industry and Idleness tells the contrasting stories of two apprentice weavers, Goodchild and Idle. Starting out in the same workshop, they follow different routes, Goodchild rising to become Lord Mayor, Idle ending up at Tyburn; their paths cross only once more, when Idle appears before Goodchild in the latter's role as magistrate. The series was aimed unabashedly not at the polite but the ordinary people, at the masters who would hang these prints in their shops and the apprentices who would have to stare at them there, week in week out. Hogarth explained without irony that they were 'calculated for the use & instruction of those young people wherein everything necessary to be convey'd to them is fully described in words as well as figure'.[15] He put aside fine engraving and concentrated on character and expression so that 'the purchase of them became within the reach of those for whom they were chiefly intended'.

The subject would hardly appeal to the connoisseur, so there would be no paintings to sell, as there had been for the *Harlot* and *Rake* and *Marriage A-la-Mode*. Instead Hogarth worked from rough sketches, refined into careful drawings.[16] He kept his style direct and his price low, a shilling a print, or 12s for the whole set, and 14s for those who came to Leicester Fields to buy a special set on superior paper. He asked for no subscriptions, put no advance notices in the press, introduced no heavily coded emblems or works within works. The story was simple, too, a version of the old ballad fairy-tale of Dick Whittington, combined with the exhortations and warnings of the common ''Prentice's Guides' which poured out in profusion, with titles of alarming sanctimoniousness, like *The Apprentice's Faithful Monitor: directing him in the Several Branches of his Duty to God, his Master, and Himself, and shewing the fatal Consequences of his Neglect thereof, with Regard both to his Temporal and Eternal Happiness, with Prayers adapted to his Station*.[17] The theme had achieved dignity: even Samuel Richardson, before he became a fêted author, had written *The Apprentices' Vade Mecum*. In the theatre, Lillo's *London Merchant*, with its story of George Barnwell's fall to crime and death, was staged every Christmas and Easter as an outing for London youth. (Hogarth must have been thinking of Lillo when he scribbled the name 'Barnwell' on the back of one drawing, before changing it to 'Idle'.)

The series had a solid bourgeois moral: hard work, clean living and honesty will bring success; laziness and profligacy are a sure way to doom.

438

This was a comfortably safe orthodoxy which would appeal to the merchants, and as a Foundling Hospital Governor it was the teaching he felt right. But it is hard to imagine, looking at Hogarth's work as a whole, that he actually *believed* it – he knew that contacts and 'interest' were a far surer way of getting on than hard work and virtue. And in his black-and-white contrasts one 'after' perspective was carefully kept out – or at least hidden from the didactic surface – Hogarth's own memory. He himself had never separated industry and idleness so tidily. With luck and hard graft he had edged towards the good apprentice's successful career but when he was a lad at Gamble's he had certainly registered the more chaotic delights of dressing to the nines and going out on the booze. The fifty-year-old Governor was a long way from young William, and the series could not help but be an oblique, and rather complacent, form of self-reflection. And by now he had also picked up – which would not be clear to his teenage self – the adult awareness of the gulf a child can fall into. Hence the simplified Awful Warnings.

Like the Statute of Artificers, which regulated the apprentice life, the story looked back to Tudor times, to the comedy of *Eastward Hoe* by Chapman, Marston, and Jonson, in which the apprentice Golding marries his master's daughter and becomes a justice of the peace while his partner Quicksilver turns to the bad. At one point Quicksilver, like Tom Idle, reaches 'Cuckold's point', a famous landmark on the Thames, and he ends in the dock before Golding, just as Idle stands before Goodchild. *Eastward Hoe* had been republished three years earlier, in Dodsley's *Old Plays*, and Hogarth's prints would soon lead to its stage revival. All Hogarth did was to take the tale a stage further, following Idle in the cart to the gallows and Goodchild in the Lord Mayor's coach.

He made his plates up to date by choosing as his subjects the Spitalfields weavers, much in the news in the last decade, especially during the riots against the Irish workers who undercut local rates in 1736. Since the Huguenot immigration half a century before, the weavers of Spitalfields and Bethnal Green had grown into a large community. In times of prosperity, when work came thick and fast, master weavers would take on several apprentices only to find themselves in trouble a year or two later – when fashions changed, or the import of silk was stopped by war, or Court mourning cast a blight upon the Town. Men who never made it past journeyman status, like Tom Idle, were always at risk since women and children could be taken on cheaply instead.

The extremes that were a feature of Spitalfields life made it an obvious setting for Hogarth's fable. The erratic nature of the trade encouraged either

439

great thrift or desperate negligence; some men became wealthy masters, owning and renting out numberless looms, but far more fell into poverty and debt and ended in the crammed and filthy workhouses. In despair, one young weaver, Thomas Bonney, first tried life at sea then turned to crime; he was executed for highway robbery in 1744.[18] For almost a century, these wild weavers were held up as examples. Many years after Hogarth showed Idle gambling in the churchyard a local vicar described 'bullock-hunting' in Bethnal Green, where the overflowing population of Spitalfields had settled:

'Every Sunday morning, during the time of divine service, several hundred persons assemble in a field adjoining the churchyard, where they fight dogs, hunt ducks, gamble, enter into subscriptions to fee drovers for a bullock . . . "This on the Sunday?" At all times, chiefly on Sunday, Monday and sometimes Tuesday; Monday is the principal day; one or two thousand men and boys will on these occasions leave their looms and join in the pursuit, pockets are frequently picked, persons are tossed and torn.'[19]

Each step in the parallel *Progresses* was starkly clear. Each plate had a title, sonorously stern, whether it be 'The Industrious 'Prentice Performing the Duty of a Christian' or 'The Idle 'Prentice Returned from Sea and in a Garret with a Common Prostitute'. Like the paintings at the Foundling Hospital each picture had a text, apparently chosen by Hogarth's friend the Reverend Arnold Quin, and these too were brutally apt. And Hogarth added emblematic borders, like old-fashioned teaching books, to hammer points home. In the first plate, 'The Fellow 'Prentices at their Looms', the border on Idle's side is decorated with a whip, chains and a rope, and beneath his feet is the inscription, 'Proverbs Chap: 23, Ve: 21. *The Drunkard shall come to Poverty, & drowsiness shall cloath a Man with rags.*' In contrast, Goodchild's emblems are an alderman's chain, a sword, and the mace of the City of London, while his text is 'Proverbs Ch: 10. Ver: 4. *The hand of the diligent maketh rich.*' On the final plates the border emblems change to flowing cornucopia for lucky Goodchild and dangling skeletons for poor Tom.

Within the pictures the lines are strong and dramatic – the uprights of the looms, the curves of the church roof – and the details, although still there to linger over, are realistic rather than intricately symbolic. In the workshop, Goodchild's ''Prentices' Guide' is clean and whole and the ballads pinned up above his head are 'Whittington Ld. Mayor' and 'The London' (a tale of a good apprentice); by the snoring Tom Idle, a tankard labelled 'Spittle Fields' rests on the loom and a cat plays with the shuttle; his ballad is 'Moll Flanders'

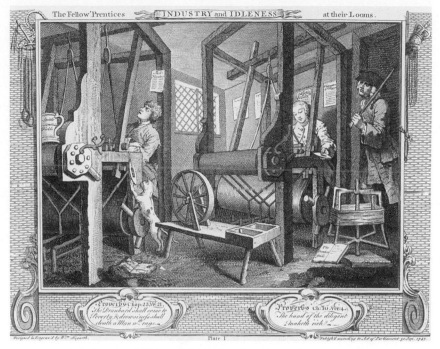

128 *Industry and Idleness*, 'The Fellow 'Prentices at their Looms' (1747)

and his 'Guide' lies crumpled on the floor. In the doorway their master stares at him thoughtfully, like Gonson entering Moll Hackabout's garret.

There is little pretence that Goodchild has his heart on rewards in the next life and not in this: to the good, the goods are given. In church, he and his master's daughter look so enamoured as they sing the psalm together that the text '*O! how I love thy Law it is my meditation all the day*' seems double-edged. In fact each religious text sounds more and more secular. The one beneath Tom Idle and his ragged gang playing dice on the grave while the earth yawns and skulls lie at their feet, conjures the magistrate rather than the deity: '*Judgments are prepar'd for Scorners, & Stripes for the back of Fools.*' And when Goodchild wins the trust of West, his master, the words from Matthew's Gospel have a worldly tinge too: '*Well done thou good and faithfull Servant, thou HAST BEEN FAITHFULL OVER A FEW THINGS, I WILL MAKE THEE RULER OVER many things.*' As West gestures like a conversation-piece host towards the working women, we begin to wonder what these 'many things' are. The strange clasped gloves on the table, an emblem of contract, suggest that master and man are 'hand in glove'.

The story runs its course. Tom Idle is sacked and goes to sea like Tom

441

129 'The Industrious 'Prentice Performing the Duty of a Christian'

130 'The Idle 'Prentice at Play in the Church yard during Divine Service'

131 'The Industrious 'Prentice a Favourite, and Entrusted by his Master'

132 'The Idle 'Prentice Turned away, and Sent to Sea'

Bonney, as he sails past the windmills of Cuckold's Point. The brawny oarsman pulls on his oar and sucks his pipe, the sailors point to the gibbet with its hanging man and dangle a toy cat-o'-nine-tails over Tom's shoulder, and his mother weeps, holding her handkerchief to her eyes like Sarah Young crying over Rakewell. Tom pays no heed; he drops his indentures in the sea just as he abandoned his written guide on the floor. But although he is banished, it is impossible to oust all the wild elements he represents. When Goodchild finishes his seven years' time he marries his master's daughter ('*The Virtuous Woman is a Crown to her Husband*'), but as he pays the drummer and she sips her expensive tea, they recall the enraged musician, assailed rather than cheered by the street music. The footman gives crumbs to the begging woman at the door; like Lazarus and Dives, the poor are always with them.

Hogarth's tart humour is more dead-pan in this series than in any other, but it could not be kept out. In his second plate he packed the good folk of St Martin-in-the-Fields into cell-like pews, and his congregation contains a snoring boy, a beaky old woman with her keys and a busty self-righteous matron. The wit crept in as he worked. In his preliminary drawing for the scene when West shows off his workshop, he had included a peaceful, sleeping hound; in the print this turned into a spitting cat and snarling dog. In the rough sketch for the married scene, he drew the street band being watched by a woman and child, playing happily with a doll; in the second stage this cheerful duo gives way to butchers with bones and cleavers (used in 'rough music' to drum out infidelity, and in City protests) and by the legless 'Philip in the Tub', a well-travelled beggar and 'a constant epithalamist at weddings in London'.[20] The butchers are about to hit the cellist and Philip's song, 'Jesse or the Happy Marriage', is a ribald ballad on how to keep a wife under your thumb.

Many of the changes Hogarth made between drawing and print stress the anarchy and crudeness of the lower orders, but they also suggest that the people have an energy that the polite lack. The bland faces of the two 'good' men in the third plate seem curiously lifeless compared to the blob-nosed porter and scrapping animals. Hogarth did not want to subvert his message – he cut a scene showing Goodchild furnishing his house and hanging pictures, probably because the old hints of imitation and luxury would cast doubts on Goodchild's integrity. But he drew back, too, from painting Tom as an out-and-out villain, choosing not to engrave two drawings, of Tom stealing from his mother at her cookhouse, and of Goodchild giving money to his.

As things begin to go wrong, Hogarth's sympathy for his villain seems to

133 'The Industrious 'Prentice Out of his Time, and Married to his Master's Daughter'

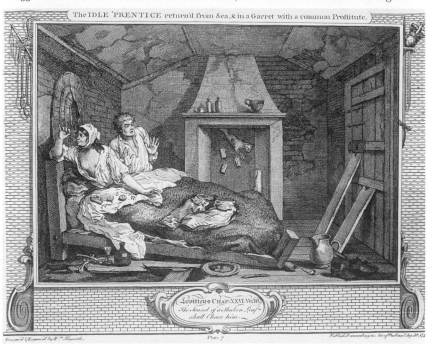

134 'The Idle 'Prentice Return'd from Sea, and in a Garret with a Common Prostitute'

increase: he makes us share Tom's fear rather than scorn him. We next see him, returned from sea, in a shabby garret bed with his mistress, 'a common prostitute'. But while she gloats over his highwayman's loot he is terrified by every sound, as the text tells us: '*The sound of a Shaken Leaf shall Chace him.*' The cat chasing a rat down the chimney makes him start; the door is wedged by planks; the rat darts over a pair of crossed pistols. Meanwhile Goodchild is a sheriff, presiding over a City banquet. But even here Hogarth's applause is not wholehearted; he showed the common people held back at the door and added a black servant and a portrait of William III, to heighten the note of dominion.

Increasingly, as if Hogarth could not hold back his feelings, even at his most didactic, Tom's fall wins sympathy as much as condemnation. The fault was his own, but, once fallen, he becomes the victim of a progress as ruthless and inexorable as that experienced by Moll and Tom Rakewell. The next scene is set in the cellar of 'Blood Bowl house' which was 'down by the fishmonger's, near Water-lane, Fleet-street'.[21] The name, some said, came from a countryman who was taken there and had his pocket picked; when he complained, he was told that if he did not shut up, the blood bowl would catch the flow from his slit throat.[22] Nichols, however, was told that it derived 'from the various scenes of blood that were almost daily exhibited, and where there seldom passed a month without the commission of the murder'.[23] Men are fighting, a soldier is pissing against the wall and a dead body is being shoved down through a trapdoor. Tom and his accomplice, dividing their pickings, are too busy to notice. But Tom is as doomed as the corpse: behind him his mistress is betraying him to the watch, just as Jenny Diver betrayed Macheath.

When Tom appears before the Justice, the betrayals – real and perceived – continue; his accomplice swears against him and his fellow apprentice is the judge who must condemn him. Between drawing and engraving Hogarth changed their poses: at first he made Goodchild point accusingly at Idle, but gradually he changed the positions round, with Tom leaning forward in appeal as Goodchild turns his head away – in horror, despair, or guilt? Although he is in the right, it is hard not to hear the dual texts as ironic: 'The Wicked is snared in the work of his own hands' and 'Thou shalt do no unrighteousness in Judgment'. Tom is a felon, who spills no blood; Goodchild is a model citizen, whose judgment slays his fellow.

As the climax approaches, each plate becomes livelier and fuller and the drama that began with two boys and their master in a workshop ends with the chorus of all London on stage. The last two plates are the public apotheosis

135 'The Industrious 'Prentice grown Rich, and Sheriff of London

136 'The Idle 'Prentice Betray'd by his Whore, and Taken in a Night Cellar with his Accomplice'

137 'The Industrious 'Prentice Alderman of London, the Idle One brought before him
and Impeached by his Accomplice'

of the two men's careers, a grand finale before the city crowds. They are slightly larger than the rest of the series, and Hogarth packed them as full of incident as *Southwark Fair* or the crowd scenes of *Hudibras*. Tom Idle's procession comes first, the long road from Newgate, stopping at the designated places like the Stations of the Cross. This is the vision Polly Peachum saw so vividly in *The Beggar's Opera*:

'Methinks I see him already in the Cart, sweeter and more lovely than the Nosegay in his Hand! – I hear the Crowd extolling his Resolution and Intrepidity! – What Volleys of Sighs are sent from the Windows of Holborn, that so comely a Youth should be brought to Disgrace! – I see him weep at the Tree! The whole Circle are in Tears! – even Butchers weep! Jack Ketch himself hesitates to perform his duty, and would be glad to lose his Fee, by a Reprieve.'[24]

There will be no reprieve for Tom. The cart has halted at the corner of Tyburn Lane by the great triple gallows. In the covered carriage in the middle, the Ordinary of Newgate waits to see Tom to the noose and hear his last words.

448

138 'The Idle 'Prentice Executed at Tyburn'

The 'Ordinary's Account', published later, was always a bestseller, but an alternative story is already being sold here, even before he swings. At the front of the 'stage', engaging the viewer's eyes as directly as the Ordinary, the official story-teller, stands a ballad-seller with her baby, holding 'The last dying Speech and Confession of Tho. Idle'.[25] The Ordinary's tale – like Hogarth's series – always emphasized the way that early misdemeanours had led irrevocably to crime and the gallows. But the ballad rescued the sinner and made him heroic. Tom's story, bitter though it is, has a touch of romance, rather like Macheath's, or like that of Jack Sheppard – Cockney hero of ballad and pantomime. Sheppard's father was a Spitalfields carpenter. He died soon after Jack was born and his impoverished mother sent him first to a workhouse and then apprenticed him to a carpenter – when he travelled to the gallows, girls threw bouquets into the cart. There are two ways of seeing this scene, Hogarth implies – take your pick.

The scene is harsh, none the less. Around the ballad centre, the chaos of life spreads and sprawls: a man swings a dog by its tail, perhaps to hurl at the Methodist preacher haranguing Tom in the cart. A woman punches a man; a

449

baby falls on the ground; an orange-seller tweaks a young boy's nose and pickpockets steal cakes from the flamboyant 'Tiddy-Doll', who attended executions as often as 'Philip in his Tub' did weddings, and whose candles show that he has been here since before dawn, to satisfy the hunger of the mob. In a high cart on the right, raising her eyes piously, but raising her glass too, stands 'Mother' Douglas, the Covent Garden bawd. In the next cart to her, the one that will carry Tom's corpse, his real mother weeps. Wheeling above them, a carrier pigeon bears the news that her son has reached the gallows: another will fly when he dies.

Surrounded by people, when Tom faces death he stands alone. Hogarth's terrible text, from the first chapter of Proverbs, reads less like a statement of faith than profound unbelief: *'When fear cometh as desolation and their destruction cometh as a Whirlwind; when distress cometh upon them. Then they shall call upon God, but he will not answer.'*

On the left of this scene, ignoring the hanging but enjoying the day out, are two ragged boys – future apprentices no doubt. All London apprentices had 'Tyburn holidays', and one for the Lord Mayor's Procession. A few days later, the same boys might watch Goodchild ride in triumph, with the Marshal peering out from beneath his high fur hat, shut in like the Ordinary in his coach at Tom's death. Before him would march the constables and representatives of all the guilds, then the magistrates and the aldermen in scarlet robes trimmed with fur, then the sheriffs and officers. 'You cannot imagine the quantity of people there are at the windows, balconies and in the streets to see the pageant pass,' wrote Saussure. 'The Lord Mayor's Day is a great holiday in the City.' Yet the crowds were not always respectful:

'The populace on that day is particularly insolent and rowdy, turning into lawless freedom the great liberty it enjoys. At these times it is almost dangerous for an honest man, and more particularly for a foreigner, if at all well dressed, to walk in the streets, for he runs a great risk of being insulted by the vulgar populace, which is the most cursed brood in existence. He is sure of not only being jeered at and being bespattered with mud, but as likely as not dead dogs and cats will be thrown at him, for the mob makes a provision beforehand of these playthings, so that they may amuse themselves with them on the great day.'[26]

Just as Tyburn was the end of one old City story, so the Mansion House was the end of another. A modern Dick Whittington, Goodchild plunges down Cheapside through hallooing, hat-waving, billowing crowds while the Prince of Wales and his attendants smile down from the balcony of the King's

450

139 'The Industrious 'Prentice Lord Mayor of London'

Head Tavern. Everything is promised to him, *'Length of days is in her right hand, and in her left hand Riches and Honour,'* says the text. Everyone is here, roadsweepers and beggars, soldiers and lovers, ballad-sellers and gin-sellers. But there have always been unnerving outsiders in Goodchild's progress and here too there is a spectre at the feast. The last figure we see as we read from left to right across the print is an old pedlar, holding up a broadside, ' A full and true Account of ye Ghost of Tho; Idle. Which . . .'

The ghost of Tom Idle will always haunt his righteous *alter ego*. The story is finished, yet unfinished. Generations of boys have passed, and more will come, choosing the routes of labour or idleness.

Vertue thought *Industry and Idleness* crude, done in 'a slight poor manner'. Hogarth's genius, he added 'seems very strong & Conversant with low life as heretofore' and this fresh instance of his skill, engraved so roughly, was 'rather to compass or grip the whole advantage of his Inventions & to prevent the shop print sellers any benefit'.[27] True, the money rolled in and the prints proved popular with employers and schoolteachers, if not with apprentices.

451

Londoners, as usual, saw their own lives reflected in the conventional story. One pamphleteer, prefacing a pious explanation of the prints, described how he walked from Temple Bar to the Exchange and was 'interrupted at every Print-Shop by a Croud of People of all Ranks gazing at Mr Hogarth's Prints'. A beadle was staring at Plate 3, of Tom Idle in the churchyard:

'G—d Z—ds Dick, I'll be d—n'd if that is not Bob —, Beadle of St. — Parish; it's as like him as one Herring is like another; see his Nose, his Chin, and the damned sour Look so natural to poor Bob. G—d suckers, who could have thought Hogarth could had hit him off so exactly. It's very merry; we shall have pure Fun tonight with Ned; I expect to see him at our Club; I'll roast him. I'll buy this Print, if it was only to plague him.'[28]

Hogarth had once more played a good double game, winning the bourgeoisie with his morals and the crowd with his 'merry' truth to life.

His own life, too, had something of the contrasts of *Industry and Idleness*: his early 'laziness', his ambition, his marriage to his master's daughter, his sweeping moods which made him feel sometimes that his progress was a triumph and sometimes a ride to rough music, a passage to hell. He had been both the industrious and the idle apprentice.

22

'Seized, and carried before the Governor'

The chief captain came near, and laid hold on him, and commanded him to be bound with two chains; and inquired who he was, and what he had done.

And some shouted one thing, and some another, among the crowd: and when he could not know the certainty of the uproar, he commanded him to be brought into the castle.

Acts 21:33–4

ALTHOUGH HE WAS now closely implicated in the polite world of benevolence, before Hogarth turned to *Industry and Idleness* he published a small print which suggested that his cynicism about the *political* world was as strong as ever. A General Election was announced on 18 June 1747, to take place at the end of the month, and on the 26th he issued *The Country Inn Yard at Election Time*. This little scene, a pattern of comic rotundity squeezed against straight lines, showed the stagecoach setting out for 'Lundun' from the old Angel Inn (misspelt, perhaps deliberately, as the 'Old Angle'), with a stout victualler chivvying hungover drunks and parting lovers.

The central focus is the backside of a fat woman trying to wedge herself into the coach, her 'broad-bottom' an easy dig at the Pelham administration. Precariously perched on the roof of the coach, while the smug lady heads for an inside place, a sailor from Anson's battleship *Centurion*, cock-a-hoop after the navy's victory off Cape Finisterre, is mocking a miserable French footman.[1] Like all the survivors of Commodore Anson's voyage round the world the British tar had earlier gone home with a phenomenal amount of prize money – hundreds of pounds – the share of the loot from a Catholic Spanish treasure ship which the navy of free, Protestant Britain allotted even to ordinary seamen. No wonder the sailor's duffel bag is tied to his arm – no wonder the footman looks so wound up.

The inn-yard is noisy and chaotic. In the background a cross spinster ticks off a mother with a crying baby, while an Election parade holds up a sign saying 'No OLD BABY', a jibe at young bucks leaping into safe parliamentary

453

Price one Shilling. — Design'd and Engrav'd by W. Hogarth. — Publish'd According to Act of Parliament. 1747.

140 *The Stage Coach; or A Country Inn Yard at Election Time* (1747)

seats. The phrase dated from 1734 when the twenty-year-old John Child (then Viscount Castlemaine, and now Earl Tylney) was a candidate in Essex and 'a man was placed on a bulk with an infant in his arms, and exclaimed, as he whipt the child, "What, you little *Child*, must you be a member?" '[2] Since Hogarth was then painting Castlemaine's assembly at Wanstead House, and could hardly attack him, one wonders if this little plate, or at least the idea, hadn't been gathering dust waiting for the opportune moment – which arrived smartly in 1747 when the cry of 'No old Baby' could refer just as well to the Stuart Pretender or the bloody Duke of Cumberland.

Hogarth was currently preoccupied with ideas of law, figures of authority, ambiguities of justice, issues of nationalism. *Industry and Idleness* was published on 30 September and three months later Hogarth embarked on another illustration of a biblical text, this time of 'justice' on a grand scale. Two years before, Lord Wyndham, the former Lord Chancellor of Ireland, had left a legacy of £200 for the decoration of the Chapel or the Great Hall of Lincoln's Inn. In the autumn of 1747 William Murray, the powerful judge who later became Lord Mansfield, proposed that this should be spent on a painting by Hogarth, whom he knew well. The commission was agreed in early December.

The subject Hogarth chose was *Paul before Felix*, an incident from Chapter 24

454

of the Acts of the Apostles. This seemed particularly apt: it showed a famous trial; it featured the patron saint of London, honoured by St Paul's Cathedral, and it gave Lincoln's Inn a history-painting in the great tradition. (St Paul was the subject of the Raphael cartoons, which British art lovers had admired for many years.)[3] To some, however, the choice of this particular scene might have seemed ironic, since Paul's trial before Felix was often cited as a lesson in the need to resist unjust judges.

In Acts, the trial is the culmination of a dramatic sequence of events which begins with Paul's arrival in Jerusalem. First he is attacked by the Jewish authorities and the crowd for bringing his disciples, whom they believe include Greek foreigners, into the Temple. Paul responds by saying that he himself is a Jew, and telling the stirring tale of his experience on the road to Damascus, but the mob will have none of it: 'they lifted up their voice, and said, Away with such a fellow from the earth, for it is not fit that he should live' (Acts 22:22). When Paul finds himself facing Roman justice, however, he appeals to his legal rather than religious identity, this time claiming he is a Roman and should be tried as such. He is eventually taken before the Governor, Felix, and accused by the Jewish High Priest, speaking through a Roman orator, Tertullus.

Tertullus describes Paul as 'a pestilent fellow, and a mover of insurrections among all the Jews throughout the world, and a ringleader of the sect of Nazarenes'. But Felix, who feels unable to judge, procrastinates. Some days later, he returns with his Jewish wife, Drusilla, to hear Paul speak 'concerning the faith in Christ Jesus':

'[25] And as he reasoned of righteousness, and temperance, and the judgment to come, Felix was terrified, and answered, Go thy way for this time; and when I have a convenient season, I will call thee unto me. [26] He hoped withal that money would be given him of Paul: wherefore also he sent for him the oftener, and communed with him. [27] But when two years were fulfilled, Felix was succeeded by Porcius Festus; and desiring to gain favour with the Jews, Felix left Paul in bonds.'

Hogarth shows the moment in the first verse, where Felix reels terrified before Paul's words, but he packs the resonance of the whole story into the scene. Felix and Drusilla appear as a judge and a great court lady, but men familiar with the classics (and what lawyer eating his dinner in Lincoln's Inn was not?) would know that Felix was a tyrant and Drusilla an adulteress, who had left her husband for this powerful man. As a Jewess she should help Paul yet she remains silent, colluding with the oppressors: Paul's outstretched hand leads

455

141 *Paul before Felix* (1751–2)

our eyes to her breasts, suggesting Felix's and Drusilla's mutual sin. No wonder Felix blenches as he hears talk of 'righteousness, and temperance, and the judgment to come'. Disappointed of the hoped-for bribes from Paul, he curries favour with the Jews by leaving him to rot in prison.

In his apparently reverential, Raphaelesque canvas Hogarth threw the much vaunted impartiality of the law into question, just as he had questioned the inequalities of medicine at St Bartholomew's and the presumption of charity at the Foundling Hospital. Seeing this new painting some people might remember that his last scene of 'justice' was Idle before Goodchild. As in those prints, where the suave engraving of the good contrasts with the rough cross-hatching of the bad characters, and as in the different textures of paint in the figures of Moses and Pharoah's daughter at the Foundling Hospital, so the smooth 'society' finish of Felix, Drusilla and Tertullus shows up the rough brushstrokes of Paul's face, hair, and gesturing hands.

Hogarth was no wrathful 'man of the people' – as a thrusting professional he was keener to distance himself from the mob than from the lawyers – but he was certainly ready to warn them against corruption and the abuse of power.

456

His critique was sharpened by the picture's placing. He chose a huge canvas, fourteen foot by ten, although he must have known that this was too large to hang in the Chapel as his commission required. In June 1748, he took the picture to show the Benchers, anxious to learn if it met with their approval, and was asked to dine with them in the Hall, a rare honour for a layman and an outsider. At the end of that month, in tones of utmost innocence, he wrote to the Treasurer, John Wood, enclosing a sketch of his proposed frame: 'According to your order', he began,

'I have consider'd of a place for the Picture, and cannot think of any other than over the sound board, in the hall, all advantage to be gained for Light can only be by setting the bottom near the wall, and inclining the Top forward as much as possible.'⁴

The next day a fee of £200 was agreed, and the money was his within the week.

Ostensibly Hogarth simply wrote to Wood to say why the frame he was ordering from Gosset's would have to be plain, without side ornaments, because of the angle against the wall. In practice he was ensuring that his painting would not only hang in the Old Hall – the heart of the Inn since the fifteenth century – but would *lean* forward, physically, overlooking the assembled company. Even on ordinary days this company would include all the lawyers and Benchers at their dinner, but the Court of Chancery also regularly sat in the Hall; this meant that during its sessions the Lord Chancellor himself would sit facing the crowd, with Hogarth's picture of a corrupt Roman judge and his accuser staring out above his head. The subject of *Paul before Felix* was so correct that no one would be able to find fault, yet those who noticed its situation could hardly fail to get the point. On 28 April 1751 George Vertue wrote,

'this large peece was done for to be placed in Lincolnns Inn chappel but there being no propper room for it is placed in Lincolnns Inn hall over the Seat where the Lord chancellor sitts'.⁵

A further issue related to the rules of art, not the role of law. In *Paul before Felix*, a Jew is denounced by other Jews as a rebel, a defier of convention, a troublemaker who is both Roman and Jew, insider and outsider. (And although Paul is the victim of powerful interests only a devout Christian reading can make him seem *entirely* innocent.) Hogarth did not exactly identify with Paul, but he knew what it felt like to be embattled, to confront a mixed bench of foreign authorities and fellow countrymen. The painting was his own declaration of faith, and Vertue suggests as much in his first mention of it in May 1748. Immediately after a long, sardonic account of the career of William Kent, who had died on 12 April at Burlington House, he wrote this entry:

'Some new designs of Mr Hogarth – painting. much bigger than the life. the story of St Paul at Ephesus – the greatness of his *Spirit* (tho a little man) to out vye. all other painters.'[6]

The phrases 'bigger than the life' and the 'greatness of his spirit' float loose as if applying equally to the canvas, Paul and the painter. Hogarth, the 'five-foot man', 'the little man', had also had his accusers. In his own terms he had turned the tables on them and kept the faith, repeating his self-justification over and over again – as Paul retold his tale of the Damascus road – and, he hoped, making his judges tremble.

After he received his fee in 1748 Hogarth worked on the picture for several more months. In February 1749 it was hung in Lincoln's Inn Council Room, and was finally placed in its great frame in the Hall in 1750. When he noticed its telling position, Vertue felt it was hung too high '& not so well to the light as it should be', but he thought it 'great and noble'. Grudgingly, he swung back and forth between an admission – at last – of Hogarth's greatness, and a familiar shudder at the practices of this 'little man', who had won the commission 'by means of his Friends & there interest' and been richly paid for both the picture and its frame:

'it is a great work and shows the greatness and magnificence of Mr Hogarths genius . . . this really is a great work & much honor so that raises the character of that little man – tho not his person – who additional cunning & skill. and a good stock of assurance every way of the acutest kind possible – to be well paid beyond most others of the same profession –'[7]

At the time, Hogarth was particularly susceptible to criticism, following the London publication of the letters of Abbé Le Blanc, one of which, containing his impressions of a visit a decade before, was 'On the State of Painting and Sculpture in England'. The criticisms flowed: Britain plundered Europe's treasures, yet had not bred a single native painter; foreign artists could not plant the seeds of inspiration in this stony soil; Paris reigned supreme because, unlike London, it had an official academy which taught drawing; Thornhill had attempted history-painting, but remained mediocre; all London offered was an endless stream of portraits (which was why a feeble painter like Kneller had flourished here). And if English painters, Le Blanc concluded with a flourish, could not rise to the majesty of the sublime, nor could they truly understand the other extreme, the 'oddities' of burlesque, 'which indeed is what they have practised most'. Here followed his remarks on the great popularity and national moral impact of *A Rake's Progress*, a work in the 'grotesque manner', produced by 'a man of genius in this way, but who is as bad a painter, as he is a good subject'.[8] This judgement, which thrust Hogarth back into the role of a burlesque, if moral and patriotic, printmaker, was circulating just as he was trying to show that he *could* produce a sublime history-painting at Lincoln's Inn.

Stout men sprang to the defence of British art. In his treatise on physiognomy, Hogarth's friend James Parsons cited the fine native works to be seen at St Paul's and Greenwich, St Bartholomew's and the Foundling Hospital. But Parsons still implicitly conceded inferiority, insisting that if Britain had 'the same academical Endowments that other Nations can boast of', it would produce as fine artists and sculptors as they did;

'for it is notorious that our Youth have made as good a Figure in foreign Academies as any that were educated at them; and we have even had some, who, by dint of Genius, have born away the Prizes from those of every other Nation'.

As Hogarth looked back on his efforts at St Martin's Lane and the Foundling Hospital, he must have felt he could not win. His response to Le Blanc affected his Lincoln's Inn painting. Although *Paul before Felix* was praised, he was not satisfied and in February 1751 he was given permission to take it away and retouch it. He simplified the scene, removing some figures, cutting out realistic effects and emphasizing the architectural elements to strengthen the focus on the central drama.[9] He reworked it, in fact, as if to prove that he could be a 'classical' history-painter. Anxiety and anger were intermingled. Yet that same year – in what was to become a characteristic pattern of behaviour – he turned on himself, almost in an act of self-mutilation. He chose this very picture to prove that he was 'a genius in his way', and that his way *was* burlesque, as the Abbé had said.

In May 1751, when he announced the proposed prints of *Moses Brought to Pharoah's Daughter* and *Paul before Felix*, he used his subscription ticket to attack yet another fashion among the connoisseurs, the vogue for Rembrandt prints. To do so, however, he caricatured his *own* work, reworking his painting of St Paul 'in the true Dutch taste', parodying the way Dutch artists reduced all subjects to the everyday (presumably refuting the innuendo that this was what he always did himself). *'Paul before Felix' Burlesqued* is

142 *'Paul before Felix' Burlesqued* (1751)

grotesquely exaggerated and crammed with visual jokes. The powerful figure of the Lincoln's Inn Paul is crumpled into a bearded, fur-hatted, long-nosed ranter. Because Paul is so small he has to stand on a stool supported by a snoozing angel (a portrait of young Luke Sullivan, who was engraving the painting), while a tiny imp is sawing the stool's leg. Drusilla, with a lap dog on her knees, is turning away as Felix, instead of 'trembling', shits himself in fear. Everyone can smell the result. Court officials hold their noses; vacant-faced burghers look on; Tertullus tears up his speech in rage; a fat, sozzled Justice with a butcher's knife and money bags at her waist wobbles on her pedestal.

Hogarth's fierce, scatological ticket attacked the 'boorish' Dutch paintings collected by the Alderman in *Marriage A-la-Mode*. It cleverly burlesqued Rembrandt's realism, his highly individual characters and use of light and shade. The lines were made deliberately 'scratchy' and Rembrandt-like and Hogarth even stained his first version with coffee to make it look like an old etching, a standard forger's trick. As a ticket, it proved so popular that he first raised the subscription for the two biblical prints from fifteen shillings to a guinea, then sold it as a separate print. Yet he was taking an extraordinary risk.

460

His burlesque stressed the gulf between high and low art – but used as a receipt for his own 'high' efforts, it might also lay Hogarth – far more than Rembrandt – open to ridicule and derision.

Hogarth was already a figure of fun in some quarters. In the summer of 1748, with the *Paul*, as he then thought, finished and accepted, he was tired and in need of a change. That spring, the peace of Aix-la-Chapelle had reopened the Continent to the English: the gates of Calais were flung wide to a throng of curious travellers, heading for Paris and beyond. Among them was Hogarth. In August, with the £200 from Lincoln's Inn in his pocket, he set off for France with a group from St Martin's Lane. As it happened, while he was there he had his own encounter with a Governor, itself an absurd and undignified burlesque.

The War of the Austrian Succession had ground on since 1743, when Hogarth had gone to Paris to find engravers for *Marriage A-la-Mode*. Henry Pelham had been trying to find a way to end this expensive, damaging conflict since 1746, when British interests looked dangerously threatened. By then French armies had gained control of Flanders and Belgium; the Duke of Cumberland's forces were thrashed at Lauffeld, and when the fortress of Bergen-op-Zoom fell the following year it looked as though Holland might be lost too. The tentacles of war spread wide, and the issues were trade and empire as much as European crowns. As far away as India the fall of Madras left the British East India Company perilously weak. The only light shone from the sea, in Anson's great victory off Finisterre, and Hawke's off Belle-Ile, which allowed the British navy to control the Atlantic and the Channel. The two sides were in a position where neither could give way – France was winning in the Low Countries, and Britain in the Americas.

Pelham, however, was both adroit and determined. After calling an early Election, and securing a sound Whig majority to scupper any alliance between the Prince of Wales's Opposition and the Tories, he steered firmly towards peace. Tortuous diplomacies finally led to an armistice between the English, French and Dutch on 29 April 1748, with the other powers following later. Among the many intricate dealings, European acceptance of the Protestant succession was finally secured: 'The Pretender is to be renounced with all his descendants male and female . . . and the cessation of arms to take place in all other parts of the world.'[10] The government was jubilant and costly festivities were the order of the day:

'Stocks rise; the ministry are in high spirits, and *peu s'en faut* but we shall

461

admire this peace as our own doing! . . . We had last night the most magnificent masquerade that ever was seen: it was by subscription at the Haymarket: everybody who subscribed five guinea had four tickets. There were about seven hundred people, all in chosen and very fine dresses. The supper was in two rooms, besides those for the King and Prince, who, with the foreign ministers, had tickets given them.'[11]

Hogarth set out for France in this mood of jubilation, with his old friends Frank Hayman and Henry Cheere, the sculptor, accompanied by the portraitist Thomas Hudson and the drapery painter Joseph Van Aken and his brother. They had 'resolvd and agreed', said Vertue, 'to go to Paris'.[12] Unfortunately, despite his visit to Paris five years before and his friendships with men such as Roubiliac and Grignion, Hogarth's mental baggage was still crammed with the rhetoric of wooden clogs and slavery, despotism and foppery. According to all accounts of his trip, he behaved badly. A nightmare to travel with, he sounds like a man on the edge of a breakdown, irrational, erratic.

When they arrived in Paris – to Hogarth the source of all affectation as well as the refuge of skulking Jacobites – his scorn was ripe. George Steevens, Nichols's sanctimonious, slander-loving collaborator, relished yet another instance of Hogarthian barbarity, as related by another English engraver who was in the city at the time:

'While *Hogarth* was in *France*, wherever he went, he was sure to be dissatisfied with what he saw. If an elegant circumstance either in furniture, or the ornaments of a room, was pointed out as deserving approbation, his narrow and constant reply was, "What then? but it is *French*! Their houses are all gilt and be—t." In the streets he was often clamorously rude. A tattered bag, or a pair of silk stockings with holes in them, drew a torrent of imprudent language around him. In vain did my informant (who knew that many *Scotch* and *Irish* were often within hearing of these reproaches, and would rejoice at least in an opportunity of getting our painter mobbed) advise him to be more cautious in his public remarks. He laughed at all such admonition, and treated the offerer of it as a pusillanimous wretch, unworthy of a residence in a free country, making him the butt of his ridicule for several evenings afterwards.'[13]

From this uncomfortable scene, Cheere, Hudson and Van Aken went north to Flanders and Holland, returning to London a month later having 'visited all the Curious & most famous Artists in those cittys were they went'.[14] Meanwhile, Hayman and Hogarth turned straight home. Hogarth's alarmed and exasperated colleagues had manoeuvred him through Paris without his

462

being mobbed but in Calais, as Steevens righteously put it, 'his unreasonable pleasantry was at length completely extinguished'. As he himself described it, he was innocently 'santering about', observing the town and the people, when he paused at the ancient gateway, taking characteristic pleasure in the fact that it was 'built by the English, when the place was in our possession' and seemed to have the English arms on the front. This feature, and 'idle curiosity', prompted him to make a sketch. But as he drew, he felt his shoulder firmly gripped from behind, and was marched off to the Governor's residence, where he was formally denounced as an English spy.

Hogarth himself later made good capital out of the disaster, and to avid collectors of gossip it was a priceless gift. Vertue quickly jotted it down, asserting that both Hogarth and Hayman 'attempting to draw some views of Fortifications &c were surprizd and clapt into the Bastile'.[15] Hogarth's friend the Reverend William Gostling, the versifier of the *Peregrination*, who put him up in Canterbury on his first night back, later told Dr Ducarel (who told Nichols) that he had been 'committed as a prisoner to Grandsire, his landlord', who promised he should not go out until he embarked. According to this version, when the English packet was ready to sail he was bustled on board ship by two guards, who watched him closely until they were three miles offshore, outside modern territorial waters:

'they then spun him round like a top, on the deck; and told him that he was at liberty to proceed on his voyage without further attendance or molestation. With the slightest allusion to the ludicrous particulars of this affair, poor Hogarth was by no means pleased.'[16]

That final shipboard humiliation – a small middle-aged Englishman being twirled like a toy by a couple of burly Frenchmen – was one that Hogarth would not have wished to record but, if true, would neither forget nor forgive. Fifteen years later the very memory of Calais produced a stream of venom – a written assault on the 'face' of France as the index of the nation:

'The first time any one goes from hence to france by way of Calais he cannot avoid being struck with the Extreem different face things appear with at so little distance as from Dover a farcical pomp of war, parade of riligion, and Bustle with little with very little bussiness in short poverty slavery and Insolence <with an affectation of politeness> give you even here the first specimen of the whole country nor are the figure less opposed to those of dover than the two shores. fish women have faces of leather and soldiers . . . raged and lean.'[17]

*

A few months after Hogarth's return, Horace Walpole passed on the tale to entertain Horace Mann in Florence, with some embellishments describing how the artist, when hauled before the Governor, was

'forced to prove his vocation by producing several caricaturas of the French; particularly a scene of the shore, with an immense piece of beef landing for the Lion d'Argent, the English inn and several hungry friars following it'.[18]

The Governor, allegedly diverted – and admitting that Hogarth's sketch would be useless to an engineer – dropped the charges but warned him that 'had not the peace been actually signed, he should have been obliged to have hung him up immediately on the ramparts'.[19] Instead, he was put under guard.

Hogarth's own later account resembled Walpole's, and he also made it sound as if the moment he was back on English soil he whipped out his canvas and paints to take his revenge. Taken before the Governor, he wrote in a tumbling rush,

'I conceild none of the memorandum I had privately taken and they being found to be only those of a painter for own use it was Judged necessary only to confine me to my lodging till the wind changed for our coming away to England where I no sooner arived but I set about the Picture wherein I introduced a poor highlander fled thither on acount of the Rebelion year before brozing on scanty french fair in sight a Surloin of Beef a present from England which is opposed the Kettle of soup meager. my own figure in the corner with the soldier hand upon my sholder is said to be tolerably like.'[20]

This painting, *The Gate of Calais*, is dark and comic, admirable and dislikeable, rich and desolate. Like a genuine spy penetrating French defences Hogarth peered in towards the town through the gloomy arch in the seventeenth-century ramparts, an outer ring encircling the old city walls. Plane by plane his painting works backwards, the action framed in the darkness of one gate, like the proscenium of a stage, and set against the backdrop of another. The whole is cut across by a sharply defined diagonal shadow as the evening sun flashes from a cloud-flecked sky of brilliant blue, picking out the English arms on the Porte du Havre. The sun shines on history, reminding viewers that Calais was in English hands from 1347 to 1558, but it also illuminates the present. It falls on the raven perched on the tower and on the glinting white robes of priests, processing to give the sacrament to the sick beyond the jagged portcullis. Above them, the dove of the holy spirit flies – on a tavern inn sign.

The main action takes place on the broad cobbles between the two gates. Here are the stock French comic characters: the servants in clogs, carrying the

143 *The Gate of Calais* (1749)

kettle of grey *soupe maigre*; the scrawny ape-like *monsieur*, spoon halfway to his mouth, with toes poking through his socks; the death-head soldier spilling his soup. They are all electrified, jealously transfixed by the sight of a huge side of beef on its way to Grandsire's hotel to feed the British visitors. The cook's boy (with 'affected' clocks on his stockings) staggers under the ton of good red meat and the gross, lascivious friar strokes its waxy fat with drooling greed. The extremes of fat and thin make their own point, about just who, in this land of superstition and fear, is living off the fat of the land.

Hogarth made shameless use of every ancient stereotype that could fuel religious and national antipathy. In the shadowy foreground, like an emblematic figure holding back a stage curtain, lies the cringing Jacobite in his tartan, with mouldering shoes and nothing but an onion to eat. Opposite him three wizened crones huddle like the witches in *Macbeth*, their toothless grins mimicked in the dead face of the skate. With their wimples and crosses round their necks they could also be seen as barefoot nuns, idiotically ecstatic at finding Christ's image in the features of the fish.

*

465

Calais Gate was painted with such careful detail that even the bunch of onions and the glinting copper soup kettle had a kind of beauty. As if obsessed, Hogarth had worked fast and over the winter he made a print of his painting, helped by another engraver, Charles Mosley. On 7–9 March 1749 the *London Evening Post* was able to announce that 'for 5s, at the Golden Head in Leicester-Square, and at the Print Shops', Londoners could buy:

'A Print design'd and engrav'd by Mr. HOGARTH, representing a PRODIGY which lately appear'd before the Gate of CALAIS
'O the Roast-beef of Old England, &c.'

No coloured print survives (although Hogarth did sometimes use coloured ink for effect) but Vertue, perhaps confusing it with the painting, grumpily complained that the print itself was a 'prodigious' blunder, because the meat was so obviously raw, not roasted, 'only coloured red and yellow'.[21]

The print was a huge success, absolutely in tune with one powerful vein of national feeling. Anti-French prejudice had always been strong, but in the aftermath of the ''45' – which Hogarth now began to re-create in *The March to Finchley* – Francophobia soared. French artists such as Gravelot and Philip Mercier left England, understandably, in 1745–6. Old fears of papist superstition, despotic laws and standing armies joined hands with the moral fight against luxury and affectation – and with mercantile self-interest. Rather bizarrely, even the promoters of rococo began to argue that this was now a native style rather than French-influenced and that rococo wares should be manufactured at home; they too joined the Anti-Gallican Society, founded in 1745 with the specific aim 'to extend the commerce of England and discourage the introduction of French modes and oppose the importation of French commodities'.[22] From the late 1740s the fashionable classes and the government were berated by a flock of writers, dramatists and pamphleteers for corrupting national life by their indulgent French tastes. If the leaders of society adopted Paris fashions, spoke French among themselves, had their hair curled and their dancing corrected by simpering *monsieurs*, British trade as well as culture would suffer, national distinction would be eroded and national fibre relaxed.

> Trulls, toupees, trinkets, bags, brocade and lace,
> A flaunting form, and a fictitious face.
> Rouse! Reassume! Refuse a gallic reign,
> Nor let their arts win that their arms could never gain.[23]

Calais Gate echoed this rallying cry: war with France might be over, but the battle must go on. It was a warning, a shout of 'Beef and Liberty!' In its downright, detailed style the painting eschewed the polite, proudly asserting red-blooded Britishness. Even *looking* at French life, it suggested, could deprive an Englishman of his freedom – and within both painting and print, everyone could see how the artist sketching in its midst, Hogarth himself, had been caught off his guard as a hand fell on his shoulder and a pike loomed above his head. The print helped to establish him as a prime representative of the dauntless, innocent, beef-eating Brit. His self-portrait, engraved as a frontispiece for his folios and grandly inscribed *Guilelmus Hogarth*, was on sale for 3s 6d at the same time, but it was the simple profile by the gate of Calais that caught the public imagination. From late 1749, this detail (minus the arresting hand) was extracted and widely copied: 'Hogarth's Head' was used 'as a shop card or sign for professions ranging from printseller to tailor'.[24] If he was held in low esteem by critics, Hogarth as artist–spy was the Englishman's hero.

467

23

Town and Country

Unnumbered suppliants crowd preferment's gate,
Athirst for wealth, and burning to be great;
Delusive Fortune hears the incessant call,
They mount, they shine, evaporate and fall.
SAMUEL JOHNSON, *The Vanity of Human Wishes* (1749)

Such easeless toil, such constant care,
Is more than human strength can bear.
One may observe it in your face –
Indeed, my dear, you break apace:
And nothing can your health repair,
But exercise and country air . . .
ROBERT LLOYD, *The Cit's Country Box* (1756)

A STRANGE MOOD ran through the nation after the peace of Aix-la-Chapelle. It was at once relieved and disturbed, calling for decorum yet turbulent with emotion. 'Our King is returned and our Parliament met,' wrote Horace Walpole on 2 December 1748. 'We expected nothing but harmony and tranquillity and love of the peace; but the very first day opened with a black cloud, that threatens a stormy session.'[1]

In every sphere it seemed that an old order had slipped suddenly into a new, taking people by surprise. In an earlier letter Walpole remarked caustically to Horace Mann that it was very difficult to make a lasting impression on the town and people were forgotten as soon as they were out of sight:

'Ministers, authors, wits, fools, patriots, whores, scarce bear a second edition. Lord Bolingbroke, Sarah Malcolm, and old Marlborough, are never mentioned but by elderly folk to their grandchildren, who had never heard of them.'[2]

Even if not forgotten, the men whose names had been on everyone's lips in the 1720s were now gone: Pope had died at Twickenham in 1744; Swift, after

468

years in a sad mental twilight, in 1745; William Kent in 1748. New names would soon be buzzed around the town, and wit would soon give way to sentiment. Among the writers, Thomas Gray was now finishing the 'Elegy in a Country Churchyard'. In Dublin, aged twenty, Edmund Burke had just taken his degree; he would enter the Middle Temple in London the following year, and had already given notice of his power, brooding on the swollen Liffey in flood before his windows: 'It gives me pleasure to see nature in those great but terrible scenes. It fills the mind with grand ideas, and turns the soul in upon herself.'[3] Working in a very different mode and mood, the twenty-seven- year-old Tobias Smollett had published *Roderick Random* in 1748, drawing on his days as a penniless Scot in London, training in medicine, joining the navy and enduring the grim Cartagena campaign of 1741. Among the painters, Joshua Reynolds, now twenty-six, set out for Italy in early 1749. A still younger group stood in the wings. In Ipswich, Thomas Gainsborough, at twenty-two, was already sought for his landscapes and portraits. As a student in Oxford, Bonnell Thornton was writing his 'Ode on St Cecilia's Day', full of the demotic music and instruments of Hogarth's *Enraged Musician*; the next year he would translate Rouquet's notes on *The March to Finchley*.

The thirst for fame was just as great and the public taste as fickle but the cast list was changing and so was the tone: the time of the Heart had come. In 1748, the novel had come of age with Richardson's *Clarissa*. Even more than in *Pamela*, Richardson appealed to feeling: Clarissa's virtue burned like fire, defying the greed of her family and the lust of the rake. In October, Fielding finished the fifth volume. Deeply moved, he wrote to his old rival:

'Shall I tell you? Can I tell you what I think of the latter part of your Volume? Let the Overflowings of a Heart which you have filled brimful speak for me.

'... her Letter to Lovelace is beyond any thing I have ever read. God forbid that the man who reads this with dry Eyes should be alone with my Daughter when she hath no Assistance within Call.

'Here my Terror ends and my Grief begins which the call of all my Tumultuous Passions soon changes into raptures of Admiration and Astonishment ... This Scene I have heard hath been often objected to. It is well for the critick that my Heart is now writing and not my Head.'[4]

But wit and comic reason were far from dead, as Fielding himself proved. When he wrote this letter his own *Tom Jones* was in the press, the sexy, quixotic adventures of its foundling hero providing a rumbustious counterpoint to Richardson's emotional drama. By September 1748 three of its six volumes had been printed but not released. The delay allowed anticipation to build to an unprecedented pitch, fuelled over the winter by assiduous 'puffing' from friends and by press announcements. The general public, in fact, did not get its hands on the novel until the end of February 1749, since, in a rush unheard of in publishing history, the whole first edition of 2,500 copies was sold before it even reached the shops. By the end of March a cheap third edition appeared, then a fourth, and soon 10,000 copies were out.

It was a portentous spring. The winter had been strange, excessively stormy but so warm and free from frosts that honeysuckles bloomed on Christmas Day and tender nectarines bore blossom.[5] At the turn of the New Year, another voice made itself heard whose sonorous tones would govern public taste and judgement for the rest of the century. On 9 January 1749, Samuel Johnson published *The Vanity of Human Wishes*, the first work whose title page carried his name, a thrumming, condensed imitation of Juvenal's tenth satire. Weighty and emotional, Johnson's poem was an exercise in tragic irony, a powerful restatement of a familiar theme, 'the helpless vulnerability of the individual before the social context, the tangled, teeming, jungle of plots, follies, vanities and egoistic passions in which anyone – the innocent and the virtuous no less than the vicious – is likely to be ambushed'.[6] This description could equally apply to *Clarissa* and *Tom Jones*, and to the inexorable plots of Hogarth's *Progresses* and his coruscating *Marriage A-la-Mode*. And for Johnson, the portrait ripped off the wall and despatched to the servants' quarters or the auction rooms stood for the fickle moods and debased values of the whole scrabbling, desperate town:

> Love ends with hope, the sinking statesman's door
> Pours in the morning worshipper no more;
> For growing names the weekly scribbler lies,
> To growing wealth the dedicator flies,
> From every room descends the painted face,
> That hung the bright Palladium of the place
> And smoked in kitchens or in auctions sold,
> To better features yields the frame of gold;
> For now no more we trace in ev'ry line
> Heroic worth, benevolence divine;
> The form distorted justifies the fall,
> And detestation rids th'indignant wall.[7]

Since 1737 Johnson had been slaving in Grub Street. For the past three years, with six impoverished assistants, he had laboured in the garret at

17 Gough Square off Fleet Street, filling mighty notebooks with quotations to illustrate his great, innovatory *Dictionary*, which he would not complete until 1755. At first sight Johnson's *Dictionary* seems a long way from Hogarth's work, and yet both men were fired by national pride. Both were part of a driving movement in British culture in the mid-century that took its energy from commerce and informal discussion rather than prestigious patrons and academic rules, a movement that sprang from the Town and not the State. While Hogarth fought for British art, Johnson – on his own – was determined to produce a British work that would rival the national dictionary of Italy, fruit of twenty years' labour by the Accademia della Crusca, and that of France, which took the Académie française fifty-five years. And while Hogarth struggled to find exhibition space for English artists and handed on Thornhill's old equipment to the St Martin's Lane Academy, Johnson too was forced to make his own way, as best he could, with *ad hoc*, inadequate resources.

The two men had friends in common, notably David Garrick: one anecdote declares that Hogarth and Garrick first met in 1740, with Johnson looking on, at an amateur performance of Fielding's *The Mock Doctor* at the *Gentleman's Magazine* offices in St John's Gate.[8] But Hogarth and Johnson moved in different circles, and did not really meet until June 1753, at Samuel Richardson's house. Hogarth was volubly defending the King's (relative) leniency towards Dr Archibald Cameron, a rebel of the ''45' whose execution had been staved off until this June, when a new plot to restore the Pretender was uncovered. According to Boswell, while Hogarth was talking,

'he perceived a person standing at a window in the room, shaking his head, and rolling himself about in a strange, ridiculous manner. He concluded that he was an ideot, whom his relations had put under the care of Mr Richardson, as a very good man. To his great surprise, however, this figure stalked forward to where he and Mr Richardson were sitting, and all at once took up the argument.'[9]

Johnson 'burst out into an invective against George II', displaying 'such a power of eloquence, that Hogarth looked at him with astonishment, and actually thought that this ideot had been at the moment inspired'.

The ''45' continued to raise high feelings. It was there in the background of English lives, woven into the narrative of *Tom Jones*, re-created in *The March to Finchley* and evoked in Ramsay's delicate half-length portrait of Flora Macdonald, also painted in 1749 and a bestseller when engraved as a mezzotint.[10] Imprisoned in the Tower for helping Bonnie Prince Charlie escape to Skye, on her release in 1747 Flora became a romantic heroine, just as Lord Lovat had become a classic villain. But for all these popular fictions, memories of the Rebellion were shockingly recent, stiffening the resolve to create a new order, a decency and decorum that went further than 'politeness', a bulwark against the anarchy of society without and the chaos of passions within.

In London a significant group of artists, writers and actors stepped forward to meet this call. They were ranged around the cusp of middle age, across the span of a generation: in 1749 Richardson was sixty, Hogarth fifty-two, Fielding forty-two, Johnson forty and Garrick thirty-two. All these men felt, in different ways, that they must take responsibility for the culture they worked in and try, if they could, to improve it.

Garrick in particular was fired with improving zeal. In 1747 he had acquired a half-share in Drury Lane Theatre, to run for twenty-seven years. His partner, James Lacy, organized the props and the day-to-day running, but Garrick was the creative force. On the night of the opening, 15 September, he was ill and exhausted – he had acted over a hundred different parts in the previous season – but his production of *The Merchant of Venice* heralded a new epoch in the staging of Shakespeare. Garrick himself read the prologue, written for him by Johnson, comparing a past golden age to the current decline. The stage was the mirror of the age, at once reflecting and commanded by its audience:

> Hard is his lot that, here by fortune placed,
> Must watch the wild vicissitudes of taste;
> With ev'ry meteor of caprice must play,
> And chase the new-blown bubbles of the day.
> Ah! let not censure term our fate our choice,
> The stage but echoes back the public voice.
> The drama's laws the drama's patrons give
> For we that live to please, must please to live.[11]

Garrick, however, was prepared to bend only so far towards public demand; Johnson's prologue welcomed a new reign 'Of rescued Nature and reviving Sense'. Determined to refine his *métier*, beginning by breaking the theatre's association with sex, one of Garrick's first acts, announced on the playbill for John Hoadly's *The Suspicious Husband*, was to ban male visitors from the Green Room. He anticipated the fuss in his own epilogue:

472

Sweet doings truly! We are finely fobb'd!
And at one stroke of all our pleasures robb'd!
No beaux behind the scenes! 'tis innovation,
Under the specious name of reformation.
Public complaint, forsooth is made a puff,
Sense, order, decency and such like stuff.[12]

Even Garrick could not impose sense and decency at once. The theatre continued to be a scene of riots and rakes. In January 1748 'gentlemen in the boxes and pit' tore out seats and pulled up floorboards, ripped down hangings, broke partitions and smashed all the mirrors and candle-sconces, because the dance at the end of the show was cancelled. In March, at the first night of Edward Moore's new comedy, *The Foundling*, a gang of young nobles 'made a party to damn it, merely for the love of damnation'. Opposing them, law students from the Temple 'espoused the play and went armed with syringes charged with stinking oil and with sticking plasters for Bubby's [Lord Hobart's] fair hair: but it did not come to action; Garrick was impertinent, and the pretty men gave over their plot'.[13]

Garrick soothed his rowdy audiences and gave them stylish performances, often sabotaging Shakespeare in the process. He played a memorable Macbeth in scarlet coat, silver-laced waistcoat and wig, and in the 1770s would still be unrepentantly delighted at altering *Hamlet*,

'I had sworn I would not leave the stage till I had rescued that noble play from all the rubbish of the fifth act. I have brought it forth without the grave-digger's trick, Osrick & the fencing match.'[14]

It was harder, however, to tinker with plays by a living author like his old friend and teacher, Samuel Johnson. Another landmark of early 1749 was his production of *Irene*, the tragedy Johnson had carried in his pocket when he and Garrick walked to London twelve years before. There were rows. Johnson grumbled about changing the title to *Mahomet and Irene*, and about the way Garrick 'wants me to make Mahomet run mad, that he may have an opportunity of tossing his hands and kicking his heels'.[15] But on 16 February, the play reached the public. The notoriously shabby Johnson dressed up and sat in a side box in a scarlet waistcoat with gold lace and a gold-laced hat. After early cat-calls and whistles, his terse prologue soothed the house and all went well until the end, when Hannah Pritchard as Irene entered with a bowstring round her neck, ready to be strangled. This innovation, breaking the rule of offstage deaths, was too much. Amid terrific uproar, with cries of 'Murder!

473

Murder!', she had to exit and die in the wings, as custom required. Afterwards, Boswell said, when Johnson was asked how he felt, he famously replied, 'Like the Monument', firm after the fire.[16]

The Fleet Street publishers, the Drury Lane stage, the Vauxhall Gardens supper boxes – and the sign of the Golden Head which swung defiantly in Leicester Fields – all marked that margin where politeness and commerce, culture and entertainment flowed together, like tides rippling over estuary bars. On that sandy, shifting margin met men whose private worlds had very different landscapes, wild dunes or stagnant marshes, calm meadows or proud hills. Johnson was struggling, fighting guilt and love as his wife Tetty, rouged and flaring, drank herself sadly to death in a rented country house in Hampstead. Fielding had grappled his way into the magistrate's seat at Bow Street but his life still lurched into extremes. In 1747 he married his second wife, Mary Daniels, the twenty-six-year-old housekeeper who had comforted him after his beloved Charlotte died three years before; to the delight of scandal-mongerers Mary was already six months pregnant. In January 1749, when *Tom Jones* was printed, she bore their second child, Mary Amelia, but the baby died before the next year came.

In domestic as well as public life, Garrick, by contrast, was bursting with *joie de vivre*, infatuated with the enchanting, bubbly Viennese dancer Eva Maria Veigel, 'La Violette'. She was widely, but falsely, rumoured to be the illegitimate daughter of Burlington's father, and Lady Burlington publicly took her under her wing. For a long time the Burlingtons hoped for a fine match for their protégée and Garrick stood disconsolately by, but on 22 June 1749 they were finally married, with the Earl's blessing and a dowry of £6000. Though there were tiffs, Garrick's letters dance with amused love; towards the end of his life he wrote, 'I have not left Mrs Garrick one day since we were Married, Near 28 years.'[17]

From this year, too, dates the only letter found from Hogarth to his wife. When June arrived, Jane and Lady Thornhill were in the country while Hogarth was sweating in Leicester Fields, painting *The March to Finchley*. The heat was stifling, 'as hot' said the papers, 'as it usually is in Jamaica'. On 6 June Hogarth put down his brush and took up his pen, the drums and ballads of his Finchley picture weaving into his prose.

'Dear Jenny

'I write to you now, not because I think you may expect it only, but because I find a pleasure in it, which is more than I can say of writing to any body else, and I insist on it you don't take it for a mere complement, your last letter pleased more than I'll say, but this I will own if the postman should knock at the door in a weeks time after the receipt of this, I shall think there is more musick in't than the beat of a Kettle Drum, & if the words to the tune are made by you (to carry on metafor) and bring news of your all coming so soon to town I shall think the words much better than the musick, but don't hasten out of a scene of Pleasure to make me one (I wish I could contribute to it – s.t.) you'l see by the Enclosed that I shall be glad to be a small contributor to it.'[18]

Never at ease as a correspondent, he stuck to his single sheet, enclosing money as his 'contribution' to the rural holiday. His spelling was better than usual, but his strong voice remains, with its mingled note of affection and restraint. Others too remained in town, and he passed on the latest news:

'I dont know whether or no you knew that Garrick was going to be married to the Violette when you went away. I supt with him last night and had a deal of talk about her. I can't write any more than what this side will contain, you know I wont turn over a new leaf I am so obstinate, but then I am no less obstinate in being your affectionate Husband

'Wm Hogarth'

After that formal signature, along the side of the note, he wrote 'Complement as usual', sending his regards to her mother.

When Steevens sneeringly implied that Hogarth could not finish *The Happy Marriage* because 'he rarely ventured to exhibit scenes with which he was not perfectly acquainted', Hogarth's friend Thomas Morell wrote at once to Nichols.[19] Hogarth's excellencies and foibles were so universally known, said Morell, 'that I cannot add to the former, nor shall I attempt to palliate the latter'. But, he added,

'to assert, however, that he had little or no acquaintance with domestic happiness, is unjust. I cannot say, I have seen much fondling between *Jenny* and *Billy* (the common apellation of each other); but I have been an almost daily witness of sufficient endearments to conclude them a happy couple.'[20]

Hogarth's family was composed of women – his wife, his mother-in-law and his sister Anne. By now, he and Jane knew there would be no children, and the atmosphere of the house was calm, a little dull even, broken only by Hogarth's occasional outbursts. Little glimpses suggest that at home Hogarth felt easy, even playful. Although, according to John Ireland, he never played cards, Jane would make up a party of her friends to play quadrille and he would watch, taking the winner's counters which were placed in a 'pool' in the middle, and thence known as 'fish', and would 'cut upon them scales, fins, heads etc, so as to give them some degree of character'.[21] Hogarth was a responsible and careful head of the household, known for his tenderness and liberality to his family. He was liberal and fair to his servants, too, and one of his finest pictures pays tribute to them. They have no names – one may be old Ben Ives, and another perhaps a 'Mrs Chappell of Great Smith Street, Westminster', who was with the Hogarths for many years, but their personalities overcome their anonymity.[22] Hogarth simply painted their heads against a plain background – a device that combines apparent spontaneity with a carefully judged composition, a formal arrangement of two semi-circles, one above the other, lit from the left. In front are his two maids and his middle-aged footman and behind them the cook, the elderly butler and the houseboy, full-lipped and open-eyed, with his hair brushed carefully for his sitting. It is one of the most profound and tender of Hogarth's paintings, a tribute to the beauty of the 'ordinary'.

144 *Heads of Six of Hogarth's Servants* (c. 1750)

Around these private lives rolled the clamour of London, its population swelled by hundreds of ragged soldiers and sailors discharged after the war.[23] Although the treaty had long been signed, this year the government planned to celebrate in the highest style. It hired the famous Cavaliere Jean-Nicholas Servandoni, a Florentine who was now a director of the Paris Opéra, to design and build a machine for the greatest ever display of fireworks. Servandoni's 'machine' (popularly known as 'Cracker Castle') was erected in Green Park, close to St James's Palace. It was shaped like a Doric temple, 114 feet high, with wings and stylish pavilions, incorporating a musicians' gallery and twenty-three statues by the young Italian statuary, Andrea Casali – the climax of the fireworks would come when eighteen pictures, like marble bas-reliefs, were transformed with innumerable lamps into a tableau of George II handing Peace to Britannia, Neptune and Mars.

The display was planned for 27 April, and

'for a week before, the town was like a country fair, the streets filled from morning to night, scaffolds building wherever you could or could not see; and coaches arriving from every corner of the kingdom'.[24]

Galleries were built for leading citizens along the Mall, and when the great evening arrived thousands of people swarmed into the Park, the courtiers and gentry squeezing into the special enclosures to protect them from the mass. Thousands more men, women and children clustered on rooftops or packed into boats in the Thames. The royal party, including the Dukes of Bedford, Richmond and Montagu, toured the edifice and the King handed out purses of gold. At half past eight the orchestra launched into Handel's special *Fireworks Music*, grudgingly altered to comply with George's martial taste by replacing the violins with a mass of brass and wind instruments. As 101 brass cannon thundered and boomed into the dusk, the fireworks were lit.

The effect was not what was hoped. It was a hot drizzly night and many fireworks simply fizzled out or would not light. Anxious men applied torches recklessly, anywhere, and smoke began to fill the sky. A startled labourer crashed to his death from a scaffold; a woman fell overboard from a boat on the Thames; a cobbler, the worse for drink, fell into a pond and drowned; a wayward rocket whizzed into the grandstand and set a young woman's dress on fire. Before the eyes of the horrified crowd, one of the 'pavilions' burst into flames. A desperate Servandoni, drawing his sword and crying *'What, will you let my Building burn!'*, hurled himself at the organizer, Charles Frederick, Controller of His Majesty's Fireworks. Servandoni was seized, carried to the Palace guardroom and, after two nights in the cells, was discharged on providing substantial bonds for good behaviour. The magistrate was Henry Fielding.

This fiasco was sandwiched between events that suggested where cultural control really lay. Transposed to different settings, the fireworks and the music illuminated the four faces of London patronage: the State, the aristocrat, the 'projector' and the charitable public. A week before Green Park, Jonathan Tyers put on a public rehearsal of Handel's *Fireworks Music* at Vauxhall. Tyers had made a deal with the Duke of Montagu, who was paying for much of the State display, providing his skilled Vauxhall staff, illuminations and huge, back-lit 'transparencies' (like those showing the flames of *The Fall of Troy* when Hogarth was a boy) in return for staging Handel's concert. The main problem was persuading a reluctant Handel to release the score.[25] By 21 April this obstacle had been overcome, and the crowd crossing London Bridge was so dense 'that no carriage could pass for 3 hours' and 'the footmen were so numerous as to obstruct the passage, so that a scuffle happen'd in which some gentlemen were wounded'.[26] Despite these alarms, the perfomance by a band of a hundred musicians took place peacefully before twelve thousand people. Although the entrance fee was raised from 1s to 2/6d, quality and mob mingled freely. There were no fireworks but the music was excellent, the pleasure great and the profit and prestige enormous.

The Vauxhall show was public entrepreneurial culture. A different new force, public charitable culture, was evident a month later when the *Fireworks Music* was performed in the new Chapel of the Foundling Hospital on 27 May, under the direction of Handel himself, who had been elected a Governor three weeks before. The Prince and Princess of Wales were present, tickets were half a guinea and, with an audience of a thousand, the Governors were well pleased. And between these two events came a show of private, not public patronage. A week after the Green Park show (while London was enjoying a print of Cracker Castle, '*The Grand Whim for Posterity to Laugh At*') the Duke of Richmond mounted his own display from his house on the Thames, using what could be rescued from the twenty-five tons of royal fireworks. Charles Frederick once again took charge, this time successfully. The Richmond family and guests watched from the terrace and the King lounged in the royal barge with a crown on its roof. The beau monde gathered: 'Lady Burlington brought the Violette and the Richmonds had asked Garrick, who stood ogling and sighing the whole time, while my Lady kept a most fierce lookout.'[27] Everything proceeded with miraculous, shimmering magic – rockets from the river, Catherine wheels from the banks, Roman candles from the railings; '200 water mines, 20 air balloons,

478

5000 water rockets, 5000 sky rockets, 100 fire showers, 20 suns and a hundred stars'.[28]

*

The fireworks reflected on the river that night, adding a brilliant lustre to the diamonds of the rich, also flickered across alleys and night shelters, hovels and huts. In this febrile post-war mood the city's extremes seemed more striking than ever. The day after the Green Park show, a Venetian spectacle was held at Ranelagh, with maypoles and harlequins, gondolas and orange trees and little booths selling Dresden china and Japan ware: all the shopkeepers wore masks. To those who inhabited this world, the death of a labourer and cobbler the day before meant nothing. Indeed, in casualties, as in everything, Britain was best. 'Very little mischief was done', wrote Walpole,

'and but two persons killed: at Paris there were forty killed, and near three hundred wounded, by a dispute between the French and Italians in the management, who quarrelling for precedence in lighting the fires, both lighted at one and blew up the whole. Our mob was extremely tranquil, and very unlike those I remember in my father's time, when it was a measure in the Opposition to work up everything to mischief, the Excise and the French players, the Convention and the Gin Act.'[29]

But things were not so different. This year, as a magistrate, Henry Fielding came face to face daily with the disorder of the capital. In that steaming June, when Hogarth wrote to Jane and Garrick married Eva Maria, Fielding gave his 'Address to the Grand Jury' at the Westminster Quarter Sessions, calling on citizens to be 'Censors of the Nation', rooting out blasphemy and political disaffection, indecency, brothel-keeping, gaming houses and masquerades. All these were seen as pervasive diseases, 'which have so inserted themselves in the Blood of the Body Politic, that they are perhaps never to be totally eradicated'. If he could not cure them, the magistrate's duty was to 'palliate and keep down' such ills.[30]

From the moment he became Justice of the Peace in December 1748, Fielding used the press to enrol citizens in this cause. After gaoling a laid-off sailor called John Jones, who had severely wounded a girl with his cutlass, he reminded readers that carrying a weapon was an ancient offence, and added,

'It's hoped that all Persons who have lately been robb'd or attack'd in the Streets, by Men in Sailors Jackets, in which dress the said Jones appear'd, will give themselves the Trouble of resorting to the Prison in order to view him.'[31]

Fielding had trouble with sailors in 1749. On Saturday afternoon of 1 July, a group of tars claimed to have been cheated and bullied at a brothel. Gathering their shipmates, they returned at night with a mob and tore the brothel apart. Pictures, mirrors, feather beds, hoops and gowns were hurled from the windows; the women were turned naked into the street and the pyre of belongings was set alight. For two nights the pattern was repeated, and the whole Strand would have been ablaze had not Saunders Welch, High Constable for Holborn, called the garrison and arrested the looters. Fielding sent three men to the Grand Jury, but the only one to hang was a Devon man, Bosavern Penlez: Lord Chief Justice Sir John Willes rejected the jury's plea for mercy and refused, three times, to advise the King to grant a pardon. The trouble was that Penlez was probably an innocent caught up in the fray, convicted on the dubious evidence of a brothel-owner. When he swung at Tyburn on 18 October, a vast crowd, including thousands of sailors with cutlasses and bludgeons, stopped his body being taken for dissection.

A month later, in a local by-election, Fielding supported the ministerial candidate, the twenty-six-year-old Viscount Trentham, who was funded by his brother-in-law, the Duke of Bedford (Fielding's patron, owner of much property in Westminster and deeply disliked), and supported by the Duke of Cumberland. His opponent, Sir George Vandeput, a wealthy merchant, was put forward by the 'Independent Electors of Westminster' and promoted by the Prince of Wales. Trentham was attacked for his failure to intervene to save Penlez, and his sponsorship of French actors at the Little Theatre in the Haymarket, where he hired armed bullies as protection. That November electors carried banners proclaiming 'UNITED FOR OUR COUNTRY. NO FRENCH STROLLERS'.[32] In his crusade for order, Henry Fielding, 'Censor of the Nation', now found himself labelled as the tool of corrupt brothel-owners, corrupt politicians and anti-British interests.

Tripped up by politics, Fielding returned to the fight, and in 1751 he would draw Hogarth into the campaign against drunkenness and crime. But although Hogarth had been moving towards stressing the 'usefulness' of his art, especially in *Industry and Idleness*, his swerve to strictness was less drastic. And his own prejudices made him slightly out of sympathy with his friend. His engraving of *The Gate of Calais*, published in early March, had much of the crude nationalism of the banner against 'French Strollers'. His print of Tom Idle's execution and his later fierce caricature of Judge Willes in *The Bench*, make one doubt that he approved the hanging of Penlez. The painting of the grenadiers at the Tottenham crossroads that he was working on during the June riots showed that he could admire, as well as criticize, lustily anarchic soldiers and sailors.

480

Hogarth hated cliques. He judged on issues. Thus he could support Cumberland as the victor of Culloden, but recoil from his butchery and from his brutality as a disciplinarian. (In February 1748, when soldiers on three-year contracts after the ''45' finished their time and went home without waiting for proper papers, Cumberland ordered them to be shot for desertion.) And in any case, at this stage, Hogarth was closer to the opposition around the Prince of Wales than to Fielding's Bedford–Cumberland sponsors. So when the opportunity came to roast Cumberland, he took it, making sure that his joke was for private friends only. In 1749 he painted a small picture of a young hurdy-gurdy player, *The Savoyard Girl*, for George Hay, the lawyer and politician.[33] This alluded to a young woman Cumberland had chased, an enjoyable scandal that led to a rash of prints of the enormously fat Duke hot in pursuit.

Hogarth's picture also hinted at another recent embarrassment for Cumberland, the 'Bottle-conjuror' drama of January 1749. Organized by the Duke of Montagu, to see just how credulous the public could be, this was one of the most famous hoaxes of the century, food for political prints for the next seventy years. An advertisement announced that among other marvels, a gentleman would get into a quart bottle on a table in the middle of the Haymarket stage, and sing in it. The theatre was packed to suffocation and when the conjuror failed to appear the audience roared for their money back, gutted the pit and gallery, tore up benches, broke lamps, and burned the lot in a huge bonfire outside. Cumberland was one of the gullible, losing his sword in the crush: in Hogarth's *Savoyard Girl*, his broken sword lies against the mantelpiece.

City life was fraught and fevered and Hogarth meant it when he told Jane that he wished he could get out of London, for a time at least. The heatwave of 1749 continued through July and August, leaving the trees parched and the grass burned brown as rust. As it drew to a close Hogarth made a move to secure himself a more permanent refuge than the summer lodgings that he and Jane had rented since their marriage. In September he bought a house in Chiswick, a few miles upriver from London.

The village clung to the eastern side of a looping bend in the Thames, gliding down from Richmond and Staines. In fact there were three main villages on this promontory. Trailing across the top, along the busy road from London, was Turnham Green, a string of houses and livery stables and great inns which formed the real social centre of the neighbourhood with their horses and bowling greens and games. In summer the street was alive before dawn, when the market gardeners began loading their carts with strawberries and cherries, asparagus, peas and beans, to catch the early markets. Small though it was, Turnham Green had its share of the new 'scientific farmers', experimenting with techniques such as undercropping and cultivation under glass, trying to make the profit margins that would beat competitors in the rush to supply London's swelling population.[34]

On the western side of the river bend was Strand-on-the-Green, with its small dock and its own industry: five malting houses, where barley was malted on quite a large scale, the river allowing easy transport of grain in and malt out. From here, the river dipped south and then north again through beds of osiers and willows, carefully cut and harvested to weave into baskets for the market gardeners. Behind them lay broad meadows, prone to flooding in winter, providing rich pasture for the slow dairy herds; and behind these lay fields of waving corn. As the broad Thames flowed past – far wider and shallower than in later years, after the banks were built up – its slow waters divided around a long, swampy island, Chiswick eyot. Sheltering behind this lay the old village itself.

In Hogarth's day Chiswick was a sleepy, rural corner. A long lane curved down from the main road to Turnham Green, ending in a cobbled street where fine brick houses with railings jostled with weatherboard cottages. The old church of St Nicholas stood – and still stands – here, on a bluff overlooking the river: much restored in the nineteenth century, it still retains its ancient tower. Next to it the ferry pulled up to carry people over to Mortlake on the southern bank. Other boatmen were more like cab-drivers, their wherries stopping at the river steps or anywhere convenient: the traffic was constant and Hogarth was as likely to come up from town by river as by road. Where Chiswick Lane met the river front, on the sloping shingle draw-dock barges were beached on the tide to unload coal and pick up beer, corn, and fruit. Between them children and pigs roamed freely all day long. (Later a wall was constructed around the churchyard to keep out pigs, 'and other profanations'.) Further downstream, from Chiswick to Hammersmith, gardens stretched down to the water.

At the beginning of the eighteenth century only shopkeepers, small traders and watermen lived along this waterside but during the reigns of Anne and George I new houses sprang up, creating the fine Chiswick Mall.[35] For a time the old cottages squashed in cheek by jowl with the mansions, but gradually the fishermen were driven out, pushed back into the narrow alleys behind the church. Chiswick was becoming not exactly fashionable but more select. It had always had its grand houses and there were several substantial mansions and manor houses in the neighbourhood. The Prebendal Manor, where John Donne had briefly lived, stood on the Mall at the bottom of Chiswick Lane; next door was the fine College House, where boys from Westminster School were sent in times of fever in London. The medieval manor had by now been replaced with a new brick house, one of several in the area where James Ralph lived at different times, later occupied by the dazzling hostesses Mary and Agnes Berry, the 'twin wives' of Horace Walpole. Walpole House and Orford House, where Horace's relations lived, stood at the other end of the Mall. Other great houses included Corney House, the old seat of the Russell family; Sutton Court, leased to the Burlington estate by the Fauconbergs; and Grove House, which now belonged to Sir Thomas Robinson, one of the signatories to the treaty of Aix-la-Chapelle who would prove an inept Leader of the House of Commons in the 1750s.

So when Hogarth moved to Chiswick he did not leave the 'great world' behind. And in one particular sense he became its neighbour. Behind the village, bounded by the swing of the Thames, lay Chiswick House, the estate of Lord Burlington and the site of his most loving and intimate (and costly) architectural and landscaping indulgences. In the late 1720s, after the west wing of the old Jacobean mansion was badly damaged by fire, Burlington built his beautiful villa, designed by himself and based on Palladio's famous Villa Capra, near Vicenza. This was connected by the 'link-building' to the remaining part of the old house. Sneered at by Hervey as 'too small to live in and too large to hang on a watch chain', the villa was built with the finest craftsmanship, its ceilings painted by Kent. Once it was finished, Burlington bought and leased land all around and over the years, largely thanks to Kent, he created a memorable garden, with avenues and glades, a lake and cascade, a graceful Palladian bridge, temple, orangery, bath-house, aviary and Deer House.[36] Throughout, winding paths gave glinting vistas. It was a teasing, artificial Eden, where nature and art embraced at the patron's will, as Pope implied in his epistle:

> To build, to plant, whatever you intend,
> To rear the Column, or the Arch to bend,
> To swell the Terras, or to sink the Grot;
> In all, let Nature never be forgot.
> But treat the Goddess like a modest fair,
> Not over-dress, nor leave her wholly bare;
> Let not each Beauty ev'ry where be spy'd,
> Where half the skill is decently to hide.

He gains all point, who pleasingly confounds,
Surprises, varies, and conceals the Bounds.[37]

(The last couplet is very like Hogarth's aims for *his* art.)

Kent had plans for a *giardino segreto* and a Flower Garden Temple. But in 1738, when Burlington's debts reached over £200,000, the landscaping had to stop. Although Burlington went to his Yorkshire estates in the summer, Chiswick remained his best-loved retreat, where he and Kent sprawled on the grass while his wife Dorothy sketched. Here George Lambert painted a series of scenes in 1742, almost certainly with figures by Hogarth. Here Garrick spent part of his honeymoon in July 1749, and here, that September, William Hogarth bought a house that almost backed on to Burlington's grounds. It is as if he were both laying claim to the territory, like an invader, and making peace after Kent's death the year before. Peace with himself, that is, since Burlington could shrug off Hogarth's criticism as he would brush off a fly that landed on his hat.

In the parish poor-rate books for 1753, Chiswick House is listed as 'rent' £180 and 'rate' £4.10.0. In comparison, the rent for Hogarth's house was £10.00 and the rate 5s: it was really the equivalent of a weekend cottage. It may be that he and Jane had rented their property in Chiswick for several years before they bought it, on Wednesday, 13 September 1749. That day, the court of the manor was held in 'Bowling Green House'. Hogarth was there and so were Anne and George Ruperti, mother and son, the current copyhold owners of a brick house completed in 1718, with garden and orchard. Before the court Anne assigned her third of the property to George, who declared he had sold the whole, 'To the Use and Behoof of William Hogarth of Leicester Fields in the Parish of St Martin in the Fields in the Parish of Middlesex Gentln. – his heirs and Assigns for ever'.[38] Hogarth paid sixpence to Susannah Sharp, the lady of the manor, and was admitted to the copyhold.

Hogarth's house was on the very far corner of the village, the last house of all: locals would even say it was not in Chiswick at all, but in 'North End', a cluster of cottages just north of the Burlington estate. It was reached by a track leading off Chiswick Lane, which ran down to the church from the turnpike, but after Hogarth's gate this track disappeared, fading into a wheelbarrow path or bridleway cutting through the market gardens across to Little Sutton.

The house was not grand but even today, as the juggernauts and rush-hour traffic trundle over the flyover, and the airport bus stops outside on the way to Heathrow, it is oddly peaceful, cut off and quiet. Now, as in his time, the house is hidden from public gaze, blocked off from the outside world by a high brick

145 Hogarth House

wall. The doorway in the wall is unpretentious (although Garrick gave Hogarth two great lead urns to dignify his gateposts), and stepping down on to the broad flagged path, the noise drops away. Within the wall stretches a long triangular garden, with a mulberry tree said to have been there in Hogarth's day: it is said, too, that there were alleys of trees where he played skittles, and Rocque's map of 1746 does show rows of trees, perhaps an orchard. The house stands at a skewed right-angle to the road, with a glazed front door beneath an overhanging, slightly lopsided bay window. When Hogarth bought it it seems to have been a two-storey cottage, but over the years he added a new kitchen with a room above and raised the roof to provide a third storey, with a curved stairway leading to garrets above.

This is a country village house, oddly shaped, built of rough warm brick, with no claims to elegant Georgian proportions. Its back wall, hunched against London, has no opening except for two high windows: when he came there from Leicester Fields all Hogarth's views looked away from the city, north-west over the garden, and beyond that across the lane and the common fields, gardens and orchards. Inside, a small entrance hall faced a narrow curving staircase. On the left was the dining room, where guests were received, and on the right the kitchen, which would have had a scullery and pantry beyond. There were effectively four storeys. On the first floor there

485

were just three rooms: Hogarth's bedroom, above the dining room; a small parlour with the sloping bay window and another room beyond, each with wood-panelled walls and inset cupboards. Other relatives, and perhaps some of the grander servants, had rooms on the floor above, their gabled windows looking out to the open country. At the very top, the servants slept in the roof space.

When John Ireland visited the house after Jane's death, he found none of Hogarth's prints there, just framed engravings of Thornhill's paintings for St Paul's, and heads of Shakespeare, Spenser and Dryden, done by Houbraken. He added that,

'the garden is laid out in a good style: over the door is a cast of George II's mask, in lead; and in one corner a rude and shapeless stone, placed upright against the wall and inscribed

ALAS, POOR DICK!
1760
AGED ELEVEN

'Beneath the inscriptions are two cross bones of birds, surmounted with a heart and death's head. The sculpture was made with a nail, by the hand of Hogarth, and placed there in memory of a favourite bullfinch, who is deposited beneath.'[39]

Often the house was full, with Hogarth, Jane, Lady Thornhill, Anne Hogarth and later Jane's cousin, Mary Lewis, and other visitors. There was no room indoors for Hogarth to work and his studio was at the far end of the garden above the stables, a wooden building with a pointed roof, a rickety outside staircase and one large window. Here Hogarth could paint or work on his prints, listening to his bullfinch and stopping to walk with Pugg down to the Burlington Arms or the Feathers.

If he turned down the lane past Burlington's estate, he could stride over to see John Ranby, five years his junior but now Principal Serjeant-Surgeon to George II and to the Chelsea Hospital. The two men knew each other of old (indeed Ranby was alleged to have sat to him as a model Tom Rakewell) and their paths had often overlapped; Ranby was also a friend of Fielding, who took his side in the heated pamphlet disputes over the treatment of the dying Sir Robert Walpole.[40] Hogarth had sketched the rural view from the south, across the cornfields towards Ranby's house, rising above the buttressed wall of the lane, next door to the old Jacobean mansion of the Burlingtons.[41] In the 1750s he painted fresh and moving portraits of Ranby's natural children, his daughter Hannah and his son George Osborne, aged about nine and six.

a View of Mr Ranby the Surgeon's house, Taken from Hogarth's window at Chiswick

146 View of Ranby's House (1750)

Theirs was an unconventional but accepted household: George, who was brought up as Ranby's heir, always cherished the memory of their mother, who died in 1746, but her name is unknown, erased from all family documents.[42]

There were many such liaisons, frowned on by the more decorous age that followed. They rarely troubled Hogarth's friends, here or in London. At Chiswick the network of acquaintances depended less on proximity than shared interests. The professional men, writers and artists who had houses here would have met, anyway, in the coffee houses and clubs, and their focus was on the city, not the local community. But the geography of summer stays brought them closer and the web of Hogarth's contacts spun across and along the river – to Samuel Scott and Horace Walpole near Twickenham and soon to Garrick, who bought a house at Hampton five years later. One friend in the immediate neighbourhood was James Ralph, now editing a new political journal, *The Remembrancer*. Journalists abounded. Another local man was the twenty-two-year-old Arthur Murphy, who lived in Hammersmith Terrace, editor of the *Gray's Inn Journal* and soon to be a successful playwright, assistant and perpetual gadfly to Garrick. Others included the editors of the new *Monthly Review*, Ralph Griffiths of Linden House in Turnham Green, and William Rose, a classicist and headmaster of a school at Bradmore House in Chiswick Lane for thirty years.[43]

Hogarth's closest friend here was the Reverend Thomas Morell of

487

Wm Hogarth del.   James Basire.sculp.

T.MORELL, S.T.P-S.S.A.

147 *Thomas Morell*, engraved by Basire (1762)

Turnham Green, twelve years his junior. Morell was later satirized by Hogarth's opponents as a sycophantic hanger-on, but this does him an injustice. He was a classical scholar, a diligent pastor and a sympathetic man of wide interests. Since 1746 he had been the librettist for Handel's oratorios, beginning with *Judas Maccabeus*, 'designed as a compliment to the Duke of Cumberland, upon his returning victorious from Scotland'.[44] Among their collaborations was *Theodora*, completed this year, in 1749, a story of early Christian martyrdom based on the novel by Robert Boyle, the seventeenth-century scientist: it contained Handel's own favourite chorus 'He saw the lovely youth', which he preferred to anything in *Messiah*. The shabby, generous Morell 'matched intellectual catholicity with sound dramatic instincts and an alertness to Handel's idiosyncratic genius'.[45] He got on well with Handel – who left him £200 in his will – as with everyone. Remembering Hogarth, another idiosyncratic genius, he said that from the time he came to

488

Chiswick he 'was intimate with him to his death, and very happy in his acquaintance'.[46] His loyal and jovial nature was summed up in Nichols's *Literary Anecdotes*:

'He was warm in his attachments, and was a cheerful and entertaining companion. He loved a jest, told a good story, was fond of musick, and would occasionally indulge his friends with a song. In his exterior appearances, however, he never condescended to study the Graces; and unfortunately for himself, he was a total stranger to Œconomy.'[47]

In Chiswick among such friends, Hogarth, like his house, could turn his back on the town. He could plan his house, walk his pug and work above the stables, amid the scents and sounds of the market gardens. But the city was still his subject and his province. However much he prized his country box, he was a cit at heart, and could never stay away from London streets for long.

24

Cruelty

I must, I will have gin! – that skillet take,
Pawn it. – No more I'll roast, or boil, or bake.
This juice immortal must each want supply;
Starve on, ye brats! so I but bung my eye.
ANON, 'Strip me Naked, or Royal Gin for Ever' (1751)

'Heark ye, Mr. what d'ye call um . . . what is the name of the
dauber who painted that miserable performance?'
TOBIAS SMOLLETT, *Peregrine Pickle* (1751)

IN JANUARY 1750 Horace Walpole told Horace Mann, in Florence,

'You will hear little news from England, but of robberies; the numbers of disbanded soldiers and sailors have all taken to the road, or rather to the street, people are almost afraid of stirring after it is dark.'

He himself was held up, and his temple was grazed by a stray bullet; by summertime highwaymen were laying siege to coaches in broad daylight in the middle of Piccadilly. The previous year had seen the riots in the Strand and at the playhouse and the storming of the Gatehouse prison by a gang of armed ruffians. Disorder seemed to spread from street to State; the passions roused by the Westminster Elections were kept at fever pitch by a Parliamentary Inquiry, and the Dukes of Newcastle and Bedford were at loggerheads over a Turnpike Bill; even Britain's roads were ruinous and impassable.

When Hogarth arranged the auction of *The March to Finchley* in March, his painting looked like a comment on the prevailing chaos and a statement of faith in the soldiers and sailors now driven to crime. There was a narrow line between anarchy and British 'liberty', as Johnson pointed out: 'They who complain in peace of the insolence of the populace, must remember that their insolence is bravery in war.'[1] Hogarth's painting, with its free-flowing crowd in the foreground and disciplined ranks in the rear, was topical, too, since from 1749 to 1751 Parliament was fiercely debating the Mutiny Bill, promoted

490

by Cumberland and introduced by Fox, as Secretary of War, to bring greater order into the army. From *Industry and Idleness* onwards, Hogarth had been preoccupied with the difficult balance between freedom and control. Although drawn to variety and spontaneity, in his prints he argued increasingly for order and self-discipline, as if haunted by premonitions of disaster.

Londoners were prone to premonitions. They looked for omens. Some thought the 'Black Sessions' at the Old Bailey – when four judges, four barristers, the Lord Mayor and forty jurors contracted gaol fever and died – was a judgment on the bench for ordering too few executions. Others noted that the weather in January was unnaturally hot, and seeing a 'bloody cloud' overhead, brooded on storms to come. The next month their pessimism seemed vindicated. At noon on 8 February, 'the shock of an earthquake was felt over the cities of London and Westminster . . . people ran out of their houses, the chairs shaking and the pewter rattling on the shelves'.[2] Exactly a month later came a second quake, more violent than the first. Between one and two in the morning of 8 March the earth shivered, beds rose beneath their sleeping occupants, there was a violent vibration and roaring, old houses collapsed, chimneys tumbled, china crashed, bells rang.

In the aftermath, gamblers laid bets on a third quake and parsons preached sermons on sin. An article in *The Gentleman's Magazine* began, 'Earthquakes are evidently placed among those methods by which God punishes a wicked and rebellious people.'[3] Irreligious Londoners trembled. Many, anticipating a third shock on 8 April (following a monthly pattern), fled from the town: the hall for one of Handel's most popular oratorios, *Judas Maccabeus*, was virtually empty.[4] On 2 April Walpole noted that 'this frantic terror prevails so much, that within these three days 730 coaches have been counted passing Hyde Park Corner, with whole parties removing into the country'.[5] In his *History*, Smollett wrote,

'In after ages it will hardly be believed, that on the evening of the eighth day of April, the open fields, that skirt the metropolis, were filled with incredible numbers of people assembled in chairs, in chaises, and coaches, as well as on foot, who waited in the most fearful suspense until morning, and the return of day disproved the dreadful prophecy.'[6]

Five days after this scare, declaring that 'not a Fribble, Bully, Wicked, or Damned-Clever Fellow' had been left in town, the *General Advertiser* suggested that 'If Mr. Hogarth were to oblige the Town with a Print of these woeful wretches in their Fright and Flight, it could not be disagreeable.'[7] Hogarth declined, but many others seized on these alarms to berate the state of the nation. Thomas Sherlock, Bishop of London since Edmund Gibson's death in 1748, wrote a pastoral letter on the earthquake as a divine judgment. Published on 16 March, it sold two thousand copies in two days, and eventually obtained over fifty thousand subscriptions. While its theology was dubious, its analysis of prevailing ills was typical, and the print shops and publishers came in for their share of the blame:

'Have not the abominations of the public stews been opened to view by lewd pictures exposed at noonday? . . . Have not histories or romances of the vilest prostitutes been published? . . . The press for many years past swarmed with books, some to dispute, some to ridicule the great truths of religion.'[8]

Sherlock's targets were not very different from Fielding's in his *Charge to the Grand Jury*: blasphemy, sex, gambling and a general moral decline. Yet the 'lewd' books he referred to included not only John Cleland's *Fanny Hill* (banned on 16 March) but also *Tom Jones*. (Paris had not read *Tom Jones* and Paris had not suffered an earthquake; *ergo Tom Jones* was to blame.)[9] And the favourite print-shop scenes included *A Harlot's Progress*.

Fielding and Hogarth were often bracketed in the public mind. Fielding praised Hogarth in *Tom Jones*, and Hogarth provided a frontispiece for Fielding's ironic *Jacobite's Journal* of 1747–8, in which he lampooned the opposition, as the blustering John Trott-Plaid. Both were associated with 'low' art, and in June 1750 one commentator, imagining people gawping at Hogarth's *The Painter and his Pug* in a print-shop window and wondering why man and dog were on the same level, rammed the point home:

> 'Tis *Hogarth* himself and his honest friend *Towser*,
> Inseparate companions! and therefore you see
> Cheek by jowl they are drawn in familiar degree;
> Both striking the eye with an equal éclat,
> The biped *This* here, and the quadruped *That* –
> You mean – the great dog and the man, I suppose,
> Or the man and the dog – be't just as you chuse. –
>
> Great Dog! why great man! methinks you should say.
> Split the difference my friend, they're both great in their way.
> Is't he then so famous for drawing a punk,
> A Harlot, a Rake, and a Parson so drunk,
> Whom *Trotplaid* delivers to praise as his friend?
> Thus a Jackanapes a Lion would fain recommend –[10]

But in 1751 these allies turned serious. Fielding, the reformed Jackanapes, investigated crime and despair in his sombre novel *Amelia*. And Hogarth, the Lion, confronted the grimmer side of life in his prints of *Gin Lane* and *The Four Stages of Cruelty*.

A spate of pamphlets attacked lawlessness, whether punished by the earthquake or not, but Fielding was the most assiduous in searching for the cause in society, not in the individual sinner. His attitude was ambivalent. While asserting that the 'luxury' of the rich brought prosperity and employment, he blamed the ethic of emulation that encouraged men and women to live above their station, leapfrogging up the social ladder and leaving those at the bottom with no recourse – if they too were to emulate the well-off – except crime and gambling. His compassion was evident both on the bench and in his writings. He forced Members of Parliament to enter the houses of the poor, where they could see 'such Pictures of human Misery as must move the Compassion of every Heart that deserves the Name of human':

'What indeed must be his Composition who could see whole Families in Want of every Necessary of Life, oppressed with Hunger, Cold, Nakedness and Filth, and with Diseases, the certain Consequence of all these; what, I say, must be his Composition, who could look into such a Scene as this, and be affected only in his Nostrils?'[11]

Ultimately, social pressures might be to blame for this stinking squalor, but Fielding could also see that the immediate cause of misery was more concrete, the widespread, habitual drinking of gin. In his *Enquiry into the Causes of the late Increase of Robbers*, published in January 1751, he made this a central issue:

'A new kind of drunkenness, unknown to our ancestors, is lately sprung up among us, and which if not put a stop to, will infallibly destroy a great part of the inferior people. The drunkenness I here intend is . . . by this Poison called Gin . . . the principal sustenance (if it may be so called) of more than a hundred thousand people in this Metropolis.'[12]

Gin, which had arrived from Holland sixty years before with William and Mary, was a huge source of profit to farmers and distillers, and a hideous curse to the poor. To the desperate and destitute gin was cheap and warming. It silenced crying children, brought oblivion from cold and hunger, and its use 'was a passion among beggars and the inmates of workhouses and prisons'.[13] It was sold from shops and street stalls, back rooms and cellars, in quart bottles, tumblers or small dram flagons. It tasted vile, more like rubbing alcohol than subtle juniper berries, and it was horribly potent, leaving drinking dens and gutters littered with collapsed bodies.

Most gin distilling took place in London, and it was nigh impossible to regulate; like all drugs it offered a cut to small-time sellers, people with no other means of going into business. After the stillborn Gin Act of 1736, hated paid informers secured nearly five thousand convictions for illegal sale, but gin-drinking still rose. In 1743 the Act was repealed in favour of a diluted version that stopped the retail sales from small distillers: when this Act was modified after a petition four years later consumption rose again. In 1750, when the constables set out to collect information to support the campaign for a new act, they found that there were still over a thousand licensed gin shops in the City (one house in fifteen) and 1,300 licensed and 900 unlicensed in Westminster (one house in eight). Holborn, which contained a number of notorious slums, had 1,350 retailers, almost one house in five.

In the parish of St Giles alone, where Hogarth would set his print, a quarter of the houses sold gin 'besides about 82 twopenny houses of the greatest infamy where gin was the liquor drunk'.[14] Those twopenny houses were common lodging houses which were also brothels and safe houses for thieves and stolen goods. The great historian of London's poor, Dorothy George, called Hogarth's *Gin Lane* 'a historic document whose essential truth is confirmed in numberless details incidentally recorded in the Old Bailey Session Papers'.[15] One case was that of Judith Defour, who fetched her two-year-old child from a workhouse where it had been given new clothes, strangled it and left the stripped body in a ditch in Bethnal Green so that she could sell the clothes. The 1s 4d she made was spent on gin, divided with the woman who suggested the crime. Next day Judith confessed. She was, said her mother, 'never in her right mind but always roving'.

On 13 February 1751, the *General Advertiser* carried the following advertisement:

'*On Friday next will be publish'd, Price* 1s *each.* Two large Prints, design'd and etch'd by Mr. *Hogarth*, call'd BEER-STREET and GIN-LANE. A Number will be printed in a better manner for the Curious, at 1s and 6d each. And on Thursday following will be published Four Prints on the Subject of Cruelty, Price and Size the Same. N.B. As the Subjects of these Prints are calculated to reform some reigning Vices peculiar to the lower Class of People, in hopes to render them of more extensive use, the Author had publish'd them in the cheapest Manner possible. To be had at the Golden Head in Leicester-Fields, Where may be had all his other Works.'

With *Beer Street* and *Gin Lane* Hogarth helped Fielding's cause, but he also muscled in, powerfully and deliberately, on the way the city and its vices were now being portrayed in the prints, asserting himself once more as the master in his field. Published at a deliberately low price, the engravings offered the 'lower class of People' positive and negative messages which developed contemporary urban images: the city as a jolly, comic romp; the city as a ravaged desert. The central female figure, so common in Hogarth's prints, offers an equal contrast: the fashionable fat woman with her hoops, wedged into the sedan chair in *Beer Street*; the crazy, loose-armed drunk of *Gin Lane*.

In Hogarth's own ordering (always significant) *Beer Street* comes first, less because it is an idealized view than because this affectionately drawn scene is the *accepted* satire of the city, with hectic 'improvements', lazy rich and sweating workers, rotund, beer-swilling, meat-eating men and saucy, easy women – like the housemaid flagrantly swinging her key.[16] So when people turned to *Gin Lane* the shock would be doubled – this was certainly *not* the London that 'polite' prints were supposed to show.

Surely the memory of the earthquake underlay this print, with all its associations of guilt and fear, as the houses topple and the baby falls? The whole scene is deathly. A straw-hatted woman throws back her head in an open-mouthed stupor, so numb and rock-like that a snail crawls without fear from the wall to her shoulder. A beggar shares a bone with a dog. Desperate for gin, ragged citizens hand over their clothes, the tools of their trade and even their pots and pans to the pawnbroker. Livelihoods are lost, and lives. In the background lie the heaped-up slums of St Giles, with the steeple of St George's Bloomsbury behind (its spire topped by a monarch, not a cross). In the middle distance the parish beadle watches as the naked body of a woman is dropped into her coffin and her orphan child weeps on the ground.

All this apparent chaos is consummately composed. The pawnbroker's sign and the barber's pole pierce the centre of the print like spears, their straight lines offsetting the curving gin signs. The angle of the undertaker's board, a coffin on a gibbet-like pole, is echoed by the sight of the hanging man, dangling in the ruins of his house. Beneath this sign a fearful emblematic figure dances a jig, a wild cook, like Satan, with the bellows for his fire balanced on his head and a baby impaled on his spit. Allegory and hyper-realism mix. The sturdy stone building of 'S. GRIPE PAWN-BROKER' is mocked on the far side by the rickety booth of 'KILMAN DISTILLER'. In front of his numbered barrels cripples fight with begging stools and crutches, charity girls raise their glasses, and a mother tips gin into her baby's open mouth.

495

148 *Gin Lane* (1751)

The whole print is cut through by harsh, broken diagonals. Even its three planes slide sideways – the sky with the signs and spire and tumbling houses; the varied groups in the centre; the bleak wall and steps in the foreground. The wall divides life from death and the steps lead down to the abyss. At their foot sits a blind ballad-singer, dying of starvation, with the skeletal face and limbs of a medieval *memento mori*. The music of Hogarth's silent prints, which always ring with sound, is reduced to the wails and cries of the drunken

496

crowd and the protesting ballad that tells it all, 'The downfall of Madam Gin'.

James Townley provided the verses, testifying to the way the 'deadly draught' preys on mankind and fosters theft, murder and perjury; a liquid fire 'Which Madness to the Heart conveys/And rolls it through the Veins'. But the most potent verses are the commonplace lines over the cellar door:

> Drunk for a Penny
> Dead Drunk for two pence
> Clean Straw for Nothing.

Hogarth was extremely proud of these prints, and explained their 'reformist' origin carefully in his autobiographical notes:

'Bear St and Gin Lane were done when the dredfull consequences of gin drinking was at its height. In gin lane every circumstance of its horrid effects are brought to view, in terorem nothing but <Itleness> Poverty misery and ruin are to be seen Distress even to madnes and death, and not a house in tolerable condition but Pawnbrokers and the Gin shop.

'Bear Street its companion was given as a contrast, were the invigorating liquor is recommend in order drive the other out of vogue. here all is joyous and thriveing Industry and Jollity go hand in hand the Pawnbroker in this happy place is the only house going to ruin where even the smallest qantity of the linquer flows around it is taken in at a wicket for fear of farther distress.'[17]

Even he describes *Gin Lane* first.

The difference in the impact of the two scenes is heightened by the viewpoint of the artist, directing our gaze. In *Beer Street* our feet are safely on the ground, as if we were walking towards the people and on into the street beyond. In *Gin Lane* we hover dizzily, somewhere in the air, above the bony ballad-singer, above the falling child. We look across the chasm whose floor we cannot see. We are gazing down, being sucked in. We too may fall. There is something eager, intent and cold, about the way Hogarth draws every detail of this self-imposed hell. Compulsively and carefully, with deliberate crudeness and deliberate caricature, he drove his graphic art to a new pitch.[18]

In comfortable *Beer Street* a barrel, not a man, dangles from the pole and 'N. Pinch', pawnbroker, is out of business. This is Britain At Its Best, even though it is affectionately guyed, and James Townley's verses suggest that ale is a patriotic weapon, just like good roast beef:

149 *Beer Street* (1751)

Beer, happy Produce of our Isle
Can sinewy Strength impart,
And wearied with Fatigue and Toil
Can chear each manly Heart.

Labour and Art upheld by Thee
Successfully advance,

498

> We quaff thy balmy Juice with Glee
>   And Water leave to France.
>
> Genius of Health, thy grateful Taste
>   Rivals the Cup of Jove,
> And warms each English generous Breast
>   With Liberty and Love.

The nationalist note is underlined by the flag on the steeple, always raised by St Martin-in-the-Fields on George II's birthday, 30 October. The King's Speech lies on the table, next to the laughing butcher. With some fudging of dates it is marked 29 November 1748 (the opening of the first session of Parliament after Aix-la-Chapelle), and its text reads 'Let me earnestly recommend to you the Advancement of Our Commerce and cultivating the Arts of Peace, in which you may depend on my hearty Concurrence and Encouragement.' The kind of commerce Hogarth recommends is suggested by the fishwives who are studying 'A New ballad on the Herring Fishery'; this refers to Hogarth's friend John Lockman, who was currently lobbying for protective legislation as Secretary to the Society of the Free British Fishery.[19]

Hogarth slyly suggested that beer-drinking might even cure cultural follies: the hamper of books being sent as waste paper to the trunk-maker contains some modern tragedies, '*Hill on Royal Societies, Turnbul on Ant. Painting, Politicks Vol:9999*' and, wedged in sideways, *Lauder on Milton* (a scholarly fraud of 1750 suggesting that Milton was a plagiarist). But the one artist he shows – the lanky, ragged sign-painter – does not quite fit the street. Leaning back from his ladder beneath the sign of the 'The Barley Mow', a rural idyll, he beams dreamily at the bottle he is copying and we notice that it is *not* a flagon of ale but a round, unmistakable gin bottle. Between his first sketch and the print, Hogarth had replaced a fat, affable painter with this absent-minded figure.[20] Did he mean that even in this land of foaming pints, a poor painter could still be driven to painting signs, and sink into the arms of Madam Gin?

The black image of *Gin Lane* almost overpowered its laughing opposite, and its racked scene of dissolution still imprints itself indelibly on the mind. Partly as a result of Hogarth's and Fielding's propaganda a new Act was passed in the summer of 1751, forbidding chandlers, grocers and others to sell gin; the tax was doubled and police powers increased. As the rising price of wheat also affected distilling, the consumption of spirits dropped, and with it some of the crime.[21] But gin still flooded the veins and soaked the brains of poor Londoners. Eighty years later Dickens described the flourishing new gin shops in the same 'filthy and miserable' area of St Giles, confirming Hogarth's vision – and incidentally showing how strongly Hogarth's prints formed his own image of the city:

'Wretched houses with broken windows patched with rags and paper: every room let out to a different family, and in many instances to two or even three – fruit and 'sweet-stuff' manufacturors in the cellars, barbers and red-herring vendors in the front parlours, cobblers in the back; a bird-fancier in the first floor, three families on the second, starvation in the attics, Irishmen in the passage, a 'musician' in the front kitchen, and a charwoman and five hungry children in the back one – filth everywhere – a gutter before the houses and a drain behind.'[22]

'What must become of an infant who is conceived in gin, with the poisonous distillations of which it is nourished, both in the womb and at the breast?' Fielding had asked.[23] Dickens echoed the anger that underlay this cry, and Hogarth's print:

'Gin drinking is a great vice in England, but wretchedness and dirt are a greater; and until you improve the homes of the poor, or persuade a half-famished wretch not to seek relief in the temporary oblivion of his own misery . . . gin-shops will increase in number and splendour.'

Hogarth knew that poverty and gin were not the only causes, or symptoms, of human callousness but he also held that the blame did not always lie with others. He advertised his two plates on drink alongside four on *The Stages of Cruelty*, which were published six days later, on 21 February. In *Gin Lane* Hogarth had shown an 'outside' pressure on the poor, their addiction driving them to crime; in *Cruelty* he suggested that evil might come from within, from the terrible, untamed instincts of mankind. He blames both nature and nurture. On one hand he suggests that the impulse to cruelty may be innate in humans; 'imagine these things done by cruel dispositions'.[24] On the other he shows that the callousness of the criminal is fostered by the world he grows up in, and that in some degree it is not opposed to, but actually mirrors the legalized brutality of the State itself.

Hogarth was very straightforward about the aim of *The Four Stages of Cruelty*. He made them, he wrote,

'in hopes of preventing in some degree that cruel treatment of poor Animals which makes the streets of London more disagreeable to the human mind, than anything what ever. the very describing of which gives pain'.

This was certainly his starting point, reflecting the pained tenderness that sprang from his own love of animals, his dogs and his birds, whose graves he marked fondly at Chiswick.

The four prints tell the story of Tom Nero. He is a pauper, brought up by the parish (the S.G. on his shoulder – like that of the gin-drinking charity girls – stands for 'St Giles') and in this series, as in *Gin Lane*, Hogarth is concerned with the examples that the State gives to 'parentless' children. He was still closely involved with the Foundling Hospital and although the minutes show his main concern was now with its fabric – in 1750 he was discussing new altar rails for the Chapel with Theodore Jacobsen – he took his responsibility to its inmates seriously too.

Unsupervised, unloved children are fated. Tom begins his career of cruelty by torturing a dog. He is not alone, but is surrounded by other boys suspending fighting cats from a rope, swinging sticks at cocks, blinding a dove with a heated wire, tying a bone to a starving dog's tail, throwing a cat from a

150 *The Four Stages of Cruelty*, 'The First Stage of Cruelty' (1751)

501

window to test its artificial wings. These urchins are no better than the rabid cur in the corner gnawing the entrails of a living cat. And through the well-dressed 'gentler' boy (said to be based on the young Prince George) trying to extract the arrow from the dog's rear, Hogarth suggests that their 'betters' must show them the right way.

151 'The Second Stage of Cruelty'

Cruel boys become vicious men. In the second plate animals are abused at work, not in play. Tom lashes an old nag which has fallen to its knees and overturned the coach; a sheep is being beaten on its way to the slaughter. Bull-baiting is going on in the distance. But there is already a difference: the cruelty applied to animals destroys men. The sleeping carter has driven his heavy load over a boy, and the written signs posted on the wall put 'Cock-fighting' below an advertisement for Broughton's Amphitheatre. The rounds at Broughton's were notoriously rough, and the battles were not all with fists: one contemporary bill advertised that the contestants would 'fight in the following manner, viz.: to have their left feet strapt down to the stage, within reach of the other's right leg; and the most bleeding wounds to decide the wager'.[25]

Hogarth's poster announces a match between 'James Field and Geo: Taylor'. No contemporary viewer could miss the point. James Field had been hanged only two weeks before the prints came out and 'George the Barber' Taylor had died in February 1750 (Hogarth produced marvellous drawings of him, wrestling with death).[26] And less than a year earlier, in April 1750, Broughton himself fought his final match, carrying a bet of £10,000 for 'Butcher' Cumberland. He lost to his opponent, Slack, when he was blinded by a blow between the eyes: 'The Duke never forgave Broughton, whose career was finished.'[27]

The street where this disturbing scene takes place is Thavies Inn, and the overturned coach is overloaded with barristers more concerned at their plight than that of the horse. The gentle boy of the first print, now a man, is noting

152 'Cruelty in Perfection'

503

down the accident to report the driver. Hogarth suggests that by 'reporting' what happens – as he is doing – some good may come. But it will not come to Tom, who is next seen in a rural churchyard being apprehended for the murder of Ann Gill, a maidservant whom he has seduced and persuaded to steal her mistress's plate. A kneeling man holds a plaintive note from Ann arranging the fatal meeting, declaring that although her mistress has been good to her, 'and my Conscience flied in my face as often as I think of wronging her, yet I am bound Body and Soul to do as you would have me do'. Her throat gapes, her wrist is almost severed from her hand, and her swollen belly tells of two deaths, not one. Her small box spills out two books, the Book of Common Prayer and 'GODS Revenge against Murder'.

Tom's end has come. In the ghastly final print he has been hanged, cut down and brought to the Surgeons' Hall. The male body replaces the prone, murdered female. With horrific vitality Hogarth makes Tom's corpse look alive, as if jerking up in pain as the surgeons probe his eye-sockets and

153 'The Reward of Cruelty'

504

excavate the delicate sinews of his ankles. The bespectacled knife-wielder in the centre (said to be based on John Freke) almost seems to peer at Tom's reaction while he reaches into his hollow ribcage, directed by the magisterial President with his stick. Below his blade intestines snake out towards a vat that already holds another man's head. This is a moral as well as physical dissection. Tom's cursing tongue has been torn out by its roots; his lusting eyes gouged out; his loveless heart thrown to a mangy dog. Skulls and bones boil over a fire, like a cannibal rite, a visceral pagan sacrifice.

Aiming at the poor, Hogarth played on their fears of hanging and dissection: but with his characteristic, unnerving, doubleness he also invited their outrage. He condemned Tom Nero outright, but as with Tom Idle, he also allowed people to feel for him at the last. Given the riots at Tyburn when relatives attempted to rescue felons' bodies from the anatomists, Hogarth's 'ordinary' viewers might well have been on Tom's side. And such sympathy would be heightened by the way this final print brought in recent criminal lives, placing the whole scene beneath the pointing skeletons of the recently executed boxer James Field and the highwayman James Maclain (or Maclean), hanged in October 1750.

Maclain, to whom the good man – our 'gentler boy' – points in dismayed warning, was the son of a Presbyterian minister. He was a handsome, well-bred rascal, a living Macheath; on the Sunday after he was sentenced three thousand people crowded to see him and he fainted twice from the heat of his packed cell. His was the pistol that had exploded in Horace Walpole's face in December 1749, blackening it with powder and shot-marks, and Walpole (who was praised in a Grub Street ballad for not demanding his death) followed his story with interest: 'You can't conceive the ridiculous rage there is of going to Newgate,' he wrote, 'and the prints that are published of malefactors, and the memoirs of their lives and deaths set forth with as much parade as as Marshal Turenne's – we have no generals worth making a parallel!'[28] Five separate memoirs of Maclain were circulating round London when Hogarth's prints came out. While keeping a scrupulous moral tone, he need only name him to suggest a parallel between Tom Nero and this hero of the road.

This might be the 'effects' of cruelty; the end of a cruel life. But the horror comes both from the corpse and from the way we are implicated, as spectators, with the doctors and polite visitors. Some read; some dispute. All show a pitiless indifference. Hogarth brought the whole of medicine into his ambit: the niches belonged to the old Barber–Surgeons' Hall, unused since 1745, while the hall itself resembles the theatre of the Royal College of Physicians near Newgate and the President's chair bears their arms. Many commentators noted the similarity between the curved amphitheatre of a cockpit and the Surgeons' Hall. The whole scene indicts self-interested, legalized cruelty.

Yet it can be read still another way. The viewpoint is absolutely central, on a level with the corpse's rigid, pointing finger, forcing us to confront the worst. The shock is intensified – as with *Gin Lane* – by a kind of relish on Hogarth's part. The emotion is more complex than outrage: he thrills to the knife, the entrails, the cut flesh. There is pleasure here, in the artist's power to convey agony. Hogarth himself is an anatomist, performing an autopsy on a diseased society, a sharp-eyed dissection.

Hogarth's metaphorical use of the body resembles the language of Fielding's tracts. In the *Enquiry*, published a month after these prints, Fielding defined the constitution as including the laws and executive provisions but also

'the Customs, Manners and Habits of the People. These, joined together, do, I apprehend, form the Political, as the several members of the Body, the animal Œconomy, with the Humours, and Habit, compose that which is called the Natural Constitution'.[29]

Similar rhetoric lay behind a political print by George Bickham junior, two years before, showing Pelham and Newcastle standing over Britannia on the rack; they too peer at her entrails while her intestines slide down to the floor.[30] In 'The Reward of Cruelty' Hogarth's vision of the bodily punishments inflicted by, and upon, Tom Nero implicates both the people and the 'constitution' that governs them. Crime, disorder and impulse find their mirror image in punishment and law; together they tear at the collective body of the nation, leaving it in a nightmarish, dismembered state.

Hogarth was adamant that this series should be cheap enough to be bought by the poor. Before his etchings were even announced he arranged to have them made as woodcuts by John Bell, although only the last two were done, with a horrifying bluntness, dated 1 January 1750. Hogarth's own etchings themselves have the force of popular cuts. In his notes, he said he deliberately chose a direct, rough style: 'neither great correctness of drawing or fine Engraving were at all necessary'. On the contrary, fine work would make them too expensive, 'out of reach of those for whome they were cheifly intended'. He had taken care of the essential, the characters and expressions and moreover, he added, 'precious Strokes can only be done with a quick Touch'; the effect would be 'languid or lost if smoothe out into soft engraving'.[31]

Here, too, he was at one with Fielding, who later wrote a short work for the same audience, *Examples of the Interposition of Providence in the Detection and Punishment of Murder*, as deliberately crude as the booklet lying by Ann Gill's corpse, 'GOD'S Revenge against murder'. For the writer–magistrate and the artist, the teaching came first. But although their practical impact was good, the effect on their reputations was not. In such works they aligned themselves unequivocally with 'low art' and 'low subjects'. When Fielding's bitter, brilliant *Amelia* – set in the prisons and spunging houses of London in the 1730s – appeared in late 1751, some praised it for its strong moral (Samuel Johnson, who had condemned *Tom Jones* as 'immoral', liked *Amelia* even better than Richardson's *Clarissa*),[32] but many disappointed readers found the mood too grim and the underworld settings offensive.

Fielding was wearied by his work and saddened by a string of family deaths over the previous two years – his baby daughter, his eight-year-old son, and three of his sisters. He was increasingly ill, 'a poor, emaciated worn out rake, whose gout and infirmities have got the better even of his buffoonery'. Even friends like Edward Moore saw this as a judgment: 'Fielding continues to be visited for his sins, so as to be wheeled about from room to room.'[33] He never lost his wit, but he was embattled and dispirited. Defending himself in a mock-trial in the *Covent-Garden Journal* of January 1752, his spokesman, a 'grave Man', described *Amelia* as his 'favourite Child', not free from faults but the product of loving labour. His speech ended, 'I do, therefore, solemnly declare to you, Mr Censor, that I will trouble the World no more with any Children of mine by the same Muse.'[34] Fielding wrote no more novels.

One element of the Town had indeed begun to turn against Fielding. A new generation of irreverent satirists was beginning to make its mark, led by a group who had been schoolfellows at Westminster a decade ago. Bonnell Thornton, now twenty-five, was the leading spirit, soon to be joined by a younger group who included George Colman, Charles Churchill, Robert Lloyd and William Cowper. At Oxford, Thornton had teamed up with a wild Cambridge student, the poet Christopher Smart. In 1750 Kit Smart started a journal, *The Midwife: or, The Old Woman's Magazine* ('one of the most original and frenetic of the eighteenth century')[35] and in January 1752 he was touring London taverns with *The Old Woman's Oratory*, a burlesque of Orator Henley, starring 'Mary Midnight'. At the same time, Thornton started *Have-at-you-all: The Drury-Lane Journal*, an answer to Fielding's 'Covent-Garden' paper. As the title suggests, he had a go at everyone, especially periodical writers such as Johnson and Smollett, but his main target was Fielding, written off after *Amelia* as having lost his true genius for low humour.

Thornton felt that Fielding had betrayed the cause, but not Hogarth. As a student he had translated Rouquet's notes on *The March to Finchley*, and his mouthpiece in *The Drury-Lane Journal* was 'Roxana Termagant', the prostitute daughter of a clergyman.[36] The resemblance to Moll Hackabout in her defiant, independent days becomes strikingly clear when Kit Smart's Mary Midnight visits Roxana in her Drury Lane garret,

'which you could hardly stand upright in, because of its rafters that hung just as if they were going to drop upon your head. 'Tis impossible to describe the wretchedness of the place: in one corner of it there was a window, but the greatest part of the casement being broke, the vacant quarrels were supplied with proof sheets of *The Drury-Lane Journal*: over the chimney hung a VINCENT WING's almanack for the year 1737 and the bare walls were set off with five wooden pictures, half-torn, of the *Harlot's Progress*.'[37]

The missing print, one assumes, was Moll's death – for here she is alive again.

These spiky, worldly, flippant young writers relished the spontaneity of Hogarth's art and his dislike of cant and affectation. But elsewhere Hogarth, like Fielding, also found himself on trial. In February, when *Gin Lane*, *Beer Street* and *The Four Stages of Cruelty* were in the print shops, Smollett's new novel *The Adventures of Peregrine Pickle* appeared. This rollicking picaresque, a series of wild sexual and scatological scams, became a *cause célèbre* largely because of its inclusion of Lady Harriet Vane's scandalous 'Memoirs of a Lady of Quality'. It also titillated readers with its spoof Grand Tour and attacks on eminent cultural figures. Without naming names, Smollett pilloried Garrick and Quin and indicted Fielding as an abject scribbler fawning on the great;

'when he is inclined to marry his own cook-wench, his gracious patron may condescend to give the bride away; and finally settle him in his old age, as a trading Westminster-justice'.[38]

Hogarth was here too. Readers familiar with the London scene might quickly recognize the loquacious, flashy, ignorant and prejudiced 'Mr. Pallet' whom Peregrine meets in Paris, travelling with a pompous physician–poet, identified as Mark Akenside.[39] In his self-portrait Hogarth had made a feature of his palette as well as his pug, and his well-known views on foreign art made good copy. Smollett's Pallet is a mixture of 'levity and assurance'. Like Hogarth, he likes dapper clothes, and

'though seemingly turned fifty, strutted in a gay summer dress of the Parisian cut, with a bag to his grey hair, and a red feather under his hat, which he carried under his arm'.[40]

Like Hogarth, he also is violently anti-French and harbours ambitions to be a history-painter, having painted both a 'Cleopatra' and a 'Judgment of Solomon'.

At the Palais Royal Pallet encounters a Swiss tourist, who,

'looking at a certain piece, pronounced the word *magnifique!* with a note of admiration; upon which Mr. Pallet, who was not at all a critick in the French language, replied with great vivacity, "*Manufac*, you mean, and a very indifferent piece of manufacture it is; pray gentleman take notice, there is no keeping in those heads upon the back ground, nor no relief in the principal figure: then you'll observe the shadings are harsh to the last degree; and come a little closer this way – don't you perceive that the fore-shortening of that arm is monstrous – agad, sir! there is an absolute fracture in the limb – doctor, you understand anatomy, don't you think that muscle evidently misplaced? Heark ye, Mr. what d'ye call um, (turning to the attendant) what is the name of the dauber who painted that miserable performance?"' [41]

The painter's pretence of learning, a slur that anticipated critics who cast doubt on Hogarth's authorship of *The Analysis of Beauty*, allowed Smollett to make hideous jokes and puns. When the Swiss connoisseur says the picture is '*sans prix*', Pallet announces that the works of the said 'Sangpree' are little prized in England, where men have more taste, and calls the Swiss 'an ignorant coxcomb'. Making matters worse, he takes the physician's embarrassed Horatian tag, '*Mutate nomine, de te fabula narratur*' ('Change the name, and the tale is told of you') as assent: '"Very true (said he) a most sensible observation! mute aye toe numbing he, (what is't?), Deity, fable honour hate her. It is indeed a most mute benumbing piece . . ."' [42]

Pallet is a composite picture, but the Hogarthian elements are plain. These range from his dress and unstoppable love of holding forth to his interest in anatomy and disdain for the unidentifiable element in fine art, the '*je ne sais quoi*', or as Pallet has it, '*ginseekye*'. This contempt would be the starting point for Hogarth's *Analysis* two years later. Even the Calais incident is hinted at when Pallet spends a ludicrous spell in the Bastille. Yet there is no malice in the character, who is shown as a genuine, even near-hysterical, admirer of truly great art. And when he refers to Hogarth directly, Smollett pays the usual tribute to his mastery of expression: 'It would be a difficult task for the inimitable Hogarth himself', writes Smollett, when his Commodore Trunnion is aghast at a forged letter, 'to exhibit the ludicrous expression of the commodore's countenance . . . not a stare of astonishment, a convulsion of rage, or a ghastly grin of revenge, but an association of all three'. [43]

Smollett's racy, undignified, chaotic novels with their inn yards and kitchens, bedpans and brawls, drunks and dupes and incompetent seducers, are harsher and cruder than Fielding's, and have many scenes and incidents that recall Hogarth's prints.[44] In *Roderick Random*, in *Peregrine Pickle* and in *Humphrey Clinker* he makes it clear that he thought Hogarth supreme as a satirist. It is only as the would-be history-painter and arbiter of taste and judgement that he makes himself ridiculous.

Hogarth may never have read Smollett's novel; certainly he seems to have felt no animosity towards him. And in any case, he himself was not averse to making fools of others, both in his art and in practical jokes. In 1745 he made and signed a mock-etching of a newly appointed naval officer at Deal, Lancelot Burton, showing him riding 'a lean *Canterbury* hack, with a bottle sticking out of his pocket; and underneath was an inscription, intimating that he was going down to take possession of the place'.[45] This was sent to Burton, whose friends, in on the joke, told him they had seen it displayed in all the London print shops. Enraged, Burton wrote abusively to Hogarth, but after his 'tormentors had kept him in suspense throughout an uneasy three weeks', they relented and told him the truth. This too was a kind of cruelty. But it was one that a chap was supposed to accept, as Burton did: 'He then became so perfectly reconciled to his resemblance, that he showed it with exultation to Admiral *Vernon*, and all the rest of his friends.'

In 1751 Hogarth joined in an even more elaborate hoax, which had the added piquancy of ridiculing the current insatiable demand for Rembrandt etchings.[46] At the end of this year Vertue noted that these were being 'collected at any price. some particularly sold at sales very extraordinary'.[47] Buyers were pouncing on

'all the wild scrabbles skratches &c. done by him or thought to be done by him – amongst others two persons imployed their thoughts and time to immitate or mimick his manner – in which they succeeded very well'.

One of these was Hogarth's friend, the artist and scientist Benjamin Wilson, and Vertue recorded how a plate made by Wilson was sold to 'one of these collectors for an extraordinary price wherein they was deceivd, and ridiculd for there conceited knowledge –'.

According to Wilson, who later told the story to Benjamin West, the tale ran thus. It began when Thomas Hudson (a Rembrandt enthusiast and Wilson's neighbour in Great Queen Street) topped Wilson's £10 bid for a Rembrandt drawing at a sale and then attacked Wilson '*very uncourteously*' for pushing up the price.[48] Wilson bit his lip, kept quiet and brooded on 'a pleasant revenge'. Hudson had apparently boasted that no one could etch like Rembrandt and that he could always tell an imitation, 'directly he saw it'. Wilson called his bluff. In secret, he copied a rare etching attributed to the master. One difficulty was obtaining the India paper Rembrandt used,

'but Wilson's resources did not fail him; he suspected the cause of the great thickness of the paper to be that more sheets than one were pasted together and pressed. In order to test this he obtained a portion of Rembrandt's paper and soaked it in hot water, when it separated at once into four or five leaves.'[49]

Having solved this problem, he made the print and scribbled its title, 'Companion to the Coach', in Dutch. Using a Dutch aquaintance as envoy, he slipped it into a portfolio of genuine etchings to be shown to Hudson. Not only did he buy it at once, for six shillings, but declared it the *'best piece of perspective'* and the *'finest light and shade'* he had ever seen from Rembrandt.

Wilson then told Hogarth ('"who", he says, "loves a little mischief"'), who persuaded him to try the trick again with a printseller called Harding. At his shop in St Martin's Lane Harding paid the Dutchman two guineas – and added a bottle of wine to persuade him to bring more. The delighted Wilson and Hogarth then got a confidant to show a different forged print to the connoisseurs Lord Duncannon and Dr Charles Chauncey, and to Arthur Pond. All were deceived. But the hoax meant nothing without the exposure of their first victim, Hudson, who had been, among other things, a witness of Hogarth's discomfiture in Paris in 1748. 'Damn it,' Hogarth allegedly said, 'let us expose the fat-headed fellow.' The profits of their fraud were splashed out on a great supper, 'an English roast', to which Wilson invited twenty-three guests including Scott, Lambert and Hogarth's young agent in Ipswich, the artist Joshua Kirby. Hudson was seated prominently between Wilson and Hogarth. The main dish was a huge sirloin and when Scott set eyes on it, he cried out, 'A sail! A sail': the roast was decorated, Wilson recalled happily, 'not with greens or with horseradish, but covered all over with the same kind of prints', identical copies of the 'priceless' etching. At first Hudson would not believe he had been taken in; but 'Hogarth stuck his fork into one of the engravings, and handed it to him'. As proof Wilson brought out his portfolio, full of the prints in various stages. Asked what Hogarth said at this point, Wilson told West, 'He! an impudent dog! he did nothing but laugh with Kirby the whole evening – Hudson never forgave him for it.'

The victim of a 'roasting' was supposed to take the joke, as Burton had, and Wilson fully, if foolishly, expected Hudson to laugh. Instead he refused to play by the rules, and 'took serious offence'. In response to this unsportsmanlike rage Wilson then declared he would expose him publicly. He kept his word, placing a humilating notice in the *General Advertiser*, announcing the availability of two Rembrandt prints 'which were purchased by two very great Connoisseurs, as curious and genuine Prints of that Master, and at a considerable Price'. Selling at sixpence and a shilling, they went so fast that 'both plates were almost entirely worn away by frequent printing'.

Hogarth may well have planned to publicize just how easy it was to deceive the public, even those who thought they were well informed. The joke ran and ran, even featuring in Samuel Foote's comedy *Taste* at Drury Lane the following year, in this exchange between Carmine the painter and Puff the auctioneer:

CARMINE: Let us be private. What have you there?

PUFF: Two of *Rembrandt*'s Etchings by Scrape in May's buildings; a paltry Affair, a poor Ten Guinea Job; however . . . what became of you Yesterday?

CARMINE: I was detained by sir Positive Bubble. How went the Pictures? The Guido, what did that fetch?

PUFF: One hundred and thirty.

CARMINE: Hum! Four guineas the frame, Three the painting; then we divide just one hundred and twenty-three –

It was only two days after the fakes were advertised that Hogarth announced the prints of *Moses* and *Paul* – for which the ticket was his own Rembrandt burlesque. After the subscription was fulfilled, he added, the receipt would be sold separately, 'at a very extraordinary price'.[50]

The hoax was a joke among friends, but also a cruel public humiliation of a colleague. Hudson was a staid painter, but not a bad one. He was short, like Hogarth, and could be prickly and demanding (Reynolds, his pupil, left him in 1743 after refusing to carry a painting to Van Aken's studio in the rain).[51] But he could also be affable and loyal – William Hickey recalled him as 'uncommonly low in stature, with a prodigious belly and constantly wearing a large, white, bushy, perriwig. He was remarkably good tempered and one of my first rate favourites.'[52] Yet now this good-tempered man was among Hogarth's enemies.

Within weeks of the Rembrandt dinner, those who smarted under Hogarth's tongue had their chance to laugh at him, in his turn. When he announced that the final date for subscriptions to the prints of *Moses* and *Paul before Felix* would be 6 June, Hogarth added that they could be seen at the Golden Head in Leicester Fields, 'as likewise the Author's six Pictures of Marriage A-la-Mode, which are to be disposed on within the said Time, by a new Method, to the best Bidder'.[53]

Vertue thought this typical of Hogarth, 'who is often projecting scheems to promote his business in some extraordinary manner'.[54] It was a clear case of a swollen head,

'as he thought the publick was so very fond of his works. & had showd often such great forwardness to pay him. very high prices. he puffd this in newspapers for a long time before hand'.

The puffing began at the end of May, when the *Advertiser* gave details of his 'new Method'.[55] Each bidder was to sign a note, stating the sum he was offering. These notes would be put in the drawers of a locked cabinet with a glass door: the bids could be seen, but the bidder's name could not, so that fresh bids could be added as the sum rose, with advances of 'not less than three Guineas each time'. Bidding would continue until noon on 6 June, 'and no longer'. On Friday the 7th, the successful bid would be announced.

Not content with this, Hogarth launched into a statement designed to alienate the art market. No 'Dealer in Pictures' would be allowed to bid. 'As (according to the Standard of Judgment, so righteously and laudably establis'd by Picture-Dealers, Picture-Cleaners, Picture-Frame-Makers and other Connoisseurs) the Works of a Painter are to be esteem'd more or less valuable, as they are more or less scarce', he wished to announce, 'by way of Precaution, not Puff' that this would be the last series of pictures he might ever exhibit. It was too difficult, he said, to sell such a number at once to a single buyer. His works of this 'historical or humorous kind', he added, had not exceeded fifty, twenty of these being accounted for by the *Harlot*, the *Rake* and the *Marriage*.

'so that whoever has a Taste of his own to rely on, not too squeamish for the Production of a Modern, and Courage enough to avow it, by daring to give them a Place in his Collection (till Time, the suppos'd Finisher, but real Destroyer of Paintings, has render'd them fit for those more sacred Repositories, where Schools, Names, Hands, Masters, &c. attain the last Stage of Preferment), may from hence be convinced, that Multiplicity at least of his (Mr Hogarth's) Pieces, will be no Diminution of their Value.'

These were bold words: 'but alas when the time came – to open this mighty secret he found himself neglected'.[56] At 11 o'clock on the morning of 6 June, John Lane of Hillingdon arrived in Leicester Fields. To his great surprise, as he told John Nichols, 'expecting (what he had been a witness to in 1745, when Hogarth disposed of many of his pictures) to have found his painting-room full of noble and great personages, he only found the painter, and his ingenious friend Dr Parsons, Secretary to the Royal Society, talking together and expecting a number of spectators at the least, if not of buyers'.[57]

Not only was the room empty but the famous glass-fronted cabinet contained only a single bid. This was from a Mr Perry, who having heard a whisper from a friend in the City that only £75 had been offered for the six pictures of *Marriage A-la-Mode*, upped this to £120, 'with a promise never to sell them to any Picture Trader or Connoisseur-Monger, so long as you or I shall live'.[58] The sentiments were fine, but not the sum. According to Vertue, Hogarth had been expecting around £500 to £600: the current offer meant that his paintings, the fruit of so much labour, were being knocked down for £20 each.

At ten minutes to twelve, when no one else had arrived, Lane told Hogarth he would make the pounds guineas. 'The clock struck twelve; and Hogarth wished Mr. Lane joy of his purchase, hoping it was an agreeable one. Mr Lane answered, Perfectly so.' But Hogarth, who had waited tensely all morning, had dressed up, 'put on his tye-wig, strutted away one hour and fretted away two more', could not keep up this stylish calm.[59] There was an outburst on the part of Dr Parsons, and 'what more affected Mr Lane, a great appearance of disappointment in poor Hogarth, and truly with great reason'. Parsons told Hogarth he had greatly harmed his chances by setting the deadline so early, when the 'Town' were hardly up. 'Hogarth, in a tone that could not but be observed, said, Perhaps it may be so!' After a pause, Lane agreed with Parsons, adding that he thought Hogarth very poorly paid for his labour and offering to wait until three o'clock to see if he could find a better purchaser. Hogarth accepted the offer warmly, acknowledging its generosity. The excited Parsons overflowed with praise and proposed to make the offer public, but 'this was peremptorily forbidden by Mr. Lane, whose concession in favour of our artist was remembered by him to the time of his death'.

There was to be no reprieve. Another hour dragged by:

'About one o'clock, two hours sooner than the time appointed by Mr. Lane, Hogarth said he would no longer trespass on his generosity, but that, if he was pleased with his purchase, he himself was abundantly so with the purchaser. He then desired Mr. Lane to promise that he would not dispose of the pictures without previously acquainting him of his intention, and that he would never permit any person, under pretence of cleaning, to meddle with them, as he always desired to take that office on himself. This promise was readily made

514

by Mr. Lane, who has been tempted more than once by Hogarth to part with his bargain at a price to be named by himself. When Mr. Lane bought the pictures, they were in Carlo Marratt frames which cost the painter four guineas apiece.'

Subdued at the time, Hogarth soon let fly. All the achievements of this year were hollow mockeries. The great impact of *Beer Street* and *Gin Lane* and *The Four Stages of Cruelty* meant nothing; the triumph of the Rembrandt hoax was forgotten; the success of his subscription for *Moses* and *Paul* was irrelevant. The fiasco of his sale, 'so mortified his high spirits & ambition', wrote Vertue, that it 'threw him into a rage cursd and damned the publick and swore that they had all combind together to oppose him –'. The next day, 'in a pet', William Hogarth tore down the sign of the Golden Head that swung above his door.

25

'A Wanton Kind of Chace':
The Analysis of Beauty

'What! – a book, and by Hogarth! – then twenty to ten,
All he gained by the pencil, he'll lose by the pen.'
'Perhaps it may be so, – howe'er, miss or hit,
He will publish, – here goes – it's double or quit.'

WILLIAM HOGARTH (1753)[1]

EVERYONE, IN 1751, agreed it was a wretched summer. For six weeks in June and July it rained without cease. Water poured from the eaves and bounced off the cobbles, swilling rubbish down the kennels in alleys and lanes, collecting in pools, flooding into cellars. Through these sodden days Hogarth licked his wounds, brooding on the fiasco of his sale. What had gone wrong? John Lane's view – although he tried to soothe Hogarth by agreeing with James Parsons – was not that the hour was too early but that the 'nouvelle method of proceeding' had put people off. He also suggested mildly that

'there seemed at the time a combination against poor Hogarth, who perhaps, from the extraordinary and frequent approbation of his works, might have imbibed some degree of vanity, which the town in general, friends and foes, seemed resolved to mortify'.

If this was the case, Lane added, '(and to me it is very apparent), they fully effected their design'.[2]

Another source said that in his excitement, worrying that the house was small and might be overcrowded, Hogarth had warned his friends to stay away, and 'they obeyed his injunctions'.[3] This puts a kindly gloss on the picture of him dressed at his finest, fretting alone with no fellow painter for company. But Lane's version might be more correct. Hogarth had become caught up in the politics of the art world and some colleagues at St Martin's Lane were not unhappy to see him brought down a peg. In particular, many of them differed from him over the style of academy they wanted, leaning to

516

the French, hierarchical model instead of the democratic style he argued for so passionately.

This debate had never gone away. It had come to the forefront in 1749 when John Gwynn published his *Essay on Design*, whose lengthy subtitle included *Proposals for Erecting a Public Academy to be supported by Voluntary Subscription (Till a Royal Foundation can be Obtain'd for Educating the British Youth in Drawing)*. Gwynn's frontispiece was designed by Wale and engraved by Grignion, both linked to St Martin's Lane. In the same year the Dilettanti held a meeting at the King's Arms in Pall Mall to consider their own academy plan, proposed by Robert Dingley – although the outcome was a bit befogged, as the minutes confess:

'The Committee growing a little noisy and drunk and seeming to recollect that they are not quite sure whether the Report of the Committee signed by Chairman and Toast-master Holdernesse may not be so intelligible to the Society as the meaning of the Committee may be intended.'[4]

And that autumn George Vertue noted yet another gathering at the Bedford Head, of the 'Grand Clubb for promoting the Arts of drawing . . . to settle preliminarys. for the Establishment of an Academy – in London'.[5]

Nothing came of these moves. Dreams of a new academy sprang back in early 1751, when Prince Frederick spoke about it to Vertue for over an hour.[6] But that March, on his way to see his hated father, who was seriously ill, the ever hopeful Frederick caught a chill, subsided into fever and was dead within days. His demise dashed hopes of royal support for the time being: the sixty-seven-year-old George II was a notorious philistine and his new heir, his grandson George, was only twelve.

The artists looked to the future, still taking Europe for their model: Reynolds was studying in Italy and Hudson would tour there in 1752. At home, disputes rumbled among the easels. The engraver Robert Strange (who favoured a state academy) recalled that many attempts were made to 'enlarge the plan' of St Martin's Lane but they always failed 'through the intrigues of several of the artists themselves; who, satisfied with their own performances, and the moderate degree of abilities they possessed, wished, I believe, for nothing more than to remain, as they then were, masters of their own field'.[7] Hogarth was definitely master of his field. And although there were no directors, he certainly saw St Martin's Lane as 'his', and Thornhill's before him. He was proud of it, thought it worked well, and saw no need for change.

Just as he upheld the egalitarian basis of the school, so he declared the democracy of the eye, and the worth of the people's own art. One of his engraving assistants, Philip Dawes, remembered that in the early 1750s, while Hogarth was brooding over his ideas for *The Analysis of Beauty*, he often went with him to the Fleet Market and the nearby Harp-alley, the great markets for sign-painters' work:

'It was the great delight of Hogarth to contemplate those specimens of genius emanating from a school which he used emphatically to observe was truly English, and frequently to compare with, and prefer to the more expensive productions of those Geniuses whom he used to term the *Black Masters*.'

He stood in front of these signs with the same absorption that he paid the ranks of faces in his *Laughing Audience*. He loved looking at the old barbers' blocks ranged row upon row 'like the spectators in the galleries of a Theatre', and liked to note

'the different characters which the workmen had bestowed upon their countenances, to endeavour to guess from their appearances at their dates, and thence deduce the effect which they would have if decorated with the various wigs which the fashion of their different periods might have clapped upon them'.[8]

Hogarth always liked signs: his friendship with Joshua Kirby, nearly twenty years younger, was said to stem from seeing the sign of the Rose which Kirby painted in Ipswich. By now, as well as selling Hogarth's prints, Kirby was a painter with a successful sideline in engravings of local churches. He later taught perspective to the Prince of Wales, and in late 1751 he was advertising his new book, *Dr. Brook Taylor's Method of Perspective Made Easy, Both in Theory and Practice*, a reponse to the standard work on perspective. When this appeared in 1754, he dedicated it to Hogarth, who, he said, first encouraged him to write. Hogarth also provided a playful satiric frontispiece on false perspective, although he declined to write an essay at the end which Kirby said would give him protection both 'Front, & Rear' so that he 'would not be afraid of the Devil himself'.[9]

Hogarth was not afraid of any devil, or any dictators of style. In late 1751, he replaced the burlesque subscription ticket for *Moses* and *Paul*, which had proved so successful, with a new receipt, a revised version of *Boys Peeping at Nature*. This time he showed no faun peeping up Nature's skirt: the central putto who restrained the faun in earlier versions now stood alone, covering the forbidden zone with a formal classical portrait, marked in correct proportions. This could be a reference to the classical style of *Moses* and *Paul*, but it also suggested that rules obscured reality, forbidding artists to see nature's secrets clearly.

Academic rules had been preying on his mind. When he argued at St Martin's Lane about his distaste for copying he grew increasingly frustrated by the fierce opposition. 'I began to think', he wrote later, 'if I were but able to publish my thoughts in writing I might have fairer play.' Then, if there was any merit in his ideas, he said, 'I should probably reap the credit and advantage of it, instead of labouring as I then did under the imputation of a vain and obstinate opposer of established opinions.'[10] His desire to write was also prompted by the barrage of enquiries stirred up by the 'line of beauty' on his self-portrait. A book would be his next project. It would counter the failure of the sale and let him prove himself again. It would also help his cause of redefining 'artists' as part of polite culture, not as 'mechanics' or purveyors of goods, whose work was defined by the market, but as 'professionals, as men of sophistication and authority in their own fields'.[11]

As soon as the prints of *Moses* and *Paul* were finished, in February 1752, the book took priority. On 24 March he announced that he proposed to publish, by subscription

A short Tract in Quarto, called THE ANALYSIS OF BEAUTY.
Wherein Objects are considered in a new Light, both as to Colour and Form.
(Written with a View to fix the fluctuating Ideas of Taste)
To which will be added
Two Explanatory Prints, serious and comical engraved on large
Copper-Plates, fit to frame for Furniture.

The price would be five shillings down and five on delivery, and after the subscription was fulfilled, it would rise, eventually to 15s. The advertisement appeared in Fielding's *Covent-Garden Journal*, but Fielding could not help Hogarth with its writing. He was stretched to the limit, ill and cast down at the bleak reception of *Amelia*; January's *Journal* contained his bitter 'Modern Glossary' with its tart definitions: 'AUTHOR. A laughing stock. It means likewise a Poor fellow and in general an object of Contempt' and 'CRITIC. All the World'.[12]

Hogarth was prepared to defy all the world. At the same time as his notice he issued a subscription ticket: *Columbus Breaking the Egg*.[13] As told by Girolamo Benzoni,

'Columbus was at dinner with a group of Spanish nobles, one of whom announced that if Columbus had not made his voyage, "some Spaniard would have done it without fail". Without a word, Columbus placed an egg on the

154 *Columbus Breaking the Egg* (1752)

table and said, "You Sirs, will make it stand up unaided . . ." All tried, but nobody could make it stand. When it came into the hands of Columbus, he struck it on the table, flattening the point slightly. Thus they all remained confounded.'[14]

The ticket was a challenge to all sneering detractors. Hogarth, like Columbus, had discovered a new world. He too would confound his critics, and slice through conventional ways of thinking. And he would do this through concrete demonstrations.

Hogarth wanted to write a *painter's* book, not an academic treatise. He wanted his writing to speak – as his prints had – to people untrained in art theory, giving examples from practice and observation. In some ways, although he was hardly 'scientific', his empirical approach was more in tune with the public lectures and demonstrations of the natural philosophers than with art theory. Hours of intense talk, with scientists and doctors as well as artists and scholars, reverberate beneath his prose. One can see him, with his elbows on the coffee-house table, pumping acquaintances for ideas and information. He could discuss perspective with Kirby, and 'natural forces', optics, electricity, and attraction and repulsion with Benjamin Wilson. He could seek advice on botany from the naturalist John Ellis, to whom he later wrote thanking him for the

'pretty little seed-cups . . . they are a sweet confirmation of the pleasure Nature seems to take in adding elegance of form to most of her works . . . How poor and bungling are all the imitations of art! When I see you next we will sit down – nay to kneel down if you will – and admire these things.'[15]

He could beg the anatomists for casts of muscles and bones, and discuss physiology with Benjamin Hoadly or Dr Ranby. He could argue about physiognomy and muscles with James Parsons, a man as doggedly iconoclastic as Hogarth himself, his oddly mystical lectures declaring all previous theorists wrong, from Descartes onwards.[16]

If he was to confound the connoisseurs he must also take account of history and art scholarship. For advice here, he turned to Dr Morell: among Hogarth's papers there is a translation in Morell's handwriting of Socrates' discussion of beauty from Xenophon's *Memorabilia*. He also talked to the 'learned antiquary and connoisseur' and collector of coins, John Kennedy, who pointed out a relevant passage in Lomazzo (and eventually sold him the book).[17] And later he was helped by James Townley, the classics teacher at Christ's Hospital who had written the verses for *The Four Stages of Cruelty*. Now in his late thirties, Townley had written an effusive but tongue-in-cheek letter in early 1750, saying how he treasured Hogarth's works like a classic,

'from which I shall regularly instruct my children, just in the same manner as I should out of Homer, or Virgil. You will be read in your course, – and it will be no unusual thing to find me in a morning in my great chair, with my three bigger boys about me, construing the sixth chapter of the Harlot's Progress, or comparing the two characters in the first book of the 'Prentices.'[18]

He saw Hogarth as a 'great man', free from insolence or vanity, hoped to write a 'full portrait' of him and ended, 'I wish I were as intimate with you, and as well qualified for the purpose, as your friend Fielding.'

However much he relied on these friends, discussed his work, and borrowed books, Hogarth still had to write the text. And he flinched from this task. To start with he asked a friend, or friends, 'offering to furnish them with materials by word of mouth' but he soon realized it was impracticable to think that one man could express another's ideas.[19] Having gone this far, he set about it himself. He was encouraged, he said in one of his drafts, by 'a gentleman of distinction and known ability' – almost certainly Benjamin Hoadly – who offered him help. 'Nor has he been worse than his word,' he went on, and it would be ungrateful not to acknowledge 'the many hints I received from him whi[l]st I was going on with the work and the touches <and corrections> he at last gave it'.[20]

Later Hogarth amended his draft to say that he 'digested the matter as well as he could, and threw it into the form of a book', before consulting Hoadly, who then 'Ingenuously told me, *you may print it*', and seeing that he was nervous, offered to help.[21] The manuscripts suggest this version was true. Hogarth had started with a clear, straightforward axiom, 'It seems to be universally admitted that there is such a thing as Beauty, and that the highest degree of it is Grace', but his first attempt to define these ended as a tangle of crossings out, incoherent phrases and indecipherable spellings.[22]

Dipping a fine pen in the inkwell, and folding the page in half, to leave one side free for second thoughts, Hogarth wrote in a curling script, his ideas following each other in rapid succession. But then he went back, again and again, crossing out phrases and adding new ones with a darker ink and stubbier nib. Occasionally, his scorings out and notes are in pencil, or red crayon – whatever came to hand. Although he began by using only the right-hand half of the page, new thoughts flowered like exotic shrubs, clambering up the left-hand margins and colonizing the backs of pages, turning into whole new sections. A passage on Leonardo da Vinci winds round an earlier alteration; thoughts cluster and blossom, on the Hyde Park statuaries and on London steeples. A quote from Lomazzo is scribbled beside a description of Isis; a whole passage on perspectives and ships flows over the back of a page, and so does the whim that Wren might have preferred to use a pineapple shape rather than the cross and globe on top of St Paul's – if it had not been for the religious motive. A stray thought about humour bursts into a cascade of examples. A whole draft chapter on 'Dress' is written on the margins and backs of sheets, later to be discarded.

If anything stands out clearly, it is that the central ideas and examples were all his own: the rough chapter headings were hardly altered.[23] But it took longer than he hoped. After the first excited draft he wrote a second, this time using the full page, with fast sketches in red pencil on the backs of pages of the drawings he would include in his plates. This time there were fewer crossings out, except in the problematic sections on line and form – where he had to stick in a little note saying 'go back a page'. He still got carried away, and wrote rushing notes on humour and characters in plays, and strong shipboard anecdotes showing how humour can accompany horror:

'a wounded man in a see fight <who> having <first> his leg shot off had also afterwards his head shot off unknown to the bearer by a cannon ball as he carried down to the surgeon . . . the surgeon being angry <at the absurdity of> bringing a man to be cur'd <without> a head, the fellow who brought the body, returnd for answere in a pet damn him he told me it was his leg'.[24]

Eventually – perhaps persuaded it was indecorous – he struck this through, like other vivid excursions. A wild and whimsical fantasy on music, colour and French cookery was also dropped.

As he worked, Hogarth moved passages around, particularly illustrations from authorities, which ended up in the Preface. Then he had a third copy made by an amanuensis, but even now he nearly despaired, lamenting 'the Motliness of the Stile of one who never wrote before' (if indeed, he added, 'it could be call'd any stile at all'). This could not be set right without 'new writing the whole book', which 'neither the work deserv'd or time would permit'.[25] He prayed his two plates might make up for it and at least, as a practitioner, he knew more than the dealers, he said, borrowing an image from his own *Industry and Idleness*:

'Hopeing, that as the mechanick at his Loom is as likely to give as satisfactory account of the materials, and composition, of the rich Brocade he weaves (tho uncouthly) as the smooth Tongue'd Mercer <with his parade of showy silks about him> I may in like manner, make myself tolerably understood, by those who are at the Pain of examining my Book, and prints together.'[26]

Only when he had gone through this version with his friends was a fourth draft, now lost, sent to the printers.

The subscriptions had begun coming in in April 1752 and on 3 July Hogarth advertised the *Analysis* again. In November he announced the content of the prints, 'a Country Dance, and a Statuary's Yard' adding that he intended his book to be

'useful and entertaining to the curious and polite of both sexes, by laying down the Principles of personal Beauty and Deportment, as also of Taste in general, in the plainest, most familiar and entertaining Manner'.[27]

But another winter in Leicester Fields and summer in Chiswick – the first good summer for two years – would go by before the book appeared, although he had finished and signed his plates by 5 March 1753.

Despite the delay, the signs looked good. As soon as the subscription opened, the scholar William Warburton, later Bishop of Gloucester, requested two copies, saying that he hoped the book would counter 'all that worthless crew proposing *vertu* and connoisseurship, to whom all that grovel in the splendid poverty of wealth and taste are the miserable bubbles'.[28] Samuel Foote's play *Taste* took the same line, and in March 1753 Rouquet wrote from Paris, suggesting that Hogarth was surprisingly in touch with French thought:

'Free thinking upon that and other topics is more common here than amongst you if possible, old pictures and old stories fare alike, a dark picture is become a damned picture as the soul of the dealer.'[29]

By the time of this letter Hogarth had reached the final stage of revision. Now his friend, he said, 'took me by the hand, and kindly assisted in conducting more than a third part through the press'.[30] Then, because of distance and business (or, according to Nichols, because Hoadly fell ill), he lost this help and after printing some sheets himself, he appealed to others. One of these was James Ralph,

'but it was impossible for two such persons to agree, both alike vain and positive. He proceeded no farther than a sheet, and they then parted friends, and seem to have continued as such'.[31]

The rest of the book was corrected by the patient, good-natured Morell. He found some of it obscure, but, as he told Nichols, Hogarth was determined and persuasive:

'In the 13th chapter I was somewhat puzzled with the flat and round, or the concave and convex, apearing the reverse; till the sun shining in upon the cornice, I had a fair example of what he intended to express. The next chapter, with regard to *colouring*, did not go on quite so smoooth; for if I satisfied him, I was not satisfied myself with his peculiar principles; nor could I relish his laying the blame on the colourmen, &c.'[32]

Morell did make Hogarth's prose more respectable, cutting out some pungent examples and attacks, but he added nothing to the substance. When he had finished, all that remained was the Preface, which was corrected by James Townley. Townley was a true, if teasing, devotee, sending Hogarth a scrap 'From an old Greek Fragment' with this pronouncement from the Delphic oracle:

'That the Source of Beauty should never again be rightly discovered, till a person should arise, whose name was perfectly included in the name of Pythagoras, which Person should again restore the antient Principle upon which all beauty is founded.

524

Pythagoras
Hogarth'

More indulgent than Morell, and perhaps in a hurry, Townley let some slips through, telling his son that when Hogarth showed him the first sheet he found 'a plentiful crop of errors' but that these got fewer as he went on. ('Such is the power of genius, whatever its direction,' noted John Ireland optimistically.)[33]

Nichols was cooler. 'The family of Hogarth rejoiced', he wrote, 'when the last sheet of the Analysis was printed off; as the frequent disputes he had with his coadjutors, in the progress of the work, did not much harmonize his disposition.'[34] At long last, all the excited tension paid off: the last sheet was printed. By late November 1753, *The Analysis of Beauty* was bound and presented to its subscribers. On the 25th Hogarth sent a copy to Thomas Birch, for the Royal Society's library. And on 1 December it was published.

The influence of Hogarth's helpers was both good and bad: they saved him from some errors and tidied up his style, but they may also have encouraged him to tackle his opponents on their own scholarly ground, instead of sticking to what he knew. Hogarth could write brilliantly and vividly when he worked, as he said in his manuscript notes, 'by my own feeling, describing how I have felt myself upon the careful examination and enquiry into the sight of objects'. But to take on the experts, he began with a preface and long introduction, sweeping through the history of art from the Greeks to Michelangelo. Truculently anxious, he overstated his case, seized on quotations that backed up his argument, brusquely dismissed other writers and criticized great painters. These opening chapters, most of all, laid him open to the critics. His detractors could have it both ways – insisting on one hand that his ideas were narrow, eccentric and ignorant, and on the other that given his obvious lack of learning, all his 'evidence' was plagiarized or written by his assistants.

His real mistake, however, was to defy the tyranny of rules by inventing a new rule himself, and insisting that it was an absolute truth. He set out to demonstrate that the essence of beauty lay in one form, the 'serpentine line', a spiralling form that reflected the rich complexity of life itself, seen in large in the mobile contours of landscape, and in small in the structure of plants and the skeins of the skin. This was oddly percipient – he would have appreciated the confirmation of this fundamental patterning of life in the structure of DNA – but difficult to turn into a satisfying aesthetic theory.

Straight lines, he argued, could represent only the crudest apprehension of reality. Thus in terms of contemporary taste he set himself against dull

525

'sedentary' regularity, rejecting the parallels, flat fronts and balanced forms of Palladianism, and embracing 'composed variety'. At its simplest, in the form of pure line, his line of beauty was an elongated S curve. In two dimensions – in pencil or paint – this waving line could express the curving body of surfaces. Taken into three dimensions it became the key to the beauty of structure, 'the *serpentine* line' or 'the line of grace'. (He made his reader 'see' this, by describing a curving rope or wire winding round a cone from head to foot.) To create his own personal reading of the classic requisites of *grandessa* and *grazia* – greatness and grace – he asserted that if volume was added to this waving surface, as in monumental sculpture and history-painting, the resulting works could inspire awe and wonder as well as delight.

Hogarth hunted for support in all the treatises. He pounced with joy on the Mannerist writer Lomazzo, who quotes Michelangelo's advice to his pupil *'that he should alwaies make a figure Pyramidall, Serpentlike, and multiplied by one, two and three'*.[35] He welcomed Lomazzo's definition of the true grace of a picture as the expression of *motion*. He applauded Du Fresnoy's praise of the 'large flowing, gliding outlines which are in waves' in the sculpted *Antinous*, and his insistence that a fine figure 'ought always to have a serpent-like and flaming form'.[36] But he slumped with disappointment when Du Fresnoy and de Piles decided that 'grace' is indefinable. Next he turned to the artists. All deviated from Hogarth's cherished principles in some way: Rubens by his over-bold S-like swellings, Raphael in his exaggeration of Michelangelo's curve, Correggio in his proportions, Dürer by his mathematical rules and Van Dyck, oddly, by following nature untutored by any rule at all.

Still seeking confirmation, he traced his theory back in time, raiding a treatise (Hermanson Ten Kate's *Beau Idéal*, translated in 1732), that spoke of 'the Analogy' of the ancient Greeks, a secret key to the rules of harmony in all the arts brought from Egypt by Pythagoras. Hogarth then identified this lost mystery with the symbols and hieroglyphics described by Lomazzo, dedicated 'in a triangular glass unto Venus'. And on he went, adding the story of the special 'line' by which Appelles was recognized by a fellow artist, Protogenes, and pointing out the twisting cornucopia that graced every ancient deity.

There is something here of the aggressive autodidact, the crank who bores people at parties with his theories of who wrote Shakespeare or of extra-terrestrial forces building the pyramids. The accumulation of codes and symbols, the invocation of Venus and Isis, of rams' horns and serpents, had the same attraction for Hogarth as the rituals and 'mysteries' of the masons in the 1730s. His contention – as with the professional 'secrets' he demystified in his prints – was that this mystery too lay in the world, waiting to be rediscovered.

Inevitably, Hogarth's ideas were shaped by the traditions he inherited. His serpentine line, detected in classical sculpture, had been cultivated by Mannerist painters whose influence flowed on into the sumptuous curves of late Baroque: his own devotion could have been born in the days when Thornhill's paintings at Greenwich ran in his head. That, too, was the time when he developed his own habit of using abstract lines as a guide to memory, lines that did not *represent*, but *underlay* the forms and characters he saw when he strolled the streets. Hogarth acknowledged that habit can train the eye to enjoy particular things, but he still held that there are certain essential shapes and effects of light and shade and colour that have always pleased the eye. Although these are echoed constantly in different cultural forms – from sculpture to fashions – ultimately they spring from nature. It is to this primary source, not the secondary source of art that we must look first.

Despite the huffing and puffing of the introduction, *The Analysis of Beauty* was intensely original, demolishing the pillars of conventional thinking about art. In the middle of his book, Hogarth moved to a more technical analysis of line, proportion, light, shade and colour. And finally he turned to the human face, and the body in action, scouring his own social world for a living, enacted ideal of the line of grace.

The *Analysis* is, above all, about ways of seeing, starting from the eye itself – 'that great inlet of beauty'. At one stage Hogarth notes that the pupil is the only organ of the human body that remains the same size in a baby, a mature adult and a man of a hundred. He is fascinated by the *process* of perception, and struggles to put this into active, physical language. He asks the reader to experiment, while actually reading his text, by concentrating on one letter, say, 'A', in the middle of a line as if an 'imaginary ray' was drawn from the eye to the page and to note how the letters on each side fade gradually into indistinctness – but when we try to see the whole line at a sweep, 'the imaginary ray must course it to and fro with great celerity'. The eye and mind are not passive but *active* – wondrous in their 'amazing ease and swiftness'. This conjures up an early memory of his own childish delight in watching the spinning fly of a jack, always moving, and yet always the same. This 'beguiling movement', he says, gave him the same sensation as when he later watched a country dance, 'particularly when my eye eagerly pursued a favourite dancer, through all the windings of the figure, who then was bewitching to the sight'.[37]

Hogarth firmly equates 'beauty' with pleasure – with what the eye finds most delight in. And in tracking beauty to its root in physical sensation he had to jettison the Shaftesburian notion that beauty was recognized not physically, but morally. To some extent Hogarth agreed. On one draft page he noted that since our judgements are dictated by 'the mind and heart', we should consider carefully how we place moral values on appearances. Admitting that his starting point is personal ('Probably many will not agree with me'), he tries to order 'the inherent quallity of objects & the motions they excite in us'. This is how his notes look:

Fitness	uniformity and Regularity	Fitness excites a pleasure equall or similar to that of truth and Justice. uniformity and regularity, are pleasures of contentment.
Variety	Simplicity and distinctness Intricacy quantity	Variety excites the lively feeling of wantonness and play Intricacy like the joy of persute quantity excite the pleasure of admiration of wonder.[38]

The sequence is intriguing in relation to his own prints, but for the *Analysis* he eventually set aside the moral route as a false start, another evasion of the absolute question, 'What *is* beauty?' In his Preface he claimed that only an artist could answer this. The complexity of the problem must make it inexplicable to 'mere men of letters,' he wrote sardonically, otherwise the 'ingenious gentlemen who have lately published treatises' would not have become bewildered and 'obliged so suddenly to turn into the broad and more beaten path of moral beauty'.

Hogarth also abandoned the treatises' standard arrangment by genre. Instead, his opening chapters were on 'Fitness', 'Variety', 'Uniformity, Regularity, or Symmetry', 'Distinctness', 'Intricacy' and 'Quantity'. He celebrated the joy of surprise and discovery, likening the questing movement of the eye through a composition to the animal joy of the hunt for its own sake: 'The hound dislikes the game he so eagerly pursues; and even cats will risk the losing of their prey to chase it over again.' In human terms, this is both the delight of the riddle and the playful excitement of sexual pursuit. 'Intricacy in form', he concluded, '*leads the eye a wanton kind of chace*, and from the pleasure that gives the mind, intitles it to the name of beautiful.'[39] Many of his ideas – of the beauty of asymmetry, of detail, of curving lines and fluctuating light and shade – recall the delicate, restless excess of rococo. But he also saw beauty in the Gothic and the picturesque:

'Huge shapeless rocks have a pleasing kind of horror in them, and the wide ocean awes us with its vast contents; but when forms of beauty are presented to the eye in large quantities, the pleasure increases on the mind, and horror is soften'd into reverence.'[40]

The *Analysis* is redeemed from reductiveness by this open-mindedness, and by the energy with which Hogarth wrestled with ideas and tackled the hard task of translating visual sensations and techniques into words. While he dismissed the theorists, and the artists who neglected to *think* about underlying principles, he never patronized the 'ordinary' reader. After the Preface, in the main body of his book he talked more of candlesticks and corsets than of goddesses and secret signs. His writing was as colourful and forthright as his speech, shunning the language of the virtuosi, 'over-born by pompous terms of art' and 'hard names'.[41] Every time he took a famous example from classical sculpture – the Farnese Hercules, the Venus de Medici and the Apollo Belvedere, the Laocoön and the Antinous – he explained their composition and structure, and why they produced certain effects; of fitness, of beauty, of struggling power, of athletic grace.

Hogarth illustrated these statues in his first plate, adding a border of diagrams and sketches, all keyed into his text. His 'Statuary's Yard' places the sculptures in witty juxtapositions, like the smug, absurd dancing master standing next to the graceful Antinous. Each illustrates a point, but the picture as a whole also comments on the impoverished copies that stood for 'antique beauty'. The yard was based on that of Henry Cheere's brother John, one of many providing lead garden statues of goddesses, nymphs and shepherds, shells and dolphins.[42] Cultivated readers might also see Hogarth's plate as a sarcastic riposte to Arthur Pond's successful prints of *Roman Antiquities*, or as a comment on Joseph Spence's book *Polymetis*, where a dialogue takes place in a garden full of copies of classical deities.[43] But all readers knew such statues: it was easy to take Hogarth's point that the golden age had turned, literally, to an age of lead. His comic groups were in line with Garrick's prologue to *Taste*, spoken as 'Peter Puff', the auctioneer:

> 'Tis said *Virtu* to such a height is grown
> All Artists are encourag'd – but our own.
> Be not deceiv'd, I here declare an Oath,
> I never yet sold *Goods* of *foreign* growth:

155 'The Statuary's Yard', *The Analysis of Beauty*, Plate 1 (1753)

Ne'er sent Commissions out to *Greece* or *Rome*;
My best antiquities are made at Home.
I've *Romans*, *Greeks*, *Italians* near at hand
True *Britons* all – and living in the Strand.[44]

Hogarth was also making another point. In Xenophon's *Memorabilia*, to which Morell had directed him, Socrates is discussing beauty in a sculptor's yard and adds that an object's 'beauty' is related to its use – be it a labourer's hod, or a hero's shield.[45] This text would be well known to the connoisseurs, who could relate it to Hogarth's own treatment of 'fitness', which linked form to function rather than to rules of proportion. For less educated readers he said the same thing more simply: 'When a vessel sails well, the sailors always call her a beauty.'[46]

Hogarth constantly used such examples and analogies to help readers

530

follow his argument. He delights in the 'infinite hints' nature offers the artist: the way a waterfall 'naturally' forms a curve, or the fact that 'the original of the Corinthian capital was taken from nothing more, as is said, than some dock leaves growing up against a basket'. The *Analysis* is rich with examples from the world of plants and animals, rainbows and dusty fields. As well as illustrating the text, these illuminate Hogarth's own sheer delight in *looking*. He loves the great and powerful beasts, the elephants and whales that 'please us with their unweildy greatness'. He thrills to the powerful grace of the Arabian war-horse, 'unbacked and at liberty', curvetting from side to side while his mane and tail sweep the air.[47] But he also loves the small: when writing of 'lines', he contrasts the harsh zig-zags of the Indian fig or torch-thistle to the curving lily and the Calcidonian iris. And there is an almost Ruskinian discrimination in the way he notes the intricate asymmetrical relation of parts to the whole in the natural world: the parsley leaf, for example,

'from whence a beautiful foliage in ornament was originally taken, is divided into three distinct passages; which are again divided into other odd numbers; and this method is observ'd, for the generality, in the leaves of all plants and flowers, the most simple of which are the trefoil and cinquefoil'.[48]

Hogarth asked his readers, above all, to 'see with their own eyes'. Often he took images from the London streets – the rising pyramids of Wren's steeples or the supreme 'composed variety' of St Paul's – and from the characters that peopled his city, beggars, boxers and watermen, dairymaids and cook-girls. Equally often he chose his models from ordinary household objects – chairs, candlesticks, ornaments on a grate – or from fashion and dress. Thus he uses the way whalebone stays should fit a body to demonstrate gradations from the ideal line; or the 'awful dignity' of a judge's robes to illustrate quantity; or a curling lock of hair to show our impulse to break uniformity. He enjoys shaping such things to his ideas, like the way women dress their hair with 'picturesque' intricacy:

'braided together from behind, like intertwisted serpents, arising thickest from the bottom, lessening as it is brought forward, and naturally conforming to the shape of the rest of the hair it is pin'd over'.[49]

All these images are direct, immediate, alive. But some of Hogarth's examples are harder to grasp, especially when he writes about the way an artist represents a phenomenon that the eye registers without conscious thought, like perspective. Here the untrained reader has to concentrate hard, pushing

531

the mind to 'see'. Even simple visual effects are complex, like light filtering through a door, or different shading rendering things convex or concave. Perhaps the most difficult of Hogarth's images to grasp is the most essential: his definition of 'line'. In the Introduction he says he has declared his intention of 'considering minutely the variety of lines, which serve to raise the ideas of bodies in the mind'.[50] But there is no such thing as an 'outline' in nature, only the play of light on a three-dimensional world. To understand how lines and flat paint can represent the 'real', we need to conceive 'as accurate an idea as is possible, of the *inside* of those surfaces'. He asks us to think of objects as being 'scooped out', like a shell, and to imagine lines radiating from the centre, with all the points where they meet the surface linked by another network. These invisible 'threads' will lie like an undulating web, mapping the most subtle contours. Perhaps late twentieth-century readers find this easier, since it is very like computer graphic modelling, in which an image can be revolved and viewed from within or without and from different angles, making us aware that a 'line' does not end, but always disappears around the contour of the figure. Hogarth's 'line of beauty' is not, therefore, a harsh outline but – as Edmund Burke put it, 'a waving surface'.[51]

In many ways, as with the scooped-out shell, Hogarth's whole book tries to look beneath the surface. He explores the way patterns imprinted on the lens of the eye are conveyed to the mind, sometimes tricking it with illusions. But the idea of the form *hidden* from the eye is equally important. This is evoked acutely in his detailed sections on bones and muscles, on the fat beneath the skin, or the filaments and pigments of flesh. There is something alarming as well as fascinating here, as Hogarth knows full well. Acknowledging that the thought of a flayed body makes the muscles 'lose in the imagination some of the beauty, which they really have', he hastens to add that he is not describing a quivering corpse, but a plaster-of-Paris cast, prepared by Cowper, 'the famous anatomist'.[52] Yet in his book as well as in the grim surgeon's theatre of *The Four Stages of Cruelty*, he shows that understanding nature means confronting ugliness as well as beauty, pain as well as pleasure. One senses the ruthless violence of the chase as well as its thrill.

Nature and culture combine to shield us from the knowledge that 'beauty' is literally skin deep. The hidden organs are not beautiful, says Hogarth, but nature has 'clothed' them to soften angles, to please with varying hues. We continue the process, beautifying the body with dress and rules of deportment. This returns to the 'wanton chace', as Hogarth restates the seductive mystery of the covered surface in sexual terms. While the face keeps curiosity awake because of its play of expression, he says,

'The rest of the body, not having these advantages, would soon satiate the eye, were it to be as constantly exposed, nor would it have more effect than a marble statue. But when it is artfully cloath'd and decorated, the mind at every turn resumes its imaginary pursuits concerning it. Thus, if I may be allowed a simile, the angler chooses not to see the fish he angles for, until it is fairly caught.'[53]

Hogarth often falls into such predatory language. When he quotes Milton, he cites the dances of the angels but also the ringlets of Eve and the sliding grace of the serpent. This is the text on his title page:

> So vary'd he, and of his tortuous train
> Curled many a wanton wreath, in sight of Eve,
> To lure her eye.

If Eden was created by God (although Hogarth prefers a female goddess, 'Nature'), its forms were used by Satan to beguile. The pursuit of beauty is dangerous: the ultimate desire to embrace and possess the world. This was the downfall of Faust, and of all Hogarth's own doomed over-reachers.

Against this driving desire Hogarth sets his rules of precision, of the 'composed' scene, of space and gradation. The rhetorical balance of excess and restraint is his own, but it is also of its age, invoking the elusive golden mean. We can understand why the statue of Antinous is 'perfect' he says, if we imagine it placed between an unwieldy musclebound Atlas and a slim, nimble Mercury.[54] Similarly, the beauty of the rainbow lies partly in the way that opposite colours form a third by 'imparting to each their peculiar qualities': thus yellow and blue 'visibly approach, and blend by interchangable degrees, and, as above, *temper* rather than destroy each other's vigour'.[55] As that language suggests, despite Hogarth's renunciation of the moral, he embraces ideals of decorum that are social as much as aesthetic. This is why he moves from art to 'grace' in manner and the body in action. 'Action is a sort of language', wrote Hogarth, 'which perhaps one time or other may come to be taught by a kind of grammar rules.' Ignoring his own brusque manner and short, stubby form, he advises that elegant movements,

'may be attain'd by a sensibility within yourself, tho you have not a sight of what you do by looking in the glass, when with your head assisted by a sway of the body in order to give it more scope, you endeavour to make that very serpentine line in the air, which the hands have before been taught to do . . . and I will venture to say, a few careful repetitions at first setting out will make this movement as easy to the head as to the hands and arms.'[56]

There is something comically touching about the thought of a stout, fifty-five-year-old Hogarth practising serpentine lines, with or without a mirror.[57] Even in his plates for the *Analysis*, he could not quite hit it off: in 'The Country Dance', Horace Walpole found his two 'samples of grace' to be 'strikingly stiff and affected . . . a Bath beau and a county beauty'.[58] And Hogarth himself noted wryly how 'people of rank and fortune generally excel their originals, the dancing-masters, in easy behaviour and unaffected grace', because they have the confidence to relax.[59]

Like Fielding, Hogarth saw deviations from social ease – in dress, behaviour, art and writing – as inherently ugly. Both men claimed that comedy was the best way to illustrate this; thus cleverly allowing them to pack their work with all the 'low' characters and carnivalesque extremes they ostensibly disapproved of. One of the most original sections of the *Analysis* is Hogarth's theory of visual humour, which first appears in the chapter 'On Quantity', where he notes that a full wig gives dignity, but if drawn twice as large again it immediately becomes 'a burlesque', and if 'an improper person' wears it, it also looks ridiculous. This prompted the thought, added in the margin of his first draft, that when 'improper, or *incompatible* excesses meet, they always excite laughter; more especially when the forms of those excesses are inelegant, that is, when they are composed of unvaried lines'.[60] Immediately a host of theatrical memories swam up – of the man dressed as a baby at Bartholomew Fair; of a Roman general in a tragedy wearing a peruke; of a dancing master playing a god; of the miller's sack in *Dr Faustus*, lumpily jumping across the stage. Even nature could look ridiculous, like the owl and the ass, who seem to be 'gravely musing' under their awkward forms. There is fondness as well as humour in these rushing observations:

'There is something extremely odd and comical in the rough shock dog. The ideas here connected are the inelegant and inanimate figure of a thrum mop, or muff, and that of a sensible, friendly animal; which is as much a burlesque of the dog, as the monkey when his coat is on, is of the man.'[61]

These conjunctions of ideas are not the same as the mixed forms of mythic monsters – the powerful sphinx and siren, the griffin and centaur. The comedy lies in the *inelegance*. Going over this passage, he scribbled some pencil notes on the back of a sheet, which survived in the final text as a playful acknowledgement that even religious art can be 'ridiculous' – and yet acceptable:

'I shall mention but one more instance of this sort, and that the most

534

extraordinary of all, which is an infant's head of about two years old, with a pair of duck's wings placed under its chin, supposed always to be flying about, and singing psalms.

'A painter's representation of heaven would be nothing without swarms of these little inconsistent objects, flying about, or perching on the clouds; and yet there is something so agreable in their form, that the eye is reconciled and overlooks the absurdity, and we find them in the carving and painting of almost every church. St Pauls is full of them.'[62]

When he writes on humour, Hogarth gives glimpses of how his own mind worked when he was drawing, or planning a character. Writing on 'attitude', he says that 'the general idea of an action, as well as an attitude, may be given with a pencil in a very few lines' – the backward curve of Coypel's Sancho Panza, for example, immediately conveys 'the comical posture of

156 'The Country Dance', *The Analysis of Beauty*, Plate II

535

astonishment'.[63] He includes a little sketch of this in the border to his second plate, and illustrates his theme more fully in the main picture. On the left, a courtly couple demonstrate the graceful minuet, its pattern outlined in the formal dance notation in a panel above. In contrast, all the other, more plebeian, characters are made up of exaggerated curves or straight lines. For once he actually hints at how his mnemonic visual alphabet might work: 'A curve and two straight lines at right angles, gave the hint for the fat man's sprawling posture.' To the awkward man in a bag wig, he says, he gave 'a sort of X', while the prim lady in the riding habit, 'pecking back her elbows' made 'a tolerable D, with a straight line under it to signify the scanty stiffness of her petticoat'. 'Z' stood for the angular legs and thighs of 'the affected fellow in the tye-wig', and 'O' for the upper body of his plump partner. The shapes of the old masters on the walls are similarly crude, portraits of British monarchs, good and bad, gazing down on the subjects of the present day. Here again, this is a nation dancing together: the polite are teaching 'grace' to the people, and the point is strengthened by the way that the young lord is now made to look like the Prince of Wales.[64]

If the visible world, to Hogarth, was a lexicon of shapes, it was also a pageant of moving forms. In a minuet with its twists and passes, its sinking curtseys and gentle bows, he saw 'the greatest variety of movements in serpentine lines imaginable, keeping pace with musical time'.[65] A romantic as well as a realist, he thought at once of *A Winter's Tale*:

> – What you do,
> Still betters what is done, –
> When you do dance, I wish you
> A wave o' th' sea, that you might ever do
> Nothing but that; move still, still so,
> And own no other function. –

Dances could be grotesque, like 'the wild skipping, jumping and turning around' of 'barbarians', but they could also be 'mystic' in their communal grace. He thrilled to the involved figures of the best country dances, and to the 'angular forms' of the comic peasant rounds of the Italian troupes, 'expressing elegant wantonness (which is the true spirit of dancing)'. Lately, he wrote, these have been 'most delightfully done, and seem at present to have got the better of pompous, unmeaning grand ballets; serious dancing being even a contradiction in terms'.

Even here, he was caught in the graded evaluation of 'high' and 'low', the genteel and the burlesque. Yet his chief delight was *formal*: he evokes his

536

intense pleasure watching dancing, when 'seen at one view, as at the playhouse from the gallery'. And as he looked down from there at the familiar characters of the *commedia dell'arte* he confessed he could not help but 'consider them lineally as to their particular movements':

'The attitudes of the harlequin are ingeniously composed of certain little, quick movements of the head, hands and feet, some of which shoot out as it were from the body in straight line, or are twirled around in little circles.

'Scaramouch is gravely absurd as the character is intended, in over-stretched movements of unnatural length of lines: these two characters seem to have been contrived by conceiving a direct opposition of movements.

'Pierott's movements and attitudes, are chiefly in perpendiculars and parallels, so is his figure and dress.

'Punchinello is droll by being the reverse of all elegance, both as to move-ment and figure, the beauty of variety is totally, and comically excluded from this character in every respect; his limbs are raised and let fall almost at one time, in parallel directions, as if his seeming fewer joints than ordinary, were no better than the hinges of a door.'[66]

A foreigner, Hogarth maintained, could place each character from hero to clown, simply from this mobile linear script.

The book that starts with learned quotations and assertions about the ancient mysteries of art ends by moving right away from the the studio and the canvas to the ballroom and the theatre. It closes abruptly, instructing not the painter but 'the comedian, whose business it is to imitate the actions of nature'. In these final sections we see into Hogarth's mind, caught offguard, unable to stop himself 'abtstracting' what he sees into shapes he can block out with his brush, lines he can cut with his burin into enduring copper plates. Powerful, odd, intimate and direct, *The Analysis of Beauty* leaves us with Hogarth not as would-be history-painter but as visual dramatist, the man who wrote, 'my Picture was my Stage and men and women my actors who were by Means of certain Actions and expressions to exhibit a dumb shew'.

26

Factions and Elections

Dunce Connoisseurs extol the Author Pugg.
This sensless, tasteless, impudent Hum Bugg.
PAUL SANDBY, *Pugg's Graces* (1754)

'The truth is, I look upon both candidates in the same light;
and should think myself a traitor to the constitution of my
country if I voted for either.'
TOBIAS SMOLLETT, *Humphrey Clinker* (1771)

POLITE SOCIETY WAS INTRIGUED BY *The Analysis of Beauty*. It exclaimed over it at tea tables, argued about it over dinner and joked knowingly about the serpentine line. Lady Henrietta Luxborough, Bolingbroke's daughter, wrote twice to the poet William Shenstone, begging to borrow a copy: 'I shall be glad to see the Analysis of Beauty, however described; and am sorry I have not *now* an S in my name to claim any share in it.' When she sent the book back she forgave Hogarth for not fixing the 'precise degree' of his line, 'because I think the task too hard to be performed literally; but yet he conveys an idea between his pencil and his pen, which makes one conceive his meaning pretty well'. She admitted, in a double-edged way, that she had been agreeably surprised, 'for I had conceived the performance to be a set of prints only, whereas I found a book which I did not imagine Hogarth capable of writing'.[1]

The press, too, was kind. *The Gentleman's Magazine* carried a short, positive recommendation in December and a full review in January, which concluded that the book would have a lasting life, despite the enemies Hogarth would undoubtedly win through his certainty of his own rightness. The new *Monthly Review* also praised it. Admittedly, the review was written by its editor, William Rose, Hogarth's neighbour in Chiswick, but still, it was heartening to read that he had treated his subject

'with great accuracy, and in a manner entirely new; has thrown out several curious hints, which may be of no small service to painters and statuaries, &c has fairly overthrown some long-received and deep-rooted opinions'.[2]

Abroad, where Hogarth's prints sold well, a German translation was warmly promoted by Lessing.

The connoisseurs, of course, did *not* like it. Disdainful voices were raised, scoffing at Hogarth's effort to tread on their ground. Within a week of publication, Arthur Murphy's *Gray's Inn Journal* printed some verse, supposed to come from the Bedford Coffee-House, responding to the wits who had 'exercised their Talents' on the book there, 'for a few days past.

> *Hogarth*, thy fate is fix'd; the Critic Crew,
> The Connoisseurs and Dablers in Vertu,
> Club their united Wit, in ev'ry Look
> Hint, shrug, and whisper, they condemn thy Book:
> Their guiltless Minds will ne'er forgive the Deed;
> What Devil prompted thee to write and read?[3]

Hogarth's statements on dress and stays were gently parodied in *The World*, which linked them not with beauty, but with satires on fashion and examples of 'deformity'.[4] *The World* was a new journal, started that February by Edward Moore, helped by a circle of virtuosi that included Horace Walpole and the Earl of Chesterfield, and soon a riposte came from Thornton's and Colman's counter-paper, the satiric *Connoisseur*. This was a bantering, light-hearted contribution to the long argument about taste that had gathered pace since *Marriage A-la-Mode*, and would be canvassed in a host of books in the 1750s.[5] While Thornton's *Drury-Lane Journal* had adopted Moll Hackabout, now his ironic 'Mr Town' promised that all the *Connoisseur*'s essays would represent the world in a Hogarthian spirit:

'like those painters who delineate the scenes of familiar life, we sometimes give a sketch of a marriage *à la mode*, sometimes draw the outlines of a modern midnight conversation, at another time paint the comical distresses of itinerant tragedians in a barn, and at another give a full draught of the Rake's or Harlot's progress.'[6]

In their eighth issue Thornton and Colman were quick to imply that in criticizing the *Analysis*, collectors were now getting their own back on Hogarth for the Rembrandt hoax, among other things.[7] This all made for lively, combative reading. But much of Hogarth's argument had been addressed to the artists themselves and here his reception was mixed. Some colleagues at St Martin's Lane were sneeringly dismissive, like James Wills, who had painted one of the Foundling scenes and was now translating Du Fresnoy, who wrote off the S-shaped line as a 'fine stroke' for a copper engraver, but meaningless in the wider art of painting.[8]

Many artists found individual insights useful, but even those sympathetic to Hogarth felt he had damaged his cause by his dogmatic, quotation-stuffed preface. They also, rightly, doubted whether anyone could reduce 'beauty' – a subjective apprehension – to a formal 'rule'. This was the response of Ramsay, who would point out in the *Essay on Taste*, published in March 1755, that Hogarth himself acknowledged that ideals of beauty could be local and cultural. Ramsay's judicious criticism was softened by his deep appreciation of the realism of Hogarth's art, which could speak even to the lowest and most illiterate, but his reminders of subjectivity and of beauty as constructed by convention were later echoed publicly by Burke and by Joshua Reynolds.[9] At the time, in private, Reynolds reacted with understandable irritation, complaining that Hogarth treated his fellow artists 'pretty cavalierly' by saying they did not understand beauty of line theoretically but 'only as a Labourer who makes use of his leaver'. He also objected that Hogarth, despite his 'air of superiority & self-sufficiency', gave no philosophical account of his theory himself: 'it is so only because it is so'.[10]

Many had reservations, but on the whole, this odd, original book was surprisingly well received. Yet for Hogarth the good reception was wiped out by an instant assault from his own, extremely damaging, weapon, the satirical print. That December saw not one but three devastating demolitions of 'Painter Pugg'.[11] In *Burlesque sur le Burlesque* the crowds pressing outside the print-shop windows could immediately recognize the 'history-painter' Hogarth, half pug, half human. He has *two* pugs (the second one, 'Jewel', is chewing his bone into a serpentine line) and his fat friend Hoadly is reading to him from his 'great work'. The studio windows have shutters papered with lives of the great artists, marked 'Pour Raphael', 'Pour Rubens', 'Pour Titian', 'Le Brun Vandyke' and 'Pour Rembrandt'. In the gloom Hogarth is sitting before a vast canvas – an obscene modern *Sacrifice of Isaac*, where the angel saves the boy by pissing in the firing-pan of Abraham's musket. On the wall is a magic- lantern show, in which Hogarth himself is the lantern, burlesquing and distorting nature instead of displaying it.

In the second print, *The Analyst Besh—n*, Lomazzo's ghost looms up to accuse Hogarth of plagiarism. In fear his bowels give way as graphically as those of Felix facing Paul in his own burlesque and his fans witness his disgrace: the key even includes 'His faithful Pugg finding his Master by the Scent'. In a third print, *The Vile Ephesian*, Hogarth became Herostratus, who burned down the temple of Diana at Ephesus to win immortal fame: with the temple blazing behind, he and his helpers are preparing to blow up a huge column, wreathed by a serpentine line and reliefs of great artists.

157 Paul Sandby, *Burlesque sur le Burlesque* (1753)

Compared to many scurrilous contemporary satires these were restrained, but they hit their target unerringly, suggesting Hogarth's pretensions, his narrow, exaggerated theory, his lack of learning and reliance on others, his 'natural' propensity for low subjects and his disdain for past greatness. Although they were anonymous it was well known that Hogarth's attacker was

541

Paul Sandby, a versatile, innovative young artist of twenty-four. Sandby was no insignificant foe; as well as prints he went on to produce fine work in water-colours and gouache which had considerable influence on the growing land-scape school. The son of a Nottingham frame-worker, in the 1740s he joined his older brother Thomas who worked for the Board of the Ordnance Survey, and after the ''45' he was sent on a surveying party to Scotland.[12] In some ways he was rather like the young Hogarth: in Edinburgh he made lively drawings of street vendors, people watching the executions of rebels, of 'A Scottish washerwoman, sketched on the spot' and later he made his own 'Cries of London'. Back in London he moved in the world that flowed around St Martin's Lane and in 1751 he and Thomas started a sketching class, sending a verse invitation to Theodosius Forrest

> Receive this humble sketch and scrawl
> From Poet Tom and Painter Paul
> Sent to inform you we at night
> Intend to deal in Shade and light . . .
> So you (like a good boy) prepare
> To Sit or Sketch a figure here
> We'll study hard from Six till Nine
> And then attack cold Beef and Wine
> In Brimmers we will drink and toste
> The Girl that we admire the most.[13]

The brothers sound very like the sociable, free-wheeling, ambitious young artists of the Vanderbank Academy in the 1720s. And, as Hogarth had done in his twenties, Paul now made his name by assaulting a major cultural target.

Ambition for publicity apart, it's hard to work out exactly why Sandby launched himself on Hogarth. In the early 1750s he was at Windsor, where Thomas was working on the improvements planned by the Duke of Cumberland, now Deputy Ranger of Windsor Forest. Admittedly Hogarth had targeted Cumberland in *The March to Finchley* and *The Savoyard Girl*, but the busy Duke would hardly have bothered to employ a cartoonist to demolish him.[14] It seems far more likely that the impetus (and the useful private details) came from Hogarth's opponents in the art world. But, here again, the people whom Sandby actually knew were, theoretically, Hogarth's friends – John Pine, Samuel Scott, and Theodosius Forrest, the son of his fellow traveller in the 'Peregrination' of 1732. Maybe they too felt he needed bringing down to earth.

Sandby had skill, wit, and inventive energy. By Christmas Hogarth was suffering, turning on himself in grim, self-mocking fury. In what he called 'A Christmas Gambol sent from Leicester Square to Westminster Hall' he sketched himself naked, wearing asses' ears, tied to a cart and whipped by an elderly connoisseur who sneers, 'You'l write books, will ye.' Above, he put a motto, ' 'Twere better a millstone had been tied about thy neck and (THOU) cast into the sea.' Below, he parodied his own advertisements:

'NB Speedily will be publishd an Apology in Quarto Calld Beauty's Defiance to Charicature? with a very extraordinary Frontispiece, a just portraiture, (printed on Fools cap paper) and discription of the Punishment that ought to be inflicted on Him that dare give false and unatural description's of Beauty or Charicature great personages, it being illegal as well as mean practice, at the same time flying in the Face of all regular bred Gentlemen Painters, Sculptures, Architects, in fine Arts and Sciences.'15

This self-inoculation did little to protect him.

In the New Year the subtext of Sandby's prints became clear: the long-running debate about a public academy. Just before the *Analysis* was published, a circular had summoned the St Martin's Lane subscribers to the Turk's Head tavern. The meeting was organized by a group of members including Frank Hayman, and the note, addressed from St Martin's Lane, was signed by the Academy's secretary, Francis Milner Newton:

'There is a scheme on foot for creating a public academy for improvement of painting, sculpture, and architecture; and it is thought necessary to have a certain number of professors, with proper authority, in order to make regulations, taking subscriptions, &c., and erecting a building, instructing the students, and concerting all such measures as shall afterwards be thought necessary.

'Your company is desired at the Turk's Head, in Gerard Street, Soho, on the 13th November, at five in the evening, to proceed to the election of thirteen painters, three sculptors, one chaser, two engravers, and two architects, in all twenty-one, for the purposes aforesaid.'16

This declaration of intent openly challenged Hogarth's views on directors, regulations, salaries and formal 'instruction'. He had, it seems, already drafted a pamphlet against it and Sandby's prints were a pre-emptive strike: in *The Analyst Besh—n* a classical pediment rises behind him, a 'public Academy', taking shape, 'in Spight of his endeavours to prevent it'.

The Turk's Head meeting came to nothing, but in January 1754 a new Sandby print, *Puggs Graces*, attacked the *Analysis* and Hogarth. The artist

543

was shown ogling a trio of naked grotesques, his floor cluttered with candlesticks, stays, a wooden leg and even 'rays of light' and against the table lies his pamphlet, 'Reasons against a Publick Academy', with a page marked 'No Salary'. The onslaught was unceasing. In March Sandby produced two more prints ridiculing Hogarth as an ignorant, deluded crank. One made him into a *Mountebank Painter*, flogging his wares to fairground crowds of serpentine-line-shaped hunchbacks and fools. The caption was a huckster's cry, challenging,

'The Arrogant Quacking Analist who is blinded by the darkest ignorance of ye principles of Painting . . . to produce one Piece of his either in Painting, or on Copper plate, that has ye least GRACE BEAUTY or so much knowledge in PROPORTION as may be found in common signs in every Street'.[17]

The second showed *The Author Run Mad*, tracing his own designs on the walls of Bedlam (of which Hogarth was now a Governor).

There was little Hogarth's friends could do. Thomas Burgess did produce two counter-prints, one of connoisseurs stamping on Hogarth, Milton and Shakespeare and a second called *A Club of Artists*, where Sandby's *Burlesque* is presented to Hogarth as lavatory paper, and Hayman offers him an Academy study of a naked woman, saying 'hear a Director's Academy take this'.[18] But these were feeble compared to Sandby's vigorous, acutely personal images. He caught Hogarth's stubby, broad-shouldered form and snub-nosed face, with the bags under his eyes, his strutting pose, cocked hat and awkward gestures. Even more cruelly, he used Hogarth's own work: the quack at *Southwark Fair* and the mad astronomer in *A Rake's Progress*. And in April he produced *The Painter's March from Finchley*, 'Dedicated to the King of the Gypsies as an encourager of Art'. This was packed with Hogarth signatures – the whores at the windows, the milkmaid from *The Enraged Musician*, the false-perspective horns from *Evening* – and aside from the innuendo of impotence and cuckoldry, the print turned conventional tributes upside down, making Hogarth 'our low refracting Mirror of ye age'. He was shown below the main picture, sitting glumly in the stocks. Soon all the prints were collected with a title page showing the grinning artist flanked by his buffoon-like helpers, Harlequin and a blind beggar. This, it proclaimed, was *A New DUNCIAD done with a view of fixing the fluctuating IDEAS of TASTE*, adding, as if with a final, insulting sigh of relief 'without Preface or Introduction'. At a stroke Sandby banished Hogarth back to Grub Street.

Hogarth tried to be stoical, but Sandby's prints stung him to the quick. It was a trite observation, he wrote, 'that as life is chequer'd', every success has

544

its reverse, so although his book had been 'well receiv'd both at home and abroad by the generality yet I suffered more [uneasiness] from the abuse it occations me than satisfaction from its success'.[19] It was nothing less than he expected, he added.

Deeply hurt by this attack from the artists, shaken and vulnerable, Hogarth appealed again to the public who had always applauded his 'comic history painting'. By the time *The Painter's March from Finchley* appeared, he had turned his attention with a snarl and shrug of the shoulders, to faction in the wider world.

Over the past year, the papers had been full of stories of political dealing. After the last election of 1747 Henry Pelham had managed his ministry with diplomatic skill and for a while Parliament was calm: in 1751 Henry Fox told Charles Hanbury Williams,

'There never was such a session as this is likely to be. The halcyon days the poets wrote of cannot exceed its calmness. A bird might build his nest in the speaker's chair, or in his peruke. There won't be a debate that can disturb her.'[20]

He was wrong. When Frederick, Prince of Wales, died in March the opposition that had gathered around him at Leicester House fell apart and there was a brisk reshuffle of interests. Leading anti-Pelhamites like George Bubb Dodington re-entered the government fold, and Pelham's position was strengthened when his ministerial rivals the Earl of Sandwich and the Duke of Bedford lost their posts.[21] But he still had to control 'Walpole's Whelps': Fox and his great rival William Pitt. A new opposition, which included Fox, threatened to coalesce around Cumberland, Commander in Chief of the Army and George II's favourite son. On Frederick's death, the Dowager Princess of Wales had rushed to heal the breach with the King, and Pelham made sure she was named as Regent for the young Prince George if the King died, with Cumberland – who hated her – simply as President of the Regency Council. After this Regency Act, old antagonisms crystallized. Some prints attacked Cumberland as a Richard III, longing to murder his nephew in the Tower; others attacked the Dowager Princess, whispering that the young Prince's advisers, including William Murray and Lord Bute, were Jacobite intriguers.

The shifting tides mattered for artists and writers dependent on the great. Fielding, for example, was sponsored by the Duke of Bedford in Westminster, while the turncoat Dodington was also his patron (praised in *Amelia*, ironically, for his principled opposition stance). James Ralph, too, was swept by the changing currents. Having run opposition papers, first for Dodington, then for Bedford, in November 1753 he swapped sides, bought off by the Duke of Newcastle with a hefty annual retainer.[22] Hogarth was more independent than the magistrate Fielding, or the journalist Ralph. But he too took stock. In the past, he had flirted with Leicester House, showing Frederick cheering Goodchild at the Lord Mayor's procession in *Industry and Idleness* and young George as the 'good child' in *The Four Stages of Cruelty*. With Frederick gone, he leaned tentatively towards the Cumberland camp that he had previously satirized, and especially towards his lieutenant, Henry Fox.

In 1753, while Hogarth was in the final throes of working on the *Analysis*, the somnolent Parliament was shaken into life. Pelham's opponents – Whigs as well as Tories – seized on a series of issues to mobilize 'public opinion' in the cause of their own power struggles. The ministry's troubles began in February with the Jewish Naturalisation Bill, a moderate measure to give citizenship rights to Jews born abroad now living in Britain.[23] Introduced by Bedford, who perhaps saw how explosive it was, the Bill moved easily through the parliamentary stages – the Jewish community was small, and outside London almost the only Jews seen were wandering pedlars – and the government foresaw few objections. But when the Act was finally passed in May, chaos broke out. On protective economic grounds, anti-immigration feeling ran high (two years earlier a Bill to naturalize foreign Protestants was dropped after opposition from the City and the Tories) and this time it merged with a High Church fervour as intense as in the riots of Hogarth's youth. City merchants, High Tory bishops and xenophobic Whigs joined forces; placard-bearing crowds marched and jeered. The ministry was the real target – the mob did not attack Jews or their property – but anti-Semitic scare stories filled the press, prophesying that the 'crucifiers' would take over the nation, children would be circumcised, the eating of pork would be forbidden. As Walpole noted incredulously,

'in a few months the whole nation found itself inflamed with a Christian zeal, which was thought happily extinguished with the ashes of Queen Anne and Sacheverell . . . and aldermen grew drunk at county clubs in the cause of Jesus Christ, as they used to do for King James'.

It was absurd, yet after six months, 'to this senseless clamour did the ministry give way; and to secure tranquillity to elections, submitted to repeal the bill!'[24]

More excitement came in May and June over Hardwicke's 'Marriage Bill', which outlawed clandestine marriages, insisting on the banns being read and on parental permission for the special licence for minors. This drew furious speeches from Bedford in the Lords and from a brilliant Charles Townshend in the Commons. An outraged Henry Fox also spoke out, acting from passion as well as pragmatism since he saw the Bill as an attack on his own elopement with the Duke of Richmond's daughter, Caroline Lennox. In Parliament and on the streets Fox and his followers argued, as Hogarth had done in *Marriage A-la-Mode*, against denying men and women the freedom to choose a partner counter to their parents' wishes. It was an ill-judged move: when the Act was finally passed, Fox hastily recanted, realizing he had made an implacable enemy of Lord Chancellor Hardwicke – who despised his recantation and damned him as 'a dark, gloomy and insidious genius who was an engine of personality and faction'.[25]

All summer the unrest continued. Anti-Jacobite feeling had reared up again the previous year with the discovery of another, final, plot to restore the Pretender: its leader, Archibald Cameron, was executed in June (the cause of the outburst on Samuel Johnson's part that so astonished Hogarth). In July, there was widespread trouble over turnpikes: Thomas Gray feared his journey would be stopped by the 'Mob at Leeds', where armed gangs supporting ancient 'liberties' were burning toll-houses and ripping down the turnpike-bars.[26] A different outcry had arisen much earlier when the Act abolishing the Old Style Julian calendar came into effect.[27] The last day of the old calendar was 2 September 1752, and the next day, 3 September, was arbitrarily named the 14th to cohere with the new Gregorian calendar used across Europe. It was too bewildering; muddled and angry citizens protested loudly, claiming they had been robbed of eleven days of life.

Hogarth was right to see national politics as a fruitful subject: passions ran high. A General Election was due in April 1754 and during the winter of 1753 he began working on a painting of the feasting, dealing and chicanery that would accompany it. Then, suddenly, on 6 March, only a month before the election, Henry Pelham died – of a stroke induced, it was rumoured, by one of his gargantuan meals. A popular print showed him entering Hell, with his crimes (especially the Jew Act) outdoing those of all his forebears, including Walpole, Wolsey, Judge Jeffreys and Machiavelli.[28] Immediately, omens were seized upon: after Pelham's death ten days of blizzards hit London. As Horace Walpole said in an oft-quoted quip:

'Almost as extraordinary news as our political is that it has snowed ten days successively and most part of each day. It is living in Muscovy, amid ice and revolutions.'[29]

In the freezing city, slithering across the political ice, shocked politicians hustled for position. Emissaries sped across London; urgent meetings were

547

held by night; tactics were planned, apologies were tendered for old sins, promises of future posts were hinted. Pelham's death robbed the ministry of its vital leader in the House of Commons. Although his brother Newcastle became First Lord of the Treasury and Hardwicke was still Lord Chancellor, they were both in the House of Lords and it was hard to control the unruly MPs from a distance. With hindsight, it seemed that there were really only two contenders for Pelham's successor – Fox or Pitt – but Newcastle loathed Fox, and the King and Cumberland hated Pitt. Newcastle hedged by choosing as his Secretaries of State the useless Sir Thomas Robinson and the far abler Solicitor-General, William Murray. The former was Hogarth's neighbour in Chiswick and the latter had commissioned *Paul* for Lincoln's Inn. But if Hogarth hoped for interest, he was out of luck; the battle for influence still raged.

In the next few weeks Fox badly mishandled things, turning down offers of posts, retiring in despair to Holland House and, to the alarm of his wife, taking badly to drink. Soon Pitt, who had decided to bide his time and stay loyal to Newcastle, also began to feel overlooked and chagrined. To outsiders it seemed as if the two most brilliant men in the House of Commons had been ignored, while Newcastle shored up his own power. For a short time the two rivals joined forces, a ferocious alliance which destroyed Robinson and silenced Murray.

With his old, opportunistic bravura, Hogarth seized the moment. On 19 March, within a fortnight of Pelham's death, he opened his subscription for his new print, *An Election Entertainment*. It would cost half a guinea, with 5s 6d to pay now, and the same on publication. (Sandby took note, and his *Author Run Mad* showed the Election plate lying on the floor, labelled 'a New Scheme to Humbug the Public'.) While the bitter cold struck deep and hard, lasting well into April, Hogarth planned his work, deciding that the *Entertainment* would be the first of a set, *Four Prints of an Election*. The other scenes, he said in an advertisement in late April, would be 'Canvassing for Votes, Polling at the Hustings, and Chairing the Members'.[30]

As his friend Rouquet said sardonically in *The State of the Arts* in 1755, no artist could get ahead 'if he has no right to vote at elections, or no protectors possessed of such a right'.[31] Hogarth, though, was looking for a protector who was *above* the voters, who manipulated them and rewarded them. His own self-interested shifts were suggested by his subscription ticket for the Election series, 'Crowns, Mitres, Maces, Etc' which had a lengthy caption of gratitude for the Engravers Act of 1735. When he opened the subscription for the

Entertainment alone, this ticket showed the sun beaming on the Prince of Wales's crown: the first names in his subscription ledger were Prince George, Princess Augusta, and the youngest brother, Prince Edward. But Henry Fox was also on the list and in May, when he produced a ticket for all four prints, Hogarth changed the crown of the Prince of Wales to that of the Duke of Cumberland. Even better, he continued to use both tickets, carefully hedging his bets.

Rouquet had also noted with astonishment that in politics and even in matters of taste the British jumped at any chance of confrontation. 'Every thing is conducted in England in the spirit of party,' he wrote, and 'to arouse an Englishman there must be a party to defend or oppose.' A sure way to appeal to that spirit of party was to suggest that 'liberties' were threatened: 'slaves to the love of liberty they live in a perpetual fear of losing the least branch of it'. With this, went a hatred of being policed that allowed freedom to degenerate easily into licentiousness.[32] Not surprisingly, although the real power-broking took place behind the scenes, no eighteenth-century Election could ever be entirely calm.

Planning his first painting, Hogarth – like all avid readers of the press, pamphlets and broadsides – had been following the Election battle already raging in Oxfordshire. It was unusual for two reasons, first because it brought back to life the old party divisions of Whig and Tory, and secondly because in the counties parliamentary seats, in the pockets of powerful landowners, were traditionally unopposed – handed straight to candidates or parcelled out on a compromise basis behind doors.[33] This was largely because in the counties all forty-shilling freeholders were entitled to vote and wooing them involved enormous cost; it was not worth an opposition candidate risking his purse. Voters had to be bribed with feasts and promises or coerced with threats of eviction and lost trade, and to bully them further, mobs of non-voters had to be organized, paid and copiously plied with drink.

In Oxfordshire the unspoken agreement had been that the Whig landowners, Lord Guilford and the Duke of Marlborough, controlled Banbury and Woodstock while the County and City seats were left to the Tory gentry, the 'Old Interest': no one had actually fought the seats since 1710. For the past decade the County MP had been a local squire Sir James Dashwood, a mighty drinker, feeble speaker and satirists' dream, with his great belly rolling over his breeches. Dashwood's cousin, Lord Wenman, was the Member for the City. But in 1752, egged on by Fox, Marlborough upset the balance. 'Prodigal and never judicious in his extravagance', as Walpole put it, and too impatient to wait until his son was of age and could take the County seat, the Duke decided to attack this 'little kingdom of Jacobitism'.[34] He would field two Whig 'New Interest' candidates – Sir Edward Turner and Lord Parker – for the County and the City.

Both sides poured money into the county: in the end the Tories spent over £20,000. Their supporters wore bright cockades, and soon events were as colourful as their hats. In December 1752 Dashwood and Wenman held a grand dinner at Henley, leading a procession of servants, trumpeters, drummers, freeholders and 'fifteen coaches and banners bearing the legends *Pro Patria*, *No Bribery*, *No Corruption* and *Liberty, Property, Independency*'. Oxford itself had always had strong Tory and Jacobite loyalties and in February 1753, when the Whigs summoned a mob to endorse their candidates they were assailed with loud cat-calls as they assembled outside Christ Church, one of only two Whig colleges in the city. One Christ Church Whig, Thomas Bray, was unmercifully lampooned when a local prostitute – later convicted of slander – swore he was the father of her baby. Both parties pursued freeholders with votes, right to the doors of their houses and shops, and great 'treatings' were held in London, as well as Oxford. Broadsheets plastered the walls, pamphlets spewed forth, verses and caricatures filled the press. The whole campaign was a raucous, drunken, violent procession. Heady with drink, a Tory gang at Banbury insulted a gentleman who had dared to go to a Whig 'New Interest' dinner, and at the White Hart in Chipping Norton a Whig mob attacked an innocent Tory.

These great dinners, and the rowdiness that went with them, epitomized the Election campaigns. Metaphorical greed was matched by the provisions consumed. As for a ritual sacrifice, herds were slaughtered and barrels emptied. In 1761, the *St James's Chronicle* listed the order placed for just one Election breakfast:

31	Pigeon Pies
34	Sirloins of Beef
6	Collars of Beef Diced
10	Cold Hams
244	Chickens to the Hams
6	Dozens of Tongues sliced
10	Buttocks of Beef
56	Pounds of Cheese
8	Pounds of Chocolate
5	Pounds of Coffee
20	Dozen Bottles of Strong Beer

10 Hogsheads of ditto
3 Ditto of Wine
2 Ditto of Punch.[35]

No wonder Hogarth named his town 'Guzzletown'.

Instead of the much-lauded ideal of a representative government, where gravely responsible property owners cast their votes on principle, Hogarth saw a scramble of self-interest on all sides – parties, candidates, electors and mob. In his paintings he did not depict Oxford or its candidates specifically. He changed the blue and green party colours to blue and orange, and set his series in a generalized country town. But Oxford gave him details, and a focus for issues. All the old tricks were used here, summed up cynically by the *Oxford Journal* in 1754 as

'A receipt to make a vote by the cook of Sir JD [Dashwood] – take a cottager of 30 shillings a year, tax him at 40; swear at him; bully him, take your business from him; give him your business again; make him drunk; shake him by the hand; kiss his wife; and HE IS AN HONEST FELLOW.'[36]

Oxfordshire Tories smeared the Whigs as tax-mongering, interfering Republicans; the Whigs had called the Tories closet Jacobites. As the accusations flew, the controversial Bills of 1752 and 1753 were hauled up as ammunition; these included the calendar reform, which had special local interest as the father of the Whig candidate Parker was Lord Macclesfield, the astronomer and President of the Royal Society (painted by Hogarth in 1740), who had helped Chesterfield draw up this Bill. In *An Election Entertainment* a Whig bruiser (said to be based on a local boxer, Teague Carter, paid to fight in the Oxford campaign) has seized a Tory banner, 'Give Us Back Our Eleven Days'. It lies beneath his feet and he still grasps his stout stick while a colleague pours raw gin on his broken pate. Another banner waved by the Tory mob outside the window reads 'Marry and Multiply in spite of the Devil', attacking the Marriage Act, and a bearded effigy wears a placard, 'No Jews'. Wenman and Dashwood had both spoken vehemently against the Jewish Naturalisation Bill, and when the Act was repealed church bells pealed across the county.

Hogarth's paintings are pervaded by the feeling of crowds almost out of control. The mood is subtly different to that of his early satirical prints where the 'great' manipulate a gullible populace. Here they still try to, but the useless, corrupt and greedy leaders, having bribed and bullied and whipped up the crowd for their own ends, now find themselves dependent on a mob pressing against the bounds of decency and sanity.

551

158 *An Election Entertainment*, from *Four Prints of An Election* (1755)

The first scene of the Election paintings showed a great feast in an inn. This is currently the Whigs' headquarters, although judging by the slashed portrait of William III, the Tories were there the day before. Pushing tables together, men sprawl and whisper, sweat and cajole and there is a sense of imminent dissolution and menace. A Tory brick has just missed the mayor, who is being bled by an apothecary after overdoing the oysters, and has knocked out the Election agent himself, who crashes back on to pewter plates and uneaten lobster. A second brick is flying through the window, and in return men are hurling stools and emptying chamber pots, while others armed with staves are beating off a crowd hammering on the door. As so often in Hogarth's work we know the sound is deafening and confusing: the cries of the mob outside mingle with the scraping of the fiddle and bass viol, the screeching of the bagpipes, the chortling and whispering and muttering of private deals.

552

The candidates themselves are almost lost in the scrum: at the far end of the table young 'Sir Commodity Taxem', said to be based on Pitt's handsome supporter, Thomas Potter, warily lets a fat old woman embrace him, while a little girl covetously fingers his ring.[37] Behind him, his fellow candidate, looking very battered and wearily smoking his pipe, is being pressed by a cobbler and a barber. But the orange Whig flag of 'Liberty and Loyalty' above him is less to the point than the escutcheon on the wall, with its motto 'Speak and have'. Coins and promises are being exchanged in all corners. In front of the candidates a grey-clad Quaker sourly reads a note for fifty pounds, payable in six months; behind the swooning mayor, a tailor resists the agent's gold coins, but his wife shakes her fist and gestures to their needy son, kneeling at her side. And in the foreground of this corrupt scene stands a Hogarthian innocent, akin to the drummer boy in *The March to Finchley*, filling up the vat of wine and anxiously watching his back.

Hogarth's composition helped to make his point. He created a 'low' Dutch scene of drunken excess which parodied Leonardo's Last Supper, with its implicit theme of betrayal – 'He that dippeth his hand with me in the dish, the same shall betray me' – echoing Leonardo's trio of Judas, Peter and John in the group around the older candidate.[38] But the circle of diners is only just pent in by the verticals of the walls, window and heavy ceiling; it threatens to burst its bounds, linked by the curling missiles to the open street outside the window. After this first indoor scene Hogarth swept his characters out into the world. His sequence bursts out of the closed room, as if the smoke-filled, boozy fumes of the *Midnight Modern Conversation* had suddenly given way to the smells and sounds and public theatre of *Southwark Fair* and *The March to Finchley*. In his next three paintings individualized groups in the foreground are set against a central band of action which fades backwards, above the buildings, into empty spaces of blue sky.

Behind the next scene, *Canvassing for Votes*, for example, the eye is drawn down the incident-packed street to a sunlit village on a green hill, its church spire pointing to the perfect heavens of an English spring, with great cumuli rolling against the blue. After the boozy table comes the relief of space and slower pace. This time Hogarth did not opt for a curving line of fetid, eager men, but for an arrangement of carefully spaced groups, each with its own tale. Both parties have taken over local inns. The Tories have settled into the 'Royal Oak' (hiding place of the Stuart Charles) and their rivals into the stoutly Hanoverian 'Crown' farther down the road. Levies on wine and tobacco were often collected at pubs and an anti-government excise riot rages outside this one; but Hogarth suggests that the man hacking the crossbar of

159 *Canvassing for Votes* (1757)

the inn sign is going to be brought down himself if he makes the Whig 'Crown' fall.

Centre stage, a bright farmer takes bribes and dinner invitations simultaneously from the Whig waiter and the Tory innkeeper. Two men already eating free dinners watch from the window as the Tory agent leers up at women on the balcony, offering them trinkets from the Jewish pedlar; though he attacks the Jew Bill he has no qualms about doing deals with Jews that will further his own cause. Across the street, outside the shabbier 'Portobello' a cobbler with a heap of boots sits with his wig askew sucking on his pipe. He is listening to a skinny barber who has left his basin and towel on the ground and is grasping a huge quart pot, earnestly demonstrating with bits of broken pipe exactly how Admiral Vernon – with only six ships – won his famous victory of 1739, the sole British triumph of the War of Jenkins' Ear.

554

These two alehouse politicians, chewing over ancient days, are balanced on the opposite side by the red lion chomping on a fleur-de-lys: a figurehead from a proud British ship now fixed to an inn door, where a landlady counts her takings under the eyes of a lurking grenadier.

The scene is like one of Fielding's, where realism and allegory meet. In some ways the whole series, with its inn yards and brawls and overflowing action, feels like a tribute to Hogarth's old friend, who sailed to Portugal in search of health in the summer of this Election. He died in October 1754, at the age of forty-seven, and was buried in the shady English graveyard gazing out over the roofs of Lisbon, far from home.

The journey, the inn – and the stage – had been Fielding's key images for human life, and Hogarth's too. And both men, like other satirists, used the motif of puppets, emblems of manipulation by the great, cleverly used against them by the people. In *An Election Entertainment* a bright-faced man in a gold-frogged coat tries to cheer his neighbour (in agony from gallstones) by making his fist into an old woman's face. But puppets have more to do than cheer the sick. Arguing in the inn kitchen in *Tom Jones* during the ''45', the master of the puppet show is cynically pragmatic, not minding who wins as long as they pay for his shows. And his art, like his politics, ignores the old values. A man of up-to-date polite taste, he defends the moral teaching of his new, 'genteel' puppets, but Tom begs to differ:

'"I would by no means degrade the ingenuity of your profession," answered Jones, "but I should have been glad to have seen my old acquaintance, Master Punch, for all that."'[39]

'Always avoid what is low,' cries the puppeteer, citing a performance of *The Provoked Husband*, damned by the gentlemen in the gallery, because

'"there was a great deal of low stuff in it about a country gentleman come up to town to stand for Parliament-man; and there they brought a parcel of his servants upon the stage"'.

Hogarth always brought the servants upon the stage. And in *Canvassing for Votes*, the kneeling porter has two packages, one labelled 'By Your Votes and Interest' and the other 'Punch's Theatre Royal Oak Yard'. The farmer's parodic Choice of Hercules in the centre of this scene (what is there to choose between these two parties?) takes place beneath a showcloth which announces that Mr Punch, a familiar image of Whig corruption since Walpole's days, will appear as 'Candidate for Guzzletown'. In the bottom half of the cloth we see him flinging coins to the voters; above him is a picture of the Treasury spewing

555

gold, and the Horse Guards (designed by Kent) with the royal coach stuck in its inadequate gateway. But although the sign is political, it is beautifully and powerfully painted. To Hogarth, signs and showcloths such as these were the rich, unpretentious iconography of the common people – both innkeepers here have hung their signs in gilt frames worthy of old masters. Brilliantly, like Fielding, he set the democratic politics of his art at the heart of his satire on the politics of the nation.

Despite his fear of the 'mob', Hogarth insisted that it was the people, the nation, who were losing out. His third painting, *The Polling*, showed the blind and the crippled, deaf lunatics and dying men being herded to the polling booth, while self-important lawyers argue as to whether they can accept the oath of man who has lost his leg and his hands for his country and can now only swear with his hook on the Bible. In the background, the shafts of

160 *The Polling* (1758)

556

Britannia's coach have broken and her cries of distress are unheard by the coachmen, cheating each other at cards. And yet this distressing allegory takes place beneath a vast sky of luminous softness, before a distant sunlit village that recalls the mystical landscapes of Poussin and Claude Lorraine. Although Hogarth was firmly of this world, his sky is a cry of hope that above the bustle and misery of the world there must, somewhere, be harmony and beauty and peace.

In *The Polling*, this landscape is divided from the coach and the crowd by a bridge, across which rolls a carriage followed by a stave-holding mob, all on their way to the hustings. But Hogarth's series did not end when the votes were cast – and nor did the the fuss over the Oxfordshire Election. The Tory candidates won narrowly, but immediately the Whigs called for a scrutiny. After the High Sheriff's tame, inconclusive investigation ended, the matter was referred to the Commons and the Inquiry ran for weeks before the result was overturned and the Whigs were declared the winners.

At one point in this process, in fury at the Sheriff's vacillation, a riotous Whig crowd led a procession over Oxford's Magdalen Bridge and when a pushing, shoving Tory mob, hurling abuse and garbage, tried to tip their carriages into the river a certain Captain Turton leaned out of his chaise, fired, and mortally wounded a local chimney-sweep. Hogarth remembered this juvenile victim in his final scene, *Chairing the Members*, painting a sweep with a blue Tory cockade pissing down on a monkey whose gun points up at him. The monkey is riding a bear decked with an orange Whig ribbon. On the wall, another young sweep holds mock spectacles over the empty eye sockets of a skull and crossbones, ornamenting a gatepost; like the soldier deputed to whisper of death to a Roman emperor riding in triumph, the sweep's grin, and the skull, tell the toppling MP that all men are mortal.

This final painting was flamboyantly mock-heroic, a shambolic parody of the triumph of Alexander the Great in Le Brun's *Battle of Granicus*, as Nichols pointed out. The turbulence of Hogarth's crowd is exaggerated by the regular proportions of the buildings that frame it; the square Georgian houses, the sober parish church and the staid town hall. With wilful symmetry, Hogarth makes the arched window in the new brick house mirror one in the town hall opposite, while the unglazed square window above where the lawyer pens his deeds mimicks the sundial, marking the hour of noon. But the setting is not as regular and solid as it seems. The sundial's inscription reads 'Pulvis et umbra sumus' ('We are dust and shadows'), and a blasted tree is withering beneath it. The new house is a stylistic mess with a classical-Chinese door frame, and its neighbour is already collapsing.

557

161 *Chairing the Members* (1758)

The procession, which seems to progress so purposefully, has in fact ground to a halt, sabotaged by animal spirits. An ass, crossing its path, has stopped to eat a thistle; this gives the dancing bear the chance to drag tripe out of the ass's panniers; a sow has knocked down one of the men carrying the Member's chair, and her piglets are leaping into the stream in panic. These animals are very real, but also emblematic, suggesting the greed and wild folly of the voters. The ass recalls the old story of a man who never smiled, until he laughed aloud at a donkey choking on a thistle; and the pigs are the Gadarene swine, possessed by the demons cast out by Christ, who now rush to their destruction. In their pathos, and in their violence, the beasts also describe specific men near them – the stumping peg-leg sailor, 'unmanned' and reduced to a travelling entertainer like his monkey; the bold-faced thresher who attacks him with his flail and whacks the chair-man behind; the bloodstained soldier stripped down for a fight.

558

In the chaos, the victorious new Member is almost unseated. His hat flies off. His legs jerk up. He clutches the arms of his woodwormy, old-fashioned chair. Directly in front of him a black servant gawps as the candidate's wife swoons – perhaps at his fall, perhaps at the sweep's obscene pissing. At the head of the procession, the blind fiddler hobbles on, following his own intoxicating tune. And over the MP's head, instead of the eagle who soared above Alexander, swoops a single stupid goose, a downgrading of classical grandeur that may also be a blasphemous joke about the descending dove of the Holy Spirit – this MP definitely not being the Lord's Anointed.

Hogarth's four paintings were prescient and disillusioned. They were also extremely powerful – as if his art had leapt on to a new plane. His canvases were large, three feet by five, but the busy scenes were all controlled, almost choreographed, by a marvellously theatrical composition. They were a demonstration, too, of the principles of his book. In his very first scene, *An Election Entertainment*, his blocking was a consummate example of his ideals of 'composed variety' and 'intricacy', with its receding planes and open spaces, encrusted with detail after detail, encouraging the eye in pursuit of innumerable stories. He made pinpoints of light flash round the room from white stocks and lace, gloves and shirts, oyster shells and the shining blank page of a book. And the beauty of his brushwork and colour gave it a curious, haunting detachment – the glow on the perfect still life of plates and jug, the blue Tory flags and orange Whig favours, the carefully balanced splashes of bright scarlet.

Looking at them 'abstractly', when the four pictures were hung together, viewers would see how the curving sweep of the crowd in the first and third painting – the entertainment and the hustings – were balanced by the spacious perspective of the street and the triangular groups of the second and last scenes – the canvassing and the procession. Yet within these large compositions, Hogarth still conveyed an acute sense of individual characters and relationships.

He managed this by adopting an entirely new and strangely beautiful style of painting: flat planes of colour, clearly outlined shapes, tingling touches of detail. In *Chairing the Members* (plate XII), for example, the slanting sunlight picks out the formal shapes of the high verticals and diagonals of shadows, roofs and walls. In the centre, the pyramid of the candidate teetering on his chair ironically echoes the triangular church pediment topped with the belltower. And cutting right across the action runs a dazzling pattern of light, curling round from the skull and crossbones to the white cap of the old servant and the pale face and breasts of the swooning woman, bouncing from the wig and coat and kicking legs of the Member – and leaping up the white goose that floats above him – then running down again to the thresher's white shirt and the creamy pigs, to be picked up, finally, by the sharp burst of brilliant flowers beneath the arch of the bridge.

If this series of paintings displayed Hogarth's deep weariness with canting factions, national and artistic, his disdain for the content was redeemed by his passionate care for his medium. It is as though he were looking down on the crowds, the voters and the candidates as he had looked down from the gallery at the Italian dancers. He might despise their art of politics, but he could resolve even this into unforgettable lines and formations.

The date on the sundial in *Chairing the Members* is 1755 and, although the Election was then over, Hogarth kept his work piquant by making his terrified MP on the 'bridge' look very like the incorrigible George Bubb Dodington, the unseated MP for Bridgwater, soon Member for Weymouth.[40] He also painted a group of nobles, idly amused by the scuffles as they wait for the delicacies being carried in by the cooks. The candidates, dignitaries and voters who think they wield power are deluded. Real power lies in discussions behind doors, in the lawyer scribbling above, and in the decisions of the aristocratic Whig in the window, turning his back on the crowd – widely taken to be Newcastle. It lies too, in the ability of such men to manipulate 'the fourth estate', the mobile, unfranchised crowd. Hogarth's paintings suggest a country teetering on the edge of anarchy, a nation rendered ungovernable.

The mood of suspense after this Election, of being on the brink, was heightened by the long petitions against the results, as well as by the murmuring of the crowds. Cabals gathered and planned, alliances were made and hidden deals sealed. Oxford was not the only Election where mobs were used, nor the only one whose result was challenged. Another seat settled by petition was that of Berwick on Tweed, where the defeated candidate – at the polls and after the Inquiry – was the twenty-five-year-old John Wilkes, later to play a significant part in Hogarth's life, first as an ally, then as a deadly opponent.

Wilkes had grown up in the square behind St John's Gate, Clerkenwell, where Hogarth had lived as a boy. The son of a distiller and a staunchly Presbyterian mother, he shared Hogarth's background of dissent, Smithfield dust, St Bartholomew crowds. And although Wilkes had privileges Hogarth missed – money and schooling and a spell at the University of Leyden – he took up the banner of 'Liberty' and would be far more a conscious 'man of the people' than Hogarth ever was. Married off by his parents to a wealthy widow ten years his senior, Wilkes settled on her Buckinghamshire acres, ignored her and energetically played a double role of diligent local magistrate and hell-bent London rake. In the city, he pushed gradually into the town circles that Hogarth knew, joining the Beefsteak Club in January 1754, acting as a country agent for the Foundling Hospital and mixing with the St Martin's Lane artists. In the country, he was taken up by Pitt's brother-in-law, Richard Grenville, Earl Temple, who lived near by at Stowe, and formed an exuberantly dissipated alliance with Thomas Potter, son of the late Archbishop of Canterbury: it was now that they collaborated on the scurrilous 'Essay on Woman' that would almost undo Wilkes in the 1760s.

Potter was famously handsome while Wilkes was notoriously ugly, with a squinting, sexy, off-balanced look that Hogarth would exploit to the full when they fought almost a decade hence. But his ugliness was offset by his elegant slimness and irreverent, dashing wit – he claimed he could easily 'talk away his face' in half an hour. In 1754, when Wilkes became High Sheriff of Buckingham – helped to his post by Potter and by Temple's brother, George Grenville – Pitt sized him up as an ideal recruit and persuaded him to stand as a candidate for Berwick, in Northumberland. Wilkes could almost be the invisible hero – or anti-hero – of Hogarth's Election series. Since many of Berwick's freehold voters did not live there, Newcastle sent a shipload of them up from London and Wilkes (allegedly) bribed the captain to land them in Norway instead of Northumberland. When he himself arrived, he announced that he came in the spirit of Liberty and his only desire was to serve his country. Offering himself to the voters, he declared, 'Gentlemen, I come here *uncorrupting*, and I promise you I shall ever be *uncorrupted*. As I never will take a bribe, so I will never offer one.'[41] He then paid out £4000 in bribes and spent the rest of the campaign fishing.

561

27

To Encourage the Others

If your enemy's obstinate, and will not stir,
You may be assur'd, he's an old fashioned cur,
But for fear he should see into this your new art,
Tack about, bear away boy, for you've done your part.

How much to this conduct my countryman owes,
There's no one can tell, 'cause there's no one yet knows
But this I'll affirm to the blood thirsty crew,
'Tis the saving of Lives, give the devil his due.

POPULAR BALLAD on Admiral Byng (1757)

IN HOGARTH'S LATE FIFTIES, his equilibrium briefly returned. Age had not mellowed him but he put the humiliations of the *Marriage A-la-Mode* sale and Sandby's prints behind him and veered away from confrontations. He was preoccupied and busy, working energetically on several different fronts (including a major commission for the altarpiece of St Mary Redcliffe, Bristol), and angling for fame, security, and income for his later years.

Four Prints of An Election were a bid for all of these. They reaffirmed his position as the great recorder and allegorist of modern life; many of his fellow artists subscribed, including George Knapton and Joshua Reynolds. They appealed indirectly to political patrons who might find him a post. And they looked sure to turn a good profit. By May 1754 there were 461 subscribers to *The Entertainment*, and 127 to the set. When the first print came out on 24 February 1755, he opened a new book for the last three alone, adding 165 more names: by then the Election itself was long past and a subscription to the whole series was less attractive. But still, over three years Hogarth's takings from subscriptions were well over £800, and many more copies were then sold separately.

The subscribers to the set, however, had to wait a long time: after the first print appeared, the remaining three were not published until early 1758. Engraving the *Entertainment* took long enough: the intricate detail was hard

562

to translate to the copper plate, and Hogarth made it even more difficult by deciding not to reverse his painting, which meant he had to engrave the scene backwards. Then, according to Nichols, 'Our artist, who was always fond of doing what no man had ventured to do before him, resolved to finish this plate without taking a single proof.'[1] The result was a disaster:

'When he discovered his folly, he raved, stamped, swore he was ruined, nor could he be prevailed on to think otherwise, till his passion subsided, and a brother artist assisted him in his efforts to remedy the general defect occasioned by such an attempt to perform an impossibility.'

This is not quite the truth. He did issue his first version to subscribers – William Hunter had a copy, 'Painted and the Whole Engrav'd by William Hogarth'[2] – but he seems to have been anxious that the contrasts were too strong, and tried to tone them down himself, before calling in another engraver (copies can be found with 'the Whole' in the signature crossed out). To make the tones more even, in some places the assistant lightened the plate by burnishing it to make the lines shallower and in others he added depth and shading by incising and adding cross-hatching. But Hogarth was not satisfied; he took the plate back and tried to regain the sharp brilliance he had lost. Altogether eight states of this print can be found and it was retouched so often that the difference between the first and last impressions, said Nichols unkindly, was the same as the stockings of a fabled character, John Cutler, 'which, by frequent mending, from silk degenerated into worsted'.[3]

By the summer of 1755 Hogarth was beginning work on his Bristol altar-piece, so for the next three plates he summoned help from the skilled French engravers, an expensive move. The second plate was engraved entirely by Grignion; François Morellon de la Cave, who had engraved his letterhead for the Foundling Hospital, helped with the third, and François Aviline with the fourth. For over two years he hustled and hurried and worried them. And as the political situation changed and Britain was drawn once more into war with France, he altered the detail of his prints to keep pace with events.

To begin with, Hogarth's dedication of the first print to Fox seemed shrewd. When Newcastle decided that he must break up the dangerous Fox–Pitt alliance, Fox accepted a minor place in the cabinet, deciding that this was his best chance. Pitt meanwhile waited cannily, playing a tactical game by moving closer to the Prince of Wales and to the Tories. But soon both men were tested in positions of power, for by now Britain was sliding into war. Since the peace of Aix-la-Chapelle in 1748, antagonism with the French had flared in the Caribbean, in Canada, in Virginia and in India, and in May 1755 the departure of a fleet under Admiral Boscawen, to prevent reinforcements reaching French Canada, effectively signalled the start of the Seven Years War.

Hastily hunting for allies, the government made treaties with the German states and with Russia. At this point, in the autumn of 1755, Newcastle made Fox Secretary of State, to Pitt's lasting fury. (In Hogarth's Punch showcloth, people could read Fox as Punch and Newcastle as his Joan.) But Fox faced a stormy Commons. The Members were still hostile to his sponsor Cumberland, and resentful of the alliance with Prussia and of the threat to bring Hanoverian mercenaries to protect Britain. The quarrels in Parliament were likened to the shocks of the Lisbon earthquake that November. By the start of 1756, a 'regular opposition' had emerged (including Hogarth's friend, George Hay). Pitt, mortified that his loyalty to Newcastle had been overlooked, began a virulent campaign: as Walpole reported, 'Pitt has rode in the whirlwind and directed the storm with abilities beyond the common reach of the genie of a tempest.'[4]

All this time, keeping a close eye on events, Hogarth worked on the Election prints and, increasingly, on his Bristol altarpiece. Then, in March 1756, news spread of large-scale movements of French troops to Le Havre and Brest. Rumours leapt across Britain. Quickly, Hogarth produced two prints of *The Invasion*: 'proper to be stuck up in public Places, both in Town and Country, at this juncture'.[5] These were crude, popular propaganda, far more optimistic and vigorous than the other prints and broadsheets, which reflected a universal gloom.[6] Their rousing mood was heightened by ringing verses from Garrick, who needed to prove his patriotism after facing rioters at Drury Lane the previous November, when the crowds thought his troupe of Swiss dancers was French.

Almost with tongue in cheek, the *Invasion* prints bought back all the glib visual slogans of *The Gate of Calais*. The first showed the French preparing their ships, and a monk bringing the idols and torture instruments of Popery, watched by frightened, scrawny soldiers. Behind them an inn with the sign of a wooden shoe, 'La Sabot Royal', sells the inevitable 'Soup Meagre'. At one side an officer is roasting frogs on his sword, gesturing at a banner that reads 'Vengence et le Bon Bier et Bon Beuf d'Angleterre'. Garrick exuberantly bashed the point home:

> With lanthern jaws, and croaking Gut,
> See how the half-starved Frenchmen strut,
> And call us English Dogs!

162 *The Invasion*, Plate I, 'France' (1756)

But soon we'll teach these bragging Foes,
That *Beef & Beer* give heavier Blows,
Than Soup & Roasted frogs.

Hogarth's second print showed the lusty, beef-eating British, with two girls measuring a grenadier's broad shoulders and a sailor waving his hat. 'Rule Britannia' lies under a plate near by, and the fifer is playing 'God Save the King'. Another grenadier is drawing a caricature of the French King with sword and gallows, uttering a bubble of puppet-show Frenchified English, *'You take a my fine ships, you be de Pirate, you be de Teef, me send my grand Armies & hang you all, Morblu.'* Again, the lusty call to arms was underlined by Garrick's verse:

No Power can stand the deadly Stroke,
That's given from hands and hearts of Oak,
With Liberty to back em.

565

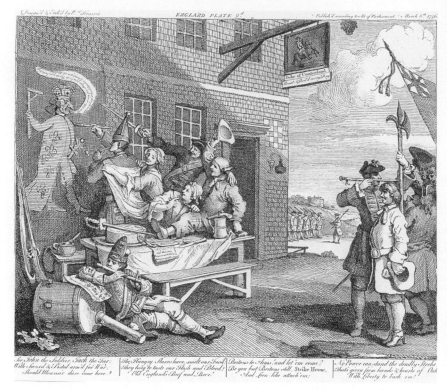

163 *The Invasion*, Plate II, 'England' (1756)

Yet the ambivalence often found in Hogarth's most obvious prints is felt even here. The British inn sign displays the Duke of Cumberland, with the motto 'Roast & Boiled every day'. Did this signal that the victor of Culloden (the last 'French' invasion) was being unjustly roasted in the popular prints? Or did it suggest that 'the Butcher's' own bloody threats (remembering Culloden in different terms) were just as tyrannical as those of the squawking French King? Or both?

The prints were timely, but instead of invading England, the French fleet sailed from Brest to North America. Meanwhile another fleet from Toulon surged through the Mediterranean to besiege the British fort in Minorca. Disaster was at hand: Admiral Byng, who was sent to defend the island, withdrew after an inconclusive engagement and the garrison fell. The City leaders, the Commons and the people howled for blood and Byng featured in over fifty prints, almost all savagely abusive.[7] Squibs, lampoons and ballads were bound in a volume of *Bungiana*; placards were posted across London, crying 'Hang Byng or look to your King.' Panicking, Newcastle

566

threw the whole responsibility on his admiral and promised a court-martial.

Hogarth referred to the Minorcan disaster in the print of *Canvassing for Votes* where the cobbler and tailor recall Vernon's old victories, and the sturdy oak of British ships is covered by the puppets' playcloth. But apart from such allusions, he steered clear of party feuds. He had always been interested in the larger picture, not the small, and the political field was, by now, extremely well covered by the print shops, most of them spread along the half-hour walk from St Paul's to Covent Garden. This summer, a new kind of print, the size of a card, came from the shop of Matthew and Mary Darly in the Strand, and a new talent appeared on the scene, the brilliant amateur, George Townshend. A lifelong collector as well as creator of political prints, he would draw anywhere, 'on tablecloths, scraps of paper, anything easy at hand', and his forte was a sharp, distinctive, linear caricature.[8] Townshend had served in Scotland and Flanders with Cumberland, becoming his aide-de-camp. In 1750, he left the army after a feud with the Duke and now, while his brother Charles – the flamboyant 'Champagne Charley' – attacked Cumberland, Newcastle and Fox in his speeches, George destroyed them with his pencil.

It seemed that Fox and Newcastle were cursed in the summer of 1756. In Canada, Fort Oswego was taken by a new French star, Montcalm; in India, Calcutta fell. At home Prince George came of age and chose his tutor, Lord Bute, who was sharply hostile to Newcastle, as his Groom of the Stole, his own 'first minister'. The harvest was hit by storms and floods; food prices soared and famine followed; hungry colliers stormed Nottingham and Coventry and mobs burned down mills across the Midland counties. Under this pressure, in October Fox resigned, swiftly followed by Newcastle and Hardwicke. Pitt's hour had come.

But not for long. Although Pitt formed a new administration with the Duke of Devonshire (the former Marquis of Hartington), most Whig MPs were place-men, firmly tied to Newcastle. Pitt managed to push through some measures; sending the hated Hessian troops home, founding new English and Highland regiments, and finally passing the Militia Bill, originally introduced in January by Charles and George Townshend. But although this Act pleased the Tory squires who felt their country would be defended by stout local stock, not foreign mercenaries, it also caused problems, and indeed riots, since the £10 fee required to find a substitute for militia duty was clearly impossible for the poor. (In *The Polling*, the Bill lies near a crippled soldier.)

Pitt's popularity was further eroded when he tried bravely to reprieve Admiral Byng, opposing both the King, and the people, who were adamant for his death. Over the spring, Pitt's nerves and health collapsed and in April

George II, testing public opinion, felt secure enough to dismiss him. But no sooner was Pitt out, than the tide turned once more: London and seventeen other towns offered him their freedom. So strong was the swing of popular feeling that by June Pitt was back in office, in an uneasy – but lasting – alliance with Newcastle. A humbled Henry Fox returned to his old post as Paymaster-General, and a defeated Cumberland, worsted by the French at Hastenbeck, was recalled and stripped of his command as Captain-General. Pitt, it seemed, had triumphed.

In February 1757, Hogarth dedicated his second print to Fox's friend Charles Hanbury Williams. But after all these lurches of political fortune, as if throwing up his hands, he dedicated his third print to someone with no links to government at all, Edward Walpole, a patron of the arts and Horace's older brother. And, for his fourth plate, he edged towards Pitt, dedicating it to George Hay, a member of Pitt's Admiralty Board.

As ministries came and went, the politics of art took their own troubled course. In 1753, although it then seemed that the drive for an academy had failed, other moves were already afoot. That year William Shipley, a painter and drawing master from Nottingham, founded a drawing school at Craig's Court, Charing Cross. Shipley was keen to encourage training for the applied rather than the fine arts – tapestry weaving, calico printing, embroidery, decorative carving. Remembering how the Nottingham horse fair was boosted by sponsored races, and inspired, too, by the Dublin Society for Promoting Husbandry, he persuaded aristocrats and merchants to fund prizes for research into technical problems such as new dyes, and for promising young artists and designers. In March 1754, at Rawthmell's Coffee House in Covent Garden, he and his patrons had formed what became known as the Society of Arts, its full, resonant title being the 'Society for the Encouragement of Arts, Commerce and Manufactures in Great Britain'.[9] As judges for the drawing competition they drew in men such as Henry Cheere, Richard Dalton and Robert Strange.

The Society offered no real competition to St Martin's Lane, which was still going strong. When Kirby's book on perspective appeared in 1754, its subscription list was marked with asterisks to show the St Martin's Lane members.[10] But the list also showed that many members had withdrawn, including Highmore, Hoare, Wills and Hudson, Knapton, Luke Sullivan, and even George Lambert and Roubiliac. Of course not all the artists connected with the school subscribed every season, but this was a substantial group and some of them were Hogarth's old friends.

Hogarth knew, too, that other colleagues from the 1720s and 1730s hoped to change St Martin's Lane from within. Frank Hayman's name headed a committee listed at the back of a new pamphlet, *The Plan of an Academy*, published in early 1755.[11] The pamphlet used the tactics that Hogarth himself had always approved, keeping royal patronage in reserve and appealing directly to the *public* to create an academy, with a charter like that for the Foundling Hospital. This time, the painters suggested, the Academy itself was the child that might perish at its birth for lack of help. Their introduction was as urgent and direct in its appeal as Hogarth might have been, although the rolling phrases were alien to his style:

'As then the Undertaking is of a Public Nature; as the Expence to the Public will be inconsiderable in Comparison to the Advantages to be expected from it; as one distinguish'd set of Noblemen and Gentlemen, long ago convinced of the Necessity of such a Plan, set apart a Sum of Money to be apply'd to a similar Use, when Opportunity should offer; as pecuniary Rewards have been offer'd by another Society of Noblemen and Gentlemen to stimulate and encourage young Beginners; and as no Foundation, how narrow in its Views and Purposes whatsoever, has ever yet wanted patrons and Benefactors, it would become criminal even to suppose a Possibility that such a One as This would be suffer'd to perish in the Birth for Want of Assistance only.'[12]

While Hogarth could accept the worth of Shipley's 'pecuniary rewards', he would not appreciate the appeal to the first 'distinguished Set of Noblemen' – the Dilettanti. They, in fact, were the painters' main target and the St Martin's Lane secretary, Francis Newton, arranged for the pamphlet to be read at their meeting on 2 February 1755. A month later, they replied, but in lukewarm tones, saying that as soon as the proposed scheme 'was brought to maturity and a Charter obtain'd' they would be ready to help.[13] In April the artists tried again, offering to include members of the Dilettanti on the Academy's governing body, insisting they must have support now. Once again, Hayman took the lead, and again the names of Hogarth's close friends and collaborators appeared – Lambert and Scott, Roubiliac and Grignion, Henry Cheere and John Pine – as well as his critics, like Hudson, Wills, Thomas Sandby.[14] Ramsay was in Italy and played no part, but Joshua Reynolds signed his name, and it has been suggested that he, or his friend Samuel Johnson, wrote that sonorous introduction.

In May the Dilettanti sent their own plan, and arrogantly proposed that the President of the Academy should always be chosen out of their Society.[15] After this, a silence fell. In December Hayman coolly urged their support again. A row had obviously taken place among the painters; this time there were fourteen fewer signatories and not even those who remained could stomach the thought of letting the connoisseurs take control. When Robert Strange, oozing obsequiousness, approached the Earl of Bute twenty years later, he blamed the artists for the collapse of the project. He had been to the Dilettanti's meetings, he said, where he

'observed that generosity and benevolence, which are peculiar to true greatness; but on the part of the majority of the leading artists, I was sorry to remark motives apparently limited to their own views and ambition, diametrically opposed to the liberality with which we were treated'.[16]

Once the 'liberal' Dilettanti realized they would not be allowed to dominate negotiations ceased.

A few years later, Hogarth looked back on this episode with derision. Patrons, he said, always wanted to be greater than those they helped and could not bear it if artists deprived them of honour, by presuming to 'make themselves without their assistance'. The Dilettanti, 'had all this in their heads when they propose a Drawing school at their expense for here they would be Lords and masters'. But when the 'schemers' among the artists wanted to 'carve for themselves', the Dilettanti kept their money, the artists 'were rejected with scorn and the whole castle came to the ground and has been no more heard of –'.[17]

Hogarth was right to think this particular castle in the air had collapsed, but wrong to suppose that the whole scheme had gone away. At the time he stayed out of the argument. His own views were known, and when he drafted an account of the history of academies in this country, he still fought for his democratic model. The habit of electing directors and having salaries he regarded as a 'ridiculous imitation' of the French academy. Louis XIV might have won honour by setting up 'a pompous parading' one in Paris, but Voltaire, Hogarth noted, said that, after its establishment, 'no work of genious appeard for says he they all became imitators and mannerists'.[18]

This was almost the only point on which he disagreed with Rouquet, who published his *State of the Arts in England* in France in late 1754, and in his own English translation in October 1755. For the last two years this lively, observant Frenchman had been living in Leicester Fields, and Hogarth's voice sounds clearly in his text: describing the history of St Martin's Lane; saluting the public basis of the work at the Foundling Hospital; praising the Engravers Act and the *Analysis*. But Rouquet, who was himself a member of the French

Academy, began by lamenting the low status of artists and suggesting that English artists, subject to the whims of patrons, *did* need the protection of an academy.[19]

He related this to the British class system, which he mocked with the impatience of an outsider who had lived in London for thirty years, noting the way that all aldermen wished to be knighted because their wives wanted to be called 'Lady'. Every Englishman, he wrote,

'constantly holds a pair of scales wherein he exactly weighs the birth, the rank, and especially the fortune of those he is in company with, in order to regulate his behaviour and discourse accordingly; and on this occason the rich tradesman is always sure to outweigh the poor artist'.[20]

But the real obstacles to an artist's progress he said – sounding just like Hogarth – were the dealers, who cornered the market and decreed the taste for these eager social climbers.

Rouquet was writing in part to defend English art against the strictures of Le Blanc, but he had his reservations: the British, he felt, suffered from too much judgement, too much 'geometrical rigour' – a good quality for commerce, but one that removed the vital 'happy delirium' of imaginative creation.[21] None the less they had an insatiable curiosity, a passion for things new, and an exquisite sensibility. There were fine artists here such as Hayman, Ramsay and Hogarth, superb colourists, with a 'large', simple manner. While Rouquet disdained aldermen and aristocrats, he respected artisans and craftsmen. His concept of the 'Arts' extended far beyond painting and sculpture, miniatures and enamels. It took in all the arts of living: architecture and printing, oratory and music, acting and shop decoration, silver, porcelain and toy-making, and even medicine – perhaps because all doctors, he said, 'affect some art'.

Hogarth too shared this breadth of view and commercial awareness. In December 1755, while Hayman was issuing his ultimatum to the Dilettanti, Hogarth was nominated for membership of Shipley's Society of Arts, perhaps opting for a lesser evil than a formal academy. He was elected, paid his two-guinea subscription and joined the judges' committee of the Society, with Henry Cheere, Dalton, Strange, and two significant non-members, Arthur Pond and Frank Hayman himself.[22] At first, the Society suited his determined mix of trade and art. As Rouquet said, the 'poor artist' – or writer, or actor, or musician – was often glanced at askance in fine company. Hogarth made an aggressive virtue of his business role, as did Samuel Johnson: in 1756, Johnson took offence when neither he nor Reynolds was introduced to the duchesses at a party. Determined to 'shock their supposed pride', Johnson called out to Reynolds loudly, 'I wonder which of us two could get most money by his trade in one week, were we to work hard at it from morning to Night.'[23]

Improving trade, as well as art, was the basic rationale of the Society, with a stress on helping British products to beat French competition. The focus was artistic but the association was typical of the many patriotic societies founded in the 1750s: nationalistic, impatient with lack of State initiative and solidly bourgeois.[24] While awards were given nationally, the Society of Arts was very much a London club, based around the Strand and Covent Garden; its members included John Fielding, now principal magistrate for Westminster, and Saunders Welch, the Bow Street chief constable. Hogarth dutifully walked down to the Wednesday night meetings at Craig's Court and sat on committees to audit accounts and create new rules. At the end of December, he was appointed to another committee to follow up a talk on 'some Hints for the Improvement of the Paper manufacture, in regard to the printing of Fine Prints', and eagerly took a copy home to read. This was a subject close to his heart since engravers were so dependent on expensive Continental sources, but a week later his 'report' was postponed (he invariably missed deadlines, and it was never heard of again). However, when the publisher Robert Dodsley suggested sponsoring a project 'for making Paper like the French proper for Copper Plates', Hogarth was among those who drew up an advertisement.

At the meeting where the paper issue was raised, on 28 January 1756, Hogarth himself gave a speech, 'containing some Hints relating to the Premiums for Drawings for the future'. Concerned for the interests of the more mature pupils at St Martin's Lane, he was trying to elbow his way into control. He attended meetings in the spring, but most of the summer was taken up with his work in Bristol on the altarpiece for St Mary Redcliffe. Then, suddenly, at the end of the year, full of vigour, he agreed to sit on so many committees that the list looked as if it had been drawn up by a South Sea Bubble projector. There was a committee for producing 'cocoons' in Georgia; for raising 'the largest and best roots of Madder' for dyes; for refining English cobalt; for making borax; for encouraging drawings – and for 'paper for Copperplates'.

This enthusiasm did not last. In 1757 he went to the February meetings and one in March, but then, with no explanation, in the subscription book for that year, his name was violently struck out. He never attended the Society again.

*

572

Hogarth's departure was obviously the result of a row. He was disillusioned partly because he felt that the emphasis on commerce and industry – which he had liked to begin with – was swamping other aims. He began to suspect that the whole programme was designed to help merchants and manufacturers, not artists at all. Though proud of his position as a tradesman, he disliked the new expansionist mood that had come with the war and distrusted the eager imperial ambitions of Pitt and the City. Although he felt no more warmly towards the French, he was not alone in his suspicions that the war in the colonies was fuelled by mercantilist greed. Samuel Johnson criticized the government strongly on these grounds in the new *Literary Magazine, or Universal Review*, claiming, for example, that the war between the British and French in America was the squabble of 'two robbers' over land stolen from the Indians.[25] And a different suspicion of trade was expressed in 1757 in a doom-laden (and interminable) polemic by the Anglican cleric John Brown, *An Estimate of the Manners and Principles of the Times*, which went through seven editions within the year. Brown claimed Britain was corrupt, divided and lacking in 'public spirit' and culturally degenerate. A friend of Garrick and acquaintance of Hogarth, he lamented the fashionable triumph of the fantastic and grotesque: 'neither the comic Pencil, not the serious pen of our Ingenious Countryman have been able to keep alive the Taste of nature, or of Beauty'.[26] But Brown too doubted whether trade was the answer. Did it not, in itself, encourage luxury and decadence?

Hogarth's grudges against the Society of Arts were both general and specific. For one thing, he failed to get them to extend the age range of artists eligible for prizes, so that it would cover the young painters at St Martin's Lane (Ramsay eventually won this in 1759).[27] He also felt increasingly strongly that the unthinking encouragement of so many young artists was not wise. This was not a new view: he had responded in a similar way in 1751 when Humphrey Senhouse, a wealthy landowner from Cumberland, asked him to take his thirteen-year-old son George as an apprentice. He never took pupils, and despite long urging, he refused, adding that there were now so many painters that it had become 'an uncertain Profession: and till a Man has distinguished himself, he is in Danger of wasting such employment as any Friend to him could wish'.[28] Engraving was more promising, since you could earn a guinea and a half a week, the minute you finished your apprenticeship. 'Besides this,' Senhouse's intermediary added, 'shou'd your son ever become eminent in History-Painting, his being able to Engrave his own Designs (as Mr. Hogarth does himself) will more than double his Profit'.

Towards the end of the decade Hogarth's views hardened: in 1758 he told

573

a Norfolk friend who brought some drawings by the son of a local clergyman, that 'if he had a Son he believes he should not bring him up that way'.[29] Competition had become more intense, 'especially since the Establishment of the Society of Arts & Sciences'. Hogarth's papers contain a draft of a speech he gave at the Society itself. This began with his sketch of art in relation to society, from its ideal stage in Greece, when 'the arts were politically considered and encouraged' and 'spoke to the eye in a language every one understood', to the valuation of art by Catholic countries in distinction to Protestant abhorrence; 'pictures and statues are now only wanted for furniture'. Even in this role, paintings had to be sanctioned by a grand name and warranted original by a connoisseur. Finally he spoke of the hard place of the artist today.[30]

Yet what could one expect? he asked sarcastically. Indeed, since Britain was a trading nation,

'it is a proof rather of the good sense of this country that the encouragement has rather been to trade and mechanics than to the arts <for it is likely the> artist who must be a man <such> uncommon parts <as Shakespear or Swift> to excell in that part of painting that to arive at the hight is capable of being carried <forego the pleasure of youth> will waste his life in a laborious <tedious> study for empty fame when his next door neighbour perhaps a brewer <or porter> or haberdasher of small wears shall acumulate a large fortune become Lord Mayor member of parliament and at length get a title for his heirs. I say must not <such> a man be mad?'[31]

If you read this aloud, even stumbling through Hogarth's rushing, unpunctuated, phonetic draft, with all its scribbled insertions, you can hear the passionate belief that art is worth caring about, the real feeling that animated the painter's rage.

He turned vehemently against the Society's schemes:

'To what end are premiums given to entice such numbers of children into employing their minds in so useless a study . . . surely did their parents enquire into those facts they <would> put their ingenious <youth> upon what would be more safely attained and beneficial to themselves and the public.'[32]

Earlier, he told how he had seen so many struggling artists and 'such misery among the unsuccessful', that they often 'wished they had been brought up cobblers'. The cruel speech of one Society member, who said that competition would make goods cheap, was 'groundless and absurd'. In an overstocked market, such thinking reduced artists to 'labourers in coal mines',

574

sending coals to Newcastle.[33] It was all very well 'setting all the boys and girls in the kingdom to drawing' on the grounds that this would make British manufactures rival the French, but the plain fact was that taste and prejudice would always favour France. What was the *point* of training so many artists if there would never be demand for their work?[34]

Hogarth spoke as much from angry compassion as from a desire to keep the world of artists small and profitable. This was the man who had drawn poets dreaming while their wives could not pay the milk bill, penniless flautists, skeletal ballad-singers. He knew how bewitching the arts were: the 'distressed artist' was the one picture that he did not, or could not bear to, make. In March 1757, the month when Hogarth finally left the Society of Arts, Admiral Byng was executed on the quarter deck of HMS *Monarch*. He dropped his own white handkerchief to give the signal for the firing squad – and his death gave rise to Voltaire's quip that the British have to execute an admiral from time to time, '*pour encourager les autres*'.

28

Pulpit and Portraits, Art and Life

Without hope there can be no endeavour . . . it is necessary to hope, though hope should always be deluded; for hope itself is happiness and its frustrations, however frequent, are less dreadful than its extinction.

SAMUEL JOHNSON on *Don Quixote*, *The Rambler* (1750)

WHEN HOGARTH HELD FORTH in the Society of Arts, his voice was louder and more assured, partly because his work on the altarpiece for St Mary Redcliffe had put him once again in a position of eminence. It is not clear how he won this commission (perhaps through contacts, perhaps through the prints of *Paul before Felix*, on sale in provincial print shops), but after a meeting on 28 May 1755, the church council invited him down to make an estimate. He agreed without hesitation, negotiating a fee of £525 – the exact sum paid to Kent thirty years earlier for his altarpiece in St Clement Danes.

Hogarth's work in Bristol was undoubtedly one of the reasons why the prints of the Election series took so long. It was a huge task. The great Gothic church had been remodelled in 1709, when a bay was created for the high altar, cutting off the Lady Chapel. This was draped on both sides with long tassled curtains: another curtain covered the Gothic window and on this hung a painting of 1710, by a London painter, John Holmes. Hogarth's plan was to replace this and to provide scenes for each side – a baroque triptych, with an arched, central panel. The shape of this panel, like the whole scheme, was unusual, more like the works of Rubens and his contemporaries in the Netherlands than the conventional English rectangular altarpiece. Hogarth departed from national custom too when he chose to paint the Resurrection, rather than the favoured Last Supper. It was an imaginative choice: the Last Supper suited the associations of the altar and the Communion service, but the Resurrection fitted the soaring arches of the church itself. It also meant that he could paint the story as a series, exploiting his talent for narrative: on the left he painted *The Sealing of the Tomb*; in the centre *The Ascension*; on the right, *The Three Marys*.[1]

576

He began work on these huge paintings in the summer of 1755 and continued through the winter. It was in the forefront of his mind as Pitt and Fox and Newcastle fought in Westminster, the artists argued with the Dilettanti, and he joined the Society of Arts. He painted in his studio, or perhaps in the painting room of Covent Garden or Drury Lane, since the three canvases were seventeen feet high, with a total length of over fifty-one feet – certainly as huge as a theatre set. Week after week he stood in front of them or balanced on his ladder, stepping down and walking back to check his progress, blocking out the scenes, moving across each picture, filling in background, highlighting robes and raised arms, catching the glint of light in an eye, the touch of shadow on a vase.

He pressed on into the spring of 1756. In March, he took time off to produce the two *Invasion* prints but by May his paintings were virtually finished.[2] As the countryside greened outside the city, the great canvases were rolled and cased and carefully transported by cart. Hogarth followed them, rattling down the Oxford road to the west to finish them on the spot.[3] In Bristol workmen were busy. An upholsterer had made new red drapes to cover the wall. Great frames had been built by a master joiner, Brice Steed, then passed to the woodcarver, Thomas Patty, who created their formal scrolled borders. Finally, at a cost of £100, John Simmons painted, gilded and varnished them. Hogarth had heard of Simmons when he drove down Redcliffe Street the year before and admired the sign of the Angel Inn: Bristol legend has it that when he knew this was by a local artist he said, 'Then they need not have sent for me.'[4] For a few weeks, Hogarth stayed in Bristol, and in Bath with Walter Chapman, who was married to a noted beauty, the daughter of Robert Dingley, the merchant who had first proposed an academy scheme to the Dilettanti. The connections of the London art world spread wide: the rector of St Mary's Redcliffe was a nephew of John Wootton, the sporting painter to the royal family for whom Hogarth had painted heads as long ago as 1732.[5] It was a strange mix of worlds – the streets of Bath, crowded with fashionable beaux, and the quays of Bristol, made rich by the slave trade.

Finally, on 8 July, his triptych was installed, and the rector, churchwardens and parishioners crowded into the choir to see it. This was not altogether easy. The shape of the bay, with pillars in front, meant that the side paintings could hardly be glimpsed from the nave. Even standing within the choir, the right-angled walls made it difficult to see all three paintings together – looking straight at *The Ascension* made the two wings mere planes at the side of your eyes. But on the other hand, when the Bristol citizens entered the church from the main west door, they would raise their eyes to see Christ radiant at the end of the nave, hovering above the dark clouds that cut him off from the tumultuous disciples and women below, and from the kneeling congregation.

As in his work for St Bartholomew's and Lincoln's Inn, Hogarth's inspiration came from Raphael. And as in those earlier pictures, the effort to create an 'ideal' type meant that he diluted his true strength, the denotion of individual character.[6] He tried instead to create an effect through melodramatic gesture, bold diagonals, vivid effects of colour and shade, and flowing drapery in the old baroque style, solving the problem with groups that were operatically expressive and had a tremendous sense of movement. Above all he painted 'the passions', the emotions of those involved.

His *Ascension* expressed shock and grief, wonder and awe: thunder rolls down the mountain and a jagged flash of lightning throws the towers of the distant city into sudden relief. This looks back to the moment of Christ's death, as described in Matthew 27:50–51:

'And Jesus cried with a loud voice, and yielded up his spirit.

'And behold, the veil of the temple was rent in twain from the top to the bottom; and the earth did quake; and the rocks were rent.'

The sudden flash of beauty and threat illuminates an ambivalence at the heart of the triptych. Each panel is dramatic, and even the weeping trio of women at the tomb has a dynamic energy. The text could not have been followed more expressively, yet Hogarth still managed to introduce a personal reading. Every time he painted a religious subject – the miracle at Bethesda and the Good Samaritan, Moses with Pharoah's daughter or Paul's passionate defence – he went back to the text, noting the telling details as well as the accepted meaning. This time he was very selective. In three of the Gospels, Christ's body is simply laid in the tomb, and a great stone is rolled across its door. In Matthew's version, however, the chief priests and Pharisees then go to Pontius Pilate and remind him of Christ's prophecies that he would rise again:

'Command therefore that the sepulchre be made sure until the third day, lest haply his disciples come and steal him away, and say unto the people, He is risen from the dead, and the last error will be worse than the first.

'Pilate said unto them, Ye have a guard: go your way, make it as sure as ye can.

'So they went, and made the sepulchre sure, sealing the stone, the guard being with them.'

This version let Hogarth express the anger he always felt towards priests and self-interested magistrates, often shown in league against the visionary

164 The St Mary Redcliffe Altarpiece, Bristol, *The Ascension* (1757)

individual, as in *Paul before Felix*. He made the scene harshly comic, showing the pompous Pharisee giving his orders while the 'guard' absurdly try to seal the tomb with wax, fetter it with chains, and lever the great boulder into place. But to a cynic, the priest's anxieties in the text might also raise the faintest of doubts – *did* the disciples come and steal Christ away and say, 'He is risen from the dead'? Was the whole story a myth?

Myths have their place, and Hogarth illustrated this one with conviction and power, but the lingering query remains. As if to question scripture, he showed two versions of the discovery of the empty tomb. On the right-hand

579

165 *The Sealing of the Sepulchre*

panel he chose that of Mark (replacing Mark's third woman, Salome, by the Virgin Mary), where the three women, bringing spices to anoint the body, find the great stone has already been moved and see 'a young man sitting on the right side, arrayed in a white robe'. This is certainly Hogarth's angel, telling the women, 'He is risen; he is not here; behold the place where they laid him.' But in their faces Hogarth also implies their response: when the angel sent them to tell the disciples, 'they went out, and fled from the tomb; for trembling and astonishment had come upon them; and they said nothing to any one; for they were afraid'.

The central picture, too, shows a moment of panic and uncertainty. This

580

166 *The Three Marys*

time the source is St John. Mary Magdalene has come to the tomb 'while it was yet dark' and seen that the stone has gone:

'She runneth therefore, and cometh to Simon Peter, and to the other disciple, whom Jesus loved, and saith unto them, They have taken away the Lord out of the tomb, and we know not where they have laid him.'

The risen Christ as an idea illuminates the heavens, but those left on earth are in suspense and doubt – 'we know not'. The people of Bristol, worshipping in a church dedicated to the Virgin, might also find it strange that the figure who dominates the earthly plane of that picture is not Christ's mother, or a saint, but Mary Magdalene – a harlot – Hogarth's symbol of the questing, fallen world.

By mid-August Hogarth was back in London, with the fee in his pocket. He could join Jane and Lady Thornhill and his sister Anne at Chiswick, with time to saunter by the river with Pugg as the late summer sun filtered through the willows. But by the end of the month such walks were impossible. The downpour that ruined the British harvest swelled the Thames to such a height that all the low-lying meadows were drowned: a few miles away Strawberry Hill was 'like a little ark, surrounded by many waters'.[7] Hogarth had his own ark, his workroom above the stables. From this retreat he could hear the foundling children playing on his lawn under the mulberry tree, the villagers trudging down the track to the swamped market gardens, the rumble of coaches on the distant road. Garrick was often in the area, engaged in complicated business on behalf of the Countess of Burlington, and there were other friends close by, Ranby and Morell, James Ralph and Arthur Murphy.

Briefly Hogarth could sit back, and bask in his great – if provincial – achievement. But if he hoped that his work would, in a positive sense, 'encourage the others', he was wrong: no great religious works followed, and he himself received no more commissions. A few years later he linked his work in Bristol – as he did so many things – to the demise of all he had hoped for:

'To shew how little it may be expected that history painting well ever be requird in the way it has been on account of religion abroad[,] there have been but two Public demands in within the forty years one for Lincoln Inn hall the other for St Mary Church at Bristol for both which I was applied to, and did them and as well as I could recollected some of these Ideas that I had pickt up when I vainly Imagind history painting might be brought into fasheon.'[8]

Sometimes time and fate both seemed to thwart him. Even his works were fragile. In February 1755, a fire ravaged Fonthill, Alderman Beckford's country house; among the treasures lost were the paintings of *A Harlot's Progress*. Those of *The Rake* were saved, although Hogarth always thought they had gone too. Recording the loss drily in his autobiographical notes, he said that what was most remarkable was the report 'that a most magnificent clockwork organ in the house being set agoing by some accident was heard in the midst of the flames to play of a great variety pleasing airs'.[9]

The tunes in the fire were the ghosts of youth. After the plateau of 1756, Hogarth's calm disappeared. He swerved between elation and anxiety, becoming more prone to anger or melancholy in times of stress. He advanced, then as suddenly withdrew. He won favours and commissions, then mocked himself and his patrons. He worked with his fellow artists, then turned on them again, feeling isolated and misunderstood. All the time he nervously assessed his achievement, judging it sometimes confidently by his own standards, sometimes miserably by the response of critics, sometimes resignedly, simply by the money he made. Pleading the cause of writers in 1758, James Ralph wrote, 'Mr Hogarth will tell you like an Honest Man, that, till Fame appears to be worth more than Money, he will always prefer Money to Fame.'[10]

Hogarth's sense of being pushed to the margins was more perceived than real. He was respected by British artists as the visionary who created St Martin's Lane and organized the display at the Foundling Hospital, and to the public he was a hero, whose prints sold across the land and across Europe. And all the evidence suggests that until he stubbornly put himself in positions that meant he *had* to be attacked in the battles of art or party, his weaknesses were regarded with affection by those who knew him. He could be impossibly aggravating, but his unselfconscious zest remained curiously attractive: when he asked his friend Dr Arnold King (who chose the texts for *Industry and Idleness*) to dine with him at the Mitre in Fleet Street, he sent a drawing of a plate like an armorial shield. It was 'supported' by a knife and fork, with a mitre on top, and a scribbled mock-Greek invitation 'Eta Beta Pye'.[11]

Nichols cites this, rather disapprovingly, as an example of Hogarth's 'propensity to merriment, on the most trivial occasions'. Despite his worries, at sixty he was no sour recluse. His acquaintance ranged from aldermen to actors, doctors to merchants, writers to rakes, and he was found at dinner tables across town. Men and women valued his directness, however blustery, and children responded to the openness that made him so vulnerable to attack. Hester Thrale remembered how Hogarth and her father, John Salusbury, 'were very intimate, and he often dined with us'.

'One day when he had done so, my aunt and a group of young cousins came in the afternoon, – evenings were earlier things than they are now, and 3 o'clock the common dinner-hour. I had got then a new thing I suppose, which was called the Game of the Goose, and felt earnest that we children might be allowed a round table to play at it, but was half afraid of my uncle's and father's grave looks. Hogarth said, good humouredly, "I will come, my dears, and play at it with you". Our joy was great, and the sport began under my management and direction. The pool rose to five shillings, a fortune to us monkeys, and when I won it, I capered for delight.'[12]

This led to Hogarth's amused request, the next time the Salusburys visited Leicester Fields, that Hester model for *The Lady's Last Stake*, begun in 1757. 'Many indeed were the lectures I used to have in my very early days from dear Mr Hogarth,' she wrote, remembering him giving 'odd particular directions about dress, dancing, and many other matters interesting now only because they were his'.[13] This time, the matter was gambling:

'"And now look here," said he, "I am doing this for you. You are not fourteen years old yet, I think, but you will be twenty-four, and this portrait will then be like you. 'Tis the lady's last stake; see how she hesitates between her money and her honour. Take you care; I see an ardour for play in your eyes and in your heart; don't indulge it. I shall give you this picture as a warning, because I love you now, you are so good a girl."'

Hogarth's fond attention to individuals appears here. But other stories from this time show him as assertive yet distrait, as if his mind was elsewhere. 'At table,' wrote Nichols, 'he would sometimes turn round his chair as if he had finished eating, and as suddenly would return to it and fall to his meal again.'[14] Another anecdote describes him just after he had 'set up his carriage' as a prosperous businessman, visiting the Lord Mayor in the City (thought to be Beckford). 'When he went, the weather was fine; but business detained him till a violent shower of rain came on. He was let out of the Mansion-house by a different door from that at which he entered; and seeing the rain, began immediately to call for a hackney-coach.'[15] When none could be found in any nearby street he walked home in the storm to Leicester Fields, 'without bestowing a thought on his own carriage, till Mrs. Hogarth (surprized to see him so wet and splashed) asked where he had left it'. His vagueness became legendary: Benjamin Hoadly's favourite example was a letter Hogarth sent him, addressed only 'To the Doctor at Chelsea'.

The stories proliferated. Twenty-five years later Benjamin Wilson was talking to George III, who assumed Hogarth 'told a story very well'.

'"Pretty well, but he was apt sometimes to tell the *wrong story*." "How is that?" said the King. "Sir", he answered, "Mr Hogarth was one day dining with Sir George Hay, Mr Garrick and others, when he said he had a excellent story to tell which would make them all laugh. Everybody being so prepared he told his story, but instead of laughing all looked grave, and Hogarth himself seemed a little uncomfortable. After a short time, however, he struck his hand very suddenly upon the table and said that he had told the wrong story. This caused no small amusement, and when he told the right one at last it was so good in its way that all the company laughed exceedingly.'[16]

*

In life, Hogarth often found himself in the middle of a course that he had thought right, then decided was emphatically the 'wrong story'. This happened at least twice in 1757. One instance was his change of mind about the Society of Arts, and just before that he also sharply turned his back on his most profitable trade – his printmaking. The second Election print was finished and signed (although probably not issued) on 20 February 1757, and on 1 March he closed his subscription book. In between, in the *London Evening Post* of 24–26 February, he placed this notice:

'Mr HOGARTH is oblig'd to inform the Subscribers to his Election Prints, That the three last cannot be publish'd till about Christmas next, which Delay is entirely owing to the Difficulties he has met with to procure able Hands to engrave the Plates; but that he may neither have any more Apologies to make on such an Account, nor trespass any further on the Indulgence of the Publick by increasing a Collection already grown sufficiently large, he intends to employ the rest of his Time in PORTRAIT PAINTING chiefly. – This Notice seems the more necessary, as several spurious and scandalous Prints have lately been publish'd in his name.'

His last sentence referred to his early *Punishment Inflicted on Lemuel Gulliver*, which had been adapted as *The Political Clyster* that January, showing Pitt as Gulliver being 'purged' of his enemies, including Newcastle.

Hogarth's declaration to reject the art that made him famous seemed like cutting his own throat. It was an act of impatience, and he did not keep his word. It was also a sign of his old competitive spirit; he was jealous of Reynolds's success as a portrait painter. He approached Benjamin Wilson, suggesting a partnership in portraiture, even asking Garrick to press Wilson to say yes.[17] He apparently suggested that the work would be much easier if less time was demanded of the sitters, whose busy lives often made it hard for them to find the time to pose.

'He therfore proposed to paint a Portrait in four sittings, allowing only a quarter of an hour to each; and on that plan actually finished a portrait in oil of his very old and much-esteemed friend Saunders Welch. Esq. a Magistrate of Westminster.'[18]

Hogarth had known Welch for years as the Constable attempting to keep order in the patch around his home, taking a particular interest in the

585

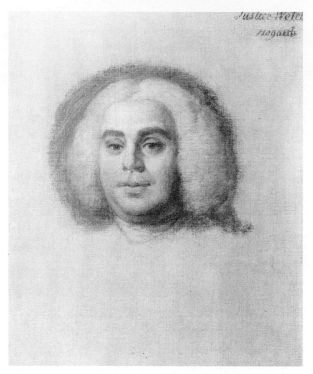

167 *Saunders Welch* (late 1750s)

'abandoned women and pickpockets who frequented Hedge lane, the Haymarket, Cranbourne-alley and Leicester-fields'.[19] The Welch portrait was typical: for much of this year he retreated into painting portraits of his friends. He never liked to let these go, and even when he did, he sometimes retouched them. An undated letter a few years earlier from John Hoadly about the portrait of his brother Benjamin (who died this year, 1757) reflects Hogarth's frequent retouchings, as well as their easy friendship.

'Dear Billy

'You were so kind as to say you wou'd touch up the Doctor, if I wou'd send it to town. Lo! it is here. – I am at Alresford for a day or two, to sheer my Flock & to feed 'em (money you know is the sinews of War,) and having this Morning taken down all my Pictures, in Order to have my Room painted, I thought I might as well pack up Dr Benjamin, & send him packing to London. My love to him, & desire him, when his Wife says he looks charmingly, to drive immediately to Leicester Fields (Square I mean, I beg your pardon) & sit an Hour or two, or three, in your Painting Room. Do not set it by, and

586

forget it now, don't you. My humble service waits upon Mrs Hogarth, & all good Wishes upon your Honour, and

'I am, dear Sir,
'your oblig'd and affectionate
'J Hoadly.'[20]

Although he was bear-like in public, in private Hogarth was always more diffident. Through his switches of mood – and through more difficult times to come – his close friends stayed loyal. He was supported by a network of allies, whose work increasingly brought them together: John Hoadly and Benjamin Wilson had just collaborated on their *Observations of a Series of Electrical Experiments*; Garrick would soon stage James Townley's highly successful farce, *High Life below Stairs*. Sometimes, blindly touchy, Hogarth began to complain that these friends too were deserting him. They had a great deal to put up with, as this affectionate admonition from Garrick suggests:

'Jany 8th [1757]

'Dear Hogarth

'Our friend *Wilson* hinted to me this Morning, that I had of late been remiss in my visits to You – it may be so, tho upon my Word, I am not conscious of it, for Such Ceremonies are to Me, mere Counters, where there is no Remission of Regard & good Wishes – As Wilson is not an Accurate Observer of things, not Ev'n of those which concern him most, I must imagine that ye Hint came from You, & shall say a Word or two to You upon it – *Montaigne*, who was a good Judge of Human Nature, takes Notice, *that when Friends grow Exact, & Ceremonious, it is a certain Sign of Coolness, for the true Spirit of Friendship keeps no Account of Triffles* – We are, I hope, a Strong Exception to this Rule –'

He reminded Hogarth of their friend Somerset Draper ('Poor *Draper*, whom I love'd better than any man breathing'), who had died last year. Draper once asked him, smiling, he said, how long it was since Garrick had visited him? It was over a year, but Draper had not kept an account: his wife had told him that morning, and 'bid me Scold You for it':

'now if Mrs Hogarth has observ'd my Neglect, I am flatter'd by it, but if it is *Your* observation, Woe betide You – Could I follow my inclinations I would see You Every day in ye week, without caring whether it was in Leicester Fields or Southampton Street, but what with an indifferent State of health, & ye Care of a large family, in which there are many froward children, I have

587

scarce half-an hour to myself – However Since You are grown a Polite Devil, & have a Mind to play at Lords & Ladies, have at You, – I will certainly call upon You soon & if you should not be at home, I will leave my *Card*.

'I am Yours Dear Hogy Most Sincerely
'D: Garrick'[21]

In January, Garrick's froward children at Drury Lane were throwing their own tantrums: his adaptation of *The Taming of the Shrew* ended in real rather than stage fights when the long-standing hostility between Woodward and Kitty Clive erupted. As Petruchio, Woodward hurled Kitty violently on the ground, and she was 'so enraged at her fall that her talons, tongue and passion were very expressive to the eyes of all beholders'.[22] Warm and diplomatic, Garrick was used to soothing fractious egos.

The most important portrait Hogarth undertook this year was of this friend, in a domestic rather than theatrical pose: *David Garrick and His Wife* (plate XI). 'Hogarth has again got into portraits, and has his hands full and at a high price,' John Hoadly told Joseph Warton on 21 April.

'He has almost finished a most noble one of our sprightly friend David Garrick and his wife: they are a fine contrast. David is sitting at a table smilingly thoughtful over an epilogue or some composition (of his own you may be sure) his head supported by his writing hand, & Madam, archly enough stealing away his pen unseen behind. It has not so much fancy to be affected or ridiculous and yet enough to raise it from the formality of a mere portrait.'[23]

Even at this stage in his career, Hogarth was inventive, unifying his large double portrait by a small action that expressed the couple's relationship. The couple are tenderly linked, by the flowers in Violette's hair and David's buttonhole and by the miniature, nestling among the pearls of her bracelet, in which he wears the same blue-green coat as in the main portrait.[24] Violette is Garrick's muse, tiptoeing with a dancer's silent step, rising behind him like the sun in her golden dress. But if she inspires him, she also wants to stop him writing. Furthermore, the paper on the desk is his prologue to Samuel Foote's comedy *Taste*, in which he had played the shady auctioneer, and which dramatized Hogarth's arguments. But his wife is stopping him writing it. Thoughts cluster suggestively: that Violette's worldly elegance (note her wondrous lace) and her Burlington connections might put her on the other side to Hogarth in his fight against the connoisseurs;[25] that she wants to steal her husband back from his friend, and possess him like the miniature; that an artist must always choose between love and work, pleasure and 'virtu'.

There are plenty of private jokes – and questions – here. Hogarth caught Garrick at a moment of surprise, of the opposite kind to the shock of *Richard III* confronted by the ghost. In that portrait, ten years before, he had complained of the mobility of Garrick's face, and this time, according to a well-known anecdote, Garrick deliberately played up to the story. As Hogarth painted, 'he mischievously altered his face with gradual change, so as to render the portrait perfectly unlike'. Thinking it was his fault, Hogarth tried again, without success:

'After swearing a little, he began a third time, and did not discover the trick until after three or four repetitions. He then got into a violent passion, and would have thrown his pallet, pencils, and pound brushes at Garrick's head, if the wag had not made his escape from the *variegated* storm of colours that pursued him.'[26]

There were other similar tales. One was of Garrick helping Hogarth conjure a true memory of Fielding, for the frontispiece to Murphy's edition. In one account, Garrick and Hogarth were in a tavern, bemoaning the lack of a portrait of Fielding: '"I think," said Garrick, "I could make his Face," which he did accordingly. "For heaven's sake hold, David," said Hogarth, "remain as you are for a few minutes."'[27] Hogarth sketched the outline and they pieced the rest together from memory. Garrick's own version of this story was naturally more theatrical: he 'helped' by appearing as Fielding's ghost, declaring: 'Hogarth! take thy pencil, and draw my picture.'[28] A trembling Hogarth did just that: 'Vastly well, Hogarth, Adieu! retire to thy chamber; and on leaving the room, beware that thou dost not look behind thee!' Hogarth questioned his staff, but did not say why, in case they should be afraid, or he look a fool. When he told Garrick, Garrick admitted all – but promised not to mention it in Hogarth's lifetime.

The Fielding profile was difficult (Murphy said Hogarth's prompter was a lady who cut out a silhouette profile), but no one could be as hard to catch as Garrick himself. Nichols reported that Garrick disliked or joked about the new likeness, and in a fury Hogarth 'struck his pencil across the face, and damaged it' (recent cleaning has indeed shown repair to the left eye).[29] The portrait looks so wonderfully assured, profound, at ease with itself, yet Hogarth certainly suffered over *David Garrick and His Wife*. To begin with he created an elaborate background, a room with mirrors, candlesticks, bookcases and prints, and then washed these out to emphasize the couple

589

168 *Henry Fielding*, engraved by Basire (1762)

themselves, against a rich olive background. Such revisions suggest the same wrestling to realize ideas visually, as the drafts of his writing do verbally. In this case, for instance, it has been argued that Hogarth was deliberately 'rewriting' a portrait of Colley Cibber and his daughter by Van Loo, implying that just as Garrick's naturalism displaced Cibber's rant so his relaxed art bettered Van Loo's formality.[30] And his difficult reworkings also suggest the fraught heart of portraiture, the problem of how to make a picture 'natural' and yet convey a meaning behind the surface of the canvas, or the face.

This was one of those paintings – like *A Performance of 'The Indian Emperor'* and *The Strode Family* – that Hogarth kept for years: Jane handed it over to Violette, as a gift, only after his death.[31] There was no breach in their

590

friendship, which stayed strong to the end. By now Garrick too had a suburban retreat: in 1754 he had bought Fuller House at Hampton. The following summer – when Hogarth was inscribing '1755' on the sundial in his painting of *The Polling* – Garrick was enlarging his new house with Robert Adam's help and was 'head over Ears in dirt and Mortar', worrying about laundry maids and dairy maids and chickens.[32] It was a Thames-side arcadia: when he asked Samuel Johnson how he liked it, Johnson answered, 'Ah, David, it is the leaving of such places as these that makes a death-bed terrible.'[33] The gardens, designed by Capability Brown, contained an octagonal Shakespeare Temple. In October 1756 Horace Walpole and his gardener brought 'a grove of cypresses' to plant around it and inside Garrick later placed a statue by Roubiliac and 'a great chair', said Mrs Delany confidently, 'which was Shakespeare's *own* chair, made for him on some particular occasion'.[34] In fact the chair was designed for Garrick, as President of the Shakespeare Club, by Hogarth. It was richly carved in mahogany, 'on the back of which hangs a medal of the poet carved by Hogarth out of the mulberry-tree planted at Stratford by Shakespeare'.[35] And in later years, when guests passed through the house before they took tea in the temple by the river they could also admire Hogarth's four paintings of the Election: Garrick bought them in 1762, and they hung on his walls until he died.

In 1757, while Hogarth worked on the painting of Garrick and Violette, he was also painting their mutual friend George Hay. Again, John Hoadly was impressed, but in a different way. 'There is an admirable head of Dr Hay of the Commons,' he told Warton,

'which if I were like, I would not have my picture drawn: I should not like to meet that figure alive in the fields going to Chelsey, for fear of dying that night in a ditch – With twenty gaping gashes on my crown'.[36]

This portrait, so tantalizingly described, has disappeared. But others of politicians survive, like the machinating, neurotically suspicious Samuel Martin, in league with Lord Bute and vehemently opposed to Newcastle, even though he was his Secretary to the Treasury. Soon, too, Hogarth began a striking portrait of Henry Fox himself, the jovial young man of *Lord Hervey and His Friends* now sliding into middle age, with quizzical eyes and down-curving eyebrows that carry the weight of public life, and of the world.

These men belonged in public life, but at this time of his life Hogarth preferred more intimate subjects, old friends and family. He painted an oval

591

169 *Samuel Martin* (*c.*1757)

portrait of William Huggins to match the one of his unscrupulous father painted about fifteen years earlier, incorporating references to Huggins's translations of Ariosto and Dante. Other works were not commissioned, but painted simply for himself, labours of love. There is a dignity and warm humanity in all these late portraits, whether Hogarth was painting the heads of his servants, the wrinkled, open face of an elderly man, or the thoughtful gaze of the *Boy in a Green Coat*, ruffling the head of his shock-haired dog. He was not painting 'servants' or 'artists' or 'children' but individual people, whose worth had nothing to do with class. Perhaps this, too, he learned from Rembrandt. In a darker, later mood, he wrote that as current taste decreed that in portraits 'the life must not be strictly followd', so his characterful works 'met with the like approbation Rembrandt's did, they were said at the same time by some Nature itself by others exicrable'.[37]

Among the gallery of friends was a vivid oval of the engraver John Pine (his friar in *The Gate of Calais*), painted like a late Rembrandt self-portrait. Pine had died in 1756 and Hogarth's painting was his memorial. But the historical portrait was currently very popular (innumerable Court beauties posed in the dress of models for Van Dyck or Velázquez) and it was typical of Hogarth to personalize the vogue. He followed it in two more portraits, one of Mary Woffington, Peg's sister, as Mary Queen of Scots,[38] and one of young Mary Lewis in a Jacobean ruff. Mary, whose father, David Lewis, was harper to

170 *Henry Fox* (*c.*1758)

171 *John Huggins* (pre-1745)

172 *William Huggins* (1758)

173 *John Pine* (late 1750s)

George II, was Jane's cousin and by now a permanent member of the Hogarth household. On the back of the canvas she recorded how when Hogarth had finished he brought the painting to her and said,

'"There, Molly, I have finished your portrait at last, and I have taken some pains with it. I have put you in a ruff to disguise you, for you are too handsome. Now, I have been offered twenty guineas for it. Therefore, if you like, I can let you have that instead of the picture." I replied, "No, Sir! I thank you for the pains you have taken to oblige me, and I shall keep the picture for your sake."'39

Mary Lewis took her portrait away, but Hogarth usually liked to keep such paintings in his studio – of Jane and his sisters, of Sir James and Lady Thornhill and his brother-in-law John. Like family photos in an office they reminded him that he had another self, valued for reasons other than his stature as an artist.

*

594

174 *Mary Lewis* (*c.*1758)

He was still, however, concerned about that stature, and the stories of his stubborn self-importance rival those of his vagueness. In March 1757 he received a letter supposedly from a German admirer, Reiffenstein, inviting him to become an honorary member of the 'Imperial Academy of Augsburg', which paid its directors not through regular salaries but 'a kind of lottery, consisting of annuities for life'.[40] The style was outrageously flattering, resembling Townley's daft note about Hogarth/Pythagoras. It acknowledged the nuisance his 'Universal reputation and undisputed title to superiority' must bring, from people 'ambitious of an acquaintance with men of genius' and, in a virtual parody of the *Analysis*, went on to mention the sages who had searched so fruitlessly for beauty: 'To you alone it was reserved to unravel her windings, reveal her charms to open view, and fix her hidden, though genuine excellence.' Hogarth accepted in the same tenor, 'being much elated'. The letter looked authentic (research has uncovered a Rieffenstein in Cassel, and a dubious academy in Augsburg, funded by lotteries) but its tone, and Hogarth's reply, suggest another elaborate spoof.

Hoax or not, Hogarth's strivings and vanity, so cruelly burlesqued by Paul

Sandby, were all too real. Since the middle of the previous year he had been brooding over a remark in Joseph Warton's essay, *The Writings and Genius of Pope*. Warton was Professor of Poetry at Oxford, a good friend of Johnson, and his thesis was that most writers and artists can achieve the heights only in a single field; Pope, he said, excelled in the secondary field of 'ethical' rather than 'sublime' poetry. To illustrate this he cited Hogarth: the 'nicer virtuosi', held that in his serious paintings, Hogarth had 'deviated from the natural bias of his genius'. Furthermore, he had brought undignified touches of the ridiculous into the paintings of Paul and Pharaoh's daughter, 'a dog spitting at a cat' and the infant Moses, 'who expresses archness rather than timidity'.[41] They showed that Hogarth, 'unrivalled in his own walk, could not resist the impulse of his imagination towards drollery', although he had managed to do so in *Garrick as Richard III*, which represented pure 'terror and amazement'.

This was the most annoying sort of criticism, since it was based on inaccuracy – the dog and cat were in *The Four Stages of Cruelty*, and Moses was all too plainly 'timid'. Friends stepped in to salve Hogarth's pride. In April 1757, John Hoadly told Warton that he had seen Garrick and Hogarth, and had told them that Warton acknowledged his mistake and promised 'an amende honourable'. He then reported (in terms as formal as if they had been about to fight a duel) that Hogarth had replied, 'you have more than conquered any resentment he might have harboured by your handsome acknowledgment; and your amende honourable is a supererogation he neither expected or desired'.[42]

He did desire it though, and badly. The corrected essay failed to appear, and in 1759, at a time when he felt particularly vulnerable, Hogarth published Warton's inaccurate comments under new issues of his prints of *Moses* and *Paul*. In 1762 he was shamefaced when he realized that Warton had not only erased all his criticism but had added a footnote confessing his mistake and offering a noble compliment (perhaps ironic in view of Hogarth's need for flattery). 'Justice obliges' the author to declare, Warton wrote,

'the high opinion he entertains of this inimitable artist, who shines in so many different lights, and on such very dissimilar subjects; and whose works have more of what the ancients called the HΘΟΣ [manners of the age] in them, than the compositions of any other Modern'.[43]

In 1762 Garrick described to Warton what happened when he showed this to Hogarth. First, when he pretended that Warton had resented his reprinting his comments under the reissued prints, 'confusion and shame overspread his face – he was much hurt'. Then when Garrick relented and told the truth about Warton's apology, this hurt Hogarth even more: 'thoroughly disconcerted', he offered 'to destroy the plate in which your name is mentioned, for he declared that he would not be outdone in kindness'.[44]

Hogarth, recalled Steevens, was 'highly delighted' with Warton's apology, but totally foxed by his Greek HΘOΣ. When he rushed to ask his friends they found the opportunity irresistible.

'All, in their turn, sported with his want of skill in the learned languages: first telling him it was Greek for one strange thing, and then for another, so that his mind remained in a state of suspense; as, for aught he knew to the contrary, some such meaning might lie under these crooked letters, as would overset the compliments . . . No short time, therefore had passed before he could determine whether he ought to retract or continue his charge against his adversary; but it was at last obliterated. For several months afterwards however, poor Hogarth never praised his provision or his wine, without being asked what proportion of the HΘOΣ he supposed to be in either.'[45]

Such anecdotes show an insecure man, but they also show teasing and affectionate friends.

To the world at large, in 1757, Hogarth would seem to have no reason to feel insecure. He was on the verge of receiving a solid honour, although accompanied by sadness. That spring his brother-in-law, John Thornhill, was so ill that he gave up his post as Serjeant-Painter to the King. The Duke of Devonshire became Lord Chamberlain in May, and among his duties was the appointment of Court officers: in early July, the *London Chronicle* was able to report, 'We hear that John Thornhill Esq; Serjeant Painter to his Majesty, has resigned his Place in Favour of Mr Hogarth.'[46] In August, John visited Chiswick to see Hogarth, Jane and his mother Lady Thornhill, who was very ill herself. He died the next month, leaving bequests to his family, to the old friends of the 'Peregrination', Ebenezer Forrest and George Lambert, and money for a mourning ring for all members of the Beefsteak Club.

Hogarth took up his post actively in September, the month of John's death. Now at last he felt he was 'landed as it were and secured from tugging any longer at the ore'.[47] Serjeant-Painter was a title he had coveted – it had belonged to his father-in-law, Sir James, and to his brother-in-law – and he felt it right that it should remain in the family. And although it carried only a nominal salary of £10, in practice it was extremely lucrative. From now on, Hogarth was in charge of all royal commissions for painting and gilding, from palaces to flags and boxes: at a quick reckoning, five years later, he estimated

597

it had brought him at least £200 a year, boosted by a Royal Funeral and Coronation. It may well have been more – the amounts paid him rose from £400 for his months in 1757 to nearly £1000 in 1761, and even after he had paid his deputy and his workmen, a tidy sum was left.[48]

This was a good financial cushion, but was it really an 'honour'? It was far from the most prestigious artist's appointment at Court, coming under the auspices of the Board of Works, which paid the plumbers and masons and bricklayers. In his heart Hogarth might have preferred the different kind of honour Reynolds was receiving, painting the leading members of the Court, and charging higher and higher prices.[49] Almost as soon as Hogarth received the royal patent he began to belittle his office and its importance, defensively drawing up his own mock-patent, rather as he had drawn his own version of Sandby's prints. The official patent rambled grandiosely through all the duties graciously entrusted to 'Our Trusty and wellbeloved William Hogarth Gentleman', down to the Office of the Revels and 'Our Navys and Shops Barges and Close Barges Coaches Chariots Charoches Litters Wagons and Close Carrs Tents & pavilions Heralds Coats Trumpets Banners'. Hogarth's version, embellished with a huge, flowery, royal-crowned initial letter, was a Fielding-like piece of theatrical and scatological debunking:

'Punch by his order (Grace) and Deportment of all theatres in the world Nabob know ye that I for divers good causes and considerations as hereunto especial moving of our especial grace and our certain knowledge and meer motion have given and granted and by these presents to give and grant to my trusty and wellbeloved WH gentleman the office of scene painter and corporal Painter to all my whatsoever as well as in any wise belonging to my . . .'[50]

With this went a title page for designs to 'be exhibited at Punches Theatre . . . Representing the true form of his Lownesses Patent'.

In something of the same mood he began a small self-portrait. His last one had been a representation of an image, already framed, with the pug and the line of beauty. This was a picture of a painter *creating* an image. Hogarth placed himself in front of his easel – almost dwarfed by it – painting his muse. This was a traditional pose, but instead of painting the muse of history or poetry, Hogarth is touching in an outline of Thalia, the muse of comedy. In the engraving you can just make out the title of Thalia's book, marked '*Suadere*', implying that his prints have the persuasive power of rhetoric.

With a self-portrait more than any other Hogarth faced the problem of a balance between naturalism and an expected ideal, this time of 'the artist'. In *Hogarth Painting the Comic Muse*, as with *David Garrick and His Wife*, he

598

175 *Hogarth Painting the Comic Muse* (1758)

changed his mind as he worked.[51] To begin with his easel was behind him on the other side, and he was painting a heroic male model; a prouder, more defiant statement; but the shadowy outlines revealed by cleaning show some self-mockery – his pug pissing on framed paintings on the floor. In the finished painting, the dog has gone and Hogarth is alone with his palette and his canvas. It is an intimate, self-exposing picture: with his shaven head, his rounded plebeian legs and turned-out feet, he looks unassuming, even humble, concentrating intently on his work. Once again, the model of Rembrandt – this time his early self-portraits – may have been in his mind.[52]

When he engraved this in March 1758, to replace *Gulielmus Hogarth* as the frontispiece to portfolios of his prints, he altered the title to *William Hogarth as Serjeant-Painter to the King*. Yet the grandiose tone is ironic. In the print,

599

he placed *The Analysis of Beauty* against his easel with 'The Statuary's Yard' folded out, but behind his chair stands a large paint pot like that in *Strolling Actresses*, or the one used by the sign-painter in *Beer Street*. He knew that the creations of a Serjeant-Painter were as low grade and ephemeral as those of a garden statue-maker, a theatrical decorator – or a street sign-painter.

In profile in this print, Hogarth looks almost as pug-like as Sandby's caricatures: the exposed shaven head and passionate gaze of the painting are replaced in the engraving by a larger silk cap and a resigned, but smiling, expression. In later states of the print, the smile vanished.[53] In the last version, of 1764, the corners of his mouth are turned down, his eyes have sunk into his skull and the furrows on his brow have deepened. His title, and the name of 'Comedy' are both erased. The white lines of his muse have turned to black, her face is lined and tragic and her horned mask has a satyr's grin: even the palette knife he holds looked less like an artist's tool than a blunted weapon. Dark times are upon him.

29

Gambling to Excess

To Risque, you'll own, t' was most absurd,
Such labour on a rich man's word;
To lose at least an hundred days,
Of certain gain, for doubtful praise;
Since living artists ne'er were paid;
But then, you know, it was agreed,
I should be deem'd an artist dead.
Like Raphael, Rubens, Guido Rene,
This promise fairly drew me in;
And having laid my pencil by,
What painter was more dead than I?
WILLIAM HOGARTH AND PAUL WHITEHEAD (1759)

IN THE YEAR that he became Serjeant-Painter, Hogarth's household was saddened by the deaths of John Thornhill in August, and then of Lady Thornhill on 12 November. After her burial in the graveyard of the parish church, Hogarth stayed in Chiswick to console Jane. But on the 28th, when he thanked the naturalist John Ellis for some botanical specimens, he ended, 'I shall be in town in two or three days for good, and will take the first opportunity of waiting on you.'[1]

He had already been in town briefly earlier in the month. On 4 November 1757 he was sixty, and next day he went to the annual artists' dinner at the Foundling Hospital. A flourishing society had grown from the small group who exhibited at the Hospital twenty years before. This year a hundred and fifty-four men were at the dinner, including forty-nine painters, thirteen sculptors, eight architects and thirteen engravers, as well as doctors such as John Freke and Governors and supporters ranging from Alderman Beckford, Francis Fauquier and Saunders Welch to the singer John Beard and Langford the auctioneer.[2] Among the artists, Hayman, Hudson, Highmore and Scott sat with the new stars, Ramsay and Reynolds; sculptors such as Henry Cheere, Roubiliac and Rysbrack mingled with the architects Gwynn and Payne and

601

with old and young engravers such as Grignion and Basire, Luke Sullivan and Robert Strange.

Their entertainment included an ode by Boyce on the theme of patriotism and art. Britannia, Boyce wrote, though free and powerful, had bewailed her lack of culture: she prayed for artists and the Almighty responded:

> Diffuse, He cried, o'er Britain's isle,
> Let there the Soul of Painting Smile
> Transcendent, all refin'd.[3]

The first to catch the divine fire was Hayman, acknowledged leader of the artists, praised as a history-painter. Others named were Lambert, Scott and Reynolds (whose painting 'breathes at his command'), while Hogarth was ranked second only to Hayman:

> The spirit glow'd in HOGARTH's heart,
> He rose Cervantes of the art,
> And boasts unrival'd praise.

The tribute was fine, but frustrating – still placing him firmly as a literary painter, a story-teller, a comedian.

At the end of this decade, Hogarth was as forthright as ever but more emotional, slightly off balance, lacking a protective skin. He tired easily, and with weariness came depression, alternating with high activity and volubility. The edge of danger in him that defied his years made him welcome among those who valued his oddity and fire: his old theatrical friends; the new generation of attacking writers; young aristocrats and art collectors cutting a dash, and older, eccentric sub-groups of the polite and political worlds.

Despite the growing power of the sober 'middling' classes, Hogarth's century had always embraced excess – in patriotism and prejudice, consumption and crime, drinking and gambling. And although his acquaintances in commerce and the professions were solidly respectable, Hogarth's early reputation for risqué pictures and sardonic portraits never quite disappeared under the mantle of the moralist. Sometimes he was asked to paint a 'moral' picture of a curious kind. This, at least, is the story behind *Francis Matthew Schutz in Bed*, showing Schutz with a vile hangover, puking into a chamber pot.[4] It was supposedly commissioned by the spirited Susan Baker when she married Schutz in 1755, to fill him with disgust for his debauched bachelor days: Horatian inscriptions remind him of the days when he kept trim for the girls. The image was too strong for a Victorian descendant, who had the chamber pot and stream of vomit painted out, and a

176 *Francis Matthew Schutz in Bed* (*c*.1758)

journal substituted – although it was read at a most peculiar angle. Now that the picture is cleaned and restored, it still makes people start. And the effect is greater because Hogarth painted it almost tenderly, in such warm, delicate colours.

Matthew Schutz was the son of Colonel John Schutz of Sion Hill, in Middlesex, along the river from Horace Walpole. The Schutz family – second cousins of George II, and welcome at Court – often entered Walpole's letters and Hogarth could have met them through him, or through his new post as Serjeant-Painter. It was a good commission and he would have been amused, rather than shocked by the subject: sensual or unconventional behaviour, when it did not exploit others, rarely bothered him. He accepted the indulgence of the male social world with its clubs and societies and massive drinking.

Hogarth also understood the way the closeness of that world brought its own erotic charge. His own friendships (and his abusive rivalries) with other men often seem more intense than his stable, affectionate marriage. This acceptance had been evident in his picture of the Hervey set twenty years before and, with an ironic edge, in his commissions for Lord Boyne, such as

Charity in the Cellar, where the Dilettanti posed in their blasphemous flow of wine. Several of Hogarth's patrons, dedicatees and friends belonged to supposed homosexual circles – Hanbury Williams, George Hay, Samuel Martin and Edward Walpole (who had fought a lengthy campaign to clear his name in 1751 against a gang of blackmailers). Aristocratic society left space for individual preference, unless men or women were foolish enough to court publicity, when everyone tut-tutted and enjoyed the scandal. And although Hogarth slated social follies and scorned connoisseurs, he was still happy to accept their commissions. It was around now that he painted Francis Dashwood as a friar, worshipping Venus in the palm of his hand. Dashwood was one of those characters who make simplistic placings of eighteenth-century 'types' so impossible. A contemporary of Pitt at Eton, he had been a great traveller in his youth, touring Europe, visiting Russia and (more unusually) Asia Minor. He was one of the founders of the Dilettanti and a leader of negotiations with the painters. As an independent MP, opposed equally to Walpolian Whigs and old-fashioned Tories, he was wooed by Fox but won by Pitt, and in the mid-1750s became first Colonel of the Buckinghamshire militia.[5]

From the outside then, Dashwood looked thoroughly respectable – an MP, a magistrate, a moderate reformer. But he was also the founder of the Medmenhamite Brotherhood. Since 1751 he had been slowly converting Medmenham Abbey, his rented house on the Thames at Marlow, into a lavish folly. According to rumour, labourers worked at night and servants took vows of silence. It has been persuasively argued that this new 'hell-fire club' was no more than a 'country club' where close friends went boating, but that was not the picture given by Wilkes (a member by 1760) nor by Charles Johnstone, Dashwood's tutor on the Grand Tour, in his sensational novel *Chrysal*.[6] Over Medmenham's door was carved 'Fay ce que voudras', the motto of Rabelais's imaginary abbey on the Loire, which admitted both men and women and abolished monastic rules in favour of individual judgement. Rabelais had envisaged order and self-discipline; Dashwood something else.

Later myths fed the notion that the rituals that took place within his ruined towers, cloisters and cellars, caves and grottoes, between walls covered with pornographic murals and punning graffiti, ranged from pagan rites to a blasphemous Black Mass. Those taking part included leading Dilettanti such as John Montagu, Earl of Sandwich, politicians such as George Bubb Dodington, and younger rakes such as Churchill and Wilkes. The Brother-hood hardly sounded like holiday boatmen. And if they dressed like watermen, in 'a white hat, a white jacket, & white trousers', they also aped the

604

177 *Sir Francis Dashwood at his Devotions* (c. 1757)

Church – 'the Prior has a red hat like a Cardinal's, and a red bonnet, turned up with a coney skin'.[7]

Medmenham's excesses were yet another version of elaborate rules and dressing up of any Georgian club, part of that tradition of irreverent counter-rituals and acting out seen in the *Peregrination* and in Hogarth's own hoaxes. This upper-class version combined Enlightenment Deism with Enlighten-ment advocacy of 'natural pleasures' – boating, music, chess, wine and women, the 'nuns' (slang for prostitutes) imported from London brothels. Dashwood was happy to gamble with loss of reputation, protected by his private circle. One of his closest confidants was the satirist Paul Whitehead, Hogarth's former neighbour. (When Whitehead died in 1770 Dashwood brought out the Bucks militia, with fife and muffled drum, to carry his embalmed heart in a marble urn to be entombed in the mausoleum beneath: the heart was displayed proudly to visitors until it was stolen, in 1833.)

605

Whitehead could well have brought Hogarth this strange commission. However it came about, in his portrait of Dashwood Hogarth entered into the religious burlesque with zest.[8] His painting had a fair tang of irony at the exploitation of women (and artists), but Dashwood's mixture of anti-clericalism, burlesque ceremonies, drink and sex might also have attracted him.

Hogarth's irreverence was often mixed with anger. It is as if he wanted order, but resented authority; as if he revered mystery, but would not be commanded to believe what he could not see. He would not be bullied by threats, or cajoled by cant. This determination coloured all his work, from portraits to prints, and affected his approach to all aspects of life, whether it be medicine, politics, religion or art itself. He would not be *told*.

In the late 1750s this obstinate anger forced its way out under pressure in different places, as through vents in a volcano. At the end of 1757, for example, he made a small painting called *The Bench*, a brilliant, schematic oil sketch of four judges, whose voluminous red robes and heavy white wigs stand out

178 *The Bench* (1757)

606

solemnly against the olive-green ground. The portly, mean-eyed judge wielding his quill pen like a scalpel is Sir John Willes, Lord Chief Justice. No stranger to excess, in his younger days Willes had supposedly modelled for Hogarth's indoor *Before* and *After*, and was later notorious as the bloody judge of the Penlez case. Behind him Hogarth placed the black-clad Sir Edward Clive, and beside him the snoring figures of Mr Justice Bathurst and the Hon. William Noel. This tribunal sits beneath a royal arms whose inscription, cleverly truncated, is no longer 'Honi soit qui mal y pense', but simply 'mal y pense', reinforced by 'semper eadem' (Queen Elizabeth's motto: 'Always the same').

The painting damned the self-important indifference of the law, acting too as a mocking illustration of 'quantity' as described in the *Analysis*, where Hogarth had written that the judge's robes

'have an awful dignity given them by the quantity of their contents . . . The full-bottom wig, like the lion's mane, hath something noble in it, and adds not only dignity, but sagacity to the countenance.'[9]

And when he engraved the painting in September 1758, he used it to defend his own case as a comic history-painter, adding a long inscription that continued the argument begun in *Characters and Caricaturas* fifteen years earlier. *The Bench*, he claimed, was comedy drawn from life as opposed to the *outré* forms and childish scribbles of caricature. Placed below *The Bench*, his tirade also implied that the dangerously crude judgement of caricature had something in common with the reductive, inhumane laws administered by the dignitaries above.

Hogarth first dedicated the print of *The Bench* to George Townshend, whose caricatures had entranced the town in 1756. Townshend was both a personal enemy – he was said to have suggested Sandby's *The Painter's March from Finchley* – and a factional one, a devout Pitt supporter. Hogarth was courting danger – when he saw the print the hot-tempered William Windham, who helped Townshend promote the Militia Bill in 1755, called Hogarth 'an ignorant conceited puppy' who should be punished 'since he has the impudence to attack my friend the Colonel'.[10] But Windham's chief reason for calling Hogarth ignorant was that he 'has no idea of a caricature, which the blockhead writes caracature', and in fact the attacks on *The Bench* did not come from political foes or disgruntled judges, but from the familiar detractors who slammed Hogarth's lack of learning, his hopeless spelling and his harping on old issues. Back in the world of the print, he was back in the midst of the fray. In response to a critical article in the *Monthly*

Review, refuting his distinction between character and caricature he drafted still more notes.[11] When James Townley questioned the difference too, he grabbed an old pen from the kitchen inkwell, saying, 'I'll shew you, master Townley', and drew a rapid sketch, then exaggerated it into caricature.[12] He reworked *The Bench* until his death, adding a line of faces and caricatures to make his point more strongly.

Hogarth's vehement defence of character was also a defiant insistence that his comic histories were not 'low'. The fact that even at sixty he was striving, as he had striven all his life, either to prove that his arguments were right and that he was the equal of artists valued by those connoisseurs whose judgement he affected to despise, suggests how insecure he was beneath his blustering show.

His old irritation at the high value placed on dead foreign artists was exacerbated in the spring of 1758 by the auction of pictures belonging to the late Luke Schaub, once connoisseur-adviser to Frederick, Prince of Wales. One of the first paintings sold was a 'Correggio', which Hogarth was convinced was not genuine but by a 'freinch master' (in fact it was by the Florentine, Francesco Furini). Its subject was *Sigismunda weeping over the heart of Guiscardo* and it sold for £404 5s. All the prices seemed inflated, but this picture in particular obsessed Hogarth – he felt, at one point, like giving up altogether.

Although he had declared in February 1757 that he was quitting engraving for portraits, a few months later he vowed equally firmly to abandon painting for engraving, 'partly on account of Ease and retirement', he wrote,

'but more particularly because he had found by thirty years experience that his Pictures had not produced him one quarter of the profit that arose from his Engravings, except in the instance of two mentioned hereafter'.[13]

These instances were the Bristol *Resurrection* and a new painting, *Picquet, or Virtue in Danger* (plate XIII; later known as *The Lady's Last Stake*), commissioned by an Anglo-Irish aristocrat, James Caulfield, the thirty-year-old Earl of Charlemont.[14]

Charlemont had wandered through Europe on the Grand Tour and then lived in Rome, where he joined the circle of young aristocrats who patronized the artist Thomas Patch (later expelled by the Pope for his 'sodomitical practices'), and was an active supporter of John Parker's 'Academy of English Professors of Liberal Arts'; Charlemont was one of this Roman circle satirized by Reynolds in *The School of Athens* in 1751.[15] A good friend of the Duke of Devonshire, he finally returned in 1755 and divided his time between

608

London and Dublin, where he had one of the best collections of paintings in the city; he was also much sought after by the women and apparently invented a diplomatic affliction, claiming he was 'incapacitated' by a love potion taken in Italy. In London, he sat to Reynolds for his portrait and soon met Hogarth, who picked out the best impressions of his prints for him, and made an oil sketch which vividly suggests his easygoing charm.

179 *James Caulfield, 1st Earl of Charlemont* (1759)

Before he 'entirely quitted the pencil', Hogarth recalled, Charlemont asked him to paint a last picture,

'leaving the subject to me and any price I asked . . . the subject of which was a virtuous married lady that had lost all at cards to a young officer wavering at his suit whether she should part with her Hon[ou]r or no to regain the loss which was offerd to her'.[16]

Hogarth could make his painting a comedy of manners rather than a potential

609

tragedy because of its clear reference to Colley Cibber's *The Lady's Last Stake*, revived in 1756. In this play the card-obsessed Lady Gentle agrees to one last game of picquet with Lord George Brilliant but – as all playgoers would know – Lord George is tricked in his turn by Mrs Conquest, who arrives disguised as her brother, pays the debt, challenges to him to a duel, and (of course) emerges as his real love.

So Hogarth was painting a classic moment of choice, but one where his viewers knew the outcome. His lady would gamble, but she would not lose all. And in any case, she seems to find cards and sex equally alluring. Despite the emblematic details – the Cupid with Time's scythe, the cut flowers, the painting of the Penitent Magdalen in the Desert and the harpies on the grate – the scene is intensely human and intimate. In this fine drawing room with its green damask hangings, the woman in her rich yellow satin is in control. Her assessing gaze, her half-open mouth and flushed cheek and the casual way she taps her satin slipper against the fire screen and rests her hand on its scene of offered fruit are all suggestive. Far from the sharp morality of *Marriage A-la-Mode* this is a moment of indecision to enjoy. The cards burn in the fire, the moon rises through the sunset, and the motto on the clock heightens the suspense. NUNC N.U.N.C. Now, it says, *n-o-w*.

The Lady's Last Stake had many admirers. Among them was the fabulously wealthy Richard Grosvenor, whose estates included acres in Cheshire and the richest streets and squares in London. At twenty-six, he was an MP and a known collector who had garnered a clutch of old masters at the Luke Schaub sale in May, and in mid-1758 Charlemont sent him to Hogarth's studio. Hogarth's own terse note takes up the tale.

'A Gentl[eman] now a noble man seeing this Picture being infinitly Rich Prest me with more vehimence to do what subject I would, upon the same terms much against my inclination. I began on a subject I once wish to paint.'[17]

That subject would be Sigismunda, grieving 'over her lovers heart'. This would be his chance to ease his rage over the Schaub sale. He had recently been painting portraits like that of John Pine in the style of Rembrandt and had copied Van Dyck's portrait of Inigo Jones for Sir Edward Littleton.[18] Could he now emulate the Italians, too? Could he – remembering Joseph Warton's criticism – show that he could paint tragedy as well as comedy? He saw no reason why he should not, like Garrick, or even Shakespeare, excel in both modes. Grosvenor, of course, did not want anything of the sort: he wanted a sprightly comedy of modern manners, in the French or Dutch style; trouble lay ahead.

Hogarth worked simultaneously on *The Lady's Last Stake* and *Sigismunda* (plate XIV) throughout the summer and autumn, moving between comedy and tragedy. Time was pressing and he had other work on hand, including his portrait of William Huggins. In November, in the burst of affectionate correspondence that accompanied this commission, Huggins sent his translation of Dante. He tried to persuade Hogarth to illustrate it, teasing him about his desire for 'glory'. 'My Dear Warm Friend', Hogarth replied:

'What you propose would be a noble undertaking which I believe ten or a dozen years ago I should have embraced with joy and would have pleased the public if I could have done the author any degree of justice; but consider now my dear Friend Sixty is too late in the day to begin so arduous a Task, a work that could not be compleated in less than four or five years.'[19]

Somewhat unconvincingly, Hogarth pleaded indifference to fame as well as age and lassitude:

'The Bubble glory you hint I have no antipathy to, weighs less and less with me every day, even the profit attending it. I grow indolent, & strive to be contented with what are commonly called Trifles, for I think otherwise of what best produces the Tranquility of the mind. if I can but read on to the end of the Chapter I desire no more. this is so truly the case with me, that I have lately (altho I enjoy and love this world as much as ever) hardly been able to muster up spirits enough to go on with the two Pictures I have now in hand because they require much exertion, if I would succeed in any tolerable degree in them.'

Yet if Hogarth was weary he was also enjoying his work and his friendship with Charlemont. This month Charlemont bought an alleged Rubens, entitled *Old Man's Head*, and showed it to Hogarth, who, 'perhaps under the Influence of Good Breeding, and perhaps of Friendship', seemed to approve. Next day, however, Hogarth confessed he had to unburden his conscience: no politeness would allow him to let his young friend be fooled. He had his doubts about the Rubens. Indeed, he clearly thought it was a fraud, the kind sold constantly by auctioneers like Langford: 'if that head I saw yesterday is not done as follows I am mistaken':

'Recipe an old bit of coarse cloth and Portray an old bearded Beggars head upon it with the features much in shaddow make the eye red and row some slurrs of the Pencill by way of freedom in the beard and band clap a vast splash of light upon the forehead from which gradate by degrees from the

611

Blacking pot, varnish it well, and it will do for Langford or Prestage. I scarce ever knew a fizmonger who did not succeed in one of these masterpieces. one old Peters famous for Old Picture making use to say, even in contempt of those easiest parts of Rubens productions that he could sh—t old mens Heads with ease consider my lord he was a dutchman.'[20]

Forgery was a ripe old trade. Here Hogarth was looking back to his youth, when the kindly, ebullient John Peeters, Kneller's chief assistant, was known as 'the Doctor' for his skill in restoring famous Italian and Dutch masters. George Vertue, who had been taught drawing by Peeters, said that when he retouched old works, 'he woud give them the masterly stroak & Air of genuine drawings. that many of the Prime Connoisseurs, or vertuose purchasd at great prices. & to thes day are well preserv'd'.[21]

A collector's zeal had its pitfalls. But if Hogarth had hoped to exploit Richard Grosvenor's enthusiasm, he was to be sorely disappointed. Whereas *The Lady's Last Stake* had the heady feel of sex free of love, *Sigismunda* showed love itself, loyalty unto death. The story came from Boccaccio, and Hogarth illustrated Dryden's version in his *Fables*. Against the will of her father Tancred, Sigismunda marries Guiscardo, Tancred's lower-class protégé, whom he has brought up as his page and then his squire. The vengeful Tancred, doubly betrayed, pursues the couple and kills Guiscardo, sending his heart to Sigismunda in a jewelled cup. Wracked with grief, she fills the goblet with poison, drinks and dies before her father's eyes.

The triangular melodrama touched something deep in Hogarth's own life, made more poignant by the use of Jane as his model; he even worked in a tiny self-portrait on the carved table leg. He cared deeply about this operatic painting. His Sigismunda sits at a marble table, against a dark green curtain. Her costume is exotic and vaguely historical; a flowing red skirt and wide, full sleeves, topped with a blue overdress. A gold band, with a sapphire and a rope of pearls, holds down her soft green scarf. On her wrist more pearls clasp her father's portrait (reminiscent of Violette wearing Garrick's miniature, and of Jane holding Thornhill's portrait in Hogarth's painting of 1738). As she holds the goblet with Guiscardo's heart, her expression is haunted, exhausted as if with hours of tears. The composition is simple and classical, devoid of any intricacy, but behind it lie echoes of Continental paintings, of penitent magdalens, stricken Cleopatras, tragic stage heroines. It is highly theatrical, recalling Hogarth's words, 'I had ever been flatterd as to expression my whole aim was to fetch Tear from the Spectator my figure was the actor that was to do it.' Having seen 'many living ladies especially that shed involuntary tears I was to be convinced that Peoples hearts were as easily touched at a Tragedy'.[22]

Yet it was not Hogarth's staginess that offended his viewers, but his realism. In one way, this is very moving – Sigismunda looks less like a great beauty or great lover than an ordinary woman suffering an unendurable sorrow. (It was said that Hogarth had worked from sketches of Jane grieving after her mother's death in 1757.) But at the time the picture's literal, not emotional, veracity seemed grisly and even comic. In the first version Sigismunda's hands were stained with gore and the heart was all too real, rumoured to have come from a corpse freshly dissected by Hogarth's surgeon friend Sir Caesar Hawkins.[23] In 1761 Horace Walpole damned Hogarth with this detail. Talking of current outbursts, he wrote:

'The true frantic estro resides at present with Mr Hogarth; I went this morning to see a portrait he is painting of Mr. Fox – Hogarth told me he had promised, if Mr Fox would sit as he liked, to make as good a picture as Vandyke or Rubens could. I was silent – "why now", said he, "you think this very vain, but why should one not speak truth?" This *truth* was uttered in the face of his own *Sigismonda*, which is exactly a maudlin whore tearing off the trinkets that her keeper had given her, to fling at his head. She has her father's picture in a bracelet on her arm, and her fingers are bloody with the heart, as if she had just bought a sheep's pluck in St James's market.'[24]

To describe the heroine thus, especially if he knew that Jane was the model, shows Walpole in his least delightful light – but strong emotion, unmediated by classical politeness, always seemed tasteless to a true connoisseur. To call her 'a maudlin whore' removed her from the category of people whom one had to be bothered with, and shoved the picture firmly back into the comic career that produced *A Harlot's Progress*.

Walpole was not alone in his distaste. In the face of this startling sight, Grosvenor paled and procrastinated: it was like ordering *Tom Jones* and receiving the dismaying *Amelia*. Goaded by Grosvenor's silence, in mid-June Hogarth announced that his commission was now completed. 'Being seen and fully approved by his lordship whilst in hand,' he wrote firmly, presumably referring to the first viewing, 'I have done all I can to the Picture of Sigismunda.' He reminded Grosvenor of their terms:

'you was pleased to say you would give me what price I should think fit to set upon any Subject I would Paint for you, and at the same time you made this generous offer, I, in return, made it my request, that you would use no

613

ceremony of refusing the Picture, when done, if you should not be thoroughly satisfied with it. This you promis'd should be as I pleased which I beg now you will comply with without the least hesitation, if you think four hundred guineas too much money for it.'[25]

Hogarth thus impudently turned the price of the Schaub *Sigismunda* from pounds into guineas. But he also inadvertently offered Grosvenor a loophole:

'One more favour I have to beg, which is, that you will determine on this matter as soon as you can conveniently, that I may resolve whether I shall go about another Picture for Mr Hoar the banker on the same conditions or stop here.'

This could have meant simply that he did not wish to take such a risk again, but Grosvenor adroitly read it as saying that Hoare, who was currently creating a picture gallery, might take the painting. He took four days to answer, apologizing smoothly for the delay due to his 'being out of town'. Then he slid out of his promise, oiling the rejection with brilliantly equivocal praise. He understood, he said,

'that you have a Commission from Mr Hoare for a Picture. If he shou'd have taken a fancy to the Sigismunda, I have no sort of objection to your letting him have it; for I really think the Performance so striking, & inimitable, that the constantly having it before one's eyes, wou'd be too often occasioning melancholy ideas to arise in one's mind; which a Curtain being drawn before it wou'd not diminish in the least.'[26]

Hogarth still hoped. He sent a further ultimatum, noting that as the response 'did not seem to be quite positive', he assumed – if he did not hear again within the week – that Grosvenor would comply with the original terms. But Grosvenor was silent. Finally, Hogarth admitted himself beaten: 'I kept my Picture he kept his money.'[27] He still protested that his price was fair. Whereas the forgers and 'cheats in the traffick of pictures' made ample earnings (because the great 'love to be cheated') he had spent more time and anxiety upon this work, 'than would have got me double the money in any of my other way and not half what a common face painter got in the time'.

In his distress Hogarth fell back on *The Lady's Last Stake*, which had *not* been rejected. He wrote to Charlemont and instead of naming his sum, this time he asked his purchaser to name his. In return came a highly flattering letter – but no cash. Charlemont said that of course the true price of *The Lady's Last Stake* was 'inestimable'. Pleading business and lack of funds, he

614

promised to send as much as he could afford when he got to Ireland. Eventually, in January 1760, £100 arrived, with assurances of his being

'ashamed to offer such a trifle in recompence for the pains you have taken and the Pleasure your picture has afforded me . . . Were I to pay your deserts I fear I shoul'd leave myself poor indeed.'[28]

Hogarth should regard this merely as a token, in return for a gift. He accepted happily. Easily wounded now, Hogarth was genuinely fond of Charlemont and any snobbish pleasure in their friendship was mixed with a real appreciation of his easy, responsive politeness. The affection was genuine, and Charlemont remembered Hogarth as a man 'with whose friendship my youthful days were honoured and delighted'.[29] Once again, the money mattered less than the tone: Charlemont's warmth could be set against Grosvenor's chill rejection. And, as the last resort of a hurt man, Hogarth could twist the language of both men to vouch for his artistic power.

Hogarth talked obsessively about Grosvenor's rebuff. He asked advice, retouched the canvas, and responded to praise with pathetic gratitude. In August 1759, after an evening with George Hay at a friend's house near Chiswick, he was even prompted to put his feelings in verse, 'turned into English' by Paul Whitehead, bemoaning his foolish 'Risque' and seizing ironically on Grosvenor's suggestion that *Sigismunda* was almost too 'striking and inimitable'. If he was going to be valued as 'dead',

> Then dead as Guido let me be,
> Then judge, my friend, twixt him and me.
> If merit crowns alike the piece.
> What treason to be like in price;
> Because no copied line you trace,
> The picture can't be right, you're sure;
> But say, my critic connoisseur,
> Moves it the heart as much or more
> Than picture ever did before?
> This is the painter's truest test,
> And this Sir *Richard's* self confess'd.
> Nay, 'tis so moving, that the knight
> Can't even bear it in his sight;
> Then who would tears so dearly buy,
> As give four hundred pounds to cry?[30]

Hogarth's gamble to be treated like an old master had failed. He had boasted of his commission and now – as with the non-sale of *Marriage A-la-Mode* in 1751, and Sandby's caricatures in 1753 – his enemies had another chance to crow. 'Ill nature spread so fast now was the time for every little dog to bark in there profession and revive the old splene which appeard at the time my analysis came out.'[31]

One of the quickest critics off the mark was Joshua Reynolds. Asked by Johnson, 'on a sudden emergency' to produce some copy for *The Idler*, Reynolds sat up all night to write and his first paper appeared on Saturday, 29 September. Brilliantly turning Hogarth's own Britophil essay against him, Reynolds posed as the man of common sense and in this Hogarthian guise, he attacked the worst kind of critic,

'who judges by narrow rules, and those too often false, and which, tho' they should be true, and founded on nature, will lead him but a little way towards the just estimation of the sublime beauties in works of genius'.[32]

Without naming names, the Hogarth of the *Analysis* was himself now caricatured as the 'Bubble-man', the canting connoisseur who traipses through the gallery, criticizing Van Dyck and Raphael's *St Paul* for lacking 'the flowing line'. Next he reaches Raphael's *Charge of Peter*:

'"Here", he says, "are twelve upright figures: what a pity it is that Raffaelle was not acquainted with the pyramidall principle . . . Indeed", added he, "I have often lamented that so great a genius as Raffaelle had not lived in this enlightened age, since the art has been reduced to principles, and had had his education in one of the modern academies; what glorious works might we then have expected from his divine pencil!"'[33]

The jibe went home. A month later, Reynolds returned to the attack, redefining the universal injunction to 'Imitate nature', and then came a third essay, turning on the relativism of beauty and the side issue of 'novelty'.[34] The ideal painter cited in both these pieces was the Italian, who 'attends only to the invariable, the great and general ideas'. Hogarth and his like, one deduces, are at the other end of the spectrum:

'To conclude then, by way of corollary, if it has been proved that the painter, by attending to the invariable and general ideas of nature, produces beauty, he must, by regarding minute particularities, and accidental discriminations, deviate from the universal rule, and pollute his canvas with deformity.'

The magisterial final six words were added by Samuel Johnson.

All Hogarth's minute, careful, graphic details from daily life were thus dismissed as the 'petty particularities' of Dutch painting. To Reynolds these meant nothing beside the sublimity of Michelangelo: 'all genius and soul'. And if his opinion, he declared, should be thought 'one of the wild extravagancies of enthusiasm', he could only say that those who censured enthusiasm did not know the old masters: 'One may very safely recommend a little more enthusiasm to the modern painters; too much is certainly not the vice of the present age.'[35]

'Enthusiasm' was a slippery term in the 1750s. It had been one of Shaftesbury's favourite words, and to Reynolds it meant the fire of imaginative creation. It had been used thus for several years by poets, as in Warton's 'Ode to Fancy' of 1746:

> O warm, enthusiastic maid
> Without thy powerful vital aid,
> That breathes an energy divine,
> That gives a soul to every line,
> Ne'er may I strive with lips profane,
> To utter an unhallowed strain . . .[36]

Hogarth, however, found 'enthusiasm' perilous – in religion, in politics and in art. It breathed the dubious zeal of fanaticism, recalling the tumults of his youth: the Sacheverell riots; the Jacobite ''15'; the fever of the South Sea Bubble; the wild superstition surrounding the 'rabbit woman', Mary Tofts. But he may also have feared intensity and pushed it away partly because it was a part of his own nature. Passionate aspiration, even more than modish imitation, had led his Tom Rakewell to lose his fortune, his values and his mind. Hogarth needed to pin his own soaring imagination down to the mundane world. Enthusiasm led to risks, cliffs and thresholds: his own attempt at the sublime, his *Sigismunda*, had brought nothing but shame.

In 1759 Hogarth's misery was profound. Yet while he sank into himself, craving reassurance, the country was rejoicing around him. The tide of war had turned, and Pitt was hailed as the nation's saviour. A comet flared across the sky in May, and from then on England enjoyed a glowing sun by day and a soft moon every night. Month after month, news arrived of more triumphs: on 1 August, after the Battle of Minden, London was packed with rejoicing crowds, and at dusk the city was illumined by bonfires, made beautiful by hundreds of twinkling lanterns on the railings of all the great houses. People of fashion gathered in the middle of the street and every wit in town was drunk. The same month, the French fleet from Toulon was defeated off Cape Lagos; three months later, the Brest fleet was demolished at Quiberon. In India Robert Clive was driving the French down the Coromandel coast. In North America General Amherst seized the key forts, and the dying Wolfe's assault on the heights of Quebec secured the way to Montreal. The British now held Canada with its rich fur and fish trade; and Guadeloupe and Martinique, the rich sugar islands. And still the sun shone.

In late October, Walpole wrote to George Montagu:

'Can one easily leave the remains of such a year as this? It is still all gold . . . Instead of the glorious and ever-memorable year 1759, as the newspapers call it, I call it this ever-warm and victorious year. We have not had more conquest than fine weather: one would think we had plundered East and West Indies of sunshine. Our bells are worn threadbare with ringing for victories.'[37]

It was a year of extremes: 'an *annus mirabilis* for victories, a "South Sea Year" for expenditure'.[38] A year before, Pitt had stunned the Commons by boasting of the millions he was spending on the war. Now, in November 1759, proposing a monument to Wolfe, he proclaimed himself as the real hero: he had done more for Britain, he said, than any orator for Rome. Called 'blind' and 'a reckless gambler' by opponents, Pitt had staked all. And won.

At the end of this year, Hogarth produced one of the most electric of all his prints, *The Cockpit*. Apart from the obvious pun of cock-pit(t), the print was a clear political comment: the 'Cockpit' was the name of a Whitehall building where politicians gathered and a synonym for the Treasury itself. Hogarth shows a blind gambler, tense and still before the pit. Around him the crowd presses and screams, shoves and whistles, but the unmoved central figure deflects the uproar without a tremor.

Emblematic as it was, this was also a realistic scene, full of 'petty peculiarities'. The blind gambler was recognized as Lord Albermarle Bertie, second son of the rich and powerful Duke of Ancaster. The figures in the crowd include a Quaker and a newspaper-seller, a Negro servant and a rich tradesman, a jockey and a hangman (or perhaps his victim, with a gibbet drawn on his back). Yet the detail is arranged like a series of distorting mirrors, endless reflections of solipsistic fury. A French noble taking snuff on the left is balanced by a dandified chimney-sweep on the right, also taking snuff. On each side, too, men yell into each other's ears. And on left and right, the toes of the men who feed and cajole the cocks poke into the mat-covered ring.

The hubbub in the Royal Cockpit in Birdcage Walk, St James's, always struck newcomers as bewildering, even terrifying: and also as somehow

180 *The Cockpit* (1759)

typically English. Four years later, the young James Boswell, having heard that enemies of the English 'always represent them as selfish, beef-eaters, and cruel', decided to be 'a true born Old Englishman'. First he had dinner alone at Dolly's in the City, making sure it was indeed a fat beefsteak. Then, filling his pockets with apples and gingerbread (but taking care to leave his pocket book behind), he went to the pit. Once inside, he found 'a circular room in the middle of which the cocks fight', with rows of seats gradually rising:

'The cocks, nicely cut and dressed and armed with silver heels are set down and fight with amazing bitterness and resolution. Some of them were quickly dispatched. One pair fought three-quarters of an hour. The uproar, and the noise of betting, is prodigious. A great deal of money made a very quick

619

circulation from hand to hand. There was a number of professed gamblers there . . . I was sorry to see the distraction and anxiety of the betters. I was sorry for the poor cocks. I looked round to see if any of the spectators pitied them when mangled and torn in a most cruel manner, but I could not observe the smallest relenting sign in any countenance. I was therefore not ill pleased to see them endure mental torment. Thus did I complete my true English day, and came home pretty much fatigued and pretty confounded at the strange turn of this people.'

Hogarth's picture, too, is a critique of Englishness as it now appeared to him – the blindess of its leaders and the fury of its crowd, in which every lonely, driven soul pursues his own, rather than a collective, interest. Each man pits himself *against* the other, as the cocks do. And as the cocks fight on, weakening and regaining strength, so the bets change. In a way this powerful print, whose amphitheatre so recalls the dissecting room of *The Four Stages of Cruelty*, could be Hogarth's answer to the enthusiasm of Reynolds, and also to the dark 'sublimity' of terror in Burke:

'Of feeling little more can be said, than that the idea of bodily pain, in all the modes and degrees of labour, pain, anguish, torment, is productive of the sublime; and nothing else in this sense can produce it.'[39]

*

Such words alert us to the uneasy sense of Hogarth's own aesthetic pleasure in portraying cruelty; elsewhere, Burke wrote, 'I am convinced that we have a degree of delight, and that no small one, in the real misfortunes and pains of others.'[40] But there is identification here too – the pain in *The Cockpit*, inseparable from the exhilaration, also seems personal.

To elucidate this print, Nichols and Steevens quoted a later essay describing the Battle Royal, in which an unlimited number of fowls were pitted against each other: 'and when they have slaughtered one another for the diversion of the otherwise generous and humane Englishmen the single surviving bird is to be esteemed the victor, and carries away the prize'.[41] The cocks and the sightless gambler are the equal focus of Hogarth's circling mob. At the heart of *The Cockpit* sits a man, charismatic yet unseeing. He thinks he has power, but he has none. While he takes people's bets, his own notes are stolen from beneath his nose. A centrifugal force seems to pull the darkness of the crowd towards him, pressing in as he gambles higher and higher. Lord Albermarle Bertie is blind, and the cocks before him will try in their frenzy to peck out each other's eyes. The print is all about *eyes*, with everyone looking

620

quickly, intently, fiercely some way or other – while the artist, and through him his audience, look *down* on them all, pulled into the circle.

The Cockpit is the last in a long line of Hogarth pictures of men gathered round a table: the Committee of the House of Commons; the *Midnight Modern Conversation*; the surgeons' dissecting room; *Columbus Breaking the Egg*; the Election banquet. Even when they are celebratory these scenes have a sinister quality. The date on Hogarth's engraving is 5 November. It was Guy Fawkes' Day, a day of Protestant bonfires, a second night of excess after the anniversary of the Glorious Revolution. It was also the day after Hogarth's sixty-first birthday. And it was the day when – had he not been ill – he would have been seated at the next annual dinner at the Foundling Hospital, in the midst of the artists.

30

Sickness, Societies and *Sigismunda*

When a man gives himself up to the government of a ruling passion, – or, in other words, when his HOBBY-HORSE grows headstrong, – farewell cool reason and fair discretion!
LAURENCE STERNE, *Tristram Shandy* (1759)

THE NATION HOGARTH HAD KNOWN was slowly changing around him: when Handel died in 1759, it seemed an age had ended. The great composer left the score of *Messiah* to the Foundling Hospital, and £1000 for poor musicians and their families, and was interred with full pomp in Westminster Abbey before a crowd of three thousand people. Around the Abbey, the city itself had changed. Even the river winding through London's heart was altered. Westminster Bridge had opened in 1750 and another crossing was planned at Blackfriars. In 1757 all the old houses left on London Bridge had been pulled down – the view from the Alderman's window in *Marriage A-la-Mode* was a glimpse of history. Then in 1760 the City applied to Parliament to widen its 'inconvenient avenues': seven medieval gateways were demolished, Newgate and Ludgate, Aldersgate and Cripplegate, Moorgate, Bishopsgate, and Aldgate. Only the names remained.

To the north, the streets spread relentlessly outwards; the New Road from Edgware to Islington was built in 1756, and the spur linking it to the City was nearly finished. To the west, the great estates around Grosvenor Square and Berkeley Square had quite taken the lustre from St James's. And along Piccadilly, where all the livery stables used to cluster, huge new mansions had risen. 'When do you come?' Horace Walpole asked George Montagu in November 1759. 'If it is not too soon, you will find a new town. I stand today at Piccadilly like a country squire: there are twenty new stone houses; at first I concluded that all the grooms that used to live there, had got estates and built palaces.'[1]

Far away from the capital and the coasts of Britain, colonies had been gained and trading posts established. And in the British Isles themselves new industrial ventures were under way, their implications still unknown. In 1759

622

Jebediah Strutt invented a machine frame for cotton goods, and the chemist John Roebuck set up an iron foundry in Stirlingshire. In 1760 the Duke of Bridgewater's Canal Act was passed, Josiah Wedgwood leased a pottery in Burlsem – and Arthur Guinness opened a brewery in Dublin.

At times, as he had never done in the past, Hogarth felt out of touch with his country, and even with his city. His mood was low. He later wrote that the anxiety *Sigismunda* brought, 'coming at a time when perhaps nature wants a more quiet life and something to chere it', brought on an illness that lasted a year.[2] It is hard to say what this illness was – it could have been a mild stroke or heart attack. It could, although it seems unlikely, have been the result of some venereal disease caught when he was young, an affliction that might also explain his childlessness and violent mood swings. Or it might simply have been a long-lasting respiratory illness, stemming from the infections that killed so many Londoners that winter. He himself put it down to the stress surrounding *Sigismunda*, and to 'exercise after long sedentary proceeding for many year'. His hand was shaky and his line unsure. When William Huggins finally finished his translation, Hogarth congratulated him ('The Dante finishd! well I can never enough admire your Resolution and constancy . . .') but felt unable to make a print of his 1758 portrait. He had always found faces difficult to engrave, he said:

'it is a thing I never did nor shall be able to succeed in witness the two damn'd things I labour'd at of my own Fiz for the Frontispiece to my works, the copying my own works is the devil. I am sure the poorerest graver will do it better than I should.'[3]

If the burin was beyond him, occasionally friends coaxed him to put pencil to paper. One instance was his work for Laurence Sterne. The first two volumes of *Tristram Shandy*, which had been rejected by the London publisher Robert Dodsley, were published in a small run in York in 1759, bringing Sterne fame at forty-seven; the London edition came out on New Year's Day, 1760. Hogarth had long been Sterne's favourite artist, and his brilliantly digressive novel – 'curvetting and frisking it away'[4] – was in tune with Hogarth's taste for the 'wanton kind of chace' and the shaping power of passion. Its narrative circled like a Hogarth print, where we choose our starting point, pause on details and fill in gaps. And Sterne appreciated Hogarth's supreme ability to express personality through the body. With a grin, he adapted Hogarth's technique of exaggerated line and contrast, although he might not have pleased Hogarth when he called this 'caricature'. In this scene, for example, the man-midwife approaches:

'Imagine to yourself a little squat, uncourtly figure of a doctor Slop, of about four feet and a half perpendicular height, with a breadth of back, and a sesquipedality of belly, which might have done honour to a serjeant in the horse-guards.

'Such were the outlines of Dr Slop's figure, which – if you have read Hogarth's analysis of beauty, and if you have not, I wish you would; – you must know, may as certainly be caricatured, and conveyed to the mind by three strokes as three hundred.'[5]

The two men met in March 1760, when Sterne asked Richard Berenger (a lively, effervescent man, much liked by Garrick) to 'sally at Leicester Fields' and demand a frontispiece.[6] When Sterne drafted his letter he wrote, 'What would I not give to have but ten Strokes of Howgarth's witty Chissel, at the front of my next edition of Shandy.'[7]

181 Frontispiece to *Tristram Shandy*, vol. I (1760)

His first drawing, as Sterne had hoped, showed Corporal Trim reading the sermon on 'Conscience', taking up his position at the 85° angle, 'which sound orators . . . know very well, to be the persuasive angle of incidence', balancing and swaying, with 'his knee bent, but that not violently, – but so as to fall

624

within the limits of the line of beauty'.[8] This, in itself, is a splendid jab at the culture of politeness, the arguments about genius and imitation, the manuals of deportment and the rules of art:

'How the deuce Corporal Trim, who knew not so much as an acute angle from an obtuse one, came to hit it so exactly; – or whether it was chance or nature, or good sense or imitation, &c. shall be commented upon in that part of this cyclopædia of the arts and science, where the instrumental parts of the eloquence of the senate, the pulpit, the bar, the coffee-house, the bed-chamber and the fire-side, fall under consideration.'

In Hogarth's drawing Walter Shandy and Uncle Toby are smoking in the background, against Toby's map of the Namur fortifications, and he also fitted in Dr Slop, looking on. The plate, engraved by Ravenet, was ready for the second edition on 2 April 1760. The following January, when the next two volumes of *Tristram Shandy* appeared, Sterne used another illustration by Hogarth, showing Tristram's christening, with his father 'with his breeches held up by one hand, and his night-gown thrown across the arm of the other',[9] arriving too late to forbid the fearful name.

Sterne was not rigidly of the Hogarth camp; the frontispiece for the *Sermons of Mr Yorick*, in 1760, was his portrait by Reynolds. But he shared Hogarth's defiance of rules and suspicion of organizations: as a Yorkshire priest he had satirized the ecclesiastical coterie, just as Hogarth set himself against a 'salaried' academy. From their very different backgrounds they understood frustration and despair – *Tristram Shandy* jumped out from the blackness of Sterne's failing marriage and his wife's madness. Both flagrantly courted greatness ('I wrote not to be *fed* but to be *famous*', said Sterne)[10] and they subverted texts and sermons, schools and models by setting them against chaotic, bawdy, illogical, preposterous spontaneity. And both, beneath the comic disorder and unfairness of life, felt the lure of desire and the call of compassion.

Sterne could see, however, that a deep preoccupation could easily turn into an obsessive hobby-horse – like Uncle Toby's fortifications, or Hogarth's *Sigismunda*. That summer, Hogarth still brooded, unrelieved, upon his painting. It became a notorious point of weakness, which people did not fail to exploit. 'A word in favour of *Sigismunda*', wrote Steevens, cruelly depicting Hogarth as avid for flattery,

'might have commanded a proof print, or forced an original sketch out of our artist's hands. The furnisher of this remark owes one of his scarcest performances to the success of a compliment, which might have stuck even in Sir *Godfrey Kneller's* throat.'[11]

Hogarth brooded, too, on the current moves in the art world. The artists associated with the Foundling Hospital and St Martin's Lane were now caught up in a new venture, to hold an annual exhibition. The impetus went back to early 1759 when the Society of Arts, which ran exhibitions for its young premium winners, first considered hiring a room for established artists, and then moved into grander premises in the Strand, opposite Beaufort Buildings. Although this Society included many leading artists such as Ramsay and Reynolds, Hudson and Hayman who also belonged to the St Martin's Lane–Foundling Hospital group, it was dominated by aristocratic Dilettanti and wealthy merchants, and was really more concerned with cultural 'improvement' and commerce than with promoting the fine arts. In contrast to this, there was a sense that the artists themselves, as a body, should now make a move. At the annual dinner of the Foundling Artists on 5 November 1759, the celebratory ode invited them 'nobly to think on Hayman's thought' of founding 'A great Museum all our own'. According to the *Royal Magazine*, what Hayman proposed was 'a public receptacle to contain the work of artists for the general advantage and glory of the Nation and satisfaction of foreigners'.[12]

As agreed at the dinner, a public meeting took place a week later at the Turk's Head. The invitation was signed by Francis Newton, as Secretary, and also by John Wilkes, Honorary President of the Artists' Committee, a close friend of Reynolds, and Treasurer of the Foundling's Aylesbury branch (he was later discovered to have embezzled the funds). At this gathering the artists decided to hold their own exhibition the next April. Theoretically, at least, the aim was to encourage artists who might not otherwise be noticed, while a shilling entrance fee would raise funds for the old and sick in their profession. The diplomatic and hard-working Hayman had already been unanimously elected Chairman and Reynolds was on the Governing Committee.

Hogarth was not part of these plans. In November he was smarting under Reynolds's *Idler* essays; his print of *The Cockpit* appeared on the day of the dinner, when Hayman made his proposal. But that winter, while he was ill, the other artists went ahead. In December they voted to ask the Society of Arts for use of their 'great Room' in the Strand, a perfect exhibition space, forty feet long. Their letter, written by Johnson, was discussed by the Society's Committee, including Allan Ramsay, in late February when they agreed to share the exhibition. The Society of Arts would carry the cost, but rejected the idea of an entrance fee (6d was charged for the catalogue instead) and demanded control over the hanging of the pictures.[13]

When the first public exhibition of British art opened on 21 April 1760, it was packed from wall to wall; over six and a half thousand catalogues were sold, at times the crowds threatened to get out of control; 'liveried servants' and others broke windows, to the tune of 13s 6d. The single review of this exhibition, published in *The Imperial Magazine*, noted the work by Roubiliac – including his model for Garrick's *Shakespeare* – and lavished praise on Hayman's *Garrick as Richard III*. The visitors liked Richard Wilson's large landscapes, and rushed to buy Paul Sandby's small ones. But the crowds saw no pictures by Hogarth, or by Ramsay, who apparently preferred to exhibit privately, or by the young Gainsborough. Reynolds – who showed two busts and two full-length portraits – was undoubtedly the star of the show. The *Imperial Magazine* thought his work 'perfect', finding

'copious and easy invention, the most graceful attitudes, great truth, sweetness and harmony of colouring . . . in short one living proof that genius is of all ages and countries and that Englishmen need not travel abroad to see fine things, would they but study to cultivate and encourage genius at home'.[14]

It looked as though Reynolds, the Italian-trained, pro-academy artist, had seized the torch from Hogarth's hands to light the way for an 'English school'.

The irony was harsh. Reynolds was now accepted as London's leading painter. He was earning up to £6000 a year and bought a large house on the western side of Leicester Fields, virtually opposite Hogarth, which he adapted at vast expense. He gave a ball, dressed his servants in livery and set up a carriage, smartly gilded and painted: when his sister Fanny, required to ride in it, complained that it was 'too shewy', he answered, 'What, would you have one like an apothecary's carriage?'[15]

Never wholly immune – to put it mildly – to envy, Hogarth was piqued. And Reynolds's presence was felt, too, in mid-May, when the Artists' Committee proposed that the catalogue profits from the exhibition should not go to needy artists as intended, but towards plans for an academy. The democratic, Hogarthian camp retaliated fast: a week later it was resolved that more time should be taken, and that the Artists' General Meeting, not the high-handed Committee alone, should decide how the money was spent.[16] In the end, the money was invested, and the artists vacillated and havered.

So by the summer of 1760, when Hogarth was slowly recovering, rumblings and divisions of opinion were already evident. His illness had not cut him off entirely. As soon as he was able to ride and get out and about, his strength and spirits revived. He went to the Artists' Annual Meeting at the Foundling Hospital on 14 May, where his name was put down as a steward for the anniversary dinner. Then, in June, he produced another frontispiece design, for the first volume of Kirby's *Perspective of Architecture*, eventually published in April 1761. And soon he was drawn back inexorably into the public debates when Kirby's pupil the Prince of Wales became King, prompting ferments among the artists, as among the politicians.

On 25 October 1760, Horace Walpole reported that the night before, George II had gone to bed well,

'rose at six this morning as usual, looked I suppose if all his money was in his purse, and called for his chocolate. A little after seven he went into the water-closet – the German valet de chambre heard a noise, louder than royal wind, listened, heard something like a groan, ran in and found the hero of Oudenarde and Dettingen on the floor, with a gash on his right temple by falling against the corner of a bureau – he tried to speak, could not and expired.'[17]

The King's last wish was more dignified than his end, but still intimate. In his will, George had asked that his coffin be placed next to Caroline's: a side was to be opened in each, so that their dust would mingle in death.

For Hogarth, the politics of the new reign were less immediately vital than his position as Serjeant-Painter. Although the practical work was done by his deputy, Hogarth was officially in charge of arrangements for any painting needed for the funeral on 11 November. This was a lavish ceremony. From the Prince's Chamber at Westminster where the coffin lay beneath a canopy of purple velvet, lit by vast silver chandeliers on tall stands, the procession wound across to the Abbey, so brightly lit that the naves and aisles and arching fretwork stood out clearer than in daylight. But within days, it seemed, the mourning gave way to magnificent balls and royal trips to the playhouse, in celebration of the accession to the throne. (Rather ominously, for his first command performance, George chose to to see Garrick's *Richard III*.)

Pyne, colourfully confusing dates and incidents, placed Hogarth's collapse in this autumn, saying he became

'seriously ill of an inflammatory disorder, caught at one of the windows of the Old Golden Cross, where he stood too long exposed to a current of air, making sketches of the heralds and the sergeant trumpeter's band, and the yeoman guard in their splendid liveries, who rendezvous'd at Charing

Cross. He purposed to paint a picture of the ceremony of proclaiming the new king.'[18]

This could have been a relapse. The kind, eccentric Messenger Monsey rushed at once to Hogarth's bedside, angry he had not been called before (but knowing how Hogarth hated doctors), and found him in a high fever, which broke just before dawn leaving him dozing and dreaming, rambling fitfully about his picture.

Pyne's story does suggest how keenly interested Hogarth was, like all the artists, in the accession of the young King. For some, their place was already secure: when he returned from Italy in 1757 Allan Ramsay had painted portraits of the Prince of Wales and of his tutor Bute. On George's accession, he painted two full-length official portraits – one for Hanover and one for St James's Palace – and after some confusion he was appointed Principal Painter in Ordinary to the Court: over the next few years he was so bogged down in royal portraits that Sterne was driven to remark, 'Mr Ramsay, you paint only the Court cards, the King, Queen and Knave.'[19] But the artists as a group also wanted to press their interests. The Society of Arts employed Samuel Johnson to compose an 'Address to the Throne', which was presented at the end of December and published in the *London Gazette* in January 1761. Signed by over sixty artists, it expressed their appreciation of George's support of the 'politer Arts', their sorrow at his father's death and their joy at his accession. This read like the forerunner of more precise requests, reviving the academy hopes, and Hogarth saw battles ahead.

As if edging himself back into position, on 15 December, before the Address was presented, Hogarth attended a meeting of the Foundling Governors, his first for eighteen months. At some point, wearily pleading his age ('upward of sixty'), he also drafted a letter to a nobleman, probably the Earl of Bute, asking for an audience to explain his point of view. Samuel Martin, he said, had informed him that his lordship would consider a plan if put in writing, but he would rather discuss particular points first, which 'will not take up more than half an hour of your lordships time'.[20] His notes were full of anxiety, and a longing to wipe off certain 'prejudices which I am assured stick to my character' and would prevent him carrying through his plans. 'My lord', his draft ended, 'I am almost af[r]aid there is a scheme on foot already the author of it will naturally defend [h]is own in opposition to mine which will breed a controversy.' This was something he must 'possitively avoid for my health sake for as I am circumstanced I had rather lose a most favorite point than break one nights rest'. In particular, he did not want to cross

629

swords with Ramsay, now his firm friend, whose skill in controversy and opposing views he openly acknowledged.

Significantly, Hogarth's note was headed 'My Lord, for a Royal academy', with 'Royal' crossed out, and 'Public' written in above. But the letter was never sent. It lay unread, jumbled among his papers, with the notes for his earlier hot-tempered speech to the Society of Arts and his rejected sections from the *Analysis*. A draft advertisement showed that he was planning a new edition and a supplement on architecture, perhaps prompted by Kirby's book.[21] Mixed with these were large, crammed sheets containing the beginnings of his treatise on 'The Present State of the Arts of painting, Sculpture & Engaving', which became known, from a phrase he used to Horace Walpole, as his *Apology for Painters*. Fast, furious and careless, he flung on to paper all his thoughts and plans and snapping resentments.

This winter Hogarth sat at his desk rather than his easel. But he was planning ahead, and in the spring of 1761 he stepped back into action. His campaign against the connoisseurs would be conducted on two fronts, via the Society of Arts and his own painting. In mid-February, he showed *Sigismunda* at Langford's auction room, announcing that he would have it engraved, 'in the manner of Drevet' if it met with public approval.[22] In some quarters it did, prompting a (bad) poem by the actor John Havard, who claimed that Hogarth had caught all his subject's passion and 'living woe':

> At length he just – throw Prejudice aside –
> The *Modern* SHEWS what the GREEK could but HIDE:
> Then from the Antient take the Palm away,
> And crown the greater Artist of this Day.[23]

At the start of March Hogarth announced his print of *Sigismunda*. Opposing his work to the old masters with deliberate bravado, as a subscription ticket he engraved *Time Smoking a Picture*, with his waving forelock, foul-smelling pipe and fat pot of varnish. Below it he put the lines, 'To nature and your Self appeal,/Nor learn of others, what to feel.' This was straightforward, but the references above the easel had a neat double edge. Hogarth referred his purchasers to *The Spectator*, where the forelocked Time visits the gallery, and to the comic dramatist Crates. In the source, the Greek quotation, translated by John Ireland, runs, 'Time has bent me double; and Time, though I confess he is a great artist, weakens all he touches.' That would be apt, but inadequate; with an added negative, Hogarth made his carefully mangled Greek read differently: 'Time is *not* a great artist . . . but weakens all he touches.'[24]

630

182 *Time Smoking a Picture* (1761)

Time took his revenge. On 2 March Hogarth opened his subscription book and placed notices in the press. But in March he collected only forty-one names, including Kirby, Garrick, John Hoadly, and his own doctor, Isaac Schomberg; and on 16 April, after adding three more, he finally closed the book. The print was destined not to be. On the back of the page after the list of subscribers, Hogarth explained that Ravenet had agreed to engrave the painting, but on discovering that he was bound by contract to work solely for the printseller Boydell for the next three years, 'the Subscription was put a Stop to, and the Money return'd to the Subscribers, there being no other engraver at the time capable of doing it as it should be done'.[25] It was another case of 'he kept his money, I kept my Picture'. Only Hester Thrale's father, John Salusbury, declined to recoup his subscription.

631

Above Hogarth's note, stuck to the page, is a torn corner of paper, all that remains of a larger sheet. One can just make out that on it he had copied Iago's lines from *Othello*:

> But he that filches from me my good name
> Robs me of that which not enriches him
> And makes me poor indeed.

*

After this setback it was even more urgent that his cherished, much abused painting should be shown to the world again. It was his bid to be accepted as a history-painter and its rejection had only strengthened his determination to win approval. By now this had become an fixed obsession, in which it is hard to disentangle hurt pride from something deeper, *within* the picture itself.

His chance, he thought, would come in May with the next public art exhibition. The 1760 shows had proved beyond a doubt that there was a huge public hungry to see modern British work, but since then the Artists' Committee had broken away from the Society of Arts. The artists had not liked the press of the 'idle and tumultuous' crowds, nor the rejection of an admission charge, nor the indignity of sharing the space with the prize-winning work of juvenile amateurs, which confused the public – to their fury, several senior artists, including Reynolds, received commiserations for not winning prizes. When the Society would not hear their appeals, the two groups split and from now on, leading artists who had been active in the Society of Arts, like Ramsay, Reynolds and Hayman, ceased to go to its meetings. Reynolds and James Paine were delegated to find a site for an independent exhibition and eventually the Artists' Committee rented Cock's auction room in Spring Gardens. They would take it for the whole of May 1761, and asked for pictures to be in by 27 April.

Now that the artists were on their own, Hogarth seized the chance to put forward his ideas about how they should work and what they should fight for. *Sigismunda* had challenged the connoisseurs' judgements and made bold claims for English painting, but he knew the struggle must be carried on at an organizational level as well. Those who came to the general meeting on 7 April heard him speak in his old challenging voice, appealing to liberty, property and patriotism. He proposed, first, that the artists should now formally associate as a society, to be called 'The Free Professors of Painting, Sculpture & Architecture'. Secondly, this society should 'enter into an amicable union' to promote measures that would 'best establish these Arts on a right Footing suitable to the Genius of this Country'. Finally, 'as absolutely necessary to that aim', they must resolve on ways 'to explore those Errors & Prejudices which have thitherto misguided the Judgments of true Lovers of Arts as well as discouraged the Living Artists in the Progress of their Studies'.[26]

Free from the taint of association with the Society of Arts, Hogarth was acknowledged as leader by a substantial number of artists, including the influential Roubiliac. In the end, the name chosen was 'The Society of Artists of Great Britain' (as opposed to the impersonal, commercial 'Arts'): but even this name proved that Hogarth had made his mark. He and his supporters wanted a society that would not dictate taste, but help *artists*. It would be more like the professional bodies of other trades, democratic and open to all practitioners, organizing exhibitions, teaching pupils, setting up funds for indigent artists and their dependants.[27] To these ends, exhibitions were important, indeed vital, because they would open up a new market and allow artists to appeal directly to a large body of people without the intervention of middlemen, dealers and jobbers.

Hogarth could see that this was a crucial moment, a chance to guide, or push, or bully British artists in the direction he favoured. There was a spirit of collective effort, as there had been in the mid-1730s when he pressed for the Engravers Act, the Foundling Hospital paintings and the starting of St Martin's Lane. If he was to exploit it, he must speak out now. His ringing proposal was both a reaffirmation of a long-held vision and a declaration of hostilities.

The Society of Arts planned to open its exhibition in the Strand on 27 April, while the Artists' breakaway show would begin in Spring Gardens on 9 May. This time Hogarth was determined to play a prominent part: he would show seven pictures, outdoing Reynolds's five. He painted no new works, but borrowed back *The Lady's Last Stake* from Charlemont, adding two more comic modern histories, *The Gate of Calais* and *An Election Entertainment*, and three portraits, including his *Bishop Hoadly*. All demonstrated his belief that native art, even history-painting, could flourish without a Frenchified or Italianate academy. But his centrepiece, of course, would be *Sigismunda*.

As the time drew near Hogarth became increasingly strained. After the Society of Arts opened its doors in the Strand in late April, only two weeks remained before the crowds rushed to Spring Gardens. It was now, in early May, that Horace Walpole visited Hogarth's studio and decided that here was 'the true frantic oestrus', when he heard Hogarth boast he could paint like Van Dyck, while all the time his *Sigismunda*, the 'maudlin whore' with bloodstained hands, stood in the background. But Hogarth also had more general worries: he had heard that Walpole was writing a book (his *Anecdotes of Painters*), based on the notes he had bought from Vertue's widow three years earlier. Writing to Montagu, Walpole re-created their conversation, unwittingly revealing his own casual complacency as much as Hogarth's nervous aggression. 'As I was going,' he wrote, 'Hogarth put on a very grave face, and said, "Mr. Walpole, I want to speak to you"; I sat down, and said, I was ready to receive his commands. For shortness, I will mark this wonderful dialogue by initial letters.' It deserves to be heard:

'H. I am told you are going to entertain the town with something in our way. W. Not very soon, Mr Hogarth. H. I wish you would let me have it, to correct; I should be sorry to have you expose yourself to censure. We painters must know more of those things than other people. W. Do you think nobody understands painting but painters? H. Oh! So far from it, there's Reynolds, who certainly has genius; why, but t'other day he offered £100 for a picture that I would not hang in my cellar; and indeed, to say truth, I have generally found that persons who had studied painting least, were the best judges of it –'

Hogarth then jumped abruptly to his main point – he was intensely anxious to know what Walpole might say about Sir James Thornhill: 'I would not have you say anything against him.' Old loyalties spurred him on. He insisted that Thornhill was the first to attempt history in England, 'and I assure you some Germans have said he was a very great painter'. Walpole soothingly explained that he was writing only about this century, and was unsure whether 'Thornhill will come within my plan or not; if he does, I fear you and I shall not agree upon his merits'. But Hogarth would not give up:

'H. I wish you would let me correct it, besides, I am writing something of the same kind myself, I should be sorry we should clash. W. I believe it is not much known what my work is; very few persons have seen it. H. Why, it is a critical history of painting, is not it? W. No, it is an antiquarian history of it in England; I bought Mr Vertue's MSS, and I believe the work will not give much offence. Besides, if it does, I cannot help it: when I publish anything, I give it to the world to think of it as they please. H. Oh! if it is an antiquarian work, we shall not clash. Mine is a critical work; I don't know whether I shall ever publish it – it is rather an apology for painters – I think it is owing to the good sense of the English, that they have not painted better. W. My dear Mr Hogarth, I must take my leave of you, you grow too wild – and I left him – if I had stayed, there remained nothing but for him to bite me.'[28]

Walpole promised the conversation was literal, adding that perhaps, 'as long as you have known Englishmen and painters, you never met with anyone so distracted'. He had intended, he concluded, to devote a line of his preface to Hogarth's genius '(I mean for wit)'; 'I shall not erase it, but I hope nobody will ask me if he was not mad.'

Londoners were highly entertained by the rivalry between the two Societies, which quickly became recast as a war between the connoisseurs and the pro-Hogarth camp. Sides were taken, pamphlets issued, arguments aired in the press. An added piquancy was given by the unstated fight within the new Society of Artists itself, between the dignified, fashionable Reynolds and the tiny but unvanquished fighting cock Hogarth. The struggle was not only one of ego – for both men were mightily vain – but also one of principle. Hogarth was certainly concerned for his own reputation which is why *Sigismunda* was so vital, but he was also upholding ideas he had stuck by for over a quarter of a century. Giving way would be a betrayal, not only of himself but of the idols of his youth, such as Wren and Thornhill.

Hogarth's standing was underlined when he was asked (although designs had already been put forward) to contribute two designs for the exhibition catalogue. His drawings, and Grignion's engravings of them, were given free to publicize the exhibition but he also used them to continue his campaign. His frontispiece was a bid for royal patronage, with a Latin motto implying that hope lay only in the ruler. It featured a sweet-faced Britannia, with a very real watering can, tending the intertwined trees of painting, sculpture and architecture; the water flows from the mouth of the British lion beneath a benign profile bust of the new King. The tailpiece, however, showed a dandified monkey with an evil wink, 'fantastically dressed in the Pink of the Mode',[29] with eye-glass and sword. He is trying to revive three long-dead 'Exoticks', marked 'Obit 1502', '1600' and '1604'. The motto reads: 'How shall I explain this – that fame is denied to the living?'[30]

Hogarth had his allies, notably Bonnell Thornton who stoutly upheld his claims in a new paper, the *St James's Chronicle*. Backed by the printer Henry Baldwin, with a group of ten investors including Garrick and George Colman, the *Chronicle* was a useful mouthpiece for Hogarth's theatrical friends and for Thornton's own informal group of ex-schoolfriends, the 'Nonsense Club' that he had formed in the mid-1750s with George Colman, Robert Lloyd and William Cowper. These two groups, the theatre and the ex-Westminster scholars, moved closer after 1757, when Colman published a eulogy to Garrick. Soon he began to edge out Arthur Murphy as Garrick's lieutenant at

183 Frontispiece to the Catalogue for the Exhibition of the Society of Artists (1761)

184 Tailpiece

Drury Lane; his first play, *Polly Honeycombe*, did well there in December 1760, and in February 1761 *The Jealous Wife* (based on *Tom Jones*) went even better. Lloyd, lurking gloomily in the background, also supported Garrick in a current feud in *The Actor*,[31] a poem that also illustrates how close the Nonsense Club's ideal of the 'natural' in acting came to Hogarth's model in art:

> ACTING, dear Thornton, its perfection draws
> From no observance of mechanic laws:
> No settled maxims of a fav'rite stage
> No rules deliver'd down from age to age . . .[32]

The intimacy of 'dear Thornton' was also typical. The members of the club were always writing to one another, in verse or prose. Lloyd's *Familiar Epistle* to Colman on the eve of *The Jealous Wife* shows how they shared each crisis, and also brings the nerves of a Drury Lane first night vividly to life:

> The coach below, the clock gone five,
> Now to the theatre we drive:
> Peeping the curtain's eyelet through,
> Behold the house in dreadful view!
> Observe how close the critics sit,
> And not one bonnet in the pit.
> With horror hear the galleries ring
> Nosy! Black Joke! God save the King!
> Sticks clatter, catcalls scream, Encore!
> Cock's crow, pit hisses, galleries roar.[33]

These friends thrived on the theatrical, on heightened nerves, controversy, cat-calls, hisses and applause. In 1760 their other great ally, Charles Churchill, with his lumbering physique and rapier wit, also exploded into print. Ridden with debts, on the brink of a formal separation from his wife, Churchill too made the theatre his home.[34] Night after night he sat transfixed in the first row of the pit, next to the orchestra, his piercing gaze bearing fruit in the devastating *Rosciad* in March 1761, which demolished Murphy and every leading actor – except Garrick. At one blow, the poem paid Churchill's debts and made his name.[35] As yet his dangerous wit posed no threat to Hogarth, whose prints, like Garrick's expressive acting, mirrored Churchill's 'fascination with the immediate impression, the unpremeditated expression, and the visceral reaction'.[36]

Satires from the Murphy camp and attacks from Smollett's *Critical Review* soon assaulted the *Rosciad*, but in April, while the theatrical war rolled on,

Thornton turned his attention to art. The *St James's Chronicle* was a real newspaper, appearing three times a week, listing appointments at Court and battles abroad, winnings at Newmarket and bankruptcies in London, drownings at sea and murders at home, fires and cricket matches and outrageous bets. It reviewed new books, and to fill its four pages ran correspondence columns, mostly invented, on controversial issues: the arguments for peace, the plight of fallen women, the excesses of Methodism – and the state of the arts.

Thornton, Colman and Garrick all wrote essays, letters and puffs for the paper. In late April, just before the exhibition of the Society of Arts, one of their spoof letters was from a stout, commonsensical Englishman, 'John Oakly'. (This was also, one notes, the name of Garrick's character in *The Jealous Wife*.)[37] Describing himself as 'an old Fellow, and a cross old Fellow too', Oakly stepped forward as a lover of the polite arts, angered by the comparison of 'their slow Progress amongst us, and of their flowering State in other countries'. He found himelf 'growing quite warm', indeed furious, to think that 'our living men of Merit should be neglected and starved, because Connoisseurs forsooth, as they are called from Conceit, and picture Jobbers from Interest, are leagued together to destroy all genius'. Many painters were labouring for a small pittance, while others were 'absolutely starving'. Of course, all this mimicked Hogarth, who soon appeared: 'as a great a genius as any Time or Nation produced', an artist who 'stands by himself as the great Original of Dramatic Painting'.[38] It was shocking, the letter continued, that this artist's work (presumably *Marriage A-la-Mode*) should go for a pittance at an auction, while Rembrandt drawings, Teniers paintings, 'and the scarce visible Productions of some antiquated dauber, have been bought up with a kind of religious Enthusiasm'.

Now that the artists had formed their own association and forgotten their petty squabbles, Oakly proclaimed, the future looked bright:

'for what may we not expect from the Merit of many I could name among them, cordially assisted by the Author of the analysis of beauty, in this free Country, under such a Government, and protected by such a King'.

Over the next month, the *Chronicle* chased up the topic. In early May it announced that Oakly's letter would be reprinted, as 'a considerable Demand for it still continues'.[39] Spread over the next two issues was a full catalogue of the Society of Arts exhibition. Even Roubiliac published a poem, attacking the virtuosi.

The issue of 7–9 May, for the Spring Gardens' opening, advertised a pamphlet entitled *A Call to the Connoisseurs*, by 'T.B.', and a few days later the paper carried a long extract from this, defending the British artists. All the old names were there, Hayman, Ramsay, Hudson, Benjamin and Richard Wilson, Roubiliac, Lambert and one woman, Catherine Read. Reynolds reigned supreme ('the powers of Mr Reynolds are perfect in the highest degree'), but Hogarth was also elevated as 'the most perfect Master of all the Characters and Passions, expressed by the human Countenance, that ever existed' and indeed, as 'the Wonder of the World'. A second Oakly letter now appeared and the stream of exuberant copy continued into mid-May. Garrick and Thornton both had a share in these letters, whose hyperbolic self-parody reminds one both of the way Hogarth's friends teased him and of the Nonsense Club's plain delight in stirring. They were bound, sooner or later, to provoke a reaction. Sure enough, the *London Chronicle* of 14–16 May reprinted Reynolds's *Idler* essays.

The *St James's Chronicle* then capped this with a spoof letter from an 'Admirer, but, thank God, no Encourager of the Polite arts', a young ex-Etonian brought up by a scholarly uncle in the country. Arriving in London recently, he explains, the first man he met was 'Lord Brillus', an old schoolfriend and a member of the 'Society for the Encouragement of the Arts'. Brillus invites him to come and 'despise the wretched English Dawbs at Spring Garden'. But why, asks the Admirer, does he despise the artists, if he is supposed to be 'encouraging' them?

'"Lord!" says he, "why you know nothing. There is a wretched fellow, one Hogarth, has . . ." "Hold," said I. "I know that Hogarth is the best painter of Life and manners in the Universe, and I know that I gave £12 or £14 for his prints and would not take five hundred for them." "Lord!" said he again. "Hogarth! an absolute Bartholomew Droll, who paints Country Elections and pretends to laugh at the Connoisseurs, for prizing."'

Inside the exhibition, however, the painting itself wins the day: face to face with *Sigismunda*, the Admirer cries aloud to see Dryden's thoughts so powerfully expressed: '"Who did it my Lord?". "Hogarth," said he, "and he is quite out of his Walk."' The letter praised the other artists too and ended by neatly identifying Brillus with the monkey in Hogarth's tailpiece. But its championing of *Sigismunda*, however brave, had come too late.

The exhibition of the Society of Artists at Spring Gardens had opened as planned in the second week of May. In some ways, from the point of view of the artists, it was almost too great a success. The shilling catalogue, with its preface by Johnson and prints by Hogarth, sold so well that the plates were worn down and the prints had to be re-engraved.[40] A spat of jealousy had meant Hogarth's name was left out of the press advertisements, but his reputation brought in crowds of admirers, many from a class that was hardly Polite. The room became 'a scene of tumult and disorder', recalled John Gwynn,

'crowded with menial servants and their acquaintance; this prostitution of the fine arts undoubtedly became extremely disagreeable to the Professors themselves, who heard alike, with indignation, their works censured and approved by kitchen maids and stable boys'.[41]

Hogarth, however, listened desperately to the approval or censure of all and sundry, particularly with regard to *Sigismunda*. After Grosvenor's reaction, he had made numerous small changes, altering the background, and overpainting the face. Thomas Morell was horrified:

'it was so altered, upon the Criticism of one Connoisseur or another; and especially when, relying no longer upon strength of genius, he had recourse to the *feigned* tears of *fictitious* woe of a female friend, that, when it appeared at the exhibition in 1761, I scarce knew it myself'.

Morell had never seen 'a finer resemblance of flesh and blood, while the canvas was warm, I mean wet'.[42]

Yet Hogarth was still avidly, self-punishingly, eager for comments. A later anecdote told that he posted a man to '*write down*' all the objections to his painting. There were, apparently, at least a hundred but only one that he took seriously,

'and that was made by a madman! and perceiving the objection was well founded, he altered it. The madman, after looking steadfastly at the picture, suddenly turned away saying *D—n it, I hate those white roses*. Hogarth *then*, and not till *then* observed that the foldings of Sigismunda's shift-sleeves were too regular, and had more the appearance of roses than of linen.'[43]

Apocryphal or not, this story suggests the strain, even the mania, the exhibition induced. He had hoped for triumph and found humiliation. Two years later, at another time of crisis, Thomas Birch wrote that Hogarth's

'vanity with his success always made him impatient of any mortification, so that Lord Grosvenor's refusal to take his *Sigismonda*, and the contempt shown it at the exhibition, were a shock that near upset him'.[44]

By 20 May, only ten days after the opening, Hogarth had withdrawn *Sigismunda*.[45] He replaced it with *Chairing the Members*, a picture that no one could say was 'quite out of his Walk'.

640

31

Signs and Symbols

Whilst, in contempt of all our pains,
The tyrant SUPERSTITION reigns
Imperious in the heart of Man,
And warps his thoughts from Nature's plan;
Whilst fond CREDULITY, who ne'er
The weight of wholesome doubts could bear,
To Reason and Herself unjust,
Takes all things blindly up on Trust;
Whilst CURIOSITY, whose rage
No Mercy shews to sex or Age,
Must be indulg'd at the expence
Of Judgment, Truth *and* Common Sense;
Impostures cannot but prevail,
And when old Miracles *grow stale,*
JUGGLERS will still the art pursue,
And entertain the World with New.

CHARLES CHURCHILL, *The Ghost* (1762)

GEORGE III WAS THE FIRST Hanoverian king to be born in Britain; when he met the Privy Council on his accession he spoke proudly of 'this my native country'.[1] It seemed a glorious time for a young man of twenty-two to ascend the throne. The years of war had revived Britain's industries and won it an empire: what had once been 'a private little island, living upon its means', was now 'the capital of the world'.[2] The mood was euphoric; tributes to the King's youth and talents filled the press, with promises of a golden age.

As spring gave way to summer, and the art exhibitions in the Strand and Spring Gardens were dismantled (and Hogarth hung *Sigismunda* in his studio once again), gossip swung back to the Court and the King. George III, though determined, was immature – he could not read until he was eleven and at twenty his writing looked like a child's.[3] He was also passionately dependent on those close to him, notably his mother's friend, and rumoured

641

lover, the Earl of Bute. Together, George felt he and Bute could cleanse the nation of its unscrupulous politicians: even Pitt was an enemy because he had not stayed with the Prince's Leicester House opposition. But although Bute was handsome, stylish and ambitious he was also 'politically inexperienced, diplomatically maladroit, unpopular and a disturbing influence'.[4] Almost immediately, he encouraged George to refuse the traditional Hanoverian compact with the Whigs; after their long exile, Tory country gentlemen, clergymen and dons were embraced at Court and the Old Corps of Whigs was thrown into panic.

The King's priority, however, was finding a wife. Bute had earlier stamped on George's infatuation with the ravishing fifteen-year-old Sarah Lennox, daughter of the Duke of Richmond, and sister-in-law of Henry Fox. Now he chose more diplomatically, opting for Princess Charlotte of Mecklenburg-Strelitz, 'not tall, nor a beauty; pale and very thin, but looks sensible and is genteel'.[5] The marriage, announced in early July, took everyone by surprise: 'It has been carried on with as much secrecy as if it had been really a love affair.'[6] Within days Garrick was hunting for printed forms for the wedding, so that he could put on a stage presentation of the ceremonies; at Covent Garden, sparing no expense, Rich was doing the same.[7]

As soon as it was known that the marriage would take place on 8 September at St James's Palace, and the Coronation a fortnight later, the capital sprang into action. Carpenters and painters, carvers and gilders moved in *en masse* and the city was completely taken over: streets were blocked by scaffolds for spectators; arguments went on about where fire engines should be posted; landlords whose houses overlooked the route advertised their rooms. There was money to be made from a Coronation: one street platform, let for £400 when George II was crowned, now cost £2,400; front seats in the Abbey galleries were ten guineas each; a small house opposite was rented for the day at £500, and a single room for 150 guineas.[8]

By mid-August 1761, the work in the Chapel Royal was finished and attention turned to Westminster Hall. This was emptied completely for a new floor to be laid and covered in matting. Fifty-two huge chandeliers were hung and three tiers of galleries were built on each side, the top one virtually perched under the roof and the lowest one 'accommodated with a curious Sluice of an admirable Contrivance for the Reception of Urinary Discharges'.[9] A regular 'correspondent' in the *St James's Chronicle* (the 'Cobbler from Cripplegate') suggested the Coronation was yet another fashionable exhibition, and could perhaps have its own catalogue – with a tailpiece by Hogarth.[10] Hogarth's task as Serjeant-Painter seemed even more like that of

642

the puppet-show scene-painter in his mock-patent. The painting required was on a huge scale. Facing the throne in Westminster Hall, there would be a grand triumphal arch with Virtues and Classical gods, royal portraits, lions and unicorns and the British arms: 'The whole interspersed with Hiero-glyphical Ornaments and Pillars of the Corinthian Order'.[11] One story has Hogarth and Hayman, all academy differences forgotten, mercilessly teasing a sweating William Oram, who was painting the enormous arch.[12]

Eventually the day came. 'All the vines of Bourdeaux, and all the fumes of Irish brains,' wrote Walpole to Montagu in Dublin,

'cannot make a town so drunk as a royal wedding and coronation. Oh! the buzz, the prattle, the crowds, the noise, the hurry! . . . The multitudes, balconies, guards and procession made Palace Yard the liveliest spectacle in the world.'[13]

Pyne, putting several good stories together, said that at nine o'clock the night before, Hogarth and Jane, and Allan Ramsay and Hayman, all arrived at his uncle's house in the city to join a party going to Palace Yard; the evening ended in the back parlour, where a long table was spread with 'ham and chicken and pigeon pies'.[14] The women were flustered about their dress for the next day and the business of leaving took for ever:

'"Od's bobs!" said my father, "we shall never set off: what are all these band-boxes for Ned?" "For the ladies, Sir." . . . "Aye", said Hogarth, the "baggage-wagons are always the last on a march." My aunt unluckily overheard this and boxed Master H's ears with her fan, and away went all in high spirits.'[15]

To avoid the blocked streets, they crossed London Bridge and drove along the south bank, along the rough track through St George's Fields, where they stopped to help a German indigo-trader, whose coach had overturned. While the passengers were being extracted, Hogarth – 'knowing the landlord' – dashed across to the nearby pub, the Dog and Duck to get a lantern.[16] After a reviving session there, they piled back into their coaches, crossed back over 'the new Westminster Bridge' and arrived at their positions not at two o'clock, as planned, but at five.

This account requires more than a few pinches of salt, but Hogarth almost certainly did see the Coronation in his capacity of Serjeant-Painter. The arrangements, however, were chaotic. Dignitaries staying in Palace Yard were kept awake the whole night before the wedding by the hammering of scaffolds, shouting of people, marching of guards and jangling of bells. Neither the Heralds nor the Earl Marshal – supposed to be in charge – were familiar with

643

the procedure. The morning procession did not leave till noon and the return procession was so late that the spectators in the streets could hardly see anything, 'the whole was confusion, irregularity and disorder'.[17] The gentry and leading citizens had sat patiently in Westminster Hall for six hours. Lord Talbot took such care to manoeuvre his horse down Westminster Hall without showing its rump to the King that it entered backwards; when he went out everyone clapped, 'a terrible indecorum, but suitable to such Bartholomew Fair doings'.[18] The Duke of Cumberland allegedly laughed until he shook.

Hogarth did not intend, at least too obviously, to laugh at the King. This year he had made a good profit from his office (£982) and in December his patent was renewed; royal patronage and Bute's good will were essential.[19] But despite his dependence on the Court, he remained cynical about majesty and pomp and over the next two years he increasingly linked the use of symbols and signs to a critique of pomposity, power and manipulation. His work on the royal arms and emblems, the allegorical figures and devices, may have reminded him both of the potency of that old emblematical style and of his resentment at the 'Somebodies' – like William Kent, who had so firmly shut him out of the Chapel Royal long ago. Found among his papers, perhaps intended for the *Apology*, was a dedication, or rather a non-dedication:

> The no Dedication
> Not Dedicated to any Prince in Christendom
> for <fear> it might be thought an Idle piece of
> Arrogance
> Not Dedicated to any man of quality for
> <fear> it might be thought too assuming
> Not Dedicated to any learned body of
> Men, as either of <the> universitys, or the Royal Society
> <for fear> it might be thought an
> uncommon piece of Vanity.
> Not dedicated to any <one> particular Friend
> for fear of offending another.
> Therefore Dedicated to nobody
> But if for once we may suppose
> nobody to be every body, as Every body
> is often said to be nobody, then is this work
> Dedicated to every body
> by their most humble
> and devoted –[20]

644

Hogarth's first hit at the new Somebodies was a print published in November 1760, whose engraved title was '*The five orders of* PERRIWIGS *as they were worn at the late* CORONATION, *measured* Architectonically'. This brilliant return to the hieroglyphic mode managed simultaneously to satirize the Coronation yet flatter the Queen, sneer at the dignitaries, mock the elaborate hairstyles of the beaux and debunk the pretensions of the Society of Arts.

In a manner reminiscent of the old joke of the *Peregrination*, *The Five Orders of Periwigs* was presented as a mock advertisement for an expensive antiquarian work, the result of decades of research:

'*In about* Seventeen Years *will be compleated, in Six Volumes, folio, price* Fifteen Guineas, *the exact measurements of the* PERRIWIGS *of the* ancients; *taken from the Statues, Bustos & Baso Relievos, of* Athens, Palmira, Balbec, and Rome, *by* MODESTO Perriwigmeter *from* Lagado. N.B. *None will be Sold but to* Subscribers.'

The principal targets of this Swiftian announcement were James 'Athenian' Stuart and Nicholas Revett, who had just announced the imminent publication of their book, *The Antiquities of Athens Measured*. (This took even longer than Hogarth suggested: it was begun in 1748, subscribers received the first volume in 1762 and had to wait until 1789 for the second.)[21] Instead of the five orders designated by the Palladians, Hogarth invented a new social hierarchy, as worn 'at the Coronation': Episcopal, Old Peerian, or Aldermanic, Lexiconic (for the lawyers), Composite or Half Natural, Qeerintian or Queue de Renard (for the Beaux). Across the bottom is an unofficial sixth order for the women, all wearing coronets except the Queen, who is shown at the end of the line, looking simple and pure. The key continues the conceit, linking the parts of the 'capital' of a column to those of the wig perched on the 'capita' of a human, from crest to final curl: Architrave, Corma, Triglyph, Caul, Foretop, Necklock. And the exaggerated wigs are also, of course, inescapably bawdy.

There were plenty of in-jokes here, addressed to different audiences and friends. The catalogue for the Society of Artists exhibition, for example, had listed several architectural drawings, including 'The Corinthian Order' and 'The Composite Order' by Kirby.[22] The satire of individuals also played its part. The 'Episcopal' line showed the Bishops of Chichester and St David's and William Warburton, now Bishop of Gloucester – whose intellectual part 'A' is noticeably small, a rather unkind dig as he had supported the *Analysis*. Among the peers was Hogarth's butt in *Chairing the Members*, Bubb Dodington, who had become Lord Melcombe in April. And the barber-block

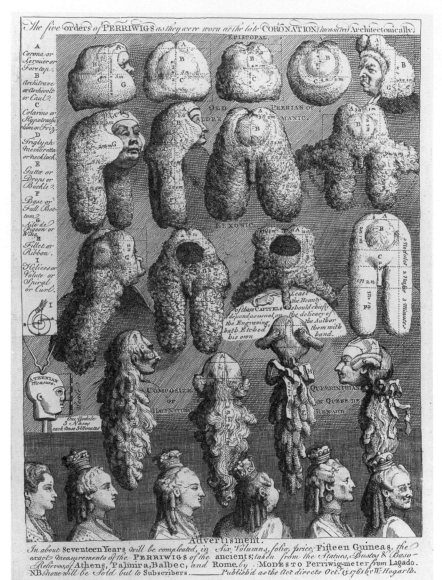

185 *The Five Orders of Periwigs* (1762)

profile of James Stuart, marked 'Athenian measure', was so lifelike, it was said, that Hogarth had to cut the nose off. In fact Stuart enjoyed the fame and kept the print on his fire screen to show off to guests.[23]

This was the Hogarth that Horace Walpole liked. He sent *Periwigs* to Montagu, telling the story of Stuart's nose and relishing its pungency: 'The enclosed print will divert you, especially the Baroness in the right-hand corner – so ugly and satisfied.'[24] *The Five Orders of Periwigs* showed that Hogarth had never lost his sharp, irreverent originality, however ill he felt, however introspective and moody. There was more amusement and enjoyment here than anger.

Hogarth's new vigour and iconoclasm coincided with his growing closeness to Thornton, Colman, Churchill and Lloyd, a group who had always been intrigued by cultural signs – of dress, language and taste. Noting the Coronation preparations, including the Queen's dresses in gold and silver, the *St James's Chronicle* reported that 'A very curious Wig is making for his Majesty, with a Tail, called by the Peruke-maker a Spanish Fly, being a Flow of Ringlets almost down to the Waist'.[25] In May 1762 a correspondent to the paper ironically reiterated Hogarth's point:

'a Wig is as much a Mark of Distinction as any other Point of Dress, or any other Circumstance in Life: It is not more ridiculous, in my opinion, for a Commoner to fix Coronets upon his Coach, than for a person to wear a Queue-Wigg, or Tye-Wig, that is not entitled to it from his Station'.[26]

And later Thornton mockingly bemoaned the breakdown of such distinctions under the name of 'an Anti-Perukist'.

Thornton and his friends had set aside respectable wigs and callings. Thornton had once trained in medicine and Colman had studied law, Churchill was a curate and Lloyd taught at Westminster. In 1760 their rejection of these professions looked right, but precarious. The *St James's Chronicle* was thriving and Thornton, at thirty-six, was at the hub of the newspaper world: when Boswell met him in 1763 he found 'a well-bred, agreeable man, lively and odd. He had £15,000 left him by his father, was bred to physic, but was fond of writing. So he employs himself in that way.'[27] The younger trio, now verging on thirty, were flaring across the London scene. Colman was firmly ensconced at Drury Lane. Churchill had capitalized on the *Rosciad* with the *Apology*, a blistering onslaught on his detractors, especially Smollett's *Critical Review*. Thought to have made £2000 by these two poems alone, the 'Bacchanalian priest' was hailed as the heir to Pope. But Walpole noted that while Churchill advertised his poems, he never actually began them until 'the bookseller, or his own want of money, forced him to thrust out the crude but glorious sallies of his uncorrected fancy'.[28]

Churchill's wit inspired fear. He had turned on Garrick in the *Apology*, accusing him of being an arrogant puppet-king – as with so many satirists, including Hogarth, his attacking impulse seemed to operate almost independently of his other judgements, attacking people he admired, simply because he *could*. An alarmed Garrick had sent a mollifying message via Lloyd and they were now firm friends (at least Churchill borrowed money from Garrick, with increasing desperation). Lloyd was also sending plays to Drury Lane and scurrying in Churchill's orbit. The threesome flaunted their power. They looked odd, and flaunted this too: Colman was tiny, with a boy-like figure, another ambitious 'little man'. Lloyd was a saturnine, hard-drinking Welshman:

> His meagre cheek, 'midst his nocturnal sport,
> With envy pale, and his lips black with port.[29]

Churchill was a giant, with a powerful, burly figure, built for a bear garden:

> In body, clumsy, heavy, big,
> With hat all pinch'd and rusty wig.[30]

Together they looked like a reprise in another generation of that older odd couple, tall Fielding and stubby Hogarth – perhaps a slightly bitter, as well as appealing, thought.

The group now included Wilkes, Churchill's constant companion, whom Hogarth later bitterly called 'formerly my friend, a flatterer'. And matching Wilkes's recklessness, there was a dangerous edge to the lives of Churchill and Lloyd, sliding into self-destructive dissipation. This aura of nihilistic risk may also have been attractive to Hogarth. The younger men were pleased to enrol him in their cause, admiring his wit, his vernacular bent, his exposure of shams. They put up with his opinionated views, and listened to his groans about *Sigismunda*; Lloyd's poem *Genius, Envy and Time* even envisaged a future when critics would own 'HOGARTH first of every clime,/For humour keen, or strong sublime'.[31] But they offered Hogarth more than flattery. Their scepticism was like the irresponsible craziness of the young Fielding, the friend whose portrait he was drawing for Arthur Murphy's edition with Garrick's 'help'. Half Hogarth's age, they evoked his own youthful energy and anger.

One of the targets of the Nonsense Club and of the other satirical writers associated with Drury Lane, was the upsurge of Methodism in the capital since George Whitefield had opened his Tabernacle in Tottenham Court Road in 1756: even Thomas Secker, Archbishop of Canterbury, had Methodist leanings. In July 1760, Foote had put the cross-eyed Whitefield into his farce

The Minor, as Mr Squintum converting a drunken bawd, Mrs Cole, a caricature of the renowned Mother Douglas. Whitefield was also a prime target of the Thornton and Churchill, and one of the longest running articles in their *Chronicle* was a discussion of 'Similes, metaphors, and familiar Allusions made use of by Dr Squintum'.[32]

During the winter, Hogarth joined this campaign, with a print called *Enthusiasm Delineated*, ironically dedicated to the Archbishop of Canterbury. The subject was clever, since it allowed him to attack two subjects not usually combined, 'low' religion and 'high' art. Although he had painted an altarpiece himself, by satirizing religious art Hogarth could strike at Catholicism as well as at Methodism. He could also ridicule the 'enthusiasm' of Reynolds for Michelangelo and the almost 'religious enthusiasm' with which, as the *St James's Chronicle* said, people bought Rembrandt drawings and Teniers paintings. On a proof sheet, in shaky, blotted writing, Hogarth wrote another mock advertisement:

'The intention of this print is to give a lineal representation of the strange effects of litteral and low conceptions of sacred beings as also of the Idolatrous Tendency of Pictures in churches and prints in religious books &c.'[33]

Yet there is something deeper still in this print: like so many of Hogarth's late works, it seems to have a personal as well as a social weight. The more you look at it, the more terrifying it becomes. We are made to feel as bewildered as the turbanned Muhammadan, puffing at his pipe as he peers through the window. At first it seems merely a reversal of the old latitudinarian *Sleeping Congregation* of the 1730s, this time showing a convulsed, crippled flock before a hysterical preacher, whose Nonconformist wig flies off in a sunburst, revealing a papist tonsure, and whose open robes expose Harlequin colours. But the details are insistent and grotesque. Puppets of God and the Devil dangle from the preacher's hands. More puppets hang like bodies at Tyburn around his pulpit: Adam and Eve, Peter and Paul, Moses and Aaron – the icons of Renaissance and Dutch art. Out of a vulval, bug-like brain, a thermometer soars from Madness and Despair to a point above Revelation, where 'Joyful' and 'PLEASED' only just outride 'ANGRY' and 'Wrathful'. Above it hangs a scale to measure the preacher's rant. It is suspended by a ring through a nose, and the gaping mouth foams with the accented words, 'Chroist, Blood blood Blood Blood!'

Any notion of love in the congregation, or in Whitefield's hymn, is cancelled out by the nobleman groping the girl, who stands parallel to 'Lust-Hot' on the scale. As he arouses her, the Christ-doll she holds folds and bends like paper.

649

186 *Enthusiasm Delineated* (*c.* 1761)

A branded thief sniffles into a bottle of tears held by a tiny Christ figure. A howling dog has 'Whitefield' on his collar. A converted Jew cracks a flea between his nails as he leans on the Bible, open at an illustration of Abraham and Isaac, the near-sacrifice of a son. On the floor, convulsed with ecstasy like a baroque saint, lies a woman who resembles Mother Douglas of *The March to Finchley*, cradling her Christ like a dead child.

650

This was all very topical: in June 1761, when Mother Douglas died, the papers were full of the wealth and pictures the pious bawd left. But as the women of Hogarth's congregation munch, gnaw, chew and gulp at the limbs and body of the rigid images of Christ, the irruption of the surreal moves the satire into a realm of tormented unreason. Even the poor box is a steel-sprung mousetrap. And over the whole scene, with its air of a feverish Black Mass, swings a lamp with the face of despair, like an unholy censer, mapped with the regions of Hell. Its mouth is marked 'Eternal Damnation Gulf'.

Earlier that year, Leicester Fields had its own drama of despair and damnation. A Swiss enamellist, Theodore Gardelle, well known to the crowd at Old Slaughter's, lodged on the square's southern side with a Mrs King, 'a showy woman of bad reputation'.[34] In February 1761, after a row – allegedly because she would not pay him for a picture – he struck her and she fell, hitting her head. In panic, as she raged and spat blood, Gardelle hit her again, and found that he had killed her. Desperate, he left the body there for days, dismissing the maid to avoid discovery, and finally decided to carry the corpse up to the garret, cutting it up and burning 'the larger limbs'. Eventually a woman who came in to clean discovered blood-stained linen, and John Fielding issued a warrant for Gardelle's arrest.

The crime was seen as an instance of artist's mania, and the ghoulish populace loved it. William Hickey, then a boy, remembered that one of the severest floggings he ever had was for staring at this house:

'For many weeks after the discovery of the murder, a large mob assembled in front of the house, every person in turn putting their noses to the keyhole of the front door when each individual went away perfectly satisfied that they smelt the burning of the flesh and bones.'[35]

As in the case of Sarah Malcolm, Gardelle was condemned to hang near the scene of his crime, at the junction of Panton Street and the Haymarket. When the cart passed his old house, he sighed and wrung his hands. Young John Richards was sketching this moment from Hogarth's window, he said, when Hogarth came in, snatched the paper and a pen from the ink-stand, corrected it with a few swift strokes and returned it.[36]

The murderous madness of *Enthusiasm Delineated* seemed symptomatic. By early 1762, all the work was done on the plate, apart from the caption, but it was never published. John Hoadly allegedly dissuaded Hogarth, convincing him it would be seen as an attack on all religion, not just on Methodism. Nothing was wasted, however. Part of the attack on 'Dr Squintum' and his followers, particularly in the *Chronicle*, had been an assault on superstition in

651

all its forms. And now London was offered a supreme example of superstition – the Cock Lane Ghost.

The story began in 1759, when a certain William Kent (a name with resonance for Hogarth) and Fanny Lynes, the sister of Kent's dead wife, took lodgings with Richard Parsons, the clerk of St Sepulchre's in Newgate Street. The house was in Cock Lane, just down the road from where Hogarth was born. Kent later sued Parsons for the loan of £12 and he and Fanny moved to Clerkenwell, where she died of smallpox. In January 1762, mysterious knockings and scratchings were heard in the Parsons' house, especially in the room of the eldest daughter, aged eleven. By a system of knocking the Vicar of St Sepulchre's questioned the spirit whose 'responses', 'interpreted' by a friend, Mary Fraser, identified it as the ghost of Fanny Lynes, who was claiming Kent had poisoned her.

As with Mary Tofts years earlier, polite society rushed to see. Every night Cock Lane was wedged with crested carriages and up to fifty people – dukes and duchesses among them – crammed into the girl's room, with no light but a tallow candle, almost suffocating her with the stench. At this point, the Vicar of Clerkenwell, encouraged by the Lord Mayor, assembled a small investigating committee, which included Samuel Johnson. After a vain night-time foray to the vault of St John's, Clerkenwell, where Fanny was buried, Johnson soberly reported their conclusion, 'that the child has some art of making and counterfeiting a particular noise, and that there is no agency of any higher cause'.[37] Three weeks later, she was seen to hide a piece of wood, with which she knocked at night. Once the hoax was exposed, Kent brought a case to clear the libel.[38]

In February, when the knockings were at their height, the Cock Lane Ghost seemed everywhere. Oliver Goldsmith published a pamphlet, *The Mystery Revealed*, and a month later Churchill published the first two books of *The Ghost*, in which politics and religion, trade and war, were all interwoven with the ludicrous happenings in Cock Lane. Covent Garden revived Addison's *The Drummer, or the Haunted House*, and Drury Lane staged a new farce by Garrick, *The Farmer's Return*, in which a yokel described the London craze. Hogarth designed the frontispiece to this play, and Garrick dedicated it to him.

Hogarth also adapted the unpublished *Enthusiasm Delineated* to make his own comment on the affair. Even better, he could still make his original point, since the Parsons were Methodists, and Whitefield and Wesley supported their cause. All Hogarth had to do was to change the religious images into occult ones. This was not difficult: the eucharistic images of Christ became Fanny of Cock Lane; the convulsed Mother Douglas became Mary Tofts with her

187 *Credulity, Superstition and Fanaticism* (1762)

rabbits; God with his triangle became a witch on her broomstick; the hanging puppets were transformed into famous ghosts, such as Julius Caesar, Sir George Villiers and Daniel Defoe's Mrs Veal. An image of Cock Lane now stood atop the thermometer of madness, balanced on 'Wesley's sermons' and 'Glanvil on Witches'. When he published his print in April 1762, and called it *Credulity, Superstition and Fanaticism*, the terror of the underlying vision of

653

enthusiasm – which no one except a few friends would have seen – had merely been shifted into a topical form. Horror seeped through the satire. This was the 'damned melancholy picture' that gave a sick Keats 'a psalm-singing nightmare'. When he recovered he wrote, 'I know I am better, for I can bear the Picture.'[39]

The print's oddity increased its power, although a sour Bishop Warburton (he of the large periwig and small brain) thought obscurity its only virtue:

'It is a horrid composition of lewd obscenity & blasphemous prophaneness for which I detest the artist and have lost all esteem for the man. The best is, that the worst parts of it have a good chance of not being understood by the people.'[40]

Horace Walpole, however, who had joined the post-opera rush to Cock Lane but disdained fraud and detested Methodism, thought this one of Hogarth's best works. It had 'a mixture of humorous and sublime satire', he wrote later, 'that not only surpassed all his other performances, but which would alone immortalise his unequalled talents'.[41]

The members of the Nonsense Club always satirized exploitation of the gullible, but they themselves loved hoaxes, and practical jokes. Their work also had a demotic, if not exactly egalitarian strain, which was part of the reason they liked Hogarth. Thornton, in particular, was a skilled decoder of 'high' and 'low' culture; it was he who picked up and ran with Hogarth's imagery of wigs. In his pamphlet *City Latin*, ridiculing the pompous inscriptions on the foundation stone of Blackfriar's Bridge, he also showed himself alert to the nuances of common English names, which at once labelled and stigmatized their owners – '*Mangey, Rag, Belcher, Gorge, Grub, Trollope, Nanney, Hussey, ,&c, &c*'. It was affectation to neglect the vigour of the vernacular, in comparison to the 'dignity' of Latin: '*Pitt! Pitt!* a low English Word! *Sink, Ditch, Bog, Quagmire*, would sound equally noble. But if, instead of this, it had been written *Fossa*, how grandly that would have sounded!'[42]

Thornton was similarly interested in popular visual language, and his next hoax – an exhibition of street signs – involved Hogarth directly. Towards the end of the 1761 art exhibitions the *St James's Chronicle* promised that 'An Account of the Exhibition designed by the Brokers and Sign-Post Painters of Knaves-acre, Harp-alley &c, shall be in a further Paper.'[43] The next issue announced that, alas, the projected exhibition was postponed until a big enough room could be found, as the collection of signs would be so large. In

654

the meantime, the artists '(Natives of Great Britain)', were kindly requested to send lists of potential submissions: 'NB No Foreigners, and *Dutchmen* in particular, will be admitted.'[44]

Many of the signs listed as already received were indisputably Hogarthian. 'The Hen and Chickens' and 'Adam and Eve' were both from *The March to Finchley*, one of Thornton's favourite prints. So was the sign 'designed for the Duke of Cumberland, but Converted into the King of Prussia, with very little Alteration' – hinting at the betrayal of English art by its proper patrons, and also, perhaps, that Butcher Cumberland was as much of a military despot as Frederick the Great. The *Chronicle*'s next issue included a list from 'Timothy Coarse-brush', including 'A Hand and Jaw, after the manner of Hogarth' and 'a crooked Billet, formed exactly in the *Line of Beauty*'. The joke, like much double-edged writing in this paper, could of course also be read as affectionately *against* Hogarth. He had, after all, incorporated signs in his work from the beginning and was known to admire them, while his emblematic details often operated like 'signs' in themselves. But there was also a serious point in Thornton's irony. Where was true 'English' art to be found, in comparison with pricey foreign imports and fakes? More to the point, as Thornton had said as early as 1752, and Hogarth had often implied, foreign competition left sign-painting as almost the only work for a native artist.

Promises of the sign-painters' exhibition, endlessly 'postponed', trickled on into June 1761, and subsided when the art exhibitions were forgotten. But the burlesque was too good to drop. When the societies began to plan their next shows, the hoax sprang to life again.

In the intervening year, Hogarth became gradually detached from the Society of Artists, more ready to join Thornton's parodic venture. After the humilia-tion over *Sigismunda*, he retired to Chiswick to escape the heat of June and July. He still worried about his picture and its reception, and brooded openly to friends near by, but he took things more easily and his strength and determination slowly returned. Then came the work for the Coronation, and the winter months when he worked on his prints.

His friends still feared lest he suffer further rebuffs from the critics and the virtuosi: in the following summer, hearing that Hogarth planned to sell his Election pictures for 200 guineas, to be raised by a raffle with tickets at two guineas each, Garrick stepped in to protect him. He had called at Leicester Fields and subscribed, he told Benjamin West,

'but on leaving his House, reflected on what he had done as unworthy to so great an artist, went back, gave him a draft for 200 guineas & took away the pictures, thus relieving Hogarth from further trouble abt. them'.[45]

It was in this year, too, that Hogarth designed Garrick's 'Shakespeare' chair.

As far as the art exhibitions were concerned, for a time Hogarth seemed to want to battle on within the Society of Artists.[46] On 15 December 1761 he was elected to a new, enlarged committee. At this point Hayman resigned as Chairman, and George Lambert was elected; the vote was split and there were clearly dissensions. It transpired that private resolutions had proposed that the committee should have total control over choice of pictures and the election of a president and secretary, and that their doings be 'kept a profound secret from the society, except when it was indispensably necessary to act otherwise'.[47]

This empire-building and top-down government signalled an attack by the pro-academy group, whose ambitions to direct public taste were 'higher' than those of the mass of members. In their view an academy 'could not be a professional association which embraced all practitioners; it had to be a smaller élite, singled out for their special skills, knowledge and taste'.[48] Such an approach, filtering through the Society, was sharply at odds with Hogarth's passionately held views. After this December the minutes mention him no more. When the next catalogue was planned, the frontispiece was by Hayman, and when the show finally opened in April, it contained no paintings by Hogarth. Once more he was on the outside looking in, like the virtuous infidel in *Enthusiasm Delineated*, or like Nobody snarling at Somebody.

Not surprisingly, Hogarth joined forces with the self-appointed outsiders. As the exhibition of the Society of Arts approached in March 1762 the *St James's Chronicle* again began to promote a Sign Painters' Exhibition, this time for real. It was very much Thornton's joke, but Hogarth was associated with it from the start in the public mind, and undoubtedly had a part in the planning and the painting of the signs.

The *Chronicle*'s first advertisement appeared on 15 March (the week that Hogarth signed *Credulity*), in an issue that also advertised Churchill's *The Ghost*, Garrick's *The Farmer's Return*, and Lloyd's *Poems on Several Occasions*. The paper simply announced that the 'GRAND EXHIBITION' of the 'Society of SIGN-PAINTERS' would take place next month, and invited suggestions for exhibits.[49] A week later the *Chronicle*'s regular column of 'INTELLIGENCE EXTRAORDINARY' contained three straight-faced notices. The first, headed '*Strand*', announced the Annual Exhibition of the

656

Society of Arts, ending with the pious hope that the arts would no longer be seen as 'Exoticks' (as in Hogarth's tailpiece) but would flourish in native soil. The second, headed *'Grand Exhibition'* announced 'the most magnificent collection' of the sign-painters, where the Virtuosi would have the chance to distinguish the *'Stile'* and *'Hand'* of individual masters. 'A remarkable *cognoscente'*, it added,

'has already piqued himself on discovering the famous Painter of the *Rising Sun* (a modern Claude Lorraine) in an elegant Night-piece of *the Man in the Moon*. He is also convinced, that no other than the famous Artist who drew the *Red Lion at Brentford*, can be equal to the bold Figures in the *London 'Prentice* . . .'[50]

The third notice, which set the others in perspective, praised the prologues at the Drury Lane Theatre.

Letters and puffs grew apace. Thornton denied any money-making scam, or any suggestion that the sign exhibition was meant to ridicule the Society of Arts. It was merely entertainment for those

'who can enjoy the Humour of a Hogarth, without thinking they do a Violence to their Taste for the Works of Raphael; and can laugh at Garrick's Abel Drugger, without losing a relish for his Lear or Hamlet'.[51]

The show was then put off for a week until 22 April, by which time the Town was thoroughly prepared to be entertained.

The *St James's Chronicle* writers enjoyed the episode. When the show opened a 'Plebian' (probably Thornton) wrote that although it might seem 'rather a Catchpenny' it offered an innocent laugh while exposing fraudulent auctioneers and fools who valued no picture that 'has not been *funkt*, as the Boys call it at Westminster, with Smoke and Time'.[52] The next issue quoted the *London Register*, whose approving report, without identifying them openly, praised Hogarth for 'enriching pictures with Humour, Character, Pleasantry, and Satire' and Thornton for his 'whimsical drollery'. The exhibition, it said, was wholly free from malice.[53] As the show made news it provoked inevitable satires, including *The Combat*, with Hogarth as Don Quixote tilting at the artists, and *A Brush for the Sign-Painters* where he paints *Sigismunda*, stung by Envy's snakes. He is sitting on a commode (his Idea Box) using the *Chronicle* for paper, and round him are more 'retailers of Stale Wit': tiny Colman, huge Churchill, solemn Lloyd, and Thornton as an ass.[54]

Outrage always creates good publicity, and the *Chronicle* published its own letter, calling the exhibition 'a most impudent and scandalous Abuse and

Bubble: an Insult to Understanding, and a most pickpocket imposture'.[55] The only fun to be had, it declared, came from standing in the street and seeing how ashamed people looked when they came out. In fact, people seemed far from ashamed. They came in droves to Thornton's rooms at the top of Bow Street, almost opposite Covent Garden Playhouse, and bought their 1s ticket, plus catalogue. Some neighbouring girls were cross not to be let in free, and other visitors complained that the ticket was torn from the catalogue on entry, meaning they had to pay to come a second time.[56] The exhibition, which was open from ten to four daily, 'continues very much crowded', the paper said, 'and the *Exhibition* of Gentlemen's coaches at the Door, shows that Newmarket has not carried away all the People of Fashion'.[57] Impudently, Thornton extended the run almost to the end of May, so that it overlapped with the exhibition of the Society of Artists, as well as the Society of Arts.

In April the *Chronicle* printed the catalogue, and later reprinted sections, with annotations. A guide was certainly needed. Turning in from Bow Street, you walked through the passageway and across the paved courtyard into a large apartment. All were crammed with signs: thirteen in the passage room, eight in the passage and seventy-six in the main room, plus twenty-five carved figures. The 'grand room' was hung with green baize on which the large wooden signs were fixed flat, like pictures in a gallery. By them swung 'Keys, Bells, Swords, Poles, Sugar-Loaves, Tobacco Rolls, Candles' – all the 'ornamental Furniture, carved in Wood', that normally dangled above shops in the street.

Many signs were real, borrowed from shops and inns and sign-painters' workshops. Several, however, were obviously painted specially: but the names of the artists, listed in the catalogue, just happened to be those of the *Chronicle*'s printers. The one prominent exception was one 'Hagarty', who contributed at least eleven signs. There was a local painter called Hagarty,[58] but one suspects that someone else borrowed his name: his signs included The Ghost of Cock Lane, Horn Fair, John the Baptist's Head on a charger (as in *Noon*), and the Hen and Chickens, Adam and Eve, and 'The Light Heart', as opposed, one presumes, to 'The Heavy Heart' of *Sigismunda*. And, almost inevitably, Hagarty/Hogarth had painted 'Nobody, alias Somebody' and 'Somebody, alias Nobody'.

As the *Chronicle* itself said, the juxtaposition of signs was as telling as the individual images: apothecaries next to coffins, for example. Like individual words in a sentence, the relationship created new meaning. Under the Saracen's Head and Queen Anne, hanging side by side, Hogarth supposedly wrote 'The Zarr' and 'Empres Quean' (the Tsar and the Queen of Hungary,

658

Maria Teresa, Empress 'whore'). On a board over their heads, he wrote 'The Present State of Europe': their tongues are hanging out and their eyes seek each other.[59]

The Signpainters' Exhibition was a carnival burlesque, replacing the polite exhibition with the shows of the street, the bewildering iconography that Addison had described, angels and bells, blue boars and red dragons, swans and half-moons, dogs' heads, geese and gridirons. But in 1762 this wealth was threatened by an Act to 'improve' Westminster streets, removing the signs.[60] The joke against the connoisseurs was also an elegy for popular art. Through his involvement with the Signpainters' Exhibition, Hogarth dipped back into his own work, and into the inventiveness of anonymous artists. It was a collective effort, with younger, rebellious men, and a culmination of his revived interest in emblematic statements after the Coronation. But one Hagarty sign was called *View of the Road to Paddington, with a presentation of the Deadly Never-green that bears Fruit all the year round*. That Never-green tree was the Tyburn gibbet – Nobody did not always win.

NIGHT

1732–1764

32

'That Devil Wilkes'

To laugh, and riot and scatter firebrands,
with him was liberty.

HORACE WALPOLE ON JOHN WILKES[1]

Lurking, most Ruffian-like behind a screen,
So plac'd all things to see, himself unseen,
VIRTUE, with due contempt saw HOGARTH stand,
The murd'rous pencil in his palsied hand.
What was the cause of Liberty to him,
Or what was Honour? let them sink or swim . . .

CHARLES CHURCHILL, *An Epistle to William Hogarth* (1763)

IT WAS GEORGE III who called Wilkes a devil, but it could just as easily have been William Hogarth. In 1762, Hogarth made a fatal miscalculation, and Wilkes and politics were at its heart.

The harmony promised at George III's accession never materialized. After 1760 a new kind of instability reigned. The first thing George and Bute aimed at was peace. The Seven Years War had been the triumph of Pitt and Newcastle and, whatever the victories, it must be stopped. The royal view, which seemed at times to run counter to British interests, did reflect a general alarm at the expense of the war which averaged over £13 million a year, double the cost of previous wars this century.[2] Taxes rose, even the smallest (there was rioting in London when beer increased from 3d to 3½d a quart) and contractors were accused of making huge fortunes. But as peace negotiations began, Pitt and his allies saw hard-won territories and trading routes being swept from their grasp. Behind Pitt's rhetoric of war, glory and gain, stood the financiers and merchants, the professional men, the common people: when the peace-seeking George drove through the City to dine with the new Lord Mayor a week after his marriage, his coach was hissed and Pitt's was cheered.

It was accepted, for example, that Britain would give back Caribbean gains in exchange for Canada and the return of Minorca, but Pitt wanted to ensure that the French were also kept out of the rich cod fisheries of the North Atlantic – marine gold. Arguing this, with increasing hopelessness, he then seized on rumours of a French alliance with Spain, proposing an immediate pre-emptive attack on the Spanish treasure fleets.[3] In October 1761, when the Cabinet would not accept this, Pitt resigned. A few days later, Temple resigned as Lord Privy Seal, and was succeeded by the Duke of Bedford. Although he was criticized for accepting a pension and a peerage, Pitt was proved right – when Spain did declare war in January 1762, Britain had lost the initiative. Disagreeing over the tactics of this new war, Newcastle too resigned in May 1762, and the Tory Bute, at last, became First Lord of the Treasury.

As Hogarth watched, he estimated where his interests lay, and how these fitted with his principles. His official post depended on Bute and the King. His influential contacts – the affable Kirby and the sinister Samuel Martin – were either in the royal pay or of their party. His many Scottish friends, Ramsay among them, were the target of constant abuse as Londoners reacted against the Scots 'invasion' in Bute's wake. Hogarth saw no need for the war to continue and lives to be lost, simply so that rich contractors could hang on to contracts and dominate trade. He deeply disliked the imperial, mercantile demands, the warmongering tone and the mob-rousing power of Pitt's words.

Increasingly, this outlook alienated him from at least one member of the Nonsense Club, Churchill, who was now almost inseparable from Wilkes: in June 1762 they were discussing ghosts, sex and politics and arranging to meet at Medmenham.[4] In 1757, Wilkes had become MP for Aylesham through what he called 'palmistry', spending over £7000 of Temple's money, and as far as his career was concerned, Pitt's resignation was disastrous. Although Wilkes defended Pitt powerfully in the Commons, his debts were mounting and he had to find other ways of making himself indispensable to his patrons. In June 1762, in answer to Smollett's *The Briton* and Murphy's *Auditor* which were both sponsored by Bute, he became editor of a new opposition paper, *The North Briton*, backed by Temple. Churchill was his deputy, soon bringing Robert Lloyd in tow.[5]

Swaggering, brilliant and audacious, *The North Briton* harried the government, praised Pitt and abused the Scots, both the nation as a whole and its notable individuals: David Hume, Adam Smith, Ramsay, Smollett, the Adam brothers. Like the numerous prints of 'the jackboot and petticoat' the paper also ran constant innuendoes about Bute's relationship with Princess Augusta.[6] Deliberately tempting fate, the fifth issue hinted at the parallel

664

between Bute and Mortimer, lover of Queen Isabella, who murdered her husband, Edward II, and dominated her son. When no prosecution followed, Wilkes felt he could get away with anything.

The North Briton made even its allies nervous. Pitt, whose favour Wilkes hoped to win, was unshakeably hostile to the paper. Lord Temple, who sponsored the paper and supplied intelligence, was alarmed by the open naming of targets: 'the sooner this scene of indiscriminate and excessive personality is closed, the better'.[7] Horace Walpole, although he loathed Bute, described it as 'virulent', having 'an acrimony, a spirit, and a licentiousness unheard of before even in this country'.[8] Rivals and critics were ruthlessly dealt with. Arthur Murphy, running another pro-government paper, *The Auditor*, was tricked into publishing a hoax letter; Samuel Johnson was pilloried for accepting a State pension after he had denigrated the word 'pension' in his dictionary. (Johnson was probably thinking of Wilkes when he defined 'patriotism' in his 1775 edition as the last refuge of a scoundrel.)

Wilkes, who so enjoyed fighting, was a dangerous person to annoy. Few would willingly enter the ring against him. Yet in the summer of 1762, Hogarth was working on a new print which placed Wilkes firmly in the opposite corner. In *The Times, Plate 1* the subterfuge of *The Cockpit*, or even of the demagogic clergyman in *Credulity*, had disappeared. It was Hogarth's only directly party-political statement in all his long years. And it was the only one totally at odds with the national mood. Among the topical prints that survive from this time, only four, including Hogarth's *The Times*, support Bute, while four hundred oppose him.[9]

In August Wilkes was in Winchester, guarding French prisoners as a Colonel of Dashwood's Buckinghamshire militia, when he heard that Hogarth was planning a print that would ridicule Pitt, Temple, Churchill and himself. Shocked, combining threats with flattery, he asked two friends to advise Hogarth

'that such a proceeding would not only be unfriendly in the highest degree, but extremely injudicious; for such a pencil ought to be universal and moral, to speak to all ages, and to all nations, not to be dipt in the dirt of the faction of a day, or an insignificant part of the country, when it might command the admiration of the whole.'[10]

Although this was self-interested, it was also wise advice, but Hogarth took no heed, replying that neither Wilkes nor Churchill were caricatured, only Temple and Pitt. But that was enough. Wilkes replied that he did not care about himself, 'but if his friends were attacked, he should then think he was wounded in the most sensible part, and would, as well as he was able, revenge their cause'. His ultimatum could not have been plainer: 'if he thought the North Briton would insert it' (which of course it would, since he was editor), he would 'make an appeal to the public' on the Saturday after the print appeared.

188 *The Times, Plate 1* (1762)

The Times, Plate 1, was dated 7 September 1762, the day after Bedford left for Paris to negotiate the peace treaty. The print is a scene of fire and chaos. In a city square, firemen rush to collect water while the tall buildings blaze behind them. The fire has just reached the house on the right, and is catching the globe over the door – a version of the familiar 'World's End' sign. But the firefighter directing his hose at the globe is being knocked down by jets of water sprayed through clyster pipes from the opposite side. In the foreground, a poor fiddler plays while the city burns, surrounded by the poor and the sick, and the mothers with their babes in arms.

This is a stagey scene, that old emblem-filled triangular space that Hogarth had used at the very start of his career, for the *South Sea Scheme* or the *Taste of the Town. Plus ça change*, it seems to say. But the references are all contemporary, a polemical version of current history.[11] In the clouds above floats a hopeful dove of peace. The street signs in the background, of the double eagle and fleur-de-lis show the burning houses to be Germany and France; out of the flames comes a wagon labelled 'Hermione', a Spanish ship captured by the British. Although Steevens (who thought Hogarth made the print to get a rise in his Serjeant-Painter's salary) assumed that the heroic figure on the fire engine marked UNION OFFICE was Bute, many immediately decided it 'can only mean his M—j', the King, with GR on his arm, trying to extinguish the blaze of the Seven Years War.[12] The fire of war is still being fanned by Pitt with his bellows, disguised as Henry VIII, weighed down by the 'millstone' of his £3000 pension. His stilts raise him above a fawning crowd of aldermen, merchants and mob with marrowbones and cleavers, 'worshipping the idol they had set up'.[13] And the fiddler with his pathetic crowd is Frederick of Prussia, his country ravaged by battle.

On the left of the print Hogarth suggests the damage Newcastle and Pitt have inflicted on Britain. The houses are collapsing and the 'Newcastle Inn' is crumbling and neglected, while on one sign George Townshend's militia dance to a 'Norfolk Jig', signed G.T. like Townshend's caricatures. The sign 'Alive from America' reminds people of the Cherokee chiefs who came to London in June after signing a peace treaty: they saw all the sights, went to Vauxhall twice, sat to Reynolds, met the King and returned to Carolina in late August. Such alliances meant increased wealth for merchants: pointing up at this sign is the West Indian merchant William Beckford, soon to be Lord Mayor. And seated comfortably on a huge bale, a Dutchman who has profited from his country's neutral trade puffs steadily on his pipe. But a new sign, the Patriot Arms, showing a bunch of clenched fists, is being levered up the ladder by a slaughterman with a candle in his hat and a knife stuck in his breeches. Near by, a little fox (or Fox), pokes his nose warily out of his secure kennel 'waiting the issue'.[14] What kind of patriotism is this?

Hogarth also showed his support for the pro-Bute, pro-Scottish camp by his inclusion of the 'loyal highlander' carrying the bucket (as opposed to the 'beggarly Scot' of *The Gate of Calais*) who is being rammed by a wheelbarrow containing *The North Briton* – fuel for the fire. And whatever Hogarth may

667

have said, the faceless figures in the 'Temple Coffee-House' plying their hoses to topple the King were taken by all to be Churchill and Wilkes.

The papers, even the pro-Pitt ones, at first treated the print as a fair contribution to a political fight, only unusual in that it was Hogarth's first direct statement. The *Royal Magazine* thought a single print from him was worth volumes of *North Britons*, *Britons* and *Auditors*:

> His mimick genius triumphs o'er the pen;
> One Hogarth's worth an hundred scribling men.

But the scribblers were not appeased. On 9 September Wilkes wrote to Churchill from his house in Great George Street, Westminster. 'Hogarth has begun the attack today – I shall attack him in hobbling prose, you will I hope in smooth-pac'd verse.'[15]

Churchill had not yet seen the print, and was in any case far more concerned about a painful dose of VD. But he soon saw it, and made his own threats. In a letter to Garrick, squeezing him for a loan because, he said, his ex-wife was making huge demands, he went on to mention the coming duel between Wilkes and Lord Talbot, who had been attacked in an August *North Briton*. The only good thing about his own clergyman's gown, he added, was 'the exemption from challenges'. Then he continued:

'I have seen Hogarth's print, sure it is much unequal to the former productions of that Master of Humour. I am happy to find that he hath at last declar'd himself, for there is no credit to be got by breaking flies upon a wheel. But Hogarth's are Subjects worthy of an Englishman's pen.
> 'Speedily will be published
> 'An Epistle to W. Hogarth by C. Churchill
> 'Pictoribus et Poetis.'[16]

Garrick, ever protective, tried to fend off disaster:

'I must intreat of you by ye Regard You Profess to Me, that You don't tilt at my Friend Hogarth before You See Me – You cannot sure be angry at his Print? there is surely very harmless, tho very Entertaining Stuff in it – He is a great & original Genius, I love him as a man & reverence him as an Artist – I would not for all ye Politicks & Politicians in ye Universe that You two should have the least Cause of Illwill to Each other. I am sure You will not publish against him if You think twice – I am very unhappy at ye thoughts of it, pray Make Me quiet as soon as possibly by writing to me at Hampton or Seeing Me here
> 'I am Dr Churchill Y^{rs} most Sincer[ely]
> 'DG —'[17]

668

The appeal was in vain. Churchill's poetic epistle was delayed by some months but it was he who took charge of seeing Wilkes's deadly *North Briton* No. 17, through the press.

The whole issue of Saturday, 25 September 1762, was devoted to William Hogarth, '*house*-painter' to the Court, 'the *supposed* author' of the *Analysis*. 'We all titter the instant he takes up a *pen*,' Wilkes wrote, 'but we tremble when we see the *pencil* in his hand. I will do him the justice to say, that he possesses the rare talent of gibbetting in colours.' Hogarth's forte was as a moralist and he should have stuck to it: whenever he strayed from '*his own peculiar walk*' he made himself ridiculous, as with *Sigismunda*. (It is fascinating how this 'out of his walk' phrase recurs, as if artists, writers, actors, are only safely praised for what they have already done, and Hogarth was perpetually straying, trespassing, pushing on to rough unbroken ground.) But now Wilkes's slurs became personal – if Sigismunda's bizarre expression could in any sense be called 'real', it could only come from what Hogarth had seen: 'his own wife in an agony of passion; but of what passion no connoisseur could guess'.

On Wilkes went, exposing Hogarth's 'insufferable vanity', his tiresome loquacity, his attraction to darkness and deformity, his 'rancour', 'malevolence', 'envy', 'relentless gall'. All objects were 'painted on his retina in a grotesque manner': he never caught a single idea of 'beauty, grace or elegance'. Hogarth's sun was setting, his light was dim, all he could do was copy others. This dig referred to a print called *John Bull's House sett in Flames*, showing Pitt and Churchill quenching a fire in St James's Palace started by Bute and Smallwit (Smollett), which had come out just before *The Times*, perhaps organized fast by opponents who knew Hogarth's design.[18]

Wilkes was grieved to see Hogarth descend to party politics:

'Whence can proceed so suprizing a change? Is it the frowardness of old age? Or is it that envy and impatience at resplendent merit in every way, at which he has always sickened?'

Hogarth had been seen to droop, he said, even at praise given to a friend:

'What wonder then that some of the most respectable characters of the age become the objects of his ridicule? It is sufficient that the rest of mankind applaud; from that moment he begins the attack, and you never can be well with him, till he hears a universal outcry against you, and till all your friends have given you up. There is besides a silly affectation of singularity, joined to a strong desire of leading the rest of the world: when that is once found

669

impracticable, the spleen engendered on such an occasion is discharged at a particular object, or ends in a general misanthropy. The public never had the least share of Hogarth's regard, or even good-will. *Gain* and *vanity* have steered his little bark through life.'

Although Wilkes turned things around, representing Hogarth's fight with the societies as a matter of mere spleen, for example, there was enough truth here to hurt, and hurt badly. And when he condemned Hogarth as 'the enemy most to be feared, I mean a treacherous friend', he brought to the surface the note of real shock and distress that had sounded through the whole outburst. It did not help that the jibe could be applied to Wilkes himself. Wilkes went on to take apart the details of the print, and to slate its political argument. Hogarth was used to that, but not to the ringing, painful, public denunciation.

Hogarth, oddly, had not been unduly apprehensive. A week after his print appeared, happening to be in Salisbury (probably visiting the Hoadlys near by), he called on Wilkes at his militia base 'with the good-natured intention of shaking hands'.[19] Hogarth's reason for publishing *The Times*, given in his notes, is astoundingly naïve: the loss of time through his illness, 'and the inattention to Prints occationd by the wars and abroad and contentions at home made it necessary to do some timed thing to stop a gap in my income'.[20] With his Serjeant-Painter's profits and portfolio sales, there was no such gap. His print, he said, 'tended to Peace and unanimity and so put the opposers of this humane purpose in a light which gave offence to the Fomentors of distruction in the minds of the people'. The attack on him was so infamous that even Wilkes 'when pushd by even his best frinds would not stand it, (wonderfull)' and was driven 'to so poor an excuse as to say he was drunck when he wrote'.

Wilkes may well have been drunk – he often was – but his performance was not impaired. Hogarth knew him well and must have known what he would do. He must have known too that his old critics would leap in with delight: at least thirteen slashing prints now attacked him.[21] Even before *The North Briton* appeared, Paul Sandby had produced *The Fire of Faction* (in which Hogarth, not Pitt, holds the bellows) and *The Butifyer: A Touch upon the Times*, with a 'Line of Booty', Hogarth's reward for kowtowing to the Court.[22] Other satires included *Tit for Tat*, showing Hogarth painting a shining boot and defacing Pitt's portrait: 'anything for money,' he says.[23] Later George Townshend published *The Boot and the Blockhead*, showing a doddering Hogarth next to a huge jackboot with a barber's block inside, topped by a Scotch bonnet. As Churchill holds a whip, Hogarth cries 'Dam it Charles, what have you done to me you'l make me run mad.'[24]

670

The most unnerving element of the attacks, reminding one of Horace Walpole's doubts of 1761, was this suggestion that Hogarth was unbalanced. Everyone could see that his paranoia, his tirades and his impulsiveness had become more intense. *The Times* seemed like a wilful, knowing courting of danger, like a man jumping into a lions' den with his eyes wide open. He was indeed on some precarious edge. Being, he said, in a kind of 'slow feaver', the controversy 'could not but hurt a feeling mind'.[25] By the end of October he had collapsed. Allan Ramsay, hearing he was dying, even suggested to Bute a successor for his post of Serjeant-Painter.[26] In late November, Wilkes wrote to Temple:

'Mr Hogarth is said to be dying, and of a broken heart. It grieves me much. he says that he believes I wrote that paper, but he forgives me, for he must own I am a thorough good-humoured fellow, only *Pitt-bitten*.'[27]

Wilkes enjoyed rows for their own sake, as games. Blithely, cruelly imperceptive, he thought Hogarth might too.

On 6 December 1762 the *North Briton* duo was due to go to the Shakespeare Club. 'Hogarth is too ill to attend,' said Wilkes.[28] But ten days later Hogarth was on his feet, spotted, of all places, at a public execution in Golden Square with Garrick: 'horrible scene' wrote the West Indies lawyer John Baker in his diary.[29] When Hogarth encountered horror, he stared it in the face.

In the course of the year, the peace terms had been settled by Bedford in Paris and the Preliminaries were debated in November. Pitt, pale and emaciated, was carried into the House by his servants: dressed in black velvet, his legs wrapped in flannel, he crawled on crutches to his seat, with the help of his friends and to the sneers of Fox's party. Allowed to sit from time to time, an unusual privilege, he spoke against the Peace for three and a half hours. When he left, he was cheered through the streets to his home. Fox, Pitt's enemy, was persuaded to come out of his kennel at the Pay Office to push the deal for peace through Parliament. Ruthlessly, he bought the votes needed, dishing out bribes and places on a scandalous scale and advising the King to make his position secure by stripping his opponents of offices and fees. Although Fox was left friendless, the vote was won – and when she heard, the Princess Dowager cried, 'Now my son *is* King of England.'[30]

The Peace of Paris was finally signed in February 1763. That month *The Auditor* and *The Briton* ceased publication, but *The North Briton* fought on. Its new victims included Hogarth's friend Samuel Martin, who was attacked

671

(justifiably) for distributing Fox's bribes and conniving to aid profiteers, and was called 'the most treacherous, base, selfish, mean, abject, low-lived and dirty fellow that ever *wriggled* himself into a secretaryship'.[31] Hogarth was still seen as a Bute supporter, and Churchill, deeply rankled, was still aiming to attack him. On 16 March he wrote to Wilkes,

'My Head is full of Hogarth, and as I like not his Company I believe I shall get him on Paper, not so much to please the Public, not so much for the sake of Justice, as for my own ease – a motive ever powerful with indolent minds. I have began already – and seem to like the Subject . . . I have laid in a great stock of gall, and I do not intend to spare it on this occasion – he shall be welcome to every drop of it, Tho' I Thought, which I can scare think, that it would never be schew'd.'

The only thing that might divert this 'gall' was 'an obliging Gonorrhea' which was at present ravaging him, 'playing the Devil with your humble'.[32]

Given the analogy with his illness, it sounds as though he had been harbouring a long-festering resentment, kept under wraps. But although Churchill's threat still hung over Hogarth's head, by now they were not really political enemies. Over the winter Hogarth had become as sick of Bute's faction as Pitt's. He made a print in the form of a ticket, never used, captioned *Jack in Office*; 'in office' meaning both in power, and using the pot. It showed a foxy-capped man piled with chamberpots, heading for the back door of St James's, or at George III's other palace at Kew. Following him is a closed sedan chair, presumably carrying Bute sneaking in to an assignation with the Princess Dowager: he may have 'resigned', but he still gets in round the back.

This spring Hogarth also worked on *The Times, Plate 2*, never issued to the public. His subtitle '*Plate 1*' implies that he had always intended a companion piece, presumably to show the benefits of peace, when it came. Here the fire-hoses are turned into a fountain, and the blazing square to a city garden in the Strand. But he was now sick of both camps, and his royal fountain is isolated on a kind of brick island. The city has been 'Butifyed': old buildings are being demolished and new ones built, the signs have vanished and the wide street ends in a vista of Robert Chambers's new pagoda at Kew.

This print feels curiously inert compared to *Plate 1*, with all the action packed away to the sides. While George III stands in a portrait pose (the plinth reads 'A Ramsay del'.) Bute, as head gardener, is diverting the flow of largesse on to a few favoured trees – mostly Scotsmen and ex-Jacobites. These are the new royal placemen, and Fox, the second gardener, is dumping the favoured trees of the previous regime into the ditch. The hustings on the left

189 *The Times, Plate 2* (1762)

is packed with Members of the Commons and Lords: half are asleep and the others are firing, trying to bring down the dove of peace. Those who peered hard could find Temple and Newcastle, Melcombe and Pitt, staggering on his gouty leg and looking over his shoulder while his long gun fires. On the other side of the street, a group of men are hoisting a large palette to the roof of the Society of Arts. And at street level, in front of a bunch of men crippled by the war, 'Fanny' of Cock Lane shares a pillory with Wilkes.

As if Hogarth had achieved it through the power of will and the black magic of caricature, Wilkes was indeed soon tried for defamation. By the spring, confidence in the ministry was so undermined that on 8 April Bute resigned. For two issues *The North Briton* ceased publishing. Then on 19 April the King made a speech in praise of the peace, and on 23 April *The North Briton* sprang back, with the famous 'Number 45'. Although Wilkes was careful to say that the King's speech was regarded as being that of his ministers, he doubted

673

whether the 'imposition is greater on the sovereign or the nation' and went on to regret that so honourable a prince could give 'the sanction of his sacred name to the most odious measures and the most unjustifiable public declarations from a throne ever renowned for truth, honour and unsullied virtue'.[33] The King, he implied, was either an idiot or a liar.

Three days later, a general warrant was issued for seditious libel against the 'authors, printers and publishers' of *The North Briton*. The printers were arrested and after newsworthy scenes, cheerful insults from Wilkes, and the ransacking of his house, Wilkes was committed to the Tower.[34] The town was in an uproar. Had he been wrongfully arrested? On 3 May he was brought to the Court of Common Pleas in Westminster Hall. Insouciant, he insisted, to deafening cheers from the gallery, that an Englishman's liberty should 'not be sported with impunity'.[35] His defence was threefold: that there was no evidence, that general warrants against unnamed people were illegal and that he was anyway covered by parliamentary privilege. Proceedings were adjourned for three days, and as he left the crowd roared 'Liberty! Liberty! Wilkes for ever!'

Wilkes's second appearance on 6 May was even more sensational. This time he appealed not only to the liberty of peers and gentlemen but

'to what touches me more sensibly, that of all the middling and inferior Class of People, who stand most in Need of Protection . . . A Question of such Importance as to determine at once whether ENGLISH LIBERTY be a Reality, or a Shadow'.[36]

The court must decide whether this vaunted liberty really had substance. From now on, his standing as radical hero was ensured. Chief Justice Pratt, as it happened, owed his place to Pitt and the judges found that the Pittite Wilkes *had* been entitled to the privilege of Parliament: he must therefore be discharged. As thousands escorted him home the slogans merged into the simple, enduring cry, 'Wilkes and Liberty!' Instead of ending as Tom Idle at Tyburn, Wilkes rode through the streets like Goodchild, in a coach of glory. He at once began a successful counter-attack, getting the printers to sue and bringing his own action for false arrest and illegal seizure of papers.[37]

When Wilkes made his great speech, Hogarth was watching him, 'skulking' (Wilkes's term) in a gallery. While the Chief Justice, wrote Wilkes,

'with the eloquence and courage of old Rome, was enforcing the great principles of *Magna Carta*, and the English constitution, while every breast from him caught the holy flame of liberty, the painter was wholly employed in *caricaturing* the *person* of the man'.

674

Back in Leicester Fields Hogarth went over his shaky crayon sketch with a pen, and then etched it – a savage likeness and a stunning slur. The jesting arrogance and sexy defiance of Wilkes were caught for posterity. His squint is just slightly exaggerated to turn his grin into the leer of a cynic; his wig is just slightly curled back into the horns of a devil. He twirls the cap of liberty on its pole, a laughing man who would exploit the very people he seduced.

190 *John Wilkes Esq.* (1763)

John Wilkes Esq., 'Drawn from the Life', was ready by 17 May. It was a private revenge, showing *The North Briton* No. 17, the attack on Hogarth, lying next to No. 45. But it was also a general denunciation of manipulative leaders who would undermine order. Hogarth's advertisements ran 'The Print is in direct Contrast to a print of SIMON Lord LOVAT, first published in 1746', linking Wilkes, the English patriot and abuser of all Scots, with a Scottish rebel – two cunning traitors in contrasting colours. And this print was just as successful as its forerunner. The first run rose to four thousand copies, and once again the presses worked constantly to keep up with demand.

Publicly, Wilkes shrugged it off. He found it, he said wryly, 'an excellent compound *caricatura*, or a *caricatura* of what nature had already *caricatured*'.[38] After all, he did not make himself, and 'never was solicitous about the *case* of his soul, as Shakespeare calls it'. His form did not pain him because it was

'capable of giving pleasure to others . . . While the share of health and animal spirits which heaven has given him shall hold out, I can scarcely imagine he will be one moment peevish about the *outside* of so precarious, so temporary a habitation, or will even be brought to own, *ingenium Galbae male habitat – Monsiur est mal logé.*'

Wilkes had forgotten Hogarth's belief that a portrait, well done, was the index of the mind. This was not the '*case*' of the soul, but the soul itself, a complete embodiment of Wilkes's 'animal spirits'. Hogarth had needed to retaliate, and 'my best was to return the complement & turn it to som advata[n]ge'. Hence the portrait, 'done as like as I could to feature at the same time some indication of his mind'. This, Hogarth wrote in his rushed, unpunctuated, mis-spelt scribble,

'fully answered my purpose the ridiculous was apparent to every Eye a Brutus a saviour of his country with such an aspect was arrant a Joke that tho it set every body else a laughing gauld him and his adherents to death this was seen by the papers being every day stuffed with evectives till the town grew sick of seeing my always.'[39]

*

The press was certainly crammed with comment. And Wilkes's adherents were certainly galled, none more so than Churchill. On 19 May, two days after *John Wilkes* appeared, Churchill announced his coming poem in the *Public Advertiser*, where Thornton was now installed. Again it was 'Speedily to be Published'. Three weeks later, as no poem had followed, the *Advertiser* published its own poem, presenting Hogarth as a monkey imitating his master shaving, pressing the blunt side of a knife against his throat. Hogarth has rashly begun playing with politics – 'that *cutting* Tool' – and has cut his own throat. The poem promised, however, that worse was in store: Churchill's exposure of Hogarth's folly and 'quick Decline'.[40] This warning also appeared

676

in the *St James's Chronicle* with an ironic commentary that the poem lowered the price of Hogarth's prints, while raising the subscriptions for the publication of Wilkes's case – a smart way of paying his debts.

The *Chronicle* would not take sides, but there was no rift in the Nonsense Club. If Hogarth was nervous, they were not. On 24 May, James Boswell, who had now been in London for six months, called on Thornton, whose style he greatly admired and took for his model. They were not alone:

'In a little, Mr. Wilkes came in, to whom I was introduced, as I also was to Mr Churchill. Wilkes is a lively, facetious man, Churchill a rough, blunt fellow, very clever. Lloyd too was there, so that I was just got into the middle of the London Geniuses. They were high spirited and boisterous, but were very civil to me, and Wilkes said he would be glad to see me in George Street.'[41]

From 'this chorus, which was rather too outrageous and profane', Boswell went to call on Samuel Johnson, whom Wilkes had attacked and Churchill had satirized as 'Pomposo'. Johnson's view of Churchill, as expressed a few weeks later, was curt. He thought him a 'blockhead' and 'talked very contemptuously of Churchill's poetry, observing, that "it had a temporary currency, only from its audacity of abuse, and being filled with living names, and that it would sink into oblivion" '.[42] Time would prove Johnson right, but not everyone was so long-sighted – and the prospect of his future oblivion offered little consolation to Churchill's living victims.

For another month, Hogarth waited. Towards the end of June, Thomas Birch described him as 'extremely unhappy', full of apprehension about the threatened poem, which 'it is imagined, will be almost a Death's wound to him'.[43] Meanwhile, Churchill sent Wilkes a draft of the opening section. He was stricken with the pox again, 'confin'd to my room with an Eruptio Veneris', but he *was* writing, he promised; 'I will – positively will – have it out by the twentieth.'[44] It seemed as though something more than illness and idleness, some old bond, some lingering admiration still held him back. In the finished version, he argued with 'Candour' about the justification for personal satire for three hundred lines before homing in on his prey. And the opening section that he sent to Wilkes ended with these ringing lines:

> How vain is worth! how short is glory's date!
> Then shall thou find, whilst Friends with Foes conspire,
> To give more proof than Virtue would desire,
> Thy danger chiefly lies in Acting Well;
> No Crime's so great, as daring to excell.

Curiously, and poignantly, this seems almost to describe Hogarth himself.

Finally, on 29 June, *An Epistle to William Hogarth* was advertised as ready. By the end of the first week of July it was on sale in the bookshops, price 2s 6d. In coffee houses and taverns, parlours and studies, salons and shops, Londoners could pore over the long-awaited denunciation of Hogarth's vanity and pride. In the poem, Candour challenges Churchill to produce one man whose destruction will justify the use of satire as a weapon: and at this dramatic moment, Churchill turns to his victim:

> HOGARTH stand forth – I dare thee to be tried
> In that great Court, where Conscience must preside.

When Churchill focused closely, he was deadly. He made no new charges, but followed Wilkes's essay. He asked Hogarth to review his life: had he ever put self aside? Had he ever given due praise to genius and merit?

Like Wilkes, Churchill hit a disturbing note that suggests he knew his man very well. His partial vision does fit the darker side of Hogarth, the air of the hanging judge, the sensual depiction of pain and ridicule:

> Hogarth, a guilty pleasure in his eyes,
> The place of executioner supplies.
> See how he glotes, enjoys the sacred feast,
> And proves himself by cruelty a priest.[45]

Hogarth had turned on weaker artists who had once flattered him and then dared to be independent. He had turned on Wilkes, lurking 'most ruffian-like' behind his screen in the gallery while Liberty was on trial. He had turned on the arts and artists themselves, trampling on established rules, condemning great works he had never seen, and setting up in their stead the pathetic *Sigismunda*, 'the helpless victim of a Dauber's hand!'. Churchill's portrait is made crueller by the intimacy it claims:

> Oft have I known thee HOGARTH, weak and vain,
> Thyself the idol of thy aukward strain,
> Thro the dull measure of a summer's day
> In phrase most vile, prate long long hours away,
> Whilst Friends with Friends all gaping sit, and gaze
> To hear a HOGARTH babble HOGARTH'S praise.

This meandering babble, Churchill continues, would be broken only by near-insane rage at the mention of 'some Antient's name'.

The pain Churchill imparts is also his own. Here too, as in Wilkes's essay, is a sense of deep personal betrayal. And here too is the difficult, intelligent struggle to separate the artist and the man: Hogarth *is* owed the praise due to a great artist, 'which rightly understood,/May make us great, but cannot make us good'. In the middle of the catalogue of failings of the man, comes a tribute that is unerringly accurate in its appreciation of Hogarth's narrative, comic and formal skill. Hogarth had always wanted to do *more*, to excel in every field, but Churchill was correct to see that it was his satirical story-telling greatness that time would endorse:

> In walks of Humor, in that cast of Style,
> Which, probing to the quick, yet makes us smile;
> In Comedy, thy nat'ral road to fame,
> Nor let me call it by a meaner name,
> Where a beginning, middle and an end
> Are aptly joined; where parts on parts depend,
> Each made for each, as bodies for their soul,
> So as to form one true and perfect whole,
> Where a plain story to the eye is told,
> Which we conceive the moment we behold,
> HOGARTH unrivall'd stands, and shall engage
> Unrivall'd praise to the most distant age.

*

Churchill's poem did not exactly cause a storm. Reviewers sighed over its length, the diplomatic *Chronicle* published verses supporting both sides and on 9 July a pro-Hogarth pamphlet appeared, *Pug's Reply to Parson Bruin*. But Churchill's phrases hung in the air, adding gusto to the new flight of prints assailing Hogarth. In a second *Tit for Tat*, for example, with bulging eyes, wearing the Cap of Liberty, he sits in the shadow of a lewd *Sigismunda*.[46]

Garrick was immediately anxious. On 10 July, he wrote to Colman:

'Pray write to me, & let me know how ye Town speaks of our Friend Churchill's Epistle – it is ye most bloody performance that has been publish'd in my time – I am very desirous to know the opinion of People, for I am really much, very much hurt at it – his description of his Age and infirmities is surely too shocking & barbarous – is Hogarth really ill, or does he meditate revenge? Every article of news about these matters will be most agreeable to me – pray write me a heap of stuff for I cannot be Easy till I know all about Churchill, Hogarth, &c'[47]

Colman himself, although one of Churchill's oldest friends, worried that the

679

poem might have 'snapped the last cord of poor Hogarth's heart-strings'.[48]

He was ill, and he did meditate revenge. He may even have had a second slight stroke, being reported as 'much indisposed of a paralytic Disorder, at his House in Leicester-Fields'.[49] But he seemed numb to the *Epistle*. When Thomas Morell, so often his buffer against the world, took a copy of the poem round to him, he hardly blenched:

'he seemed quite insensible to the most sarcastical parts of it. He was so thoroughly wounded before by the *North Briton*, especially with regard to what related to domestic happiness, that he lay no where open to a fresh stroke. Some readers, however, may entertain a doubt on this subject.'[50]

Hogarth worried, though, about the effect of the row on Jane, always in the background of his life. From time to time a little glimpse of her appears, relieved when the *Analysis* is finished, wearied by the difficulties with the Election prints, spending the summer days with Mary Lewis and visiting relatives such as Julien Bere. Yet he felt her distress at this juncture. Their lives were not quite so separate after all: in the middle of a draft description of his prints comes a stray note ringed with a circle, 'their Malice so great as they could not . . . it that they endeavourd to wound the peace of my family'.[51]

Elsewhere in his notes, Hogarth wrote as if he was indeed insensible:

'Churchill W— toadeater put the North Briton into verse in an Epistle to me, but as the abuse was the same except a little poetical heightening which alway goes for nothing, it not only made no impression but in some measure effaced the Blacks stroke of the NB.'[52]

But whatever Hogarth said, he suffered. Revenge would only increase the attacks, and hurt his wife more – but he took it just the same.

Since Hogarth's pencil was his only weapon, he planned to etch a portrait of Churchill, just as he had done of Wilkes. It would be the visual equivalent of Pug's reply to Bruin. But this time he did not make a new portrait or work from a sketch. Instead he took the copper plate of his own portrait, *Gulielmus Hogarth*, and erased his own face. Pug remained, guarding the frame, in which a great bear with a torn clergyman's collar now appeared, grasping a huge club with 'Lye' written on the knots, and drooling into a quart of beer. Pug is pissing on Churchill's *Epistle*, and a poor box stands on *The North Briton* with a 'comedy' of Wilkes's subscription, 'A new way to pay old debts'. The caption reads,

'THE BRUISER, *C. Churchill (once the Rev^d!) in the Character of a Modern*

191 *The Bruiser* (1763)

Hercules, *Regaling himself after having Kill'd the Monster* caricatura *that so sorely Gall'd his* Virtuous *friend, the Heaven born* WILKES.'

The satire is clear, but why did he reuse that plate? Hogarth's own explanation was simple, and given his poor health, on the surface it was probably true:

681

'having an old plate by me with some parts ready such as the background and a dog, I thought how I could turn so much work laid aside to account so patch up a print of Mr Churchill in the character of a Bear'.[53]

Still, it was an extraordinary act, to replace his own face with that of the man who had tried to destroy him, especially when he produced such a strong, powerful, almost attractive image. To some it might seem less of a revenge than an unconscious surrender: a suicide, even. In the midst of his anger, Churchill saw this. 'I take it for granted You have seen Hogarth's print – was ever anything so contemptible,' he wrote to Wilkes, '– I think he is fairly *Felo de se*.'

Had Hogarth, and all he stood for, been obliterated by Churchill and Wilkes? Perhaps not. In a later state of the print he began to fight back, to return the argument to its political context. Propped on the palette is a small framed picture. It shows a planned tomb for Pitt very like Rysbrack's for Newton in Westminster Abbey, but while the sculpted Newton props himself up on the tomes of his works with a globe over his head, here Pitt reclines beneath the 'millstone' of his pension. (It does, as Nichols said, also look like a cheese, reminding people of Pitt's claim that he 'would rather subsist for a week on a *Cheshire* cheese, and a shoulder of mutton, than submit to the implacable enemies of his country'.)[54] On each side are the emblems of his City supporters, the 'Guildhall giants' Gog and Magog, one of whom is crowning the hero: but Pitt is borrowing a match from them to fire a cannon at the dove of peace. In the centre, as Nichols explained, stands Hogarth himself, whipping a dancing bear (Churchill) on a string.[55] The monkey beside him is Wilkes, riding a mop-stick topped by the cap of liberty as a hobby-horse. In the background stands Lord Temple, their faceless patron.

Focusing on the detail of the poor box and the comedy, Churchill could see that the print was aimed at Wilkes's subscription to clear his debts as well as settling old scores with himself. Vowing not to let Hogarth off by pretending Wilkes was the target, Churchill exploded: 'he has broke into the pale of private Life, and set that kind of illiberality, which I wish'd – of that kind of attack which is ungenerous in the first instance, but justice in the return.' 'I intend an Elegy on him, supposing him dead,' he continued, but his mistress, at his elbow, 'tells me he will be really dead before it comes out. Nay, she tells me with a kiss that I have kill'd him, and begs I will never be her enemy.'[56]

It is typical of Churchill to boast of his sexual potency in the same breath as he trumpets his destructive power; just as he pleads a sexual disease when unable to finish any work. Wilkes was just as bad. 'I have not yet seen Hogarth's print,' he replied. 'I wish you wou'd cut off the margin, and send it to me by the post – I have a rod steeping for him.'[57] Both men made much of Hogarth's impotence, in all senses. He felt the contrast with their vitality and youth, no doubt about it. But by attacking these virile young enemies through their images, he seemed to suck power and strength back into his veins. He could ride the trouble out. In his notes on this episode, he ended casually, 'the satisfaction <and pecuniary advantage> I receivd from these two prints together with constant Riding on horse back restored me as much health as can be expected at my time of life'.[58] But then, turning the page, he wrote,

What may follow god knows
Finis

33

The End of All Things

Pale quiv'ring lips, lank cheeks, and falt'ring tongue,
The Spirits out of tune, the Nerves unstrung,
Thy Body shrivell'd up, thy dim eyes sunk
Within their sockets deep, thy weak hams shrunk
The body's weight unable to sustain,
The stream of life scarce trembling thro' the vein . . .

Hence Dotard, to thy closet, shut thee in,
By deep repentance wash away thy sin,
From haunts of men to shame and sorrow fly,
And, on the verge of death, learn how to die.

CHARLES CHURCHILL (1763)

'It is in the tranquillity of decomposition, that I remember the
long confused emotion which was my life . . . To decompose is
to live too, I know, I know, don't torment me.'

SAMUEL BECKETT, *Molloy* (1951)

OVER AND OVER AGAIN in Churchill's long poem Hogarth was made to see himself declining. The year before, he had 'complained of an inward pain, which, continuing, brought on a general decay that proved incurable'.[1] In the rainy August of 1763, while the trees greened under the deluge and the Chiswick market gardens turned to mud, he pondered mortality. But the last thing he was thinking of was deep repentance.

While he reworked *The Bruiser* and satires, squibs and poems still pursued him, he consoled himself with the profit from his prints of Churchill and Wilkes. Among his papers are pages from a small notebook, often blank except for pencilled accounts in a shaky hand, upside-down in relation to the rest of his writing. One entry is dated 'August 26 – 1763':

Painting   120–0–0
Remainder of 200

684

G—ks m	15– 0–0
W—ks m	4– 2–0
C—ll m	30–15–0²

The first sum is from his work as Serjeant-Painter, the 'remainder' after paying his assistant. The next is from Garrick, perhaps towards his portrait. The last two are from recent sales of his prints of Wilkes (still going strong, with over 80 new sales) and Churchill (around 600).

A little later, taking a new page, he wrote a couple of lines before pencilling another rough set of domestic outgoings, the high cost of his carriage:

'When a man is cruelly and unjustly treated he naturally looks round and appeals to the standers by

'My Phylosophical friends bid me laugh at the Abusive nonsense of party writers But I cannot rest myself

C—	
Coach maker	27
Taylor	14
Chandlers	20
Corn	20
Hay straw &c	30
Carpenter	4
	115
Car	120
Due from P to C	180 ³

Jane kept the notebooks and loose papers, which Hogarth would have swept away, and the letters from supporters, which gave him heart.

Wilkes and Churchill were still in the news. On 15 August, in Paris, Wilkes was challenged to a duel by a young Scotsman, the son of a Jacobite *émigré*: he had recognized his target from Hogarth's print. Later that year, a mad Scottish marine crept into his London house, bent on assassination, although armed only with a penknife. But if Wilkes escaped assassins he could not dodge the law. After the failed trial of *The North Briton*, George III was determined that Wilkes should not go unpunished. Spies were set, and government agents bribed a printer at his private press to hand over a proof sheet of the gross parody of Pope, the *Essay on Woman* with its jovial, cynical invitation to lust, '. . . since life can little more supply/Than just a few good fucks and then we die.' Although the verse was probably written by

685

Potter years earlier, Wilkes had recently annotated it with acutely witty notes, parodying the pedantic Bishop Warburton, and had begun to print it in June.

The *Essay* was the perfect ammunition. On 16 November, when Wilkes tried to raise the question of his parliamentary privilege again, his enemies were ready. In the Commons Grenville spoke to a motion to expel him. In the Lords, his old Medmenham allies, Francis Dashwood, now Lord, and the Earl of Sandwich turned against him: Sandwich lacerated him in a speech containing extracts from the *Essay on Woman*, which caused much mock horror and private mirth, the poem was voted an outrageous attack on a member of the Lords, Bishop Warburton, and the leaders of the Commons, notably Pitt, were quick to denounce the blasphemy and expel its 'author'. Wilkes now faced a possible double trial, for reprinting No. 45 and for obscenity: this time the judge would not be Chief Justice Pratt, but the pro-Bute Mansfield.

During the debate, Samuel Martin rose to his feet. He had waited to avenge the *North Briton*'s attack, choosing this moment to call Wilkes 'a cowardly, scandalous and malignant scoundrel'.[4] Trembling with rage, he repeated the words twice. Next day, when Wilkes sent a note admitting authorship of the article, Martin challenged him to meet 'in Hyde-park immediately with a brace of pistols each'.[5] The morning was misty, but at the second shot Martin struck Wilkes a deep wound in the groin. Believing he was dying, Wilkes followed the old code of honour impeccably; he urged Martin to flee, attempted to destroy the incriminating challenge and would not speak of the matter until assured his life was safe: 'My antagonist behaved very well,' he told his daughter Polly. Others thought differently, noting how long Martin had waited, how he had deprived Wilkes of the choice of weapons and had been seen practising target-shooting all summer. In *The Duellist*, in January, Churchill portrayed him as a hired assassin, the tool of the ministry, and later Wilkes added damning financial evidence:

'Under the head of *secret and special service* I find that between October 1762 and October 1763, a most *memorable year*, there was issued to Samuel Martin, Esq., £40,000.'

At the end of the memorable year, Wilkes's fortunes swooped. Pitt turned against him, a blow more painful than Martin's pistol shot. On 3 December, when *The North Briton* was due to be burned by the public hangman as a seditious libel, 'a great riot ensued, the paper was forced from the hangman, the constables were pelted and beaten',[6] but Wilkes still feared trial and imprisonment and on Christmas Eve he slipped away secretly for Dover and

Paris. When illness stopped him returning in January 1764 he was expelled from the Commons. In February he was tried in his absence before Lord Mansfield and a warrant was issued for his arrest. By November, he was formally an outlaw. He would stay in France for the next four years.

In December 1763, Churchill had also travelled to Flanders and Paris, perhaps fearing prosecution. He had personal problems: that autumn he had eloped with the daughter of a London stonemason, Elizabeth Carr (rumoured at the time to be 'Elizabeth Cheere', daughter of Hogarth's sculptor friend Henry Cheere); her family threatened lawsuits and rumours spread that they were planning to ambush and shoot him. Elizabeth returned home, but soon ran away to live with Churchill again. In 1764, back in England, Churchill furiously wrote poetry in support of Wilkes's cause.[7] His rush of energy was in marked contrast to Bob Lloyd's collapse: after sliding into alcoholism, Lloyd was arrested for debt and sent to the Fleet in February.

But if Hogarth's enemies were scattered and preoccupied, so were his friends. Poor Rouquet, grief-stricken by the death of his wife, had died raving in a hospital in Charenton, in 1758.[8] William Huggins had died in 1761, James Ralph and Louis-François Roubiliac in 1762. And in September 1763, having handed over the management of Drury Lane to Colman, Garrick and Violette left for Paris, and then Italy: they would not return to London until April 1765. Among the artists, Hogarth remained close to old companions of his youth such as Frank Hayman and George Lambert, despite their differences.[9] But he had lost the academy battle. On 24 January the Society of Artists decided to petition the King to incorporate them as a formal Society by royal charter; this was granted a year later. Just over the horizon, in 1768, lay the founding of the Royal Academy – with Joshua Reynolds as its first President.

Over the autumn and winter of 1763 Hogarth began to set his affairs in order. One project he had been working on since the summer, for example, was updating and completing Rouquet's notes on his prints. This was a sensible idea. Rouquet's commentary had proved invaluable for foreign sales and Hogarth included it with every portfolio he sold abroad. And if he added a biographical note, the updated version could also be his own vindication, his explanation of himself and his work to posterity:

'As an entire collection of Mr Hogarths prints, are considered (by some) as discriptive of the peculiar manners & characters of the English nation, the curious of other Countries frequently send for them in order to be informed and amused with What cannot be conveyed to the mind with Such precision

687

and truth by any words whatsoever. but as strangers to the singular humour and customs of England may be at a loss for the authors meaning in many material parts of Such of his designs as have been published since Mr. Roquet's discription in the year – a discription of these also may not be unacceptable. to which if we add a short account of the author himself perhaps we may be forgiven.'[10]

So far so good. But as with the *Analysis* Hogarth found writing difficult. He began again and again, writing careful drafts on loose sheets of paper, before taking up the small notebook which is interrupted, in late August, by his pencilled sums. He picked it up and left it, returning a couple of months later. He rewrote and added, he crossed out and corrected, he dodged from the third person to the first person and back again. He looked back to his childhood, to his earliest memory of watching the spiralling jack, his delight in 'shews of all kinds', in drawing the alphabet with care, in spending long hours at the neighbouring artist's studio. He wrote of his studies and his pleasures, the long hours of apprenticeship when the paintings at St Paul's and Greenwich were running in his head. He spoke of his struggle to find 'the shorter way'. And he remembered his father's death, blamed on the booksellers and great men's promises, and his own battles against the printsellers.

At every stage, as Hogarth recalled his marriage and his conversation pieces, his progresses, portraits and history-painting, emotional arguments leapt in. He presented himself carefully as a self-taught artist, a champion of the English people and of the rights of the 'ordinary man' against connoisseurs, printsellers, dealers. But a thread of paranoia vitiated his account. Above the heading 'Story of Coram', for example, he noted, 'The three things that hav brought abuse upon me are 1st the attempting portrait painting 2^d the analysis 3^{rly} the Prints of the times.'[11] Attempting a neutral description, he launched into repeated barrages of opinion: on other painters, on the evils of copying, on printsellers, dealers and more 'persecution'. His hobby-horse rode him and he could not, would not, achieve a smooth final version.

At the same time as he was writing about his career, Hogarth was still working on his *Apology*. These different strands merged with other notes, new beginnings and headings, such as, 'Painting & Sculpture considered in a new manner differing from every author that has as yet wrote upon the subjects'.[12] The reason for this 'hardy attempt', he goes on, is the injury which the arts have laboured under 'by the Prejudices imbibed from the bookes hitherto written on this subject': then he launches into a definition of still life, portrait painting and landscape. His energy and conviction, and determination to clear away the clutter of convention, showed no sign of dying.

In odd bursts, Hogarth began to define the nature of his own art, writing of the moral power of comedy, the neglected 'intermediate species of subjects' between the sublime and the grotesque, the power of the print and the instinctive judgement of the untutored eye:

'ocular demonstration will convince and [word illegible] man sooner than ten thousand Vols for this purpose this plate is published and the decision left to evry unprejudiced Eye, let figure be consider as Actors dresed for the sublime genteel comedy or same in high or low life.'[13]

His insights were trapped in the almost illiterate, indecipherable jumble. As the notes piled up, the three separate 'works' – the explanations of the prints, the autobiography and the *Apology*'s argument about art in general and in England in particular – became hopelessly entangled. Future generations, sifting through the sheafs of papers and notebooks, would see only the ramblings of an ailing, unbalanced man. And sometimes that is what they were.

Hogarth left chaos, but he was aiming at order: a final, definitive portfolio with a commentary. And if the text needed writing, the prints also needed revising. If the future were to judge his work rightly, worn lines must be sharpened and details clarified. He had begun this process three years earlier in a casual way when Luke Sullivan engraved *The March to Finchley* in 1761, continuing with *The Sleeping Congregation*, which was reissued to balance *Credulity* in 1762. Both these prints were inscribed as 'Retouched & Improved' by himself. But the changes he made now were different, angrier, more pessimistic. In *Canvassing for Votes*, he made the British lion toothless. In *A Rake's Progress* he added a huge coin to the walls of Bedlam, the reverse face of a halfpenny. It shows Britannia with her hair flying, driven mad by the state of her country, with the date firmly inscribed beneath her feet, '1763'. Other details in this plate were also changed: the man grasping Rakewell's shoulders lost his pale wig and flowing shirt and became a dark-haired, bony-fingered figure of death.

It was now that he wiped the smile off his last self-portrait, and darkened the lines of the Comic Muse. Instead of the bold claim 'SERJEANT PAINTER *to His* MAJESTY' the caption was simply '*William Hogarth – 1764*'. He had destroyed *Gulielmus Hogarth* to create *The Bruiser* – a bully, a thug, a fighter – and now this dark, intense, final self-portrait would replace it as the frontispiece to his prints. All that he needed to complete the portfolio was a tailpiece.

689

In his tailpiece, Hogarth extended the death of self to encompass the whole world. It was claimed that the idea arose one evening 'while the convivial glasses were still circulating':

' "My next undertaking," says Hogarth, "shall be the End of all Things". "If that is the case," replied one of his friends, "your *business will be finished*, for there will be *an end of the painter*". "There *will* so," answered Hogarth, sighing heavily, "and therefore the sooner my *work is done*, the better." '[14]

Accordingly he began the next day, and continued his design with a diligence

192 *Tailpiece: or The Bathos* (1764)

690

which seemed to indicate an apprehension (so the report goes) that he should not live till he had completed it.[15]

Tailpiece, or The Bathos declared itself a satire, a *Dunciad* landscape. It was a bitter answer to those carpers who claimed Hogarth's sun was dim, like the 'special friends' Swift imagined in his mock obituary:

> For poetry, he's past his prime:
> He takes an hour to find a rhyme;
> His fire is out, his wit decay'd,
> His fancy sunk, his Muse a jade.
> I'd have him throw away his pen; –
> But there's no talking to some men!

Hogarth was thinking of those giants of his youth, Swift and Pope, when he drew this print. He evoked Pope's *Peri Bathous*, or 'the Art of Sinking' in his caption, 'The Bathos, or Manner of Sinking in Sublime Paintings, inscribed to the Dealers in dark Pictures'. His footnote wittily reapplied the old attack against himself: 'See the manner of disgracing ye most Serious subjects, in many celebrated Old pictures, by introducing Low, absurd, obscene & often prophane circumstances into them.'

The tone of that footnote is lively and sharp and the long inscription beneath the print is also proud and combative. On the left is the pyramidal shell (part of the crest on his carriage), the 'conic' form in which Aphrodite, 'the Goddess of Beauty', was worshipped at Paphos. This is supported by two quotations, from Tacitus and Maximus Tyrius. On the right is the cone around which the Line of Beauty twines in the *Analysis*, with a note saying that the resemblance between the two forms, 'did not occur to the Author' until two or three years after his book was published.

Even at this point Hogarth was not merely defending his ideas, but excited by them. His search for the mystery of beauty had defied time and language. It reached back to Classical and pre-Classical eras, into a realm of abstraction where the goddess of love could be inscribed in pure form. The brash artist from Smithfield whose greatest work was born of sharp observation in London streets and salons had become the votary of an ideal. This, too, was like a shedding of life. Perhaps Auden and Kallman felt this when they wrote the libretto for *The Rake's Progress*; in Bedlam, their lustful gambler becomes the artist as lover, a weary Adonis awaiting the goddess who will lull him into death: 'Venus, my queen, my bride. At last. I have waited for thee so long, so long, till I almost believed those madmen who blasphemed against thy honour.'[16]

In the light of the inscription, one could read this print as an indictment of

691

the 'awful' Sublime, in contrast to the true Line of Beauty. But the image is almost at odds with the inscription. There is no aesthetic goddess here. Hogarth's scene leaps beyond polemic into a tragic realm, a cry of self-destructive negation. The print is packed with references: to funerary tombs, to the littered images of Dürer's *Melancholy*, or Salvator Rosa's baroque print of the philosopher Democritus.[17] It recalls *Peri Bathous* in another way, as a mordant acceptance of Pope's mock science, which decrees poetry (and by analogy, art) to be

'a natural and morbid Secretion from the brain . . . I have known a man, thoughtful, melancholy, and raving for divers days, who forthwith grew wonderfully easy, lightsome, and cheerful, upon the discharge of the peccant humour, in exceeding purulent metre.'[18]

Hogarth's setting is a wasteland; the time, 'A late evening in the future'.[19] Outside a long-gone tavern, the broken sign of 'The World's End' slants like a gibbet against two dead trees, their branches fingering the sky like tresses of hair. In the angle of the sign is a real gibbet, where a hanged pirate swung above the margins of land, sea and sky: now only the chains that held his decaying body remain. Even the fecund sea is an ocean of death, with its sinking ship. Even in the breathing sky the light is fading – Apollo and his steeds are dead, and the sad-faced moon is waning.

Time himself, with his gnarled face and Christ-like body, gasps a last 'Finis'. His scythe is useless, his pipe broken. The sands have run out from his cracked hour-glass. Below his limp hand is a scrolled will, in which he leaves 'every atom thereof to – '. The beneficiary's name is crossed out and replaced by Chaos, his executor, and the witnesses are the three Fates, Clotho, Lachesis and Atropos. At Time's feet, a candle end is setting *The Times* smouldering. As he leans against the broken column, in the shadow of the ruined church tower, the ground around him sprawls with finality: a playscript, open at 'Exeunt Omnes'; a bankruptcy deed with the Pale Rider on its seal, marked 'H. Nature Bankrupt'; a punning shoemaker's last, with a 'waxed end' curled round it. All must die, cobbler and king, soldier and poet. No one will come after them to sweep up these endings: the bent crown, the broken serpentine line of the unstrung bow; the musket butt; the rope end and used broom; the shattered gin bottle mirroring the cracked church bell.

The word broken, broken, recurs and recurs if we try to turn the images to words. And in the centre of these shattered relics, beneath the feet of Time, leaning against Hogarth's *Times*, lies a broken palette. So strong was the impact, that anecdote demanded the painter's voice:

'"So far, so good," cried Hogarth; "nothing remains but this," – taking his pencil in a sort of prophetic fury, and dashing off the similitude of a *painter's pallet broken* - "*Finis*," exclaimed Hogarth, "*the deed is done – all is over*."'[20]

The pessimism of *Bathos* is matched only by its desperate, despairing egotism. The apocalyptic hints in Hogarth's work, from the whore setting fire to the map of the world in *A Rake's Progress* to the war-inflamed globe of *The Times*, coalesce in the exploding, fiery globe in the tavern sign of the World's End. Conscious of coming death, Hogarth would bring everything down with him. If he was not there to see it and record it, the sun would fall from the sky. Yet for all the sad, startling pain there is also something weirdly comical about the print in its extreme travesty of all the familiar, dignified images of '*O tempora, O mores*' and '*Tempus fugit*' – making Time the last inebriate at the pub to end all pubs.

On 1 April 1764, All Fool's Day, there was a total eclipse. The sun was indeed darkened and the air was suddenly chill.[21] Hogarth had time to draw in this convenient element of apocalypse by including the death of Apollo, for although the publication date on the print is 3 March 1764, it was not advertised as finished until the second week in April. The announcement had an air of finality: 'It may serve as a Tail-Piece to all the Author's engraved Works, when bound up together.'

It was as if he had died already. When he saw the print soon after it appeared, Churchill wrote with ironic ambiguity:

> All must old Hogarth's gratitude declare,
> Since he has nam'd old *Chaos* as his heir:
> And while his works hang round that anarch's throne,
> The connoisseur will take them for his own.[22]

The final 'his own' rings with ironic ambiguity: does the pronoun apply to Hogarth, the connoisseur, or Chaos? The last is strongest. Churchill, who knew Hogarth so well, could see that in this careful composition he was almost embracing the anarchy he loathed. This was not 'order from confusion sprung' but confusion itself, brilliantly and terribly composed. Instead of Venus, Hogarth had seen the dreadful muse that Pope beheld:

> She comes! she comes! the sable Throne behold
> Of *Night* Primaeval and of *Chaos* old!
> Before her, *Fancy*'s gilded clouds decay,
> And all its varying Rain-bows die away.
> *Wit* shoots in vain its momentary fires,

The meteor drops, and in a flash expires . . .
. . . Nor *public* Flame, nor *private*, dares to shine;
Nor *human* Spark is left, nor Glimpse *divine*!
Lo! thy dread Empire, CHAOS! is restored!
Light dies before thy uncreating word:
Thy hand, great Anarch! lets the curtain fall;
And Universal Darkness buries All.[23]

*

After that spring, Hogarth made no new engravings. In May came the two rival exhibitions, now annual fixtures: the Society of Arts in the Strand, and the Society of Artists in Spring Gardens, the sites of past battles, and the object of past hoaxes. The memory of his humiliation over *Sigismunda* still rankled; he wanted it engraved, if only for his intimate circle. At the start of the year, on 2 January, he had reopened his subscription book, writing a note in his shakiest hand: 'All efforts to this time to get the Picture finally engraved proving in vain, Mr Hogarth humbly hopes his best endeavours to engrave it himself will be acceptable to his friends.' But by June he had managed no more than the head, and had asked the young artist Edward Edwards – who was currently making drawings of old masters for the printseller Boydell – to draw a clear outline for other engravers.

On 12 June, for a friend, he copied the history of the painting that he had written in his subscription book, adding that the final work:

'was after much time and the utmost efforts finished, BUT HOW! the Authors death as usual can only positively determine.

'Wm Hogarth'[24]

That day he also sent Edwards's drawing to George Hay. The print, he said, would be more delicate and would be engraved by George Basire, 'who has the surest command of the Burin being determin'd to make it his masterpiece in order [to] show what he can do'. In a postscript, he said he would take care of the head himself. According to Nichols, Hogarth's first choice had been Grignion, but he then turned to Basire, who came from a family of engravers and had already etched the drawing of Fielding and *The Farmer's Return*; he had a clear, flowing style derived from the severe old English school. Basire was in his mid-thirties and got on easily with people, including Hogarth: six years later, when the fourteen-year-old William Blake became his apprentice, he found him a kind master.

Hogarth's letter to Hay also noted that the drawing can be spared for some

694

time, 'the Engraver being out of town'.[25] In addition, when he commissioned him, Basire was already working on two plates of an antique bronze for the Society of Antiquaries, 'so remarkably grotesque that Mr. Hogarth very readily consented that his plate should be postponed, and declared, "he could not have imagined that the Ancients had possessed so much humour."'[26] By the autumn, the work on *Sigismunda* had only just begun. Twenty years later Nichols saw the unfinished plate, 'etched by Mr. Basire, but not bit-in, and from which consequently no proof can have been taken. The outlines in general, and particularly of the face, were completed under the immediate direction of Mr Hogarth'.[27] In this rough state it was issued by Basire in 1790.

Although frail, Hogarth was still sending out portfolios of prints as requests came in, with Jane or his sister Anne sometimes acting as his agent. In June he received a letter from Benjamin Franklin, who wanted to order a complete set of prints for the Philadelphia Library Company. But in mid-September the publisher William Strahan told Franklin that soon after he had delivered his letter Hogarth was taken ill, 'and continues so dangerously bad, that he could not yet comply with the order'.[28]

That summer Hogarth wrote a new will. His first act was to 'release and Aquit and Discharge my sister Ann Hogarth of and from all her Claims and Demands which I have on her at the time of my Decease on any account whatsoever'.[29] Having cleared Anne of loans and debts he left her a small independent annuity of £80, to be paid quarterly by Jane out of the sale of his prints and, to protect their staple income, the precious copper plates were not to be sold or disposed of without the consent of both women. The plates were to belong to Jane unless she married, when she would be provided for; at that point the three most important sets 'called Mariage Alamode, the Harlots Progress and the Rakes Progress shall be delivered to my said sister'. If Jane died, Anne would inherit the plates and profits from the prints.

There were other individual bequests. Mary Lewis, the youngest member of the household, who undertook the hard work and looked after them when they were ill, was to have £100, 'for her faithful Service'. Samuel Martin was 'requested to accept of the portrait which I painted of him for my Self'. His principal doctor, Isaac Schomberg, should have a ring worth ten guineas, 'in remembrance of me' and Julien Bere a ring worth five guineas. The remaining money, securities and moveables and the two houses: 'I do give and bequeath the same and every part thereof unto my Dear Wife Jane Hogarth whom I do Ordain Constitute and Appoint my Sole Executrix of my Will.'

The will was signed and dated on 16 August 1764.[30] Gradually, the business of Hogarth's life was being concluded – in September, his deputy, Samuel

695

Cobb, began to take over his work as Serjeant-Painter. But he still worked on, retouching his prints, 'with the assistance of several engravers whom he took with him to Chiswick'.[31] Much of his last year was spent in his workshop above the stables, among the familiar smells of varnish and lamp-black, nut-oil and ink, and the litter of needles and gravers, paper and plates.

At the beginning of October Charles Churchill published *Independence*. In this poem comes a strange, moving recognition of how close he felt to his old adversary. In rolling, urgent verse, Churchill drew his own self-portrait as the Bard of the people, a Bruiser, an unlicked Bear abandoned by his Dam, a huge figure of untamed energy emerging from a wasteland like that of Hogarth's *Bathos*: 'An utter *Chaos*, out of which no might/But that of God could strike one spark of light':

> O'er a brown Cassock, which had once been black,
> Which hung in tatters on his brawny back,
> A sight most strange, and aukward to behold
> He threw a covering of *Blue* and *Gold*.
> Just at that time of life, when Man by rule,
> The Fop laid down, takes up the graver fool,
> He started up a Fop, and fond of show,
> Look'd like another HERCULES turned Beau.
> A Subject, met with only now and then,
> Much fitter for the pencil than the pen;
> HOGARTH would draw him (Envy must allow)
> E'en to the life, was HOGARTH living now.[32]

Earlier Churchill had sworn angrily that he would write an elegy on Hogarth, 'supposing him dead'. But Hogarth was living and drawing still.

On Thursday, 24 October, Churchill left to meet Wilkes in France. On the same day, in Chiswick, Hogarth was working on *The Bench*. He had burnished away a thin section across the top of the plate. With a clean rag, he dusted away the copper slivers and dust. He polished and smoothed and cleaned it with charcoal, and chalk, and varnished the empty strip. When the plate was dry, he took the familiar tool, feeling the smooth round of the handle in the hollow of his hand and stretching his finger towards the cutting point, as he had done almost without thinking for over forty years. On the empty strip, he etched in a frieze of heads to illustrate caricature and character. To the end, he wanted to make his ideas live through his images. The judge came from his own print; the other heads looked back to Raphael and to Leonardo's *Last Supper*. Under the caption, where the ironic dedication to George

Townshend once appeared, one of his assistants engraved: 'This plate would have been better explain'd had the Author lived a Week longer.'

The next day Hogarth was too unwell to work. He was taken from Chiswick to Leicester Fields, very weak, 'yet remarkably chearful'. On his arrival he found a pleasant letter from Benjamin Franklin, and drew up a rough draft of an answer. He felt fine, and 'boasted of having eaten a pound of beef-steaks for his dinner, and was to all appearance heartier than he had been for a long time before'.[33] Although this meal was later disputed – 'Misinformation. He only eat an egg or some such trifle,' wrote one commentator – it remained solidly part of the myth.[34] But whatever he ate, on going to bed:

'he was seized with a vomiting, and rang his bell with such violence that he broke it, and expired about two hours afterwards in the arms of Mrs Mary Lewis, who was called on his being taken suddenly ill.'

Despite all his preparations, death ambushed him.

34

'Finis'

*Having dispatched the herd of our painters in oil, I reserved
to a class by himself that great and original genius, Hogarth.*
HORACE WALPOLE, *Anecdotes of Painting* (1780)

JANE WAS IN CHISWICK when Hogarth died – of an aneurism, a ruptured
artery, the doctors said. His body was taken back to the Thames-side village
and buried in the graveyard of St Nicolas' Church. Notices of his death were
conventional, and only the *London Evening Post* attempted an immediate
judgement. In Hogarth, the paper declared, were 'happily united'

'the utmost force of human genius, an incomparable understanding, an
inflexible integrity and a most benevolent heart. No man was better
acquainted with the human passions, nor endeavoured to make them more
subservient to the reformation of the world, than this inimitable artist. His
works will continue to be held in the highest estimation, so long as sense,
genius and virtue, shall remain among us; and whilst the tender feelings of
humanity can be affected by the follies and vices of mankind.'[1]

Hogarth's death was marked as a significant event, but the passing of an
elderly, irascible artist, who had been known to be ill for some time, offered no
great gossip. Horace Walpole simply slotted it into his news of the week:
'Hogarth is dead, and Mrs. Spence, who lived with the Duchess of
Newcastle.'[2] It took time to register. Garrick learned of Hogarth's death in
Rome, at the same time as that of Hubert, the young Duke of Devonshire. 'I
heard nothing of Hubert & Hogarth before your letter told me of their deaths,'
he told Colman. 'I was much affected with your news, the loss of so many of
my acquaintance in so short a time is a melancholy reflection.' Then he wrote,
'Churchill I hear, is at ye point of death in Boulogne.'[3]

It was true. After a week with Wilkes, planning a journey to Italy, Churchill
had collapsed with a high fever. It was not, as was thought, the result of heavy
drinking, but typhus: he worsened, and died on 4 November. Wilkes was
distraught, wept for three days in agonies of despair, and plunged into the task

698

of editing his friend's work. The two adversaries, the artist of sixty-six and the poet of thirty, were bracketed by death. Churchill's *Epistle* was even blamed for killing Hogarth, breaking his heart-strings, as Colman said. But as the *Public Advertiser*, with Thornton now closely involved, retorted, Hogarth's pencil could be said to be just as deadly as Churchill's pen, 'since neither long survived the contest'.[4] The following January, the same paper ran a 'Dialogue of the Dead' (a favourite eighteenth-century form) between them, bringing in Bob Lloyd, who had died in December. Wilkes would weave Lloyd, too, into his legend of Churchill's death: 'Mr. Lloyd soon after died in the Fleet prison, absolutely of a broken heart.'[5] In their imaginary dialogue, the tone is amicable, the quarrel forgotten. But 'Churchill' makes the point that although it was said that the wounds he gave Hogarth proved mortal, 'from your own account of the Matter, I am rather disposed to think you died a Suicide'.[6]

It was an odd coincidence, as Walpole remarked, that the two deaths should be so close. Churchill's

'meteor blazed scarce four years . . . and what is as remarkable, he died in nine days after his antagonist Hogarth. Was I Charon, I should without scruple give the best place in my boat to the latter, who was an original genius.'[7]

All deaths bring such private testimonials, brief appraisals, passing nods to something long unrecognized and now acknowledged. When Hogarth died, in city mansions and country houses people might raise their eyes to the portraits in the dining room – a salute to men and women now dead, like the artist: to Mary Edwards, to John and William Huggins, to John Pine. Or their glance might bring back childhoods caught in passing: the Graham children with Time's scythe on their clock, the Ranby children with their clear gaze, little Caroline Lennox acting in *The Indian Emperor* thirty years earlier, now the matronly wife of Henry Fox. Other paintings would recall a marriage, an appointment, an anniversary, an assembly. And over those old conversation pieces might hover a memory of a stocky, ambitious London artist whose social graces never quite matched his skill. Many of these paintings, hung proudly in the salon or the dining room, would soon be consigned to murkier corners in the corridor or swept upstairs by the next generation. 'As a *painter*,' Horace Walpole decided, 'Hogarth has slender merit.'[8] Art critics have never rated Hogarth with his contemporaries Reynolds, Ramsay or Gainsborough, although his colours and marvellous sketches – *The Shrimp Girl*, *The Happy Marriage*, the *Servants' Heads* – made some see him as Britain's first Impressionist. His influence simmered on in European art.[9] As a boy, lying ill in St Petersburg, Whistler was given a Hogarth folio: he stayed loyal all his

699

life, and in old age his voice crackled through the National Gallery, declaring, 'Why! Hogarth! he was a great painter.'[10]

Even in the late eighteenth century, when the prices of his canvases were low, people admired the directness of his portraits, the rough, fast oil sketches for the *Rake* or the flat, packed, formal beauty of the *Election*. Ten years after Hogarth's death Benjamin Wilson was talking to George III, who owned a substantial collection of Hogarth prints and had kind memories of his Serjeant-Painter. 'The King', Wilson said, 'made repeated inquiries respecting the personal history of Hogarth, and his paintings of which he was a great admirer.' They talked of *Marriage A-la-Mode* and *The Happy Marriage*, and the King borrowed the painting of breaking the bride-cake from Garrick, deciding that 'the bride was a handsome likeness of the Queen'.[11]

Royal approval came too late, but however much he had aimed to please the Court and win patrons – and he tried very hard to do both – Hogarth had also always reached towards the public. Lesser folk, as well as great, were affected by his death. When the news reached a country vicarage or merchant's redbrick house, for example, someone might leaf through the portfolio of prints which they had bought recently for a sizeable £15. This was where his fierce, lasting life was – in Moll Hackabout smiling and dangling her stolen watch; in Tom Rakewell raising his fist to heaven; in the actresses shaking out their shabby finery; in the open mouth of the falling baby in Gin Lane; in the gold coach of Goodchild, the dice-playing of Tom Idle, the curling entrails of Tom Nero.

Generations grew up with these prints, their detailed references becoming mistier as time passed. In 1736 Abbé le Blanc had been amazed to find *A Rake's Progress* in ordinary houses across the country; in 1996 people still tell you that the *The Country Inn Yard* hung in their grandmother's hall, or that when they were young they looked every evening at *The Four Times of the Day* as they climbed the stairs.

In the winter of 1764 Jane and Anne, helped by Mary Lewis, took over the business of selling the prints. There were immediate practical problems to deal with. For some of the earlier works, the term of protection given by Hogarth's own Engravers Act had now run out and the pirates quickly moved in. Printsellers' practices had not changed, and even the names were the same; John Bowles had copied Hogarth in his time, and now his son Carington produced a pirated copy of *The Sleeping Congregation*.[12] Jane made a stand. By the beginning of February 1765, she had organized the printing of new impressions when needed and began to advertise again:

700

'The Works of Mr Hogarth, in separate prints or complete sets, may be had, as usual, at his late dwelling-house, the Golden head, in Leicester Fields; and NO WHERE ELSE . . . Commissions from abroad will be carefully executed; and particular regard had for the correctness of the Impressions.'[13]

The advertisement was repeated a month later. To keep the popular market, Jane also sold cheap copies of the prints herself.

In the immediate aftermath, the praise of Hogarth the moralist who 'reproved, instructed and delighted' his age was frequently repeated. It was heard in the obituaries, in the epitaph by James Townley in the *Public Ledger*, in the essay, probably by Morell, in the *Public Advertiser*.[14] Jane was a shrewd business woman, or she had good advisers. Building on Hogarth's 'moral' reputation, she commissioned the Reverend John Trusler to write a commentary, to be sold from the Golden Head. This was announced in August 1766:

'As many beauties in the late Mr. HOGARTH'S prints have hitherto escaped Notice for want of a minute Explanation, Mrs Hogarth has now engaged a Gentleman to explain each Print, and moralize on it in such a Manner as to make them instructive as well as entertaining.'[15]

Trusler's *Hogarth Moralised* appeared in 1768 with small copies of the prints, its subtitle presenting it as 'Calculated to improve the Minds of youth, and Convey Instruction, under the mask of Entertainment'. In the mid-nineteenth century, new editions of Trusler appeared, with gold-tooled bindings and commentaries starring heroines with throbbing hearts and villains who say 'Ha! Ha!' Turned into melodrama, cleaned up, with all excrement and nastiness removed, Hogarth became a Victorian. The *Cornhill* applauded:

'The anchor which held Hogarth fastest to the public favour, was the sincere and deliberate belief – prevalent among the more serious of the substantial orders – that his Works were in the highest degree moral, and that they contributed to the inculcation of Virtue and Piety.'

He was also, the magazine declared, 'The Philosopher who ever preached the sturdy English virtues that have made us what we are.'[16]

Yet I doubt whether anyone ever learned a direct moral lesson from Hogarth. People valued his prints as entertainment, of a peculiarly 'English' kind. In 1772 Lord Grantham, who was then Ambassador Extraordinary at the Court of Madrid and feeling his exile, told George Selwyn that he had 'sent for Fielding's works; for Tristram Shandy; and have even spoken about a set of Hogarth's prints; so precious do I hold English humour to be, especially in a place where a hearty laugh is really a cordial!'[17]

Hogarth prints accompanied colonists and settlers to America, Africa, India and later to New Zealand and Australia.

For most people, the grim side of Hogarth was subsumed under the comic. Other elements in his work faded too. The satire of individuals no longer had meaning, except perhaps for those two great rebels, Lovat and Wilkes. The ancient common language of emblems and signs became hard to decipher. Hogarth became part of the past, like the fashions and habits of the London he knew. On New Year's Eve 1818, when Keats wrote about passing fashions and taste, he asked 'With what sensation do you read Fielding? – and do not Hogarth's pictures seem an old thing to you?'[18]

But although they were old, the prints still had life. As Hogarth guessed, it was the detail, the vivid observation of the everyday, that never failed to fascinate – the pointed shoes, the decorative clocks on torn silk stockings, the cool gaze of a black servant, the easy way a fishwife carries a laden basket on her head. As they had in his lifetime, people continued to respond to Hogarth's extraordinary immediacy, to the caught gestures, perceived in a flash and retained in the mind. His pictures portrayed a whole age through individuals, as Hazlitt saw when he called them, in the strictest sense, 'Historical', or even, by analogy with Tom Jones, 'Epic Pictures':

'When I say that Hogarth treated his subjects historically I mean that his works represent the manners and humours of mankind in action, and their characters by individual expression. Everything in his pictures has life and motion in it. Not only does the business of the scene never stand still, but every feature and muscle is put into full play; the exact feeling of the moment is brought out, and carried to its utmost height, and then instantly seized and stamped on the canvas for ever.'[19]

Beneath this active, alluring surface Hogarth's work drew on fast-flowing currents of drama and story, sometimes explicit, sometimes elusive. It was for this reason that he was so often ranked with authors, not with artists. His prints, wrote Charles Lamb, 'are indeed books; they have the teeming, fruitful, suggestive meaning of words. Other Pictures we look at – his Prints we read.'[20] Hogarth said himself that his pictures were his stage, with actors who 'exhibit a dumb shew'. Yet his mute pictures spoke. They told of ambition and its pitfalls, of imitation and affectation, of striving egotism, of the greed for power. They spoke of fellowship, of families, streets and fairs and of the lonely individual in the crowd. They told of triumph and of death, not through great allegories of gods, princes and generals, but the small triumphs and forgotten deaths of aldermen and thieves, harlots and rakes and charity children.

Because he looked with acute perception at the lives of the common people, Hogarth's work – like an urban *Lyrical Ballads* – appealed to Romantics and Radicals. Wordsworth was overjoyed when he was sent a set of prints, 'there are perhaps few houses to which such a collection would be more welcome'.[21] Coleridge, too, thought Hogarth one of England's great men, absolutely *sui generis*.[22] Garibaldi, passing Hogarth's grave, was heard to mutter, 'il pittore del populo'.[23] Dickens, whose own father was imprisoned in the Marshalsea for debt, immersed himself early in Hogarth, 'from whom his greatest visual debt comes' and later hung *A Rake's Progress* all the way up his staircase at Gad's Hill: 'The Soul of Hogarth has migrated into the Body of Mr Dickens,' wrote Sydney Smith when he read *Sketches by Boz*.[24] And Hogarth lived on, too, on the popular stage. A Drury Lane playbill of 1880 announced a whole evening devoted to 'the Story of the '45':

Part I
A semi-Country Road in the Outskirts of London, with the
'ADAM AND EVE' TAVERN
Song and Chorus . . . ' Which nobody can Deny'
TABLEAU - HOGARTH'S
'MARCH TO FINCHLEY'[25]

Hogarth fed the imaginations of those that followed him.

In the early years, while the business of distributing the prints was being dealt with, Jane had also sorted through the canvases in Chiswick and Leicester Fields. She gave Samuel Martin his portrait, and Garrick and Violette theirs. But many paintings remained, hung on the walls or stacked away in safety. Leicester Fields remained the commercial base, and during the 1780s Mary Lewis arranged the sale of prints from there. Jane also rented rooms to lodgers, like the portrait painter and engraver Richard Livesay, and Thomas Cheeseman, engraver of *The Lady's Last Stake*. But from the early 1780s Chiswick was her principal home.

Life there was changed, but there was continuity. When the Directors of the Foundling Hospital decided that the children who had been under their

703

supervision in Chiswick should be sent back to the hospital, Jane replied indignantly. She wanted to keep them near by at least until the end of the year:

'imagining that if the Children which are under my inspection was Brought to the House when the Year was expired which is but a few months to come; it would be but a trifling expence to the House; but perhaps a Material Difference to the Children as they would enjoy the benefit of a run in the Country for the Summer Season, which in all probability would quite establish their Healths'.[26]

The Hogarths' house had never been quite childless. Another story told how Jane regularly asked the children of the village to come each summer and eat the mulberries from the tree on their lawn, 'a custom established by her husband'.

On 13 August 1771, aged seventy, Anne Hogarth died. She was buried near her brother William in Chiswick churchyard. That year it was decided to raise a proper monument to Hogarth, with a classical urn. Jane asked Garrick to write the epitaph and after much thought he produced the following –

> Farewell, great painter of mankind,
> Who reached the noblest point of art;
> Whose *pictur'd morals* charm the mind,
> And through the eye correct the heart.
>
> If *Genius* fire thee, reader, stay,
> If *Nature* touch thee, drop a tear;
> If neither moves thee, turn away,
> For *Hogarth*'s honoured dust lies here.

Perhaps his style was cramped by the occasion, or the widow's approval of Dr Trusler. But the poem is touching and Garrick was proud of it, sending a copy to John Hoadly: 'I have done it, as well as I can, & am lucky Enough to have it approv'd by those I wd wish to please – here it is for You.' Replying, Hoadly said, 'I have given it a Niche in my Temple of Immortality.'[27]

Garrick's decorous lines were cut into the stone beneath a design with a mask, laurel wreath, mahlstick, palette, pencils and a book, 'Analysis of Beauty'. The whole episode seemed comically un-Hogarthian – or at least far removed from the desecrator of the *Peregrination*. But while Garrick was mulling miserably over his verses, he had turned to Samuel Johnson for help.

VIEW FROM HOGARTH'S TOMB. CHISWICK.
London Pub: by D Walther Bryddges St. Covent Garden Aug.st 1823.

193 Hogarth's tomb in St Nicholas' Churchyard, Chiswick, with the Thames beyond

After one try, he sent Johnson his verses again, suggesting he simply ran his pen through the lines he liked least. Johnson's suggested emendation was simple and powerful:

> The hand of Art here torpid lies
> That traced the essential form of Grace:
> Here Death has closed the curious eyes
> That saw the manners in the face.[28]

The end of this decade saw other moves to 'place' Hogarth in history. The passion for collecting his prints began with Horace Walpole, who boasted 'the most complete collection of his prints that I believe exists', most of it assembled by Arthur Pond.[29] In October 1780 Walpole produced the fourth small, fat volume of his *Anecdotes of Painters*. It contained a shrewd chapter on 'that great and original genius, Hogarth' and a catalogue of his prints. To Walpole, Hogarth was a 'writer of comedy with a pencil', a Molière, 'catching the manners and follies of an age *living as they rise*'. He felt that Hogarth had no model, but 'created his art' on a plane of his own, between the sublime Italian and the Flemish burlesque, an art illuminated by the telling use of detail. Like Swift, wrote Walpole, Hogarth

705

'combined incidents that divert one from their unexpected encounter, and illustrate the tale he means to tell. Such are the hens roosting on the upright waves in the scene of the Strollers, and the devils drinking porter on the altar'.

Walpole was sympathetic and acute, but when he recounted Hogarth's life, he set his progress from obscurity to fame against his collapse into obsession, ending with *Sigismunda*. Such frankness did not please Jane, guardian of Hogarth's reputation. In pique she let herself be pressed into helping the editor, printer and inveterate collector of anecdotes John Nichols and the splenetic George Steevens – best known for his endless Shakespeare commentaries – only to find that their *Biographical Anecdotes* and catalogue of 1781 was more unacceptable still.[30] A second and a third edition of the *Anecdotes* soon appeared: Edmond Malone wrote to Charlemont of 'Hogarthomania' and William Cole (who sat to Hogarth in the 1730s, and whose sister was Jane's close friend) complained to Walpole, 'Mr Nichols is so quick in his publications that he hardly gives one time to read one before another pops upon you . . . this is sad, pickpocket stuff!'[31] Within the next thirty years, with the works of John Ireland, and Samuel Ireland, and Nichols's and Steevens's *Genuine Works*, Hogarth was given a 'life'.

In her lifetime Jane had sensibly kept Hogarth's late papers unpublished, preferring to let the public judge him by his work. For two decades, while she guarded and hallowed his reputation, it seemed that Hogarth's desire to support her after his death would be fulfilled. In June 1767, a revised Engravers' Act carried a special clause, securing her the copyright for a further twenty years. When this expired in 1787, although she had arranged for copies, and for engravings of Hogarth's drawings to be made by Richard Livesay, her income shrank. She appealed, of all places, to the Royal Academy, and was given an annual pension of £40. A dignified figure, she was remembered progressing slowly up the aisle of Chiswick Church, wearing a black silk sacque, raised head-dress and black calash, and carrying her crutched cane, accompanied by Mary Lewis. In front of her went her grey-haired servant Samuel, who would wheel her to church in her bath chair, carry in the prayer books and shut the pew door.[32]

Jane Hogarth died at the age of eighty, on 10 November 1789. She had lived to see the return of Wilkes, his imprisonment and triumphant popular re-election to Parliament in 1774, while still technically an outlaw. She witnessed Garrick retire from Drury Lane in 1776, and his death three years later. The world her husband had known was passing fast: Britain lost the

706

American colonies; London suffered the terrible Gordon Riots; Pitt's son, another William, became prime minister of a Tory government; the Channel was crossed in an air balloon; James Watt perfected his steam engine. Four months before Jane died came the fall of the Bastille, the start of the French Revolution.

When the time came to open up the Hogarth tomb to receive Jane's coffin, there was a macabre moment. Hogarth's corpse was nowhere to be seen. It took a second to remember that the vault had been built long after he was buried. His body lay deeper still, beneath the stone floor, beneath the imposing monument with Garrick's solemn verse, deep in the Thames-side earth.

After Jane's death, Mary Lewis sold her right in Hogarth's copper plates for an annuity of £250, on which she lived in Chiswick until she died in 1808. The purchaser was John Boydell, who produced a new folio, with additional plates, in 1790: among the newly made prints of Hogarth's paintings was *The Beggar's Opera*, Act III, etched and engraved by William Blake.[33] Other reissues appeared up to 1850, when the plates were laid by. (In the end many were given to the British government to be melted down for copper for bombs in the First World War – a rather Hogarthian fate.)[34]

Mary also disposed of the household's prints and paintings. From time to time, Jane had sold odd paintings, but never *Sigismunda*; she would not let this go for less than the £400 Hogarth had demanded. In 1790, it was included in the auction of the remaining works. At twelve o'clock, on Saturday, 24 April, when the curious turned up at the Golden Head, *Sigismunda* was knocked down to John Boydell for £58 16s.

Jane had kept other paintings: the portraits of herself and her mother, of Anne and Mary Hogarth, Hogarth's own self-portrait, the heads of their servants and *The Shrimp Girl*, which she showed so proudly to visitors. These too went in the sale, as did Roubiliac's bust of Hogarth and of his pug, and a mass of prints and drawings. Among these were academy figures and studies dating from Hogarth's youth, and prints by other artists conjuring up the world he inherited, studied from and worked in. Here were Vandergucht's engravings of Thornhill's paintings in St Paul's and a book containing sixty-one prints, engravings of the Kit-Cat Club portraits and of paintings by Van Dyck, Rubens, and Kneller. The catalogue amounted to a small library of predecessors, colleagues and rivals: plates from Watteau's *Receuil*; Pine's engravings of the Armada Tapestry; Pond's and Knapton's *Imitations of Drawings of Old Masters*; Ghezzi caricatures; prints by Vivares and Strange.

At the end, after the paintings were sold, and the colour cabinet and the

707

mahogany cupboard from Hogarth's painting room, came odd lots. Horace Walpole bought lot 66: twelve Delftware plates, painted in August 1711, 'by Sir James Thornhill, representing the sciences, *very curious*'. But no record survives of who walked away with 'half a ream of French printing paper' or 'sundry frames and odd articles'.[35]

With this sale, Hogarth's working world was finally dismantled. And although Turner later donated Hogarth's palette to the Royal Academy and Whistler recognized him as a forebear, his legacy was not the founding of 'an English school of painting'. That was left to the classicists, Reynolds and his heirs. Instead Hogarth's spirit flowed on through the popular graphic arts, into the cartoons of Gillray and Rowlandson and the graphic narratives of Cruikshank.[36] Although imbued with imagination and emotion, his was a punning, witty, *thinking* art: he would have liked the eclecticism and multiple references of much modern art and writing, the special effects of films, the acid narratives of modern newspaper cartoonists and graphic artists. When David Hockney brought his sketchbooks back from America as a student in 1961, he thought of *A Rake's Progress*. It seemed natural to transpose the story of a young man in London in the 1730s to modern New York, transforming himself with a bottle of Lady Clairol, drinking in gay bars, and ending in a Bedlam of T-shirted robots. Hogarth continues to cross boundaries, to explore the lonely individual in the city.[37]

Although he played a part in the eighteenth-century project of politeness, Hogarth was never quite polite himself. Many of his battles were foolish, spurred by wounded vanity. But his prints challenged people to see clearly and control their fates, to defy passions within and oppressive powers without. As an artist, too, he battled for autonomy. He fought for the exhibition at the Foundling Hospital, for the Academy at St Martin's Lane, for the Engravers Act. And he knew – as Reynolds did – that it was vital for artists, not connoisseurs, to dictate taste.

Hogarth was driven by vision as well as ambition. Whether arguing for the true line of beauty or the best way to run his profession, he never confessed himself beaten. After the sale of 1790, the lease on the house in Leicester Fields ended and the 'Golden Head' was no more. But from time to time someone would recall seeing Hogarth there, or in St Martin's Lane, or Covent Garden, or the maze of streets in between. The painter James Barry, who came to London the year before Hogarth died, remembered walking through Cranbourn Alley with Joseph Nollekens, the sculptor. Suddenly Nollekens called out,

708

'"There, There's Hogarth." "What!" said I, "that little man in the sky blue coate?" Off I ran, and though I lost sight of him only for a moment or two, when I turned the corner into Castle Street, he was patting one of two quarreling boys on the back.'[38]

But Hogarth was not promoting peace. He had dived into the fight, and now, 'looking steadfastly at the expression in the coward's face, cried, "Damn him! if I would take it of him; at him again!"'

NOTES

Abbreviations in the Notes

Details of other works are given the first time they are cited in each chapter; thereafter short titles are used. Place of publication is London, unless otherwise specified.

A   William Hogarth, *The Analysis of Beauty*, ed. Joseph Burke (Oxford, 1955). This includes the 'Autobiographical Notes'.

Allen (1984)   Brian Allen, *Francis Hayman and the English Rococo* (Ph.D. thesis, University of London: Courtauld Institute of Art, 1984)

Allen (1987)   Brian Allen, *Francis Hayman* (1987)

Antal   Frederick Antal, *Hogarth and His Place in European Art* (1962)

Ap   'Hogarth's "Apology for Painters"', ed. Michael Kitson, *The Walpole Society*, XLI (Oxford, 1968), 46–111

Atherton   Herbert M. Atherton, *Political Prints in the Age of Hogarth: A Study of the Ideographic Representation of Politics* (Oxford, 1974)

Baldini   *L'Opera Completa di Hogarth pittore*, ed. Gabriele Baldini (Milan, 1967)

Barrell   John Barrell, *The Political Theory of Painting from Reynolds to Hazlitt: 'The Body of the Public'* (New Haven, 1986)

Battestin   Martin C. Battestin, with Ruthe R. Battestin, *Henry Fielding: A Life* (1989)

Beckett   R. B. Beckett, *Hogarth* (1949)

Bertelsen   Lance Bertelsen, *The Nonsense Club* (Oxford, 1986)

Bindman   David Bindman, *Hogarth* (1981)

BL   British Library

BM   British Museum

BM Sat.   *Catalogue of Political and Personal Satires in the British Museum*, 11 vols; vols I–V ed. F. G. Stephens (1873–83); vols VI–XI ed. D. M. George (1938–54)

Boswell *Journal*   *The London Journal of James Boswell, 1762–3*, ed. Frederick A. Pottle; *Yale Editions of the Private Papers of James Boswell*, I (New Haven, 1950)

Boswell *Life*   *Boswell's Life of Johnson*, ed. G. B. Hill, revised and enlarged by L. F. Powell, 6 vols (Oxford, 1934–50)

Brewer   John Brewer, *Pleasures of the Imagination: English Culture in the Eighteenth Century* (1997)

Charlemont   *The manuscripts and correspondence of James, first Earl of Charlemont*, Historical Manuscripts Commission, 12th report (1891)

Churchill   *The Poetical Works of Charles Churchill*, ed. Douglas Grant (Oxford, 1956)

Colley   Linda Colley, *Britons: Forging the Nation 1707–1837* (1992)

DA   Daily Advertiser

Dabydeen *Commercial Britain*   David Dabydeen, *Hogarth, Walpole and Commercial Britain* (1987)

Dabydeen *Hogarth's Blacks*   David Dabydeen, *Hogarth's Blacks:Images of Blacks in Eighteenth-century English Art* (Kingston-upon-Thames, 1985)

DC   Daily Courant

Delany   *The Autobiography and Correspondence of Mary Granville, Mrs Delany* , ed. Lady Llanover, 6 vols (1861)

Deutsch   Otto Eric Deutsch, *Handel: A Documentary Biography* (1955)

DJ   Daily Journal

Dobson   Austin Dobson, *William Hogarth* (1907)

Donald   Diana Donald, *The Age of Caricature: Satirical Portraits in the Reign of George III* (New Haven and London, 1996)

DP   Daily Post

Edwards   Edward Edwards, *Anecdotes of Painters who have resided or been born in England* (1808)

Fielding *Joseph Andrews*   Henry Fielding, *Joseph Andrews and Shamela*, ed. Douglas Brooks-Davies (Oxford, 1966)

Fielding *Tom Jones*   Henry Fielding, *Tom Jones*, ed. R. C. Mutter, (Harmondsworth, 1966)

Fitzw.   Fitzwilliam Museum, Cambridge

Garrick   *The Letters of David Garrick*, ed. D. M. Little and G. M. Kahrl, 3 vols (1963)

Gay *Dramatic Works*   John Gay, *Dramatic Works*, ed. John Fuller, 2 vols (Oxford, 1983)

Gay *Letters*   *The Letters of John Gay*, ed. C. F. Burgess (Oxford, 1966)

Gay *Poetry and Prose*   John Gay, *Poetry and Prose*, ed. Winton A. Dearing, 2 vols (Oxford, 1974)

George *Caricature*   Dorothy M. George, *English Political Caricature to 1792: A Study of Opinion and Propaganda* (Oxford, 1959)

George *London*   Dorothy George, *London Life in the Eighteenth Century* (1925); references are to the 1966 edition.

GI   Samuel Ireland, *Graphic Illustrations of Hogarth*, 2 vols (1794–9)

Gilmour   Ian Gilmour, *Riot, Risings and Revolution: Governance and Violence in Eighteenth-Century England* (1992)

GL   Guildhall Library

GM   Gentleman's Magazine

Gowing   Lawrence Gowing, *Hogarth*, Tate catalogue (1971)

GSJ   Grub-Street Journal

GW   John Nichols and George Steevens, *The Genuine Works of William Hogarth*, 3 vols (1808–17)

Hallett   Mark Hallett, *The Spectacle of Difference: Graphic Satire and Urban Culture in London, 1700–1751* (unpublished Ph.D. thesis, University of London: Courtauld Institute, 1996). A book is forthcoming.

Hammelmann   Hans Hammelmann (edited and completed by T. S. R. Boase) *Book Illustrators in Eighteenth-Century England* (1975)

Hazlitt   *The Complete Works of William Hazlitt*, ed. P. P. Howe, 21 vols (1931)

Hervey   John, Lord Hervey, *Some Materials towards Memoirs of the Reign of King George II*, ed. Romney Sedgwick (1931)

HGW   Ronald Paulson, *Hogarth's Graphic Works* (New Haven, 1965; rev. edns, 1970, 1989); references, unless otherwise specified, are to the 1989 edition.

HI   John Ireland, *Hogarth Illustrated*, 3 vols (1791–8; 3rd edn, corrected, 1806, 1812)

HLAT   Ronald Paulson, *Hogarth, His Life, Art and Times*, 2 vols (New Haven, 1971)

Hogarth the Painter   Elizabeth Einberg, *Hogarth the Painter*, Tate catalogue (1997)

Jarrett   Derek Jarrett, *The Ingenious Mr Hogarth* (1976)

Keates   Jonathan Keates, *Handel: The Man and His Music* (1985)

Kerslake   John Kerslake, *Early Georgian Portraits*, 2 vols (1977)

Klingender   F. D. Klingender, *Hogarth and English Caricature* (1944), including the catalogue of the Artists International exhibition, 1943.

Langford   Paul Langford, *A Polite and Commercial People: England 1727–1783* (Oxford, 1989)

LC   London Chronicle

LDP   London Daily Post

LEP   *London Evening Post*

Lichtenberg   Georg Christoph Lichtenberg, *Lichtenberg's Commentaries on Hogarth's Engravings*, (1784–6; rev. edn, 1794–9), trans. and ed. Innes and Gustav Herdan (1966)

Lindsay   Jack Lindsay, *Hogarth: His Art and His World* (1977)

Lippincott   Louise Lippincott, *Selling Art in Georgian London: The Rise of Arthur Pond* (New Haven, 1983)

LJ   *London Journal*

LM   *The London Magazine*

The London Stage   *The London Stage*, 11 vols (Southern Illinois, 1968); Part 2, *1700–1729*, ed. Emmett L. Avery

Lonsdale   *The New Oxford Book of Eighteenth Century Verse*, ed. Roger Lonsdale (Oxford, 1984)

Manners and Morals   Elizabeth Einberg (ed.), *Manners and Morals: Hogarth and British Painting 1700–1760*, Tate catalogue (1987)

Millar   Oliver Millar, *Tudor, Stuart and Early Georgian Pictures in the Collection of Her Majesty the Queen* (1963)

Mitchell   Charles Mitchell (ed.), *Hogarth's Peregrination* (Oxford, 1952)

Moore   Robert E. Moore, *Hogarth's Literary Relationships* (Minneapolis, 1948)

NG   National Gallery, London

N   John Nichols, *Biographical Anecdotes of William Hogarth with a Catalogue of His Works* (1781, 1782, 1785); references are to the 3rd edn, facsimile reprint, introduced by R. W. Lightbown (1971).

NPG   National Portrait Gallery, London

Omberg   Hildegard Omberg, *William Hogarth's Portrait of Captain Coram: Studies in Hogarth's Outlook around 1740* (Uppsala, 1974)

Oppé   A. P. Oppé, *The Drawings of William Hogarth* (1933)

P   Ronald Paulson, *Hogarth*, 3 vols (Rutgers, 1991–3): I *'The Modern Moral Subject'*, *1697–1732*; II *High Art and Low, 1732–1750*; III *Art and Politics, 1750–1764*

Pears   Iaian Pears, *The Discovery of Painting: the Growth of Interest in the Arts in England, 1680-1678* (New Haven, 1988)

Pointon   Marcia Pointon, *Hanging the Head: Portraiture and Social Formation in Eighteenth-Century England* (New Haven and London, 1993)

Pope *Poems*   *The Poems of Alexander Pope*, ed. John Butt (1963)

PA   *Public Advertiser*

Pye   John Pye, *Patronage of British Art* (1845)

Pyne   [Walter Pyne], *Wine and Walnuts; or After Dinner-Chit Chat* by Ephraim
Hardcastle, Citizen and Dry-Salter, 2nd edn, 2 vols (1824)

Quennell   Peter Quennell, *Hogarth's Progress* (1955)

Richardson   *The Works of Jonathan Richardson* (1793)

Rococo   *Rococo: Art and Design in Hogarth's England*, V&A catalogue (1984)

Rouquet *Lettres*   Jean André Rouquet, *Lettres de Monsieur** à un de ses amis à Paris* (1746)

Rouquet *State of the Arts*   Jean André Rouquet, *The Present State of the Arts in England*
(1755)

SJC   *St James's Chronicle*

Saussure   César de Saussure, *A Foreign View of England in the Reigns of George I and
George II* (1725), trans. Madame de Muyden (1902)

Shawe-Taylor   Desmond Shawe-Taylor, *The Georgians: Eighteenth-Century Portraiture
and Society* (1990)

Simon   Robin Simon, *The Portrait in Britain and America* (Oxford, 1987)

Smart   Alastair Smart, *Allan Ramsay: Painter, Essayist and Man of the Enlightenment* (New
Haven and London, 1992)

Smith   J. T. Smith, *Nollekens and His Times* (1828), ed. Wilfred Whitten, 2 vols (1917)

Solkin   David H. Solkin, *Painting for Money: The Visual Arts and the Public Sphere in
Eighteenth-Century England* (Newhaven and London, 1993)

Spectator   *The Spectator*, ed. Donald F. Bond, 5 vols (Oxford, 1965)

Sterne *Tristram Shandy*   Laurence Sterne, *The Life and Opinions of Tristram Shandy*
(1759), ed. Graham Petrie (Harmondsworth, 1967)

Swift *Corr.*   *The Correspondence of Jonathan Swift*, ed. Harold Williams, 6 vols (Oxford,
1963)

Swift *Poems*   *Jonathan Swift: the Complete Poems*, ed. Pat Rogers (New Haven and London,
1987)

Tate   Tate Gallery, London

Tate Coll.   Elizabeth Einberg and Judy Egerton, *Tate Gallery Collections*, II: *The Age of
Hogarth, British Painters Born 1675–1709* (1988)

V&A   Victoria and Albert Museum, London

Vertue   George Vertue, *Notebooks*, 6 vols, *The Walpole Society* (Oxford, 1934–50):
I, vol. XVII (1929–30); II, vol. XX (1931–2); III, vol. XXII (1933–4); IV, vol. XXIV (1935–6);
V, vol. XXVI (1937–8); VI, vol. XXX (1948–50)

Waterhouse *Painting* Ellis Waterhouse, *Painting in England, 1530 to 1790* (1953)

Waterhouse *Three Decades* Ellis Waterhouse, *Three Decades of British Art* (1965)

Walpole *Anec.* Horace Walpole, *Anecdotes of Painting in England*, 4 vols (1771–80); references are to vol. IV (1780), 1786 edn.

Walpole *Corr.* *Horace Walpole's Correspondence*, ed. W. S. Lewis, 44 vols (New Haven, 1937–83)

Walpole *Memoirs II* Horace Walpole, *Memoirs of King George II*, ed. John Brooke, 3 vols (New Haven, 1985)

Walpole *Memoirs III* Horace Walpole, *Memoirs of the Reign of King George III*, ed. Denis le Marchant, 4 vols (1845)

Weatherly *The Correspondence of John Wilkes and Charles Churchill*, ed. Edward H. Weatherly (New York, 1954)

Webster Mary Webster, *Hogarth* (1979)

Whitley W. T. Whitley, *Artists and Their Friends in England, 1700–1799*, 2 vols (1928)

Notes

PREFACE: Picturing a World

1 'The Work of Hogarth', in *Lectures on The English Comic Writers* (1819), Hazlitt, VI, 140–41.
2 A Bristol mob in 1754; Colley, 155–6.
3 See N, *HI*, *GI* and *GW* in the list of abbreviations.

CHAPTER 1: Smithfield Muses

1 For the quotations, and the area destroyed by the Fire, see Felix Barker and Peter Jackson, *The History of London in Maps* (1994); see also W. G. Bell, *The Fire of London* (1923).
2 GL MS 6778/1. For archival sources, see *HLAT*, and P, I, 340–50.
3 John Stow, *A Survey of the Cities of London and Westminster, 1698. Corrected, improved and very much enlarged, 1720 by John Strype . . . brought down to the present by careful hands*, 2 vols, 6th edn (1754–5), I, 714.
4 Ibid., I, 719.
5 Nonconformist Register (no. 4), GL 6780.
6 *HI*, I, vii, accepts St Bees, as does Dobson, 11.
7 For the press, see F. Siebert, *Freedom of the Press in England, 1476–1776* (Urbana, 1952); Michael Jarris and Alan Lee, eds., *The Press in English Society from the Seventeenth to Nineteenth Centuries* (London and Toronto, 1986), and Jeremy Black, *The English Press in the Eighteenth Century* (1987).
8 Jonathan Keates, *Purcell* (1995), 201.
9 *Thesaurum Trilingue Publicum: Being an Introduction to English, Latin and Greek*, (1689); Sold by Randal Taylor, nr Stationers-Hall. This book was found in the BM and credited to Richard Hogarth by Dobson, 14. A facsimile reprint (Menston, 1971) of a Shrewsbury School copy cites it as a 'valuable and hitherto unrecognized source' for seventeenth-century pronunciation. The first part teaches spelling and punctuation, with twice-daily lessons. The second teaches Greek, 'so plain that an *English* Scholar may (for the most part) *Accent* any *Greek* truly according to Grammar'.
10 Ibid., 71.
11 *Gazophylacium Anglicanum*. Quoted in P, I, 4–5.
12 For topography, culture and literary treatment, see Pat Rogers, *Grub Street: Studies in a Sub-Culture* (1972).
13 Henry Fielding, *The Author's Farce* (1730), ed. Charles B. Woods (1967), 30.

717

14 Lewis Maidwell, *Essay upon the Necessity and Excellence of Education* (1705); Keates, *Purcell*, 173.

15 Richard corrected the *Opera Posthuma* of Marcello Malpighi. See Latin letters, N, 4–5, and *HLAT*, II, app. C, 484–5. He also approached Thomas Gale (former Cambridge Professor of Greek, now head of St Paul's School), ran errands for the Countess Dowager of Carlisle (Thomas Noble was her Chaplain) and contacted with Lord Carlisle. See P, I, 11–13.

16 George, *London*, 94.

17 'A Description of a City Shower', Swift *Poems*, 114.

18 *A*, 204.

19 Ned Ward, *The London Spy* (1702), ed. Ralph Straus (1924), 239–40. For Bartholomew Fair, see Sybil Rosenfeld, *The Theatre of the London Fairs in the Eighteenth Century* (Cambridge, 1960), 9–11. See also W. Boulton, *The Amusements of Old London* (1900), and R. D. Altick, *The Shows of London* (1978).

20 Lord Mayor's ordinance; Henry Morley, *Memoirs of Bartholomew Fair* (1880).

21 Morley, *Bartholemew Fair*, 262.

22 Ward, *The London Spy*, 269.

23 Morley, *Bartholomew Fair*, 290–91.

24 To the Countess of Burlington, 28 August 1726, Gay *Letters*, 53–4.

25 Ward, *The London Spy*, 263–4.

26 For a well-argued warning about generalizations concerning children in eighteenth-century art, and a reading of Hogarth's paintings, see Pointon, ch. v, 'The State of the Child'.

27 George Rude, *Hanoverian London: 1714–1808* (1971), 75.

28 *Post-Man*, 8–11 January 1704; reproduced in Bryant Lillywhite, *London Coffee Houses* (1963), 269–70.

29 Aytoun Ellis, *The Penny Universities: A History of the London Coffee-Houses* (1956), 44.

30 Ward, *The London Spy*, 11.

31 Pamphlet of 1665, in Ellis, *The Penny Universities*, 256.

32 *Spectator*, I, 3–4; no. 1, 1 March 1711.

33 Jonathan Swift, *Journal to Stella*, ed. Harold Williams, 2 vols (Oxford, 1948), I, 167; 16 January 1711.

34 Daggastaff, *DC*, 23 June 1701: Lillywhite, *London Coffee Houses*, 270.

35 P, I, 5, n. 23. and ch. 1 *passim* for Hogarth relations.

36 His facility is implied by his work with Rouquet and by a translation of a chapter from Watelet's *Art de Peindre* (1760), University of Illinois library. See John Dussinger, *William Hogarth's Translation of Watelet on Grace* (Chicago, 1983), and Dussinger's article in *Burlington Magazine* 126 (1984) 691–4.

37 Suggested in Jarrett, 19–21. Comenius' chief works, *Orbis Sensualium Pictus* and *Janua Linguarum Trilingua*, appeared in English editions from the late 1650s.

38 *A*, 204.

39 See Gilmour, 41–56.

40 Jarrett, 24.

41 *The Picture of Malice or a true Account of Dr. Sacheverell's Enemies*, in George, *Caricature*, 66. For Sacheverell portraits and prints, see also Hallett, 27–35.

42 In George, *London Life*, 297.

43 See *The Rumours of the Fleet* (1739), 2–5, and John Ashton, *The Fleet: its Rivers, Prison*, 2nd edn (1888), 260–71.

44 Swift, *Journal to Stella*, I, 171; 21 January 1711.

45 *DC*, 13 January 1709.

46 BL, Portland Loan: Harley Papers 26 (1710), 172; *HLAT*, II, app. C, 485–6.

47 Ibid. He adds that it is 'in the manner of Elisha Coles', i.e. based on Coles's Latin–English, English–Latin dictionary, 1677.

48 *GW*, I, 67.

49 *Disputationes Grammaticales*, with English and Latin dialogues, published by William Taylor in 1711; *New School Dialogues*, 1713, 'composed and digested by R.H.', appeared from the competing firm of John Wyatt.

50 P, I, 31.

51 *A*, 204–5.

52 For the original painting (Birmingham Art Gallery), see Beckett, 65, plate 82, and Baldini, 97, plates 70 and XIV. See *HGW*, 101–3, for Elisha Kirkall's frontispiece to *The Works of Tom Brown* (1708 edn) and the description of a poet in *GSJ*, 2 May 1734. Hogarth's 1736 print has a caption from *The Dunciad*, Book I:

> Studious he sate, with all his books around,
> Sinking from thought to thought, a vast profound!
> Plung'd for his sense, but found no bottom there:
> Then write, and flounder'd on, in mere despair.

CHAPTER 2: Mapping the Town

1 *A*, 201.

2 Dobson, 15, noted the marriage of Edmund Hogarth to Sarah Gambell, 12 August 1707, at All-Hallows-in-the-Wall. Also P, I, 38 9.

3 Gladys Scott Thomson, *The Russells in Bloomsbury, 1669–1771* (1940), 257.

4 John Richardson, *London and Its People* (1995).

5 George Augustus Sala, *William Hogarth* (1866), 59.

6 John Nichols, note to *Tatler*, no. 16. (See *Spectator*, I, 61, n. 2.) Powell was at Covent Garden from 1711 until his death in 1729.

7 John Evelyn, in John Summerson, *Georgian London*, rev. edn (1988), 25.

8 *The Foreigner's Guide* (1729), 8.

9 Daniel Defoe, *A Tour Through England and Wales*, (1724; London: Everyman, 1962), 329.

10 Sterne, *Tristram Shandy*, 73–4.

11 Christopher Hibbert, *London, The Biography of a City* (1969; Harmondsworth, 1980), 145.

12 Saussure, 204–5, 207.

13 'A Description of the Morning' (1709), Swift *Poems*, 107.

14 'Trivia, Or, The Art of Walking the Streets of London', Gay *Poetry and Prose*, I, 135.

15 Ibid., 150–51.

16 Defoe, *Tour*, 292.

17 Saussure, 81.

18 *The Tatler*, ed. Donald F. Bond, 3 vols (Oxford, 1987), I, 145; no. 18, 21 May 1709.

19 Tom Brown, *Amusements Serious and Comical*, in *Works*, 3rd edn (1715), III, 67–8.

20 *Spectator*, I, 115–18; no. 28, 2 April 1711.

21 Although they endured until the 1760s, the signs were finally banished by statute and only those over the pubs were left.

22 By the 1720s there were about 12,000 permanent employees in government service. Geoffrey Holmes, *Augustan England: Professions, State and Society, 1680–1730* (1982), 255.

23 John Brewer, *The Sinews of Power: War, Money and the English State, 1688–1783* (1989), 118.

24 Harley aimed to raise £9 million investment in the South Sea Company, to fund the debt and create an independent check on the power of the Bank of England; profits were to come from trade with Spanish America after the war.

25 [Daniel Defoe], *The Villany of Stock-Jobbers Detected* (1701), 21–2, quoted in Dabydeen *Commercial Britain*, 16.

26 Defoe, *Tour*, 336.

27 Jonathan Swift, *The Examiner*, no. 13, 2 November 1710.

28 'Trivia', Gay *Poetry and Prose*, I, 138.

29 Daniel Defoe, *Review*, II, 9; 6 March 1705.

30 *Spectator*, I, 295; no. 69, 19 May 1711.

31 Richard Steele, *The Conscious Lovers*, Act IV, scene ii, in *The Plays of Richard Steele*, ed. Shirley Strum Kenny (Oxford, 1971), 359.

32 See Gilmour, 65–72.

33 John Stow, *Survey of London*, 2 vols, 6th edn (1754–5), I, 58.

CHAPTER 3: Pleasures and Studies

1 Rejected passage from *The Analysis of Beauty*; *A*, 185.

2 One attributed piece (dubious) is a snuffbox with vignettes from *The Rape of the Lock*; *HGW*, 198, plates 244, 245.

3 D. Jocelyn Dunlop, *English Apprenticeship and Child Labour* (1912), 118.

4 Steven Rappaport, *World Within Worlds* (Cambridge, 1989), 236, 327; Ilana Krausman Ben-Amos, *Adolescence and Youth in Early Modern England* (New Haven and London, 1994), 130.

5 Daniel Defoe, *The Family Instructor* (1715), II, 262.

6 Dunlop, 182, 189; Ben-Amos, 293.

7 'Trivia', Gay *Poetry and Prose*, I, 153.

8 Saussure, 162; for cockfights and gladiators, see 276–82.

9 In George Rude, *Hanoverian London 1714–1808* (1971), 92.

10 Oppé, 31, catalogue and plates 6–7.

11 Lord Macaulay, *The History of England from the Accession of James II*, 6 vols (1913), I, 410.

12 *Weekly Register*, 9 June 1731, 'The Grub-Street Ballad Singer'.

13 Roy Palmer, *A Ballad History of England from 1588 to the Present Day* (1979), 8.

14 *London Journal*, 7 May 1726, in A. D. Harvey, *Sex in Georgian England* (1994), 133.

15 Ibid., 124. For context, see Rictor Norton, *Mother Clap's Molly-House: the gay subculture in England, 1700–1830* (1992) and Kent Gerard and Gert Hallma (eds), *The Pursuit of*

Sodomy: Male Homosexuality in Renaissance and Enlightenment Europe (New York and London, 1989).

16 Henry Fielding, *Jonathan Wild* (1741), ed. David Nokes (Oxford, 1982), 110. With thanks to Lucy Moore.

17 Ben-Amos, 199–200.

18 *Spectator*, I, 10; no. 2, 2 May 1711.

19 *The London Stage*, 2, xviii.

20 To Pope, January 1717; Gay *Letters*, 31–2.

21 John Macky, *Journey Through England* (1714), 2nd edn (1722), 170–71.

22 *A*, 201, 205.

23 The only men held in any esteem were Simon Gribelin, and Michiel Vandergucht.

24 Vertue, III, 7–8.

25 See Donald, 1–3; Richard Godfrey, *Printmaking in Britain* (New York, 1978), 24, and Lippincott, 128. For a general overview, see Timothy Clayton, *The English Print, 1688–1802*, (1997).

26 For the context sketched in this paragraph, see Hallett, 3–35.

27 Precursors, including Francis Barlow (1626–1704), Francis le Piper (1640–1698) and Egbert van Heemskerk (1634/5–1704), are noted in the typescript catalogue, BM exhibition of prints and drawings, 1964 (Paul Mellon Centre). For Barlow, see also David Kunzle, *History of the Early Comic Strip*, (Berkeley, 1973/London, 1974), 133–6.

28 Le Piper also produced paintings of Samuel Butler's *Hudibras*, engraved for an edition of 1702 that Hogarth later copied.

29 Brewer, 455.

30 *A*, 201.

31 *A*, 185.

32 N, 15; *GW*, I, 24.

33 N, 7; *GW*, III, 13–14.

34 *A*, 206.

35 Ibid., 208.

36 Ibid., 210.

37 N, 63.

38 *A*, 211.

39 Oppé, 12.

40 See Lindsay, 15, on *The Invasion* and caricature.

41 *GW*, I, 15; see also N, 8.

42 Donald, 4–5.

43 Donald, 56; and 42–58 *passim*.

44 *Gulliver's Travels* (1726), irresistibly quoted in this context by Klingender, ix. (In this passage Swift ridicules the government hysteria over the Jacobite Atterbury plot of 1723.)

45 For this blending of traditions, see Klingender, iii–v, and for Hogarth's use of the classical emblematic tradition, and eighteenth-century reading structures, in art, sculpture and landscape gardening, see R. Paulson, *Emblem and Expression* (1975).

46 *A*, 42.

47 The standard work was Cesar Ripa's *Iconologia, or Moral Emblems*. Advertised as of special use to orators, painters and sculptors, this heavy tome offered 'various images

of virtues, vices, passions, arts, humours, elements and celestial bodies', taken from Egypt, Greece and Rome as well as 'Modern Italians'; see Jarrett, 28–30.

48 Ibid., 147.

49 Ibid., 108.

50 E.S. Lumsden, *The Art of Etching* (1924), 51.

51 *A*, 210.

52 *HI*, III, 321.

CHAPTER 4: Meeting the Artists

1 Joseph Highmore to Sir Edward Walpole, 28 February–3 March 1764, *GM*, 86, April 1816, 300–304; paraphrased in Whitley, I, 23–4.

2 Vertue, III, 7.

3 The French Academy laid down rules both for technical training and aesthetic hierarchies; no non-members could apply for Court or royal patronage. Rica Jones, 'The Artists' Training and Techniques' in *Manners and Morals*, 19; also, Nikolaus Pevsner, *Academies of Art, Past and Present* (Cambridge, 1940) 25–93.

4 *Ap*, 93.

5 Whitley, I, 18.

6 See Hammelmann, 79–86.

7 Vertue, III, 11.

8 Walpole *Anec.*, 67.

9 For Chéron's possible influence on Hogarth, see Omberg, 25–30.

10 Walpole *Anec.*, 10.

11 Ibid., 11, and Pyne, II, 134.

12 William Cheselden (1688–1752) published *The Anatomy of the Human Body* (1712), with drawings by Highmore for the 2nd edition in 1722, and is most famous for *Osteographia, or the Anatomy of the Bones* (1733), with drawings by G. Vandergucht and J. Schinvoet made by means of a 'camera obscura'.

13 Walpole *Anec.*, 125.

14 Pyne, II, 37–8.

15 Review of Northcote's *Life of Reynolds*, *European Magazine*, LXIV, 1813, 415; in Allen, 21.

16 Lord Radnor to Dr Cox Munro (n.d.); Whitley, I, 81.

17 Vertue, III, 6.

18 Ellis Waterhouse, *Painting in Britain, 1530 to 1790*, 2nd edn (1962), 107.

19 Edwards, 19–20.

20 Pyne, I, 112–13.

21 *GI*, I, 115; for the bookcase, see Elisabeth Einberg, *George Lambert* (1970), 6.

22 See Robin Simon, 'Hogarth and the Popular Theatre', *Renaissance and Modern Studies*, 12 (1978), 13–25.

23 Vertue, III, 105. See also Lippincott, 21.

24 Walpole *Anec.*, 236.

25 *Ap*, 86–7.

26 William Kent to Burrell Massingberd (n.d.), quoted in James Lees Milne, *Earls of Creation* (1962), 122. For Kent, see also Margaret Jourdain, *The Works of William Kent*

(1948); John Harris, *The Palladians* (1981), and Michael Wilson, *William Kent* (1984).

27 To Burrell Massingberd, 19 January 1720, quoted in John Harris, *The Palladian Revival: Lord Burlington, His Villa and Garden and Chiswick* (1995), 41.

28 Anthony Ashley Cooper, 3rd Earl of Shaftesbury, *Characteristics of Men, Manners, Opinions, Times* (1711), 2 vols in one, ed. John M. Robertson (Indianopolis and New York, 1964), 146.

29 'Epistle to the Right Honorable Paul Methuen, Esq', Gay *Poetry and Prose*, I, 216–17.

30 *A*, 63.

31 Vertue, III, 139.

32 John Locke, *An Essay concerning Human Understanding* (1690), ed. Peter H. Nidditch (Oxford, 1975), 163.

33 'The Science of a Connoisseur', Richardson, 196.

34 *A*, 215.

35 The long debate on consumption and taste can only be indicated here. In recent years, many studies from different perspectives have redefined the territory; see, for example, Barrell, Brewer, Pears and Solkin, and earlier studies: Lance Lipking, *The Ordering of the Arts in Eighteenth-Century England* (Princeton, 1970); John Sekora, *Luxury: the Concept in Western Thought from Eden to Smollett* (Baltimore and London, 1977); Neil McKendrick, John Brewer and J. H. Plumb, *The Birth of a Consumer Society: the Commercialisation of Eighteenth-century England* (1982); J. G. A. Pocock, *Virtue, Commerce and History* (Cambridge, 1985).

36 Shaftesbury, 'Concerning Virtue or Merit', *Characteristics*, 279.

37 John Closterman, *The 3rd Earl of Shaftesbury and the Hon. Maurice Ashley-Cooper* (*c.*1700–1701), and *Anthony Ashley Cooper, 3rd Earl of Shaftesbury* (*c.*1701–2) – both NPG. The double portrait is in a classical–rural setting; the second portrait, in which Shaftesbury retains his toga but wears a wig, has more contemporary reference. See Solkin, 4–13, 23–6.

38 Ibid., 94–6.

39 Jules Lubbock, at the Tate conference, 'Is there a British Art?', 2 May 1996. I am grateful for his notes on this argument.

40 *A*, 131.

41 One (which Hogarth refers to specifically in his *Analysis of Beauty*) was the Latin poem *De arte graphica* by Charles Alphonse du Fresnoy, translated by Dryden as *The Art of Painting*, reissued in 1716, introduced by Pope and dedicated to Burlington.

42 'The Theory of Painting', Richardson, 63.

43 Ibid., 93.

44 Ibid., 7.

45 'The Science of a Connoisseur', Richardson, 275.

46 Paul Monod, 'Painters and Party Politics in England, 1714–60', *Eighteenth-Century Studies*, 1993, 26, no. 3 (spring), 389.

47 See Jennifer Montagu, *The expression of the passions: the Origins and influence of Le Brun's Conférence sur l'expression générale et particulière* (New Haven and London, 1994).

48 *A*, 191.

49 *Spectator*, I, 288; no. 67; 17 May 1711.

50 Brewer, 203.

51 See Lippincott, 113–14.

52 The Italians Ricci and Pellegrini, the French Goupy, the Fleming Tillemans, worked in the King's Theatre at the Haymarket in the 1720s, and the Italian John Devoto at Drury Lane. See Allen, 11; also S. Rosenfeld, *Short History of Stage Design in Great Britain* (Oxford, 1993), and *Georgian Scene Painters and Scene Painting* (1981).

53 'Theory of Painting', Richardson, preface, v. See also, Stephen Copley in John Barrell (ed.), *Painting and the Politics of Culture: New Essays on British Art 1700–1850* (Oxford, 1992), 20–21.

54 Quoted in Whitley, I, 4–5.

55 Walpole *Anec.*, 29–30.

56 Brewer, 211.

57 *Spectator*, I, 39; no. 9, 10 March 1711.

58 Vertue, III, 120.

59 Rica Jones, *Manners and Morals*, 20, quoting John Gwyn, *An Essay on Design* (1749).

60 'The perfect measure of a man taken from the antique' in John Elsum, *The Art of Painting after the Italian Manner, with practical observations on the principal colours, and directions how to know a good picture* (1714), 26. The comparison with Hogarth's periwigs is made by Rica Jones, *Manners and Morals*, 21.

61 *A*, 184.

62 *Ap*, 106.

63 Vertue, III, 124.

64 *A*, 211.

65 Ibid., 185.

66 Ibid., 212.

67 *A*, 209.

CHAPTER 5: Stocks, Operas and Satires

1 John Carswell, *The South Sea Bubble* (Stanford, 1960), 137.

2 *London Journal*, 7 May 1720.

3 'The Hubble Bubble' (1720); in Roy Palmer, *A Ballad History of England from 1588 to the Present Day* (1979), 46–7.

4 Pat Rogers analyses this rhetoric in 'This Calamitous Year', *Eighteenth-Century Encounters* (Brighton, 1985).

5 Allan Ramsay, 'The Rise and Fall of Stocks, 1720', *The Works of Allan Ramsay*, ed. Burns Martin and John W. Oliver, 6 vols (Edinburgh, 1945–74), I, 180. For the South Sea in relation to Hogarth and contemporary satire, see Dabydeen *Commercial Britain, passim.*

6 *Applebee's Weekly Journal*, 29 April 1721. See Rogers, *Eighteenth-Century Encounters*, 157.

7 A failed Jacobite coup, engineered by Sunderland, who trapped the Pretender into thinking an invasion was safe; supporters such as Bishop Atterbury of Rochester assured him of victory.

8 Gilmour, 76.

9 See *GI*, I, 4, and *HGW*, 40, plate 4.

10 *Funeral Ticket* (between 1721 and 1736), made for 'Humphrey Drew, Undertaker, in King-street, Westminster'; *HGW*, 41, plate 22.

11 *Letterhead for Blundell's School, Tiverton* (September 1726); *HGW*, 68, plate 104.

12 See Antal (who compares Hogarth's shop cards to cards from the Netherlands, such those of Bernard Picart), 78, and *HGW*, 69.

13 *A. de la Motraye's travels through Europe, Asia, and into Part of Africa; with Proper Cutts and Maps*, 2 vols (February 1724). One plate is dated 'Rome, 1716' and another (by George Vertue) is marked '1718'. Other engravers were then called in and more names appear: R. Smith, D. Lockley, W. Nutting, W. Hogarth.

14 The booksellers (listed on title page) were in Cornhill, Little-Britain, Fleet Street, Temple Bar and Paternoster Row. The subscription list includes Burlington, Chandos and Steele. (Subscription publishing ventures were often indirect patronage; subscribers ordered several sets and never collected them.)

15 *Recueil de cent estampes représentant différentes nations du Levant* (1712–13), as reissued with an explanation of the plates (1715). See *HGW*, 43, and plates 28–42.

16 See *HGW*, 56, plates 58–62 ; 57, plates 64–5; 57, plates 66–79 (all 1725).

17 Pat Rogers, *Literature and Popular Culture in Eighteenth-Century England* (Brighton, 1985), 44.

18 Keates, 86, and *passim* for a vivid account of opera content, music and professional rivalries.

19 Richard Steele, *The Theatre*, ed. John Loftis (Oxford, 1962), 82; no. xix, 5 March 1720.

20 To Pope, 10 January 1721; Swift *Corr.*, II, 368.

21 Bishop Berkeley, *An Essay towards Preventing the Ruin of Great Britain* (1721), in Dabydeen *Commercial Britain*, 43; *The Theatre*, no. xx, xxi (March 1720); Swift *Corr.*, III, 116.

22 To Swift, 3 February 1723; Gay *Letters*, 43.

23 *Weekly Journal or Saturday's Post*, 6 April 1723, on Rich's *Jupiter and Europa*; *The London Stage*, 2, cx–cxi.

24 *Universal Journal*, March 1723. *The London Stage*, 2, cxi.

25 La Motraye, *Travels*, 2nd edn (1732), III, 278.

26 Keates, 104; Deutsch, 53–4.

27 Rogers, *Literature and Popular Culture*, 54.

28 In an early version, the texts in the barrow were joined by the satirical paper *Pasquin*, no. xcv (27 December 1723), attacking rigid 'orders' in architecture; *HGW*, 49.

29 *A*, 205.

30 *DC*, 24 February 1724; see also 27 February, and P, I, 90.

31 *DC*, 4 March 1724; *HGW*, 49.

32 Pointon, 90; and 85–9 for discussion of this tradition.

CHAPTER 6: Great Men and Fools

1 *GW*, I, 15.

2 Vertue, III, 15.

3 *Ap*, 93.

4 Vertue, III, 20.

5 Vertue, VI, 170; *Ap*, 93.

6 The old artisan members were known as 'operative' masons, the incomers as 'accepted

masons'. For the social and intellectual tradition see Margaret C. Jacob, *The Radical Enlightenment: Pantheists, Freemasons and Republicans* (1981); D. Knoop, G. P. Jones and D. Hamer, *Early Masonic Pamphlets* (Manchester, 1954), 157–76.

7 Jacob, *The Radical Enlightenment*, 279.

8 Jarrett, 54.

9 Antal, 244, n. 39. See also Hallett, 75–90, for an interesting reading of this print, and a discussion of the popularity of Coypel's *Don Quixote* illustrations.

10 P, I, 114, but there is no evidence to suggest, as Paulson does, that Hogarth was a Mason by the time he engraved the *Gormagon* print.

11 Jacob, *The Radical Enlightenment*, 281.

12 Paul Monod, 'Painters and Party Politics in England, 1714–60', *Eighteenth-Century Studies*, 1993, XXVI, no. 3 (spring) 389–90.

13 *Evening Post*, 5–7 October 1725. See *HGW*, 58–65, plates 82–93. For drawings, see Oppé, plates 4–10.

14 Samuel Butler, *Hudibras*, ed. John Wilder (Oxford, 1967), 45; Part I, Canto II, 565–71.

15 Ibid., 38; Part I, Canto II, 321–30.

16 Ibid., 149; Part II, Canto II, 815–19, 830–31.

17 Antal, 88.

18 Ibid., 87; argued in P, I, 124–31.

19 Butler, *Hudibras*, 273–4; Part III, Canto II, 1505–9.

20 'The Theory of Painting', Richardson, 9–10.

21 Ibid., 10.

22 *A*, 206.

23 Smart, 5.

24 Alastair Smart, *Allan Ramsay, 1713–1784* (catalogue for Scottish National Portrait Gallery, Edinburgh, 1992), 95.

25 N, 435. See also Hammelmann, 81–5. The edition was published, with Vanderbank's designs, engraved by G. Vandergucht and du Bosc, in 1738. Hogarth's plates were published by Boydell in 1790; see *HGW*, 65–7, plates 94–9.

26 Nicholas Amhurst, *Protestant Popery: or, the Convocation* (1718) and *The Protestant Session, a Poem* (1719). See Ronald Paulson, 'Putting Out the Fire in Her Imperial Majesty's apartment: Opposition Politics, Anticlericalism and Aesthetics', *English Literary History*, LXIII (1996), 79–107.

27 See *HGW*, 67, plate 101.

28 See *HGW*, 51–2, plate 54, and, for different readings, Jarrett, 58–9, and Dabydeen *Commercial Britain*, 18–19.

29 To Swift, 17 November 1726; Gay *Letters*, 60.

30 See John Howard's account, *Tracts relating to Mary Toft*, BM. For narrative plus gynaecology, see Fiona Haslam, *From Hogarth to Rowlandson: Medicine in Art in Eighteenth Century Britain* (Liverpool, 1997), ch. 3.

31 Richard Manningheim, *An Exact Diary of What was Observed during a Close Attendance upon Mary Toft, The Pretended Rabbit Breeder of Godalming in Surrey from Monday, November, 28th., to Wednesday December, 7th., following, Together with An Account of her Confession of the Fraud* (1726).

32 Robert Halsband, *Lord Hervey, Eighteenth-Century Courtier* (Oxford, 1973), 16.

726

33 N, 146–7, reprints letters to Onslow.

34 *HGW*, 69.

35 John Maubray, *The Female Physician* (1724), 325. (Nichols opts for another surgeon, Sainthill; Paulson chooses Ahlers; Haslam argues for Maubray.)

36 Sterne *Tristram Shandy*, 129.

37 'The New Whim Wham' is reproduced in Peter Wagner, *Eros Revived: Erotica of the Enlightenment in England and America* (1988), 44–5. See N, 147–51 for other responses.

38 To Horace Mann, 9 December 1742; Walpole *Corr.*, XVIII, 124.

39 Quennell, 46.

40 *A Paviour's Sign* was dated in this period by Gowing (1971), who also attributed *The Carpenter's Yard* and *A Doctor's Visit* to Hogarth: the date and the attributions of the last two pictures have been much disputed: see P, I, 305–6, II. 40.

41 *GW*, I, 44.

42 The South Sea Commissioners noticed Thornhill had demanded £1,500 for 'a stair case & little hall' for the absconded Robert Knight. Thinking this high, they demanded estimates and eventually paid only the '25 shillings p yard' he earlier received at Blenheim; Vertue, III, 27.

43 Court Deposition, 20 December 1727, reproduced in N, 23–6; *GW*, I, 39–42, and *HLAT*, II, app. D, 487–8.

44 Vertue, III, 35–6.

45 Hervey, I, 22.

46 Ibid., I, 22.

47 Ibid., I, 26.

48 Ibid., I, 69. (The half-mad Philip V of Spain was dominated by his second wife, Elizabeth Farnese.)

49 Walpole to Pelham, 20 October 1743; quoted in Geoffrey Holmes, *The Age of Oligarchy, 1722–83* (Harlow, 1993), 32, n. 4.

50 To Gay and the Duchess of Queensberry, 29 June 1731; Swift *Corr*, III, 471.

51 Gay and Pope to Swift, 22 October 1727; Gay *Letters*, 68.

52 Hervey, I, 107.

53 Ibid., 89.

54 Ibid., 66.

55 To Lady Mar, [October 1727]; *The Complete Letters of Lady Mary Wortley Montagu*, ed. Robert Halsband (Oxford, 1966), II, 85–6.

56 Ibid., 85–6, n. 2, quoting Walpole's notes (Walpole *Corr.*, XXXIV, app. 9, 260).

57 Henry Fielding, 'The Masquerade' (1728), *The Female Husband and Other Writings*, ed. Claude E. Jones (Liverpool, 1960), 7.

58 Henry Fielding, *Miscellanies I*, ed. Henry Knight Miller (Oxford, 1972), 155.

CHAPTER 7: Imitation Games

1 The play opened in February 1727, with John Harper as Falstaff, Cibber as Shallow and Josiah Miller as Silence. *Henry IV, Part II* was frequently performed; as the paper is the same as that used to sketch *The Beggar's Opera*, Hogarth could have sketched a production in early 1728. See *Manners and Morals*, no. 82, 102.

727

2 *Daily Journal*, 24 October 1727; *London Stage*, 2, cxix.

3 W. H. Wilkins *Caroline the Illustrious* (London, 1904), 350–51 (following a pamphlet of 1760); in Pat Rogers, *Literature and Popular Culture in Eighteenth-Century England* (Brighton, 1985), 131.

4 *HGW*, 72, plate 113.

5 *The Craftsman*, 29 July 1717.

6 Broadsheet of 1725, in A. S. Turbeville, *English Men and Manners in the Eighteenth Century* (Oxford, 1926), 209.

7 Joseph Spence, *Observations, Anecdotes, and Characters of Books and Men*, ed. J. M. Osborn, 2 vols (Oxford, 1966), I, 107.

8 Benjamin Victor, *The History of The Theatres of London and Dublin*, 2 vols (1761), II, 154.

9 Boswell *Life*, II, 368; 18 April 1775.

10 *The Beggar's Opera* (1728), I, x; Gay *Dramatic Works*, I, 18.

11 Ibid., I, iii, and II, iv; 6, 27.

12 Ibid., I, iii; 6.

13 Ibid., III, ii; 47.

14 Quoted in Keates, 137.

15 Hervey to Stephen Fox, 13 June [1727]; Earl of Ilchester (ed.), *Lord Hervey and his Friends* (1950), 19.

16 *British Journal*, 10 June 1727; *London Stage*, 2, lxxx.

17 Oppé 32, catalogue 24, plate 21. For the Falstaff scene, see Oppé, 32, catalogue 23, plate 20. Hogarth also used *The Beggar's Opera* for a benefit card for the actor Milward (who took the role of the Player) in 1728, even though the benefit was for a play by Susanna Centlivre at Lincoln's Inn Fields (*HGW*, 71–2, plate 112).

18 *The Beggar's Opera*, III, xi; Gay *Dramatic Works*, I, 58.

19 See Christopher Swan, 'Hogarth's Painting of "The Beggar's Opera"', in *Among the Whores and Thieves: William Hogarth and The Beggar's Opera*, ed. David Bindman and Scott Wilcox (New Haven, 1997), 17–23; also Bindman's Foreword, 5–6. In 1994, the version at the Lewis Walpole Library in Farmington, referred to in all previous works as *The Beggar's Opera* (I), was proved by X-ray, and by evidence given by David Bull, Chairman of Painting Conservation at the National Gallery in Washington, to be a contemporary copy by another hand. This copy had been bought by Horace Walpole from John Rich in 1762. In *Tate Coll.*, 74–81 the various versions are illustrated (with the 'copy' as first version) including the sketch; figs 26–31. Also *Hogarth the Painter*, 22, catalogue 2, for version VI. An engraving, by William Blake, was published in 1790.

20 Keys later identified figures in the audience: Sir Robert Fagg, a famous horse-breeder, with his back turned; Sir Thomas Robinson of Rokeby, amateur architect, on his left; Major Robert Paunceford between them. These identifications were made by Horace Walpole, and are attached to the stretcher of the Rich painting (Lewis Collection, Yale). Other versions are thought to include portraits of Rich and Gay himself. See P, I, 176, n. 33.

21 To Swift, 6 July 1728; Gay *Letters*, 76.

22 To Thomas Tickell, March 1728, quoted in David Nokes, *John Gay* (1994), 419.

23 To Swift, 6 July 1728; Gay *Letters*, 76.

24 See *HGW*, 73–4, plate 114.

25 Quoted in Battestin, 284.

26 Walpole *Anec.*, 112.
27 *The Craftsman*, 1 February 1729.
28 For the trials of *Polly*, see Nokes, *John Gay*, 435–69.
29 John Arbuthnot to Swift, 19 March 1728/9; Swift *Corr.*, III, 326.
30 *Polly*, I, i; Gay *Dramatic Works*, I, 77.
31 Ibid., I, i; 77–8.
32 Ibid., I, vi; 85.
33 Ibid., I, iv; 81.
34 Kerslake, I, 330–38, fig. 942.
35 For the report of the Committee and the sequence of events, see John Mackay, *A True State of the Proceedings of the Prisoners in the Fleet-Prison* (1729); William Cobbett, *A Parliamentary History of England*, 36 vols (1806–20), VIII, 708–31, 744–54; and John Ashton, *The Fleet: its Rivers, Prison*, 2nd edn (1888), 230–35.
36 Cobbett, VIII, 744.
37 Ibid.
38 Ibid., 747–8.
39 Ibid., 716–17.
40 For a personal response, see A. N. Newman (ed.), *The Parliamentary Diary of Sir Edward Knatchbull, 1722–30* (Camden Third Series, XCIV, 1963), 88. An extract is quoted in Jarrett, 76.
41 P, I, 195; *Weekly Journal of the British Gazeteer*, 21 June 1729.
42 Walpole *Anec.*, 153–4.
43 Cobbett, VIII, 718.
44 *GW*, I, 46.
45 *The Craftsman*, 5 April 1729.
46 N, 27.

CHAPTER 8: Painting the Polite

1 *The Craftsman*, 5 December 1730.
2 See Hugh Phillips, *Mid-Georgian London* (1964), 146–8. Betty Careless's brothel was taken over by 'Mother Douglas' in 1739.
3 For the difficulty of dating, see *HGW*, 51–2, plate 54.
4 To Pope, 6 March 1729; Swift *Corr.*, III, 313.
5 Vertue, III, 38.
6 Ibid., 38–9.
7 *A*, 215.
8 Rouquet, *State of the Arts*, 42–3.
9 *GW*, I, 23.
10 Vertue, III, 40–41.
11 For the influence of Shaftesbury and Addison on the conversation piece in the debate about culture and luxury, see Solkin, and also John Mullan, *Sentiment and Sociability: The Language of Feeling in the Eighteenth Century* (Oxford, 1988). For the origins and popularity of the genre, see Ellen d'Oench's catalogue, *The Conversation Piece: Arthur Devis and his Contemporaries* (New Haven, 1980).

729

12 Richardson, *The Theory of Painting* (1715), quoted by Brian Allen, 'The Age of Hogarth, 1720–1760', Antique Collectors' Club, *The British Portrait, 1660–1960* (1991), 132.

13 Ibid., 142, quoting Kellom Tomlinson, *The Art of Dancing* (1735).

14 *Spectator*, I, 365; no. 86, 8 June 1711.

15 Richardson, 190; Solkin, 31–2.

16 In Bainbrigge Buckeridge, *Essay Towards an English School of Painting* (1706). See d'Oench *The Conversation Piece*, 2.

17 Mercier's early paintings in England include *A Hanoverian Party on a Terrace, with the Schutz Family* (1725) and *Viscount Tyrconnel and his Family* (1725/6); his most famous work is *Frederick Prince of Wales and his Sisters at Concert* (1733) (NPG).

18 Joseph van Aken, *A Sportsman and a Man of Fashion in a Park* (private collection) and *An Elegant Company on a Terrace* (Collection of Nathaniel Robertson, Connecticut, US), both mid-1720s; illustrated in Solkin, 58–9, with detailed discussion.

19 *Tate Coll.*, 82–3; catalogue 88; *Hogarth the Painter*, 23, catalogue 3. Ashley Cowper married Dorothy Oakes *c.* 1730; the child is probably their daughter Thordora, baptized 1731, and added to the picture later.

20 The tapestries are hard to decipher. Paulson suggests that the bust, and the portrait behind Child (of Brutus' wife Portia and Pompey's wife Julia) were of loyal women who killed themselves after their husbands' deaths; P, I, 207–8.

21 N, 49. *Manners and Morals*, no. 53, 73–4.

22 *The Ashley and Popple Families* (Collection of Her Majesty The Queen).

23 *Captain Woodes Rogers and his Family* (National Maritime Museum, Greenwich). See Webster, 28–9.

24 For identifications, see Webster, 23–4. The setting could be either their town house in St James's Square, or their country home, Finborough Hall, Suffolk.

25 For an interesting analysis, see Solkin, 84–90, 92–4.

26 Vertue, III, 46.

27 Mary Pendarves to Anne Granville, 13 July 1731; Delany, I, 283. Mrs Delany was then Mrs Pendarves.

28 *The Jones Family* was acquired from Fonmon Castle by the National Museum of Wales in July 1996; see the entry by Mark Evans, *National Art Collections Fund Magazine* (1996). Cleaning has now made its colours and details far more vivid; I am grateful to Juliet Carey of the Museum for information and discussion of her research into the Jones family. See also *Manners and Morals*, no. 66, 86–7.

29 Family letters in Glamorgan County Record Office, quoted in Sotheby's catalogue *British Painting, 1500–1850*, 10 July 1996, 38–9. For the family, see P. Jenkins, *The Making of a Ruling Class: the Glamorgan Gentry, 1640–1790* (Cambridge, 1983).

30 See Pointon, 210–11, for a careful reading.

31 *The Indian Emperor* (1665–7), IV, iv; *The Works of John Dryden*, ed. John Loftis, 12 vols (Berkeley, 1966), IX, 88–9. For the painting, see *Manners and Morals*, 89–90, catalogue 68; *Hogarth the Painter*, 24, catalogue 4; P, II, 1–4.

CHAPTER 9: Impolite Conversations and Probing Ideas

1 *The Highland Fair* was performed at Drury Lane, in March 1731. For the frontispiece, engraved by Vandergucht, see *HGW*, 188, plate 221.

2 Joseph Mitchell, *Three Poetical Epistles. To Mr. Hogarth, Mr. Dandridge, and Mr. Lambert, Masters of the Art of Painting* (1730); see P, I, 234-5.

3 *Spectator*, V, 28; no. 593, 13 September 1714.

4 Mary Pendarves to Anne Granville, 13 July 1731; Delany, I, 283. For *The Wesley Family* (Apsley House), see Baldini, catalogue 40, 93.

5 For Arthur Pond's cultivation of women patrons, see Lippincott, 38-41.

6 *A*, 202.

7 Ibid., 216.

8 See *Manners and Morals*, no. 68, 89-90; Webster, 79-80, 84-5; P, I, 276-7.

9 Walpole *Anec.*, 161; *GW*, I, 19-20.

10 See Derek Jarrett, *England in the Age of Hogarth* (New Haven, 1974), 66.

11 *GM*, 1731, 15; Jarrett, *England*, 65.

12 G. Midgley, *The Life of Orator Henley* (1973), 144.

13 Vertue, III, 41.

14 Ibid., 50.

15 N, 15-16; P, I, 218; *PA*, 18 July 1781.

16 See Bindman, 81.

17 For the wigs, see Pointon, 112-13.

18 N, 202-7; *HI*, I, 98; *GW*, III, 223; II, 112n.; *HGW*, 84-5.

19 Antal, 95, 161, compares them to Jean François de Troy's *La Surprise, La Proposition, La Jarretière* (all mid-1720s). See also *Rococo*, catalogue 20, 47-8.

20 For *A Harlot's Progress* in relation to women, the law and literary images, see Ian A. Bell, *Literature and Crime in Augustan England* (1991), 92-146. For a general survey, see Bridget Hill, *Eighteenth-Century Women: An Anthology* (1984).

21 Captain Alexander Smith, *The School of Venus* (1715), quoted in John Richetti, *Popular Fiction before Richardson, 1700-39* (Oxford, 1969), 40.

22 Tom Brown, *Amusements Serious and Comical*, ed. Arthur L. Hayward (1927), 99.

23 Quoted in Peter Wagner, *Eros Revived: Erotica of the Enlightenment in England and America* (1988), 57.

24 *The Complete Letters of Lady Mary Wortley Montagu*, ed. R. Halsband, 3 vols (Oxford, 1966), III, 66.

25 Battestin, 131.

26 For the frontispiece, engraved by Vandergucht, March 1731, see *HGW*, 187-8, plate 220.

27 Fielding, *Joseph Andrews*, 185.

28 Ibid., 189.

29 Dr William Harris, Preface to Simon Brown, *A Defence of the Religion of Nature and the Christian Revelation*, III, quoted in G. R. Cragg, *Reason and Authority in the Eighteenth Century* (Cambridge, 1964), 382, and Geoffrey Holmes, *The Making of a Great Power: Late Stuart and Early Georgian Britain 1660-1722* (1993), 370.

30 Holmes, *The Making of a Great Power*, 369.

31 Thomas Woolston, *Discourses on the Miracles of our Saviour* (1727-30).

32 See Thomas Woolston, *Defence of his Discourses* (1729); P, I, 288–92.

33 E.g. Thomas Cooke (for whose translation of Hesiod he drew a frontispiece in 1728), who upheld freedom of religious debate in an open letter to the Archbishop of Canterbury in 1732. See R. Paulson, *The Beautiful, Novel and Strange* (1995), 316, n. 9.

34 By Paulson, in the revised biography and more substantially in *The Beautiful, the Novel and the Strange*.

35 The triangle of the Trinity is inverted, and emptied of its mystic tetragrammaton, while the *'Dieu'* of *Dieu et mon droit* is lost behind a curtain. See *HGW*, 98–9.

36 Geoffrey Holmes and Daniel Szechi, *The Age of Oligarchy; Pre-Industrial Britain 1722–83* (1993), 107.

37 Bernard de Mandeville, *The Fable of the Bees: or Private Vices, Publick Benefits*, 2 vols (1723, 1729), ed. F. B. Kaye (Oxford, 1924), 7. For Hogarth, Mandeville, and the conversation piece, see Solkin, 78–105.

38 *The Champion*, 26 January 1740, in *The Works of Henry Fielding*, ed. Leslie Stephen, 10 vols (1882), V, 229.

CHAPTER 10: *A Harlot's Progress*

1 Vertue, III, 58. This sketch is discussed in P, II, 237–8.

2 See John Richetti, *Popular Fiction before Richardson, 1700–39* (Oxford, 1969), 35–9.

3 I am grateful to Felicity Riddick for setting off this train of thought. The line quoted is from Robert Henryson, *The Testament of Cresseid*, ed. Denton Fox (1968), 63, ll. 63–4.

4 David Kunzle, *History of the Early Comic Strip* (Berkeley, 1973; London, 1974). Kunzle describes and illustrates religious sequences and moral tales from Germany, Italy, France, the Netherlands and Russia. See in particular his chapter 'Rakes and Harlots', and the picture strips from Rome and Venice, 287–91.

5 *The Tryal of Colonel Francis Charteris* (Dublin, repr. London, 1730), 2.

6 *Select Trials* (1734–5), II, 200.

7 Ibid., 15.

8 *Some Authentic Memoirs of the Life of Colonel C—s Rape-Master of Great Britain* (1730), 10.

9 *The History of Col Francis Ch—rtr—s* (1730), 42.

10 Ibid., 5.

11 Ibid., 37; see also *The Life of Colonel Don Francisco* (1730), 47–8.

12 *DC*, 31 April 1730.

13 *HGW*, 81, citing *A History of Executions* (1730), no. I, 81.

14 For newspaper reports, see P, I, 241–55.

15 *DP*, 1–2 August 1730.

16 For the latter view, see W. A. Speck, 'The Harlot's Progress in Eighteenth Century England', *British Journal of Eighteenth-Century Studies*, 3 (1980), 127–39.

17 Daniel Defoe, *Some Considerations Upon Streetwalkers* (1726); Bernard de Mandeville, *A Modest Defence of Publick Stews; or, an Essay upon Whoring, as it is now Practis'd in These Kingdoms* (1724).

18 *Spectator*, II, 534–5; no. 266, 4 January 1712.

19 Boswell *Journal*, I, 249.

20 Dryden, *King Arthur* (1691).

21 Brewer, 9, 16–17.
22 *A View of London and Westminster, or the Town Spy* (1725), in Speck, 'The Harlot's Progress', 128.
23 Swift *Poems*, 453–5.
24 *A*, 209.
25 Webster, 34.
26 Tom Brown, *Works*, II, 282; *Amusements*, 99.
27 Gay, *The Beggar's Opera*, I, iv; Gay *Dramatic Works*, II, 7.
28 N, 195; *GSJ*, 24 September 1730.
29 Saussure, 301–2.
30 *The Harlot's Progress, being the life of the noted Moll Hackabout* (1733); Hallett, 106–7.
31 Lichtenberg, 49. Dabydeen, in *Hogarth's Blacks*, 131, calls this scene 'the earliest example of anti-slavery sentiment in English painting, if not in English art, anticipating the more detailed images of Blake, Morland, Gillray, Cruikshank and Turner by several decades'.
32 Vertue, III, 53.
33 N, 216.
34 Theophilus Cibber, *Lives of the Poets of Great Britain and Ireland*, 5 vols (1753), V, 339; and *Weekly Register*, 21 August 1731, quoted in *The Dramatic Works of George Lillo*, ed. James L. Steffensen (Oxford, 1993), 123.
35 *DJ* and *DP*, 14 January 1732; P, I, 305.
36 Vertue, III, 58.
37 N, 29–32.
38 *DJ*, 19 April 1732.
39 Vertue, III, 58.
40 *The Harlot's Progress; or the Humours of Drury Lane* (1732).

CHAPTER 11: Nobody and Somebody

1 N, 27.
2 Sir James Thornhill, *Sketch of His Family* (Rt Hon. the Marquess of Exeter).
3 Vertue, III, 58.
4 James Ralph, *The Weekly Register*, no. 112, 3 June 1732.
5 Prologue (spoken by Theophilus Cibber) to *The Covent-Garden Tragedy* (1732); *The Works of Henry Fielding*, ed. Leslie Stephen, 10 vols (Oxford, 1882), IX, 175.
6 Vertue, III, 61.
7 'Memoir of William Tothall' by the Reverend J. Lyon of Dover, given to Nichols by Dr Ducarel, in N, 116–18n.
8 Ebenezer Forrest, *Momus turn'd Fabulist: or, Vulcan's Wedding*, 1729.
9 The bound folio account, written by Forrest, now in BL, was edited by Charles Mitchell as *Hogarth's Peregrination* (Oxford, 1952). All quotations are from this edition, 3–17.
10 Walpole *Corr.*, x, app. 2, 330. (Horace Walpole's note on a letter from his brother Edward to Mrs Scott.)
11 N, 97.
12 Richard Graves, *The Spiritual Quixote*, ed. C. Tracy (1967), 140; in Langford, 66.
13 See Mitchell, Introduction, xxiv–xxxi, tracing popular traditions back to Odysseus telling

Polyphemus to shout 'Nobody' when asked who is attacking him, and to the medieval 'nemo'.

14 *The Craftsman*, no. 345, 10 February 1733.

15 *Britannia Excis'd*, broadsheet satire; in J. H. Plumb, *Sir Robert Walpole: The King's Minister* (1960), 245.

16 Hervey, I, 133.

17 Plumb, *The King's Minister*, 252–3.

18 Hervey, I, 165.

19 Langford, 31.

20 N, 173n.

21 *GM*, 3, March 1733, 534–5; *HGW* 86.

22 *HI*.

23 *The Royal Family* (1732–3): indoor (National Gallery of Ireland, Dublin), and outdoor (Collection of Her Majesty The Queen); see Millar, 559, plate 209.

24 Hervey, I, 193.

25 Ibid., 232.

26 Vertue, III, 68.

CHAPTER 12: The Fair and the Rake

1 *DA*, 18 December 1732; P, II, 5.

2 Ibid.

3 *DA*, 25 January 1733. The advertisement was repeated as late as 24 February in *LJ*; *HGW*, 84.

4 *Dorking Inventory* (1869), 157; P, II, 49.

5 J. T. Smith, *The Streets of London* (1845); see also Tom Taylor, *Leicester Square; Its Associations and its Worthies* (1874).

6 *A*, 169.

7 N, 102.

8 John Hoppner, quoted in Shawe-Taylor, 14.

9 J. Holden Macmichael, *Charing Cross and its Immediate Neighbourhood* (1906), 189.

10 Smith, *Streets*, 76.

11 Macmichael, *Charing Cross*, 187: *LEP*, 20–23 October 1733.

12 *LJ*, 22 December 1733; *HGW*, 86.

13 Sybil Rosenfeld, *The Theatre of the London Fairs in the Eighteenth Century* (Cambridge, 1960), 94.

14 *The Rake's Progress* (1947–8), I, i, in W. H. Auden and Chester Kallman, *Libretti*, ed. Edward Mendelson (Princeton, 1993), 50.

15 P, II, 16. Other accounts in N, 180–86, mention the death of flyers at Shrewsbury and Bristol.

16 *The Fall of Troy* had not been played at Southwark since 1726, but *The Fall of Bajazet* was performed in 1732, with performances of Fielding's *The Miser*; Rosenfeld, *London Fairs*, 93–4.

17 N, 183.

18 Edward Phillips, *The Stage Mutineers: or, a Play-House to be Lett* (1732), 37, in Battestin, 168. See N, 180.

19 *GI*, I, 110–11.
20 'Hercules MacSturdy', in David Coke, *The Muse's Bower: Vauxhall Gardens, 1728–1786* (1978), n.p.
21 This correct way of holding a glass is illustrated in Gerard de Lairesse, *The Art of Painting in All its Branches* (English translation, 1738); see Smart, 49–50.
22 Pointed out by Robin Simon in his stimulating essay, 'Poses' (Simon, 68–70). Watteau's painting was engraved by Lepicie in 1734. Simon notes that in its brief vogue the pose was adapted by Hayman in *David Garrick and William Windham of Fellbrigg* (*c.*1750; private collection) and by Gainsborough in *John Plampin* (1753–4; NPG).
23 John Gay, *The Beggar's Opera*, II, iv; Gay *Dramatic Works*, 27.
24 Saussure, 93. For contemporary accounts see Max Byrd, *Visits to Bedlam: Madness and Literature in the Eighteenth Century* (Columbia, SC, 1975), and, for general context, Roy Porter, *Mind Forg'd Manacles: a History of Madness in England from the Restoration to the Regency* (1987).
25 Donald F. Bond (ed.), *The Tatler*, 3 vols (Oxford, 1987), I, 224; no. 30, 18 June 1709.
26 Whiston is mentioned in *GW*, II, 126; see 'The Longitudinarians', Larry Stewart, *The Rise of Public Science: Rhetoric, Technology, and Natural Philosophy in Newtonian Britain, 1660–1750* (Cambridge, 1992).
27 See Henry Fielding, *Amelia*, ed. David Blewett (Harmondsworth, 1987), 36.
28 *GM*, 7, May 1737, 289–90, cited in the clear account of humours, English melancholy and suicide in Derek Jarrett, *England in the Time of Hogarth*, 207–12.
29 Rouquet, *Lettres*, as translated in Webster, 60.
30 'The Legion Club', Swift *Poems*, 550.
31 W. H. Auden, Note in *La Biennale di Venezia* (1951), translated in *Libretti*, ed. Mendelson, 608. For the legacy of the *Rake* in prints and theatre design, see *A Rake's Progress: From Hogarth to Hockney*, ed. Robin Simon and Christopher Woodward, catalogue to exhibition at Sir John Soane's Museum (1997).

CHAPTER 13: Clubs and Cabals

1 Vertue, III, 91.
2 David Coke, 'Vauxhall Gardens', *Rococo*, 80.
3 See Pyne, I, 112–50.
4 *Rococo*, E 10, 69. Old Slaughter's was demolished in 1843 to make way for Cranbourn Street.
5 *GI*, I, 118.
6 See *The Complicated Richardson*, *HGW* (1970 edn), I, 314.
7 *GW*, III, 134.
8 Vertue, III, 40.
9 See Elaine Barr, 'Rococo Silver: Design', and Philippa Glanville, 'Patrons and Craftsmen', for discussion of Paul de Lamerie, Paul Crespin and George Wickes, *Rococo*, 100–102, 103–7.
10 For Vanderbank's drawings, see Hammelmann, 76–86.
11 For Roubiliac, see Katharine Esdaile, *The Life and Works of Louis-François Roubiliac* (Oxford, 1928), and David Bindman and Malcolm Baker, *Roubiliac and the*

Eighteenth-Century Monument: Sculpture as Theatre (1995).

12 Vertue, III, 105. For Gravelot's book illustrations, see Hammelmann, 38–46.

13 Vertue, III, 91.

14 The incident was remembered by Gravelot's pupil Grignion; see *The Diary of Joseph Farington*, ed. Kathryn Cave, 10 vols (New Haven, 1978–82; continuing), VIII, 2801.

15 Hammelmann, 38.

16 Rouquet *State of the Arts*, 104.

17 Smith, II, 92.

18 See *HGW*, 112, plate 155.

19 P, II, 56.

20 Smith, II, 346.

21 *HI*, II, 295–6. See also *HGW*, 83–4.

22 *The Prompter*, 24 December 1734.

23 P, II, 63, and see Keates, 156.

24 *The Weekly Register*, 207, 23 February 1734; see also 216 (27 April) and the reprint of his 1732 essay in 228 (8 June).

25 *GSJ*, 27 June and 19 September 1734; P, II, 79.

26 Vertue, III, 146.

27 Quoted in P, II, 42–3.

28 In 1753 the printseller Thomas Jeffreys brought a case against a bookseller, Richard Baldwin, who had copied for the *London Magazine* a view originally comissioned by Jeffreys, and assigned him by the artist. The case was dismissed, by Lord Chancellor Hardwicke, as Jeffreys had only an assignment and was not 'the original inventor', see P, III, 54.

29 *A*, 216.

30 Battestin, 228, quoting Chesterfield's *Miscellaneous Works* (1777), I, 228ff.

31 Walter Arnold, *The Life and Death of the Sublime Society of Beefsteaks* (1871), 2.

32 Pyne, I, 109–12.

33 *GW*, III, 160, dated 1733.

34 For Steele on Estcourt, see *Spectator*, IV, 156–8; no. 468, 27 August 1712. (These early Beefsteaks were said to have a gold gridiron hung on a green ribbon.) There was also a Rump-Steak Club (or Patriots Club) in 1734: see Robert J. Allen, *The Clubs of Augustan London* (Hamden, Conn., 1967), 56, 136.

35 Fielding's song was included in the suppressed *Grub-Street Opera* (1731), and repeated in *Don Quixote in England* (1733). Richard Leveridge's version and setting, with slightly altered lyrics, was included in *The British Musical Miscellany*, III, 1735.

36 Lionel Cust, *History of the Society of Dilettanti*, ed. Sidney Colvin, 28, 37.

37 W. Arnold, *Beefsteaks*, 16.

38 Lord Middlesex, quoted in Joseph Spence, *Anecdotes, Observations and Characters of Books and Men* (1858), 304–5.

39 Lindsay, 94.

40 Jarrett, 118.

41 Roy Porter, 'Consumption: Disease of the Consumer Society' in John Brewer and Roy Porter (eds), *Consumption and the World of Goods* (1983), 59.

42 Henry Fielding (1731); see n. 35 above.

43 *The Connoisseur*, no. 19; Allen, *Clubs*, 144.

44 *Ap*, 93.

45 Vertue, III, 76. For the site, and the equipment, still depicted in Zoffany's painting of 1761, see Martin Postle, 'The St Martin's Lane Academy: true and false records', *Apollo*, 1991, 134, no. 353 (July) 33–8.

46 *Ap*, 94.

47 These links are made clear in numerous catalogue entries in *Rococo*, from painting, sculpture and print to architecture and interiors, silverware and porcelain. See also Mark Girouard, 'English Art and the Rococo': *Country Life*, 1966 (13 and 27 January and 3 February), 58–61, 188–90, 24–7.

CHAPTER 14: Allegories of Healing

1 A large portrait exists of an elderly woman, 50 × 40 inches, signed 'W.H. ft' (the form Hogarth used in his 1745 portrait), in the James D. Hamlin Collection, Panhandle-Plains Historical Museum, Canyoun, Texas. This was long thought to be of Hogarth's mother between 1735 and 1740, painted from memory, or a reworking of an earlier portrait, but it is now thought to be by another hand (Brian Allen to the author, 1995). The sitter's lips are closed, her cheeks sag, her eyes are thoughtful. Although her hands and arms are elegantly placed, her dark dress and white muslin bands beneath the black widow's hood give her a stoic dignity.

2 *A*, 202–3.

3 Robert Nelson, *Address to Persons of Quality and Estate* (1715); in David Owen, *English Philanthropy 1660–1960* (Oxford, 1965), 13.

4 Fielding *Tom Jones*, 583.

5 George *London*, 71.

6 See V. C. Medvei and J. L. Thornton (eds), *The Royal Hospital of St Bartholomew's 1123–1973* (Ipswich, 1974), 134, and Norman Moore, *History of St Bartholomew's Hospital*, 2 vols (1874), 531.

7 Robert Seymour, in Webster, 72, and Medvei and Thornton, *St Bartholomew's*, 288.

8 Vertue, III, 78.

9 Ibid., 77–8.

10 Journal of the Meetings of the Governors of St Bartholomew's Hospital, 21 July 1737; Moore, *St Bartholomew's*, 364.

11 Walpole *Anec.*, 164.

12 Fielding *Joseph Andrews*, 47.

13 *GW*, II, 190. For diagnoses, see Haslam, ch. 4, who agrees with P, II, 87, that the infant with curved spine has rickets, first described by a doctor in the hospital in 1650 and also discussed by Freke; see also Moore, *History of St Bartholomew's Hospital* (1918), II, 850.

14 *A*, 137–8; Hogarth was writing in 1753. Francis Hayman also illustrated twelve heads from Le Brun's *Treatise on the Passions*, engraved by Grignion for Dodsley's *The Preceptor*, 1748; Allen (1987), 20.

15 Hogarth's medical friends shared these interests; see Shearer West, 'Polemic and the Passions: Dr James Parson's *Human Physiology Explained* and Hogarth's Aspirations for

British History-painting', *British Journal of Eighteenth-Century Studies*, 1990, XIII, no. 1 (spring), 73–89.

16 *A*, 177.

17 Ibid., 70–82.

18 Ibid., 71.

19 Ibid., 81.

20 Ibid., 126.

21 Martin Hopkinson, 'William Hunter, William Hogarth and the "Anatomy of the Human Gravid Uterus"', *Burlington Magazine*, CXXVI, 1984, 10. Hunter lectured at St Martin's Lane and became first Professor of Anatomy at the Royal Academy in 1768. His first uterine specimen was dissected in 1750, and drawings of his studies were engraved by Grignion, Ravenet and Scotin, all associated with Hogarth. He subscribed to both the *Analysis of Beauty*, and *Four Prints of an Election*. For background, see W. F. Bynum and Roy Porter (eds.), *William Hunter and the Eighteenth-Century Medical World* (Cambridge, 1985).

22 The motto from the *Aeneid* II alludes to the Greeks and Trojans who killed each other amid the ruins of Troy (*HGW*, 100–101). For the heraldic terms see ibid. and source, N. B. Gwyn, 'An Interpretation of the Hogarth Print "The Arms of the Company of Undertakers"', *Bulletin of the History of Medicine*, 8, 1940, 115–27.

23 N, 239.

24 Hervey, III, 877–915. Hervey felt strongly about Ward; the incompetence of medicine in the 1730s is graphically illustrated in his description of the lingering death of Queen Caroline.

25 N, 241.

26 *The London Stage*, 3, 1, 736–7.

27 *Scene from 'The Tempest'* 31½ × 40 in. (*c.* 1736), St Oswald Collection, Nostell Priory, Wakefield.

28 Jonathan Richardson, *Explanatory Notes and Remarks on Milton's 'Paradise Lost'* (1735), 71–2. See *Tate Coll.*, 88–90; catalogue 95, and D. Bindman, 'Hogarth's "Satan, Sin and Death" and its influence', *Burlington Magazine*, CXII, 1970, 153–8.

29 John Milton, *Paradise Lost*, II, ll. 650–726.

30 These artists would know it through Charles Townley's print of 1767.

CHAPTER 15: City Spaces

1 *St James' Evening Post*, 14 September 1736.

2 Austin Dobson, *A Paladin of Philanthropy* (1899), 246.

3 *St James' Evening Post*, 31 August 1734; for the 1738 incident, see J. Holden Macmichael, *Charing Cross and its Immediate Neighbourhood* (1906), 255.

4 Smith, II, 215–16.

5 *The Craftsman*, 8 September 1733, and *DA*, 15 June 1742.

6 *DA*, 18 February 1742.

7 Ibid., 4 February 1742.

8 Laurence Stone, *The Family, Sex and Marriage in England 1500–1800* (1977), 537.

9 *A*, 120–21.

10 Ibid., 99–100.

11 N, 215.

12 Ibid., 254.

13 Ibid., 255.

14 The description that follows is a brutal encapsulation of Sean Shesgreen's fascinating *Hogarth and the Times-of-the-Day Tradition* (Ithaca and London, 1983).

15 Shesgreen, *Hogarth*, 85–6.

16 Ibid., 105–14.

17 Hazlitt, VI, 137.

18 Walpole to Horace Mann, 21 July 1742; Walpole *Corr.*, XVII, 504.

19 See Lichtenberg, 155–6.

20 First performed 1731 (*HGW*, 108) and based on *The Devil to Pay* by Jevon, 1686; Lichtenberg, 156; see Christina H. Kiaer, 'Professional Femininity in Hogarth's *Strolling Actresses Dressing in a Barn*', *Art History*, XVI, 2 (June 1993), 239–65. Paulson (*HGW*, 108) also suggests the title may refer to a pamphlet, *The Devil to Pay*, at St James's (1727, attributed to Arbuthnot), a witty account of the fights between Faustina and Cuzzoni.

21 Walpole *Anec.*, 156.

22 Battestin, 213.

23 BM cutting, quoted by David Coke, *Rococo*, 75.

24 Solkin, 121.

25 W. Wroth, *The London Pleasure Gardens* (1896). See the excellent essays, quotations and plates in the exhibition catalogue, T. J. Edelstein *Vauxhall Gardens* (1983). This material is developed by Solkin (102–44) in relation to refinement, and the incorporation of, and resistance to, carnival elements.

26 Newspaper clipping, Warwick Wroth Papers, III, Museum of London; Solkin, 111.

27 *A Trip to Vaux-Hall: Or, a General SATYR on the Times of 1737*, by Hercules Mac-Sturdy, of the County of Tipperary, Esq. Quoted in full in David Coke, *The Muse's Bower: Vauxhall Gardens 1728–1786* (1978).

28 François Gravelot, 'The Invitation to Mira requesting her company to Vaux-Hall Garden', 1738, illustrated in *Rococo*, F 11, 87–8.

29 Solkin, 137.

30 'An Evening at Vaux-Hall' by S. Toupee, *Scots Magazine*, August 1739; extended quotation in David Coke, 'Vauxhall Gardens', *Rococo*, 77–8.

31 Gowing (53, plate 26) believed Hogarth contributed *The Fairies Dancing on the Green by Moonlight*, but the attribution is disputed.

32 Edelstein relates several of the pictures – like sliding on the ice – to the old emblem books, often turned into children's picture and reading books. A selection of the paintings, engraved 1744, were second in popularity only to Hogarth's *Progresses*; *Rococo* 79, 92–6, F 25–39.

33 *DP*, 18 April 1738.

34 Illustrated in *Rococo*, F 12, 87–8.

35 Keates, 215.

36 Allen, 34–6, points out that Hogarth used this pose as early as 1731, in *Sir Robert Pye* (Marble Hill House).

37 Keates, 268.

38 N, 57, and *GW*, I, 237; told by the surgeon Dr Belchier, of an occasion when Hogarth dined with William Cheselden.

CHAPTER 16: Country, Coram and Children

1 See *HLAT*, II, app. F, 491–3.
2 Ibid., 492.
3 Hervey, II, 627–8.
4 Ibid., 671, 681.
5 In 'Dissertation on Parties' (1733–4), and *Idea of a Patriot King*, circulated privately before it was published in 1738.
6 W. Cobbett, *The Parliamentary History of England*, 36 vols (1806–20), X, 341–2.
7 George *Caricature*, 86.
8 Fielding *Tom Jones*, 56.
9 Contemporary report, in J. P. Malcolm, *Anecdotes of the Manners and Customs of London during the Eighteenth-century*, 2 vols, (1808), I, 26.
10 *Journals of the House of Commons*, 8 March 1715, quoted in Ruth K. McClure, *Coram's Children: The London Foundling Hospital in the Eighteenth Century* (New Haven and London, 1981), 14.
11 Quoted in R. H. Nichols and F. A. Wray, *The History of the Foundling Hospital* (1935), 14.
12 Joseph Addison, *Guardian*, no. 105, 11 July 1713; McClure, *Coram's Children*, 3.
13 Coram to Dr Benjamin Colman, 22 September 1738; McClure, *Coram's Children*, 20.
14 Petition to the King in Council, 21 July 1737. Coram Foundation Library, reproduced in full in Nichols and Wray, *History*, 16–17.
15 Nichols and Wray, *History*, 19.
16 *LDP*, 11 February 1740; see Deutsch, 494–5.
17 *A*, 217.
18 Ibid.
19 See Brian Allen for *Sir Christopher Wren* by Verrio and Thornhill, in Antique Collectors' Club, *The British Portrait 1660–1960* (1991), 176; and Antal, 45–6, for Rigaud's *Samuel Bernard*. Omberg, 46–7, less convincingly, also suggests Van Dyck's portrait, *Frances Brydges, Countess Dowger of Exeter*.
20 Omberg, 64. Brocklesby's account (1751) is included in John Brownlow, *Memoranda or Chronicles of the Foundling Hospital* (1847).
21 Shawe-Taylor, 85. See A. A. Ettinger, *James Edward Oglethorpe, Imperial Idealist* (Oxford, 1936), 110–12.
22 *Theory of Painting*, Richardson, 8.
23 Rouquet *State of the Arts*, 25.
24 Minutes of the Governors of the Foundling Hospital, 1 April 1741; P, II, 329.

CHAPTER 17: The Index of the Mind

1 Vertue, III, 82.
2 Ibid., 83.
3 Ibid., 84.

4 Rouquet *State of the Arts*, 37-8.

5 Vertue, III, 84.

6 *A*, 217.

7 Ibid., 98-9

8 Vertue, III, 106–7.

9 Vertue, III, 111; the trick advertisment appeared in *LEP*, 21–23 October 1742.

10 Ibid., 98.

11 Walpole *Anec.*, 123.

12 Vertue, III, 85.

13 *Ap*, 98.

14 Vertue, iii, 93–4.

15 Robert Campbell, *The English Tradesman* (1747), 97.

16 Smart, 43.

17 *A Night Encounter* (*c.*1740?), 28 × 36 in. (The Right Hon. the Viscount Boyne). The note is quoted in the Burwarton House sale catalogue, 17–20 July 1956, and cited in P, III, 270 71.

18 *Charity in the Cellar*, 39 × 49 in. (The Right Hon. the Viscount Boyne). Paulson places this in the 1750s but Gowing (1971; 38) notes that a copy by R. Livesay (Huntington Library and Art Gallery) dates it 1739, presumably on information from Mrs Hogarth.

19 See Jill Campbell's interesting article, 'Politics and Sexuality in Portraits of John, Lord Hervey', *Word and Image*, 1990, VI, 4 (October–December) 281–97.

20 For Hervey's urgent efforts to advance his friends, see Hervey, III, 667–9.

21 *Epistle to Dr Arbuthnot* (1735), Pope *Poems*, 608.

22 See Alastair Laing, *In Trust for the Nation: Paintings from National Trust Houses*, Tate Gallery catalogue (1996). Webster and Paulson both decide on Willemin but Alastair Lang sees no reason to doubt Walpole. In the Ickworth painting, the stuck-on paper had lost its design before restoration in 1966, and was reconstructed from a copy made for Thomas Winnington.

23 To Horace Mann, 19 October 1741; Walpole *Corr.*, XVII, 171.

24 To Mann, 23 November 1741; ibid., 211.

25 To Mann, 22 January 1742; ibid., 298.

26 *LEP*, in George *Caricature*, 92–3.

27 *A*, 138.

28 See *Tate Coll.*, 91–7, catalogue 96.

29 *A*, 136–7, 140.

30 Harriet Cowper to William Hayley, 1802; in *Tate Coll.*, 82

31 *The Grey Children*, (1740), 41 × 35¼ in. (Washington University, St Louis).

32 Until recently the baby was thought to be Anna Maria, but it is now known to be Thomas (born 1740; died February 1741). See Mary Webster, 'An Eighteenth-Century Family: Hogarth's Portrait of the Graham Children', *Apollo*, September 1989, 171–3. The children are identified in *Hogarth the Painter*, 41, catalogue 18.

33 Another instance is *The Mackinen Children* (*c.*1742; Dublin, National Portrait Gallery of Ireland). This double portrait of Elizabeth and William, aged about thirteen and ten, the grandchildren of a Scottish sugar-plantation owner in Antigua, can also be read as a symbolic study of transience.

741

34 *Theodore Jacobsen* (1742; Allen Memorial Art Museum, Oberlin College, Ohio).

35 N, 99; *Joseph Porter* (*c.*1740; Toledo Museum of Art, Ohio).

36 Richard Cumberland, *Memoirs* (1807), I, 80.

37 *The Rosciad*; Churchill, 31. For the painting, see *Tate Coll.* 98, catalogue 98.

38 *Thomas Pellett M.D.* (*c.*1735-9; Tate), see *Tate Coll.* 96, catalogue 97; *Sir Caesar Hawkins* (*c.*1740; Royal College of Surgeons, London); *Edwin Sandys* (*c.*1741; Bristol City Art Gallery).

39 For the paintings, see *Hogarth the Painter*, 35-6, catalogue 12, 13. For a concise account of Macclesfield and the Royal Society, see Sir Henry Lyons, *The Royal Society, 1660-1940* (1944), chs. 5 and 6.

40 I am grateful to Elizabeth Einberg for this suggestion, made in a conversation with me in February 1997.

41 A connection made by Einberg, *Hogarth the Painter*, 36.

42 C. R. Weld, *History of the Royal Society* (1848), 424.

43 *Bishop Hoadly* (*c.*1738) and *Mrs Hoadly* (*c.*1745), both 24 × 19 in. (Huntington Library and Art Gallery, San Marino, California).

44 *Tate Coll.*, 101-3, catalogue 99.

45 See *Hogarth the Painter*, 36.14, where Einberg suggests that his gesture echoes that of Aristotle in Raphael's *School of Athens*, 'to indicate the Aristotelian roots of this philosophy'.

46 Shawe-Taylor (81-98) traces a line from *George Arnold* through Ramsay, Reynolds and Raeburn to Sir Thomas Lawrence's *George IV* (1822), 'the most interesting', Lawrence said, 'from its being so entirely of a simple domestic character'.

47 See *Hogarth the Painter*, 40, catalogue 17, 'Unknown Gentleman in Grey, Holding Gloves'. This painting came to light in an auction in 1989, bears a striking resemblance to the Arnold portraits in style, pose and colouring, and it has been suggested that it shows the barrister Lumley Arnold (1723-1781) although the connection is unproven.

48 Simon (86-92) suggests this pose was a response to the argument about the superiority of sculpture to painting.

49 *The London Tradesman*, 1747, 139; Allen, 35.

50 *Mrs Catherine Edwards* (1739; Geneva, Musée de l'Art et Histoire). Probably a celebratory portrait on her marriage to John Nodes in 1739, painted at his house, Shephall Manor, Hertfordshire. (Catherine Vaslet/Nodes became Mrs Edwards on her second marriage in 1761.)

51 *Lavinia Fenton* (*c.*1740), *Tate Coll.* 106-9, catalogue 102.

52 See *Manners and Morals*, 118-19.

53 *Hogarth the Painter*, 43, catalogue 20. The Macclesfield connection was also unearthed by Einberg.

54 *Tate Coll.* 104, catalogue 101.

55 See W. F. N. Noel, 'Edwards of Welham', *The Rutland Magazine and County Historical Record*, IV (1909-10), 209. Mary held land in Leicestershire, Northampton, Middlesex, Essex, Hertford, Kent and the City as well as substantial shares. Her mother came from a rich Huguenot family, who had orginally come over to drain land in Lincolnshire for the Crown in the early seventeenth century. (See also P, II, 421, n. 2.)

56 Mary Edwards to Mary Tooke (Mrs Constantine Vernatti), Emilia F. Noel, *Some Letters*

and Records of the Noel Family (1910), 130; see also 30–31.

57 *Gerard Anne Edwards in His Cradle* (1732), 12½ x 15½ in. (National Trust, The Bearsted Collection, Upton House, Edgehill).

58 *The Edwards Hamilton Family* (1733–4), 26 × 33⅛ in. (private collection).

59 Walpole *Corr.*, XVII, 439, n. 51.

60 *Rutland Magazine*, 243.

61 For the costume, see Aileen Ribiero, *A Visual History of Costume: the Eighteenth Century* (1983), 52.

CHAPTER 18: *Marriage A-la-Mode*

1 *A*, 216.

2 Ibid., 216.

3 *The Champion*, 10 June 1740.

4 'Honour, A Satire' (1747), in Edward Thompson, *Poems and Miscellaneous Compositions of Paul Whitehead* (1775), 54–61. See P, III, 272.

5 Fielding *Joseph Andrews*, 4.

6 Ibid., 5–6.

7 Suggested by Martin Battestin, 'Pictures of Fielding', *Eighteenth-Century Studies*, 17 (1983): 9–13; P, II, 422, n. 9.

8 *Shamela* (in Fielding *Joseph Andrews*), 330.

9 *A Marriage Contract* (*c.*1733), 24½ × 29¼ ins. (Oxford, Ashmolean Museum).

10 Mary Granville Pendarves to Mrs Dawes, 10 November 1743; Delany, II, 221.

11 To his burlesque of Richardson Fielding added a parody of Colley Cibber's autobiography and the dedication of Conyer Middleton's life of Cicero (both 1740), and 'reviews' and letters.

12 *Taste in High Life, or Taste à la Mode* (1742; private collection). Because this was a private commission, Hogarth produced no print, but one was made covertly after Mary's death by her servants in 1746.

13 To Horace Mann, 18 May 1741; Walpole *Corr.*, XVII, 45.

14 Sir Charles Hanbury Williams (1708–1759), *Isabella: or, The Morning*, written 1740, published 1765.

15 Deutsch, 580.

16 'Philogamus', from *The Present State of Matrimony* (1739); see Vivien Jones (ed.), *Women in the Eighteenth Century: Constructions of Femininity* (1990), 77–81.

17 'Epistle to a Lady'; Pope *Poems*, 308.

18 Ibid.

19 *The Dramatick Works of John Dryden*, 6 vols (1735), see Hammelmann, 42.

20 In 1740, Garrick wrote a short plotless piece for Drury Lane called *Lethe*: it has been cited as a possible prompt to Hogarth because it shows different modern types being quizzed by Aesop before they crossed the Styx, among them the newly wed Lord Chalkstone, who declares, 'I married for fortune; she for a title. When we had both got what we wanted, the sooner we parted the better.' As far as I can see, neither this character, nor the lines, appear in the 1740 or 1745 version, but only in the 1757 script, which is advertised 'With the additional character of Lord Chalkstone'. Garrick's debt

743

is to Hogarth, not vice versa. David Garrick, *Lethe* playscripts, BL.

21 R. Blunt and M. Wyndham, *Thomas, Lord Lyttleton* (1936), 85; in Lawrence Stone, *The Family, Sex and Marriage in England 1500–1800* (1977), 273.

22 Hervey to Mrs Digby, 13 November 1735; The Earl of Ilchester (ed.), *Lord Hervey and his Friends*, (1950), 232.

23 Ibid., 233.

24 *The Irish Register: or a List of the Duchess Dowagers, Countesses, Widow Ladies, Maiden Ladies and Misses of Large Fortunes in England* (Dublin, 1742).

25 To Mann, 12 January 1748; Walpole *Corr.*, XIX, 456–7.

26 Wetenhall Wilkes, *A Letter of Genteel and Moral Advice to a Young Lady*, 1740.

27 See the reading in Dabydeen *Hogarth's Blacks*, 74.

28 Smart, 50, quoting François Nivelon's *Rudiments of Genteel Behaviour: An Introduction to the Method of Attaining a Graceful Attitude, an Agreeable Motion, an Easy Air and a Genteel Behaviour* (English translation, 1737; engravings after Bartholomew Dandridge).

29 The first published attack, by Abbé le Blanc, came in 1745 (translated 1747); Michael Snodin, 'English Rococo and its Continental Origins', *Rococo*, 28.

30 Claude Prosper Jolyot de Crebillon *fils*, *The Sopha. A Moral Tale*, 2 vols. (1742), 32, 60–61; see Dabydeen *Hogarth's Blacks*, 79.

31 To Horace Mann, 26 November 1741, and to Conyers Middleton, 9 April 1743; Walpole *Corr.*, XVII, 213, and XV, 15.

32 Walpole *Anec.*, 159–60.

33 Charles Lamb, 'On the Genius and Character of Hogarth', *Poems, Plays and Miscellaneous Essays*, ed. Alfred Ainger, II (1899), 134.

34 N, 275. Ravenet settled in London in 1750. He engraved Hogarth's drawings for *Tristram Shandy*, and later *The Pool of Bethesda* and *The Good Samaritan*. Louis Gérard Scotin the younger engraved plates 1 and 6; Bernard Baron plates 2 and 3, Ravenet plates 4 and 5. Mrs Ravenet was said to have engraved the background of plate 5.

35 Vertue, III, 120.

36 *DA*, 8 November 1744; P, II, 210.

37 See N, 263–6.

38 Prologue to *The Clandestine Marriage* (1766) in *Plays by David Garrick and George Colman the Elder*, ed. E. R. Wood (Cambridge, 1982), 114.

CHAPTER 19: Public Stage, Private Art

1 Rouquet *State of the Arts*, 119–20.

2 Ibid., 123–4.

3 Ibid., 126.

4 Vertue, III, 124.

5 Ibid., 123.

6 Ibid., 124.

7 Hester Thrale Piozzi, *Anecdotes of the late Samuel Johnson, LL.D.* (1786), ed. S. C. Roberts, (Cambridge, 1925), 89.

8 To Lady Ossory, 3 April 1773. Walpole *Corr.*, XXXII, 114 and n. 9; in his commonplace

book Walpole identified the 'cripple' as 'a Mr Wood, who had much more of the air of a coxcomb than a rake'.

9 Vertue, III, 124.

10 *Thomas Herring* (1744), 50 × 40 ins. (Tate).

11 In 1749 Daniel Wray passed on a recommendation from Hogarth of Quentin de la Tour's pastels to Philip Yorke; Whitley, I, 31.

12 *GW*, I, 193.

13 *Letters from the Late Most Reverend Dr Thomas Herring, Lord Archbishop of Canterbury, to William Duncombe, Esq* (1777), ed. John Duncombe, 88–9; P, II, 183.

14 Elizabeth Einberg, to the author, 1996.

15 Joseph Knight, *David Garrick* (1894), 29.

16 To Horace Mann, 26 May 1742; Walpole *Corr.*, XVII, 434.

17 To John Hoadly, 29 December [1744]; Garrick, I, 46.

18 To Frank Hayman, [post 10 October 1745]; Garrick, I, 54.

19 To Somerset Draper, 23 October and 1 December 1745; Garrick, I, 65, 70.

20 Vertue, III, 130.

21 Quennell, 190.

22 Vertue, III, 123, 127.

23 Ibid., 126.

24 *Hogarth the Painter*, 20, catalogue 8; see also fig. 9, for the X-ray, and fig. 10, for a miniature by Roquet, *c.* 1735, clearly based on the original bewigged portrait.

25 *A*, X–XI.

26 Robin Simon makes the interesting suggestion that this may also be a statement of Hogarth's Masonic loyalties: the pug was adopted as a Masonic symbol in Germany after 1738, the same date that Roubiliac sculpted both Hogarth and his pug. See 'Panels and Pugs: reflections and speculations', *Apollo*, 1991, 133, no. 352 (June) 370–73.

27 The maulstick and shovel-shaped palette are in the Royal Academy, donated by J. M. W. Turner.

28 Jane Hogarth's sale catalogue of 1790 (nos. 59, 60). See *HLAT*, II, app. L, 511–13.

29 See W. G. Constable, *The Painter's Workshop* (Oxford, 1954).

30 Rica Jones, 'Changes in Technique of Painting, 1700–1760', *Manners and Morals*, 23, quoting Marshall Smith *The Art and Practice of Painting according to the Theory and Practice of the Best Italian, French and German Masters* (1692), 77.

31 *A*, 129.

32 Ibid., 130.

33 Ibid., 127–30. For Hogarth's palette, see John Gage, *Colour and Culture: Practice and Meaning from Antiquity to Abstraction* (1993), 178–80. For pigments in general, and their history, see Max Doerner *The Materials of the Artist*, translated by Eugen Neuhaus (New York, 1934), and R. D. Harley, *Artists' Pigments c. 1600–1835* (1990).

34 Ibid. See Roy Ashok, ' "Marriage à la Mode" and Contemporary Painting Practice', in *National Gallery Technical Bulletin*, VI (1982), 59–67.

35 The painting chair was described by Alfred Dawson in 1867; Warwick Draper, *Chiswick* (1923).

36 *Ap*, 100.

37 James Northcote, *The Life of Sir Joshua Reynolds* (1819), I, 17–18.

38 *The Happy Marriage*, 'The Wedding Banquet' (*c.*1745), 28 × 36 ins. (Cornwall County Museum, Truro).

39 Benjamin Wilson reported this to George III. See Randolph, 31.

40 See *Tate Coll.*, 118–22, plate 105, which suggests persuasively that this series begins with marriage, and family life, including *The Staymaker*, rather than presenting a courtship leading up to the wedding, as Nichols and John Ireland had thought.

41 *A*, 5.

42 Ibid., 107.

43 Ibid., 110.

44 Ibid., 159–60.

45 *The Staymaker*, Tate. See *Tate Coll.*, 114–17, which suggests the young wife is being fitted for her dress to wear at the dance.

46 *A*, 207. See also Gowing, 31.

47 V&A Forster collection cutting: P, III, 439.

48 *A*, 82.

CHAPTER 20: The Forty-Five

1   To Montagu, 13 July 1745; Walpole *Corr.*, IX, 17.

2   *The Mitred Champion:, or, the Church Militant* (BM Sat. 2634). For more print responses see George *Caricature*, 95–7.

3   *GA*, 14 November 1745; Deutsch, 624.

4   Colley, 44, and Percy A. Scholes, *God save the Queen! The History and Romance of the World's First National Anthem* (1954), 7–15.

5   Henry Fielding, *The True Patriot and Related Writings*, ed. W. B. Coley (Oxford, 1987), which also includes his three pamphlets of 1745.

6   John Wesley, *Journal*, III, 211–12; Gilmour, 110.

7   Colley, 77.

8   See W. Speck, *The Butcher*, 145–7, 161, and A. Youngsson, *The Prince and the Pretender* (1985), 258–9.

9   Langford, 211; 'Essay on Ballads', *LM*, 1769, 580.

10 Tobias Smollett, 'The Tears of Scotland, Written in the Year 1746'; Lonsdale, 407–8.

11 See Gilmour, 126.

12 The first three were tried under the Treason Act of 1696; Lovat by impeachment.

13 To John Hoadly, July [1746]; Garrick, I, 78–9.

14 Memoir, *Annual Register*, 19, 1776: 39–40.

15 An extract is in P, II, 259–60: transcribed from a manuscript belonging to the late R. W. Ketton-Cremer, a descendant of William Windham; see Garrick, I, 85, n. 1. The 'little bawdy play' is mentioned briefly – 'though very dull it is quite unprintable' – in R. W. Ketton-Cremer, *Early Life and Diaries of William Windham*, 1930.

16 N, 58.

17 To John Hoadly, 19 August 1746; Garrick, I, 84.

18 Ibid., I, 86. (The phrase in italics is a near quote from *Hamlet*, I, ii, 187.)

19 N, 58.

20 To Montagu, 16 August 1746; Walpole *Corr.*, IX, 47.

21 Quoted in Quennell, 182.
22 N, 282, citing *Archaeologia*, iv.
23 Ibid., 282; Sir William Young, *State Trials*, IX, 627.
24 N, 282.
25 To Mann, 20 March 1747; Walpole *Corr.*, XVIII, 382.
26 N, 283.
27 Vertue, III, 131.
28 To Mann, 20 March 1747; Walpole *Corr.*, XVIII, 380–81.
29 *DA*, 10 and 11 April 1747.
30 E. Charteris, *William Augustus, Duke of Cumberland* (1913), 230.
31 *DA*, 6 December 1745.
32 Fielding, *Tom Jones*, 336.
33 Ibid., 339.
34 Ibid., 337–8.
35 Rouquet, *Description du Tableau de Mr. Hogarth qui représente la Marche des Gardes à leur rendez-vous de Finchley, dans leur route en Ecosse* (1750), 2; translated by Bonnell Thornton in *The Student*, 20 January 1751; and *The Old Woman's Magazine*, 1751, I, 182.
36 For example, *Escorte d'équipage, Retour de campagne, Camp volant* and *Le Départ de Garnison*. See Marianne Roland Michel, 'Watteau in England', in Charles Hinds (ed.), *The Rococo in England: A Symposium* (1986), 46–59.
37 *HI*, II, 141–2.
38 Ibid.
39 N, 302; Bonnell Thornton in *The Student*, 20 January 1751, II, 162–8.
40 *HI*, II, 153.
41 N, 311.
42 Vertue, III, 153.
43 N, 299n.

CHAPTER 21: Bible Stories: Foundling and Apprentice

1 See *Rococo*, L15, 166. The sculptor remains anonymous.
2 *The Admission of Children by Ballot*, reproduced in R. H. Nichols and F. A. Wray, *The History of the Foundling Hospital* (1935) facing 45. Solkin (161–3) reproduces and discusses Wale's other prints, *A Perspective of the Foundling Hospital I, II*.
3 See Vertue, III, 132.
4 *Rococo*, 166. And see M. I. Webb, *Michael Rysbrack, Sculptor* (1984), 131–5, 141.
5 P, II, 337–8, suggests Hogarth was also illustrating a Masonic theme, since Moses, 'founder of Masonic symbolism', learned Egyptian hieroglyphics from his adoptive mother.
6 General Court I, 149; Ruth K. McClure, *Coram's Children: The London Foundling Hospital in the Eighteenth Century* (New Haven and London, 1981), 66–7.
7 Vertue, III, 135.
8 Argued by Solkin, 168–9.
9 David Hume, 'Of the Delicacy of Taste and Passion (1741) in *Essays* (1777 edn), 6; see Solkin (169), who develops this argument, in relation to George Turnbull's *Treatise on*

Ancient Painting, Containing Observations on the Rise, Progress, and Decline of that Art Amongst the Greeks and Romans (1740). For private and public 'virtue' and the arts, see also Barrell, 54–63.

10 Sarah Markham, *John Loveday of Caversham 1711–1789: The Life and Tours of an Eighteenth Century Onlooker* (Salisbury, 1984), 377, 505; in Solkin, 173.

11 Rouquet *State of the Arts*, 26–7.

12 Nichols and Wray, facing 151.

13 McClure, 193, quoting Foundling Hospital's Library, 39; and *GM*, 17 June 1747.

14 George *London*, 227–9.

15 *A*, 225.

16 For the rough sketches, and second stage of careful drawings with ink wash, see Oppé, 40–44; catalogue 40–63, 41–64.

17 *HGW*, 129.

18 George (*London*, 187), who gives a detailed and vivid analysis of the trade, 178–91.

19 Ibid., 191–2, quoting *Report on the Police of the Metropolis* (1816), 151.

20 N, 285.

21 Ibid., 285–6.

22 *LEP*, 21 March 1745; *HGW*, 135.

23 N, 286.

24 *The Beggar's Opera*, III, xii; Gay *Dramatic Works*, 20.

25 See Peter Linebaugh, 'The Ordinary of Newgate and his Account', in J. S. Cockburn (ed.), *Crime In England, 1550–1800* (1977), 246–69, and *HGW*, 137.

26 Saussure, 111.

27 Vertue, III, 136–7.

28 *The Effects of Industry and Idleness Illustrated* (1748), shilling pamphlet; P, II, 290–91.

CHAPTER 22: 'Seized, and carried before the Governor'

1 The *Centurion*, under Captain Denis, took part in the Battle of Cape Finisterre despite having its mainmast shot away; in 1742 it had captured the great Spanish galleon *Acapulco*; *HGW*, 127.

2 N, 284. (Child's name was changed to Tylney by deed poll in 1735, and by 1747 he was Earl Tylney.) For the 'warming-pan baby' story connected with James II's desire for an heir, for possible links to Samuel Child, a Jacobite candidate of 1747, and connections with Fielding's propaganda, see *HGW*, 126–7.

3 Antal, 153; Hogarth copied Raphael's figure from *Paul Preaching at Athens*, and echoed his composition of a different judgment in a Roman court, from *Paul and Elymas before Sergius Paulus*, also copied by Thornhill in St Paul's.

4 Reprinted in Dobson, 106–7n., from Lincoln's Inn archives.

5 Vertue, III, 155.

6 Ibid., 141.

7 Ibid., 155.

8 Abbé Le Blanc, *Letters on the English and French Nations* (Dublin, 1747), 162–3.

9 For the complicated retouching and engraving of *Paul before Felix*, see *HGW*, 152–6. In a second version of the print, engraved by Hogarth himself and not Sullivan he removed

748

the figure of Drusilla, focusing on the confrontation between Paul and Felix.

10 To Mann, 29 April 1748; Walpole *Corr.*, XIX, 482.

11 Ibid., 483.

12 Vertue, III, 141-2.

13 N, 50. Of the two possible informants, Robert Strange was in Paris, 1748-50, and Thomas Major, 1745-48; P, II, 446n.

14 Vertue, III, 142.

15 Ibid.

16 Ibid.

17 *A*, 227-8.

18 To Mann, 15 December 1748; Walpole *Corr.*, XX, 13.

19 N, 50.

20 *A*, 228.

21 Vertue, VI, 200.

22 Quoted in *Rococo*, 16.

23 Colley, 88.

24 P, II, 55.

CHAPTER 23: Town and Country

1 To Mann, 2 December 1748; Walpole *Corr.*, XX, 3.

2 To Mann, 26 January 1748; ibid., XIX, 460.

3 Edmund Burke to Richard Shackleton, 25 January 1745; *The Letters of Edmund Burke* (Cambridge, 1958), I, 39.

4 Fielding to Samuel Richardson, 15 October 1748; Battestin, 442-3.

5 To Mann, 26 December 1748; Walpole *Corr.*, XX, 16.

6 Walter Jackson Bate, *Samuel Johnson* (1978), 281.

7 *The Vanity of Human Wishes*, from Samuel Johnson, *Poems*, ed. D. N. Smith and E. L. McAdam (Oxford, 1964) 56.

8 Sir John Hawkins, *Johnson* [1787], 45; J. L. Clifford, *Young Samuel Johnson* [1955], 235.

9 Boswell *Life*, I, 146-7.

10 *Flora Macdonald* (1749; Ashmolean Museum, Oxford). The engraver was James McArdell.

11 'Prologue Spoken at the Opening of the Theatre Royal, Drury Lane, 1747'. Samuel Johnson, *Poems*, ed. E. L. McAdam (New Haven, 1964), 89.

12 David Garrick, Epilogue to *The Suspicious Husband*, quoted in Joseph Knight, *David Garrick* (1894), 109.

13 To Mann, 11 March 1748; Walpole *Corr.*, XIX, 468.

14 To Sir William Young, 10 January 1773; Garrick, II, 846.

15 *Correspondence and Other Papers of James Boswell*, ed. Marshall Waingrow (New York, 1969), 22; W. J. Bate, *Samuel Johnson* (1978), 264-5.

16 Boswell *Life*, I, 196-8.

17 Garrick, I, introduction, xxxv.

18 Published as *Hogarth to His Wife*, Houghton Library Brochures, no. 5 ([Cambridge, Mass.], 1946); reprinted in P, II, 274. The manuscript is in the Houghton Library, Harvard University.

19 For Steevens's remarks, see N, 48.

20 *GW*, I, 127n., amplifying N, 74.

21 *HI*, I, 205.

22 *Heads of Six of Hogarth's Servants*, c.1750–55, see *Tate Coll.*, 132–4, catalogue 109.

23 In 1748 one of Pelham's first moves towards economic retrenchment was to cut military expenditure: by 1751 the navy was reduced from 51,550 to 8000, and the army from 50,000 to 18,850. See Geoffrey Holmes and Daniel Szechi, *The Age of Oligarchy: Pre-industrial Britain, 1722–1783* (1993), 271.

24 To Mann, 3 May 1749; Walpole *Corr.*, XX, 47.

25 Keates, 287–8.

26 *GM*, 21 April 1749.

27 To Montagu, 18 May 1749; Walpole *Corr.*, IX, 81.

28 Quoted in Stella Tillyard, *Aristocrats: Caroline, Emily, Louisa and Sarah Lennox, 1740–1832* (1994), 79.

29 To Mann, 3 May 1749; Walpole *Corr.*, XX, 48.

30 'A Charge to the Grand Jury' in *An Enquiry into the Causes of the late Increase of Robbers and Related Writings*, ed. M. R. Zirker (Oxford, 1988), 14.

31 *General Evening Post*, 17–18 December 1748; Battestin, 461.

32 Battestin, 488.

33 *The Savoyard Girl* (1749; 16½ × 13 ins; private collection – as Leger Galleries, London). When this came up for auction (Phillips, 19 November 1991) it was identified as Hogarth's by Elizabeth Einberg: see 'Music for Mars, or the Case of the Duke's Lost Sword', *Huntington Library Quarterly*, 56, May 1993. (See also *The Politician*, painted for Theodosius Forrest: Ralph Lillford, 'Hogarth's Politician', *Apollo* 97 (1983), 100.)

34 For all aspects of Chiswick life, I am indebted to James Wisdom and Valerie Box, who generously shared their detailed knowledge of local history.

35 For the history of Chiswick, see Gillian Clegg, *Chiswick Past* (1995); Thomas Faulkner, *History of Brentford, Ealing and Chiswick* (1845), Lloyd Sanders, *Old Kew, Chiswick and Kensington* (1910); Warwick Draper, *Chiswick* (1923).

36 See John Harris, *The Palladian Revival: Lord Burlington, his Villa and Garden at Chiswick* (Royal Academy Catalogue, 1994).

37 'Epistle to Richard Boyle, Earl of Burlington', Pope *Poems*, 112.

38 Court Roll of the Prebendal Manor of Chiswick, Archives of the Church Commissioners, 205.418; P, 269, n. 48.

39 *HI*, I, cvi.

40 In this dispute, in 1745, Ranby criticized the handling of the case by James Jurin, Sir Edward Hulse and William Chiselden in *A Narrative of the Late Illness of the Right Honourable the Earl of Orford*, and Fielding supported him in a lively satire, *The Charge to the Jury: or the Sum of the Evidence, on the Trial of A.B.C.lD. and E.F. All M.D. for the Death of one Robert at Orfud . . .*, in which Ranby appears for the prosecution as 'Dr John Narrative'.

41 The location of Ranby's house was identified by James Wisdom; it was previously thought that this sketch was the view north from Hogarth's own windows.

42 See *Manners and Morals*, 204–5, where both portraits are reproduced. *Hannah, Daughter of John Ranby* (c.1748–50; 25⅛ × 22⅝ in; private collection); *George Osborne,*

750

later John Ranby (*c*.1750; 25⅛ × 22¾ in.; private collection).

43 See B. C. Nangle, *The Monthly Review, First Series, 1749–89* (Oxford, 1934), and Faulkner, *History*, 349ff.

44 Deutsch, 851, quoting an extract from Morell's manuscript memoirs, written *c*.1764. Morell's Handel librettos included *Judas Maccabeus* (1747), *Joshua* (1748), *Theodora* (1749–50), *Jephtha* (1752) and *The Triumph of Time and Truth* (1757).

45 Jonathan Keates, 'A Saintly Dignity', review of the Glyndebourne production of *Theodora*, *Times Literary Supplement*, 14 June 1996, 19.

46 *GW*, I, 127n.

47 John Nichols, *Literary Anecdotes*, 9 vols (1812–15), I, 655–6.

CHAPTER 24: Cruelty

1 Samuel Johnson, *Selected Writings*, ed. R. T. Davies (1965), 257; in Derek Jarrett, *England in the Age of Hogarth*, 41. Jarrett (53), reads the Strand riots as a clash between sailors – 'champions of a free country' – and soldiers – 'instruments of a despotic king'.

2 *DA*, 9 February 1750.

3 *GM*, 1750, 20, 169.

4 Deutsch, 683–4.

5 To Mann, 2 April 1750; Walpole *Corr.*, xx, 137.

6 Tobias Smollett, *The History of England from the Revolution in 1688, to the Death of George the Second* (1827), 317–18; Langford, 284–5.

7 *GA*, 13 April 1750.

8 Thomas Sherlock, *A Letter . . . to the Clergy and People of London and Westminster on Occasion of the Late Earthquake* (1750).

9 See *Old England*, 7 April 1750, and Henry Fielding, *Tom Jones*, ed. R. P. C. Mutter (Harmondsworth, 1966), Introduction, 11.

10 *The Scandalizade* (1750); N, 296.

11 Henry Fielding, *Proposal for Making an Effectual Provision for the Poor* in *An Enquiry into the Causes of the late Increase of Robbers and Related Writings*, ed. M. R. Zirker (Oxford, 1988), 230.

12 Fielding, *Enquiry*, 88–9.

13 George *London*, 52.

14 Ibid., 54.

15 Ibid., 53.

16 For the iconography of the London street, and 'acceptable' satires of fashion by Bickham, June, Boitard, Walker and Gravelot, see Hallett, 230–50.

17 *A*, 226.

18 Jarrett (146–7) points out that John Baillie's *Essay on the Sublime*, stressing the link with catharsis, appeared in 1747. Lamb also called *Gin Lane* an exercise in the 'Sublime'.

19 Ibid., 147. The Society was incorporated in late 1750, with the Prince of Wales as Governor; in 1751 Lockman wrote *The Shetland Herring and Peruvian Gold-Mine*, on the profits of the first as opposed to the fantasies of the second.

20 See Oppé, 48, catalogue 76, plate 73.

21 The price of wheat rose by almost a third, from under thirty shillings a quarter in the

1730s and 1740s to thirty-eight shillings in the 1750s. Langford (149) notes that total domestic consumption of spirits fell from 7,886,000 gallons in 1745 to 5,453,000 in 1752 and 3,243,000 in 1758, practically all the reduction being a fall in the consumed volume of British spirits.

22 Charles Dickens, 'Gin-Shops', in *Sketches by Boz, Illustrative of Every-Day Life and Every-Day People* (1833–5; published in volume form 1836–7), (Oxford, 1963 edn), 187.

23 Fielding, *Enquiry*, 89.

24 *A*, 226.

25 J. T. Smith, *The Streets of London* (1845), 23.

26 *Death giving Taylor a Cross-Buttock*, and *Taylor Triumphing over Death*; see Oppé, 49, catalogue 79, plates 75–6. These were allegedly designed for Taylor's tombstone: N, 412.

27 *HGW*, 150.

28 To Mann, 18 October 1750; Walpole *Corr.*, xx, 199. Walpole was one of many who compared him to Macheath: see *Among the Whores and Thieves: William Hogarth and The Beggar's Opera* (New Haven, 1997), catalogue 19, 96.

29 Fielding, *Enquiry*, 66.

30 *The Conduct of Two Brothers* [*BM Sat*]. See Hallett, 266–8, who also relates the *Cruelty* series to current anatomical iconography.

31 *A*, 226–7.

32 Samuel Johnson in Hester Lynch Piozzi, *Anecdotes of the Late Samuel Johnson* (1786); R. Paulson and T. Lockwood (eds), *Henry Fielding: The Critical Heritage* (1969), 445.

33 Quoted in Pat Rogers, *Henry Fielding; A Biography* (1979), 191.

34 Henry Fielding, *The Covent-Garden Journal*, 28 January 1752, ed. B. A. Zolger (1988), 65–6.

35 Bertelsen, 18.

36 The Rouquet translation appeared in Christopher Smart's journal *The Midwife: or, The Old Woman's Magazine*, 17–19 January 1751, and a separate explanation in Thornton's own journal, *The Student: or, Oxford and Cambridge Miscellany*, 7–9 March 1751.

37 Bertelsen, 25.

38 Tobias Smollett, *The Adventures of Peregrine Pickle*, ed. James L. Clifford (based on the first edn, not the revised and toned-down 1758 edn), (Oxford, 1964), 660.

39 The identification of Hogarth with Pallet was first made by Ronald Paulson in 'Smollett and Hogarth: The Identity of Pallet', *Studies in English Literature*, v (1965), 351–9; see P, III, 1–5.

40 Smollett, *Peregrine Pickle*, 224.

41 Ibid., 224–5.

42 Ibid., 225.

43 Ibid., 75.

44 See R. E. Moore, *Hogarth's Literary Relationships* (Minneapolis, 1948), 162–86.

45 N, 101.

46 See Lippincott, 122–3. Also Christopher White, *Rembrandt in 18th-Century England* (New Haven and London, 1983).

47 Vertue, III, 159.

48 For Wilson's remarks to West, see H. Randolph, *Life of General Sir R[obert] W[ilson]*, I, 13–15; quoted freely in P, III, 37–40. The anecdote is also told in Smith, I, 159–60;

Edwards, *Anecdotes*, 147–8; Whitley, 123–5.

49 Randolph, *W[ilson]*, and Whitley, I, 124.

50 *DA*, 9 May 1751.

51 Joseph Farington, in Edmund Malone, *The Works of Sir Joshua Reynolds* (5th edn with Memoir by Farington, 3 vols, 1819), 16–19.

52 *Memoirs of William Hickey*, ed. Alfred Spenser (1913), I, 27–8, quoted in the exhibition catalogue *Thomas Hudson* (Kenwood, 1979).

53 *DA*, 9 May 1751.

54 Vertue, III, 156.

55 *DA*, 28 May 1751, repeated twice, once in a shorter form.

56 Vertue, III, 156.

57 N, 280. All quotes referring to Lane are from this source. His account appears in a slightly different version in *GW*, I, 183–8.

58 *HI*, III, 99. The letter is in BL, Add. MS 27995.

59 N, 281, quoting 'another correspondent' (a letter in the *St James's Evening Chronicle*, 10–12 July 1761).

CHAPTER 25: 'A Wanton Kind of Chace': *The Analysis of Beauty*

1 *HI*, III, 102.

2 N, 279.

3 Ibid., 281.

4 Cust, 52, and *HLAT*, II, 505.

5 Vertue, IV, 150. See Allen (1984), 355–6.

6 Vertue, I, 10. For his own plan see II, 150–55.

7 P, III, 15–16, quoting Sir Robert Strange, *An Enquiry into the Rise and Establishment of the Royal Academy of Arts* (1775), 61.

8 *GW*, I, 416–19; Edwards, 9.

9 BL Add. MS 27995, f. 9. Dawes, sometimes described as Hogarth's pupil, was said to be the illegitimate son of a City merchant and was apprenticed to Henry Morland. Samuel Redgrave, *Dictionary of Artists of the English School* (1878 edn), 116.

10 *A*, 185–6.

11 David Bindman and Malcolm Baker, *Roubiliac and the Eighteenth-century Monument: Sculpture as Theatre* (1995), 70.

12 Henry Fielding, *Covent-Garden Journal*, 14 January 1752, ed. B. A. Zolger (1988), 35–6.

13 *A*, ix.

14 Ibid. (A version of the fable had been used, for example, by Vasari of Brunelleschi's design for the dome of Florence.)

15 Whitley, I, 156. (Ellis brought many new seeds from Carolina and elsewhere.)

16 James Parsons, 'The Crounian Lectures, on Muscular Motion', 1745; and *On the Analogy between the Propagation of Animals and Vegetables* (1752). See Robert E. Schofield, *Mechanism and Materialism: British Natural Philosophy in An Age of Reason* (Princeton, 1970), 194–6.

17 *A*, 231.

18 *HI*, I, lxxxix–lxxxiii. Like the Hoadly brothers, Townley tried his hand at poetry and the occasional play – his comedy *High Life Below Stairs* was staged with great success in

1759. In 1760, he became headmaster of Merchant Taylors'.

19 *A*, 19.

20 Ibid., 186. BL Eg. MS 3015, ff. 10–11.

21 Loose sheets in BL Add. MS 27992, ff. 17, 17b, 18. See *A*, 192–3.

22 See BL Eg. MS 1013. Each draft takes up two notebooks in the manuscript series held by the British Library, Eg. MSS 3011–16.

23 BL Eg. MS 3011. The chapter headings are listed by Burke in 'The Rejected Passages', *A*, 167.

24 *A*, 180.

25 Ibid., 186.

26 Ibid., 192; BL Add. MS. 27992, f. 11.

27 *GA*, 16 November 1752; *HGW*, 157.

28 BL Add. MS. 27995, f. 7.

29 Ibid., ff. 12–13.

30 *A*, 19.

31 N, 52.

32 Ibid., 53.

33 *HI*, I, lxxx–lxxxiii.

34 N, 53.

35 *A*, 5; citing Giampolo Lomazzo, *Tracte Containing the Artes of Curious Paintinge, Carvinge & Buildinge*, trans. Richard Haydocke, 1582.

36 *A*, 7.

37 Ibid., 43, 45.

38 Ibid., 170.

39 Ibid., 35, 41, 42.

40 Ibid., 46.

41 Ibid., 23.

42 See J. T. Smith, *The Streets of London* (1845), 11–12, and M. I. Webb, 'Henry Cheere, Sculptor and Businessman, and John Cheere, I', *Burlington Magazine*, C (1958), 236–9.

43 For Pond, see Lippincott, 142–4. P, III, 102–3 sees Hogarth's plate as a response to Joseph Spence, *Polymetis: or, an Enquiry concerning the Agreement between the Works of the Roman Poets, and the Remains of the Antient Artists* (1747).

44 Samuel Foote, Prologue, *Taste: A Comedy in Two Acts* (1757 edn), xi.

45 See Joseph Burke, introduction to the *Analysis*, *A*, xxxiv, and 'A Classical Aspect of Hogarth's Theory of Art', *Journal of the Warburg and Courtauld Institutes*, VI (1943), 151–3.

46 *A*, 33.

47 Quennell (231n.) points out that Arab horses had been in Britain since the late seventeenth century, and that 'between 1684 and 1724, three famous stallions arrived . . . the Byerley Turk, the Darley Arabian and the Godolphin Arabian, to become the progenitors of modern blood stock'.

48 *A*, 47, 150–51, 61, 62, 59.

49 Ibid., 63, 46.

50 Ibid., 26–8.

51 *A*, 1. Edmund Burke, *A Philosophical Enquiry into the Ideas of the Sublime and the Beautiful* (1757), ed. J. T. Boulton (1958; 1987), 155, section XXIII, 'Variation'.

52 *A*, 72.

53 Ibid., 53.

54 Ibid., 96-7.

55 Ibid., 98.

56 Ibid., 149.

57 P, III, 146, quotes Uvedale Price, *Essays on the Picturesque* (1798), II, 269-70n. Price's father remembered Hogarth asserting that no one with a true idea of the line of beauty could do anything ungraceful and saying that he himself, '"should not hesitate in the manner I should present any thing to the greatest monarch." "He happened", said my father, "at that moment, to be sitting in the most ridiculously awkward posture I ever beheld."'

58 Walpole *Anec.*, 165.

59 *A*, 149-50.

60 Ibid., 48.

61 Ibid., 49.

62 Ibid., 49. See BL Eg. MSS 3013 f. 42b – his first thought was that St Paul's had '4 or five hundred of them in one part or other of it'.

63 *A*, 46, 48.

64 The nationalist point is well made by Richard Dorment, 'The Genius of Gin Lane', *The New York Review of Books*, 27 May 1993, 19.

65 Ibid., 157.

66 Ibid., 158-9.

CHAPTER 26: Factions and Elections

1 *Letters written by the Right Honourable Lady Luxborough, to William Shenstone, Esq* (1755), 16 March 1754, 380-81. On 21 December 1753 she had written, ' I want to see Hogarth's Analysis of beauty', complaining she had missed the subscription date (369). For Shenstone's own response that the *Analysis* is 'really entertaining; and has, in some measure adjusted my notions with regard to beauty in general', see *Letters of William Shenstone*, ed. Marjorie Williams (Oxford, 1939), 396. For other reactions see P, III, 132-52.

2 *Monthly Review*, 10, February 1754, 100-110.

3 *Gray's Inn Journal*, 38, 7 July 1753.

4 *The World*, 13 December 1753; P, III, 144.

5 These included John Armstrong, *Taste: An Epistle to a Young Critic* (1753); J. G. Cooper, *Letters concerning Taste* (1755); Ramsay, *Dialogue on Taste* (1755).

6 P, III, 339.

7 *The Connoisseur*, 8, February 1754.

8 P, III, 149.

9 See *Idler*, 76, 29 September 1759; 79, 20 October 1759; 82, 10 November 1759.

10 D. Hudson, *Sir Joshua Reynolds, A Personal Study* (1958), 66.

11 For this series of satirical prints attacking Hogarth see *BM Sat.*, 3238-3249.

12 Survey parties went to Scotland after 1745, when it was decided that roads and military forts must be improved. For Sandby see William Sandby, *Thomas and Paul Sandby: Royal Academicians* (1892). More accurate but idiosyncratic is Johnson Ball, *Paul and Thomas Sandby: Royal Academicians* (Cheddar, Somerset, 1985); for a concise, clear

account see Luke Herrman, *Paul and Thomas Sandby* (V& A catalogue, 1986).

13 See Johnson Ball, *Paul and Thomas Sandby*, 141.

14 Paul Sandby, *Eight Perspective Views of Cities, Castles and Forts, in North Britain*, 6 December 1753.

15 *GI*, III, 112–13n.

16 *DA*, 23 March 1753, reproduced in full in P, III, 132, and in W. A. Sandby, *The History of the Royal Academy of Arts from It Foundation in 1768 to the Present Time* (1826), I, 26–7. For Hayman's involvement see Allen, (1984), 356–9.

17 *BM Sat.*, 3249.

18 *BM Sat.*, 3278; first published in Allen (1984), 359.

19 *A*, 203.

20 Henry Fox to Charles Hanbury Williams, 1751, in Stella Tillyard, *Aristocrats; Caroline, Emily, Louisa and Sarah Lennox, 1740–1832* (1994), 86.

21 Sandwich was dismissed as Secretary for the Navy, and Bedford resigned in protest.

22 In 1751, Dodington employed Ralph to attack ministerial patronage in *The Remembrancer*; when Dodington changed sides Ralph started a new opposition paper, *The Protester*, for the Duke of Bedford.

23 Pelham supported a similar Bill in 1751 to encourage immigrants (30,000 foreigners were squeezed into City lodgings) but fears of job losses led to its defeat. See Langford, 224.

24 Walpole *Memoirs II*, I, 238–9.

25 Tillyard, *Aristocrats*, 89.

26 Gray to Thomas Wharton, 14 July 1753; *Correspondence of Thomas Gray*, ed. Paget Toynbee and Leonard Whibley (Oxford, 1971), 378.

27 The Act, passed in May 1751, meant that the calendar year would now start on 1 January (instead of Lady Day, 25 March).

28 *BM Sat.*, 3202; George *Caricature*, 100.

29 Walpole *Corr.*, III, 221.

30 Advertised in *LEP*, 25–27 April, and in *PA* throughout May; P, III, 158. For subscription list, see BL Add. MS 22394, k. 1, ff. 2–28: the ledger has 19 March on the binding (28 March on title page), but subscriptions were received from mid-March.

31 Rouquet *State of the Arts*, 15.

32 Ibid., 41–2, 117–18.

33 Walpole *Memoirs II*, 23.

34 For a vivid account see J. R. Robson, *The Oxfordshire Election of 1754* (Oxford, 1949). *Humours of a Country Election* (1734) also had a frontispiece featuring an Election dinner and chairing the members; N, 334; *HGW*, 163.

35 *SJC*, 20–23 April 1761.

36 Robson, *The Oxfordshire Election*, 62.

37 N, 335, which also identifies other individuals; ' Sir Commodity Taxem' is on the woman's letter. Many details of the action in the four scenes are described in *A Poetical Description of Mr Hogarth's Election Prints* (1759), which claimed to be ' Written under Mrs Hogarth's sanction and Inspection', reproduced in N, 338–60.

38 See E. Wind, 'Borrowed Attitudes' in 'Reynolds and Hogarth', *Journal of the Warburg and Courtauld Institutes*, 1938–39, 184, cited in *HGW*, 165.

39 Fielding *Tom Jones*, 567–8.

756

40 Dodington represented Bridgwater for thirty years but lost his seat in 1754; a temporary setback as he had another safe seat at Weymouth.

41 *The Correspondence of the Late John Wilkes*, ed. J. T. Almon, 5 vols (1805), I, 25–7.

CHAPTER 27: To Encourage the Others

1 N, 361.

2 *HGW*, 164.

3 N, 361, 360.

4 To Montagu, 20 December 1755; Walpole *Corr.*, IX, 189.

5 *LC*, 20–22 September 1759, during another invasion scare; *HGW*, 169.

6 George *Caricature*, 100–110.

7 Ibid., 103.

8 Atherton, 53.

9 See D. G. Allan, *William Shipley, Founder of the Royal Society of Arts, A Biography with Documents* (1968). Founders were Shipley, Viscount Folkestone, Lord Romney, the Reverend Dr Stephen Hales: soon joined by ministers and politicians. See Sir H. Truman Wood, *A History of the Royal Society of Arts* (1913); D. Hudson and K. Luckhurst , *The Royal Society of Arts, 1754–1954* (1954).

10 Kirby's subscription list, in the back of first editions, 1754, and 1755. Volume I was dedicated to Hogarth, II to 'An Academy of Painting, Sculpture, Architecture &c'. It prompted a long, critical letter from Highmore to which Hogarth drafted a reply; *HLAT*, app. H.

11 *The Plan of an Academy for the Better Cultivation, Improvement and Encouragement of Painting, Sculpture, Architecture, and the Arts of Design in General*, 15 pp. (1755). See Allen (1984), 359–60, and P, III, 186. Also raised in John Buckeridge, *Essay Towards an English School* (1755).

12 Lionel Cust, *History of the Society of Dilettanti* (1898), 53.

13 Ibid.; Minutes of the Dilettanti, signed by the Duke of Bedford as President.

14 Ibid., 54. The signatories were Hayman, Grignion, Hudson, Lambert, Scott, John Gwynn, Moser, Wale, Richard Yeo, Robert Strange, Roubiliac, Thomas Carter, Robert Taylor, Hoare, James Stuart, Richard Dalton, Frances Newton, Joshua Reynolds, Henry Cheere, John Pine, G. Hamilton, Isaac Ware, John Astley, Nicolas Revett, Thomas Sandby. Dated 2 April 1755.

15 Perhaps Dingley's original plan, 1753, but Allen (1984), 363, suggests *An Essay, in Two Parts, on the Necessity and form of a Royal Academy of Painting, Sculpture and Architecture* (1755), which proposed the President should not be an artist but 'a Man of Consequence' and professors be recruited from abroad.

16 Robert Strange, *An Enquiry into the Rise and Establishment of the Royal Academy of Arts. To which is prefixed a letter to the Earl of Bute* (1775), 61–2.

17 *Ap*, 105.

18 Ibid., 92.

19 Rouquet *State of the Arts*, 1–2.

20 Ibid., 17.

21 Ibid., 7.

22 Hogarth was possibly nominated by Henry Cheere, who saw this as another base for the campaign: in February 1756 he presented a plan for a Royal Academy to the Society. See Allen (1984), 366.

23 Boswell *Life*, III, 304.

24 See Colley, 88–98.

25 Walter Jackson Bate, *Samuel Johnson* (1978), 328.

26 Dr John Brown, *An Estimate of the Manners and Principles of the Times* (1757), I, 47. See P, III, 182–3.

27 Ramsay was elected on 14 December 1757. The Society's Committee on Drawings, 1757–8, recommended the age limit be raised to twenty-four, and drawings for prizes could be done at St Martin's Lane, the Duke of Richmond's gallery, or before a witness in the artist's rooms. For prizes awarded in 1759, see Allen (1984), 367.

28 Senhouse correspondence, Cumbrian Record Office, quoted in P, III, 51–3.

29 Reverend Edmund Pyle, *Memoirs of a Royal Chaplain*, ed. A. Hartshorne (1905); P, III, 201.

30 *Ap*, 87–91.

31 Ibid., 89.

32 Ibid., 96.

33 Ibid., 79–80.

34 Ibid., 98–9.

CHAPTER 28: Pulpit and Portraits, Art and Life

1 The St Mary Redcliffe altarpiece remained in the church until the 1840s when the Gothic window was recovered. The paintings were then bought for the Bristol Academy, and in 1955 were left to the Art Gallery, where they were restored and cleaned.

2 See *Critical Review*, I (1756), 479.

3 M. J. H. Liversidge, *William Hogarth's Bristol Altarpiece* (Bristol, 1980), 9–10.

4 P, III, 206, and source, *The Bristol Memorialist* (1816). See also J. F. Nichols, *Bristol Past and Present* (Bristol, 1881), III, 192, and John Latimer, *The Annals of Bristol* (1893). Simmons is credited locally with helping Hogarth.

5 P, III, 202; see Ruth Young, *Mrs Chapman's Portrait: a Beauty of Bath of the 18th Century* (1926), 71–4.

6 Antal (154–5) suggests that the figures of Peter and Mary on the left derive from Raphael's *The Transfiguration*.

7 To Montagu, 28 August 1756; Walpole *Corr.*, IX, 195.

8 *A*, 219.

9 Ibid., 227.

10 James Ralph, *Case of Authors* (1758), 18.

11 N, 63–4.

12 Hester Thrale Piozzi, *Autobiography, Letters and Literary Remains*, ed. A. Hayward (2nd edn, 1861), II, 308–9.

13 Hester Thrale Piozzi, *Anecdotes of the late Dr. Samuel Johnson, LLD*, ed. S. C. Rogers (Cambridge, 1925), 89–90.

14 N, 58.

15 Ibid., 58–9.

16 H. Randolph, *Life of General Sir R[obert] W[ilson]* (1862), I, 32.

17 Ibid., I, 17.

18 *GI*, I, 155.

19 Smith (1828 edn), I, 131.

20 BL Add. MS 27995, f. 23; reproduced in *HI*, 61.

21 Garrick, I, 369–70. The date 8 January fell on a Saturday in 1757, and 1763. The editors of the *Letters* chose 1763 from references to 'ill health and managerial difficulties', but this is revised in G. W. Stone and G. M. Kahrl, *David Garrick: A Critical Biography* (Cambridge, Illinois, 1979), which opts for 1757 (more likely in view of Hogarth's illness in 1763, and the role of Benjamin Wilson in 1757). See also P, III, 286, and Joseph Knight, *David Garrick* (1894), 157.

22 Tate Wilkinson, quoted in Knight, *Garrick*, 153.

23 *GW*, I, 212.

24 See the reading in Richard Wendorf, 'Hogarth's Dilemma', in *The Elements of Life; Biography and Portrait Painting in Stuart and Georgian England* (Oxford, 1990), 171–88.

25 Argued by Lance Bertelsen, 'Garrick and English Painting', *Eighteenth-Century Studies*, XI (1978), 312–13.

26 *LC*, 9–12 November 1786; P, III, 286.

27 *LC*, 7–9 November 1786; P, III, 517, n. 14.

28 Garrick told the story to Fielding's French translator, La Place; see Whitley, I, 152–4, Stone and Kahrl, *David Garrick*, 104.

29 N, 12. For discoveries during cleaning, see Oliver Millar, '"Garrick and His Wife" by William Hogarth', *Burlington Magazine*, CIV (1962), 347–8.

30 See Wendorf, *Elements of Life*, 185–8. Also *Hogarth the Painter* (where the painting is entitled *Mr and Mrs Garrick*); catalogue 29, 51–2.

31 N, 12; BL Add. MS 27991, f. 28b.

32 Garrick, I, 223, 206.

33 Garrick, I, Introduction, xxix.

34 To Montagu, 14 October 1756; Walpole *Corr.*, IX, 198. Delany, I, 283, and Garrick, I, 205, n. 4.

35 Walpole *Anec.*, 180. *Rococo*, E 7, 67–8, points out that the chair is mahogany, although the 'Shakespeare' mulberry tree at Stratford was cut down in 1756, and some wood used to make souvenirs; Stone and Kahrl, *David Garrick* (104), note that Garrick bought six pieces.

36 *GW*, I, 212–13.

37 *A*, 212. For Rembrandt's influence see Bindman, 193–5.

38 *Mary Woffington as Mary Queen of Scots* (Petworth Collection, Petworth).

39 Inscribed on back of canvas (City of Aberdeen Art Gallery); P, III, 298.

40 For story and documentation see *HI*, III, 128–36.

41 Joseph Warton, *Essay upon the Genius and Writings of Pope*, 2 vols (1757, and revised edn, 1762), I, 122–3.

42 *GW*, I, 210–11.

43 N, 65; Warton, *Pope*, 3rd edn (1762).

44 Garrick, I, 353.

759

45 N, 65–6n.

46 Although he was paid from 6 June, Hogarth himself noted that he 'entered upon the business of serjeant painter' on 16 July; V. A. Forster Bequest, with print of Livesay's *Hogarth's Crest*; P, III, 487 n. 20.

47 *A*, 219.

48 See P, III, 214, citing PRO Works 5/61–63. The sums were: 1757, £400; 1758, nearly £700; 1759, £947; 1760, £645 and 1761, £982.

49 See 'Sir Joshua Reynolds Sitter Book, 1755', transcribed and edited by Ellis K. Waterhouse, *Walpole Society*, XLI (1966–8), 112–64.

50 P, III, 215, quotes the royal patent; Hogarth's note is in the Nichols Hogarth collection, V, Fitzw.

51 See Kerslake, I, 146; catalogue 289.

52 Movingly compared by Bindman (195–6) to Rembrandt's *The Artist in His Studio* (Boston).

53 See *HGW*, 170.

CHAPTER 29: Gambling to Excess

1 Whitley, I, 156.

2 The list is included in John Brownlow, *Memoranda or Chronicles of the Foundling Hospital* (1847), 17–19.

3 Samuel Boyce, 'The Progress of the Sister Arts', quoted in *GW*, III, 292–4. The music was by Arne.

4 See Andrew Moore, 'William Hogarth; Francis Matthew Schutz in his Bed', *National Art Collections Fund Review*, 1990, 87, 138–41.

5 He argued for a radical programme to make MPs more accountable – a Place Bill (to remove patronage from Parliament), the repeal of the Septennial Act and the Militia Bill. See Betty Kemp, *Sir Francis Dashwood; An Eighteenth-Century Independent* (1967).

6 For the 'country club' theory, see Kemp, 130–36. Wilkes was a member by at least 1760 and exposed in the *Public Advertiser*, June 1763. Its rituals were satirized by Churchill in *The Candidate* (1764). See also Wilkes's *New Foundling Hospital for Wit* (1784), III, 104–7; J. T. Almon, *Letters of the Late John Wilkes*, III, 60–63; Ronald Fuller *Hell-Fire Francis* (1939); Donald McCormick, *The Hell-Fire Club* (1958). See also N. A. M. Rodger, *The Insatiable Earl: A Life of John Montagu, Fourth Earl of Sandwich* (1993).

7 Horace Walpole, *Journals of Visits to Country Seats*, *Walpole Society*, VI (1928), 50–51.

8 For an interesting contextual approach, see Shearer West, 'Libertinism and the ideology of male friendship in the portraits of the Society of Dilettanti', *Eighteenth-Century Life*, XVI, 2 (May 1992), 76–104.

9 *A*, 47–8.

10 R. W. Ketton-Cremer, *Felbrigge, the Story of a House* (1962); *HLAT*, II, 453–4, n. 8.

11 *Monthly Review*, XIX, 318–20; 2 September 1758.

12 *GW*, I, 286.

13 BL Add. MS 22394.

14 For his time travelling and in Rome, see Maurice James Craig, *The Volunteer Ear, Being the Life and Times of James Caulfield, First Earl of Charlemont* (1948), 57–79.

15 *The Grand Tour: The Lure of Italy in the Eighteenth Century*, ed. Andrew Wilton and Ilaria Bignamini, Tate catalogue (1996).

16 *A*, 219.

17 Ibid., 219–20.

18 *Inigo Jones* (c.1757); see *Concise Catalogue of Oil Paintings in the National Maritime Museum* (1988), 209h, and the fine analysis in *Hogarth the Painter*, catalogue 31, 53–4.

19 P, III, 292, Hogarth to Huggins, 9 November 1758, The Hyde Collection, Somerville, New Jersey (location of the two Huggins portraits).

20 Ibid., 223. BL Add. MS 40015, ff. 19–20.

21 Vertue, III, 33.

22 See *Hogarth the Painter*, catalogue 30, 52–3.

23 *A*, 220.

24 To Montagu, 5 May 1761; Walpole *Corr.*, IX, 365.

25 BL Add. MS 22394, f. 32. (Extracts from this correspondence are also in P, III, 230–35.)

26 BL Add. MS 22394, f. 37.

27 *A*, 220.

28 BL Add. MS 22394, ff. 33, 35.

29 Notes in his folio of Hogarth prints (Fitzw., vol. I). He put these in order, he says, as an act of friendship, angry that Hogarth's reputation was affected by the 'indiscriminate publication of humorous trifles', ransacked from his closet after his death.

30 N, 77–8.

31 *A*, 220.

32 *The Idler*, 76, 29 September 1759, in W. J. Bate, John M. Bullitt and L. F. Powell (eds), *The Idler and The Adventurer* (New Haven and London, 1963), 237.

33 Ibid., 238.

34 *The Idler*, 79, 20 October 1759, and 82, 254–8, Bate *et al.* (eds), *The Idler*, 246–8.

35 Ibid., 247–8.

36 Joseph Warton, 'Ode to Fancy' (1746), in Lonsdale, 391.

37 To Montagu, 21 October 1759; Walpole *Corr.*, IX, 250–51.

38 Langford, 339.

39 Edmund Burke, *A Philosophical Enquiry into the origin of our Ideas of the Sublime and the Beautiful* (1757), ed. J. T. Boulton (1958, 1987), 86; part II, xxii, 'Feeling Pain'.

40 Ibid., 45; part I, xiv, 'The effects of sympathy in the distresses of others'.

41 *GW*, III, 336–7, quoting the Reverend Thomas Young, *Essay on Humanity to Animals* (1798); *HLAT*, I, 241.

CHAPTER 30: Sickness, Societies and *Sigismunda*

1 To Montagu, 8 November 1759; Walpole *Corr.*, IX, 255.

2 *A*, 220–21.

3 Hyde Collection, Somerville, New Jersey; P, III, 293.

4 Laurence Sterne, *Tristram Shandy*, ed. Graham Petrie (Harmondsworth, 1967), 296.

5 Ibid., 123–4.

6 *Letters of Laurence Sterne*, ed. L. P. Curtis (Oxford, 1935), 99.

7 Ibid., 101.

8   Sterne *Tristram Shandy*, 138.

9   Ibid., 288.

10 Ibid., quoted in the introduction by Christopher Ricks, 10.

11 N, 56.

12 Whitley, 165, and Allen (1984), 368–70, who includes Boyce's ode in full. See also P, III, 307; *Minutes of the General Meetings of the Artists and of the Committee for managing the Public Exhibition* (opened 12 November 1760). See *Walpole Society*, VI (1917–18), 116.

13 For these negotiations, see Wood, *Royal Society*, 228; *Walpole Society*, VI, 118 (and Society of Arts Minutes books, vol. IV, 27 February 1760); Pye, 95–7; Waterhouse *Three Decades*, 47–52.

14 Whitley, I, 167.

15 *Reynolds* (exhibition catalogue, Royal Academy of Arts, 1986), ed. Nicholas Penny, 24; quoting J. Northcote *The Life of Sir Joshua Reynolds*, 2 vols (1818), I, 183.

16 Artists' Committee minutes, 15 and 23 May 1760; *Walpole Society*, VI, 120.

17 To Montagu, 25 October 1760; Walpole *Corr.*, IX, 311.

18 Pyne, I, 162–3.

19 Smart, 161–4.

20 For quotations in this paragraph see *A*, 223–5.

21 BL Add. MS 27993/4. See Michael Kitson's introduction to *Ap*, 48–9, 60–62.

22 *DA*, 16 February 1761.

23 *PA*, 7 March 1761; and P, III, 323. (See also *HI*, III, 3; 207, for Kirby's defence of *Sigismunda*.)

24 *HI*, I, xcvi. For the mistranslation, see *HGW*, 173 (the emphasis is mine). For *The Spectator*, see ch. 4. (Some subscribers may have had *Hymen and Cupid* as a ticket; see *HGW*, 110.)

25 BL Add. MS 22394, ff. 29–31; P, III, 323.

26 *Walpole Society*, VI, 128; P, III, 319, adds the final paragraph.

27 The distinction is made clearly in Brewer, ch. 6.

28 To Montagu, 5 May 1761; Walpole *Corr.*, IX, 365.

29 *SJC*, 7–9 May 1761.

30 The frontispiece motto is from Juvenal's *Satires*, the tailpiece from Martial's *Epigrams*: *HGW*, 194.

31 *The Actor* (1760) supported Garrick in a long-standing quarrel with Thady Fitzpatrick, whom Garrick satirized as 'Fribble' in a farce of 1757, and in *The Fribbleriad* (1761).

32 'The Actor', *The Poetical Works of Robert Lloyd, A.M.*, ed. W. Kenrick, 2 vols (1774), I, 10. See Bertelsen, 71–3.

33 Robert Lloyd, *Poetical Works*, I, 109.

34 Churchill and his wife separated in February 1761: his two sons lived with her. In 1760 he was rescued from debtors' prison by Dr Pierson Lloyd, Robert Lloyd's father. See Weatherly, vi–viii.

35 Bertelsen, 120.

36 Ibid., 118.

37 Garrick to George Colman, [December 1760]; Garrick, I, 333.

38 *SJC*, 23–25 April 1761.

39 *SJC*, 2–5 May 1761.

40 *HI*, III, 96, and 100. Ireland claims 13,000 were sold, compared with 6,582 in 1760. Hudson and Luckhurst (37), estimate 6000 catalogues, and 20,000 visitors.

41 John Gwynn, *London and Westminster Improve'd, illustrated by Plans, to which is prefix'd, a discourse on Public Magnificence, with Observations on the State of the Arts and Artists in this Kingdom* (1766), 24.

42 N, 74.

43 Letter to *SJC*, 8–10 April 1790. Whitley (175–6) ascribes it to Philip Thicknesse (one of the subscribers to *Sigismunda*).

44 Thomas Birch to Lord Royston, BL Add. MS 35400, f. 75; partly transcribed in Whitley, 175–6.

45 See Horace Walpole's 'Notes . . . on the Exhibition of the Society of Artists and the Free Society of Artists, 1760–61', ed. Hugh Gatty, *Walpole Society*, XVII (1938–9), 55–88.

CHAPTER 31: Signs and Symbols

1 Langford, 340.

2 To Horace Mann, 23 July 1761; Walpole *Corr.*, XXI, 518.

3 J. H. Plumb, *The First Four Georges* (1956), 96.

4 John Brewer, *Party Ideology and Popular Politics at the Accession of George III* (Cambridge, 1976), 11.

5 To Mann, 10 September 1761; Walpole *Corr.*, XXI, 529.

6 To Mann, 1 August 1761; ibid., 520.

7 To Thomas Birch, 13 July 1761; Garrick, I, 341–2.

8 *LC*, 3–6 January 1761; *GM*, 1761, XXXI, 414; Walpole *Corr.*, XXI, 536 (to Mann, 28 September 1761).

9 *SJC*, 15–18 August 1761.

10 *SJC*, 11–13 August 1761.

11 *SJC*, 5–8, 12–15 September 1761.

12 Pyne, II, 6–11.

13 To Montagu, 24 September 1761; Walpole *Corr.*, IX, 386; see also XXI, 534 (to Mann, 28 September 1761).

14 Pyne, II, 25.

15 Ibid., 32–3.

16 Ibid., 42.

17 *LM*, XXX (1761), 448.

18 Ibid., 389.

19 For the 1761 patent see *HI*, III, 139–41.

20 *Ap*, 49.

21 See *HGW*, 174.

22 *SJC*, 7–9 May 1761 (nos. 197, 198 in the catalogue).

23 Ibid. For the fire screen, see Smith, I, 35.

24 To Montagu, 4 November 1761; Walpole *Corr.*, IX, 401.

25 *SJC*, 15–18 August 1761.

26 Ibid., 25–27 May 1762; and Bertelsen, 144.

27 Boswell *Journal*, 239.

28 Walpole *Memoirs III*, 181. Walpole also said of Churchill that 'Imagination, harmony, wit, satire, strength, fire and sense crowded on his compositions'.

29 Arthur Murphy, *The Examiner*, 1761.

30 Bertelsen, 85–7; anon., *The Triumvirate* (1761).

31 *Genius, Envy, Time: a Fable, addressed to William Hogarth, Esq* (1761), *Poetical Work of Robert Lloyd, A.M.*, ed. W. Kenrick, 2 vols (1774).

32 *SJC*, throughout April–May 1761.

33 BM 1858–4 17–582; *HGW*, 175.

34 See Tom Taylor, *Leicester Square* (1874), 493–5.

35 Roger Hudson, *Covent Garden, Trafalgar Square and the Strand* (1996), 120 (misdating this as 1757).

36 *GI*, I, 172.

37 *GM*, XXXII, 1762, quoted in Boswell *Life*, I, 407, n. 3.

38 The trial was in July 1762, but sentence was deferred until January: Parsons was sentenced to the pillory and two years in prison, his wife to a year in gaol, and Mary Fraser to six months hard labour in Bridewell.

39 John Keats, *Letters*, ed. Hyder Rollins (Cambridge, 1958), II, 260, 271.

40 *Pope's Literary Legacy: The Book Trade Correspondence of William Warburton and John Knapton*, ed. Donald W. Nicoll (Oxford, 1992), in P, III, 366.

41 Walpole *Anec.*, 145. For his visit to Cock Lane see Walpole *Corr.*, X, 6 (to Montagu, 2 February 1762).

42 [Bonnell Thornton] *City Latin, or Critical and Political Remarks on the Latin Inscriptions on laying the First Stone of the intended New Bridge at BLACKFRIARS* (1760; 2nd edn, 1761), 24. Quoted Bertelsen, 133–5, and P, III, 340. Beneath the foundation stone for Blackfriars Bridge were placed inscriptions in English and Latin, 'in large plates of pure tin', paying tribute to the Mayor, the architect and Pitt. They had 'a very Roman air, though very unclassically expressed' remarked Walpole (the inscription praising Pitt 'talked of *the contagion of his public spirit*'); to Mann, 1 November 1760, Walpole *Corr.*, XXI, 449.

43 *SJC*, 21–23 May 1761.

44 *SJC*, 23–27 May 1761. This issue also contained the Admirer versus Brillus letter.

45 *The Diary of Joseph Farington*, V, ed. K. Garlick and Angus Macintyre (1755); 7 March 1802.

46 In 1761, the catalogue profits *were* distributed to poor artists and their dependants: Hogarth arranged for a sum to go to the widow of Henry Weldon, a fellow pupil at the Vanderbank academy.

47 *Conduct of the Royal Academicians* (1771), 13. See P, III, 348. (The committee had been enlarged from sixteen to twenty-four members.)

48 Brewer, ch. 6.

49 *SJC*, 13–16 March 1762.

50 Ibid., 23–25 March 1762.

51 Ibid., 3–6 April 1762.

52 Ibid., 22–24 April 1762.

53 Ibid., 29 April–1 May 1762.

54 *BM Sat.*, 3481. See Bertelsen, 146, and Allen (1984), 377.

55 *SJC*, 22–24 April 1762.

56 The history and layout of the exhibition is vividly evoked in successive issues of the *SJC*. Some background details are given in Jacob Larwood and John Camden Hooten, *The History of Signboards* (1866), and Bertelsen, 142–5.

57 *SJC*, 20–22 April 1762.

58 An Irish painter, James Hagarty, lived in Queen Street, Golden Square; R. Paulson, *The Beautiful, the Novel and the Strange* (1996), 327–8, n. 35.

59 *Works of Cowper*, ed. Robert Southey (1836–7), I, 37.

60 This became law in June 1762: the signs were taken down and placed flat against the walls of the houses.

CHAPTER 32: 'That Devil Wilkes'

1 Walpole *Memoirs III*, II, 180.

2 Langford, 346.

3 When Carlos III became King of Spain in 1759 the Bourbon family compact implied an alliance between France and Spain.

4 Wilkes to Churchill, 15 June 1762; Weatherly, 3.

5 See Weatherly, xii–xiii, and George Nobbe, *The North Briton; a Study in Political Propaganda* (New York, 1939), 12–14. The first issue of *The Briton* appeared on 29 May; *The North Briton* on 5 June, and *The Auditor* on 12 June. Wilkes wrote most numbers; Churchill wrote several, but was generally the manager, supervising printing, etc.

6 For the relationship with contemporary anti-Bute, and anti-Scottish, prints, see George *Caricature*, 118–31, and Atherton, 208–27.

7 Quoted by George Rude in *Wilkes and Liberty: A Social Study* (Oxford, 1962), 21.

8 Walpole *Memoirs III*, I, 176, 178.

9 George *Caricature*, 121.

10 *The Correspondence of the Late John Wilkes*, ed. J. T. Almon, 5 vols (1805), III, 24–5; N, 80.

11 See *HGW*, 179–80.

12 N, 376–7.

13 Ibid., 377.

14 Ibid.

15 Wilkes to Churchill, 9 September 1762; Weatherly, 15.

16 For Churchill's begging letters, see John Forster, *Historical and Biographical Essays* (1858), II, 262, n. 1, and Joseph Knight, *David Garrick* (1894), 199.

17 To Churchill [*post* 7 September 1762]; Garrick, I, 366.

18 *BM Sat.* 3890 (sometimes attributed to Sandby).

19 *HI*, I, xcii.

20 *A*, 221.

21 George *Caricature*, 129.

22 *BM Sat.* 3955 and 3971.

23 Ibid., 3978: the inscription continues, 'I'll gild this Scotch Sign & make it look Glorious, & I'll daub the other sign to efface its beauty & make it as black as Jack Boot.' Other satires of this winter included *A Sett of Blocks for Hogarth's Wigs*, *The Vision on M-n-st-al*

Monster (*BM Sat.* 3916 and 3983) and *The Hungry Mob of Scriblers and Etchers* (including Johnson and Hogarth).

24 Ibid., 3977. George *Caricature*, 129, attributes this to Sandby. She quotes Darly's explanation: 'This caricature shews the exaltation of a Scotch Blockhead, which infatuated the greatest droll genius in the World to fall down and worship and even daub his own Character to whitewash the Black Boot; and forgot himself so far as to aim at injuring the most exalted *English* Patriot that ever was, till the bold and honest North Briton nipped him in the Bud. But they say he has Scotch fitts at intervals.'

25 *A*, 21.

26 Ramsay was anxious to clear up the muddle that deprived him of his proper salary as Principal Painter in Ordinary. See Smart, 172–3.

27 Peter Thomas, *Wilkes: A Friend to Liberty* (Oxford, 1996), 22; See W. J. Smith (ed.), *The Greville Papers*, 4 vols (1852–3), I, 469–73.

28 Wilkes to Churchill, 5 December 1762; Weatherly, 36–7.

29 *The Diary of John Baker*, ed. Philip C. Yorke (1931), 164. Baker had dined with Samuel Martin, Hogarth and his wife and their relation Julien Bere in February 1759; 120.

30 See Walpole *Memoirs III*, I, 223–35.

31 *The North Briton*, 19 March 1763.

32 Churchill to Wilkes, 16 March 1763; Weatherly, 48.

33 *The North Briton*, 45 (April 1763), 228, 231.

34 For the ensuing events, see Thomas, *Wilkes*, 23–45.

35 *PA*, 7 May 1763; Almon, *Correspondence*, I, 109–12.

36 Ibid., 122–3.

37 Ibid., 28–34.

38 Postgate, 36.

39 *A*, 221.

40 In full fraught Humour every Line
   Shall descant on thy quick Decline:
   In lively Colours shall be shewn,
   (Colours, more lasting than thine own,)
   That *mimic* wit has no Pretence
   To trespass on the Ground of Sense.
   PA, 14 June 1763; *SJC*, 12–14 June; reprinted in *LC*, 5–7 July 1763; P, III, 401.

41 Boswell *Journal*, 239; 24 May 1763.

42 Boswell *Life*, I, 419; see also Boswell *Journal*, 255; 1 July 1763. Churchill satirized Johnson in *The Ghost, Book II* (Churchill, 97–8).

43 Quoted in Whitley, I, 177, and P, III, 402 (BL Add. MS 35400, f. 75).

44 Weatherly, 55.

45 All quotations from the *Epistle* are taken from *The Poetical Works of Charles Churchill*, ed. Douglas Grant, (Oxford, 1956), 213–30.

46 *BM Sat.* 4054, subtitled *Wm Hogarth Esqr Principal Pannel Painter to his Majesty*.

47 Garrick to George Colman, 10 July 1763; Garrick, vol. I, 378.

48 In his satirical *Terrae-Filius* essays, written 5–8 July 1763; George Colman, *Prose on Several Occasions* (1787), I, 237–8. See Garrick, 379, n. 1.

49 *SJC*, 2–5 July 1763.

50 N, 90.
51 A, 230.
52 Ibid., 221.
53 Ibid., 221–2.
54 N, 92.
55 Ibid.
56 Churchill to Wilkes, [3 August] 1763; Weatherly, 59.
57 Wilkes to Churchill, 29 August 1763; ibid., 64.
58 A, 222.

CHAPTER 33: The End of All Things

1 N, 93.
2 BL Add. MS 27991, f. 42b (not in A).
3 BL Add. MS 2991, f. 42b; A, 222.
4 Walpole Memoirs III, I, 317.
5 Martin's letter, quoted in Raymond Postgate, 'That Devil Wilkes', (1930), 79.
6 Walpole Memoirs III, I, 330.
7 Churchill's poems of 1764 included The Duellist, the long, idealistic poem Gotham, then The Candidate, The Farewell and Independence.
8 See the touching account by R. W. Lightbown in his introduction to Rouquet State of the Arts.
9 See the 'Dialogue of the dead' in the Gazetteer, 14 November 1764, in which Hogarth is presented as calling them his 'friends' and speaking of them in the highest terms.
10 A, 201.
11 Ibid., 213.
12 Ibid.
13 Ibid., 215.
14 GM, 1785, 344; GW, 259f.
15 Letter to GM, 55 (1785); N, 403.
16 The Rake's Progress, in W. H. Auden and Chester Kalmann, Libretti, ed. Edward Mendelson (Princeton, 1993), 89.
17 Antal, 168.
18 Alexander Pope, The Art of Sinking in Poetry (Peri Bathous), ed. E. L. Steeves (New York, 1968).
19 Samuel Beckett, Krapp's Last Tape.
20 N, 403.
21 SJC, 3–5, 5–7 April 1764.
22 'On Hogarth's print of Bathos, or the Art of Sinking in Painting. Written by Mr. C. Churchill when at Mr. Dell's, in Kew-foot Lane, April 18, 1764'; Churchill, 453.
23 The Dunciad (1742 edn), Poetical Works, ed. Herbert Davis (Oxford, 1966), 583–4.
24 P, III, 428; BL Add. MS 22394. The note was explained thus: 'Things having been represented in favour of his Lord much to Mr Hs dishonour, the foregoing plain tale is therefore submitted to Such as may at any time think it worth while to see the whole truth, of what has been so publicly talked of.'

767

25 Despite his claim in January that he would do the work himself, Hogarth may have engaged his engraver provisionally before that since Basire went to Italy to study in 1763.

26 N, 75.

27 *GW*, I, 329–31.

28 David Hall to William Strahan, 25 June 1764; P, III, 433.

29 P. C. C. Simpson 427, PRO, London; *HLAT*, II, app. J, 508.

30 His three witnesses were Richard Loveday, a Chiswick doctor, and George Ellsom and Mary Graham.

31 N, 93.

32 '*Independence*'; Churchill, 417.

33 N, 94.

34 [Samuel Badcock], review of John Nichols, *Biographical Anecdotes of William Hogarth*, *Monthly Review*, December 1781. See N, Introduction, n.p.

CHAPTER 34: 'Finis'

1 *LEP*, 28–30 October 1764. See the interesting collection, 'Eulogies of Hogarth' in *HLAT*, II, app. K, 508–11.

2 To the Earl of Hertford, 1 November 1764; Walpole *Corr.*, VI, 139.

3 To Colman, 10 November 1764; Garrick, II, 429.

4 *PA*, 8 December 1764.

5 Bertelsen, 249.

6 *PA*, 30 January 1765; *HLAT*, II, 510.

7 To Mann, 15 November 1764; Walpole *Corr.*, XXII, 261.

8 Walpole *Anec.*, 160.

9 See Antal, 196–217.

10 Roy McMullen, *Victorian Outsider: A Biography of J. A. M. Whistler* (1973), 32.

11 H. Randolph, *Life of General Sir R[obert] W[ilson]*, I, 30–32.

12 P, III, 533, n. 47.

13 *LC*, 31 January–2 February 1765.

14 *Public Ledger*, 19 November; *PA*, 8 December; for obituaries see e.g. *PA*, 29 October; *SJC*, 25–27 October; *Lloyd's Evening Post*, 26–29 October; *Gazetteer*, 9 October; *LM*, 32 ; *Annual Register*, 7 (all 1764).

15 *PA*, 5 August 1766. See Reverend Doctor John Trusler, *Hogarth Moralised* (1766–8).

16 Quotes from the *Cornhill Magazine* on the title page of *The Complete Works of William Hogarth*, with Introductory Essay by James Hannay and Descriptive Letterpress by the Reverend J. Trusler and E. F. Roberts, New and Revised Edition (n.d.).

17 J. H. Jesse, *George Selwyn and his Contemporaries, with Memoirs and Notes*, 4 vols (1882), II, 34. I am grateful to Stella Tillyard for this reference.

18 To the George Keatses, 31 December 1818; John Keats, *Letters*, ed. Hyder Rollins (Cambridge, 1958), ii, 18.

19 William Hazlitt, *The Examiner*, 1814, reprinted in The Round Table, ed. Catherine Macdonald Maclean (1906). See also a slightly different version in Hazlitt, VI, 133–49.

20 Charles Lamb, 'Essay on the Genius and Characters of Hogarth', *The Reflector*, no. III,

1811. Quoted by David Bindman in *A Rake's Progress: From Hogarth to Hockney*, Sir John Soane's Museum (1997), Introduction, 3.

21 Wordsworth to John Kenyon, 26 January [1832], *The Letters of Dorothy and William Wordsworth*, ed. E. de Selincourt, (2nd edn, Oxford, 1975), v, part II, 482.

22 *Coleridge on the Seventeenth Century*, ed. R. F. Brinkley, 463, 567. The context is Coleridge's note on Thomas Fuller for 'English Worthies': 'Shakespeare! Milton! Fuller! De Foe! Hogarth! – As to the remaining Host of our Great Men, other countries have produced something like them – but they are uniques . . . these are *genera*, containing each only one individual.' For the ludicrous juxtaposed to beauty see *The Friend*, ed. Barbara E. Rooke, 2 vols (1969), II, 213; no. 16, 7 December 1809.

23 Warwick Draper, *Chiswick*, 105; Antal, 216. See also Dabydeen *Hogarth's Blacks*, 15–19.

24 Peter Ackroyd, *Dickens* (1990), 462 and *The Letters of Charles Dickens*, ed. M. House and G. Storey, 8 vols, I (1965), 431n.

25 Fitzw. Hogarth Collection, v. This volume is full of fascinating images of Hogarth himself, often completely unrecognizable, from popular editions, lists of 'British Worthies', etc.

26 Archives of the Foundling Hospital; P, III, 533, 49.

27 Garrick, II, and 783, n.5. See also 778, 782, and *The Letters of Samuel Johnson*, ed. Robert W. Chapman (1953), I, 273. Garrick also sent a copy to the Reverend Evan Lloyd. For Hoadly see *The Private Correspondence of David Garrick*, 2 vols, ed. James Boaden (1831–2), I, 470.

28 *Thraliana, the Diaries of Hester Lynch Thrale (later Mrs Piozzi) 1776–1809*, ed. Katharine C. Balderston, 2nd edn, 2 vols (Oxford, 1951), I, 41; also see *Anecdotes of the late Samuel Johnson, LLD*, ed. S. C. Roberts, (Cambridge, 1925), 239–40.

29 All Walpole quotations are from Walpole *Anec.*, 146–93.

30 Nichols compiled the catalogue and wrote much of the life and Steevens provided the critical, and often malicious, commentary; Isaac Reed gave general assistance and provided theatrical anecdotes. For their roles, and the complicated genesis of this work, see the very clear introduction by R. W. Lightbown to the 1971 facsimile reprint of the 1785 edition.

31 Charlemont papers, 382–3; and Walpole *Corr.*, II, 330; Cole to Walpole, 29 June 1792.

32 Sir Richard Phillips, cited in Dobson, 182.

33 *The Original Works of William Hogarth. Sold by John and Josiah Boydell, at the Shakespeare Gallery, Pall Mall, and no 90, Cheapside, London, 1790.* The plates were not retouched. In addition to previous folios, this contained *Boys Peeping at Nature, Martin Folkes, The Times*, Plate II, *Battle of the Pictures, Ranby's House, Time Smoking a Picture.*

34 As *Genuine Works of William Hogarth* (1820–22), published by Baldwin, Cradock and Joy (who bought the plates at some point after Boydell's death, and sale of 1818) and subsequent issues, with additional plates after Hogarth's designs, and commentary. Three new editions appeared betwen 1828 and 1840. In 1835 the plates were bought by Henry G. Bohn, who issued a new edition in 1849. For the different editions, the plates, and the principal collections, see *HGW*, 16–24.

35 *Catalogue of the pictures and Prints; The Property of the late Mrs Hogarth.* Sold by auction at '*the Golden Head, Leicester square, On Saturday the 24th April, 1790, At twelve o'Clock.* Reproduced in *HLAT*, II, app. L, 511–13.

769

36 See Duncan, *passim* and Klingender, vi–xiii and catalogue, which shows how Gillray adapted or parodied several of Hogarth's designs and subjects for his own political caricatures, e.g. in *The Morning after Marriage* (1786), *A March to the Bank* (1787), *The Gin Palace* (1815), *The Stage Coach* (1816) and Rowlandson also often refers to him, e.g. in the title page of the *Caricature magazine* (1806).

37 David Hockney, *A Rake's Progress* (1963); Editions Alecto, limited edition portfolio of sixteen etchings.

38 Smith, II, 270.

Acknowledgements

Like all who work on Hogarth, I owe much to Ronald Paulson, whose biographical researches, catalogue of the prints and later writings cleared the way for modern Hogarth studies. His work is acknowledged in my notes, but I would also like to thank him for his personal interest.

When I began I was diffident about venturing into the specialized field of art history: in the event I have been received as a welcome guest, not a trespasser, and I am extremely grateful to the experts who have encouraged and assisted me. My greatest debt is to the Paul Mellon Centre for Studies in British Art, and to its Director, Brian Allen. The Mellon Centre library has been a haven as well as a resource: Brian Allen generously invited me to use it, answered queries, set me straight about attributions, talked with passion and humour about eighteenth-century art and finally – in the middle of a packed schedule – found time to read and correct my draft. I owe him many thanks.

Several other art historians and curators generously shared their time and expertise, and in particular I would like to thank David Bindman, Elizabeth Einberg, Mary Webster, Juliet Carey – who explained her research into *The Jones Family* – and Jules Lubbock, who sent his conference notes on Addison as a cultural ideologue. Special thanks are due to Mark Hallett, for invigorating discussions of Hogarth's engravings in the context of other city prints and for his helpful comments on the text.

From an early point, John Brewer's draft study of eighteenth-century culture (now published as *Pleasures of the Imagination*) was an invaluable map against which to track Hogarth's individual path; his encouragement also spurred me on. Stella Tillyard sent references and her lively interest was a tonic. Simon Schaffer graphically outlined the role of scientific lecturers and instrument-makers. Jeremy Barlow played me the music in the background of Hogarth's work, especially *The Beggar's Opera* and Handel's *Julius Caesar*. Fiona Haslam kindly sent her type-script on graphic satire and medicine; Fran Hazleton shared her knowledge of London localities and history; Jack Skelton-Wallace helped me to find maps, and Roger Lonsdale's anthologies of eighteenth-century verse often provided inspiration. With regard to places, I should like to thank Alan Downend, of the Friends of Hogarth House, and James Wisdom and Valerie Box, whose con-versation made Georgian Chiswick come alive and who carefully checked passages on the village.

I wanted people to see as much of Hogarth's work as possible, and would like to acknowledge the great generosity of Carol and Kate Machin, who lent me their Hogarth portfolio: it was marvellous to have such a vivid, direct source. I am also grateful to those who helped with the illustrations, including Janet Allan, Robin Bloxsidge of Liverpool University Press, Alison Balfour-Lynn of The Print Room, Carolyn Hammond of Chiswick Local Studies Collection. I would especially like to thank Emma Scrase of the Paul Mellon Centre, and the unflappable Luke Vinten of Faber. I am also greatly indebted to the designer Ron Costley and the copy-editor and type-setter Jill Burrows, for their skill and warm-hearted enthusiasm.

ACKNOWLEDGEMENTS

A key person throughout has been my editor Julian Loose; his energetic dedication made the book possible and his wry humour kept its author going. Others kept me going too. To my delight, Hogarth interested the Uglows: Steve provided information on law, crime and punishment; Tom's research shone light on *Strolling Actresses*; Jamie made me see medical and political aspects; Hannah and Luke pored over prints and paintings. So – thank you all (or thanks to Hogarth) for more than wry domestic toleration. Friends have also been important: deep gratitude goes to Francis Spufford for reading the draft over so many cups of coffee and commenting with his usual wayward genius. And to John Barnard, who lent me books and was always ready to listen and question. Finally I would like to thank Hermione Lee, who has followed the book's progress, responding warmly and in detail, and who has supported me with her friendship from start to finish.

With regard to picture permissions, the author and publishers are particularly grateful to Carol and Kate Machin for permission to reproduce a large number of engravings. They would also like to thank The Print Room, Museum Street, London, for generously allowing them to use film for reproduction of prints from *Hogarth's Graphic Works* (revised edition, 1989). Thanks are also due to the following institutions and individuals for permission to use their archives, or to reproduce individual prints, drawings and paintings as noted in the List of Illustrations: Her Majesty The Queen, for pictures from the Royal Collection, St James's Palace and the Royal Library, Windsor Castle; The Albright-Knox Art Gallery, Buffalo, New York: City of Aberdeen Art Gallery and Museums Collections; The Governors of the Royal Hospital of St Bartholomew; The Beaverbrook Foundation, The Beaverbrook Art Gallery, Fredericton, New Brunswick, Canada; Henry W. and Albert A. Berg Collection, New York Public Library; Birmingham Museums and Art Gallery; City of Bristol Art Gallery; Bonham Ltd; The Rt Hon. the Viscount Boyne; The Bridgeman Art Library; The British Library; The British Museum Department of Prints and Drawings; Chiswick Local Studies Library, The London Borough of Hounslow; The Rt Hon. the Marquess of Cholmondely; Christies Images; Columbus Museum of Art, Ohio; The Fitzwilliam Museum, Cambridge; Lincoln's Inn; Simon Foyle; The Frick Collection, New York; Hogarth House, Chiswick; The Horne Collection, Florence; The Hyde Collection, Somerville, New Jersey; Ickworth House (The National Trust); The Earl of Iveagh: M. C. Jones-Mortimer, Esq.; Koriyama City Museum of Art, Japan; The Earl of Macclesfield; The Metropolitan Museum of Art, New York; The Trustees, The National Gallery, London; The National Gallery of Ireland; The National Maritime Museum, London; Philadelphia Museum of Art: The John H. McFadden Collection; The National Portrait Gallery, London; The National Museum and Gallery, Cardiff; The National Trust; Norfolk Museums Service (Norwich Castle Museum); The Earl of Rosebery; The Royal Society; The Simon House Collection; Smith College Museum of Art, Northampton, Massachusetts; The Trustees of Sir John Soane's Museum; Sotheby's Ltd; The Trustees of the Tate Gallery; The Trustees of the Thomas Coram Foundation; The Victoria and Albert Museum; The Board of Trustees of the National Museums and Galleries on Merseyside (The Walker Art Gallery, Liverpool); The Lewis Walpole Library, Farmington, Connecticut; Executors of the Estate of the late H. C. Wollaston; Yale Center for British Art, New Haven, Connecticut.

The author and publishers apologize for any errors or omissions in the above list and would be grateful to be notified of any corrections that should be incorporated in the next edition or reprint of this volume.

772

Illustrations

This list notes size (to ⅛ in.), source or location; the city is London, unless otherwise stated. My gratitude to the galleries and individuals is recorded in the Acknowledgements. Unless otherwise specified, photographs were provided by the institutions.

Colour Plates

Illustrations in the Text

774

ILLUSTRATIONS

775

777

Index

779

785

787

791